"*Unprecedented* is a tour de force of enormous importance for our planetary future. In his superb analysis of climate change through the lens of science, politics, economics, energy, morality, and religion, Griffin has provided a wealth of insight for how to move forward. This will be an indispensable book for raising awareness that civilization itself is at stake."

—MARY EVELYN TUCKER
Forum on Religion and Ecology at Yale University

"Theologian David Ray Griffin brings to bear his considerable skills of synthesis to lay out, from the best current sources including Lester Brown and Bill McKibben, a comprehensive snapshot of the climate crisis, its dark threat of planetary desertification, and the urgent need for us all to act swiftly to close the era of fossil fuels and switch to clean energy. This would require as much moral will as it does political skill: Griffin makes a strong case that humanity's differing faiths, world views and ethical creeds, including the secular, have enough in common to allow us to act now on behalf of the next generations if we can only begin to act from our full humanity and face the climate challenge squarely."

—VINCENT STANLEY
co-author, *The Responsible Company:
What We've Learned From Patagonia's First 40 Years*

"Myths and Big Lies proliferate about global warming. Griffin's new book is must reading. It explains what everyone needs to know. It does so responsibly. In lucid detail like everything he writes. Global warming is one of the most important issues of our times. Survival may depend on resolving it responsibly."

—STEPHEN LENDMAN
author of *Banker Occupation: Waging Financial War on Humanity*

In 1995, Nobel Prize-winning scientist Sherwood Rowland asked,

"What's the use of having developed a science well enough to make predictions if, in the end, all we're willing to do is stand around and wait for them to come true?"

UNPRECEDENTED

CAN CIVILIZATION SURVIVE THE CO2 CRISIS?

David Ray Griffin

Clarity Press

ISBN: 978-0-9860769-0-9
EBOOK ISBN: 978-9-9860769-1-6

In-house editor: Diana G. Collier
Cover: R. Jordan P. Santos
Cartoon: Steve Sach, Courtesy Cagle Cartoons

Library of Congress Cataloging-in-Publication Data

Clarity Press, Inc.
Ste. 469, 3277 Roswell Rd. NE
Atlanta, GA. 30305 , USA
http://www.claritypress.com

TABLE OF CONTENTS

Preface
8

PART I: UNPRECEDENTED THREATS

Introduction
11

1 Extreme Weather
24

2 Heat Waves
33

3 Droughts and Wildfires
40

4 Storms
54

5 Sea-Level Rise
68

6 Fresh Water Shortage
80

7 Food Shortage
94

8 Climate Refugees
106

9 Climate Wars
118

10 Ecosystem Collapse and Extinction
134

PART II: UNPRECEDENTED CHALLENGES AND FAILURES

11 Climate Change Denial
153

12 Media Failure
181

13 Political Failure
200

14 Moral Challenge
227

15 Religious Challenge
244

16 Economic Challenge
264

PART III: WHAT IS TO BE DONE

17 The Transition to Clean Energy
303

18 The Abolition of Dirty Energy
362

19 Mobilization
391

Conclusion
421

Endnotes
425

Acknowledgments
503

Index
504

To Ann and our six grandsons
Michael, Matthew, Nicolas, Van, Dakota, and Dylan

This book is also published in memory of Tod Fletcher.

PREFACE

What to do about global warming and climate change has become the most contentious issue on our planet.

This is strange, given the fact that virtually all climate scientists – between 97 and 99.8 percent of them, depending on which criteria are used – agree that the climate is changing, that this is because of global warming (the planet's average temperature is rising), and that global warming has been caused almost entirely by greenhouse gases, primarily CO2 (carbon dioxide), which are emitted by fossil fuels: coal, oil, and natural gas.

In spite of this scientific consensus, the issue has become contentious, because the fossil-fuel industries, wanting to prevent government regulations that might decrease their profits, have used their enormous wealth to create a false debate. Even as some of the effects of climate change have become too obvious to deny – such as unprecedented extreme weather, wildfires, and melting glaciers – the fossil-fuel corporations have considered their profits more important than the planet's welfare. Even after multiple warnings by scientists that climate change now threatens the very survival of civilization, the coal, oil, and natural gas industries show no willingness to accept a reduction of profits simply to save a climate that can support the continuation of human existence.

This book tells the story about what has been going on and what needs to be done if we are to save humanity (along with millions of other species). Physicist Joe Romm has said: "One of the greatest failings of the climate science community (and the media) is not spelling out as clearly as possible the risks we face on our current emissions path, as well as the plausible worst-case scenario, which includes massive ecosystem collapse."

After the Introduction, which discusses the relation between global warming and climate change and the threat to civilization, Part I deals with various dimensions of climate change, focusing on what they will mean for those of us alive today, our children and grandchildren, and all future generations.

Part II explains ways in which the fossil-fuel industries have created the false debate, and ways in which their greed has been supported by politicians, the media, bad morality, bad religion, and bad economics.

Part III, while showing why the fossil-fuel industries should be put out of business, shows that doing so is possible, because solar, wind, and other types of clean energy are now capable of replacing fossil-fuel energy. The book concludes with a discussion of the full-out mobilization needed to save civilization.

PART I

UNPRECEDENTED THREATS

INTRODUCTION

"The world is now experiencing unprecedented challenges."
– U.N. Secretary General Ban Ki-Moon, January 2013

"It's the unprecedented speed with which
we're changing the climate that is so worrisome."
– Michael Mann, 2013

Global Warming and Climate Change

The term "global warming" refers to the phenomenon of the Earth's average temperature becoming warmer, which occurs because the planet's energy has been out of balance. "This energy imbalance is the difference between the amount of solar energy absorbed by Earth and the amount of energy the planet radiates to space as heat," explained the world's best-known climate scientist, Dr. James Hansen, who had long headed NASA's Goddard Institute for Space Studies. "If the imbalance is positive, more energy coming in than going out, we can expect Earth to become warmer in the future."[1]

This positive imbalance began with the industrial revolution. It initiated the heavy use of fossil fuels, which emit gases that are called "greenhouse gases" (GHG), because they trap heat from the sun, preventing it from returning to space. To grasp the importance of the current warming of our planet, it is necessary to reflect upon the context in which this is occurring.

Civilization and the Holocene

The most recent glacial period (popularly called an "ice age") began about 110,000 years ago. About 19,000 years ago, the Earth started to warm up, because of changes in the Earth's orbit around the sun. By 11,700 years ago, these changes brought about a transition from the glacial epoch to an "interglacial" one, called the Holocene epoch, which brought the partial melting of glaciers, the formation of lakes, and the spreading of forests across much of the planet. It was in this context, about 10,000 years ago, that human civilization began.

The Holocene climate was remarkably stable. It never become warm enough or cold enough to bring human civilization to an end and, in most places, it was even suited for humans to thrive. The Holocene thereby "enabled the development of modern civilization, global agriculture, and a world that could sustain a vast population."[2]

Within this stability, to be sure, there were changes. After being relatively warm during the early Holocene – 11,700 to 5,000 years ago - the climate started cooling, due primarily to decreased solar radiation. It continued to cool until the end of the 19th century. But then, this long-term cooling "ended abruptly with the rapid warming of the 20th Century," wrote physicist Stefan Rahmstorf of the Potsdam Institute for Climate Impact Research. "Within a hundred years, the cooling of the previous 5000 years was undone." In the words of Oregon State University's Shaun Marcott – who headed the study about which Rahmstorf was commenting – "What we found is that temperatures increased in the last hundred years as much as they had cooled in the last six or seven thousand."[3]

This analysis of the unprecedentedly rapid increase in the global temperature corroborated the 1999 graph by physicist Michael Mann, which became known as the "hockey stick," because, after showing a long period of decline in global temperature, it showed an extremely sharp uptick in the 20th century. This unprecedented increase can be plausibly explained only by the corresponding rapid increase in fossil-fuel emissions in the 20th century. "[W]ithout the increase in greenhouse gases caused by humans," Rahmstorf said, "the slow cooling trend would have continued."[4]

Some people claim that this reversal of the planet's temperature can be explained by increased radiation from the sun. However, the increase in solar radiation leveled off after 1950, leaving greenhouse gases clearly the main contributor since 1970. In fact, since the 1970s the sun and climate have been moving in opposite directions: While the sun has had a slight cooling trend, the climate has been getting warmer and warmer. As another scientist put it, "We should be cool, but we're not."[5]

In fact, the planet's temperature has been getting so warm, says Rahmstorf, that "[w]e are catapulting ourselves way out of the Holocene."[6] To mark this transition, some scientists have suggested that human civilization has initiated a new epoch, the "Anthropocene," signifying "the human-dominated geological epoch." Indeed, a vote on whether to adopt this name as officially designating a new epoch may be taken in 2016.[7]

Realization of the CO$_2$ Threat to Civilization Emerges

In most fields, humanity seeks to rely on the best science of the day. In 1998, an international organization of climate scientists - the Intergovernmental Panel on Climate Change (IPCC) - was formed. Since then, members of this panel have been warning that continued global warming will have disastrous consequences for civilization.

For several years, climate scientists discussed these consequences mostly in scientific journals, relying on the press to make their concerns known. But in recent years, because of the failure of that strategy, some of the leading scientists have been speaking out publicly, joining other well-informed people to warn that the very survival of human civilization is threatened:

- In 2005, Canadian lawyer and Minister of Parliament Elizabeth May entitled her Killam Lecture "Can Civilization Survive Climate Change?"[8]

- In 2006, well-known *New Yorker* writer Elizabeth Kolbert concluded her book, *Field Notes from a Catastrophe*, with this oft-quoted statement: "It may seem impossible to imagine that a technologically advanced society could choose, in essence, to destroy itself, but that is what we are now in the process of doing."[9]

- In 2007, Nobel laureate scientist Paul Crutzen said: "Global warming . . . [is] raising concerns about the [ability] of Earth's environment . . . to maintain viable human civilizations."[10]

- In 2009, Lester Brown, who founded the institute that has published the annual *State of the World* books, released an updated version of his 2003 book entitled *Plan B*, this time subtitled *Mobilizing to Save Civilization*.[11]

- Also in 2009, Brown published an article in *Scientific American* asking, "Could Food Shortages Bring Down Civilization?"[12]

- In 2010, National Medal of Science recipient Lonnie Thompson, explaining the new outspokenness of climate scientists, wrote: "Climatologists, like other scientists, tend to be a stolid group. We are not given to theatrical rantings about falling skies. . . . Why then are climatologists speaking out about the dangers of global warming? The answer is that virtually all of us are now convinced that global warming poses a clear and present danger to civilization."[13]

- Also in 2010, Pulitzer Prize-winner Ross Gelbspan wrote: "[A] growing number of scientific findings are focusing on the increased likelihood of abrupt and catastrophic changes. . . . [T]his problem is real. It threatens the survival of our civilization."[14]

- In 2011, former Vice President Al Gore, speaking of the climate crisis, said: "What hangs in the balance is the future of civilization as we know it."[15]

- In 2012, the 20 previous winners of the prestigious Blue Planet Prize issued a statement saying: "In the face of an absolutely unprecedented emergency, society has no choice but to take dramatic action to avert a collapse of civilization."[16]

- In 2013, Noam Chomsky wrote that "we are moving toward what may in fact be the ultimate genocide - the destruction of the environment."[17]

- In 2013, Paul and Anne Ehrlich, saying that an array of environmental problems, especially climate disruption, is threatening human civilization with collapse, added: "Humankind finds itself engaged in what Prince Charles described as 'an act of suicide on a grand scale.'"[18]

- In 2014, Tom Engelhardt said that climate change, besides being a "crime against humanity," is also a crime "against most living things," hence "terracide." And Naomi Oreskes and Erik Conway, who wrote *Merchants of Doubt* (which will be central to Chapter 11), published *The Collapse of Western Civilization: A View from the Future.*[19]

All of the above-named writers reflect Lester Brown's sentiment expressed in 2009: "Within the environmental community, we have talked for decades about saving the planet. But now we have a new challenge: to save civilization itself."[20] Suspecting that this idea would be ridiculed, Brown added:

> For most of us, the idea that civilization itself could disintegrate probably seems preposterous. Who would not find it hard to think seriously about such a complete departure from what we expect of ordinary life? What evidence could make us heed a warning so dire . . . ? We are so inured to a long list of highly unlikely catastrophes that we are virtually programmed to dismiss them all with a wave of the hand: Sure, our civilization

might devolve into chaos - and Earth might collide with an asteroid, too![21]

Those who ridiculed Brown's warning would seem to have been guilty, in Al Gore's words, of "confusing the unprecedented with the improbable."[22]

This book, entitled *Unprecedented*, provides reasons why we should be worried that civilization might be destroyed by changes in our climate. The discussion begins with establishing the relation of global warming to climate change, and of climate to weather.

Distinguishing Between Global Warming, Global Climate Change, and Weather

The terms "global warming" and "climate change" have often been used as if they were synonymous. However, as the website Skeptical Science has pointed out, these terms "refer to two different physical phenomena." The term "global warming" properly refers to the "long-term trend of a rising average global temperature," while "global climate change" refers to changes in the global climate that result from the global warming. Instead of being synonyms, "these [two terms] are related as cause and effect": Global warming causes global climate change.[23]

Failure to acknowledge, or consistently to employ, the distinction between "global warming" and "global climate change" can lead to confusion. This confusion has allowed critics – writing with sarcasm or intended humor - to say that global warming is disproved if Europe or the United States has an extra cold winter. One author even suggested that the 2010 winter showed "God's sense of humor."[24] However, such writers reveal only that they misunderstand the difference between *global warming*, *climate change*, and *weather*.

- "Global warming" refers to the mean (average) temperature of the planet as a whole.

- "Weather" refers to various phenomena created by atmospheric conditions in a limited region during a brief period of time (a few hours, a day, or a week) – phenomena such as sunshine, temperature, humidity, rain, and wind.

- "Climate" refers to a weather pattern that is characteristic of some area, such as Great Britain, southern France, or the American Southwest, during a longer period - perhaps 40 years, a century, a millennium, or even longer. Climate change occurs when the weather pattern that had been characteristic of that area changes to a different pattern. *Global* climate change concerns the planet as a whole.

The *weather* can be extremely variable, even within a few hours, whereas the *climate*, being the weather pattern of an area during an extended period, generally changes only slowly. Climate change can be detected, therefore, only by looking at fairly long periods. Accordingly, "a single bout of cold weather," as one writer put it, "doesn't actually say diddly squat about long-term climate patterns." Indeed, far from contradicting climate change, colder European winters are actually predicted by global warming science (due to the increased melting of Arctic ice).[25]

A closely related misconception is that the only indicator of climate change is a rise in air temperature. As White House science advisor John Holdren has pointed out: "The changes are not limited to increased average temperatures or warmer weather – they also mean more extreme and unstable weather conditions, more storms and floods, more droughts and more coastal erosion - as well as warmer weather in parts of the world."[26]

The tendency to equate "warming" with an increase in air temperature has led many people to say that, because the air temperature has not increased much over the past 15 years, global warming has hit a "pause button." This is a mistake, because about "90 percent of the warming of the planet is absorbed in heating the oceans." So, while "global surface air warming has slowed . . . the overall warming of the Earth's climate has sped up." All that has happened during the "faux pause," as some scientists call it, is that a higher percentage of the warming than previously went into the deep ocean.[27]

Moreover, if there was a pause in the surface temperature, it did not last: NASA reported that the surface temperatures during November 2013 were the warmest November temperatures on records.[28]

More Accurate Terminology: Climate Disruption, Breakdown, and Collapse

Although "climate change" has been the standard term for the effect of global warming, various people have expressed unhappiness with the term. British journalist George Monbiot called it a "ridiculously neutral term for the biggest potential catastrophe humankind has ever encountered." Holdren has long advocated that we instead speak of "climate disruption"; Monbiot suggested the term "climate breakdown"; and American academic David Orr has spoken of "climate collapse."[29]

The term "climate disruption" is certainly more descriptive of the kind of climate change being caused by global warming. But the terms "breakdown" and "collapse" should be used for only the most extreme types of climate change. Accordingly, I alternate between "climate change" and "climate disruption," except where ecosystem collapse is in view.

CO_2: The Primary Cause of Climate Change

Climate change is now primarily anthropogenic (human-caused) and has been fueled by greenhouse gases, the most important of which has been CO_2 (carbon dioxide). The concentration of CO_2 in the atmosphere has been increasing since the rise of the industrial age. From the beginning of civilization until the industrial revolution in the middle of the 18th century, CO_2 constituted only 275 ppm (parts per million) of the atmosphere. Since then, however, the planet's CO_2 has been rising at an ever-increasing rate. Between 1958 and 1968, it rose from 316 to 324 (as measured at the Mauna Loa Observatory in Hawaii). In each of the following decades, it rose more than the previous decade.

- By 1978, it had risen to 336.

- By 1988, to 352.

- By 1998, to 367.

- By 2008, to 386.

Then in only six years – from 2008 to 2014 – it rose from 386 to almost 400 ppm, on some days going over 400. By mid-2014, it had risen to 401.30. It has recently been rising, therefore, at about 2.5 ppm per year.[30]

In this entire period – from the pre-industrial age to the present - the planet's average temperature rose over 0.8 degrees Celsius ($0.8\,^{\circ}$C), which translates to over 1.4 degrees Fahrenheit ($1.4\,^{\circ}$F). This means that our planet has now reached, and probably surpassed, the "Holocene maximum" (the warmest period of the Holocene), which occurred about 8,000 years ago. We have no historical basis, therefore, to assume that civilization could continue under much higher temperatures.[31]

While the anthropogenic increase in the level of CO_2 in the atmosphere had long been suspected to be the primary cause of this global warming,[32] this suspicion became scientifically very probable by 1990. Since 2001, it has been considered an established scientific fact (even if some individuals and organizations, funded by fossil-fuel companies, have denied this).

This global warming has been significantly responsible for the various types of extreme weather that have recently been experienced. Although global warming is generally not the immediate cause of heat waves, droughts, and storms, it does make these phenomena more intense.

As suggested by George Lakoff: Global warming is a *systemic cause* of extreme weather events and, by analogy, "Smoking is a systemic cause of lung cancer. . . . Working in coal mines is a systemic cause of black lung disease. . . . Sex without contraception is a systemic cause of unwanted pregnancies."[33] Although these behaviors do not always produce such consequences, they make them more likely. Likewise, global warming is a systemic cause of extra-severe weather, making its occurrence more likely.

Moreover, CO_2 is also the main cause of some of the other negative consequences of global warming discussed in Part I: sea-level rise and the creation of climate refugees, along with the threats of ecosystem collapse and climate wars. Global warming also contributes to shortages of food and fresh water.

Drawing Red Lines for Increases of Temperature and CO_2 Concentration

Given the fact that the approximately 0.8 °C (1.4°F) rise from pre-industrial times has already had devastating consequences, it would seem obvious that we should, if possible, prevent climate disruption from becoming even worse.

But can we? Not completely: Because of a 30-year lag between CO_2 emissions and the manifestation of their effect on the climate,[34] another increase of at least 0.2°C in the planet's average temperature is already in the pipeline. So a total rise of at least 1°C is assured. As a result, there will be increasingly severe weather events, along with the other consequences of global warming, even if CO_2 emissions could be suddenly reduced to zero.[35]

Unfortunately, although politicians and some scientists have considered an increase of no more than 2°C (3.6°F) to be the "guardrail" against excessively dangerous global warming, James Hansen, generally regarded as the world's expert on these matters, has never accepted that view. In 2011, in fact, he declared that "a target of two degrees (Celsius) is actually a prescription for long-term disaster."[36] In support, journalist-turned-activist Bill McKibben has said, "the one degree we've raised the temperature already has melted the Arctic, so we're fools to find out what two will do."[37]

Although it was widely said, on the assumption that a CO_2 concentration of 450 ppm would keep the temperature below 2°C, that 450 ppm would be safe, Hansen in 2008 had already said that the concentration of CO_2 in the atmosphere needed to be brought back down to "350 ppm or less."[38]

Speaking to both issues in 2013, Hansen and 17 other scientists said that civilization should have the twofold aim of (1) returning to 350 ppm or lower, and (2) stabilizing the temperature at an increase of 1 ° C.[39] Although this view is sometimes seen as a radical lowering of the safe limit, it is simply a return to the original position.[40]

The Budget Approach

There has been a growing conviction among climate scientists that stating the target in terms of a concentration of CO_2 is insufficiently precise, because of the lag between a given concentration and the eventual temperature change and because scientists have an imperfect understanding of "climate sensitivity" (meaning the temperature increase to be caused by a doubling of the preindustrial CO_2 concentration of 275 ppm to 550 ppm).[41]

A more precise approach, they say, deals with "the climate response to emissions, rather than concentrations, of carbon dioxide," which works because "global temperature change is approximately linearly related to a given amount of cumulative carbon dioxide emissions." Hence, by calculating emissions, scientists can tell policy-makers the amount of total CO_2 emissions that must not be exceeded to prevent unacceptable climate disruption. Just as families or state governments must live within a budget, the world must live within a carbon budget, which indicates the maximum amount of additional CO_2 that can be put into the atmosphere without going beyond a given temperature.[42]

Even if the temperature to stay below is set at 2°C, staying within the carbon budget will be difficult, because "past greenhouse gas emissions [roughly 500 gigatons, meaning 500 billion tons, of CO_2] have already committed us to warming of around 1°C," and another 500 billion tons would put the warming above 2°C. That being too high, the cumulative emissions of CO_2 by 2050, climate scientists say, must be no more than 750 billion tons, which means that there can be no more than an additional 250 gigatons between now and 2050.[43]

Moreover, once the global fossil CO_2 emissions are capped in 2050 at 750 gigatons, there could be "only a small residual amount being emitted post-2050," meaning that "a virtually zero-emission economy must have emerged." There is no time to waste, because at current emission rates, "this CO_2 budget will be exhausted within around 25 years – and even sooner if emissions continue to rise."[44] Indeed, one of the authors of this approach admitted that, when he first saw the numbers, he was "terrified." The IPCC in 2013 endorsed this budget approach.[45]

Even more terrifying is the need to reduce emissions sufficiently to keep the temperature increase close to 1°C. In terms of not exceeding a CO_2 concentration of 350 ppm, Bill McKibben has argued in "Global Warming's

Terrifying New Math" that there can be no more than "roughly 565 more gigatons of carbon dioxide into the atmosphere by midcentury." However, "carbon emissions are now growing at about 3% a year, so "at the present rate, we'll blow through our 565-gigaton allowance in 16 years."

Accordingly, the final chapter of this book, which describes the need for *unprecedented mobilization*, is no exaggeration.

Looking Ahead

Warnings such as those quoted at the beginning of this chapter - that civilization itself will likely be destroyed unless the world is mobilized immediately - have been repeatedly enunciated, by people and organizations of the highest credibility. But no such mobilization has occurred. None of America's major media have expressed the urgency for such mobilization and only a few of its political leaders. Why has America not launched a mobilization to save civilization comparable to the American mobilization for World War II?

A complete answer would include many elements. One of these is that there has been an effective campaign, financed by coal, oil, and gas lobbies, to discredit the reality of global warming, at least human-caused global warming (to be discussed in Chapter 11, "Climate Change Denial"). Another factor is that the fossil-fuel industry has convinced many politicians, usually by means of more-or-less subtle bribes, to deny that climate change is a problem requiring strong legislation (see Chapter 13, "Political Failure"). But the most important reason for American complacency is the fact that the major media have failed to convey the seriousness of the problem (see Chapter 12, "Media Failure").

There are still other reasons. One is that the most powerful type of American religion generally denies that climate change is a serious religious and moral issue (see 14, "Moral Challenge," and Chapter 15, "Religious Challenge"). Another is that America's economic establishment has portrayed steps to address climate change as a threat to continued economic growth (see Chapter 16, "Economic Challenge").

As a result of these blockages, most Americans, including national politicians, have not yet understood just how disastrous climate disruption will increasingly be for themselves and, especially, for their children, grandchildren, and all future generations. These features determine this book's focus:

- The dimensions of climate change from which human beings will directly suffer.
- The threat of climate change to human beings (although I have long taken a non-anthropomorphic point of view, emphasizing the intrinsic value of all creatures).[46]

- The threat to America, not because its welfare is more important than that of other countries, but because America has made the greatest contribution to the global-warming threat and also has the greatest potential – along with China – for leading the world in mitigating it. Although people in other countries understandably bristle at America's self-description as "the indispensable nation," any hope for getting out of the CO_2 crisis will certainly require American leadership.

America's Response to the Crisis: Three Possibilities

As Americans become more aware of the seriousness of global warming, with its potential to cause a complete climate breakdown, the next question is: How will American leaders respond to the threat? This could be discussed in terms of three possible responses: Plans A, B, and C. The term "Plan B" is used as Lester Brown uses it in his book *Plan B*, along with his follow-up book, *A World on the Edge*.[47] In the latter book, Brown described Plan B as the goal of cutting carbon emissions rapidly "to avoid civilization-threatening climate change. This is not Plan A, business as usual. This is Plan B - a wartime mobilization, an all-out effort to restructure the world energy economy."[48]

However, although I use "Plan A" and "Plan B" in basically the same way, I discuss them in reverse order, plus adding a third possibility, Plan C, the wait-and-see approach.

Plans B, A, and C

An outline that closely approximates our three responses was provided in 2008 by Vicky Pope, the head of the Met Office Hadley Centre, which is the UK's leading climate change organization. She wrote: "The latest climate projections from the Met Office Hadley Centre show the possible range of temperature rises, depending on what action is taken to reduce Greenhouse gas emissions":

- "Even with large and early cuts in emissions [similar to our Plan B], the indications are that temperatures are likely to rise to around 2°C above pre-industrial levels by the end of the century."

- "If action is delayed or not quick enough [similar to our Plan C], there is a large risk of much bigger increases in temperature [beyond those in Plan B], with some severe impacts."

- "In a worst-case scenario [similar to our Plan A], where no action is taken to check the rise in Greenhouse gas emissions, temperatures would most likely rise by more than 5°C by the end of the century. This would lead to significant risks of severe and irreversible impacts."[49]

Plan B

Our Plan B is the same as Vicky Pope's first possibility, except that, in light of Hansen's declaration that a 2°C (3.6°F) rise would be a "disaster," we should have a target significantly below 2°C. This might be possible if the United States, China, and the other nations move into full and rapid mobilization, beginning in 2015, to deal radically with the CO_2 crisis.

However, because of changes that have already occurred or are impossible to prevent, the Earth will never be the planet on which civilization arose, and into which most people alive today were born. For example, the melted mountain glaciers will not come back, the sea level will not go back down, and the weather will not return to what had long been considered normal – at least in the foreseeable future. To symbolize this difference between the present planet and the one on which civilization was built, Bill McKibben entitled his 2010 book *Eaarth*. This new planet will be quite difficult for people, compared with the planet of the 20th and preceding centuries. But if Plan B is carried out, living in our world will be, while unpleasant, not hell – physicist Joe Romm has called it "Planetary Purgatory."[50]

Plan A

A second possibility is that the world's political leaders simply continue with business as usual indefinitely. It can rightfully be called Plan A, because it is the plan the world has followed thus far. If we continue this plan, the world *will* become what David Roberts has called "hell on earth." The hellish existence will then be followed – if business as usual continues – by the extinction of civilization. This would likely lead to the need for the angels to write - in Australian writer Clive Hamilton's phrase – a "requiem for a species."[51]

Plan C

A third possibility, which we can call Plan C, is that the present political leaders of the United States – along with those of China, the other chief emitter of CO_2 – will delay. Thinking that the scientists' predictions might be wrong, they take a wait-and-see approach. Not wanting to cut back on fossil fuels for fear that this would needlessly reduce economic growth, they do not begin an all-out switch to clean energy until seeing unambiguous evidence that human-caused global warming will result in intolerably extreme weather and shortages of fresh water and food. If later experience shows that the scientific warnings were correct, society can quickly quit adding emissions, then reverse the process. But this plan involves several problems:

- There is a lag of about 30 years between the emissions of CO_2 and the climate-change effects. By the time the wait-and-see advocates have seen, for example, that a CO_2 concentration of 450 ppm, or an average temperature increase of 1.5 °C, has intolerable consequences, their wait-and-see approach will have set in motion climate changes that their children and grandchildren will find *beyond* intolerable. This problem was already stated in 1979 by Verner Suomi of the National Academy of Sciences, who wrote: "A wait-and-see policy may mean waiting until it is too late."[52]

- Plan C assumes that, if we simply eliminate any new emissions, the carbon in the atmosphere will dissipate, just as smoke does. However, recent scientific studies have shown that carbon is nothing like smoke. Instead, as the title of an article puts it, "Carbon is Forever" – with "forever" meaning at least 1,000 years.[53]

- Americans who take the wait-and-see approach may assume that the effects of global climate change will not be very serious for the United States, compared with most other countries. However, the Climate Vulnerability Monitor says that, among the so-called Umbrella Group (Australia, Canada, Iceland, Japan, New Zealand, Norway, the Russian Federation, the United States, and Ukraine), only the vulnerability of the United States is "acute."[54]

Conclusion

It is possible that, although Plan C would result in a hellish existence, it might allow us, if we are lucky, to avoid extinction. More likely, however, the results would ultimately be no different from those of Plan A. The only rational option, therefore, is Plan B. As Princeton climate scientist Michael Oppenheimer has said: "We still have a choice, even if it's only a choice between pain and disaster."[55] Whether we choose Plan B, A, or C will determine whether humanity in future decades will experience life as unpleasant, hellish, or not at all.

1

EXTREME WEATHER

In the ten years from 2001 to 2010, the planet
"experienced unprecedented high-impact climate extremes."
— World Meteorological Organization, 2013

"The climate has shifted to a new state capable of delivering
rare and unprecedented weather events."
— Jeff Masters, Weather Underground, 2012

The first part of this book deals with a number of features of climate change — better called "climate disruption" — that constitute unprecedented threats to human civilization, even human existence itself.

The first four chapters deal with extreme weather, sometimes called "climate gone wild." Chapters 2, 3, and 4 treat three types of extreme weather: heat waves, droughts, and extreme storms of various types (hurricanes, tornadoes, extreme rain, and extreme snow storms). The present chapter discusses extreme weather in general, which in 2012 was called "Climate Story of the Year" by physicist Joe Romm, who founded the website Climate Progress.[1]

The New Normal

In recent years, extreme weather has become increasingly common. Indeed, commentators have come to refer to such weather as the "new normal":

- In 2011, Bill McKibben wrote an article entitled "Weather Extremes: Are You Ready for the New Normal?" and paleoclimatologist Curt Stager published an article entitled "The 'New Normal' Weather," in which he said: "It seems like there is a new flood, tornado, or hurricane every day. Is this the kind of meteorological insanity we need to learn to expect?"[2]

- In 2012, after Hurricane Sandy hit New York, Governor Andrew Cuomo declared: "Extreme weather is the new normal," and the acting director of the U.S. National Weather Service, said: "The normal has changed, I guess. The normal is extreme."[3]

- By 2013 and 2014, there were many similar stories, with names such as "Wild Weather: Extreme is the New Normal," "Fasten Your Seatbelt – Weather Whiplash is the New Normal," and "Abnormal is the New Normal." A CNN story in 2014 said, "Welcome to another a typical day in America, a day marred by weather-related carnage. Ponder the new normal."[4]

This new normal did not come about gradually. Joe Romm spoke instead of a "quantum jump in extreme weather" – a phenomenon requiring an explanation.[5]

The Connection to Global Warming

For a long time, climate and weather commentators said that, due to natural weather variability, no particular extreme event could be attributed to global warming. In 2011, however, Kevin Trenberth, who at the time headed up the Climate Analysis Section at the U.S. National Center for Atmospheric Research, told the *New York Times:* "Global warming is contributing to an increased incidence of extreme weather because the environment in which all storms form has changed from human activities." And in 2012, James Hansen argued that some extreme anomalies can be attributed to global warming in this sense: "We can say with high confidence that such extreme anomalies would not have occurred in the absence of global warming."[6]

Global warming causes these events, Hansen argued, by virtue of having "loaded the dice." This loading can be seen by comparing the 1951-1980 period, when extremely hot summers covered only one percent of the Earth's land, with the 1980-2010 period, when the area covered by heat waves was 10 percent. So whereas there was a 1-in-300 chance of extreme summers in the earlier period, there was a nearly 1-in-10 chance in the later period.[7]

Another metaphor for global warming is "steroids for the atmosphere."[8] A baseball slugger who would normally hit 40 home runs in a season might, after taking steroids, hit 73. Of course, a baseball player who cannot even make contact with the ball will not, by taking steroids, start hitting home runs; nor will global warming create hurricanes where the minimal conditions do not exist. But just as steroids can help sluggers hit more balls with sufficient intensity to clear the outfield wall, a tropical storm might turn a hurricane or an ordinary heat wave into a once-in-a-thousand-years hurricane or heat wave due to an increase in the energy in the atmosphere.[9] That extreme weather in recent years has been influenced by global warming is strongly indicated by the fact that increases in the level of CO_2 in the atmosphere have been followed by increases in extreme weather events.

In recent decades, as the concentration of CO_2 in the atmosphere has been increasing dramatically, there have also been dramatic increases in extreme-weather events.

- In 2010, Jeff Masters said: "In my thirty years as a meteorologist, I've never seen global weather patterns as strange as those we had in 2010. The stunning extremes we witnessed gives me concern that our climate is showing the early signs of instability."[10]

- In 2011, the IPCC published a special report on extreme weather, saying: "A changing climate . . . can result in unprecedented extreme weather and climate events." The report's lead author said: "It's really dramatic how many of the patterns that we've talked about as the expression of the extremes are hitting the U.S. right now."[11]

- In March 2012, Michigan and surrounding states had "a ten-day stretch of unprecedented record-smashing intensity," which was dubbed "Summer in March," as temperatures reached almost 90°F.[12] Jeff Masters said that this event "ranks as one of North America's most extraordinary weather events in recorded history."[13]

- In 2013, the *Guardian* entitled its story about the year in review, to prove that climate change is here to those who still doubted: "A Year of Increasing Extreme Weather Events."[14]

Then in 2014, it was as if the weather gods decided to prove to those who still doubted that climate change is here:

- In February, the *Guardian's* John Vidal wrote: "There have been heatwaves in Slovenia and Australia. . . . Britain has had its wettest winter in 250 years but temperatures in parts of Russia and the Arctic have been 10°C above normal. Meanwhile, the southern hemisphere has had the warmest start to a year ever recorded, with millions of people sweltering in Brazilian and southern African cities. . . . [T]he first six weeks of 2014 have seen an unusual number of extremes of heat, cold and rain – not just in a few regions as might be expected in any winter, but right the way around the world at the same time."[15]

- In May, the *San Diego Free Press* said: "The last week in April saw extreme weather over as much as half the nation. Over 20 states were affected. In some places a month's worth of rain fell in a day. In New York City there was close to 5 inches of rain in one day. In Pensacola, FL there was over 20 inches of rain in 24 hours, 6 inches in one hour alone, more rain than Los Angeles saw all last year. More rain fell in Pensacola than during Hurricane Ivan. There were nearly 6000 lightning strikes in fifteen minutes. . . . Two trillion gallons of water fell on the south and the east coast in just one day."[16]

More examples of 2014's extreme weather are provided in Chapters 2-4. In the meantime, one specific kind of extreme weather requires discussion here.

Extreme Snow and Global Warming

Critics of the scientific community's view about global warming and climate disruption often write as if cold, snowy weather contradicted this view. For example, Steve Doocy of Fox News pointed out one morning that New York City had received a lot of snow the previous night, after which he said: "I wonder where Al Gore is this morning? . . . That global warming is really taking its toll. Isn't it?" In the middle of the extreme cold spell of January 2014, Donald Trump tweeted: "This very expensive GLOBAL WARMING bullshit has got to stop. Our planet is freezing, record low temps, and our GW scientists are stuck in ice."[17]

But these comments, rather than being wickedly clever, simply reflect a failure to understand that global warming and climate change have a *cause-effect relationship*. To repeat points made in the introduction:

1. Talking about global warming is not the same as talking about the weather or even the climate of some time and place. Rather, "global warming" refers to a gradually increasing average temperature of the planet as a whole.

2. Global warming has been bringing about climate disruption of various types: It can make hurricanes and tornadoes more intense; it can cause, or at least intensify, drought; it can make summers hotter; it can bring about downpours, or at least make them heavier; it can make snowstorms heavier. In an article asking, "Does Record Snowfall Disprove Global Warming?" Skeptical Science answers:

> Warming causes more moisture in the air which leads to more extreme precipitation events. This includes more heavy snowstorms in regions where snowfall conditions are favorable. Far from contradicting global warming, record snowfall is predicted by climate models. . . . As climate warms, evaporation from the ocean increases. This results in more water vapor in the air. . . . The extra moisture in the air is expected to produce more precipitation, including more extreme precipitation events. . . . Snowstorms can occur if temperatures are in the range of -10°C to 0°C. . . . In northern, colder regions, temperatures are often too cold for very heavy snow so warming can bring more favorable snowstorm conditions.[18]

Extreme Weather and Global Warming: Some Arguments

There are many arguments for the idea that climate disruption is being caused by global warming, some of which are based on extreme weather events. Here are three:

The Experiential Argument

It was long predicted that a lot of people would not accept the connections between CO_2, global warming, and climate change until the latter becomes serious climate disruption. And now, polls and interviews have shown that, among people who had not accepted statements by scientists, a growing percentage have been changing their views because of recent extreme weather events. Suzanne Goldenberg of the *Guardian* wrote an article entitled "Extreme Weather More Persuasive on Climate Change than Scientists."[19] And right after Hurricane Sandy, Bill McKibben said:

> It's experience that changes people: the summer's drought left more than half of American counties as federal disaster areas, and meteorologist Jeff Masters estimates Sandy hit 100 million Americans with 'extreme weather.' Add in the largest forest fires in Colorado and New Mexico, the hottest month in US history, and the completely absurd summer-in-March heatwave that kicked off our year of living sweatily, and you can begin to understand why the percentage of Americans worrying about global warming has spiked sharply this year.[20]

In a 2010 article entitled "A Case for Global Warming," *New York Times* journalist Justin Gillis wrote:

> The floods battered New England, then Nashville, then Arkansas, then Oklahoma — and were followed by a deluge in Pakistan that has upended the lives of 20 million people. The summer's heat waves baked the eastern United States, parts of Africa and eastern Asia, and above all Russia, which lost millions of acres of wheat and thousands of lives in a drought worse than any other in the historical record.

Gillis then pointed out that outcomes predicted by the theory of global warming – "heavier rainstorms in summer, bigger snowstorms in winter, more intense droughts in at least some places and more record-breaking heat waves" – were starting to happen. Moreover, pointing out that Russians had previously opposed actions to limit climate change, Gillis indicated that Russia's 2010 summer – with extreme heat, drought, and wildfires – changed minds: "Everyone is talking about climate change now," Russia's then-president Dmitri A. Medvedev told the country's Security Council, "because we have never in our history faced such weather conditions."[21]

Record Highs vs. Record Lows: A Statistical Argument

Gillis then gave a statistical argument, saying:

> If the earth were not warming, random variations in the weather should cause about the same number of record-breaking high temperatures and record-breaking low temperatures over a given period. But climatologists have long theorized that in a warming world, the added heat would cause more record highs and fewer record lows. The statistics suggest that is exactly what is happening.[22]

In 2013, weather historian Christopher Burt, after reporting that "2012 has been the warmest calendar year on record for the continental U.S.," said: "What was truly astonishing, however, was the ratio of heat records versus cold records that was established over the course of the year."[23] Looking at the months in 2012 with record high temperatures and months with record lows, Burt found the ratio to have been 362 to 0, which is, Burt said, "truly astonishing."[24]

Increase in Weather-Related Financial Losses

Another argument has been formulated by Dr. Peter Hoeppe, who heads the Geo Risks Research Department of the insurance giant, Munich Re. He said:

> For me the most convincing piece of evidence that global warming has been contributing already to more and more intense weather-related natural catastrophes is the fact that while we find a steep increase in the number of [financial] loss-relevant weather events (about tripling in the last 30 years) we only find a slight increase in geophysical (earthquake, volcano, tsunami) events, which should not be affected by global warming.

Hoeppe explained: "If the whole trend we find in weather-related disaster should be caused by reporting bias, or socio-demographic or economic developments, we would expect to find it similarly for the geophysical events."[25]

The Arctic Connection

Climate scientists have for many years been concerned that the Arctic sea ice has been melting. This concern became much stronger in 2007, due to record melting that summer, in which the surface area of the sea ice floating in the ocean went down 23 percent. In 2012, a new low in the amount of sea ice resulted from an even larger ice melt, which scientists described as "amazing," "astonishing," and "unprecedented." Research showed that by 2012 there was "a 45 percent reduction in the area covered by sea ice compared to the 1980s and 1990s."[26]

Even more important is the loss of volume: A project to model the sea ice had said that the ice had evidently lost 75 to 80 percent of its volume. Although this estimate was widely considered extreme, data from a satellite created to study the polar ice caps revealed in 2013 that this estimate "may have been *too conservative.*"[27]

Climate watchers have pointed out that there are various reasons for concern. The loss of Arctic ice, recent studies have shown, is even more important than previously thought. A 2012 study led by Jennifer Francis of Rutgers University showed that enhanced Arctic warming, by producing accelerated sea ice loss, increases the probability of extreme weather events "such as drought, flooding, cold spells, and heat waves." This discovery was not simply one among others: "The story of the decade," said Romm, "is the collapse of Arctic sea ice and its impact on our extreme weather."[28]

In 2013 and 2014, the relation between the Arctic and extreme weather, especially in the United States, became widely known, because of a phenomenon known as *the polar vortex*. Indeed, news stories turned "polar vortex" into a household expression. Bloomberg BusinessWeek said that the term had "taken an uncontested lead in the competition for buzzword of 2014." The *Christian Science Monitor* said: "A bitter Arctic blast spanning the central and eastern US has propelled the phrase 'polar vortex' from the pages of dense scientific papers to headline status."[29]

The phrase was well explained by *Time* magazine's Bryan Walsh, who wrote that "global warming could be making the occasional bout of extreme cold weather in the U.S. even more likely." Explaining that a polar vortex "is pretty much what it sounds like: a whirlwind of extremely cold, extremely dense air that forms near the poles," Walsh said that its fast winds normally keep the air locked up, but "when the winds weaken, the vortex can begin to wobble like a drunk on his fourth martini, and the Arctic air can escape and spill southward, bringing Arctic weather with it."[30]

The relation of the polar vortex to the strange winter weather was explained in a Climate Progress story entitled "Hot Alaska, Cold Georgia: How the Shifted Polar Vortex Turned Winter Upside-Down," which noted:

> The polar vortex, normally tucked away much closer to the Arctic, has swept down several times this winter, bringing cold temperatures and snow to large segments of the U.S. east of the Rockies. . . . This leaves the far north [such as Alaska] much warmer than normal.[31]

The Arctic changes have also brought about what Romm calls the "quantum jump in extreme weather" in the summer, because the jet stream in the Northern Hemisphere sometimes splits into two. The weird weather in the summer of 2013, with extremely hot weather in Alaska occurring simultaneously with record flooding further south, resulted from this dual jet stream. This pattern was even more extreme in the summer of 2014, as Arctic ice continued to melt, leading NASA to say:

> In places where it should be seasonably hot – the eastern and southern United States and western Europe – it's just been warm. In places where weather is usually mild in the summer - northern Europe, the Pacific coast of North America - it has been ridiculously hot.

NASA then continued:

> Records for high temperatures . . . were approached or broken in Latvia, Poland, Belarus, Estonia, Lithuania, and Sweden in late July and early August. Searing temperatures also dried out forests and fuelled wildfires in Siberia; in the U.S. states of Oregon, Washington, and California; in the Canadian provinces of British Columbia, Alberta, and Northwest Territories; and even in Sweden. At the same time, cool air moved from high northern latitudes into much of the U.S., setting record-low daytime and nighttime temperatures as far south as Florida and Georgia. Temperatures dropped to the winter-like levels in the mountains of Tennessee.[32]

Likewise, California's drought continued while "the East Coast [saw] off-the-charts flooding." The deluges result when jet stream waves of a particular type (Rossby waves) "become virtually stalled and greatly amplified," leading to "midlatitude synchronization of extreme heat and rainfall events." Saying that this discovery of "why extreme weather has begun running amok may be one of the most important and consequential scientific findings in recent years," Joe Romm includes it in the mounting evidence "that we have entered a new regime of extreme weather thanks to our as-yet unrestricted emissions of greenhouse gas."[33]

Three Possible Responses: Plans B, A, and C

Let us now look at the three possible responses discussed in the Introduction, Plans A, B, and C, with the first two discussed in reverse order:

Plan B

The IPCC's "Special Report on Extreme Weather," which appeared in 2011, said:

> The report shows that if we do not stop the current steep rise in atmospheric levels of greenhouse gases, we will see much more warming and dramatic changes in extreme weather that are likely to overwhelm any attempts human populations might make to adapt to their impacts.[34]

But if we do stop this steep rise and also institute a crash program to cut back radically on greenhouse gases, we could prevent the extreme weather from getting terribly worse. The weather will, to be sure, become more unpleasant for the next few decades in most of the world. But it might not, in most places, become hellish.

Plan A

Plan A would be to continue business as usual. This might mean not only failing to reduce our use of greenhouse gases but also to continue increasing this use. As Bill McKibben says, "If we stay on our current path, our children will live on a super-heated planet [whose mean global temperature is] four or five degrees warmer than it is right now."[35] Moreover, there would be no stopping point. Weather will continue to become more extreme.

Plan C

According to Plan C, we would wait to see whether the dire predictions made by climate scientists start to become true: We would wait to see whether the planet's average temperature does increase to 2° or 2.5°C higher than in pre-industrial times and, if so, whether the predicted climate changes start to become true, at which point we could start instituting more-or-less radical changes. But for reasons explained earlier, this plan will have results little different from Plan A.

Conclusion

Plan B is the only possible way to prevent *extreme weather* from becoming *intolerable weather*.

2

HEAT WAVES

"A 4°C world would be one of unprecedented heat waves."
– World Bank, *Turn Down the Heat,* 2012

"The current heatwave – in terms of its duration, its intensity and its extent – is now unprecedented in our records."
– David Jones, Australia's Bureau of Meteorology, 2013

The present chapter focuses on the phenomenon that comes to mind most readily when people think of "global warming" – namely, that the world's weather will become warmer. And, indeed, it is already becoming very uncomfortable in places, even deadly.

Heat Waves in the United States

There are clear signs that summer weather in the United States has become warmer:

- In 1988, America experienced the first heat wave to be partially blamed on global warming.[1] This heat wave led to historic testimony before Congress by Dr. James Hansen, in which he stated that human-caused global warming is definitely occurring.[2]

- Starting in 1998, hotter weather appeared to be a regular phenomenon in America, with 13 of the 14 hotter years on record appearing in the 21st century.[3]

- In 2005, there was a two-week, widespread heat wave, with record high temperatures from Alaska to Colorado to Florida, and above-100 temperatures in cities from Phoenix to New York.[4]

- June 2010 had a heat wave during which cities in South Carolina, Tennessee, and Illinois reached 109°F (43°C), their hottest June temperatures ever.[5]

- The 2011 year was even hotter: The summer broke 2,000 records, and July was the hottest month that had ever been recorded in the contiguous USA.[6]

- In 2012, the temperature became still hotter in places: Kansas reached 118°F (48°C) in June, and the 48 contiguous states experienced, from January through August, the warmest eight-month period ever. July 2012 not only exceeded the temperature of the previous July, but it was "the hottest of any month on record." By the end of 2012, it had turned out to be the warmest year ever recorded for the 48 contiguous states. The record exceeded the old one, set in 1998, by a full degree.[7]

- June 2013 brought scorching weather to the Western U.S. Many flights were canceled and highway pavements buckled. It was so hot in Phoenix that "tigers at the zoo were served frozen fish treats and elephants were doused with hoses to keep them from overheating." California's Death Valley reached 129°F, tying the highest June temperature ever recorded in the country, and officials pleaded with visitors to quit frying eggs on the pavement. Alaska, moreover, was so hot that AP headlined its story "Baked Alaska." Then July brought a high-pressure "heat dome" that covered two-thirds of the country.[8]

- In 2014, California in the first eight months experienced its warmest 8-month period on record, and August was the hottest month of August since records have been kept. Indeed, being 1.35°F above the 20th-century average, August's temperature was "the largest departure from average of any month on record." Although the eastern U.S. had an average summer, this was not true of the West or of most of the world, including West Antarctica, which was 4°C to 8°C (7°F to 14°F) above average.[9]

Heat Waves Worldwide

In addition to the unprecedented heat in the United States, there has been unprecedented heat elsewhere in the world. For example:

- In 2003, a heat wave covered the Western part of Europe and lasted for weeks. It was so much hotter than previous heat waves that, for example, Great Britain reached 100°F (38.5°C) for the first time ever.[10]

- In 2010, a heat wave in Eastern Europe and Russia covered an area even bigger than the 2003 heat wave, and there was a record-breaking heat wave in the Middle East: Iraq set a new record of 52°C (126°F), and Israel had its warmest year ever, with the temperature at the Dead Sea climbing in August to 51°C (125°F).[11]

- The 2012-2013 summer in Australia, labeled the "Angry Summer," was the country's hottest season ever. Due to a "dome of heat," Australia also had its hottest day ever, averaging 40.3°C (105°F) over the entire country, while reaching almost 48°C (118°F) at places. "Never before in 103 years of record keeping," said Jeff Masters, "has a heat wave this intense, wide-spread, and long-lasting affected Australia." The Climate Commission said: "Extreme heatwaves and catastrophic bushfire conditions during the 'Angry Summer' were made worse by climate change." Moreover, the "Angry Summer" was follow by the "Abnormal Autumn," resulting in Australia's hottest two years ever recorded.[12]

- In 2013, Siberia, which typically does not get warmer than 60°F, hit 90°F. "Even Verkhoyansk, a contender for coldest continuously-inhabited city in the world, posted an 82 degree day." Europe had a very hot July, after which it became even hotter in August, with Austria having its highest temperature ever, 104.9°F (40.5°C). And China had its worst heat wave since records were kept, with 40 cities remaining above 104°F (40°C) for 31 days.[13]

- In 2014, China experienced the hottest month of May ever, and India experienced its longest heat wave and hottest May-June period ever – so hot that the streets of Delhi were virtually empty. One young professional said, "Every day, the heat seems to be getting more intense and is not bearable anymore." The fact that these and some other countries had their hottest-ever summers – although 2014 was a relatively cool summer for the USA – fits with the fact that the three months from April through June constituted the planet's warmest quarter of all time, with July not far behind.[14]

Although what has already happened is bad enough, climate scientists say that the heat is going to become far worse. In "Mother Nature Is Just Getting Warmed Up," Joe Romm reported a study showing that, whereas through the 1970s new records for cold temperatures exceeded record highs, by now the highs exceed the lows 13 to 1. Romm also quoted the statement by Stanford University's Noah Deffenbaugh that "by the middle of this century, even the coolest summers will be hotter than the hottest summers of the past 50 years."[15]

Extremely Hot Days and Heat Deaths

"What matters most to humans directly is not average temperatures, but hot extremes" in inhabited areas, a 2014 report pointed out. "Extremely hot days" are defined as ones that are above the 90th percentile for the region at issue. Over the past 15 years, this report said, the number of very hot days over land has soared: "the amount of land that saw more than 50 extreme warm days above the long-term average increased multi-fold." Extremely hot days matter most to us because of their effects on human health (as well as agriculture, infrastructure and ecosystems). The health effects often involve heat death.[16]

Although we naturally think of heat as the obvious sign of global warming, what first comes to mind when we think about weather-related deaths is usually not heat but dramatic things such as hurricanes, tornadoes, and floods. However, according to the National Weather Service, "Heat is the number one weather-related killer in the United States, resulting in hundreds of fatalities each year." Indeed, the report said, on average "excessive heat claims more lives each year than floods, lightning, tornadoes and hurricanes combined."[17]

- The aforementioned 1988 heat wave killed 5,000 to 10,000 people.

- "In 2006, a brutal heat wave that spread throughout most of the U.S. was responsible for or contributed to the deaths of 140 people in New York City alone."

- By 2013, the number of heat deaths in America had risen to 660.[18]

Other countries have, of course, also suffered many heat deaths. For example:

- The aforementioned European heat wave of 2003 was at first estimated to have killed about 35,000 people, but this figure was later revised upwards to as many as 70,000.[19]

- The final estimate of the deaths caused by Russia's aforementioned 2010 heat wave was 50,000.[20]

- In Australia's 2009 heat wave, over 375 deaths occurred (not counting the 170 who died in the resulting Black Saturday bush fires).[21]

- Although China news agencies spoke of only a few dozen deaths in its 2013 heat wave, "suspicions emerged that Chinese officials are covering up what are potentially thousands of heat-related deaths."[22]

- In 2013, a heat wave in the UK took over 700 lives, and a heat wave in the Indian state of Hyderabad killed over 500 people.[23]

Furthermore, experts say that heat deaths will surely rise dramatically. For example:

- By 2050, heat deaths in eastern U.S. cities will likely increase ten-fold, much more if greenhouse gas (GHG) emissions continue.[24]

- In Australia, where extreme heat has killed more people than any other natural hazard in modern times, an unprecedented heat wave in 2009 killed close to 400 people in Victoria alone, and Australian heat deaths are expected to quadruple by 2050.[25]

Hotter and Hotter

The increasing heat waves reflect the fact that, over the past 30 years, the planet has become warmer, and this trend continued in 2014. March-May was the warmest three-month period ever, April was tied for the highest April ever, May and June were the hottest months for those months ever, and "32 countries across every continent except Antarctica had at least one station reporting a record high temperature for July" (NOAA). Scandinavia was especially warm in July, with Norway and Latvia having their warmest months ever.[26]

Let us now look at three possible responses to the evidence that the United States, along with the world in general, is getting hotter.

Three Possible Responses

Plan B

If the world quickly mobilizes to deal with global warming, carbon emissions that have already been emitted will continue to raise the planet's average temperature, so warmer weather will make life quite unpleasant for Americans and most of the rest of the world. Heat waves will be even hotter than those since 2010, and they will occur more regularly than before. Nevertheless, life for most people , while more unpleasant than before, will not be intolerable.

Plan A

Plan A, continuing business as usual indefinitely, will have fierce consequences.

"Without a change in policy," said the International Energy Agency in 2008, the world will be "on a path for a rise in global temperature of up to 6 degrees C [11˚F]" by the end of the century. A 2009 study by MIT gave roughly the same projection, saying that business as usual would lead to an average warming of more than 5°C (9°F) by 2100. And a 2012 report by the National Center for Atmospheric Research projected that the doubling of carbon dioxide (from 270 to 550 ppm) will produce a global temperature rise of more than 7°F (4˚C). If current emission trends continue, that temperature will be reached long before the end of this century, so that by 2100, said Romm, "warming would likely exceed 11 degrees F — possibly by a few degrees!"[27]

With regard to the United States in particular, a 2009 government report said that, if we continue with business as usual, the average temperature of most of the inland USA will increase from 9 to 11°F by 2090." In an article about this report called "Our Hellish Future," Romm pointed out that these *average* temperatures for inland America as a whole would mean *extreme* temperatures in the central, southern, and western United States that would rise to 122°F (50°C).[28] How could those of us who can hardly tolerate 100°F contemplate with equanimity our grandchildren suffering temperatures 10 to 20 degrees higher?

This issue was raised in a 2010 report saying that future temperatures in the world could *exceed livable limits*. More specifically, it said that global warming would likely, sometime in the next century, lead the planet to "a 21-degree [F] warming," which "would put half of the world's population in an uninhabitable environment."[29] This would mean, of course, that half of the world's population (some five billion people) would either die or else move to those places that are still inhabitable, thereby making those places much more crowded.

More immediately, some scientists have determined that, if business as usual continues, 2047 will bring *climate departure*, "when the old maximum average temperatures become the new minimum temperatures."[30]

Plan C

According to those who advocate a wait-and-see approach, the warnings about continuing business as usual are probably exaggerations, so we should wait, perhaps 20 years, to see whether the predictions about rising temperatures start to come true. If they do, leading perhaps toward a global temperature increase of 3 or 4°C, these Plan C advocates say, we can deal with the problem at that stage. In any case, they assume, the temperatures will not be unbearable.

However, tens of thousands of people have already found the heat waves of this new century to be unbearable – they have died from them.

And yet these heat waves occurred when the global average temperature had increased by only 0.8°C (1.4°F) beyond pre-industrial times. We simply do not know how well the human race will survive additional warming that is already in the pipeline, which will make the heat waves in 20 years even worse than today, let alone the additional warming that will be caused by two more decades of business-as-usual emissions.

Moreover, insofar as our climate scientists can predict what the climate will be like if the average temperature rises 4°C (7°F), this picture is not pretty, as shown by a "snapshot of a 4°C world" provided by Kevin Anderson of the Tyndall Centre for Climate Change Research:

> A global mean surface temperature rise of 4°C equates to around 5-6°C warming of global mean land surface temperature.... [A] 4°C world would likely see the hottest days in China being 6-8°C [9-14°F] warmer than the hottest days experienced in recent heat waves with which China has struggled to cope; Central Europe would see heat waves much like the one in 2003, but with 8°C [14°F] on top of the highest temperatures; during New York's summer heat waves the warmest days would be around 10-12°C [18-21.6°F] hotter.[31]

Anderson's forecast is reinforced by a 2012 World Bank report, *Turn Down the Heat*. Warning that "a warming of 4°C could occur as early as the 2060s," it said:

> Temperature conditions experienced during [the heat waves of the first decade of the 21st century] would become the new norm in a 4°C [7°F] warmer world and a completely new class of heat waves, with magnitudes never experienced before in the 20th century, would occur regularly.[32]

Accordingly, if Plan C, with its a wait-and-see approach, leads to an increase of ("only") 3 or 4°C, it will likely condemn our children and grandchildren, beginning as early as the 2060s, to a hellish existence. They might begin to wonder, in fact, how their summers differ from the weather in the popular image of hell.

Conclusion

Bill McKibben has said, "We're hot as hell and we're not going to take it any more."[33] Not to "take it any more" means: Become very aggressive about forcing politicians to reduce and finally eliminate the fossil-fuel emissions that are making heat increasingly unbearable – which means going with Plan B.

3

DROUGHTS AND WILDFIRES

"The atmospheric conditions associated with the unprecedented drought in California are very likely linked to human-caused climate change."
– National Science Foundation, September 2014

"The common theme statewide this year is unprecedented number of fires and fire activity across the state, in many cases two to three months earlier than normal."
- Ken Pimlott, director of the California Department of Forestry and Fire Protection, May 2014

"An unprecedented combination of tree-killing insects, wildfires, and heat and dryness is disrupting the forests of the Rocky Mountains."
– Union of Concerned Scientists/ Rocky Mountain Climate Organization, 2014

The present chapter is closely related to the previous one, because extra heat increases the odds of droughts. Drought is the climate effect that has thus far been most harmful to people. Although drought occurred long before the era of global warming, it is aggravated by it and will be further aggravated if global warming is allowed to continue. As global warming develops, it will make drought increasingly important, because, says Joe Romm, "future droughts will be fundamentally different from all previous droughts that humanity has experienced because they will be very hot weather droughts."[1] The increased drought in places has already led to dramatic increases in wildfires in those places.

Drought and Global Warming

Global warming causes increased evaporation, which leads to increased precipitation, so the idea that global warming could cause drought may seem counter-intuitive. However, while there is more precipitation now than before, global warming can change when and where the precipitation falls.

Research has shown that La Niña, in its oscillation with El Niño, seems to be responsible for drought in the American Southwest. If so, how can global warming be responsible for it? The answer is that - to quote Kevin Trenberth, one of America's premier climate scientists - although La Niña has continued to be responsible for drought in the Southwest, "global warming helps make droughts hotter, and therefore drier, than they would be without a human influence." Global warming "creates stronger, more intense, and longer-lasting drought."[2]

In 2011, Aiguo Dai, a scientist at the National Center for Atmospheric Research, wrote a major study of drought over the past 1,000 years, concluding with 1950 to 2008, in which he focused on the influence of greenhouse gases [GHG] since the 1970s. He wrote:

> Since the middle 20th century, global aridity and drought areas have increased substantially, mainly due to widespread drying since the 1970s. . . . [T]he rapid warming since the late 1970s has increased atmospheric demand for moisture and likely altered atmospheric circulation patterns (e.g., over Africa and East Asia), both contributing to the recent drying over land. Since a large part of the recent warming is attributed to human-induced GHG increases, it can be concluded that human activities have contributed significantly to the recent drying trend.[3]

Climate science has reached three major conclusions about changes in droughts brought about by global warming.

- "[T]he wet gets wetter and the dry gets drier." That is, places that historically received a lot of precipitation will receive more, while places already afflicted by drought will get still drier. "For dry and poor countries, like Somalia, warming spells famine . . . . To wet nations, like Thailand, climate change brings deadly floods."[4]

- "When it rains, it pours." That is, warmer temperatures in the atmosphere cause more evaporation. With warm air sitting in the atmosphere holding more water vapor, when it does rain, it often pours.[5]

- Global warming is producing more drought that occurs "under warmer temperature conditions," which has been called "global-change-type drought." This is bad news because, as Romm says, "warm-weather droughts are worse than cooler-weather droughts." We are going to have more warm-weather droughts, "and if we don't change course soon," he adds, "they will become hot-weather droughts, then hellish droughts."[6]

Major Effects of Hot Weather Droughts

The human harm caused by droughts comes primarily through three major effects: food shortage, desertification, and wildfires.

Food Shortage: Farming in Hell

Although Chapter 7 will focus on global warming's contribution to food shortages, a chapter on drought would be incomplete without some mention of its impact on food production, which is the most serious consequence of drought. The U.N. has said: "Drought ranks as the single most common cause of severe food shortages in developing countries. Drought caused more deaths during the last century than any other natural disaster." Romm has written:

> Drought is the most pressing problem caused by climate change. . . . Feeding some 9 billion people by mid-century in the face of a rapidly worsening climate may well be the greatest challenge the human race has ever faced.[7]

More than a billion people are regularly hungry, and this problem becomes even worse when there is prolonged drought. "The U.S. is the world's largest producer of corn and 2012 was supposed to be a banner year," but in many states, the heat and drought caused the corn to "shrivel and die." Saying that the Midwest was having weather that was impossible for growing corn, a plant biologist in Illinois said: "It's like farming in hell."[8]

The drought led the U.S. Department of Agriculture to issue its most extensive disaster declaration ever, one that included almost one-third of the counties in the United States, covering 26 states. The drop in crops caused by droughts is especially hard on the poor. Besides running up prices, a year of meager crops means that, whereas the US government normally buys staples (to remove surpluses), which they then give to food banks, a drought results in there being few if any surpluses.[9] It was the devastating effect of the U.S. drought on farming, beginning in 2011, that led many Americans to begin taking climate change seriously.

Dust-Bowlification

When drought is long-lasting, it can lead to "desertification" – a process in which previously fertile land becomes desert by means of drought, poor agricultural practices, or both – as in America's Dust Bowl. Indeed, Romm has suggested that climate change appears to be leading the American Southwest to a new "dust-bowlification," in which long-standing drought leads to a loss of vegetation and a resulting increase in dust storms – a process that is already afflicting Australia.[10]

Wildfires

Big wildfires "thrive in dry air, low humidity, and high winds; climate change is going to make those conditions more frequent over the next century," wrote James West in *Mother Jones*. Indeed, according to a University of Arizona study:

> [L]arge forest fires have occurred more often in the western
> United States since the mid-1980s as spring temperatures
> increased, snow melted earlier, and summers got hotter,
> leaving more and drier fuels for fires to devour.

As a result, "the fire season now lasts two months longer and destroys twice as much land as it did four decades ago." Forty years of global warming have brought about a huge change.[11]

The media give lots of attention to big wildfires, but they have, by and large, not discussed global warming as a major cause. And yet, says climate scientist Amanda Staudt of the National Wildlife Federation, "talking about western wildfires without mentioning climate change is like talking about lung cancer without mentioning cigarettes." Explaining why climate change needs to be included in the discussion, she said:

> The frequency and extent of fires in recent decades is
> unlikely to happen under natural conditions. With one
> catastrophic fire after another, it is clear that something
> quite different is happening to our forests.[12]

As the connection between climate change and wildfires has become more obvious, news shows have mentioned it a little more often. In July 2013, for example, NBC noted:

> Tonight, 17 major wildfires are burning in seven western
> states. Today, scientists meeting in Washington said climate

change plays a factor in what's become a deadly and historic fire season.[13]

Due to 2012's drought combined with unprecedented heat, "America's wildfire activity in 2012 surged beyond the 10-year average for number of acres burned," and the fire season ended up "destroy[ing] more acres of forest than in any year on record." "Not only are more wildfires flaring up in the West this year than last," said Jennifer Smith of the National Interagency Fire Center, "the nation's fires have gotten bigger." These increases have continued a pattern that developed in earlier decades. The wildfire season in the 16-year period from 1987 to 2003 was 78 days longer than it had been in the previous 16 years, and the major fires burned nearly five times as long. By 2014, a study of wildfires in the West found that the area they burned had been increasing by nearly the size of Denver every year. As if to illustrate these points about size and earliness, Alaska in May had a fire bigger than Chicago.[14]

Global warming has brought about these wildfire changes not only by virtue of the drier conditions, increased lightning frequency, and longer fire seasons, but also by stimulating the breeding of bark beetles, which kill trees, thereby making them more combustible. Most of the roughly 600 species of bark beetles live in dead or dying hosts, but a few of them attack and kill healthy trees. Two of these are the mountain pine bark beetle and the southern pine bark beetle.[15]

These tiny creatures burrow through the bark in order to get to the layer of tissue that provides the trees with their water and nutrients. The beetles infect the trees with a fungus that prevents them from using their defenses and even from using their water and nutrients, so the trees quickly die, becoming fuel for the next wildfire. Mountain pine beetles have been devastating North American pines trees since the late 1990s. By 2013, they had "wiped out 70,000 square miles of the Rocky Mountain forests in just over a decade. Southern pine beetles have been destroying pine trees not only in many southern states but also in more northern ones."[16]

In northern US states and Canada, the beetles were always killed off every winter, but recently the winters have usually not been getting cold enough. Surviving through the winter, the beetles have started reproducing twice a year. Although healthy trees have natural defenses, the enormous numbers of beetles now overwhelm them. The warmer weather has also allowed the beetles to move to higher elevations, where the trees had developed no defenses.[17]

Droughts in the United States

Even aside from its growing wildfire problem, the United States is one of the places where drought has been serious. A list of the major droughts to hit this country in recent decades would include:

- The heat of 1988, mentioned in the previous chapter, was accompanied by the worst drought since the Dust Bowl days. (As if warning us, 1988 was the first year that the atmosphere's CO_2 level exceeded 350 ppm.)

- In 2007, many parts of the West and Southeast had their driest years since records had been kept. At the end of September, "43 percent of the contiguous U.S. fell in the moderate to extreme drought categories."[18]

- In 2011, a Reuters story noted: "Texas remained the epicenter of unprecedented drought, with climate data showing the state suffering its driest 10 months ever in over a century of data."[19]

- In 2012, a drought that began in 2011 became one of the most intense and widespread US droughts ever. About 63 percent of the lower 48 states were in drought by the end of the year, with 42 percent in *exceptional* drought. "[T]he dryness this year has been so extreme and persistent that, not only did several states rank driest for several time scales," wrote the National Climatic Data Center, "but their records were by wide margins compared to the previous records."[20]

- At the beginning of 2013, the 2011-2012 drought was continuing, with over 55 percent of the lower 48 states still in moderate drought conditions or worse. The drought even intensified in Texas and Florida.[21]

What made the US droughts from 1988 to 2014 unprecedented was that these droughts were occurring much more often. In 2012, *The New York Times* wrote:

> [T]his summer's drought is one for the record books. But so was last year's drought in the South Central states. And it has been only a decade since an extreme five-year drought hit the American West. Widespread annual droughts, once a rare calamity, have become more frequent and are set to become the 'new normal.'[22]

The present condition of American drought can best be appreciated by looking at recent developments in California and a few other states.

California

California is, of course, the most important state in the country for agriculture. After being in moderate drought since 2010, it became afflicted with serious drought in 2012. In a pattern that is becoming the new normal, the drought was followed by a deluge: "In December, it rained, and rained, and rained or, if you were in the mountains, snowed and snowed," said a blog. "But a funny thing happened as soon as 2012 turned into 2013. The rain stopped. Seriously stopped. January and February were the driest months ever recorded in California." By the end of 2013, California had experienced "its driest year since recordkeeping began in 1849." Although most of the state was in severe to extreme drought, the Central Valley, which grows much of the country's food, was hit the hardest. As a result of this long-term drought, the federal irrigation water was, for the first time ever, cut off to most of the Central Valley farm districts.[23]

In early 2014, there was another deluge, resulting in serious flooding, but then the drought continued and by mid-2014, 100 percent of the state was, for the first time since the Drought Monitor was begun, experiencing "severe drought." With 58 percent of this being in the highest category, "exceptional drought," California was experiencing the most severe drought ever recorded.[24]

California's drought could not be considered a surprise, because climate scientists had predicted "a decade ago that Arctic ice loss would bring on worse droughts in the West, especially California," due to changes in the jet stream, wrote Romm. Even prior to Jennifer Francis' work, there was Lisa Sloan's 2004 article, "Disappearing Arctic Sea Ice Reduces Available Water in the American West." Going still further back, James Hansen had been warning since 1990 about ever-worsening droughts in the Southwest. In 1995, Nobel Prize-winning scientist Sherwood Rowland asked, "What's the use of having developed a science well enough to make predictions if, in the end, all we're willing to do is stand around and wait for them to come true?"[25]

In any case, California's drought brought some huge fires, including the Rim Fire that, threatening Yosemite National Park, burned an area about the size of New York City, and the state's third-largest fire on record, which burned 400 square miles north of San Francisco. In addition, the fire season began very early in 2013, with 680 fires already by the beginning of May, and continued very late, with a big fire at Big Sur in mid-December.[26]

In 2014, the fire season again began early, with almost twice the number of fires by May as the average and, said a spokesman for the Department of Forestry at the beginning of August, "We're seeing fire behavior we wouldn't normally see until September." On the TV series "Years of Living Dangerously," former Governor Schwarzenegger was told, "Governor, you have to understand there really is no fire season. The fires are gonna be all year round." In September, a story entitled "California Dealing with Unprecedented Fire Season" stated that the state had had about 1,000 more fires than it normally had by that time.[27]

Texas

The summer of 2011 was devastating for Texas. By Labor Day, wildfires had afflicted every part of the state. Many areas throughout Texas' central and eastern regions were left scorched and barren. Texas Forest Service's information officer said: "This is a situation of historic proportions. The fuels are so dry. The winds are astronomical. . . . It's never been like this before." This led an AccuWeather meteorologist to speak of "a never-before-seen wildfire situation in Texas." Indeed, 2011 was officially named the worst fire season in Texas's history.[28]

After that, moreover, the drought did not improve. In 2013, the Water Utility Director of Austin called it "the worst drought we've faced in Central Texas, ever." Because the drought was in its third year, drinking water started running low. Near the end of 2013, Central Texas had a torrential downpour, getting over a foot of rain in one day. But this deluge did not betoken an end of the drought. Instead, the water flowing into the Highland Lakes in the early months of 2014 was less than that of 2011, "a year that had the lowest total inflows in history."[29]

Arizona

The biggest fire story of 2013 was the Yarnell Hill Fire, in which 19 of 20 members of an elite firefighting team were killed. The fire, which evidently started with a lightning strike, had gotten out of control because of erratic winds, a long-standing drought, and a heat wave that exceeded 100 degrees F.[30]

Colorado

In 2012, the Waldo Canyon Fire north of Colorado Springs burned almost 350 homes, making it the worst fire in the state's history. But in June 2013, it was superseded by the Black Forest Fire, which destroyed some 380 homes and a total of almost 490 structures. This fire's record-breaking achievement was aided by the fact that Denver thermometers had hit 100 degrees – the earliest this had ever happened.[31]

Oregon

A 500-page report in 2010 concluded that Oregon's future "looks a lot like the drought-stricken and fire-plagued Southwest." The year 2013 suggested the truth of this prediction, as "all but the Northwest corner of the state [was] mired in conditions ranging from abnormally dry to severe drought," leading to the most expensive fire season ever.[32]

Idaho

In August 2013, the Beaver Creek Fire near Sun Valley, which came to national prominence because it threatened the getaways of Arnold Schwarzenegger, Tom Hanks, and Bruce Willis, was huge, with 1,200 firefighters working to save some 10,000 endangered homes. The fire, caused by a combination of lightning, strong winds, and "drought-parched land," lasted over three weeks and burned 115,000 acres. This fire occurred at the same time as nine more fires in Idaho and the fires in Oregon Arizona, and California.[33]

Washington

In 2014, when the fire season in Washington State was only partly over, the state already had six times the number of acres normally burned for an entire year, and the state had already spent over three times its fire-fighting budget.[34]

Drought in Other Countries

Australia

The country that has had the most severe drought is Australia. A 14-year drought that began in 1997 — Australians call it the "Big Dry" — lasted until 2012. During an emergency summit in 2006, Australia was said to be facing its "worst drought in 1000 years." Although that description might not be historically accurate, it did express the depth of the drought. The South Australian premier called the drought "a frightening glimpse of the future with global warming." After 2006, the drought became even worse; by 2007, agriculture, energy, and water storage were running low; and a *New Scientist* article entitled "Australia — the Continent that Ran Dry" said the "sense of panic became palpable." That same year, with over half of the country's agricultural land in drought, Australia's Water Services Association said: "The urban water industry has decided the inflows of the past will never return." Therefore, it said, Australians should no longer speak of "drought," which suggests a temporary condition, but instead say that "this is the new reality."[35]

In 2008, Dr. David Jones, the head of climate analysis at the Bureau of Meteorology, said that the drought, which was affecting all of the country except the northern part, was "without historical precedent." Regarding Melbourne in particular, he added: "We simply have not seen anything like what we currently have, not even close." But it became worse. In 2012, stories announced that the long drought had ended. But by 2013, it had started to return to the eastern part of the country. Due to the combination of heat and drought in Australia's "Angry Summer" (see Chapter 2), there were "fires in five of Australia's six states, including at least 90 wildfires through New South Wales."[36]

By 2014, Queensland suffered the most widespread drought on record. "February, normally one of the wettest times of the year," said Queensland's agriculture minister, "has been particularly dry." Prime Minister Tony Abbott correctly called this a once-in-a-century drought, but as a climate-change denier, he resisted the conclusion of the 2014 report by Australia's Climate Council, "Heatwaves: Hotter, Longer, More Often." Although this report said that Australian "droughts are projected to occur more frequently with the ongoing increase in greenhouse gas emissions," Abbott pushed through a repeal of the carbon tax, thereby helping to make Australia's heat and droughts even worse.[37]

Brazil

Following a megadrought that began in 2005 and another that began in 2010, Brazil in January 2014 experienced the "hottest and driest month on record in much of southeastern Brazil," even though January had usually been the wettest month. The press focused most of its attention on coffee, for which Brazil is the world's leading producer. But Brazil also produces the most citrus, sugarcane, and beef, which are also affected by the drought. Because the drought had been prolonged, the hot and dry weather in the early months of 2014 led to water rationing in 140 cities, including Brazil's largest city, Sao Paolo, which by mid-February was about to run out of drinking water. The world was very aware of the drought because of the World Cup, especially the fear that the lack of water and hence lack of hydroelectric power might lead to a blackout in the stadium.[38]

Whereas most people are understandably concerned about water, food, and coffee prices, the still more serious problem is what drought is doing to the Amazon rain forest – which, besides being the most species-rich ecosystem in the world, is the planet's biggest carbon sink. If it starts dying, it will turn into "a smokestack spewing CO_2 into the atmosphere." This concern was elevated in 2013 by two reports: NASA's Jet Propulsion Laboratory reported that after 30 percent of the rainforest was damaged by the 2005 megadrought, the rainforest had not bounced back before the beginning of the 2010 megadrought, which damaged half of the rainforest. And then in 2013, a study suggested that, "If the dry season is too long, the rainforest will not survive."[39]

Canada

Like Australian Prime Minister Tony Abbott, Canada's prime minister, Stephen Harper, has denied the seriousness of global warming; in fact, he and Abbott formed an alliance around this denial.[40] But also like Australia, the western part of Canada in2014 experienced some of the hottest and driest weather ever, resulting in unprecedented wildfires. In the Northwest Territories, wildfire activity was six times higher than the 25-year average, leading to "unprecedented" burning of the boreal forests, which threatens to melt the permafrost.[41]

China

Drought has become serious for China and hence for the world, as Chinese crop losses can impact much of the world, because Chinese purchases to make up for their losses run up prices in other countries, and also because China is the world's leading wheat producer. The winter of 2010-11 was so dry that the U.N.'s Food and Agriculture Organization issued "a rare special alert." Especially hard hit was the southwestern province of Yunnan: "China has long been affected by desertification in the northern and western regions, but the drought in Yunnan marks a new high in China's troubles with the climate and environment." Ma Jun, who wrote *China's Water Crisis* – which has been compared with Rachel Carson's *Silent Spring* in terms of influence – has called the lack of water in Yunnan a "new warning signal."[42]

Unfortunately, the drought in the north continued, and by 2014 the Shaanxi Providence in Northwest China was having its worth drought for a century, perhaps ever.[43]

India

Whereas droughts are "bad for the United States," they are "catastrophic for India," as a *Business Insider* headline put it. The reason they are catastrophic is that half of India's population depends on farming for its livelihood. The monsoons normally bring 75 percent of India's annual rainfall. But in 2009, the monsoons failed, devastating the country. Saying that the intensification of drought "is one of the predictable impacts of climate change and climate instability," Vandana Shiva noted that "two thirds of India" has been impacted by the "failure of monsoon in India and the consequent drought."[44]

India was barely recovering from the effects of the 2009 drought when, in 2012, the monsoons failed again. This being the fourth drought in a dozen years, India became concerned about "the reliability of . . . the monsoon rains that typically fall from June to October." This drought, moreover, was accompanied by exceptional heat. The temperature soared in Delhi to 115°F (46°C) and even to 120°F (48.9°C) in the state of Uttar Pradesh, the heart of India's rice belt. The wheat harvest in Punjab, India's largest producer, was down 70 percent. The drought especially dealt "a devastating blow to grain crops used for animal feed" and thereby to millions of farmers, for whom their cattle is the only source of income. The intensified drought led to desperation."The farmers are depressed, feeling their lives have been left as a question mark over whether the rains will come," said the co-secretary of the All India Farmers' Union, adding that over a quarter-million famers had been driven to suicide in the past 16 year, because of the hardships and precariousness of farming. In 2013, moreover, the partial drought continued, especially in Maharashtra, India's wealthiest and second most populous state.[45]

Plans B, A, and C

In light of the fact that the problem of drought has already become unprecedented, let us look at the three possible ways to respond.

Plan B

The best response – Plan B – would involve a radical mobilization, beginning immediately, to prevent further global warming. However, insofar as drought has already been made irreversibly worse by global warming, even if all additional greenhouse emissions were stopped today, the drought will inevitably become even worse in 30 years, due to the lag. But efforts begun now could lead drought to cease becoming worse by 2045.

Drought in America, even in the Southwest, including California, has not been as bad as Australia's "Big Dry." Nevertheless, as we have seen, the global warming of 0.8 °C (1.4°F) has already been giving the Southwest increasingly severe and extensive droughts, accompanied by ever worse wildfires. But if greenhouse gases are quickly and radically curtailed, drought should not become bad enough to make the Southwest completely unlivable.

Plan A

There have been several studies about what drought will be like if business as usual continues.

- The Met Office Hadley Centre said that, if business as usual continues until 2100, one third of the planet's land surface would be in a permanent state of "extreme drought," on which agriculture would be impossible.[46]

- According to Aiguo Dai's combination of 22 climate models, "a very large population will be severely affected in the coming decades over the whole United States" as well as "southern Europe, Southeast Asia, Brazil, Chile, Australia, and most of Africa."[47]

- A 2012 *Popular Science* article predicted that people in the United States, along with Canada and Mexico, will look back to the 2000-2004 dry spell as a fairly wet period.[48]

The drought in the latter part of this century probably, moreover, would become the worst kind, in which drought is accompanied by extreme heat, with temperatures in countries such as Australia, China, and the United States becoming 16°F higher than today. Because greater heat usually results in greater drought, much of the planet would suffer what Australians call the "permanent dry."

Plan C

Plan C would be to keep the CO_2 down sufficiently to prevent the planet's average temperature from exceeding 4°C (7°F) above pre-industrial times – which, it is widely assumed, would require the CO_2 concentration to be kept 450 to 600 ppm. But the result, said the National Oceanic and Atmospheric Administration (NOAA), would be "irreversible dry-season rainfall reductions in several regions comparable to those of the 'dust bowl' era" (with "irreversible" meaning that they will continue for at least 1,000 years).[49] In a commentary entitled "New Study Puts the 'Hell' in Hell and High Water," Romm said that "in a half century, much of the United States (and large parts of the rest of the world) could experience devastating levels of drought – far worse than the 1930s Dust Bowl."[50]

In a contribution to a 2011 volume devoted to challenges of "a 4°C world" – meaning one in which there has been a 4°C rise in the planet's average temperature above pre-industrial times – Rachel Warren wrote:

- "Drought and desertification would be widespread, with large numbers of people experiencing increased water stress, and others experiencing changes in seasonality of water supply."

- "[C]limate-change induced changes in precipitation patterns and changes in climate variability would increase the area of the globe experiencing drought at any one time from today's 1 per cent to a future 30 per cent by the end of the twenty-first century."

- "[A]n increased human population might increasingly be concentrated in areas remaining wet enough for economic prosperity."[51]

In a commentary about the conference, the *Guardian* wrote:

> A hellish vision of a world warmed by 4°C [7°F] within a lifetime has been set out by an international team of scientists. . . . A 4°C rise in the planet's temperature would see severe droughts across the world and millions of migrants seeking refuge as their food supplies collapse.[52]

Those who advocate a wait-and-see approach generally hold that, if drought becomes worse, we will be able to adapt. This is true, Romm says, if by "adapt" we mean: "force the next 50 generations to endure endless misery because we were too damn greedy to give up 0.1% of our GDP each year."[53]

Conclusion

If carbon emissions are cut back quickly and drastically, droughts and wildfires will not continue to increase much past 2045. But if that does not happen, then these phenomena will continue getting worse for our children and grandchildren. Plan B is the only rational, only moral, option.

4

STORMS

"This storm was literally unprecedented."
– Bill McKibben, "Sandy's Real Name," 2012

"A slow moving storm over eastern states left areas from Maryland
to New England facing unprecedented rainfall and flooding. . . .
[P]arts of New York state saw an entire summer's worth
of rain fall in 12 hours."
– Flood List, 14 August 2014

Because of a rash of extreme weather, an increasing number of Americans have started taking seriously the idea that global warming is causing climate change. The present chapter looks at a third type of extreme weather: extreme storms. Four types of storms will be examined: (1) extreme rainstorms and resulting floods, (2) extreme snowstorms, (3) hurricanes (also called "typhoons" and "tropical cyclones"), and (4) tornadoes.

Extreme Rainstorms and Flooding

In 2010, the National Weather Service published a study, based on 60 years of reporting, showing that "extreme precipitation events" – defined as storms producing at least one inch of rain during a 24-hour period - are occurring more frequently, and that the same is true of bigger storms, which produce two or even four inches. In this chapter, storms are called "extreme" only if they drop at least three inches of moisture in a 24-hour period.[1]

Global Warming, Deluges, and Flooding

As to the reason for this increase in extreme rainstorms, commonly called "deluges," there is no mystery, given the reality of global warming. As *New York Times* writer Justin Gillis pointed out,

> basic physics suggests that warming must accelerate the
> cycle of evaporation and rainfall. . . . [A]s air warms, it can

hold more water vapor, which means that more water can then be squeezed out of the atmosphere as liquid or frozen precipitation.

Michael Lemonick added: "A warmer atmosphere can absorb more water vapor, and what goes up must come down — and thanks to prevailing winds, it won't come down in the same place."[2]

When one asks whether extreme deluges are caused by warming or natural variability, the answer is both. Joe Romm has written: "It is the compounding of 'typical' extreme weather events on top of human-caused climate change that creates the devastating, record-smashing 'global-warming-type' events."[3] While agreeing that "you can't attribute a single event to climate change," Kevin Trenberth added:

> But there is a systematic influence on all of these weather events now-a-days because of the fact that there is [more of] this extra water vapor lurking around in the atmosphere than there used to be say 30 years ago. It's about a 4% extra amount, it invigorates the storms, it provides plenty of moisture for these storms and it's unfortunate that the public is not associating these with the fact that this is one manifestation of climate change. And the prospects are that these kinds of things will only get bigger and worse in the future.[4]

From Droughts to Deluges

One of the predicted features of extreme deluges is that they will often follow upon droughts. For example:

- "Georgia's 2007 drought," wrote *The New York Times*, broke "every record in Georgia's history," but hardly had Georgia begun to recover from this "once-in-a-century drought" when in 2009, it had a "once-in-a-century flooding, during which counties around Atlanta had 15 to 20 inches of rain during a 72-hour period."[5]

- After 14 years of Australia's Big Dry (see Chapter 3), rains finally came in September 2011. But then, said a *Rolling Stone* story, "the rains kept coming. By late December, the ground was saturated and fields were flooding. . . . And still the rain kept coming. In early January, eight inches of rain fell in five days. Gas stations closed, farmers wrote off an entire season."[6]

- In October 2012, England's *Guardian* newspaper wrote, "The dramatic switch from drought to the wettest April to June ever and widespread flooding was of a magnitude never seen before, water experts said."[7]

- In 2013, the Midwestern farm belt, after suffering through one of the country's droughts, was pummeled with torrential rains, which for weeks prevented planting. One corn and soybean farmer said, "This is the worst spring I can remember in my 30 years farming." And citizens of Boulder, Colorado, after complaining about the heat, were hit by "biblical rainfall amounts" – more rain in a week than Boulder usually gets for the whole year.[8]

Recent Reports of Deluges

The fact that deluges are continuing to get bigger can be illustrated by news reports from 2009 to 2014:

- In 2009, Tennessee had an "unprecedented rain event" that "virtually paralyzed" Nashville, "thanks to that city's heaviest recorded 1-day and 2-day rainfall in its history." The manager of the Grand Ole Opry said: "If you'd been sitting in the front row, you'd have had seven feet of water over your head." Even though no hurricane was involved, Nashville's rainfall of 13.5 inches in two days exceeded Hurricane Katrina's in places.[9]

- In 2010, Pakistan experienced a deluge that flooded a fifth of the country and forced eight million people to evacuate. U.N. Secretary-General Ban Ki-Moon called it "the worst disaster" he had ever seen.[10] California suffered the heaviest rainfall since records have been kept. "Rainfall records weren't just broken," said the Associated Press, "they were obliterated."[11]

- From August to October 2011, heavy monsoon rain, with multiple typhoons, inundated parts of Thailand, Cambodia, Vietnam, Laos, Myanmar, and the Philippines, resulting in some 1,100 deaths.[12] Virginia's Fairfax County – the home of the CIA – received 7 inches of rain in three hours, which the National Weather Service described as "off the charts."[13]

- In July 2012, a downpour in southern Russia by the Black Sea caused river levels to rise as much as 23 feet. "The water came with such force that it tore up the asphalt," reported Russian Television, and "carried trucks out to sea."[14] Southwestern Australia also experienced a record-breaking deluge, more than 8 inches in 24 hour, breaking all-time records.[15]

- In 2013, extreme rain raised the Danube to its highest-ever level and the River Vlatava overflowed, forcing tens of thousands of people to evacuate. This region's previous "once-in-a-lifetime" flooding had occurred just three years earlier. Also, the river that divides northeast China from southeast Russia reached its highest level ever, forcing hundreds of thousands of people to relocate.[16]

- 2014, USA: The eastern U.S. was drenched on April 30, with Florida and Alabama receiving over two feet of rain in 24 hours – much more than during Hurricane Ivan. On May 28, the rain was so heavy for a few hours in Louisiana that in Belle Rose a dozen caskets floated away from their graves.[17] August 13 saw deluges in many places: Portland, Maine, had a rainstorm so torrential that it dropped more than 8 inches of water and even dislodged manhole covers; Detroit, Michigan, which normally has 3 inches of rain at most during a month, received almost 5 inches of rain in four hours; Greenhaven, Maryland, received almost 10 inches of rain; the airport in Islip, New York, received over 13.5 inches – 2 inches more than from Hurricane Irene; and Manning, North Dakota, received over six inches of rain in 24 hours.[18] On August 16, Kearney, Nebraska, received almost 4 inches of rain in about 2 hours; and on August 19, Phoenix and surrounding areas of Arizona received more rain than in the previous year they had received the entire summer, with one place receiving 1.75 inches in 45 minutes.[19]

- 2014, Other Countries: In February 2014, the U.K. received "biblical" rains – the most in any winter month since recording began. In April, days of sudden, heavy rains in Afghanistan caused flash floods that killed 120 people and displaced tens of thousands. In May, Serbia suffered "the biggest water disaster in Serbia's history" and, in what one meteorologist called "a pretty unprecedented event," Bosnia received three months' worth of rain in three days, causing the loss of 100,000 homes.In August, two weeks of violent storms in Central and Eastern Europe caused devastating flooding from Budapest, where the Danube River reached its highest-ever level, to northern Germany, which had to ask Denmark to send it 650,000 sand bags.[20] During that same period, southern China also experienced a two-week deluge, with daily rainfalls of 2-6 inches, which killed 40 people, destroyed 25,000 homes, and forced 500,000 people to evacuate. In early September, at the very beginning of the monsoon season, India and Pakistan had massive rains and flooding in Kashmir and Punjab, which killed almost 500 people and stranded 200,000, leaving many in several feet of standing water teeming with trash and dead animals. And Hokkaido, Japan's northern island, had a torrential rain storm that forced about a million people to evacuate.[21]

One writer summarized the weather of 2014 thus: "Weather defines our lives, but unlike most years, 2014 seems defined by weird weather."[22] However, as we saw above, other writers call this "weird" weather the "new normal." Or, in Romm's terms, there has been a "quantum increase in extreme weather."[23]

Scientific Reports about Extreme Rain

Stories such as these resulted in some major scientific reports about the growing occurrence of extreme rain.

- A 2012 report on "Extreme Rain Storms in Midwest" concluded: "A threshold may already have been crossed, so that major floods in the Midwest perhaps now should no longer be considered purely natural disasters but instead mixed natural/unnatural disasters."[24]

- "When It Rains, It Pours" was the name of a 2012 report by *Environment America*, which concluded: "The biggest rainstorms and snowstorms are getting bigger."[25]

- "Weather Gone Wild" was the title of a 2012 report by *National Geographic*, which said: "Extreme events like the Nashville flood – described by officials as a once-in-a-millennium occurrence – are happening more frequently than they used to."[26]

- In 2013, the University of Adelaide issued a worldwide study of extreme rain between 1900 and 2009, which said that "rainfall extremes are increasing on average globally [and] that there is a 7% increase in extreme rainfall intensity for every degree increase in global atmospheric temperature." Romm headed the story: "Après Nous, Le Déluge: Extreme Rainfall Rises with Global Temperatures."[27]

The description in the May 2012 report – that major floods in the Midwest should be considered "natural/unnatural disasters" — can be applied more generally to extreme weather events, which result from "the compounding of 'typical' extreme weather events on top of human-caused climate change."[28]

Extreme Snowstorms

As pointed out in Chapter 1, there is no contradiction between the theory of global warming and the fact of extreme snowfall. Indeed, the theory predicts heavier snowstorms, because they will be produced when there is more moisture in the air and it is cold enough for snow. It is true that there will be no more snowfall after the planet has heated up so much that snow will no longer form. However, as Jeff Masters said, "we're not at that point -- the Earth hasn't warmed that much yet."[29]

In the meantime, he said, "we could actually see an increase in very heavy snowstorms in some portions of the world," which seems to be "happening for winter storms in the Northeast U.S." – namely, the "Snowpocalypse" storm of December 2009 and, less than two months later, the "Snowmageddon" of February 2010.

With regard to the former: Snowpocalypse was "the largest December snowstorm on record." With regard to the latter, Masters wrote:

> The top U.S. weather story of 2010 has to be 'Snowmageddon' [a name reportedly coined by President Obama], the remarkable February blizzard that buried the mid-Atlantic under 2-3 feet of snow. Snowmageddon set the all-time record for heaviest snowfall in Delaware history.

Moreover, "'Snowmageddon' was followed just three days later by a second massive snowstorm," with the result that "Washington D.C., Philadelphia, Wilmington, and Atlantic City all had their snowiest winters on record."[30]

Moving to the far Northwest: "Snow in Alaska doesn't usually make headlines," said a writer in 2012, "but even The Last Frontier has extremes." The extremes the writer had in mind were "weeks of record snowfall [that] left the city [of Cordova] buried under 18 feet of the white stuff."[31] (The winter of 2014 was discussed in Chapter 1.)

Other countries have also had unprecedented snowfalls. For example, on 3 February 2014, places in northern Iran reportedly received two meters (over six feet) of snow.[32]

Hurricanes

Hurricanes provide one of the types of evidence informing the scientific consensus about global warming and climate change: Because the oceans have become warmer, they have more energy, which can be converted to tropical hurricane wind. Hurricanes can form once the ocean's surface temperatures reach 80°F (26.5°C). And, given the fact that hurricanes "draw their strength from heat transferred to the atmosphere when ocean water evaporates," it follows that "the warmer the ocean's surface, the more powerful the hurricane."[33]

Also, it is not surprising that, although there is thus far no consensus as to whether hurricanes have been occurring more frequently, "strong hurricanes are getting stronger," with the result that "category 4 and 5 storms have almost doubled in number and proportion since 1970."[34]

Of course, hurricanes of any category can be very destructive, because their destructiveness is based on other factors as well. All other things being equal, the strongest storms will be the most destructive. But often the other things are not equal, so some of the greatest destruction has been caused by the lower-category hurricanes. Here are a few notable hurricanes in recent years:

Hurricane Katrina

The best-known hurricane in the United States – at least prior to Hurricane Sandy in 2012 – was Hurricane Katrina in 2005. While it was over the Gulf of Mexico, it became a Category 5 hurricane, due to unusually warm waters: During the last week of August the ocean's surface temperatures "were one to two degrees Celsius above normal."[35]

After striking Louisiana and other states, Katrina was still a Category 3 and was "the largest hurricane of its strength to approach the United States in recorded history," the sheer size of which "caused devastation over 100 miles (160 kilometers) from the storm's center." Katrina was (at that time) "the costliest hurricane in U.S. history." It was also one of the deadliest, causing close to 2,000 deaths, most of which were in New Orleans. Aside from the criminal incompetence of the Bush administration, these deaths were due primarily to an inadequate levee system combined with a very strong storm surge, which breached the levees, leaving 80 percent of the city under water. "The devastation of Katrina," wrote Romm, "showed what havoc a super-hurricane can wreak when it hits a city that's largely below sea level."[36]

Tropical Cyclone Nargis[37]

In 2008, Myanmar (Burma) was hit by Cyclone Nargis, which *The New York Times* called "one of the deadliest storms in recorded history." It apparently killed almost 140,000 people. It also killed three-fourths of the livestock and "salted a million acres of rice paddies with its seawater surges." Cyclone Nargis has been called a "perfect storm" and "Asia's answer to Katrina." Although the number of deaths was magnified by the government's inadequate warnings, the high death toll was also due to the fact that for the first time, in Jeff Masters' words, a hurricane "tracked right over the most vulnerable part of the country, where most of the people live."[38]

Cyclone Giri

In 2010, Myanmar was struck again, this time by an even stronger storm - a Category 4 cyclone named Giri, which was, Masters reported, "the strongest tropical cyclone on record to make landfall on Myanmar." Although it was stronger than Nargis, it caused fewer deaths, because it struck a sparsely populated area, but it still left more than 80,000 people homeless.[39]

Cyclone Yasi

In February 2011, northeastern Australia was hit by Cyclone Yasi, "[o]ne of the most powerful cyclones ever to strike Australia." Rated a Category 5 cyclone, it reached 185 miles per hour and "ripped dozens of houses from their foundations, uprooted trees and shredded millions of dollars worth of sugar and banana crops." It also did extensive damage to the Great Barrier Reef.[40]

Hurricane Sandy

In late 2012, a conjunction of events that Bill McKibben earlier that year had suggested might happen – "a giant hurricane swamps Manhattan, a megadrought wipes out Midwest agriculture"[41] – did happen. The Manhattan-swamping hurricane was Sandy. Suzanne Goldenberg, the *Guardian*'s US environment correspondent, wrote:

> The storm on 29 October killed more than 125 people after making landfall in America, paralyzing the lower half of Manhattan, and obliterating entire neighborhoods in New York and New Jersey. . . . Sandy's brute force, in the form of a 13-foot storm surge over Battery Park that shut down New York's stock exchange and subway system for days, forced climate change on to the political agenda after months of public silence.[42]

Weather Channel meteorologist Bryan Norcross called Sandy "unprecedented and bizarre." This description was justified, said Norcross, because (1) a hurricane should weaken as it moves north over cold water, but Sandy did not; (2) every tropical storm going north in October had previously turned out to sea, but Sandy turned left into the northeast coast. This turn, said Stu Ostro (another Weather Channel meteorologist), was "unprecedented in the historical database."[43]

The word "unprecedented" was also used to describe Sandy by McKibben, who said: "This storm was literally unprecedented. It had lower barometric pressure, a higher storm surge, and greater size than the region had ever seen before" – referring to the National Hurricane Center's statement that Sandy was the "largest hurricane to ever form in the Atlantic."[44]

Sandy came to be widely called a "Frankenstorm," after this word was coined by a forecaster at NOAA. CNN banished this term for coverage of Sandy for fear that it would "trivialize" the storm.[45] But the term was entirely appropriate: As Romm said, "Frankenstein – and his monster – have become a metaphor for the unintentional consequences of scientific and technological advances."[46] This was the "right name for Sandy," added McKibben, because it involved "some spooky combination of the natural and the unnatural."[47] Regarding the contribution of global warming to Sandy, meteorologist Dan Satterfield has made the following points:

- The planet's atmosphere is a degree C warmer than it was a century ago, which means that it holds 5-7% more water vapor than it did then.

- The oceans are over a degree warmer than a century ago, and record ocean temperatures (2-3 degrees C above normal) were off the East Coast for several months before Sandy's appearance.

- During the past 60 years, the water level along the eastern coast has risen over 18 inches.

- Sandy's extremely unusual hard left turn towards the coast was due to a rare late-October high pressure cell over Greenland.

- The high-pressure block over Greenland "could very well be connected to the record melt of Arctic sea ice [in 2012]," according to Masters and other experts (see the section on The Arctic Connection in Chapter 1).[48]

With regard to this final bullet point, the IPCC's "special report on extreme weather," which appeared almost exactly a year before Sandy, had warned of "a 'poleward shift' in the pattern of the storms, which will mean severe storms are more likely to strike areas such as New York."[49]

As for what was ultimately responsible for Hurricane Sandy, McKibben wrote: "[I]f there were any poetic justice, it would be named Hurricane Chevron or Hurricane Exxon." In 2013, NOAA produced a study concluding that because of sea-level rise, Sandy-type storm surges "will occur more frequently in the future," even when storms are weaker.[50]

Super Typhoon Haiyan

In November 2013, the Philippines was hit by Typhoon (another term for hurricanes) Haiyan, with wind speeds of 190-195 miles per hour – the highest speed of a hurricane to make landfall so far on record. Haiyan's strength was partly explainable by the ocean temperature, which was as much as one degree higher than normal. Being 33 knots higher than the speed necessary for a Category 5 rating, Haiyan would have been a Category 6, if such a category had been created. But much of Haiyan's destructiveness was caused by the massive storm surge it created. Haiyan ended up killing over 5,000 people, displacing over 4 million people, and costing close to $6 billion. Speaking at the climate conference at Warsaw that was then occurring, the Philippines' delegate said: "Typhoons such as Haiyan and its impacts represent a sobering reminder to the international community that we cannot afford to procrastinate on climate action."[51]

Tropical Cyclones Ita and Amanda

In April 2014, northeastern Australia was again hit, this time by Cyclone Ita, the most powerful cyclone since Yasi. Like Yasi, Ita did extensive damage to Queensland and the Great Barrier Reef. The following month, the first-named storm of the year, Tropical Cyclone Amanda, appeared earlier than the June 1 beginning of the hurricane season and turned out to be the strongest Eastern Pacific hurricane ever recorded for May. With wind speeds of up to 145 mph, Amanda topped the previous May record holder, Hurricane Adolphi in 2011. Unsurprisingly, the ocean temperatures in both years were exceptionally warm.[52]

Hurricanes Iselle and Julio

These two storms, which struck Hawaii in August 2014, were exceptional not in terms of their strength, but because Hawaii, which is only rarely hit by hurricanes, was hit by two within a few days. Weather Channel meteorologist Kevin Roth said: "This is unprecedented."[53]

Tornadoes

Tornadoes can be as destructive as hurricanes, and even more so, as can be seen by a brief look at some of the most destructive tornadoes in recent decades.

Recent U.S. Tornadoes

- 1974: The "Super Tornado Outbreak" of April 3–4 was the most devastating U.S. outbreak of the 20th century. Lasting 16 hours and killing 330 people, this outbreak involved 148 tornadoes in or near Xenia, Ohio, six of which were EF-5 tornadoes (the strongest type there is, with wind speeds between 261 and 318 mph).

- 1999: Just outside Oklahoma City, 36 people were killed in Bridge Creek and Moore, which were hit May 3 by a tornado with the highest wind speeds ever measured, 318 mph.

- 2011: The 2011 tornado season was named "the top U.S. weather story of 2011" by Jeff Masters. In a three-month period, beginning in April, the Plains and Southeast U.S. had a tornado onslaught, during which three of the five largest tornado outbreaks on record occurred, killing 552 people. This outbreak included an EF4 tornado that struck Tuscaloosa, Alabama, on April 27, killing 44 people. Late in May, an EF5 tornado in Joplin, Missouri, which killed 122 people, was the most costly (financially) tornado in world history.[54]

- 2012: In March, a "massive tornado outbreak of stunning violence swept through the nation's midsection [during March 2-3]," wrote Masters, "with 70 tornadoes touching down in eleven states, from southern Ohio to southern Georgia. . . . The outbreak spawned two EF4 tornadoes" (which have wind speeds in the range of 207-260 mph).[55]

- 2013: Moore, Oklahoma, which had been struck by a tornado in 1999, was struck in May by a new one, which was at least a mile wide. Then in June, there was an extraordinary EF5 tornado near Oklahoma City, which was the widest documented tornado in U.S. history, with a width of 2.6 miles.[56] Finally, in November, seven Southern and Midwestern states suffered one of the biggest outbreaks ever, with 72 tornadoes, several of which were rated EF3 or EF4.[57]

- 2014: In April, there was a tornado outbreak with 75 tornadoes from Nebraska to North Carolina, one of which was an EF5. Then in June, the tiny town of Pilger, Nebraska, was virtually wiped off the map when two EF3 twisters touched down simultaneously.[58]

Is Global Warming Making Tornadoes More Powerful?

Would a more extensive study of this history show that tornadoes are influenced by global warming? The histories of previously discussed types of extreme weather - heat, drought, precipitation events, and hurricanes – have shown this influence by means of decades-long trends that correlate with increases in the Earth's average temperature. But tornadoes do not, at least as clearly, exhibit a trend.

Although there is no trend showing a greater frequency of tornadoes (indeed, some studies suggest that they have become *less* frequent),[59] there is growing evidence that with tornadoes, similar to hurricanes, the effects of global warming combine, as a NASA report put it, "to cause more continental storms to be of the strongest kind we see today, though there would be fewer storms overall."[60] This seems, in fact, to have become the dominant view among climate scientists and other experts.

- Tony Del Genio, along with other climate scientists at NASA's Goddard Institute for Space Studies, suggested in 2007 that, based on new modeling, there will be fewer tornadoes and other violent storms overall, but we can expect "stronger and more severe storms."

- Harvard's Paul Epstein wrote in 2011: "[T]ornadoes, like hurricanes, will not increase each year. . . . But it is clear that changing atmospheric and oceanic conditions underlie the changing patterns of weather - and that the stage is set for more severe storms, including even more punishing tornadoes."

- Kevin Trenberth has said: "The basic driver of thunderstorms is the instability in the atmosphere: warm moist air at low levels with drier air aloft. With global warming the low level air is warm and moister and there is more energy available to fuel all of these storms."

- In 2013, James Elsner of Florida State University reported: "Beginning in 2000, tornado intensity – as measured by a twister's damage path – started rising sharply." Accordingly, he said, the "risk of violent tornadoes appears to be increasing."

- In 2014, Elsner published new research showing that "the risk of big tornado days featuring densely concentrated tornado outbreaks is on the rise."[61]

Accordingly, we should assume, until evidence shows otherwise, that tornadoes, like the other types of extreme weather, will continue to get worse, as long as the temperature of the planet's atmosphere continues to rise. Given the fact that tornadoes have already become frighteningly destructive in the 20th century and the first decades of the 21st, we should not want to inflict on our children and grandchildren, along with future generations in general, a world that may be even more threatened by tornadoes.

Plans B, A, and C

Plan B

If we follow Plan B, making an immediate and drastic reduction in the emissions of greenhouse gases, the various types of storms would nevertheless continue to become worse until the middle of this century, due to the 30-year delayed responses to emissions already made. And in light of the serious changes that have been brought about by the 0.8°C (1.4°F) increase that has already occurred, we must anticipate that another increase of that same amount would produce much more terrible rain downpours, snowstorms, hurricanes, and tornadoes. Nevertheless, if the planet's average temperature can be kept from increasing greatly, perhaps no more than 1.5°C (2.7°F) beyond pre-industrial times, the destruction of human life and property resulting from these particular effects should be limited.

Plan A

But if the international community refuses to limit its use of fossil fuels, this destructiveness will become increasingly frightful in the second half of this century. After Hurricane Katrina, Joe Romm said: "On our current greenhouse gas emissions path, we face 100 Katrinas," and MIT's Kerry Emanuel noted that the power of hurricanes would likely "continue to increase over the next 100 to 200 years."[62] The same can be expected with regard to deluges and tornadoes.

Plan C

According to Plan C, our political leaders would wait, perhaps another 15 years before deciding whether to institute a crash program to cut back on the emissions of greenhouse gases. This plan would be insane, given Joe Romm's reminder that "lags in the climate system mean we're only now experiencing the temperature and climate changes from CO_2 levels of [many years] ago," so it would be at least 2060 before the planet's temperature could quit rising.[63] In the meantime, moreover, the planet might be brought to a point of no return and hence runaway global warming. With this eventuality, there would be no significant difference from Plan A.

Conclusion

The only rational option is Plan B.

5

SEA-LEVEL RISE

*"This is unprecedented in this area of Antarctica. . . . [N]othing in the
natural world is lost at an accelerating exponential rate like this glacier."*
— Professor Andrew Shepherd, Leeds University, 2009

*"[T]he rise in sea level in the 20th century is unprecedented
for the recent geologic past."*
— Kenneth Miller, Rutgers University, 2011

"Of all the various anticipated impacts of global climate change, sea level rise will likely be the first to produce a human catastrophe on a global scale." So said Orrin Pilkey and Rob Young in a 2009 book, *The Rising Sea*.[1] Whether sea-level rise is the impact that is most likely to produce such a catastrophe — more likely than, say, drought — might be debatable. But continued sea-level rise will certainly produce global-scale catastrophes, especially if business as usual continues.

The centrality of this issue is indicated by James Hansen's description of the Holocene as "the world of stable shorelines in which civilization developed."[2]

During the 20th century, the ocean rose about 8 inches (20 centimeters) and, during the first decade of the 21st century, most climate scientists said that, if business as usual continues, it will rise about a meter (39 inches) by 2100.[3] (The always too-conservative IPCC finally caught up to this projection in its 2014 report, albeit only as the worst-case scenario.[4]) According to a 2011 *Scientific American* article, however, some scientists expected "seas to rise 3 to 6 feet [roughly 1 to 2 meters] by the end of the century." The prior year, Pilkey and Young said that the world should even be prepared for a 7-foot rise. Many scientists considered those predicting a 6- or 7-foot rise to be out in left field, but more recently, evidence suggests that these predictions may be close to the truth if business as usual continues.[5]

In any case, even a two-to-three foot rise would be very destructive. The most obvious effect is that many islands will be partially submerged, including some favorite tourist destinations for Americans, such as the Bahamas, Bermuda, and St. Kitts. Some island nations will even become uninhabitable, leading to "climate refugees," as discussed in Chapter 8.[6]

In addition, the coastal regions of several countries, including China and the United States, would be partially submerged. With regard to China, "A 1-meter rise in sea level would submerge an area the size of Portugal along China's eastern seaboard; the majority of Shanghai - China's largest city – is less than 2 meters above sea level."[7]

Regarding the USA, *National Geographic* wrote in 2012:

> Sea level rise on the U.S. East Coast has accelerated much faster than in other parts of the world - roughly three to four times the global average. . . . [C]ities such as Boston, New York, Philadelphia, and Baltimore could face a more flood-prone future.

Although it might seem self-evident that sea-level rise would be the same everywhere, it actually varies greatly, for several reasons. Even if the global average sea-level rise were to be only three feet, New York City would likely have a rise of about four feet – leading one journalist to ask, "Say Goodbye to the Big Apple?"[8]

Thanks to Superstorm Sandy, we are now aware of how destructive a storm surge can be, especially if a storm strikes at high tide. A recent report about Boston said that "it could be even more vulnerable than New York to rising sea levels." In fact, "had Sandy's storm surge reached Boston 5½ hours earlier than it did," striking it rather than New York City at high tide, we would likely be talking more about *it*.[9]

Moreover, even apart from storm surges, many cities on the East Coast are still more at risk. *The New York Times* provided a map showing that, whereas a sea-level rise of five feet would permanently submerge (during high tide) 7 percent of New York City, it would submerge 20 percent of Miami and 94 percent of Miami Beach.[10] In "Goodbye, Miami," Jeff Goodell wrote that Miami is "on its way to becoming an American Atlantis," quoting the geology professors as saying, "If you live in South Florida and you're not building a boat, you're not facing reality."[11]

Worldwide, said World Watch founder Lester Brown, "The country where rising seas threaten the most people is China, with 144 million potential climate refugees." Next are India, Bangladesh, Viet Nam, Indonesia, and Japan.[12]

Thermal Expansion, Ice-Melting, and Sea-Level Rise

The rising sea level has two causes, both rooted in global warming: First, as the ocean gets warmer, its waters expand. This phenomenon, called "thermal expansion," has thus far been the main cause: "In the 20th century," say Pilkey and Young, "sea level rise was primarily due to thermal expansion of ocean water."[13]

Although the increase in the planet's mean temperature will continue to cause the ocean to expand in this century, a greater percentage of the sea-level rise will be due to the second cause, the melting of land ice. Indeed, melting now reportedly accounts for about 75 percent of the sea-level rise. During the 20th century, the melt water came primarily from glaciers and ice caps, but in the 21st century, it will increasingly come from the three giant ice sheets of Greenland, West Antarctica, and East Antarctica.[14] (Technically, the ice sheets are also glaciers, called "continental glaciers." But to employ that language would require us to use some adjective, such as "non-continental" or "local," for all mountain glaciers, which would be cumbersome and contrary to the meaning of "glacier" presupposed by most people. So this chapter simply distinguishes between "ice sheets" and "glaciers.")

After looking briefly at the glaciers and the melting of the Arctic sea ice, this chapter looks at why the continued melting of the three ice sheets will be disastrous.

Glaciers

Until recently, ordinary glaciers had contributed more to sea-level rise than the trio of giant ice sheets. Although the glaciers have evidently been overtaken by the ice sheets, the melting of glaciers will continue to contribute to global sea-level rise until they disappear.[15]

Part of the story about glaciers is that some of them have disappeared; this fact will be discussed in the chapter about fresh water. But there are still many glaciers that, having not completely melted, are continuing to shrink. Some glaciers are remaining the same and a few are even growing, but "the overwhelming trend in glaciers worldwide is retreat," and "the global melt rate has been accelerating since the mid-1970s."[16]

Arctic Sea Ice

A dramatic sign of global warming is the melting of the Arctic sea ice. Although scientists had previously predicted that the summers in the Arctic would not become completely ice-free until at least 2100, recent studies show that Arctic sea ice has been "disappearing at a far greater rate than previously expected." When the Arctic sea ice is completely melted in the summer, this will constitute the end of a very long era. Neven Acropolis – who founded the Arctic Sea Ice Blog – explained:

Since the start of the current ice age, about 2.5 million years ago, the Arctic Ocean has been completely covered with sea ice. Only during interglacials [several-thousand-year periods of warm weather separating glacial periods], like the one we are in now, does some of the sea ice melt during summer.[17]

For *all* the ice to melt during the summers, therefore, would indicate the crossing of a major threshold. Although scientists originally thought that this would not happen until far in the future, processes occurred much more quickly than anyone expected. "When the IPCC released its Fourth Assessment Report in 2007, it was generally thought that the Arctic could become ice-free [during summers] somewhere near the end of this century." However, that same year, which RealClimate.org called "apocalyptic for Arctic sea ice," saw the greatest amount of ice-loss ever, leading Mark Serreze, a senior scientist at the National Snow and Ice Data Center in Boulder, to say: "The Arctic is screaming." A paper of that year (2007) said that there might be "an ice-free Arctic in summer sometime within the upcoming decades."[18]

2012 was even worse: The amount of ice that disappeared, according to one calculation, was "equal to the areas of Alaska and Canada, combined." No longer merely screaming, the Arctic appeared to be in a death spiral: Cambridge professor Peter Wadhams, one of the foremost experts on the Arctic, predicted in 2012 that the Arctic would have ice-free summers by 2016. More generally, it is expected that, at the current rate of ice-melt, this will happen no later than 2020.[19]

The loss of Arctic sea ice, it is well known, has been having tragic consequences for polar bears - "the magnificent animal that symbolises more than any other our failure to safeguard the planet that every living creature calls home."[20] However, one might think sea-ice loss will have no direct effect on humans because it is irrelevant to the level of the seas (because the sea ice is already in the ocean, it raises the water level the same amount whether it is in a solid or liquid state). However, the melting is relevant for at least three reasons:

- It provides a warning: "The Arctic is global warming's canary in the coal mine. . . . Most scientists view what's happening now in the Arctic as a harbinger of things to come."

- More directly, sea ice is highly reflective: When sun shines on it, the ice reflects most of the sunlight back into space, so that it does not heat up the atmosphere. But where the ice has been melted, the sun's rays penetrate into the Arctic Sea's dark ocean water, heating it up. "The extra radiation absorbed because of the Arctic sea-ice loss," Wadhams calculated, is "the equivalent of about 20 years of additional CO_2 being added by man." Because the loss of Arctic sea ice increases global warming and thereby raises the sea level, Acropolis said that "what happens in the Arctic, doesn't stay in the Arctic."

- Third, if Arctic warming continues, it threatens to thaw permafrost - hitherto permanently frozen soil – thereby releasing an enormous amount of carbon into the atmosphere. Continued warming of the Arctic Ocean could, moreover, liberate high levels of methane – a greenhouse gas much more potent than carbon dioxide[21] - this being one of the primary examples of dangerous feedback: The warmer temperature releases millions of tons of carbon and methane, which then further raise the temperature, which in turn releases more carbon and methane. "I just don't see a happy ending for this," said Ted Scambos of the National Snow and Ice Data Center."[22]

A recent article by NASA asked: "Is a Sleeping Climate Giant Stirring in the Arctic?" Our politicians and the fossil-fuel companies seemed intent on waking this giant, as the temperatures in the Arctic, revealed a 2014 article, "have not been matched or exceeded for roughly 120,000 years" – in other words, 10 times longer than civilization has existed.[23]

Greenland

One of the reasons to bemoan the loss of arctic ice is that it "will likely accelerate . . . the disintegration of the Greenland ice sheet." In 2012, Bill McKibben wrote, "There's no place on Earth that's changing faster – and no place where that change matters more – than Greenland." Things have been changing so fast that, since the 1980s, the air temperature of Greenland has increased an astounding 3.6°F.[24]

Compared with the Antarctic ice sheets (consisting of the West and East Antarctic ice sheets), the Greenland ice sheet is rather small. Nevertheless, this ice sheet, which covers roughly 80 percent of Greenland, is still large, being three times the size of Texas, or 14 times that of England. Accordingly, as Paul Brown pointed out in 2007, melting of the Greenland ice sheet "could be catastrophic in terms of sea level rise," because if it were to melt totally, the world's average sea level "would rise seven metres [23 feet]."[25]

Not long before, climate scientists believed that the Greenland ice sheet was so stable that many thousands of years would be required for it to completely melt. But developments in recent years have shaken this confidence. It could have been shaken in the 1990s, when scientists discovered that the sheet had started to lose about 48 cubic miles a year, but that seemed a small amount, given the enormity of the sheet.[26] In the present century, however, the rate of the loss has accelerated. In 2007, Brown reported, journalists were shaken by a helicopter trip they took over Greenland at the time of the ice melt of that year:

> What they were all talking about was the moulins, not one moulin but hundreds, possibly thousands. 'Moulin' is . . . the name for a giant hole in a glacier through which millions of gallons of melt water cascade through to the rock below. The water has the effect of lubricating the glaciers so they move at three times the rate that they did previously. Some of these moulins in Greenland are so big that they run on the scale of Niagara Falls.

However, no actions were taken to slow the rise, and three years later the unusually hot summer of 2010 caused the Greenland ice sheet to lose 100 billion tons in mass. One year later, a news report was headed: "Greenland Melting in 2011 Well Above Average with Near-Record Mass Loss." Behind that headline was a drama: Thanks to satellite images, "scientists watched the sea ice that hugs the Greenland and Antarctic shores dwindle and disappear." These images revealed that "far more melt water is being added to the oceans than was previously expected." Another news report was headed: "Greenland Ice Melt Sets a Record – and Could Set the Stage for Sea Level Rise."[27]

That same year – 2011 – a team of climate scientists, having studied developments over 18 years, reported that each year, "the Greenland ice sheet lost mass faster than it did the year before," and the following year, Greenland was reported to be losing "almost 290 billion tons a year." That same year – 2012 - there was a massive, puzzling melting: Whereas there had previously been extensive melting only on about 55 percent of the ice sheet, the melting suddenly went from 40 to 97 percent in four days. Asking whether this was a fluke, a 2013 study instead concluded that it was a sign of things to come: By 2025, there would be a 50-50 chance of such rapid and widespread melting happening annually. Another 2013 story suggested that portions of the sheet "may be vulnerable to rapid ice loss through catastrophic disintegration."[28]

Still other scientists have suggested that the ice sheet may be moving into a process in which the melting becomes irreversible. A 2011 report suggested that the ice sheet "could undergo a self-amplifying cycle of melting and warming that would be difficult to halt" and that it might be close to a "tipping point." Ohio State polar researcher Jason Box, founder of the blog Meltfactor, has pointed out that the Greenland ice sheet, by virtue of losing snow, is becoming darker, thereby losing its reflectivity. "In this condition, the ice sheet will continue to absorb more solar energy in a self-reinforcing feedback loop that amplifies the effect of warming." A 2012 report said that "just losing 10% of the ice sheet can be enough to make the process irreversible."[29]

Unfortunately, a major international study published in 2012 suggested that the sheet may have been melting almost five times faster than in the mid-1990s. This rapid disintegration of the Greenland ice sheet surprised researchers, because their models did not allow for such rapid change. In response, new models have been developed. In addition to the 2011 idea of "self-amplification," a 2013 article named "Like Butter" explained that meltwater drains through cracks in the ice sheet, where it "warms the ice sheet, which then - like a warm stick of butter - softens, deforms, and flows faster."[30]

As a result of the unprecedented melting of the Greenland ice sheet, which has had a four-fold increase in its ice loss, its "contribution to global sea level has soared in the past two decades," to about one-fourth of the global sea-level rise during that period. But recent developments indicate that it will soon contribute even more.[31]

A major way in which ice is lost is for glaciers to move from land to the sea. They have usually moved, unsurprisingly, at a "glacial pace." But according to a 2014 study of Jakobshavn glacier - Greenland's largest glacier, which is believed to be the source of the iceberg that sank the Titanic – it is now moving ice from land into the ocean at a speed that appears to be the fastest ever recorded. . . , more than 10.5 miles (17 kilometers) per year, or more than 150 feet (46 meters) per day." Joe Romm quipped, "Greenland's glaciers are now moving faster than America's climate policy."[32]

In any case, an even more surprising study was published later in 2014. Whereas scientists had long known about melting in most parts of Greenland - especially the southwest, where Jakobshavn is - the northeast had always been considered stable, an international study reported that the ice in this region had been thinning since 2003, after three especially warm summers. Still more surprising, the study indicated that the largest glacier in that region, the Zachariae, had been retreating even faster than Jakobshavn: Whereas the latter had retreated 21.7 miles in 150 years (which was considered fast), Zachariae had retreated 12.4 miles *in a decade*.[33]

This calculation of the rate of the retreat was so astounding, and so out of line with previous studies, that some Greenland experts had doubted it. "Nobody else has really seen this big dynamic [ice loss] signal they're seeing," said one. "I'm not sure how they arrive at these high thinning rates," said another, "I just don't agree with the numbers they're coming up with."[34] In any case, everyone agrees that there is no longer a part of Greenland that is stable. Because the northeast region had not been included in any models of sea-level rise, moreover, the rise is likely to be higher than recent models had suggested.

In *Merchants of Doubt* (which plays a major role in Chapter 11), Naomi Oreskes and Erik Conway wrote: "Rome may not be burning, but Greenland is melting, and we are still fiddling." Hansen has said that estimations of a slow disintegration of the Greenland ice sheet are based on linear assumptions, which correspond to "paleoclimate ice sheet changes [that] were initiated by weak climate forcings changing slowly over thousands of years," whereas contemporary climate changes are being brought about by quite violent forcings, so that we should expect Greenland's mass loss to be non-linear - that is, exponential.[35]

Hansen added that this likelihood is especially serious to Europeans and North Americans: "If the world allows a substantial fraction of the Greenland ice sheet to disintegrate, all hell breaks loose for eastern North America and Europe."[36]

However, in spite of such warnings, the world is still fiddling: In 2014, 40% of the Greenland Ice Sheet melted during the summer, rather than the normal 15%, and a new study based on satellite data showed that just since 2009, the volume loss had doubled.[37]

Antarctica

The Antarctic ice sheet, which covers about 98% of the Antarctic continent, is the largest mass of ice on Earth, having 10 times as much ice as Greenland. Antarctica had been stable for at least 10,000 years, and as late as 2001 the IPCC thought that it would lose little mass by 2100. But in a 2008 article entitled "The Antarctic Ice Sheet Hits the Fan," Romm wrote that it was "losing mass much faster than anyone expected." The following year, he reported that it was losing ice four times faster than just 10 years before. Indeed, as Penn State climate scientist Richard Alley put it, the Antarctic ice sheet had been losing mass "100 years ahead of schedule."[38]

East and West Antarctic Ice Sheets

Although it has been customary to speak simply of "the Antarctic ice sheet," it is necessary to distinguish between the West and the East Antarctic ice sheets. For one thing, East Antarctica is a single continent, whereas West Antarctica is, as one writer put it, "a series of islands covered by ice," sort of "a frozen Hawaii." Also the West and East have different elevations. The East Antarctic ice sheet is on dry land, with two thirds of it being a high, cold desert, whereas the West Antarctic ice sheet is grounded below sea level, which allows it to be destabilized by increasingly warm ocean water.[39]

Finally, the two ice sheets are very different in size: The West Antarctic ice sheet, if fully melted, would raise the ocean by about 19 feet, so it is comparable to Greenland's ice sheet, which would raise it about 23. But the East Antarctic ice sheet, being about the size of Australia, "would raise global sea level by about 60 meters (197 feet)."[40]

The East Antarctic Ice Sheet

The giant East Antarctic ice sheet had long been thought to be entirely stable, but recently it has been "beginning to crumble." Since 2006, scientists have been learning from NASA's "GRACE" (Gravity Recovery and Climate Experiment) program that "there has been more ice loss from East Antarctica than previously thought." To be more specific, GRACE's satellite survey showed that the "East Antarctic ice sheet is losing around 57 billion tons of ice a year into surrounding waters" – a fact that is "raising fears that global sea levels will rise faster than scientists expected."[41]

The West Antarctic Ice Sheet

West Antarctica is entirely different. Its ice sheet has lost considerable mass following a large increase in land temperature: Since 1960, it has gone up roughly 5 degrees F (3°C), making it perhaps *the* fastest-warming region on the planet.[42]

This ice sheet's changing condition has been dramatized by the disintegration of huge ice shelves, which are "permanent floating sheets of ice that connect to a landmass." This process began with one called the Larsen Ice Shelf, which actually consisted of three shelves, named Larsen A, B, and C. Larsen A, the smallest, disintegrated in 1995. In 2002, scientists "watched in amazement as almost the entire Larsen B Ice Shelf," an area of 1,250 square miles (3,250 square kilometers) – "collapsed in just over one month." In 2013, scientists learned that "[o]ne Antarctic ice shelf has completely disappeared and another has lost a chunk three times the size of Rhode Island."[43]

But this did not stop the disintegration. In 2012, climate scientist Andrew Monaghan said: "A growing body of research shows that the West Antarctic Ice Sheet is changing at an alarming rate, with pressure coming from both a warming ocean and a warming atmosphere." Next, attention turned to the huge Pine Island Glacier, which, constituting about 10 percent of the ice on Antarctica, is its biggest contributor to sea-level rise. In 2013, an NBC story reported that an expedition to this glacier revealed that "currents of warm water beneath the glacier are melting the ice at a staggering rate of about 2.4 inches (6 centimeters) per day."[44]

Then in 2014, French scientists declared that Pine Island Glacier "has started a phase of self-sustained retreat and will irreversibly continue its decline." One of these scientists said: "We have passed the tipping point."[45]

The Antarctic Paradox: Growing Sea Ice

While the sea ice in the Arctic has been declining, the amount of ice in the ocean surrounding Antarctica has been steadily growing, making it possible for penguins to stand farther north than had previously been recorded. Some non-scientists have said that global warming is contradicted by the fact that Antarctic ice has been growing, so there is no basis for the "alarmist" worry that it will contribute to sea-level rise. But this is a confused claim, based on a failure to distinguish between sea ice and land ice. When scientists report the loss of Antarctic ice, which is raising the sea level, they are talking about ice on land, which is ice formed from precipitation. The sea ice is "entirely different," because it "forms in salt water during the winter and almost entirely melts again in the summer." So although it does increase greatly in the winter, this increase is irrelevant to the question of ice loss in Antarctica.[46]

Sometimes the charge of contradiction is based on sea ice alone. For example, climate-change denialist James Taylor, writing in *Forbes*, said: "Sea ice around one pole is shrinking while sea ice around another pole is growing. This sure sounds like a global warming crisis to me." But this is not a contradiction, for three reasons:

- The growth of Antarctic sea ice does not mean that the Southern Ocean has been getting colder.

- "The Arctic is an ocean surrounded by land, while the Antarctic is land surrounded by ocean."

- Fact Checker's Mark Robinson said, "an increase in Antarctic sea ice not only isn't contradicted by trends toward higher global temperatures but is to be expected, according to the scientists who study it."[47]

One of those scientists is Penn State's Andrew Carleton. As fresh water melts into the ocean, he explained to PBS, it decreases the salinity of the seawater. Water with less salt content freezes at a higher temperature, so even with warming air temperatures melting the glaciers, the Antarctic Ocean continues to gain sea ice. "It seems paradoxical," Carleton said, "but it makes sense." An additional explanation has been given in the *Proceedings of the National Academy of Sciences* by Jipling Liu and Judith Curry, who said: "Associated with the warming, there has been an enhanced atmospheric hydrological cycle in the Southern Ocean that results in an increase of the Antarctic sea ice for the past three decades through the reduced upward ocean heat transport and increased snowfall."[48]

In any case, the main point is that, although Antarctic's sea ice has been growing, "Antarctica is losing land ice as a whole, and these losses are accelerating quickly." Indeed, a 2014 study based on satellite data showed that the volume loss of the West Antarctic ice sheet had increased by a factor of 3 since 2009.[49]

Plans B, A, and C

It is now time to ask what the choice of one of our three plans would mean for sea-level rise.

Plan B

Acting in accordance with Plan B would mean going into immediate and complete mobilization, racing against time to prevent the kind of sea-level rise that would result from the continuation of business as usual. However, even this will not prevent continued sea-level rise from causing much distress over the next 30 years, because a great amount of further sea-level rise is already built into the system. As Romm pointed out in *Hell and High Water*, global warming has already guaranteed that while it will "feel like hell" in many parts of the world, global warming will also produce a lot of "high water" in many parts of the world. But if Plan B is followed, the high water may quit rising before it drives many billions of people to migrate or move inland.

Advocating the need for Plan B will, of course, be controversial, because explaining the need for it will require pointing out that, according to current projections, long-term investments in expensive coastal properties would no longer be wise. The North Carolina Senate dealt with this problem by passing a law in 2012 saying that state agencies would need to base all assumptions about sea-level rise solely on linear projections from historical data, meaning they must assume that the sea level will rise only 8 inches. Faux-conservative comedian Stephen Colbert reported: "Scientists predict an economy-destroying, 39-inch sea level rise, but North Carolina drafts a law to make it eight inches."[50]

Plan A

If business as usual continues, the sea level will rise by "around 1 foot by 2050, then 4 to 6 feet (or more) by 2100, rising some 6 to 12 inches (or more) each decade thereafter," said Romm. Moreover, if business as usual continues, the ice sheets of Greenland and West Antarctica will disintegrate, bringing about an additional sea-level rise of 39 feet, which would completely submerge the lands of the approximately 650 million people who live in coastal areas that are less than 33 feet above sea level.[51] Plan A, which means "continuing to do nothing," will mean simply writing off not only the island nations but also the most populous and agricultural portions of China and many other countries - and even some of America's leading cities, including Boston, New York, Washington D.C., Miami, Seattle, Los Angeles, and San Francisco. A 2014 study of the prospects for Washington, for example, said that "at least one flood reaching above 10 feet would be close to certain this century.[52]"

One of the commissioners of the San Francisco Public Utilities Commission, pointing out that San Francisco International Airport would be flooded, said that "the solution to climate change is clear: fly Oakland." But then, he added, "Oops, maybe not" – because the Oakland airport's runways, access roads, and terminals would also be underwater.[53] Gallows humor aside, it is hard to believe that American and Chinese leaders believe that there are goals more important than saving the coastal zones of America, China, and other countries.

Plan C

Following Plan C would mean doing little or nothing until political leaders realize that the climate scientists were right about sea-level rise. Although this plan might seem like a reasonable compromise between Plan A and Plan B, its impact on the lives of our children and grandchildren would likely be little different from Plan A. If, for example, political leaders in 2025 finally decide that any further sea-level rise would be intolerable, the CO_2 in the atmosphere would continue to raise the global temperature until at least 2055, and by that time the sea level would be far beyond intolerable and a tipping point for the giant ice sheets will likely have been passed.

Conclusion

Plan B, accordingly, is the only sensible plan.

6

FRESH WATER
SHORTAGE

*"Glacier retreat in the tropical Andes
over the last three decades is unprecedented."*
– Antoine Rabatel, Laboratory for Glaciology and Environmental
Geophysics, Grenoble, France, 2013

*"With [Lake] Mead's levels just as low [as Lake Powell's],
officials in Nevada and other states are predicting
an unprecedented water crisis."*
– Frances Weaver, The Week, February, 2014

In 2012, a *New York Times* article said: "More than anything else, climate change is a water problem." When we think of climate change as a water problem, we often think of the coming sea-level rise. But far more people have been worried about what is sometimes called the "other water problem": the lack of sufficient fresh water. "Among the environmental specters confronting humanity in the 21st century," said a 2002 *National Geographic* article, "shortage of fresh water is at the top of the list." At the end of 2013, the Potsdam Institute completed an international, comprehensive study of the human impacts from climate change, in which it concluded that "water is the biggest worry."[1]

In a 2002 book called *Blue Gold*, Canadians Maude Barlow and Tony Clark wrote: "There is simply no way to overstate the fresh water crisis on the planet today." Ten years later, they warned: "Unless we dramatically change our ways, between one-half and two-thirds of humanity will be living with severe freshwater shortages within the next quarter-century." That same year – 2012 - a U.S. intelligence report said that "nearly half of the world's population [is already] experiencing severe water stress." Moreover, giving support to the description of water as "blue gold," a 2012 report by the National Intelligence Council said: "Water may become a more significant source of contention than energy or minerals." Indeed, it is now often said that water is more valuable than oil.[2]

Due to overpopulation, increasing industrialization, and other factors, there would be a water crisis even if climate change were not occurring. But this change has been making the crisis worse, and it threatens in the near future to make it *much* worse. Indeed, Lester Brown wrote in 2013: "Peak oil has generated headlines in recent years, but the real threat to our future is peak water. There are substitutes for oil, but not for water." Tom Brown, co-author of a 2012 U.S. Forest Service study, said: "We were surprised to find that climate change is likely to have a much greater effect on future water demands than population growth."[3]

Climate change causes the reduction of water availability in various ways, including rainfall in the wrong places (the ocean or places with too much rain already), and rainfall at the wrong times, alternating between drought and deluge (which does not give water time to soak in). But the main cause is the warmer weather: Besides reducing water availability by requiring more water for both drinking and agriculture, warmer weather mainly does so through its melting of our "reservoirs in the sky" – glaciers and snowpack.[4]

Glaciers[5]

A glacier can be considered "a natural water reservoir. It accumulates water during the winter, and then during the summer when it melts, it lets it out at a nice consistent rate." But if glaciers melt too much – more than the winter snows will replace – the consequences will be serious because, as Lester Brown has said, "it is the summer ice melt from these glaciers that sustains so many of the world's rivers during the dry season." This fact is a problem because, as a 2011 *National Geographic* story said: "Mountain glaciers long have been known to be in retreat as the planet warms. But the process is occurring even more rapidly than previously believed." And there is no doubt that humans are the cause: While a recent study showed that humans were responsible for about one fourth of the planet's loss of glacier mass, we account for almost 70 percent of the loss over the past two decades. This human-caused loss has been occurring, moreover, in many places around the world.[6]

North America

The problem of melting glaciers is not quite as serious in North America as it is in many other places, because there are fewer people in North America dependent on meltwater from glaciers. But it is still serious.

Glacier National Park: Although at one time, Glacier National Park in Montana had 150 glaciers, there are now only 25, leading CNN to call it "the poster-child for climate change." In light of the park's name, it is nice that a few glaciers do remain. But a study in 2003 predicted that none will be left by 2030, and some scientists have even predicted that Glacier's "heat stroke" will eliminate all of its glaciers by 2020, so the park may, as one environmentalist quipped, need a name change. The dark humor is inevitable, but the complete loss of the glaciers will be devastating for the park's wildlife and vegetation.[7]

Although the glaciers of this park, unlike most of the glaciers to be discussed below, are not very important for drinking water and agriculture, the coming death of Glacier National Park, by virtue of its name, provides an especially graphic example of what global warming is doing to our beautiful world.[8]

The Canadian Rocky Mountains: The massive glaciers of Canada's Saint Elias region, which now consists of nearly 98 cubic miles (453 cubic kilometers) of ice, will probably - assuming the continuation of the present level of emissions - be only half this size by 2100. Garry Clarke, emeritus professor of glaciology at the University of British Columbia, said that some glaciers in parts of the Canadian Rockies will shrink to remnants, perhaps 5 to 20 percent of their current size, while others will disappear completely.[9]

Alaska's Glaciers: Alaska has thousands of glaciers, most of which have been retreating. One of the best known is the 12-mile long Mendenhall Glacier, which is so close to the state's capital, Juneau, that the visitor center bills it as the "drive-up glacier." But the glacier has retreated so rapidly that the director of the visitor center has said: "Right now we're using 60-power spotting scopes to find the mountain goats up on the peaks. How long is it going to be until we need to use those to find the glacier?"[10]

South America

"Glaciers, especially tropical glaciers, are the canaries in the coal mine for our global climate system," stated Lonnie Thompson of Ohio State University, one of the world's leading glaciologists. The canaries of South America are not healthy. Andean glaciers are the "natural water towers" for many South Americans, including those in the capital cities of Ecuador (Quito), Peru (Lima), Chile (Santiago), and Bolivia (La Paz). These "frozen water towers" have served as reservoirs "providing a steady summer water supply for drinking and agriculture," as a *Scientific American* article has said. These glaciers have been providing water for around 80 million people, but a recent study of the Andean glaciers shows that they have shrunk "30 to 50% since the 1970s" and that, if warming continues, many of the glaciers will completely disappear within 20 years.[11]

Peru: The home of 70% of the world's tropical glaciers, Peru has 29 million people, 60 percent of whom live in the semi-arid coastal region. Peru's glaciers have always provided water for Lima, other cities, and for farmers, who are totally dependent on glacier water during the annual dry season. But over 20% of Peru's glaciers have now disappeared and, experts say, all the glaciers may disappear within 20 years. Peruvians say that, if this occurs, they will have to change the name of the mountain range, Cordillera Blanca ("White Range").

The biggest body of ice in South America is Peru's ice cap called Quelccaya. Its Qori Kalis glacier has probably been the most rigorously tested glacier in the world, thanks to Lonnie Thompson, who has shown that it has been retreating at an ever-faster pace. Having retreated 20 feet (6 meters) a year in the 1960s, by 2007 it was retreating 200 feet (60 meters) every year. In 2009, Thompson said, "it's now retreating up the mountainside by about 18 inches a day, which means you can almost sit there and watch it lose ground." In 2013, Thompson reported that data from ice cores, which he had been gathering for many years, showed that ice that had been long accumulated on Quelccaya, at least 1,600 years, had recently melted in 25 years. Finally, in 2014, a paper reported a study, in which Thompson was not involved, that supported his long-held view that the retreat of glaciers has been driven mainly by warming (rather than a drop in precipitation).[12]

Bolivia: "In recent decades," wrote Carolyn Kormann, "20,000-year-old glaciers in Bolivia have been retreating so fast that 80 percent of the ice will be gone before a child born today reaches adulthood." Bolivia's best known glacier has been an 18,000 year-old glacier named Chacaltaya ("cold road"), an appropriate name because it provided the highest ski run in the world. By 2009, however, Chacaltaya had completely melted, leaving nothing but rocks and mud. This was sad for skiers, but the truly important tragedy is that Chacaltaya had been providing water for millions of Bolivia's people, including those of La Paz. This ex-glacier has become "the most glaring symbol of Bolivia's rapidly transforming cryosphere."[13]

Patagonia: Comprising parts of both Chile and Argentina, Patagonia lies in the southernmost part of South America. The Patagonian Icefield is, apart from Antarctica, the largest mass of ice in the southern hemisphere. But it is retreating quickly. A recent study found that, between 2000 and 2012, "the Southern Patagonian Icefield glaciers thinned by about six feet per year."[14]

Europe

The glaciers in Europe have, like most of the glaciers around the world, been melting since the 1980s at an accelerating rate. Scientists believe – said

Wilfried Haeberli, the director of the World Glacier Monitoring Service – that European glaciers have lost one quarter of their mass in the last eight years alone.[15]

The Alps: A 2009 report of the European Environment Agency said: "Since 1980, alpine glaciers have lost about 20–30% of their remaining ice. The hot summer of 2003 led to a loss of 10% of the remaining glacier substance in the Alps." These figures show that the retreat of the Alps "far exceeds the background rate that could be expected as part of natural climate variations."[16]

According to a 2012 report, "Half the volume of Europe's Alpine glaciers has disappeared since 1850," and this disappearance has not been steady: "Glacier melting has accelerated in the European Alps since 1980, and 10 to 20 percent of glacier ice in the Alps has been lost in less than two decades."[17] Continuing loss will be extremely harmful to Europe in several ways. The European Environmental Agency stated in 2010:

> The Alps are an iconic symbol of Europe. One of the continent's prime tourist destinations, the range provides much more than holiday destinations. Forty per cent of Europe's fresh water originates there, supplying tens of millions of Europeans in lowland areas. No wonder the Alps are sometimes called the 'water towers of Europe.' This fresh water is vital, not only to the eight Alpine countries [Austria, Germany, France, Italy, Liechtenstein, Monaco, Slovenia, and Switzerland] but a huge part of continental Europe.[18]

Some parts of Europe are especially dependent upon the water from the Alps. The cities of Milan and Turin, for example, get up to 80 percent of their water from them.[19]

The Pyrenees: The most rapid melting of glaciers in Europe has been happening in Spain's Pyrenees mountain range. According to a 2009 report by the World Glacier Monitoring Service, the Pyrenees have, over the past century, lost almost 90 percent of their glacier ice. At this rate, said Wilfried Haeberli, they will likely disappear completely within a few decades. This disappearance of a major source of summer water, reported a 2009 story in the *Guardian,* will have a severe impact on Spain's agriculture.[20]

Africa

Climate change is also threatening Africa's glaciers, including its most famous one.

Kilimanjaro: Ernest Hemingway, in a story called "The Snows of Kilimanjaro," made this mountain - the highest one in Africa - famous. This mountain's "snows," however, are actually glaciers, and the glaciers of Mount Kilimanjaro are headed for extinction. Lonnie Thompson, who has been going to Tanzania for several decades to study Kilimanjaro's dwindling ice, recently said that it "continues to diminish right on schedule for disappearing, unfortunately, in the next couple of decades."[21]

Al Gore's treatment of the partial disappearance of the glaciers of Kilimanjaro is one of the most impressive segments of his film, *An Inconvenient Truth*. Perhaps partly for this reason, people seeking to discredit Gore's message about global warming's effects have attempted to argue that, although the glaciers of Kilimanjaro have diminished, this has not been due to human influence. But this attempt has been a failure.

One fact that disproved Gore's (and hence the IPCC's) view, according to advocates of an alternative interpretation, was that the retreat of Kilimanjaro had begun in the 19th century, before there was any significant human-caused warming. This claim was then combined with one or another theory, especially the idea that precipitation had declined, with the result that ice could disappear because of a process called "sublimation," in which ice can, in very dry and cold conditions, vaporize without first melting. This theory, however, did not fit the facts.[22]

Mount Kenya: Although Kilimanjaro is the best known African mountain, at least to Westerners, some of the other glacier-covered mountains are more important to Africans, such as Africa's second highest, but it is in deep trouble. Lester Brown wrote: "Mount Kenya has lost 7 of its 18 glaciers. Local rivers fed by these glaciers are becoming seasonal rivers, generating conflict among the 2 million people who depend on them for water supplies during the dry season."[23]

Africa's Alps: The third highest mountain in Africa is Mount Stanley, which is part of the Rwenzori mountains in Uganda, sometimes called "Africa's Alps." The name Rwenzori in the local language means "rain-maker," but within two decades its 43 glaciers, say scientists, "will be bare rock" – leading a British mountaineer to say: "It is such a shame to think that any children I may have will never get to see the ice-capped peaks." Even more serious is the coming loss of sustainable water supplies, which is "already impacting agricultural production and cutting the output of hydroelectric power plants," said a professor at Uganda's Makere University.[24]

Asia

In terms of the sheer numbers of people who depend on them, the glaciers of Asia are the most important.

Indonesia: Puncak Jaya on the island of Papua New Guinea is the highest mountain in Indonesia, the highest mountain on an island, and the highest point between the Andes and the Himalayas. Nevertheless, when Thompson, who had studied it in the 1970s, returned to it for two weeks in 2010, he was pounded every day with rain, something he had never experienced on a glacier. "These glaciers are dying," Thompson said: "Before I was thinking they had a few decades, but now I'd say we're looking at years."[25]

This glacier further demonstrates the fact that they are melting all around the world. Like those at Glacier National Park, however, the Indonesian glaciers do not provide a lot of water for people. Asian water is supplied primarily by the glaciers of the Himalayas and those, more inclusively, of the "third pole."

Himalayan, Tibetan Plateau, and Third Pole Glaciers: The three names, Himalayan glaciers, Tibetan Plateau glaciers, and Third Pole glaciers, are used in a variety of ways.

- Some articles equate the first and third terms, saying that the "glaciers of the Himalayas are the Third Pole."[26]

- Some articles equate the second and third terms, using "Third Pole glaciers" to refer to "glaciers on the Tibetan plateau."[27]

- Some articles speak simply of the "Himalayan glaciers," as if it were an inclusive term, but then refer to the "glaciers in the Himalayas and the Tibetan Plateau."[28]

- Others use "Hindu Kush Himalayan Ice Sheet" as the inclusive term, according to which this sheet – "the largest ice mass outside the two poles" – includes both the Himalayas and the Third Pole.[29]

- Still others refer to the glaciers of "the Tibetan plateau and surrounding region."[30]

Arguably, the last of these descriptions, which is that of Thompson and Tandong Yao – the director of the Institute of Tibetan Plateau Research at the Chinese Academy of Sciences – is the most adequate. That description, explained Jane Qiu in *Nature*, is shorthand for the "Tibetan plateau and the bordering mountain ranges, the Himalayas, the Karakoram, the Pamir and the Qilian," which make up "a vast region known as the Third Pole, home to 100,000 square kilometres of glaciers that supply water to about 1.4 billion people in Asia."[31]

The term "Third Pole" refers to the fact that this region contains the third-largest mass of ice on earth, which encompasses thousands of glaciers, with estimates running from 15,000 to 45,000. These glaciers store more usable fresh water than any other mountain range (the fresh water in the Greenland and Antarctic ice sheets has not been usable). The number of people who depend on them for water range from "hundreds of millions" to Jane Qiu's "1.4 billion" to "three billion."[32]

Like most glaciers around the world, these glaciers are losing mass. However, the 2007 IPCC report erroneously said that "glaciers in the Himalaya are receding faster than in any other part of the world and, if the present rate continues, the likelihood of them disappearing by the year 2035 and perhaps sooner is very high if the Earth keeps warming at the current rate."[33]

In making its erroneous statement, the IPCC uncharacteristically relied on a comment by a scientist in a popular magazine (not in a scientific journal), and as such it had not been peer-reviewed. Although this error was found by fellow climate scientists, not denialists, the latter used it to speak of a new climate scandal, "Glaciergate," with some denialists even claiming that the Himalayan glaciers were not shrinking but growing.[34]

However, multiple scientific studies have shown that these glaciers are indeed retreating, albeit not as fast as suggested in the 2007 IPCC report. For example, the Skeptical Science website said in 2010, "Satellites and on-site measurements are observing that Himalayan glaciers are disappearing at an accelerating rate." In addition, Rajendra Pachauri, the IPCC chairperson, has said: "There is no scientific doubt on the rapid melting of the glaciers in the Himalayas, although they are very unlikely to disappear during the next few decades."[35]

In any case, given the importance of these Third Pole glaciers for such a huge number of people, their disintegration would be a disaster second to none. Besides reporting in 2012 that "the majority of the glaciers have been shrinking rapidly," Tandong Yao said that "the rate of retreat had accelerated." For Yao, this is far from merely academic: "The full-scale glacier shrinkage in the plateau region," he had said several years earlier, "will eventually lead to an ecological catastrophe."[36]

The issue of the rapid shrinking needed discussion in 2012 because, it had been reported earlier that year, "an analysis of 7 years' worth of measurements, taken by the Gravity Recovery and Climate Experiment (GRACE) satellite mission, suggested that high-altitude Asian glaciers on the whole are losing ice only one-tenth as fast as previously estimated, and that glaciers on the Tibetan plateau are actually growing." By contrast, a study led by Yao and Thompson reported on the retreat of 82 glaciers over the previous 30 years, with the retreat being the fastest in the Himalayas (understood as part of the region surrounding the Tibetan Plateau, which together make up the Third Pole).[37]

Lester Brown has said: "The world has never faced such a predictably massive threat to food production as that posed by the melting mountain glaciers of Asia."[38] One of the most important reasons to quit spewing CO_2 into the atmosphere, therefore, would be to save the water supply of the one to three billion Asians who have depended on the Third Pole glaciers for drinking and agricultural water and also hydroelectric power.[39]

Snowpack

A *New York Times Magazine* story in 2007, entitled "The Future Is Drying Up," focused on the gradual disappearance of snowpack. A 2012 study referred to snowpack as "an essential source of drinking water and agricultural irrigation for billions of people."[40] This is a problem, said Stanford professor Noah Deffenbaugh, because continued global warming could cause this snowpack to shrink significantly within the next 30 years. Mountain snowpack - layers of snow that accumulate at high altitude – has become vital to regions containing more than 50 percent of the world's people, including Europe, Central Asia, and the western United States. Roughly 70 million people in the western United States obtain 60 to 80 percent of their annual water supply from winter snowpack.[41]

Global climate models project that, with the continuation of business as usual, the western United States in general will by 2050 suffer a 70-percent reduction in the amount of snowpack (in large part because more precipitation will fall as rain, rather than snow). California, which grows much of the nation's food and is the sixth-largest agricultural exporter in the world, depends heavily on snowpack-derived water from both the Rockies and the Sierra Nevada. In fact, roughly two-thirds of California's water supply is provided by the Sierra snowpack. In the Pacific Northwest, snowpack declined between 1950 and 1997 by 15 to 30 percent.[42]

A 2011 study by the U.S. Geological Survey stated that part of the snowpack decline "can be attributed to natural decadal variability," but that "between 30-60 percent of the declines in the late 20th century are likely due to greenhouse gas emissions."[43]

Lakes and Rivers

According to a 2010 study reported in a *National Geographic* article ("Global Warming Burning Lakes?"), the world's largest lakes have, over the past 25 years, increased in temperature as much as 4°F (2.2°C). This is important, because lake ecology can be very sensitive to temperature, so that, as one of the study's authors said, "A small change in temperature can have quite a dramatic effect."[44]

Great Lakes

A prime example is provided by North America's Great Lakes - Superior, Michigan, Huron, Erie, and Ontario.

> [T]he Great Lakes basin is home to more than one-tenth of the population of the United States and one-quarter of the population of Canada. . . . Nearly 25 percent of the total Canadian agricultural production and 7 percent of the American production are located in the basin.[45]

These five lakes contain over 80 percent of North America's surface freshwater, which provides drinking and agricultural water for 40 million people. But the future of the Great Lakes does not look promising. A 2013 Associated Press story noted:

> Two of the Great Lakes have hit their lowest water levels ever recorded, the U.S. Army Corps of Engineers said, capping more than a decade of below-normal rain and snowfall and higher temperatures that boost evaporation. . . . The other Great Lakes – Superior, Erie and Ontario – were also well below average.

The watershed hydrology chief for the district office Army Corps said: "We're in an extreme situation."[46]

This extreme situation has been brought about by several factors, including dredging and natural cycles. But central causes, the Associated Press story indicated, have been two features of climate change: drought, which obviously means less precipitation, and higher temperatures, which have increased evaporation. Due to higher temperatures, only five percent of the Great Lakes' surface froze over in 2012, whereas 30 years earlier the coverage had been as high as 94 percent. This lack of ice coverage means that the lakes lose a lot more water by evaporation, because the water is directly exposed to sunlight much more than previously. In addition, the higher temperatures have also increased the evaporation rate and the growth of algae producing toxic cyanobacteria.[47]

Colorado River and Lakes Mead and Powell

"The sinuous Colorado River and its slew of man-made reservoirs from the

Rockies to southern Arizona," wrote Michel Wines in a 2014 *New York Times* article, "are being sapped by 14 years of drought." As a result, "The once broad and blue river has in many places dwindled to a murky brown trickle. Reservoirs have shrunk to less than half their capacities." The most important of these reservoirs are Lakes Mead and Powell.[48]

Lake Mead, which is the largest reservoir in the United States, resulted from the construction of Boulder (now Hoover) Dam, completed in 1936. About 180 miles upstream is Lake Powell, the second largest reservoir in the country, which was created by the Glen Canyon Dam, completed in 1966. These dams control the flow of the Colorado River, so as to have enough water to get through summers and droughts for the seven states - Arizona, California, Colorado, Nevada, New Mexico, Utah and Wyoming – for which the river is a lifeline.

They are also means for apportioning water, so that these seven states plus Mexico, where the river ends, get their fair shares, which had been settled by agreements, primarily the Colorado River Compact. This compact had worked well for 80 years. But in 2013, the Bureau of Reclamation cut the flow from Lake Powell by 9 percent, hence cutting the amount of water sent to Lake Mead, thereby reducing water for cities from Las Vegas to Los Angeles. The Bureau also said that it was likely that in 2015 it would need to cut water to downstream states.[49]

If the continued drop of Lake Mead leads to rationing, California will not immediately be affected by this move: Due to an agreement made several decades ago, Arizona will lose half of its allotment before California loses any. Nevertheless, cities and farmers have already been hurt: In early 2014, the California Department of Water Resources cut off water to "local agencies serving 25 million residents and about 750,000 acres of farmland." And then in July 2014, Lake Mead fell to its lowest level ever.[50]

Moreover, the situation is likely to get much worse, as "many experts believe," wrote Wines, "the current drought is only the harbinger of a new, drier era in which the Colorado's flow will be substantially and permanently diminished." One of those experts is Joe Romm, whose prediction of the "dust-bowlification" of the Southwest was cited in Chapter 3.[51]

The bad prognosis for the Colorado River and its lakes (there are eight more besides Mead and Powell) is to be traced back, of course, to the snowpack situation. The decline of snowpack in the Rocky Mountains could mean, said a 2009 report in the *Proceedings of the National Academy of Sciences*, that by 2050 the river will be unable to provide all of its allocated water 60 to 90 percent of the time.[52]

Aquifers

The world's natural underground reservoirs, called aquifers, have "made the deserts bloom" around the world – that is, they have allowed people to farm in places where it would have otherwise been impossible. But now the aquifers around the world are being seriously depleted.

Depletion results from a variety of causes, including overpumping because of overpopulation and wasteful irrigation practices. But climate change can also cause overpumping necessitated by a drought or drying up of a glacier-fed river, or by exceptional heat that has dried out plants and soil. Also, aquifers in various countries are being contaminated by deluge-caused flooding and by sea-level rise and greater storm surges.[53]

In addition, there is now another cause of aquifer depletion: The procedure to get oil and gas called "fracking," as discussed in Chapter 18, uses a tremendous amount of water. "Fracking is depleting water in America's driest areas," said a 2014 report. The use of water for fracking, furthermore, ruins it forever, so it is taken out of the water cycle permanently.[54]

Evidently all of these causes have led to an extreme loss of water in the Colorado River Basin, and researchers recently discovered that a "shocking" 75 percent of the loss was from underground sources.[55]

One of the greatest of the underground reservoirs is the Ogallala aquifer beneath the High Plains, running from Texas to South Dakota. "By the 1970s," wrote Fred Pearce, "there were 200,000 water wells, supplying more than a third of the U.S.'s irrigated fields." These irrigated fields provided food to markets around the world. Now, however, the Ogallala water is drawing down and many wells are going dry. A 2013 *New York Times* story said:

> Vast stretches of Texas farmland lying over the aquifer no longer support irrigation. In west-central Kansas, up to a fifth of the irrigated farmland along a 100-mile swath of the aquifer has already gone dry. And when the groundwater runs out, it is gone for good. Refilling the aquifer would require hundreds, if not thousands, of years of rains.[56]

Similar things have happened in other countries. For example, discussing water in terms of cubic kilometers (one cubic kilometer is 264 billion gallons), Pearce reported that India every year is pumping out 70 cubic kilometers more than the amount that is replenished, and Pakistan is overpumping by 35 cubic kilometers. Moreover, "Water tables are falling by more than a meter a year beneath the North China Plain, the breadbasket of the most populous nation on Earth. Saudi Arabia has almost pumped dry a vast water reserve beneath the desert in just 40 years. Libya is doing the same beneath the Sahara."[57]

In *Full Planet, Empty Plates*, Lester Brown wrote: "Faced with falling water tables, not a single country has mobilized to reduce water use so that it would not exceed the sustainable yield of an aquifer. Unless we can stop willfully ignoring the threats and wake up to the risks we are taking, we will join the earlier civilizations that failed to reverse the environmental trends that undermined their food economies."[58]

Conclusion

The water situation, which is clearly dire and destined to get worse, is a climate-change threat second to none. Besides the obvious life-and-death problems that will increasingly be caused by water shortages, they are troubling various corporations, as reported in a 2014 *Financial Times* article entitled "A World without Water."[59] These shortages will also increasingly lead to conflict. Once it is fully realized that water is more valuable than oil, we can expect that the kinds of deadly conflicts that occurred during the past century over oil will result in conflicts over water – which is one of the kinds of conflict discussed in Chapter 9. Just how bad this conflict will become will depend on whether we choose Plan B, A, or C.

Plans B, A, and C

Plan B

To follow Plan B would be to begin reducing CO_2 emissions radically and quickly - while at the same time doing the other obvious things that will protect and even increase our water supplies, such as cleaning up rivers and lakes, eliminating wasteful water practices, stopping fracking and overpumping, and adopting zero-growth population policies. Even with this plan, there will be increasing losses of fresh water availability in America and much of the rest of the world, because of climate-change dynamics that are already built into the planet's processes. But Plan B should prevent water shortage from leading to the collapse of civilization.

Plan A

To follow Plan A would mean that business as usual would continue until there will be no business whatsoever in many places. Australia and the American Southwest, including California, would become deserts, unable to support cities and agriculture. In other places, the glaciers and snowpack would virtually disappear, meaning that fresh water will not be available in the late spring and summer, when it is most needed. The lack of adequate fresh water would mean the death of billions of people and, eventually, most people.

Plan C

According to Plan C, society would wait to see if the dire predictions, such as those in the present chapter, start becoming true before any drastic action is begun. But they have already begun coming true, and more global warming will make them come even more tragically evident. According to a multinational project studying what warming will mean for human societies, the lack of water will be greatly increased by only a little warming: Whereas 4.5 percent of the world's people presently suffer from either chronic or absolute water scarcity, a global warming rise of one fifth of a degree (Celsius) will increase the figure to 19 percent, the increase of another degree to 29 percent – almost one third of the human race.[60]

If the decision to take action is delayed, furthermore, it will soon be too late to prevent the planet's average temperature from rising 4°C (or more) above pre-industrial temperatures, so that Plan C would turn out to be little different from Plan A.

Conclusion

Plan B is, therefore, the only rational, as well as the only moral, approach.

FOOD SHORTAGE

"[T]he Western United States and the semi-arid region from North Dakota to Texas will develop semi-permanent drought. . . . California's Central Valley could no longer be irrigated. Food prices would rise to unprecedented levels."
– James Hansen, *New York Times*, 9 May 2012

"The ocean continues to acidify at an unprecedented rate in Earth's history."
– Third Symposium on the Ocean in a High-CO_2 World, 2013

As we saw in the introductory chapter, Lester Brown in 2009 asked, in all seriousness, "Could Food Shortages Bring Down Civilization?" *Scientific American* took this question seriously enough to publish Brown's article. That same year, John Beddington, the UK government's chief scientist, warned that by 2030 the world will be confronted with a "perfect storm" of food shortages, scarce water, and insufficient energy, saying: "There are dramatic problems out there, particularly with water and food."[1]

In 2011, former UN Secretary-General Kofi Annan said that climate change, with its rising temperatures and water shortages, is having a devastating effect on food production. "Yet so far," he said, "our generation – my generation – of leaders, including those here in the United States, have failed to find the vision or courage to tackle it." The lack of food security for close to a billion people, said Annan, is "an unconscionable moral failing." A 2012 Oxfam report, "Climate Change vs. Food Security," noted: "Increased hunger is likely to be one of climate change's most savage impacts on humanity. . . . [T]he food security outlook in a future of unchecked climate change is bleak."[2]

In his 2012 book *Full Planet, Empty Plates*, Lester Brown began by saying: "The world is in transition from an era of food abundance to one of scarcity." The transition of which Brown spoke was remarkable. In the second half of the 20th century, "the dominant issues in [U.S.] agriculture were overproduction, huge grain surpluses, and access to markets by grain. As a result, the number of hungry people in the world was declining. But now, thanks to climate change combined with continued population growth, the number of hungry people is increasing and the excess grain stocks have been used up, so that "the world is now living from one year to the next, hoping always to produce enough to cover the growth in demand."[3]

In 2013, *Guardian* blogger Nafeez Ahmed published an essay called "Peak Soil," based on a report by the World Resources Institute. In light of the UN projection of a human population of 9.3 billion by 2050, the report noted, "available worldwide food calories will need to increase by about 60 percent from 2006 levels," but climate change will lead to a decrease, rather than allowing an increase, in food production. Ahmed concluded that "if we don't change course, this decade will go down in history as the beginning of the global food apocalypse."[4]

The 2014 IPCC report emphasized this same contrast - that climate change will lead to a decline in global agricultural production (perhaps 2 percent each decade), while at the same time the world will add two billion people to the rolls of those whose stomachs need to be filled. Focusing on this IPCC report's warning of the "breakdown of food systems linked to warming, drought, flooding, and precipitation variability and extremes," Joe Romm emphasized the report's assertion that climate change has "*already* begun to reduce food security."[5]

The thus-far unchecked CO_2 increase in the planet's atmosphere will be an increasingly important factor in the world's food shortages. Continually increasing CO_2 would do this by (1) producing further climate changes and (2) increasing the ocean's acidity.

Impact of CO_2-Caused Climate Changes on Food Production

This section looks at the implications of the previous chapters for the planet's food supply.

Extreme Weather (in general)

John Podesta, who was President Clinton's final chief of staff and later became co-chair of President Obama's transition team, wrote in 2010: "Food shortages resulting from severe crop losses will occur more frequently and take longer to recover from as more people become vulnerable to extreme weather events."[6]

In 2011, Oxfam published a report entitled "Extreme Weather Endangers Food Security: 2010-11: A Grim Foretaste of Future Suffering and Hunger?" Romm judged this report, according to which extreme weather had pushed millions of people into hunger, the "climate story of the year." Oxfam's report, Romm said, "shows how several extreme weather events have contributed to food insecurity at global, regional and local levels since 2010."[7]

In 2012, George Monbiot entitled a story, "If Extreme Weather becomes the Norm, Starvation Awaits." In 2013, Peter Kendall, president of Britain's National Farmers Union, said that extreme weather is the biggest threat to farming's ability to feed the country. "A gentle increase in temperature is fine," said Kendall, "but extreme weather events completely stuffs farming."[8]

In 2014, Bloomberg published an article headed "Extreme Weather Wreaking Havoc on Food as Farmers Suffer," which began:

> Too much rain in northern China damaged crops in May, three years after too little rain turned the world's second-biggest corn producer into a net importer of the grains. . . . U.K. farmers couldn't plant in muddy fields after the second-wettest year on record in 2012 dented the nation's wheat production.[9]

Heat

A 2009 article in *Science* noted: "Although much attention is focused on threats of increased droughts in subtropical agriculture, the potential impacts of seasonal average temperature changes in both the tropics and sub-tropics. . . are often over-looked."[10] Lead author David Battisti said, "The stress on global food production from temperatures alone is going to be huge." Because temporary heat waves have already greatly reduced crops (the European heat wave of 2003 caused crops to decline as much as 36 percent), a world in which the *average* temperatures are as high as today's hottest summers "will surely challenge the global population's ability to produce adequate food in the future."[11]

The years following the Battisti article almost seem designed to prove its truth:

- The year 2010 brought the historic Russian heat wave, in which 17 percent of Russia's total crop, including 30 percent of its wheat crop, was lost – a loss that led Russia to end grain exports for a year.[12]

- In 2011, Lester Brown reported: "Crop ecologists have found that each one-degree Celsius rise in temperature above the optimum can reduce grain harvests by 10 percent."[13]

- In 2013, the World Bank warned that in sub-Saharan Africa, the combination of increasing heat and drought will make it impossible for the staple crop, maize, to thrive in 40 percent of the current farmland, and that the heat will kill or at least degrade swaths of the savanna where livestock graze. Also, researchers at Kansas State

University concluded that the addition of another degree Celsius will lead to a 21 percent decrease in the wheat harvests of that state.[14]

- In early 2014, the heat was so extreme in Brazil that, in conjunction with the long-lasting drought, it scorched the grazing fields, leading the price of Brazil's beef – which is primarily grass fed – to go to the highest level ever.[15]

Increasing temperature can also affect food supply by making waters too warm for both ocean and freshwater seafood. For example, a 2013 study of California's native fish projected that the continuation of business as usual would lead to the extinction of 82 percent of its 121 freshwater species. In 2014, Maine's shrimp season was cancelled after the rising water temperature in the Gulf of Maine had become too warm for the tiny organisms on which shrimp feed, and in California, salmon were dying because the water was too warm, so millions of young Chinook salmon were shipped to the ocean by truck.[16]

Drought

As pointed out in Chapter 3, Romm in 2011 wrote: "Drought is the most pressing problem caused by climate change. . . . Feeding some 9 billion people by mid-century in the face of a rapidly worsening climate may well be the greatest challenge the human race has ever faced." That same year, Oxfam reported, East Africa had a drought that contributed to "over 13 million people being pushed into crisis." Oxfam also reported that, due to a serious drought in Afghanistan, people were facing food shortages, because up to 80 percent of their rain-fed wheat crops had been destroyed by the lack of rain.[17]

In 2012, a University of Leeds-led report warned that severe droughts in Asia are likely to bring food crises imminently – within 10 to 15 years. The crises will originate, it says, in China, India, Pakistan, and Turkey as they are major producers of wheat and maize. One of the co-authors said: "Our work surprised us when we saw that the threat to food security was so imminent; the increased risk of severe droughts is only 10 years away for China and India."[18]

In 2014, just as heat and drought devastated Brazil's beef cattle, this combination did the same for the corn crop of Argentina, the world's third largest supplier.[19]

According to a 2012 UN statement quoted in Chapter 3: "Drought ranks as the single most common cause of severe food shortages in developing countries. Drought caused more deaths during the last century than any other natural disaster." That same year, the US drought led the Department of Agriculture to issue its most extensive disaster declaration ever, one that included almost one-third of the counties in the United States, covering 26 states.[20]

Storms

The expected increase in frequency and severity of the two types of storms that are most destructive of agriculture - hurricanes and extreme rain with flooding - will have a major impact on food production, if the past is any guide.

Extreme Rain with Flooding: Ban Ki-Moon called the Pakistani deluge of 2010 (see Chapter 4) "the worst disaster" he had ever seen. It destroyed crops estimated to be worth over two billion dollars, reported *Time* magazine, which added: "Some 17 million acres of agricultural land have been submerged, and more than 100,000 animals have perished." This destruction was catastrophic, because "[a]bout a quarter of Pakistan's economy and nearly a half of its workforce depend on agriculture."[21]

Between August and October 2011, reported Oxfam, heavy monsoons "inundated large areas of productive rice lands in South East Asia - including Thailand, Cambodia, Vietnam, Laos, Myanmar, and the Philippines." These floods were devastating to the year's rice fields; in Thailand, which is the world's largest exporter of rice, these rains "caused that nation's most expensive natural disaster in history."[22]

Hurricanes: A summary of the damage by Hurricane Mitch in 1998 said:

> At least 70 percent of [Honduras'] crops destroyed. . . .
> Beans, sugar, and banana crops [of Nicaragua) devastated. .
> . . As much as 80% of [El Salvador's] maize crop lost. Coffee
> plantations and sugar cane crop severely affected.

In 2009, Cyclone Nargis in Myanmar (Burma) "killed three-fourths of the livestock [in the delta it struck] and salted a million acres of rice paddies with its seawater surges."

In 2012, Hurricane Isaac caused an estimated $100 million worth of crop damages in Louisiana, and Hurricane Sandy "ravaged parts of the Caribbean, sparking fears of food shortages where food insecurity was already a concern." And in Haiti "up to 70% of crops - such as corn, avocados, bananas and plantains - were obliterated."[23]

Sea-Level Rise

Three countries whose food supplies along the coastlines are especially threatened are Bangladesh, Vietnam, and Egypt.

Bangladesh: According to the IPCC, "Bangladesh is slated to lose the largest amount of cultivated land globally due to rising sea levels. A one-meter rise in sea level would inundate 20 percent of the country's landmass," because much of the country's crop-growing land is only slightly above sea level. Long before the land is inundated, moreover, seepage can make it too salty to grow food. "The once fertile land of this whole southwestern region has now turned into a huge saline swamp where no vegetation grows," said one farmer. "We cannot grow rice or any vegetables. Coconut palms and banana groves are dying. The coconut water that used to be so sweet and refreshing even a decade ago has now become bitter." A Union of Concerned Scientists report said: "By mid-century, more than 3 million people stand to be directly affected by sea-level rise. . . . Bangladesh could lose nearly 25 percent of its 1989 land area by around 2100."[24]

People cannot respond by moving to higher land, because Bangladesh has 142 million people locked in a very small space: Being about the size of the state of New York, its population is almost half that of the USA. According to an article by two German scholars: "There are no free areas left in Bangladesh; its neighbour India is already very concerned about the past and present illegal immigration of Bangladeshi."[25]

Vietnam: Orrin Pilkey and Rob Young wrote: "[I]n many parts of Asia the rice crop will be decimated by rising sea level. . . . [A] three-foot sea level rise will eliminate half of the rice production of Vietnam" (one of the world's leading producers of rice). Much of Vietnam's rice fields could be destroyed because, due to its very long coastline, "74% of the population lives in low-lying areas such as coastal plains or river deltas that are threatened by sea level rise." As a result, "Vietnam could face the most devastating consequences of global sea level rise."[26]

The chief problem is that the Mekong Delta, which is Vietnam's "rice bowl," is becoming salty. According to a 2011 story in the *Guardian*: "The vast, humid expanse of the delta is home to more than 17 million people, who have relied for generations on its thousands of river arteries. But rising sea water caused by global warming is now increasing the salt content of the river water and threatening the livelihoods of millions of poor farmers and fishermen." This salinity especially affects rice production. If the world keeps emitting large quantities of CO_2, a 2009 report noted, the sea level will keep rising and salt water could submerge almost a third of the delta.[27]

Egypt: Illustrating the fact that sea-level rise does not threaten only the food supply of Asian countries, Egypt is experiencing the same problems as Bangladesh and Vietnam. According to the UN Human Settlements Program, a rise of almost 20 inches (50 centimeters), which is expected at about 2040, will "forc[e] two million people in Egypt's north coast and delta region to abandon their homes." Besides forcing these people to move, the rising sea-level cuts into Egypt's capacity to feed its growing population:

> [F]armers throughout the delta are losing crops to the rising water table as the salty seawater contaminates the groundwater and makes the soil infertile. This is particularly worrying because nearly half of Egypt's agriculture - including such crops as wheat, rice, corn and cotton - takes place in the delta region.[28]

Water Shortage

"Of all the environmental trends that are shrinking the world's food supplies," said Lester Brown, "the most immediate is water shortages. In a world where 70 percent of all water use is for irrigation, this is no small matter." But various sources of water have been fading.[29]

Glaciers: As we saw in Chapter 6, global warming is causing the melting of South America's "frozen water towers," the "water towers of Europe," "Africa's Alps," and the "Third Pole glaciers." At some point, the continents will have trouble producing the food needed by their populations.

Snowpack: "Being an essential source of agricultural irrigation for billions of people," snowpack is providing less water each decade. While he was the Secretary of Energy, Steven Chu said that the continuation of present policies will lead to the disappearance of the Sierra snowpack, which provides most of California's water. This is a scenario, he said, "where there's no more agriculture in California." This is serious, given the fact that California's Central Valley "yields a third of all the produce grown in the United States."[30]

Ground Water: Equally serious is the depletion of ground water. "Aquifer depletion now," said Lester Brown in his 2013 article on peak water, "threatens harvests in China, India, and the United States," which "together supply half of the world's grain harvest." With regard to China, "the water table under the North China Plain, an area that produces over half of the country's wheat and a third of its corn, is falling fast." With regard to India, "The country's farmers have drilled 21 million irrigation wells, with the result that water tables are falling in almost every state."[31]

The first country "to publicly reveal how aquifer depletion will shrink its grain harvest," Brown added, was Saudi Arabia: In the 1970s, the Saudis "developed a heavily subsidized irrigated agriculture based on pumping water from a fossil aquifer over a half-mile below the surface. In early 2008, with the aquifer largely depleted, the Saudis announced that they will phase out wheat production by 2016." As a result, Saudi Arabia will start "importing roughly 14 million metric tons of wheat, rice, corn, and barley."[32]

Given Saudi Arabia's relatively small population, this development will not cause a shock too large for world markets to absorb. But what will happen if China or India do the same?

CO_2-Caused Ocean Acidification

"The CO_2 problem" has traditionally been understood as the fact that excessive CO_2 produces global warming. But near the end of the 20th century, scientists started talking about a second CO_2 problem, "ocean acidification" (although the term was not coined until 2003). Although ocean acidification is sometimes called simply "the other CO_2 problem," Jane Lubchenco - who headed the National Oceanic and Atmospheric Administration — referred to it as global warming's "equally evil twin."[33]

Ocean acidification results from the fact that about 30 percent of our CO2 emissions have been absorbed by the ocean. This absorption keeps down the warming of the atmosphere that would otherwise be produced by these emissions. Far from sounding "evil," this would seem to be a good thing, and scientists at first focused on this benefit. An article in *Discover* magazine said: "It all seemed so convenient: As our smokestacks and automobile tailpipes spewed ever more carbon dioxide into the air, the oceans absorbed the excess. Like a vast global vacuum cleaner, the world's seas sucked CO_2 right out of the atmosphere, mitigating the dire consequences of global warming and forestalling the melting of glaciers, the submergence of coastlines, and extremes of weather from floods to droughts." However, scientists now know that the oceans cannot absorb large quantities of CO_2 with no serious consequences.[34]

Ocean acidification involves the ocean's pH, changes in which make the water become either more alkaline or more acidic. Tests have shown that "for more than 600,000 years the ocean had a pH of approximately 8.2 (pH is the acidity of a solution measured on a 14-point scale)." But since the industrial revolution, the ocean's pH has dropped by 0.1 unit. That may not sound like much, "but pH is a logarithmic scale, so the decline in fact represents a whopping 30 percent increase in acidity." Moreover, the IPCC has said that if business as usual continues, the pH may drop down to 7.8, which "would correspond to a 150 percent increase in acidity since preindustrial times."[35]

Why is acidification destructive? When CO_2 is combined with water, it produces carbonic acid — which is the ingredient that, besides giving soft drinks their fizz, also eats out limestone caves. Its relevance here is that it does this to animals with chalky skeletons – that is, ones that calcify – "which make up more than a third of the planet's marine life." Elevating the percentage of carbonic acid will make it increasingly difficult for calcifying organisms to make their skeletons – organisms such as plankton, corals, sea butterflies, molluscs, crabs, clams, mussels, oysters, and snails.[36]

Most of us are, of course, especially interested in the ones we like to eat. More important for the cycle of life, however, are two tiny organisms, corals and plankton, which are at the base of the marine food web.

Phytoplankton

There are two basic types of plankton: phytoplankton, which are microscopic plants, and zooplankton, which are microscopic animals. The most basic type is phytoplankton, because they are capable of photosynthesis and are thereby the food for zooplankton (which in turn provide food for bigger animals). Besides providing about half of the biosphere's oxygen, phytoplankton also, in the words of marine biologist Boris Worm, "account for about half of the total organic matter on Earth," so they provide "the basic currency for everything going on in the ocean." We do not, of course, feast directly on phytoplankton, but they "ultimately support all of our fishes."[37]

Therefore, a reduction in the ocean's phytoplankton is extremely serious:. A major study in 2010 has already indicated that there has been an astounding reduction: 40 percent since the 1950s. "A 40 percent decline," said Worm (one of the study's coauthors), "would represent a massive change to the global biosphere." Indeed, he said, he could not think of a biological change that would be bigger. Referring to this 2010 study, Joe Romm said: "Scientists may have found the most devastating impact yet of human-caused global warming." Explaining the importance of the study, its lead author, Daniel Boyce, said that "a decline of phytoplankton affects everything up the food chain."[38]

In 2013, additional studies suggested that phytoplankton are very sensitive to warmer water. In one study, scientists at the National Oceanic and Atmospheric Administration reported on the normal spring surge of phytoplankton, which provides food for various types of fish when they are producing offspring. In the spring of 2013, the North Atlantic's water temperatures were "among the warmest on record" and the springtime plankton blooms of northern New England were well below normal, "leading to the lowest levels ever seen for the tiny organisms."[39]

Corals

Corals form coral reefs, which have been called the "rainforests of the sea," because they play host to much of the oceans' life.[40] Already threatened by bleaching, which is caused by global warming, they are now further threatened by global warming's evil twin. Corals form their skeletons by means of calcium carbonate in the sea water. As the water becomes more acidic, it is harder for the corals to calcify. In the past 30 years, calcification rates of corals on the Great Barrier Reef have declined by 40 percent. "There's not much debate," said Professor Ove Hoegh-Guldberg of the University of Queensland, "about how [the decline] happens: put more CO_2 into the air above and it dissolves into the oceans."[41]

This decline has not only occurred off Australia. A 2013 study of coral reefs in the Caribbean found that many of them "have either stopped growing or are on the threshold of starting to erode," due to difficulty in accumulating sufficient calcium carbonate.

The amount of new carbonate being added to the reefs was found to be far below historical rates, in some cases 70 percent lower. And yet the accumulation of carbonate is necessary for the reef to grow vertically, which is essential, given the rising sea level; corals, being plants, need to be close enough to the surface for sunlight to reach them. The leader of the study said: "Our estimates of current rates of reef growth in the Caribbean are extremely alarming."[42]

Marine biologist Joanie Kleypas of the National Center for Atmospheric Research said she first understood the urgency of ocean acidification in 1998, while she was attending one of the first scientific meetings on the subject. "As she realized what rapidly rising acidity could mean for coral reef ecosystems, she left the room, went to the bathroom, and threw up."[43]

A World without Seafood

Acidification, which threatens both phytoplankton and corals, has speeded up. Professor Timothy Wootten of the University of Chicago reported in 2008 that the pH level was "going down 10 to 20 times faster than the previous models predicted." The more it goes down, the more difficult it will be for organisms such as corals and phytoplankton to calcify. CO_2 in the atmosphere is now at about 400 parts per million. If it reaches roughly 500 ppm, according to Ove Hoegh-Guldberg, "you put calcification out of business in the oceans."[44]

If and when this occurs, phytoplankton and corals will die, and their death will mean that crabs, clams, oysters, and scallops will disappear. And they are already disappearing, faster every year. In the Pacific Northwest and British Columbia, the waters have become so acidic that the once-thriving shellfish industry there is on life support." In 2014, scallop growers in a location near Vancouver, B.C., reported that 10 million scallops over the past two years had died, with the mortality rate hitting between 95 to 100 percent.[45]

The disappearance of the phytoplankton will also lead to the death of sardines, which are just above them in the food chain. And "the sardine population from California to Canada is vanishing," resulting in starving sea lion and seal pups, and brown pelicans are showing signs of starvation, not raising any chicks in the past four years. Eventually, the disappearance of phytoplankton and corals will mean that all fish will go, as emphasized by a film subtitled *Imagine a World without Fish*. "Continued rise in the acidity of the oceans," the script forewarns, "will cause most of the world's fisheries to experience a total bottom-up collapse."[46]

A world without fish and other kinds of seafood is hard to imagine. It would be even harder for the planet's people to *live* without seafood: Besides being the world's largest source of protein, with over 2.6 billion people depending on it as their primary source of protein, the ocean also serves as the primary source of food for 3.5 billion people.[47] How would we survive if three and a half-billion people can no longer rely upon what has always been their primary source of food? "Global warming is incredibly serious," said Hoegh-Guldberg, "but ocean acidification could be even more so."[48]

Nevertheless, although the world's governments have been warned about acidification for many years, already in 2010 the oceans were "acidifying 10 times faster today than 55 million years ago when a mass extinction of marine species occurred." Probably not coincidentally, the NOAA in 2014 added 20 new species of coral to the list of threatened species.[49]

Conclusion

At the end of *Full Planet, Empty Plates*, Lester Brown wrote: "Food is the weak link in our modern civilization – just as it was for the Sumerians, Mayans, and many other civilizations that have come and gone. They could not separate their fate from that of their food supply. Nor can we."[50]

Plans B, A, and C

Plan B

As Brown and others have indicated, CO_2-caused climate changes have already made the planet's food shortage worse. Over the next three decades, climate changes will make it still worse. These shortages will be further exacerbated by the reduction of seafood because of CO_2-caused ocean acidification. Plan B, by bringing down CO_2 emissions as rapidly as possible, would prevent the food shortage from becoming even worse in the second half of the century.

Plan A

The continuation of the present path, in which CO_2 emissions will continue unchecked and probably even increase, will lead to unprecedented misery. Summer heat in many places will make agriculture impossible, and drought will make it even worse. More destructive rains, flooding, and hurricanes will reduce the harvests of wheat, rice, and other crops. Sea-level rise will mean that much of the world's most productive land, if not completely flooded, will become too salty to grow crops. And where the land is dry, increased droughts will mean a lack of adequate water to crow crops. Rising ocean acidification, moreover, will reduce and eventually eliminate seafood, which is the primary source of food for more than 3 billion people. This combination of changes would bring about a holocaust that would dwarf all previous holocausts.

Plan C

The third plan could be the attempt by leaders in wealthy countries to continue with present practices while planning – if evidence proves the dire predictions about food availability to start becoming true – to prevent a food holocaust. This prevention, it is assumed, can be achieved by (1) cutting CO_2 emissions back drastically, thereby allowing the extra CO_2 in the atmosphere to dissipate, while (2) using geoengineering to remove some of it more quickly and reverse ocean acidification.

However, the CO_2 will not dissipate for a very long time; there is no evidence that geoengineering could do very much about excess CO_2 (see Chapter 10); and there is a strong consensus that it would not be able to do anything about ocean acidification.[51] Plan C, accordingly, would probably have essentially the same results as Plan A.

Conclusion

If we want to prevent a civilization-threatening food holocaust, we must go with Plan B.

8

CLIMATE REFUGEES

*"[I]f allowed to progress along current trajectories, climate change will
displace unprecedented numbers of people."*
– Aaron Saad, "Climate Change, Compelled Migration,
and Global Social Justice," 2010

*"Countries first impacted by unprecedented climate change
are the ones with the least economic capacity to respond.
Ironically, these are the countries that are least responsible
for climate change in the first place."*
– Camilo Mora, October 2013

The term "climate refugees" has recently become widely used, in large part
because of three documentaries: *Climate Refugees*, *Sun Come Up*, and *The
Island President*.[1]

Whereas the term "environmental refugees" was evidently first used
in 1976 by Lester Brown, the term "climate refugees," referring to a particular
type of environmental refugees, was apparently first used in a Worldwatch
Institute paper of 1988.[2] Climate refugees are just what the term suggests:
people who had to leave their homes because of climate-influenced changes
that forced them to move to other places.

The term "climate refugees," however, is controversial, primarily
because it is not recognized in international law: The 1951 Geneva Convention
Relating to the Status of Refugees mandates protection only of people who
have fled their countries for fear of state-led persecution. The appropriateness
of the term "climate refugees" will be discussed in the second part of this
chapter. In the meantime, it will be used as if it were unproblematic.

Climate refugees can be created by almost any of the climate-
influenced changes discussed in the previous chapters. But this chapter focuses
on the primary reason for climate refugees: sea-level rise.

Countries Especially Vulnerable to Sea-Level Rise

The mass displacement of people because of sea-level rise had long been discussed as a problem likely to emerge in coming decades. But some people have already needed to move; others are making plans to move; and still others - if business-as-usual emissions continue – will need to move sometime in this century. I here discuss a few of the many countries that are especially vulnerable to sea-level rise, beginning with three island nations.

The Carteret Islands

The documentary film *Sun Come Up* is about the tiny Carteret islands, which have had at most a population of about 2,600 people. A *New York Times* article of 2009 began: "With their boundless vistas of turquoise water framed by swaying coconut palms, the Carteret Islands northeast of the Papua New Guinea mainland might seem the idyllic spot to be a castaway." However, the writer continued, the Carterets are no longer so idyllic, due to the rising sea.[3]

Beginning with these words, "The Carteret islanders are moving. Virtually all of them," a 2009 article noted:

> They are being forced to relocate their entire society, and give up much of what makes them unique as a people. Not because of war, famine or disease, but because of climate change. The Carteret islanders did not choose to be poster children in the worldwide debate over global warming, yet they are among the first climate refugees in a trend that could affect as many as 250 million by mid-century, according to the UN.[4]

Whether there are likely to be that many so soon may be debatable. But there is no doubt that the number of climate refugees will continue to grow, especially if CO_2 emissions are not radically curtailed.

The need of the people of the Carterets to leave their homes because of climate change is especially cruel, given the fact that they have made no contribution to this problem: Besides having no roads and no airstrip, "They rarely use electricity, live in huts with sand floors and survive primarily on seafood they harvest themselves and vegetables they grow in gardens."[5]

This culture's self-sufficiency, however, has been ruined by the rising ocean. Because of seepage, the people's regular food – breadfruit, bananas, and coconuts – no longer grows well enough to supplement their seafood diet. Ursula Rakova, who heads the program to help islanders relocate, said: "The sea that was once a friend to us is basically now destroying the lives of my people." Besides destroying their food, the ocean began frightening them. During what is called the "king tide" season (from November to March), the waves become higher. One health professional said: "We are so scared living on these atolls that any time soon waves will come and sweep over all of us."[6]

This fear became much greater during the king tides of 2008. As Jennifer Redfearn, who made *Sun Come Up,* explained: "Back in December they had very bad high tides that covered their land. Their gardens . . . were ruined [and] some turned into breeding grounds for malaria-carrying mosquitoes." The people of these islands were very strongly attached to them. The year before, only three families responded to the offer of help to relocate. In *Sun Come Up,* one clan chief said "he would rather sink with the islands than leave." But after the king tide season of 2008, 750 people signed up to move.[7]

The fate that has been inflicted on the Carterets provides a preview of what the world, given its current practices, holds in store for many other countries with coastlines.

Maldives

A review of a documentary about the country's president, Mohamed Nasheed, described Maldives as "an archipelago of 1,200 tiny, breathtakingly beautiful islands in the middle of the azure Indian Ocean." A *Washington Post* story said that the country was "best known for its plush resorts, its scuba diving and its reputation as an upmarket honeymoon destination." The first of these two descriptions ended, however, by saying that "Maldives is one of the nations most vulnerable to climate change." The reason is that 80 percent of the country is less than a meter above sea level. Approximately 200 of the archipelago's almost 1,200 islands had been inhabited, but by 2012, 14 of them had already been abandoned.[8]

As soon as he won the presidency of Maldives in 2008, Mohamed Nasheed began warning that the country would be swamped by rising sea levels unless action were quickly taken to reduce carbon emissions. He symbolized his government's commitment by holding an underwater cabinet meeting in scuba equipment. Nasheed supported, in particular, the movement to bring the level of the planet's CO_2 down to 350 ppm. Urging wealthy nations to lead the effort to cut carbon emissions, Nasheed said that "every rich country [needs] to understand that this is unlike any other thing that's happened before."[9]

The Island President, the documentary about Nasheed, focused on his twofold effort to establish democracy in Maldives, which had lived through three decades of dictatorship, and his attempt to save his country "from the peril of rising sea waters." Nasheed's career had begun with "his 20-year pro-democracy movement against the brutal regime of Maumoon Abdul Gayoom, during which he endured multiple arrests, torture and 18 months in solitary confinement." During this process, Nasheed earned the nickname "the Mandela of the Maldives."[10]

The highpoint of his effort to get the world to cut back on greenhouse gas emissions came in 2009 at the UN climate change negotiations in Copenhagen. Like many others, Nasheed had called success essential, saying that if the nations failed to sign a commitment to bring carbon emissions down, they would in effect have signed a "global suicide pact." These negotiations, about which scientists, environmentalists, and islanders had been very hopeful, turned out to be a great disappointment. More than anyone else, reportedly, Nasheed had worked tirelessly to make the Copenhagen meeting a success, and what little was achieved was due primarily to him.[11]

After Copenhagen, Nasheed continued a two-part plan to save his country: On the one hand, he believed the most important thing Maldives and other island nations could do would be to become carbon neutral, thereby setting an example that could be followed by bigger nations. Besides pledging to use wind and solar power to make Maldives carbon neutral within ten years, he persuaded eleven other nations to do likewise and form a Climate Vulnerable Forum.[12] "A group of vulnerable, developing countries committed to carbon neutral development," Nasheed said, would send "a loud message to the outside world." On the other hand, realizing that the effort to save low-lying nations such as Maldives might fail, he announced plans for a fund to buy a new homeland for his people.[13]

However, in 2012 he was removed from office by a coup, apparently arranged by the former president.[14] He later tried to win the presidency back, but he lost, evidently because of fraud.[15] This sad story about the crushing of Nasheed's dream illustrates the tendency of many politicians worldwide to take immediate political contests more seriously than the possible end of their countries.

The Sundarbans

The Sundarbans (also spelled "Sunderbans"), which are in the delta of the Ganges River – partly in Bangladesh and partly in the Indian state of West Bengal – constitute the world's largest mangrove forest. (In the Bengali language, "Sundarban" means "beautiful forest."[16])

Besides being home to a wide variety of animals – including spotted deer, wild boar, Indian otters, marine turtles, 260 bird species, and the endangered Bengal tiger - the mangroves serve as "a biological shield protecting coastal communities from the worst effects of storm surge." Over the past 30 years, however, 185,000 acres (7,500 hectares) of mangroves have been submerged by the rising sea (combined with some subsidence). This delta of the Ganges has a human population of nearly 4 million people, who occupy about half of the 100 low-lying islands that constitute the Sundarbans.[17] These islands are so low-lying that some are already being flooded. According to a 2009 article:

> Lohachara Island, once visible from Ghorama, two kilometres to the east, is already gone beneath the waves, succumbing to the ocean five years ago. It was the world's first populated island to be lost to climate change and its disappearance left more than 7,000 people homeless.[18]

The fate of Lohachara became known in the West because of Hollywood's 2007 Academy Awards ceremony: Each of the Oscar presenters – including Jack Nicholson, Meryl Streep, and Leonardo DiCaprio – was given a little glass model called the "Lohachara Sculpture" in memory of the island that "in December, 2006, became the first inhabited island to be lost to rising sea levels caused by global warming."[19]

In addition, neighboring Ghorama, from which Lohachara was visible, "has lost a third of its land mass in the last five years." These two islands provide previews of the fate of the Sundarbans in general: A rise of 45 centimeters [18 inches] in global sea level "would destroy 75 percent of the Sundarbans."[20] And that, especially if we remain on the present trajectory of emissions, will occur within the next 40 or 50 years, and many of the islands will become uninhabitable long before that.

The question of where the climate refugees from the Sundarbans will go is not, however, a problem that is waiting for the future. According to a school teacher in 2009, "At least 200 people are going to the mainland every day." Because most of the refugees head for the closest big city, Calcutta, the government has been putting up advertisements saying: "To save Calcutta, save the Sunderbans."[21]

Tuvalu

The island nation that has been most discussed in the media about the threat from sea-level rise is Tuvalu. Indeed, "Of all the world's nations negatively impacted by climate change, none are more threatened with total inundation than Tuvalu." Sitting only 3 meters above sea level, this nation's island is in a region between Hawaii and Australia where the sea level has been rising three times the global average. The island's 10,000 inhabitants will soon need somewhere to go.[22]

Bangladesh

According to Lester Brown, "The country where rising seas threaten the most people is China, with 144 million potential climate refugees." Next, according to Brown, are India, Bangladesh, Viet Nam, Indonesia, and Japan.[23] Easily the most threatened country on this list is Bangladesh.

In a 2012 story entitled "Rising Seas from Antarctica to Bangladesh," Al Gore said: "A one-meter sea level rise - which could happen as soon as 2050 according to some Antarctic specialists - could result in between 22 and 35 million people in Bangladesh relocating from the areas in which they now live and work." Moreover, Gore said:

> For the nation's 142 million people packed into a small space, climate change poses a nearly unimaginable challenge. The threat of sea level rise is not simply flooding, but saltwater intrusion that hurts the production of rice, the country's staple crop. Increased damage to rice farmers could soon put 20 million farmers out of work and force them into crowded cities.[24]

In 2013, John Vidal of the *Guardian* published a story called "Bangladesh's Climate Refugees," in which he said: "Many Bangladeshis have relocated from the vanishing island of Kutubdia in the Bay of Bengal to Cox's Bazaar [a city on the mainland]." In a companion story, Vidal put at 40,000 the number of people who had fled Kutubdia in the past two decades. Moreover, he added: "The 80,000 people left on Kutubdia all expect to follow [them]."[25]

However, an even larger wave of climate refugees has relocated from Bhola Island, Bangladesh's biggest island, which had over 2 million inhabitants. By 2009, a million of them had already moved to Bangladesh's capital, Dhaka.[26] The migration had begun in 1995, according to a 2007 *Washington Post* essay:

> Scientists in Dhaka, the capital, predict that as many as 20 million people in Bangladesh will become 'climate refugees' by 2030, unable to farm or survive on their flooded land. The migration has already started. In 1995, half of Bhola Island, Bangladesh's biggest island, was swallowed by rising sea levels, leaving 500,000 people homeless.[27]

Already by 2009, about 3.5 million of Dhaka's 12 million residents were slum-dwellers. This is certain to increase exponentially, given the fact that 40 million of Bangladesh's 140 million people live in coastal areas. A scientific representative of the International Union for Conservation of Nature said: "Roughly 20 per cent of our country's landmass will be under water if sea levels rise by 89 centimetres [35 inches]. Such a catastrophe would displace roughly 18 million people."[28]

"We are staring catastrophe in the face," said a leader of a group helping climate-affected refugees. They lose everything they have and they cannot recover when their land is washed away.

> They have no option but to migrate from the islands but they have no money, and when they leave they have no schools or hospitals. They have no work and no future.[29]

Given its population density, Bangladesh will create demands on other countries to take many of its people wanting to migrate. Saber Hossain Chowdhury, an important political leader in Bangladesh, said: "Due to the impacts of climate change there would be around 30 million people [in Bangladesh] that would be displaced. Since the country is already densely populated, it may not be able to accommodate the affected parties."[30]

Mozambique

To complete this selection of very threatened countries with one in Africa: In 2009, the National Disaster Management Institute of Mozambique — a country that had already been severely affected by natural disasters – released a detailed report on climate-change effects in this country. The U.N. resident coordinator in Mozambique said: "I am alarmed by many of the findings presented in this study."[31]

What is especially alarming, according to this report, is that unless immediate action be taken to mitigate global warming, the country will be severely impacted by a number of climate-change effects, including cyclones, floods, droughts, and sea-level rise. "Up to approximately 2030," said the report, "more severe cyclones will pose the biggest threat to the coast." But from then on, "the accelerating sea level rise will present the greatest danger."[32]

The reason that sea-level rise presents the greatest threat is due to a combination of factors: the country's coastline is 1675 miles (2,700 kilometers) long; 60 percent of the population (roughly 12 million people) live within 985 yards (900 meters) of the coastline; and erosion of the shore, if business as usual continues, will probably push the coastline some 550 yards (500 meters) farther inland. This scenario, said the report, is "likely to be catastrophic for Mozambique."[33]

The Appropriateness of the Term "Climate Refugees"

It has been argued that the term "climate refugees" is not appropriate. For example, one writer, criticizing the title of Michael Nash's film *Climate*

Refugees, wrote: "The 1951 Refugee Convention only provides protection to people residing outside of their country of origin, and who have a well-founded fear of persecution." Saying that "we need to get the terminology correct," this writer insisted that we should use an alternative, such as "a person displaced by climate change" or "an environmentally induced migrant."[34]

This attitude is important, because governments use this reason to withhold refugee status. A man from the island of Kiribati, for example, sought refuge in New Zealand, saying that Kiribati's coral atolls, being only slightly above sea level, made him fear for his children's future. Denying his application in 2012, New Zealand authorities cited the fact that the Refugee Convention makes no mention of environmental harm. Next the man, whose three children were all born in New Zealand, applied for asylum, because he was subject to persecution though a forced exodus induced by climate, but NZ's High Court ruled that the "legal concept of 'being persecuted' rests on human agency" (even though the Convention's definition does not mention this requirement, and even though human agency has certainly been responsible for sea-level raising climate change).[35]

It is correct that current international law regarding refugees makes no provision for people displaced for climate-change reasons. But this does not entail that the term "climate refugee" should not be used. This issue is not trivial, because assigning refugee status to people gives the international community obligations to help them. If they do not have this status, the international community has no - or at least less – legal obligation to assist them.

A wise treatment of this issue was provided in a 2008 essay by Frank Biermann and Ingrid Boas of VU Amsterdam's Institute of Environmental Studies. They began by pointing out that dealing with refugees, which is already a problem, promises to become a huge one. Although there is no agreement about how many climate-displaced persons there are likely to be, "most scenarios agree on a general trend: in this century, global warming may force millions of people - mainly in Asia and Africa - to leave their homes and migrate to other places." A 2011 *Guardian* story said that "[m]ore than 30 million people were displaced last year by environmental and weather-related disasters across Asia."[36] Warning that the number of climate refugees may become enormous, Biermann and Boas in 2008 wrote:

> According to some estimates, more than 200 million people might have to give up their homes due to climate change by 2050. . . . Climate refugees just from Bangladesh might outnumber all current [political] refugees worldwide. . . . Water scarcity and drought will also affect millions of

> Africans. . . . Water scarcity due to glacier melts in the South
> American Andes may affect . . . 50 million people in 2050.[37]

Because the United Nations High Commissioner for Refugees (UNHCR) can apply the description of refugees only to people moving to a different country, people who have to move within their own countries are called "internally displaced persons" – a designation that gives the international community less responsibility for them than for refugees. However, Biermann and Boas wrote:

> [B]ecause climate change will cause both transnational and internal flight, the UNHCR's traditional distinction between the two categories of involuntary migration does not seem germane; it is difficult to argue that a global governance mechanism for the protection of people who have lost their homes due to climate change should bestow a different status, and a different term, depending on whether they have crossed a border.

The distinction would certainly seem irrelevant to the migrants themselves, given the enormous change from being, for example, a fisherman or land-owning farmer on an island to being a slum-dweller in a huge city. Coming, in light of these considerations, to the term "climate refugees," Biermann and Boas wrote:

> [I]t does not stand to reason to reserve the stronger term 'refugee' for a category of people who earned international attention after 1945 and to invent less appropriate terms - such as 'climate-related environmentally displaced persons' - for new categories of people who are forced to leave their homes now, with similar grim consequences. Why should inhabitants of some atolls in the Maldives who require resettlement for reasons of a well-founded fear of being inundated by 2050 receive less protection than others who fear political persecution?

"Therefore," they concluded, "it seems sensible to continue using the term 'climate refugees' and adjust the outdated UN terminology accordingly by allowing for different types of refugees (for instance, political refugees that fall under the 1951 Geneva Convention and climate refugees that fall under [a to be created] climate refugee protocol."[38]

As a 2013 book, *Threatened Island Nations,* points out, there are currently no international agreements obligating any nation to take in people from countries displaced by climate change.[39] To refuse to grant refugee status to climate-induced migrants would seem to imply that they are somehow to blame for their situation. However, as a report by the Environmental Justice Foundation states, "those being forced to leave their homes and land have played close to no role in increasing the rate of climate change."[40] Climate-displaced persons exist because the international community – meaning primarily the United States and other rich nations – have refused to act on the warnings that have been coming from climate scientists for the past several decades. The rich countries have put all their focus on becoming richer and, in some cases, trying to become more powerful.

It would not only be appropriate for wealthy countries to take responsibility. It would be unjust for them *not* to do so. As Biermann and Boas stated:

> [T]he protection of climate refugees must be seen as a global problem and a global responsibility. In most cases, climate refugees will be poor, and their own responsibility for the past accumulation of greenhouse gases will be small. By a large measure, the wealthy industrialized countries have caused most past and present greenhouse gas emissions, and it is thus these countries that have the greatest moral, if not legal, responsibility for the victims of global warming. This does not imply transnational migration of 200 million climate refugees into the developed world. Yet it does imply the responsibility of the industrialized countries to do their share in financing, supporting, and facilitating the protection and resettlement of climate refugees.[41]

In 2014, there was a new development: A family from Tuvalu had moved to New Zealand in 2007. In order to be able to get work permits, the family applied for refugee status, saying that climate change had made life on the island too difficult, because coastal erosion and frequent inundations ruined their crops. Although the immigration tribunal dismissed the application in 2013, it approved it in 2014. In doing so, it did not say that climate change can be an adequate basis for receiving refugee status. But it did, in accepting the appeal on "exceptional humanitarian grounds," say that the children were especially "vulnerable to natural disasters and the adverse impact of climate change." At this writing, it remains to be seen whether this decision will open the way for other people to receive refugee status at least partly because of climate change.[42]

Conclusion

The present chapter has focused on sea-level rise, which seems destined to be, if it is not already, the primary type of climate change creating refugees. But climate refugees can also be produced by other types of climate disruption, such as droughts, hurricanes, flooding, fresh water shortage, and food shortage. When all of these possible causes of climate refugees are taken into consideration, the number of such refugees, as Biermann and Boas indicated, is likely to be enormous. International law, therefore, needs to be equipped to deal with this issue. Besides enlarging the definition of "climate refugees," the UN could complement the Convention and Protocol Relating to the Status of Refugees with – as Biermann and Boas propose – a "Protocol on the Recognition, Protection, and Resettlement of Climate Refugees."[43]

Plans B, A, and C

William Lacy-Swing, the director general of the International Organisation of Migration, has said: "What is more significant about climate change than people? I think we have to do a better job of recognizing that the most fundamental problem is that people are going to be displaced in massive numbers."[44] It would be more accurate to say that the displacement of people is *one of the most important* consequences of climate change. In any case, the international community needs to agree on ways to help people who – through the international community's failures to respond to the scientific warnings over the previous decades – have had their homes and livelihoods destroyed.

It is also important that the international community overcome "the trend to regard climate-induced migration as a security threat rather than a humanitarian challenge closely linked to aspects of vulnerability, development and justice" – a trend that led to a conference organized by Bread for the World, the Pacific Conference of Churches, and the World Council of Churches, which led to a publication on the role of the churches in relation to climate refugees.[45]

Besides responding to the needs of displaced persons immediately, the international community needs finally to deal with global warming, which is at the root of the fate of climate refugees. As with previous chapters, we can consider the likely consequences of Plans B, A, and C.

Plan B

Even if greenhouse emissions could be eliminated tomorrow, many more climate refugees will be created in the coming three to four decades, because of dynamics already in the system. However, if these emissions were to be greatly reduced by 2020, the number of new refugees who would otherwise be created after 2050 could be reduced.

Plan A

If, by contrast, the international community continues down the present trajectory, the number of climate refugees will surely continue to grow at an accelerating pace, due to the consequences outlined in the previous chapters: the most extreme weather events of today will become the "new normal"; the summers in many places will regularly be hotter than today's hottest summers, with heat waves too hot for human beings and agriculture to survive; much of the planet will be in a condition of extreme drought, making growing crops impossible; floods, hurricanes, and tornadoes will be increasingly more destructive; sea-level rise will destroy the habitats of tens of millions – eventually hundreds of millions – of people (a 2014 report warned that more than 500 million people could be flooded out by the next century[46]); and billions of people will have inadequate water and food. Given all of these reasons for making it impossible for people to remain where they are, the number of people needing refugee status will likely be even higher than today's most pessimistic predictions.

Plan C

According to Plan C, we would wait before doing any serious mitigation to see if the predictions of the scientific community start to become true. However, the predictions about sea-level rise and the displacement of people have already become true in many parts of the world. To wait for another two or three decades before beginning to curtail CO_2 emissions will likely result in consequences little different from those of Plan A.

Conclusion

In light of a statement by Steve Trent of the Environment Justice Foundation - that climate change is "not just an environmental issue; it's a human rights issue too"[47] – the only moral approach is Plan B.

9

CLIMATE WARS

"The world is entering an era of pervasive,
unprecedented resource scarcity."
– Michael T. Klare, *The Race for What's Left,* 2012

For most people, disruptive climate change is important because of the harm that it is causing, and will increasingly cause, to the ecosphere, to civilization, and to the lives of people and their communities. But for people who think about national security, climate disruption is also important because of the ways it might threaten a nation's security and, beyond that, the security of the world's political-economic order. In this century, this issue has become a growing concern and thereby an additional reason, beyond those discussed in the previous chapters, for taking seriously the need to deal with climate change.

Exemplified in a multi-authored volume entitled *Climate Change and National Security,* the issue is often discussed in terms of "climate wars," as further illustrated by Gwynne Dyer's 2010 book, *Climate Wars: The Fight for Survival as the World Overheats.*[1]

Besides being an additional reason for taking climate change seriously, this is, some would argue, one of the *most important* reasons. Joe Romm, who had long said that extreme weather, especially drought and resulting food insecurity, would probably have the worst direct impacts on people, said in a discussion in 2013 of "deadly climate impact[s]" that "war, conflict, competition for arable and/or habitable land" may well "affect far more people both directly and indirectly."[2]

The idea that climate change is a security issue has been expressed by many political and military leaders. For example, Secretary of State John Kerry, referring to a "list of shared challenges which does not get enough attention," said: "[A]t the top of that list . . . is the challenge of climate change," which is "not just an environmental issue and it's not just an economic issue. It is a security issue."[3]

Most national Republican politicians praise the U.S. military while expressing scorn for taking climate change seriously, but military and intelligence leaders share Kerry's perspective.

- Admiral Samuel Locklear, the Commander of the U.S. Pacific Command, has said that significant upheaval related to global warming "is probably the most likely thing that . . . will cripple the security environment."[4] Many similar discussions are provided in the first section, below.

- In 2009, the CIA created the Center on Climate Change and National Security, the job description for which is "not the science of climate change, but the national security impact of phenomena such as desertification, rising sea levels, population shifts, and heightened competition for natural resources." The CIA Director at that time, Leon Panetta, said: "Decision makers need information and analysis on the effects climate change can have on security. The CIA is well positioned to deliver that intelligence."[5]

- A center with a slightly different name, the Center for Climate and Security, said: "Climate change is what risk analysts would call a 'high probability, high impact' risk, meaning that it is very likely to occur (between 90 and 97%), and will have a very large and widespread impact on security."[6]

The growing concern with this issue is illustrated by the IPCC. In its first four assessments, it had not discussed the likelihood that climate change will contribute to resource wars and other forms of conflict and violence. But in its fifth assessment, *Climate Change 2014*, it finally did so, "connecting," as the AP's Seth Borenstein put it, "hotter global temperatures to hotter global tempers." There is "robust evidence," the report said, that "human security will be progressively threatened as climate changes." More concretely, the report said continued climate change will bring an escalating "breakdown of food systems linked to warming, drought, flooding, and precipitation variability and extremes," and increasing "risks of violent conflicts in the form of civil war and inter-group violence."[7]

    The first section of the present chapter summarizes some of the high-level reports that have talked about climate change as a matter of national security. The second section discusses some expressions of doubt that climate change should be regarded as a national security matter. The final section discusses four places where climate change has already contributed to war, or has the potential to do so.

National Security Reports

The growing concern in this century about the importance of climate disruption for national security has been demonstrated by a number of special reports focused on the issue.

The 2004 Pentagon Report

The first to receive significant attention was a 2004 report commissioned by the Defense Department's "Yoda," the legendary defense planner Andrew Marshall. This report was entitled "An Abrupt Climate Change Scenario and Its Implications for United States National Security."[8]

Making a point that at the time was far from commonplace, this "extraordinary new report by an elite Pentagon planning unit," Mark Hertsgaard wrote in *The Nation*, "declared that climate change is a national security threat of the greatest urgency."[9] This point was also made by articles in other publications.

Fortune Magazine: The first story about this report appeared in *Fortune* magazine, to which it had been leaked. The *Fortune* story, entitled "The Pentagon's Weather Nightmare," had this summary heading: "The climate could change radically, and fast. That would be the mother of all national security issues."

The attention of these strategic planners was "riveted," explained *Fortune* writer David Stipp, by the threat of rapid change: "Global warming, rather than causing gradual, centuries-spanning change, may be pushing the climate to a tipping point. Growing evidence suggests the ocean-atmosphere system that controls the world's climate can lurch from one state to another in less than a decade - like a canoe that's gradually tilted until suddenly it flips over." The Pentagon report, Stipp concluded, "may signal a sea change in the debate about global warming."[10]

London's Observer: A story in London's *Observer*, contrasting this Marshall-commissioned Pentagon report with the attitude of the Bush administration, was entitled "Now the Pentagon Tells Bush: Climate Change Will Destroy Us." This report, having been suppressed for several months by the Bush administration, came to light only through a whistleblower.[11]

The reason for this suppression, according to the *Observer*, was obvious: President Bush, while emphasizing national security, had "repeatedly denied that climate change even exists," whereas the Pentagon report "predicts that abrupt climate change could bring the planet to the edge of anarchy." Put more succinctly: "You've got a President who says global warming is a hoax, and across the Potomac river you've got a Pentagon preparing for climate wars."[12]

The *Stern Review* (2006)

An influential report of 2006 dealt with national security not in military, but in economic, terms. Written by Nicholas Stern, one of the world's most respected economists, it was entitled the *Stern Review: The Economics of Climate Change*.[13] All the evidence covered in his report, Stern said, "leads to a simple conclusion":

> [T]he benefits of strong, early action considerably outweigh the costs. The evidence shows that ignoring climate change will eventually damage economic growth. Our actions over the coming few decades could create risks of major disruption to economic and social activity, later in this century and in the next, on a scale similar to those associated with the great wars and the economic depression of the first half of the 20th century.[14]

National Security and the Threat of Climate Change (CNA Corporation, 2007)

In 2007, the CNA Corporation – a private nonprofit research organization previously called "Center for Naval Analysis" – published a report prepared by its Military Advisory Board composed of admirals and generals. Entitled *National Security and the Threat of Climate Change*, this report began by saying: "Global climate change presents a new and very different type of national security challenge." It continued: "The nature and pace of climate changes being observed today and the consequences projected by the consensus scientific opinion are grave and pose equally grave implications for our national security."

Using a term that would become widely used, the report said: "Climate change acts as a *threat multiplier* for instability in some of the most volatile regions of the world." In expanding on this point, it said:

> Many governments in Asia, Africa, and the Middle East are already on edge in terms of their ability to provide basic needs: food, water, shelter and stability. Projected climate change will exacerbate the problems in these regions and add to the problems of effective governance. Unlike most conventional security threats that involve a single entity acting in specific ways at different points in time, climate change has the potential to result in multiple chronic conditions, occurring globally within the same time frame.[15]

In an essay entitled "On Risk," General Gordon Sullivan – the former US Army Chief of Staff and also the chairman of the CNA Military Advisory Board – commented on the fact that many people do not want to act upon climate change until there is 100 percent certainty about it. Drawing on his military experience, he noted: "We never have 100 percent certainty. . . . If you wait until you have 100 percent certainty, something bad is going to happen on the battlefield."[16]

In managing risk, Sullivan said, military leaders give significant attention to "low probability/high consequence" events – ones that "rarely occur but can have devastating consequences if they do." During the Cold War, he continued, "much of America's defense efforts focused on preventing a Soviet missile attack – the very definition of a low probability/high consequence event." By contrast, climate change, if ignored, will become a "high probability/high consequence scenario. . . . If we keep on with business as usual, we will reach a point where some of the worst effects are inevitable."[17]

The Age of Consequences (CSIS 2007)

Also in 2007, the Center for Strategic and International Studies put out a report entitled *The Age of Consequences*, subtitled *The Foreign Policy and National Security Implications of Global Climate Change*. The title was based on Winston Churchill's famous statement in the 1930s, "The era of procrastination . . . is coming to a close. In its place we are entering a period of consequences."

In their Executive Summary, the authors said: "[H]opefully, the award of the 2007 Nobel Peace Prize to Vice President Al Gore and the Intergovernmental Panel on Climate Change is a clear recognition that global warming poses not only environmental hazards but profound risks to planetary peace and stability as well."

The *Age of Consequences* consists of three "future worlds," the first of which is the "expected" climate change scenario, according to which the average global temperature would increase by 1.3°C by 2040. In the "severe" scenario, according to which the global temperature would increase 2.6°C by 2040, "massive nonlinear events in the global environment [would] give rise to massive nonlinear societal events," with nations around the world being "overwhelmed by the scale of change and pernicious challenges." The "catastrophic scenario," according to which the average global temperature would rise 5.6°C by 2100, would pose "almost inconceivable" challenges, such as "permanent agricultural disruptions, endemic disease, ferocious storm patterns, deep droughts, the disappearance of vast tracks of coastal land, and the collapse of ocean fisheries, which could well trigger a profound loss of confidence in the most advanced and richest states."[18]

Quadrennial Defense Review 2010

The U.S. military's primary planning document, the *Quadrennial Defense*

Review, addressed global warming and the resulting climate change for the first time in 2010. While making many of the points made in the previous reports, it also said: "While climate change alone does not cause conflict, it may act as an accelerant of instability or conflict, placing a burden to respond on civilian institutions and militaries around the world."[19]

Global Trends 2030 (NIC 2012)

In 2012, the National Intelligence Council - which is in the Office of the Director of National Intelligence - produced a new edition of a report that comes out every four years, *Global Trends 2030.* "It is prudent to expect that over the course of a decade some climate events," this report said,

> will produce consequences that exceed the capacity of
> the affected societies or global system to manage and that
> have global security implications serious enough to compel
> international response.

The consequences of climate change, this report added, pose security threats greater than do terrorist attacks.[20]

Quadrennial Defense Review 2014

This new version largely repeated the earlier one. The most notable change was giving up the characterization of climate change as an "accelerant of instability or conflict" in favor of a "threat multiplier." The pressures caused by climate change, the report said, "are threat multipliers that will aggravate stressors abroad such as poverty, environmental degradation, political instability, and social tensions – conditions that can enable terrorist activity and other forms of violence."[21]

Global Warming, Conflict, and "Climate Wars"

In spite of the high-level figures and organizations who have described climate change caused by global warming as a security threat because it increases the likelihood of conflict, even war, some commentators have expressed criticism of the growing consensus that such possible consequences provide a new argument for taking climate change seriously.

Critiques of "Climate Wars"

The term "climate wars" has been criticized in a 2012 IRIN article as reflecting the "securitization" of climate change, that is, "[f]ocusing on climate change as a security threat alone," thereby turning humanitarian responsibilities over to the military.[22] The securitization of climate change in this sense should indeed be avoided. But the term "climate wars" does not necessarily have this connotation and usually is not so understood.

This IRIN article, entitled "Climate Change: Beyond the Hype of 'Climate Wars,'" criticizes the term "climate wars" as "alarmist" and "hype" – exaggerating the likelihood of wars caused by climate change, perhaps to try to get political and military leaders to take it more seriously.[23] Such exaggerations should certainly be avoided. But speaking about the threat of "climate wars" – meaning wars that are significantly influenced by climate change – does not necessarily involve exaggeration.

IRIN's article criticized "a paper by the UN Environment Programme [that] portrayed climate change-related environmental degradation as one of the root causes of the conflict in Darfur, Sudan." The IRIN article criticized this view as an "attempt to oversimplify the crisis." However, how can regarding climate change as *"one of* the root causes" be an oversimplification?

Oversimplification occurs when "both/and" is needed but "not this, but that" is declared. This kind of oversimplification is shown by IRIN itself, which quoted favorably the statement that the "Darfur crisis has been shown *not* to be a result of climate change *but* of local political and social circumstances." Surely it has been both – as stated in a different IRIN article entitled "Sudan: Climate Change – Only One Cause among Many for Darfur Conflict."[24]

It is certainly true that climate is rarely if ever the only cause for a war, whether between two nations or within a single nation. But using the term "threat multiplier" – to mean a development "that is likely to exacerbate many existing environmental and resource challenges" – avoids this problem. Indeed, since 2007, when this expression was used by the CNA Military Advisory Board, it has become widely employed, as in the 2014 version of the *Quadrennial Defense Review*."[25]

Those responsible for national security, therefore, should not be encouraged to ignore the possibility of climate wars – meaning wars in which climate change plays a significant role.

Global Warming as Inducing Conflict

Bruno Tertrais, in an article called "The Climate Wars Myth," began a critique of a connection between global warming and conflict by saying: "History shows that 'warm' periods are more peaceful than 'cold' ones." He elaborated: "Since the dawn of civilization, warmer eras have meant fewer wars. The reason is simple: all things being equal, a colder climate meant reduced crops, more famine and instability."[26] However, such reasons for conflict can equally well be caused by global warming, which reduces the availability of water and food.

Granting that "some local changes in the climate [such as drought] can increase the propensity to collective violence," Tertrais argued that "drawing deterministic conclusions from this observation would be a stretch."[27] However, few people draw deterministic conclusions from climate changes, as if the lack of water or food *always* causes conflict. The argument is merely that it may, in some situations, make violent conflict more likely.

Finally, no one argues that warm weather is always more conducive to violence than cold weather. Rather, insofar as temperature as such is an issue, the point made is that *really hot* weather tends to increase the level of violence.

This point was extensively documented in a 2013 study by three researchers at UC-Berkley based on an analysis of 60 quantitative studies of both interpersonal violence and intergroup conflict. These studies, which were drawn from archeology, criminology, economics, geography, history, political science, and psychology, indicated that, on average, unusually high temperature will increase interpersonal violence by 4 percent and intergroup violence by 14 percent. Extreme rainfall was also found to increase violence, but not nearly as much as heat. Thomas Homer-Dixon, one of the founders of the study of the influence of environmental stress on violence, told Andrew Freeman that this study "presents a compelling case for a robust link between climatic stress and violence."[28]

Of course, there is nothing new about the idea that very hot weather makes violence, including war, more likely. At the interpersonal level, Raymond Chandler, writing about the "oven-hot" Santa Ana winds in his 1938 story "Red Wind," said: "Every booze party ends in a fight. Meek little wives feel the edge of the carving knife and study their husband's necks."[29] What is new in the Berkeley-based paper is the number of studies that were analyzed and the number of fields that were included.

Some Instances of Climate Wars

In 2008, a Swedish government study said: "There are 46 countries – home to 2.7 billion people – in which the effects of climate change interacting with economic, social, and political problems will create a high risk of violent conflict."[30] This section discusses four places where climate change has already contributed to the initiation of a war or could easily do so.

Making a general point about the effect of overheating, Gwynne Dyer said in his *Climate Wars*: "There is a probability of wars . . . if temperatures rise 2 to 3 degrees Celsius." After saying that "the first and most important impact of climate change on human civilisation will be an acute and permanent crisis of food supply," Dyer added that "countries that cannot feed their people are unlikely to be 'reasonable' about it."[31]

Africa: Sudan

Dyer's observation has been illustrated by the conflict in the Darfur region of Sudan – a conflict that, a 2014 report said, "may be the first site of violence induced by climate change."[32]

The reference is, of course, to the war in Darfur, which began in 2003 with an attack on the government of Sudan by rebel groups accusing it of oppressing Darfur's non-Arab population, to which the government responded by starting a campaign of ethnic cleansing against non-Arabs. Estimates of the number of people killed have ranged from 300,000 to almost a half-million.

The view of it as a climate-change war was presented in 2006 by Jeffrey Sachs, who argued in *Scientific American* that the war had "roots in an ecological crisis directly arising from climate shocks." Those roots lay in a drought in the 1980s, when communities that depended on rainfall – both sedentary farmers and roaming pastoralists – "fought to survive by raiding others and attempting to seize or protect scarce water and food supplies." Sachs did not argue that the ensuing famine was the sole cause of the resulting war. Rather, he said:

> A drought-induced famine is much more likely to trigger
> conflict in a place that is already impoverished and bereft
> of any cushion of physical or financial resources. Darfur was
> also pushed over the edge by ethnic and political conflict,
> with ambitious, violent and unscrupulous leaders preying
> on the ethnic divisions.

But Sachs was critical of the fact that the carnage in Darfur was usually "discussed in [only] political and military terms," because our public debates "focus on politics and only rarely on the underlying environmental pressures."[33]

This perspective was then articulated the following year by the U.N. Environment Program (UNEP), which said – in the *Guardian*'s summary statement – that "the true genesis of the conflict pre-dates 2003 and is to be found in failing rains and creeping desertification." The rainfall had dropped by as much as 30 percent. And the desertification had been rapid, with the Sahara desert in northern Sudan advancing 60 miles over the previous 40 years. "It doesn't take a genius," said UNEP's executive director, to figure out that "as the desert moves southwards there is a physical limit to what [ecological] systems can sustain, and so you get one group displacing another."

> Echoing Jeffrey Sachs, U.N. Secretary-General Ban Ki-moon said:
> Almost invariably, we discuss Darfur in a convenient military
> and political shorthand - an ethnic conflict. . . . Look to its
> roots, though, and you discover a more complex dynamic.
> Amid the diverse social and political causes, the Darfur
> conflict began as an ecological crisis, arising at least in part
> from climate change.

As this statement shows, he did not say that climate change was *the* cause,
but one among "diverse social and political causes."[34]

Likewise, a 2007 article in IRIN was entitled, "Sudan: Climate Change
– Only One Cause among Many for Darfur Conflict." Nevertheless, the article
began by arguing that to consider climate change "the single root cause would
obscure other important factors," but without quoting a single commentator
who affirmed this single-cause view. The article shows its animus against this
view by quoting a writer saying that global warming "has become such a trendy
issue that everything is being packaged as climate change." The article, however,
does not deny that competition for resources has "definitely been one of the
main issues in the conflict." It was only against putting "undue emphasis on
it, at the expense of other causes," thereby trying "to simplify the crisis." But,
again, it does not give a single example of someone who does this.[35]

Rather than correcting a commonly held one-sided view, the IRIN
piece is simply repeating the consensus view - that the violent conflict in Darfur
was a climate war, in the sense of a war that was significantly influenced,
albeit not wholly caused, by climate change.

Middle East: Syria

The main reason for a shortage of food may, of course, be a lack of fresh
water, and this lack could lead to violence. In this regard, Dyer quoted General
Anthony Zinni, the former head of the US Central Command, who said:

> The existing situation [in the Middle East] makes this place
> more susceptible to problems. . . . You already have great
> tension over water. These are cultures often built around
> a single source of water. So any stresses on the rivers and
> aquifers can be a source of conflict.[36]

The conflict in Syria, which started in 2011, provides a perfect example of the
way in which climate change can serve as a "threat multiplier."

Syria suffered a terrible drought – some commentators say the worst
ever – from 2006 to 2011. NOAA pointed out in 2011 that this drought was

part of a drying of the Mediterranean countries over the previous 20 years that was "too great to be explained by natural variability alone" – a drying that confirmed the predictions of climate science that human-caused emissions would make the region drier.[37]

It has been widely agreed that the drought played a role in the initiation of the conflict. In the media, Thomas Friedman made this case in a *New York Times* piece called "Without Water, Revolution," saying that, although the drought did not cause the civil war, the Assad regime's failure to respond to the drought played a big role.[38] This evaluation agreed with analyses by many scholars, such as William R. Polk, as well as Francesco Femia and Caitlin E. Werrell, the founders of the Center for Climate and Security. In giving an extensive analysis of the Syrian conflict in the *Atlantic*, Polk argued that the war had to be understood in the context of the drought, writing:

> In some areas, all agriculture ceased. In others crop failures reached 75%. And generally as much as 85% of livestock died of thirst or hunger. Hundreds of thousands of Syria's farmers gave up, abandoned their farms and fled to the cities and towns in search of almost non-existent jobs and severely short food supplies. Outside observers including UN experts estimated that between 2 and 3 million of Syria's 10 million rural inhabitants were reduced to "extreme poverty."

The situation was aggravated, moreover, by the fact that hundreds of thousands of Palestinians and Iraqis had in previous years taken refuge there, so that the new Syrian refugees had to compete with them for jobs, water, and food.

By 2008, the representative of the UN's Food and Agriculture Organization had described the situation as "a perfect storm," which threatened Syria with "social destruction." The Syrian Minister of Agriculture, he pointed out, had acknowledged that the economic and social fallout from the drought was "beyond [its] capacity as a country to deal with." He made these comments in an appeal to the USAID program for help. However, the Bush-Cheney USAID director said (in a cable that was later published by WikiLeaks), "we question whether limited USG resources should be directed toward this appeal at this time."

Besides getting no help, the Assad government made its country even worse off. "Lured by the high price of wheat on the world market, it sold its reserves." Accordingly, Polk said, "tens of thousands of frightened, angry, hungry and impoverished former farmers constituted a 'tinder' that was ready to catch fire. The spark was struck on March 15, 2011, when a relatively small group gathered in the town of Dara'a to protest against government failure to help them."[39]

David Arnold added that this protest began after a group of children were arrested and tortured after they had "painted some anti-government graffiti on a school wall in the ancient farming community." This excessive response by the government led to protests in the city, which were then met with "harsh repression," which in turn "led to a nationwide revolt."[40] The Assad regime then tried to quell this response with military force, thus starting a civil war.

This analysis by Polk and Arnold explains why, as Femia and Werrell point out, "the role of disaffected rural communities in the Syrian opposition movement has been prominent compared to their equivalents in other 'Arab Spring' countries." Although the fact that the rural farming communities ended up "without water" was due in part to the drought, it was also partly due, as the people knew, to the Assad regime's mismanagement.[41]

This regime favored the urban elite over the farming communities. While taking subsidies away from ordinary farmers, it also subsidized water-intensive wheat and cotton farming and unsustainable irrigation techniques. It then allowed these big farmers to take all the water they wanted from the aquifer, although this was illegal. The Assad government's wasteful use of water also meant that rural people needed to drill for water. As a result, the aquifer went down swiftly – faster than in any other country except India.[42]

Accordingly, Femia and Werrell say, the primary responsibility for the civil war is Assad's criminal mismanagement of Syria's water plus his brutal repression of protest. However, they add, this is "not the whole story" – the extraordinary drought was part of the mix.

This both-and approach has been rejected in an essay by Francesca de Châtel, a graduate student in Nijmegen. She began her essay by seemingly agreeing with these other scholars, saying that "it was not the drought *per se*, but rather the government's failure to respond to the ensuing humanitarian crisis that formed one of the triggers of the uprising." However, she then questioned the helpfulness of referring to climate change as a "threat multiplier." She did agree that "climate change may have contributed to worsening the effects of the drought." But, she said, "it seems unproductive to focus on the possible role of climate change in the uprising." She ends up, in fact, saying that the possible role of climate change is "irrelevant." Why so? Because it is "an unhelpful distraction." From what? "From the core problem: the long-term mismanagement of natural resources." Scholars, therefore, should not talk about climate change as having a possible role in the uprising, because "it strengthens the narrative of the Assad regime that seizes every opportunity to blame external factors for its own failings."

It is evident, therefore, that her denial of the importance of climate change was based more on a political than a historical judgment. The statement of Brian Merchant of Motherboard is more accurate: climate change "warmed Syria up for war." Having done this, he added, climate change is "going to make basic survival for millions of its victims hell, too."[43]

Asia: China

In addition to inundation from sea-level rise, mentioned in Chapter 5, China's main national security concern is to make sure it will have adequate food and water for its population in the coming decades. This concern might lead it into serious conflicts. According to Dyer, stronger storm systems, the weakening of the monsoons, and the rising sea level will cut food production, with the result that the Chinese government "may seek to fortify its domestic position, rendered shaky by these blows, by directing popular anger outwards."[44]

However, Joanna Lewis – who wrote the chapter on China in Daniel Moran's *Climate Change and National Security* - suggests that conflict would most likely be occasioned by the melting of the Tibetan glaciers, which will, after a period in which the melting causes serious flooding, lead to less water in the rivers that cross through China. "Water scarcity could cause China," Lewis wrote, "to divert these rivers from flowing into surrounding countries, which could cause tensions with neighbors such as Vietnam, Myanmar, Laos, Pakistan, Nepal, and India."[45]

Asia: India and Pakistan

In South Asia, Dyer said, the melting of glaciers and snowpack that have provided water for the rivers that rise in the Himalayas and the Tibetan plateau – including the Ganges, Indus, Mekong, and Yangtze rivers – "will lead to food shortages and cross-border disputes over water in the Indian subcontinent, and nuclear-armed India and Pakistan will face the risk of war over the Indus River."[46]

Background information for understanding this risk has been provided in Brahma Chellaney's 2011 award-winning book, *Water: Asia's New Battleground*. Chellaney wrote: "The risk of water becoming a trigger for war or diplomatic strong-arming is especially high in Asia, which is home to three-fifths of the human population, yet has the lowest per capita freshwater availability among all continents."[47]

Chellaney's concern is well-taken, because the possibility of violent conflict is inherent in the situation. On the one hand, the Indus is essential to the Indian state of Punjab (not to be confused with the Pakistani state of Punjab), which is known as India's "bread basket." Also, India needs more hydroelectric dams "to fill in the serious energy shortfalls that crimp its economy." On the other hand, "unlike India, all of Pakistan is wholly dependent upon the Indus River system." In addition, Pakistan is an arid country, in which most of the population makes its living by farming, and yet "all of its rivers either originate in or pass through India" – so that India could at any time shut off the flow of water to Pakistan.[48]

In 1960, India and Pakistan signed the World Bank-mediated Indus Water Treaty, according to which three of the tributaries of the Indus river system would be controlled by India, while the Indus itself and two tributaries – the Jhelum and Chenab rivers - would be controlled by Pakistan, with this proviso: India is allowed to build dams on the Pakistan-controlled rivers to harness hydroelectric power, as long as these dams do not reduce the water supply to Pakistan.[49]

The treaty has remained in effect all these years, but there has been great tension, with Pakistan repeatedly accusing India of withholding water that is by right Pakistan's. This suspicion is based in part on the fact that the water issue is closely connected to the long-standing dispute about Kashmir, which led to war between the countries in 1947, 1965, and 1999. It is also based partly on the fact that India has recently been building more hydroelectric dams, creating a perception in Pakistan that India is holding water back.[50]

A 2008 article entitled "Blood in Kashmir's Water" indicated the centrality of this issue in its opening sentence: "Water is destined to be a determining factor in the regional conflicts of South Asia in the years to come, particularly between India and Pakistan."[51]

With regard to Pakistan's complaints, it has indeed had insufficient irrigation water, with the result that "Pakistan is on the brink of water scarcity. Its once-lush agricultural fields, which employ half of all Pakistanis and account for a quarter of its GDP, are now frequently parched," and its "water shortage is seen as a direct result of India's upstream dams and water projects."[52]

India, however, rejects what it calls "the myth of water theft,"[53] a rejection supported by some neutral observers and even by some leading Pakistanis, including Jamaat Ali Shah, Pakistan's then-commissioner of the Indus waters, and Shah Mahmood Qureshi, Pakistan's then-foreign minister.[54]

Pakistan, it appears, has insufficient water for two reasons (beyond those of mismanagement): Its population has increased and the rainfall has decreased, due to climate change. The annual precipitation in Kashmir, a recent study showed, has been declining since 1975. Even more important for future decades is the fact that most of Pakistan's irrigation water depends on glacial melt, but the glaciers are projected to decline greatly by 2050.[55] They are declining partly because of warmer temperatures and partly because of black carbon soot, which makes snow dirty, so that it absorbs more sunlight and hence melts faster.[56]

In 2009, Stephen Faris, the author of *Forecast: The Consequences of Climate Change*, wrote: "It sometimes seems as if Pakistan can't get any more terrifying." However, he said, "The country's troubles today pale compared with what it might face 25 years from now. When it comes to the stability of one of the world's most volatile regions, it's the fate of the Himalayan glaciers that should be keeping us awake at night." The reason is that the success of the Indus Waters Treaty "depends on the maintenance of a status quo," but this status quo is being altered by climate change.[57]

In any case, because of water tension in conjunction with other causes of tension, many observers fear that war may break out in the not-too-distant future. For example:

- In 2010, a *Financial Times* story reported: "New Delhi fears that water from the Himalayas could emerge as a new populist dispute, on a par with the contested territory of Kashmir, between the two nuclear-armed rivals that have fought three wars over the past 63 years."

- An Inter Press Service story that same year was entitled "India/Pakistan: Reduced Himalayan Snowfall Could Spark Water War."

- A 2011 essay entitled "Kashmir: The Forgotten Conflict," ends by saying: "Given that both Pakistan and India are dangerously energy and water starved and nowhere close to an agreement on Kashmir, teamed with the impact of climate change and population pressures, the prognosis on the Indo-Pak water problem involving Kashmir is anything but positive."

- In 2012, Kamal Majidulla, the Pakistani prime minister's special assistant on water resources, said: "Unfortunately, we are going towards conflict and not conflict resolution."[58]

Plans B, A, and C

This chapter has discussed climate change from the perspective of its possible implications for war. As with the issues discussed in the previous chapters, we can look at three possible responses.

Plan B

There seems little doubt that CO_2-fueled climate change, insofar as it becomes serious climate *disruption*, will tend to spark or at least exacerbate strife between countries in various parts of the world. This will be especially the case insofar as the climate disruption leads to food and water shortages and unwanted climate refugees. The best way for the international community to minimize such strife – which in some cases could lead to war – would be to initiate a crash program to keep global warming down as far as possible.

Plan A

If instead, the international community simply allows greenhouse emissions to continue unabated, in spite of all the warnings, then climate wars - wars that are at least partly due to climate change – will surely become increasingly likely. Given the tensions that have already been increased by a rise of the global temperature of less than one degree C above pre-industrial times, it is surely not "hype" to think that much stronger tensions will arise if the global temperature rises by 2°C and then, if business as usual continues, 3, 4, 5, and even 6°C – at which James Woolsey predicted that the United States and other countries would face "almost inconceivable" challenges – including security concerns occasioned by perhaps billions of climate refugees.

If we continue with Plan A, therefore, our children and grandchildren will face not only all the unprecedented problems discussed in Chapters 1-8 but also unprecedented resource wars. The only way to avoid this, it would seem, would be the possibility raised in Chapter 10 – that ecosystem collapse would put an end to their misery.

Plan C

Many political and business leaders are probably thinking in terms of the third option: that they would allow business-as-usual emissions until they have 100 percent certainty – to use General Gordon Sullivan's phrase – that CO_2-fueled climate change will have disastrous consequences, at which point they will initiate a crash program to prevent any further warming. By that time, however, the planet will, because of the lag between CO_2 emissions and global warming, probably already be fated to experience a temperature rise of at least 4°C. Therefore, insofar as Plan A will lead to unprecedented climate wars, Plan C will have largely the same results.

Conclusion

Once again, Plan B must be chosen.

ECOSYSTEM COLLAPSE AND EXTINCTION

"The scale, spread and rate of change of global drivers are without precedent. Burgeoning populations and growing economies are pushing environmental systems to destabilizing limits."
– UNEP, 2012

"If current trends continue, . . . governments will preside over unprecedented levels of damage and degradation."
– Achim Steiner, UNEP, 2012

The previous chapters have dealt with various aspects of CO_2-caused climate change – increases in extreme weather, including heat waves, droughts, and storms; sea-level rise; fresh water shortage; and food shortage, due in part to ocean acidification. Any one of these effects, especially assuming the continuation of business as usual, is sobering enough by itself. Even more serious is the fact that all of these effects would be occurring simultaneously. But there is an even worse possibility: that the effects of the increases in atmospheric and oceanic CO_2 will result in a global ecosystem collapse.

Ecosystem Collapse

An ecosystem (ecological system) is a network of living organisms (plants, animals and microbes) interacting with nonliving things (including air, water, soil, and minerals), and functioning as a unit. An ecosystem can be very small, such as a tiny lake, or very large, such as one of the oceans, or larger yet, such as the oceans as a whole. Inclusive of all local ecosystems, the planet as a whole can be considered an ecosystem.[1]

Small local ecosystems can collapse, so that they no longer provide support for animals, as when a pond no longer supports the life of its fish. Larger ecosystems, such as a lake or a sea, can also collapse, as when they no longer support plant and animal life. For example, the Dead Sea is dead because it became so salty that nothing other than microbes can live in it.

Moreover, besides the fact that some regions of the ocean have become "dead zones," some scientists have discussed the possibility, as discussed in Chapter 7, that the oceanic ecosystem as a whole might collapse, due to ocean acidification. Finally, in recent years, earth scientists have begun thinking about an unprecedented ecosystem collapse: the collapse of the *global* ecosystem.

Global Ecosystem Collapse: 2004 to 2009

From 2004 to 2009, there were some important articles directly relevant to the possibility of global ecosystem collapse. Three will be discussed.

2004: Extinction Risk: Chris Thomas, a conservation biologist at Leeds University in England, led a team studying "Extinction Risk from Climate Change." The conclusion was that if business as usual continues, 15 to 37 percent of the land plants and animals they studied would, by 2050, be "committed to extinction."[2] In an article discussing global warming and ecosystem collapse, journalist Paul Brown reported that Thomas found the conclusions reached by his team "terrifying."[3]

2007: Keystone Species: The following year brought a major article that "discusses the plight of four keystone species which are absolutely essential for human survival: plankton, edible fish, bees, and topsoil." In their conclusion, the authors wrote:

> The preservation of the fundamental cornerstones of the ecosystem must become a foremost goal in human advancement, and it is clear that their destruction must be stopped. Plankton supporting abundant sea life are dying, fish that is a staple part of the diet of many people around the world are being fished to extinction, bees pollinating crops are threatened by many factors, and topsoil sustaining agriculture is disappearing.[4]

2009: Planetary Boundaries: A major step forward in the study of the possibility of global ecosystem collapse was taken in 2009, with the publication of an article entitled "Planetary Boundaries: Exploring the Safe Operating Space for Humanity." This article was written by lead author Johan Rockström and 28 other scientists, including Paul Crutzen, James Hansen, Hans Joachim Schellnhuber, and Will Steffen.[5]

In this article, the notion of "planetary boundaries" was placed in the context of the shift from the Holocene epoch to the Anthropocene, which began with the industrial revolution. Because industrialized society has been "pushing the planet outside the Holocene range of variability for many key Earth System processes," the emergence of the Anthropocene epoch raises a new question:

> What are the non-negotiable planetary preconditions that humanity needs to respect in order to avoid the risk of deleterious or even catastrophic environmental change at continental to global scales?[6]

The authors called these non-negotiable planetary preconditions "thresholds." The idea was that, just as a local ecosystem has thresholds or "tipping points," which if reached will cause that ecosystem to undergo a sudden "state change," the transgression of one or more *global* thresholds might lead to an abrupt state change of the global ecosystem as a whole. The authors wrote:

> There is ample evidence from local to regional-scale ecosystems, such as lakes, forests, and coral reefs, that gradual changes in certain key control variables (e.g., biodiversity, harvesting, soil quality, freshwater flows, and nutrient cycles) can trigger an abrupt system state change when critical thresholds have been crossed.[7]

By extension, the authors said, scientists need to study "the dynamics of thresholds and feedbacks that operate at continental and global scales." In speaking of "thresholds," the authors meant "intrinsic features of [human–environmental] systems." Some thresholds, such as the temperature at which fresh water turns into ice, are known. However, scientists have no precise knowledge of global thresholds, such as the average surface temperature at which the planet would undergo a state change.

Rockström and his fellow authors proposed, accordingly, that we agree on estimates of "planetary boundaries within which we expect that humanity can operate safely" – meaning that if we do not transgress these boundaries, we should have no fear of "crossing thresholds that will trigger non-linear, abrupt environmental change within [the global ecosystem]."[8]

For example, many scientists and politicians had assumed that the ecosystem will be safe as long as the increase in the global temperature remains below $4\,^\circ$C (7°F). More recently, many climate scientists have agreed that we will be safe if, and only if, the temperature increase remains below 2°C (3.6°F). But Rockström and his fellow authors (including Hansen) endorsed the view that the boundary should be placed at an increase of $1.5\,^\circ$C.

In any case, the authors identified nine planetary boundaries, adding that, in their opinion, three of them - atmospheric CO_2 concentration, biodiversity loss, and changes to the nitrogen cycle – have already been transgressed.[9]

On the assumption that boundary transgressions will not be disastrous immediately, the authors said that their framework provides a twofold task for global environmental governance: do what can be done to rectify the transgressions of boundaries that have already been made, while ensuring that there are no further transgressions.[10]

Global Ecosystem Collapse: 2012 - 2014

Articles that appeared in 2012 and 2014 advanced the study of the possibility of global ecosystem collapse still further.

2012: Approaching a State Shift: In 2012, Anthony Barnosky of the University of California (Berkeley) led a team of 22 highly respected scientists in producing a major study entitled "Approaching a State Shift in Earth's Biosphere." With regard to the results, one of the team members, Arne Mooers of Simon Fraser University, said that his fellow scientists are "more than pretty worried." In fact, he added, "some are terrified." Another one of these scientists, James Brown of the University of New Mexico, said that the study's conclusion "scares the hell out of me." What terrifies these scientists is the possibility of a collapse of the global ecosystem.[11] An excellent article in the *Vancouver Observer* put it this way:

> Scientists have reached near-total consensus on climate change. But according to the new study, once you add other variables – such as population growth, over-consumption, agriculture and extinctions – to that mix, the entire ecological system may teeter on the brink. Everything could, in fact, change in the proverbial blink of an eye (at least, on the scale of earth's history). It's called a 'global state change,' and the report estimates it could begin as early as the second half of this century if we stay on our present course.[12]

These abrupt changes, the scientists said, would likely involve a massive reduction in the planet's biodiversity – not the first mass extinction, to be sure, but the first one caused by human beings - and also a massive reduction in the availability of food and fresh water. "It really will be a new world, biologically, at that point," said team-leader Barnosky. Arne Mooers concluded: "This review is dramatic – it's quite stark. The chances are that this transition would not only be extremely problematic to human society, but the new state might not be conducive to human society at all."[13]

2014: Earth on the Brink of Mass Extinction: An international group of nine scientists in 2014 carried out a comparison of historical rates of extinction with those of today. The lead author, Duke University biologist Stuart Pimm, said that "species are going extinct one thousand times faster than they should be." This means, he said, that "planet Earth is on the brink of a mass extinction event comparable in scale to the one that wiped out the dinosaurs 65 million years ago," and from which it took "5-10 million years to recover."[14]

Conclusion
In discussing the likely nature of a world in which the global temperature had risen to 4 $^{\circ}$C beyond preindustrial times, Kevin Anderson - the director of the Tyndall Centre for Climate Change in London - has said: "I think it's extremely unlikely that we wouldn't have mass death at 4°C. . . . [Y]ou might have half a billion people surviving."[15] This is a bleak scenario. But in light of the possibility that a world with a 4°C increase would lead to global ecosystem collapse, Anderson's scenario may be overly optimistic.

The Methane Threat

The previous section discussed the possibility of global ecosystem collapse apart from the greatest threat to the global ecosystem, that of methane (CH_4). Methane release from thawing permafrost in the Arctic, Romm has said, "is the most dangerous amplifying feedback in the entire carbon cycle."[16]

What has been called "permafrost" (meaning perennially frozen soils) was formed in the Arctic during the most recent glacial period. It contains an enormous amount of carbon from dead plants and animals, which the Arctic's extremely cold climate has prevented from thawing. The carbon exists in methane clathrates (also called hydrates), which are crystalline solids, looking like ice, in which water molecules form cage-structures around methane molecules.

"Over hundreds of millennia," explained a 2013 NASA article, "Arctic permafrost soils have accumulated vast stores of organic carbon - an estimated 1,400 to 1,850 pentagrams" (a pentagram is a little over two trillion pounds), and this is "about half of all the estimated organic carbon stored in Earth's soils." If so, the Arctic's frozen carbon is between four and five times larger than the 350 pentagrams of carbon that have been emitted by human beings (primarily through fossil fuels) since 1850.[17]

Four factors combine to make these figures very threatening. First, the Arctic is warming up twice as fast as the rest of the planet (except for

Antarctica). Second, if the so-called permafrost begins thawing, it will release its carbon. Third, most of the carbon is "located in thaw-vulnerable topsoils within 10 feet (3 meters) of the surface." Fourth, if the permafrost is on dry land, so the organic material is well-aerated, oxygen-breathing bacteria will break down the material into CO_2, but if the permafrost is in the bottom of a lake or wetland, the organic material will enter the atmosphere as methane, which is a greenhouse gas dozens of times more potent than CO_2.[18]

At one time, scientists thought this was only a problem for the future and even then relatively minor. But in the past decade, evidence has been accumulating that the thawing of permafrost, besides being anything but a minor matter, is already occurring.

In 2008 and 2010, Natalie Shakhova (of the University of Alaska Fairbanks) and other Arctic specialists, having for many years been investigating the Arctic shelf off the northern coast of East Siberia (which is parallel with northern Alaska), reported that the surface water showed "extreme methane supersaturation." Then in 2010, she and colleagues gave an explanation, reporting that the underwater permafrost was "losing its ability to be an impermeable cap." In response, the National Science Foundation said: "Release of even a fraction of the methane stored in the shelf could trigger abrupt climate warming."[19]

"The East Siberian Arctic Shelf," added Romm, is of special concern "because it is so shallow. In deep water, methane gas oxidizes into carbon dioxide before it reaches the surface. In the shallows of the East Siberian Arctic Shelf, methane simply doesn't have enough time to oxidize, which means more of it escapes into the atmosphere."[20]

In 2010, a study by the National Snow and Ice Data Center predicted that, if business as usual continues, the thawing of permafrost will dump 100 billion tons of carbon into the atmosphere by 2100. More immediately, it said that it expected the permafrost to switch from a carbon sink to a source during the 2020s.[21]

Also in 2011, the authors of an article in *Nature*, having pointed out that "Arctic temperatures are rising fast, and permafrost is thawing," said: "We calculate that permafrost thaw will release the same order of magnitude of carbon as deforestation if current rates of deforestation continue." Even worse, they said that, because the emissions will include a significant amount of methane, "the overall effect on climate could be 2.5 times larger."[22]

In 2012, former oilman Andy Skuce wrote in Skeptical Science that, if business as usual continues, the carbon feedback from thawing permafrost will likely "be self-sustaining and will cancel out future natural carbon sinks in the oceans and biosphere," thereby adding as much as 1.5°F to global warming by the year 2100.[23]

Prior to 2013, virtually all of the discussion about thawing permafrost was about the Arctic. But in that year, a study of coastal permafrost in the Antarctic revealed that it was melting much faster than expected – in fact, similar to the melt rate of Arctic permafrost.[24]

The Temperature and the Threat

Given the fact that a melting of much of the permafrost will have devastating consequences, a crucial question is: At what global temperature will significant thawing of permafrost begin? In 2013, Oxford University's Anton Vaks led a team that examined the 500,000-year history of stalagmites and similar rock formations in Siberian caves. Vaks learned in this study that "global climates only slightly warmer than today are sufficient to thaw extensive regions of permafrost" – to be precise, when the global temperature was merely 1.5°C warmer than it was in the Holocene era (before the rise of the Anthropocene).[25]

The main reason that allowing permafrost to thaw is so threatening – on top of the reasons given earlier – is that the thawing is likely to become self-amplifying, so that a positive feedback cycle would be initiated. The thawing of a significant amount of permafrost could, therefore, create runaway global warming – which will, of course, lead to ecological collapse.[26]

The Economic Costs of Permafrost Melting

Finally, even apart from global warming and hence ecological collapse, methane release caused by permafrost thawing promises to be extremely expensive economically. In July 2013, *Nature* published a study saying that if the permafrost in the Eastern Siberian shelf were to thaw, it could cost the global economy $60 trillion during this century and the next. Although some critics found this estimate far too high, the study had credibility due to its authorship, in which economic and management professors joined with Arctic specialist Peter Wadhams.[27]

With regard to the projected cost: Although news stories reporting the $60-trillion figure made some people gasp, the actual study indicated that the cost would be far higher. Saying that "the costs of a melting Arctic will be huge," the study predicted that "[t]he release of methane from thawing permafrost beneath the East Siberian Sea . . . alone comes with an average global price tag of $60 trillion in the absence of mitigating action." As a story in Science Daily pointed out, "methane from the East Siberian Sea . . . constitutes just a fraction of the vast reservoirs of methane in the Arctic." The total predicted cost for the Arctic thawing, reported another story, was about $400 trillion.[28]

This study is relevant with respect to those economists, discussed in Chapter 16, who suggest that strong climate abatement would not be cost-effective.

Extinction

Although the idea of extinction was mentioned a few times above, the issue deserves a section to itself. Indeed, even if it seldom makes the evening news, extinction is one of the major stories of our time, because we are in the midst of one of the six mass extinctions since the emergence of life on our planet. The previous five mass extinctions were:

- The extinction at the end of the Ordovician Period (referred to as "the end-Ordovician extinction"), which occurred about 440 mya (million years ago);

- The end-Devonian extinction, which occurred some 370 mya;

- The end-Permian extinction, which was the worst of the extinctions thus far, occurred about 245 mya, having evidently been triggered by a massive lava flow in Siberia that increased global temperatures by $6°$ C, which melted frozen methane deposits, which in turn raised the temperature even further. This "Great Dying," as it is called, evidently caused about 95 percent of the planet's complex organisms to go extinct – a catastrophe so great that "[it] took about 50 million years for life again to develop the diversity that it had prior to the event."[29]

- The end-Triassic extinction, which occurred some 210 mya (shortly after mammals and dinosaurs had evolved), and came about when "an increase in atmospheric CO_2 caused acidification of the oceans and global warming" (which is believed to have been caused by volcanoes).[30]

- The end-Cretaceous extinction, which occurred about 65 mya, eliminated (among other animals) the last of the dinosaurs.

Whereas all of those extinctions were caused by various types of natural causes, the sixth mass extinction, which may prove to be the worst ever, is unique in being caused by human beings. It began about 100,000 years ago, when humans began spreading from Africa to the rest of the world. The extinction speeded up qualitatively after agriculture began in the Holocene epoch, and even more after the industrial revolution.[31]

In fact, human beings, who now emit about 100 times more CO_2 than volcanoes, are evidently extinguishing species – according to a 2010 article in a special issue on biological diversity published by the Royal Society – at a rate that "far exceeds anything in the fossil record."[32]

Another article in the same issue, written by Jeremy Jackson of the Scripps Institution of Oceanography, discussed extinction caused by ocean acidification. Explaining that "massive influxes of carbon at the end of the Paleocene caused intense global warming, ocean acidification, mass extinction throughout the deep sea and the worldwide disappearance of coral reefs," Jackson said that unless there is immediate and decisive conservation action, "another great mass extinction affecting all ocean ecosystems and comparable to the upheavals of the geological past appears inevitable."[33]

At the end of her 2014 book, *The Sixth Extinction*, Elizabeth Kolbert asked, "In an extinction event of our own making, what happens to us?" Many people seem to think that we self-named *Homo sapiens* are so wise and powerful that nothing could drive us to extinction. However, she points out, "When a mass extinction occurs, it takes out the weak and also lays low the strong." The famous anthropologist Richard Leakey, she added, warned that "*Homo sapiens* might not only be the agents of the sixth extinction, but also risks being one of its victims."[34]

There are now some scientists who believe that human extinction, or at least *near* extinction, will happen in the near future.

Kevin Anderson, director of England's Tyndall Centre for Climate Change, said in 2009 that if the global temperature rises by 4°C, about 90 percent of the Earth's people will die - although human extinction will not be total, because "a few people with the right sort of resources may put themselves in the right parts of the world and survive."[35]

Anderson's view is considered overly optimistic by others, such as atmospheric and marine scientist Ira Leifer of the University of California Santa Barbara. Asking what portion of the population would be able to adapt to a global temperature increase of 4°C, Leifer said he believed that it would be "just a few thousand people [seeking refuge] in the Arctic or Antarctica."[36]

Even Leifer's view is too optimistic for other scientists, such as Australian microbiologist Frank Fenner - who had announced the eradication of smallpox to the World Health Assembly in 1980. In 2010, Fenner, the author of 22 books and hundreds of scientific articles, said: "Homo sapiens will become extinct, perhaps within 100 years."[37]

Some scientists who expect an imminent extinction of the human race regard methane emissions from thawing permafrost as the most likely cause. A good introduction to the thinking of some scientists about the danger of extinction from methane is provided by a 2013 video called "Mass Extinction: Let's Not," which was narrated and co-authored by Thom Hartmann.[38] Given the seriousness of the danger from methane, the present book might better have been subtitled, "Can Civilization Survive the CO_2-CH_4 Crisis?"

Probably the scientist who has written the most about the demise of the human race within the next several decades is Guy R. McPherson, professor emeritus of evolutionary biology at the University of Arizona. In various articles, at a blog called "Nature Bats Last," and in a 2013 book entitled *Going Dark,* McPherson has presented an array of scenarios through which humanity could become extinct, one of which is due to methane emissions from thawing permafrost.[39]

The prediction of human extinction through methane emissions has been central to the thinking of retired Earth-systems scientist Malcolm Light. In 2012, Light wrote that the process of significant methane release, which began in 2010, "will accelerate exponentially, release huge quantities of methane into the atmosphere and lead to the demise of all life on earth before the middle of this century." From Light's point of view, the only hope for human survival is a massive reduction in CO_2 emissions combined with the immediate use of geoengineering "as a cooling method in the Arctic to counteract the effects of the methane buildup."[40]

Is There a Geoengineering Salvation?

Geoengineering has been defined as "intentionally altering the planet's physical or biological systems to counteract global warming."[41] It has been portrayed as a way to prevent climate change from becoming catastrophic without needing to fight against the fossil-fuel industry. In a 2013 book, Clive Hamilton predicted that, "As the effects of global warming begin to frighten us, geoengineering will come to dominate global politics."[42]

Prior to 2006, very little had written about geoengineering, because it was a taboo topic. Virtually all climate scientists had feared, Hamilton said, "that the availability of an alternative to cutting emissions, even if manifestly inferior, would prove so alluring to political leaders that it would further undermine the will to do what must be done." But, fearing that the politicians would never act, Paul Crutzen wrote an article urging research into geoengineering as a back-up position.

Crutzen's article opened the floodgates. Today, journalist John Vidal reported, "there are hundreds of groups and institutions proposing experiments." Crutzen and some other scientists are making proposals for the sake of saving civilization, but some of the proposals "are being pushed hard by entrepreneurs and businessmen attracted by the potential to make billions of dollars."[43]

In any case, there are two basic forms of geoengineering (which is sometimes called "climate engineering"). On the one hand, there is *solar radiation management*, which seeks "to reduce the amount of sunlight reaching the planet." On the other hand, there are *carbon dioxide removal* technologies, which aim to extract CO_2 from the atmosphere and "store it somewhere less dangerous."[44]

Solar Radiation Management

The type of geoengineering that is best known is solar radiation management (SRM). It was the type advocated in a 2007 *Wall Street Journal* op-ed entitled "Thinking Big on Global Warming." It was written by former Reagan administration official Fred Ikle, along with a former weaponeer at the Pentagon, Lowell Wood, who had been a protégé of Edward Teller – who inspired the "Dr. Strangelove" character – and who himself has been jokingly called "Dr. Evil." Ikle and Wood wrote: "We know [geoengineering] would work, because it happens naturally all the time." That is, "Clouds routinely deflect sunlight and thereby cool the Earth. Volcanoes – when they erupt and inject millions of tons of fine particulate material into the stratosphere (mostly sulfate aerosols) – have also cooled large regions of the globe."[45]

In SRM, engineers put sulfate aerosols in the stratosphere and/or put mirrors in space to reflect the sun's rays – an approach that, Romm says, is quite literally "smoke and mirrors."[46] As Romm's quip suggests, he, like most other climate scientists, is not positive towards SRM, believing that it would be ineffective, harmful, or both.

Brightening Clouds: One of the types of SRM – the type that Romm summarized as "mirrors" - would spray stratocumulus clouds with tiny drops of seawater, thereby making them 10 percent brighter (whiter), so that they will reflect more of the sun's rays. The spraying would be done by specially constructed, satellite-controlled vessels, which would roam the oceans, pumping the drops into the air. But this project has encountered several difficulties:

- To raise the reflectivity by 10 percent, there would need to be an estimated 1,500 vessels, each of which would need 28 billion tiny nozzles – each having a diameter of less than a micron.

- The water droplets must be of just the right size. And, as one researcher pointed out, there is a flaw in the "idea that you'd inject a particular drop size, because it won't stay that size for long."

- The salty residue of the spray, which causes the brightening, will be washed out, so that spraying would need to be continuous.

- It would also need to go on forever, because "the sudden termination of any solar radiation technology could be disastrous because the heating suppressed by the intervention would rebound at a much faster rate."

- Almost nothing is known about what long-term spraying would do to climate patterns, and models suggest that, for example, cloud brightening in the South Atlantic would cause Amazon drought.[47]

Spraying Sulphur: The many problems with cloud brightening do not necessarily discourage SRM advocates, because a different type, involving sulphate particles, is generally considered the most promising. This approach was suggested, as the Ikle-Wood op-ed indicated, by cooling caused by volcanic eruptions. The proposal, said Hamilton, "is to spray tiny aerosol particles into the stratosphere in order to reflect an extra 2 per cent or so of incoming solar radiation," which would (roughly) offset the warming that would otherwise be caused by a doubling of greenhouse gases. Again, however, several difficulties arise:[48]

- Volcanic eruptions affect the climate for a few years at most, but nobody can predict the consequences of pumping sulfates into the atmospheres.

- Insofar as scientists have good ideas about what would happen, they believe that spraying sulphur would weaken the global hydrological cycle, which could mean reducing the precipitation in Asia during the summer monsoons – which could affect the food supplies of two billion people.

- Spraying sulphur could also be disastrous for Africa. A 2013 study of the four major 20th-century droughts in the Sahel showed that three of them came after major eruptions.

- Spraying sulphur could also harm the ozone layer: The most comprehensive study of this issue concluded that injecting enough sulphur to offset CO_2 doubling would delay the healing of the ozone hole by 30 to 70 years.[49]

- The problem of starting this program and then stopping it – which, Hamilton says, "is known (without irony) as the termination problem" – would cause such a rapid increase in the global temperature that,

145

for example, only a sixth of the world's forests would survive.

Final Observation: In 2014, a study providing the first major comparison of the various types of geoengineering was published in *Nature Communications*. The authors, led by David Keller, concluded that no one of the methods can be called the best, because levels of effectiveness and risk rise together. In particular, they said, SRM can be the most effective, but it also contains the greatest risks.[50]

Carbon Dioxide Removal

The other major type of geoengineering, carbon dioxide removal technologies, target the source of global warming, namely, "too much carbon in the atmosphere" (whereas SRM methods "target one of its symptoms: too much heat").[51]

Ocean Iron Fertilization: The best known of these methods is ocean fertilization. It primarily uses iron, so it is also called ocean iron fertilization (OIF). In this method, iron sulfate is put into the oceans in order to stimulate phytoplankton blooms, with the hope that they will absorb carbon dioxide and then sink to the bottom of the sea, where the carbon would remain. But there are several reasons to doubt that it will ever be helpful.

The 2010 eruption of an Icelandic volcano provided a "natural experiment." It produced so much ash that air traffic across Europe was brought to a standstill. According to a 2013 scientific report, the eruption resulted in a significant amount of dissolved iron in the Iceland Basin, but there were indications of only "minor increases in phytoplankton abundance." In addition, the eruption resulted in "a significant perturbation to the biogeochemistry of the Iceland Basin, so that overall the results were negative."[52]

In 2012, a California businessman, hoping to get rich, carried out a rogue experiment by dropping iron sulfate off the west coast of Canada. It did indeed spawn a massive plankton bloom.[53] But studies indicate that, overall, OIF would be more harmful than helpful. On the side of being less helpful than expected:

- Although OIF can be effective in short time scales, it is "less so on longer ones."

- OIF has no long-term effect: When it is discontinued, "the ocean stops taking up CO_2 at a higher rate."[54]

- OIF-produced plankton will not work in two-thirds of the Southern Ocean, because it has no silicon, so the phytoplankton do not have the shells needed to deter zooplankton predators.[55]

On the side of being harmful:

- Although OIF increases local marine productivity, the ecosystems of the fertilized regions are disrupted.

- OIF causes the pH of the regions to decline – thereby increasing ocean acidification.

- OIF also brings about a decrease in oxygen, and discontinuing OIF does not bring the oxygen back up to its previous state.[56]

- Probably most important, algal bloom artificially fertilized with iron "soaks up large amounts of other nutrients, like phosphate [and] nitrate," thereby disrupting "the great cycles that distribute phosphorus and nitrogen," which is one of the nine "planetary boundaries."[57]

In short, while OIF produces only a little long-term effect with regard to increasing phytoplankton bloom, it does have significant effects of a deleterious nature.

Liming the Seas: Whereas most of the types of geoengineering are aimed at keeping the planet's heat down, there is one type that is intended to reverse ocean acidification. The idea is to sprinkle the ocean with "lime, an alkali, so as to return its alkalinity to normal levels." Unfortunately, extracting lime from limestone (as in making cement) takes a tremendous amount of heat, which is usually provided by natural gas.

This problem can be avoided by simply putting crushed limestone into the ocean. But to do much good would "require an enormous amount of rock to be crushed, itself an energy-intensive process," and then thousands of ships. Also, it will be several decades before the crushed rock will make any difference.

Geoengineering in General: Summary

The 2013 comparative study by Keller and colleagues concluded that even the most effective methods have only "limited warming reductions, or they have potentially severe side effects."[58] As for dangers of geoengineering methods in general, three are especially worth raising.

First, testing to see if one of the types of geoengineering is helpful would require taking a completely different approach than that which is taken with regard to new medicines. The development of a new medicine, when done properly, begins with a model, which is then tested in a laboratory. If that goes well, there are then field tests with a limited number of patients. Only if that goes well is the new medicine widely implemented. But with geoengineering schemes, there is no way to test the model apart from "full-scale implementation." And so, if the implementation turns out unexpectedly to produce catastrophic impacts, even strong-supporter Ken Caldeira has said, "we'd be totally screwed."[59]

Second, Clive Hamilton, in a *New York Times* op-ed, said that "perhaps the greatest risk of research into geoengineering [is that] it will erode the incentive to curb emissions. Think about it: no need to take on powerful fossil-fuel companies, no need to tax gasoline or electricity, no need to change our lifestyles."[60]

Third, the desire to erode this incentive may be the main hope of some of geoengineering's advocates. In 2009, a long-time spokesperson for the coal industry said:

> I am firmly convinced that dangerous AGW [anthropogenic global warming] is not a problem and cannot become one. However, I do think the possibility of the geo-engineering should be supported. My reason for this is a political ploy. . . . The politicians need a viable reason if they are to back-off from [supporting constraints on greenhouse gases] without losing face. The geo-engineering option provides the needed viable reason to do nothing about AGW now.[61]

Conclusion

It seems that we cannot expect geoengineering salvation. Lowell Wood said, "We've engineered every other environment we live in – why not the planet?" But an MIT scientist has asked, "How can you engineer a system you don't understand?"[62] Given this lack of understanding, trying to engineer salvation will likely produce its opposite.

Plans B, A, and C

Plan B

As the scientists in the Barnosky-led study indicated, they have no precise knowledge of what combination of ecological changes would bring about a global ecosystem collapse. It is possible, therefore, that a collapse may already be fated to occur within the present century.

However, we must act on the assumption that this is not the case – that there is still the possibility of preventing this worst-of-all-possible scenarios. It is surely already fated that, given dynamics guaranteeing the outcomes discussed in the previous chapters – increases in heat waves, droughts, storms, sea-level rises, fresh water shortages, and food shortages (due in part to ocean acidification) - human life in the latter part of this century will be more dangerous and unpleasant. But if we immediately begin a crash program to greatly reduce our emissions of greenhouse gases, we might be able to prevent a global ecosystem collapse.

Plan A

If the world's political and economic leaders continue with Plan A, according to which the planet's average temperature will be allowed to continue to rise, a global ecosystem collapse will likely be in our future, perhaps as early as the second half of this century. The planet after this collapse, as Arne Mooers stated, might not be "conducive to human society." If so, the angels will need to write – to repeat Clive Hamilton's words – a "requiem for a species."[63]

Plan C

Discussing "Approaching a State Shift in Earth's Biosphere," James Brown, one of the co-authors, said that our society will probably respond by doing "what we seem to do best these days: cross our fingers and hope that the scientists are wrong." That description would be appropriate for Plan A. But it could also apply to Plan C, in this sense: Those who have the power to initiate a crash program to prevent global ecosystem collapse would say: "We are assuming that the scientists are wrong, so that continuing to burn fossil fuels will not bring civilization to an end. However, if we start seeing signs that these scientists are right, we will then initiate a crash program."

The problem with this response is twofold. In the first place, we already have been given ample signs that a major change is underway, such as the melting of glaciers and ice sheets, the disappearance of Arctic ice, and a 40% decline in the ocean's pH. In the second place, if we wait until the threat of a global ecosystem collapse is any clearer, then – given the lag time between CO_2 emissions and their effects - the possibility for preventing collapse will be past. Political leaders will only be able to say: "Guess those scientists were right." In effect, therefore, Plan C will be little different from Plan A. The angels will need to get ready to compose their requiem.

Conclusion

Given the fact that continued global warming, by crossing any of the planetary thresholds, could lead to an extinction that would include the human species, it should be abundantly evident that Plan B, with extremely rapid and extensive mobilization, must be followed.

PART II

UNPRECEDENTED CHALLENGES AND FAILURES

CLIMATE CHANGE DENIAL

*"Human nature makes us vulnerable to confusing
the unprecedented with the improbable."*
– Al Gore, "Climate of Denial," 2011

*"We're witnessing an unprecedented rise in climate denial in me-
dia and politics. . . . I've never seen anything like it.
. . . [H]elp keep science in the headlines."*
– Tim Flannery, Australia's Climate Council, 2014

Bertrand Russell wrote: "Since Adam and Eve ate the apple, man has never refrained from any folly of which he was capable."[1] If applied to particular follies and individual human beings, Russell's statement would be an exaggeration. A good case could be made, however, that this statement is correct about human societies.

It is true, in any case, that segments of societies have been guilty of many huge follies, some of which in our age could destroy civilization. It is certainly true of efforts to deny that climate change results from global warming due to excessive CO_2 emissions, thereby to deny that it is a crisis that requires political leaders to take action.

Those who make this denial are properly called "denialists." Although they have sometimes been called "climate skeptics," skeptics are ones who remain skeptical of particular claims until – and only until - there is sufficient evidence for them. Skepticism is the proper stance of scientists. Climate denialists, by contrast, have an anti-scientific stance. Mark Hoofnagle, who founded the Denialism Blog, has said:

> Denialism is the employment of rhetorical tactics to give
> the appearance of argument or legitimate debate, when
> in actuality there is none. These false arguments are used

when one has few or no facts to support one's viewpoint against a scientific consensus or against overwhelming evidence to the contrary.[2]

Climate denialism employs arguments based on talking points originally provided by fossil-fuel corporations. Some denialists are paid by these corporations, usually through front organizations they fund. But some denialists may believe that the denials were made in a quest for truth, being unaware, as journalist Mark Hertsgaard put it, "that they are mouthing talking points originally developed by big money interests."[3]

In any case, the denialist campaign has been so effective that many Americans believe that a lot of climate scientists reject the view that climate change results from greenhouse gas emissions, although in reality only a tiny number do.

Previous Denialist Campaigns

This chapter begins with some previous denialist campaigns. In 2010, Naomi Oreskes and Erik Conway published a book entitled *Merchants of Doubt*, subtitled *How a Handful of Scientists Obscured the Truth of Issues from Tobacco Smoke to Global Warming*.[4] As that subtitle suggests, the strategy of global warming denialism is part of a trajectory that began with an effort by the tobacco industry to deny that cigarette smoke causes cancer. Oreskes and Conway call this the "Tobacco Strategy."[5]

Cigarette Smoking

The tobacco industry realized that it did not have to prove that cigarette smoking was harmless (which would have been impossible). They needed only to plant doubt. An internal 1969 memo from a tobacco industry executive said: "Doubt is our product, since it is the best means of competing with the 'body of fact' that exists in the minds of the general public. It is also the means of establishing a controversy."[6]

However, the fact that cigarette smoking actually does cause cancer was shown by German scientists already in the 1930s.[7] In the United States, the U.S. Public Health Service determined in 1957 that smoking was "the principal etiological factor in the increased incidence of lung cancer."[8] In 1959, leading researchers declared in peer-reviewed articles that the evidence linking cancer with cigarettes was "beyond dispute."[9] In 1964, the U.S. Surgeon General issued a report, *Smoking and Health*, which was written by a committee that reviewed over 7,000 scientific studies and took testimony from over 150 consultants. The committee concluded – unanimously – that smokers were 10 to 20 times more likely to get lung cancer than nonsmokers.[10]

In fact, the tobacco industry's own scientists concluded that cigarettes caused addiction and cancer. In 1963, the vice president of Brown and Williamson had concluded: "We are, then, in the business of selling nicotine, an addictive drug." And yet as late as 1994 seven CEOs of cigarette companies would (notoriously) testify before Congress, under oath, that the nicotine in cigarettes is not addictive.[11] In 1965, Brown and Williamson's head of research stated that tobacco industry scientists were "unanimous in their opinion that smoke is . . . carcinogenic."[12]

In 1967, nevertheless, Brown and Williamson replied to the Surgeon General's report by saying: "There is no evidence that cigarette smoking causes lung cancer."[13] To support this claim, Brown and Williamson joined with other cigarette companies to invest millions of dollars in finding scientists to help with their disinformation campaign, which has been called "manufacturing uncertainty."[14]

For example, the R. J. Reynolds tobacco company gave Frederick Seitz – who at one time had been a prominent physicist and later became president of the U.S. National Academy of Sciences – $45 million to distribute to various scientists and organizations. The money was billed as being for scientific research, but the research had a very narrow focus: The money, reported Oreskes and Conway, was "for biomedical research that could generate evidence and cultivate experts to be used in court to defend the 'product.'"[15]

Seitz himself – who earned $585,000 for his services – later admitted that the interest in research was constrained, because R. J. Reynolds "didn't want us looking at the health effects of cigarette smoking."[16] What the company did want was to cultivate witnesses who "could testify to causes of illness other than smoking."[17]

Secondhand Smoke

In the 1970s, a new threat to the tobacco industry emerged. Many states in America began passing laws against smoking in public places, on the grounds that inhaling the smoke from other people might cause cancer. At that time, very little scientific evidence for this suspicion had appeared. But tobacco industry scientists had already determined privately that secondhand smoke – also called "environmental tobacco smoke" and "passive smoking" – caused cancer.[18] The industry, of course, did not reveal this to the public.

Nevertheless, scientific evidence of the danger of environmental tobacco smoke began to accumulate. Most important was a 1981 study by Takeshi Hirayama – chief epidemiologist at Japan's National Cancer Center

Research Institute – which showed that the wives of men who smoked had a much higher death rate from lung cancer than the wives of nonsmokers.

The tobacco industry launched an attack on Hirayama and his report, using scientists who had been taken on as consultants. One of these scientists, biostatistician Nathan Mantel, claimed that Hirayama's report was based on a serious statistical error. The tobacco industry publicized Mantel's work and persuaded leading newspapers to give "both sides" of the story. As a result, headlines appeared stating that a scientist had disputed the claim that secondhand smoke was deadly. The tobacco industry then ran full-page ads highlighting these headlines.[19]

The tobacco industry did this in spite of knowing, as stated above, that environmental tobacco smoke could kill people. An internal memo said: "Hirayama [and his defenders] are correct and Mantel and TI [Tobacco Institute] are wrong." Another memo said that "Hirayama was correct, that the TI knew it, and that TI [attacked] Hirayama knowing that the work was correct."[20]

Medical science in general concluded that Hirayama was correct. In 1986, the Secretary of Health and Human Services said: "Involuntary smoking is a cause of disease, including lung cancer, in healthy nonsmokers." (The Executive Summary was written by Dr. Robert Windom, the assistant secretary, who had been nominated by President Ronald Reagan.) That same year, the National Research Council reached that conclusion, and so did a report by the Surgeon General.[21]

The tobacco industry knew that scientists had spoken definitively, that the scientists were correct, and that continued exposure to environmental tobacco smoke would threaten the lives of millions of people. They also realized that environmental tobacco smoke was even more serious than smoking: "It was one thing to say that smokers accepted uncertain risks in exchange for certain pleasures," as Oreskes and Conway put it, "but quite another to say they were killing their friends, neighbors, and even their own children."[22]

These facts were not sufficient, however, to prevent the tobacco industry from sponsoring a disinformation campaign to prevent laws against smoking in public places, because, as it figured, it had its own "survival" to think about. In the words of the vice president of Philip Morris:

> All of us whose livelihoods depend upon tobacco sales – directly or indirectly – must band together into a unified force [because we face this question]: "Are we going to be able to survive and continue to make a living in this industry in the years to come?'" [The industry would shrink, because] "If smokers can't smoke on the way to work, at work, in stores, banks, restaurants, malls and other public places, they are going to smoke less."[23]

This industry's disinformation campaign to ensure its own survival and profits took some novel forms, as when Brown and Williamson paid Sylvester Stallone $500,000 to use its products in five feature films, thereby linking "smoking with power and strength, rather than sickness and death."[24]

More important than such novel forms, the tobacco industry's disinformation campaign relied on its standard methods: getting the media to report "both sides" and, in Project Whitecoat, hiring scientists to be helpful witnesses. One of those witnesses was biomedical researcher Martin Cline, who was given $3 million over 10 years. During a trial about cancer contracted by 25 young flight attendants, Cline was asked whether he had been paid for his testimony, Cline said that he had not: The money was merely a gift.[25]

Just as Frederick Seitz had helped the tobacco industry in its initiative to defeat anti-smoking regulations, another physicist, Fred Singer, helped the industry's effort to defeat regulations involving environmental tobacco smoke. With the assistance of APCO Associates, a public relations firm hired by Philip Morris, Singer had created the Science and Environment Policy Project to promote what he called "sound science" and to denounce what he called "junk science."[26]

"The rhetoric of 'sound science' is," point out Oreskes and Conway, "Orwellian. Real science – done by scientists and published in scientific journals – is dismissed as 'junk,' while misrepresentations and inventions are offered in its place."[27]

Singer, along with Seitz, became an advisor to an organization called The Advancement of Sound Science Coalition (TASSC), which had been started by Steven Milloy but launched by APCO – which was used by Philip Morris, instead of its regular public relations firm, Burson-Marsteller, to hide its affiliation.[28] Thanks to Philip Morris, therefore, both Singer and Milloy had purportedly independent organizations attacking the EPA's report on secondhand smoke as junk science (Milloy even created a website named JunkScience.com).

Singer teamed up with the Heartland Institute, which "promote[s] free-market solutions to social and economic problems" and which has long had a symbiotic relationship with Philip Morris. The Heartland Institute website featured a banner that displayed Heartland's president, Joseph L. Bast, along with other people, including Benjamin Franklin, Thomas Jefferson, and James Madison. The implication, evidently, was that these men's writings, such as *The Declaration of Independence* and *The Constitution of the United States*, were not qualitatively superior to Bast's best-known work, *Please Don't Poop on My Salad*.[29]

Be that as it may, the charge of "junk science" was leveled at the EPA, because of its 1992 report, *Respiratory Health Effects of Passive Smoking*.[30] The EPA had reviewed many studies, gathered from various countries, which concluded that, as Oreskes and Conway put it, "Lots of smoke produced lots of cancer. Less smoke produced less cancer." The EPA judged the evidence "conclusive."[31]

In trying to prevent the EPA report from leading to regulations against smoking in public places, Singer, working together with Philip Morris, employed his concept of "sound science," which was used "to support science they liked and to discredit as 'junk' any science they didn't." They, of course, did not like the EPA report, so Singer wrote an article, entitled "Junk Science at the EPA," and the tobacco industry published a book, drawing on Singer's work, called *Bad Science*.[32]

The EPA report, however, could not credibly be called bad science. "Peer review," point out Oreskes and Conway, "is what makes science science." And whereas peer review is normally carried out by three experts, the EPA report was reviewed by a committee of *nine* experts, including "a professor of medicine at Yale University; a senior staff scientist at the Lawrence Berkeley Laboratory; [and] the chief of Air and Industrial Hygiene for the California Department of Health." Moreover, the committee, after reviewing the report twice, stated: "The Committee concurs with the judgment of EPA that environmental tobacco smoke should be classified as a Class A carcinogen."[33]

Of course, having long known that passive smoking caused cancer, Singer and Philip Morris knew that the EPA report was *not* bad science. Nevertheless, they attacked the report, claiming, for example, that the report had been heavily criticized – even though the "criticism had come not from the scientific community, but from the tobacco industry and groups and individuals funded by it."[34]

The criticism was not to improve the science but merely to "maintain the controversy" in order to forestall legislation against smoking in public places. The ultimate goal was to enable people in the tobacco industry to "survive and continue to make a living." In the period in which this legislation was forestalled, cancer contracted from secondhand smoke ruined the lives of millions of people in America and, because of its influence, in other countries. But this was evidently viewed as relatively unimportant, compared with keeping tobacco company profits up.

The background of the denialist campaign against climate change legislation also includes battles about acid rain and ozone depletion.

Acid Rain

The need to pass regulations to deal with the developing environmental problems required a switch from aesthetic environmentalism to science-based regulation. This switch became institutionalized in the creation of the EPA, whose early victories included the Clean Air Act and the Clean Water Act, both of which were limited to the United States. The first *global* environmental problem to be discussed was acid rain, as scientists realized that local pollution could have global consequences.

In the early 1970s, scientists in various countries began documenting evidence that acid rain was damaging trees, fish, and other things, concluding that "anthropogenic sulfur was implicated." This conclusion led to studies to answer the question whether "we know *for sure* that the sulfur was anthropogenic."[35]

A study in 1978 answered this question by means of atomic isotopes, because "the isotopic signature of sulfur in acid rain in Sudbury [in Ontario, Canada] was identical to the sulfur in the nickel minerals being mined there."[36]

This and other studies led to a 1979 paper in *Scientific American* stating that the question had been answered: "The principal cause [of the acidity of rain] is the release of sulfur and nitrogen by the burning of fossil fuels."[37]

On the basis of these studies, the United States and Canada in 1979 issued a Joint Statement of Intent to move toward a formal agreement "that will make a real contribution to reducing air pollution and acid rain."[38]

A 1981 article in *Nature* gave even stronger evidence for anthropogenic acid rain, saying: "It has now been established beyond doubt that the precipitation in southern Scandinavia has become more acidic as a result of long-distance transport of air pollution."[39]

That same year, the National Academy of Sciences (which had been set up by President Abraham Lincoln to advise the government on scientific matters) issued a report saying that there is now "clear evidence of serious hazard to human health and the biosphere."[40]

In 1983, the EPA issued a 1200-page report, which had been compiled over two years by 46 industry, government, and university scientists, with the intention of providing a "scientifically unimpeachable assessment."[41]

The scientific consensus reflected in these reports should have quickly led the U.S. government to pass bills to reduce acid rain, including one approving a final formulation of the U.S.-Canadian agreement. However, 1981 brought to power the Ronald Reagan administration, which – in line with its commitment to reducing federal regulations – made any acknowledgment of acid rain *verboten.*[42]

An early sign of the changed attitude in the White House came in 1982, when its Office of Science and Technology Policy decided to review the evidence on acid rain. The National Academy of Sciences had just completed such a review and the EPA was in the midst of writing an even more complete review. But the new review was to be based on a panel with different personnel. For the chair of the panel, the White House chose Bill Nierenberg, "who had never worked on acid rain" but who, like his long-time associate

Frederick Seitz, "hated environmentalists." (In 1984, Seitz and Nierenberg would found, along with Robert Jastrow, a conservative think tank called the George C. Marshall Institute.)[43]

Nierenberg chose most of the members of the panel, but the White House suggested the addition of Fred Singer, who, like Seitz, worked against tobacco legislation. Nierenberg, being aware of Singer's attitude toward acid rain, accepted this suggestion.[44] The Office of Science and Technology panel included several good scientists, but the addition of Nierenberg and Singer resulted in a report that differed significantly from the earlier ones.

On the one hand, Nierenberg allowed the White House to change the panel's peer review report unilaterally. Whereas the panel had stated that legislation is needed to prevent acid rain from causing long-term damage, the White House replaced these statements with ones saying that the present knowledge was insufficient to justify controls.[45]

On the other hand, whereas the other eight panel members co-authored the report based on consensus, Singer, who had very different views, was allowed to write an appendix (which was not approved by the rest of the panel). The effect was that, whereas the consensus chapters agreed that the scientific knowledge justified legislation, the report concluded with the suggestion that the science was still in doubt and that, insofar as acid rain *was* a problem, the market could solve it.[46]

The appendix had the desired effect. *Newsweek*, for example, said that the Reagan administration had said, "Prove it," without pointing out that, as *Merchants of Doubt* said, "scientists had, in fact, proved it." Reflecting the Singer-White House view, EPA administrator William Ruckelshaus, when asked in 1984 whether the evidence on acid rain was decisive, replied: "We don't know what's causing it" – even though the EPA's 1200-page review completed the previous year had said that the evidence was "scientifically unimpeachable."[47]

Unsurprisingly, the House subcommittee on acid rain voted 10-9 against the proposed U.S.-Canadian legislation, which was based on the 1980 Memorandum of Intent to deal with acid rain. The U.S.-Canadian committee's 1983 "Technical Report" said: "The existence of a severe problem of environ-mental acidification . . . is not in doubt."[48] But the Reagan administration, with its appointment of Nierenberg and Singer, made it seem as if doubt still existed. Commenting on Ruckelshaus's statement, Oreskes and Conway observed:

> "We don't know what's causing it" became the official position of the Reagan administration, despite twenty-one years of scientific work that demonstrated otherwise. 'We don't know' was the mantra of the tobacco industry in staving off regulation of tobacco long after scientists had

proven its harms, too. But . . . the doubt message was picked up by the media, which increasingly covered acid rain as an unsettled question."

The media also picked up the White House-Singer view that trying to fix this uncertain problem would cost far too much. For example, a 1984 article in *Fortune* magazine, entitled "Maybe Acid Rain Isn't the Villain," said that, because making a major reduction in sulfur dioxide would likely cost $100 billion, "we should be more certain that acid rain is in fact a major threat to the country's environment."[49]

Trying to set the record straight, a group of scientists - including Gene Likens, who had written the 1979 article in *Scientific American* - published an article called "Red Herrings in Acid Rain Research." However, Orestes and Conway pointed out, "the scientific facts were published in a place where few ordinary people would see them, whereas the unscientific claims . . . were published in mass circulation outlets."[50] As a result of the disinformation, "Many people became confused, thinking that the acid rain issue was unsettled, that scientists had no consensus." The disinformation allowed the Reagan administration to avoid any legislation during its eight years.

Singer and the Reagan administration, echoed by *Fortune* and other publications, dismissed what they called "ecological alarmism," while engaging in *economic* alarmism. In later decades, however, it became clear that the warning about ecological devastation was justified, while the warnings of economic devastation proved to be unfounded: In 1990, legislation authorized a "cap and trade" system that, although inadequate, resulted in a 54 percent decline in sulfur dioxide levels in less than two decades, while the pollution control cost only $9 billion, resulting in benefits to the American economy of over $100 billion.[51]

Singer could not have been more wrong about acid rain, as he was about tobacco smoke, but these errors would not convince him to keep quiet: He was, after all, not interested in being right, only in fulfilling Big Tobacco's wish to have legislation delayed and weakened and, of course, the money it would pay him.

The Ozone Hole

In the early 1970s, scientists began thinking that human activities might damage Earth's protective ozone layer in the stratosphere. Some scientists who first presented evidence to this effect were accused of alarmism, thanks to a misleading summary of their work.[52]

But then a set of scientists taking a different approach showed that chlorine reaching the stratosphere might destroy ozone. A decisive 1974 paper by Sherwood Rowland and Mario Molina argued that chlorofluorocarbons (CFCs) - which were used in spray cans, refrigerators, and air conditioners - would destroy ozone after reaching the stratosphere, thereby increasing skin cancer.[53]

In response, hearings were quickly held in Congress, and a panel established by the Ford administration declared that, unless new evidence suggested otherwise, Congress should ban all CFC emissions to the atmosphere. The question about evidence was assigned to the National Academy of Sciences.[54]

Hoping to influence the National Academy, the aerosol industry set up a Committee on Atmosphere Science. Its star scientific witness denounced the idea of ozone depletion as a "scare story," arguing that human activities are too small to harm the atmosphere. But this critic lost effectiveness after being exposed as a "scientific hired gun."[55] The industry next argued that the chlorine was generated by volcanoes. However, besides having theoretical problems, this hypothesis was not empirically supported. But the industry did not give up. As a book entitled *The Ozone War* reported:

> They [the CFC industry] challenged the theory every step of the way. They said there was no proof that fluorocarbons even got into the stratosphere, no proof that they split apart to produce chlorine, no proof that, even if they did, the chlorine was destroying ozone.

But all of these hypotheses were quickly disproved.[56] In desperation, the aerosol industry tried the "we don't know" defense, arguing that all that the scientific studies have shown is that "we don't know what is going on." As an alternative, Reagan's secretary of the interior Donald Hodel proposed that no regulation was necessary thanks to a "personal protection plan," namely, people will wear hats and long-sleeved shirts.[57]

Fred Singer, who was the chief scientist for the Department of Transportation in 1987-88, denounced what he called the "ozone scare" in an article carried on page 1 of the *Wall Street Journal*. But his argument, that "ozone is not lost at all but simply moves about," falsely entails that the movement of ozone from one region would lead to increases elsewhere. Singer then tried other arguments, but they were all versions of his basic claims: Scientists have overreacted and are corrupt, so they cannot be trusted, and that changes in the ozone layer reflected natural variability, so that no regulation was needed.[58]

In 1995, shortly after Singer had argued that "stratospheric chlorine comes mostly from natural sources" and there was "no scientific consensus on ozone depletion," Sherwood Rowland, Mario Molina, and Paul Crutzen shared the Nobel Prize in Chemistry for their work on stratospheric ozone chemistry. So Singer attacked the Nobel committee.[59]

All of Singer's arguments failed, if judged from a scientific perspective. However, as Oreskes and Conway pointed out, his claim, according to which an "ozone scare" had been created by "corrupt" scientists, who could not be trusted, was picked up by others:

> Fred Seitz included [such] claims in a 1994 Marshall Institute 'report' on ozone depletion and climate change..., implying that CFCs couldn't reach the stratosphere – a claim even a freshmen physics major would know was wrong – much less a former president of the National Academy of Sciences.[60]

Eventually, Singer's argument "was proved wrong, when CFCs were banned and the ozone hole began to repair itself."[61]

Big Oil Adapts Big Tobacco's Strategy

As the campaign histories above show, the campaigns about smoking, secondhand smoke, acid rain, and the ozone hole were *disinformation* campaigns, in which people heading the campaigns knew that their claims were false.

In an amazingly similar revelation, the petroleum industry was, in 1995, told the truth about global warming by its own scientific advisors. These scientists had constituted an advisory committee for the Global Climate Coalition (GCC), which was formed in 1989 in response to the creation of the IPCC. It was led, interestingly, by Leonard S. Bernstein of the Mobil Corporation (prior to its 1999 merger with Exxon to form ExxonMobil). In its primer for the coalition, the committee wrote:

> The scientific basis for the Greenhouse Effect and the potential impact of human emissions of greenhouse gases such as CO_2 on climate is well established and cannot be denied. . . . The contrarian theories. . . do not offer convincing arguments against the conventional model of greenhouse gas emission-induced climate change.[62]

The scientific committee's primer was adopted by the GCC - but only, *The New York Times* reported, "after the operating committee had asked the advisers to omit the section that rebutted the contrarian arguments."[63] Having been secretly aware of the scientific advisors' statement that the Greenhouse Effect "cannot be denied," the GCC continued to deny it (although several of the founding members dropped out). In 1992, for example, the GCC successfully lobbied the first Bush administration to avoid mandatory emission controls at the Earth Summit in Rio and, in relation to the 1997 conference in Kyoto, it launched an advertising campaign against any U.S. agreement for international emission controls (see Chapter 13).

Just as the tobacco companies paid for disinformation campaigns to forestall legislation against their deadly products, the fossil-fuel industry has spent millions of dollars to do the same with regard to anthropogenic global warming. In 1997, for example, it launched an advertising campaign against any U.S. agreement for international emission controls. Just as the "Tobacco Strategy" regarded doubt as the industry's most valuable product, an internal American Petroleum Institute memo about its Action Plan in 1998 said: "Victory will be achieved when average citizens 'understand' (recognize) uncertainties in climate science [so that] recognition of uncertainties becomes part of the 'conventional wisdom.'" This uncertainty has been regarded as essential. In a leaked memo, Republican political consultant Frank Luntz wrote: "The scientific debate is closing [against us] but not yet closed. . . . Should the public come to believe that the scientific issues are settled, their views about global warming will change accordingly. Therefore, you need to continue to make the lack of scientific certainty a primary issue."[64]

Whereas the coal industry and many oil companies have employed this strategy, by far the most important oil corporation to do so has been ExxonMobil (previously simply Exxon). This has especially been the case since 1997, when most of the other leading oil companies dropped out of the Global Climate Coalition.[65] This discussion will, accordingly, focus on ExxonMobil, employing both *Merchants of Doubt* and a report by the Union of Concerned Scientists, *Smoke, Mirrors & Hot Air: How ExxonMobil Uses Big Tobacco's Tactics to Manufacture Uncertainty on Climate Science.*[66] ExxonMobil's strategy to create uncertainty has involved several dimensions: using front organizations, using established scientists, creating new faces, denying climate science, and using friendly politicians.

Using Front Organizations

A central feature of the ExxonMobil strategy was to create a number of front organizations, which served two purposes: to "launder" propaganda, so that it would not obviously be from ExxonMobil; and to create the impression that a large number of organizations reject the IPCC's view of climate change.

Between 1998 and 2014, ExxonMobil gave over $22 million to some 100 organizations for climate change denial. The Union of Concerned Scientists wrote:

Many of these organizations have an overlapping –

sometimes identical – collection of spokespeople serving as staff, board members, and scientific advisors. By publishing and republishing the non-peer-reviewed works of a small group of scientific spokespeople, Exxon-Mobil-funded organizations have propped up and amplified work that has been discredited by reputable climate scientists.[67]

Here are the names of a few such organizations, followed by the money they have received from ExxonMobil since 1998 and, in parentheses, the names of scientists with publications about climate change who have been affiliated with them:

Advance of Sound Science Coalition (TASSC): $30,000 (1998-2002) (Fred Singer, Patrick Michaels, Frederick Seitz)

Advancement of Sound Science Center: $50,000 (2000-2004)

ALEC:- American Legislative Exchange Council: $1,474,200 (Fred Idso)

Atlas Economic Research Foundation: 1,082,500 (evidently no scientists; discussed below)

Cato Institute: $125,000 (Patrick Michaels, Fred Singer, John Christy, Richard Lindzen)

CFACT: Committee for a Constructive Tomorrow: $582,000 (Sallie Baliunas, Patrick Michaels, Sherwood Idso, Craig Idso, Frederick Seitz)

Competitive Enterprise Institute: $2,005,000 (John Christy, Sallie Baliunas, Patrick Michaels)

Frontiers of Freedom: $1,272,000 (Fred Singer, Willie Soon)

Heartland Institute: $676,500 (Sallie Baliunas, John Christy, Richard Lindzen, Patrick Michaels, Fred Singer, Willie Soon, Roy Spencer)

National Center for Policy Analysis: $615,900 (Fred Singer, Frederick Seitz)

Science and Environmental Policy Project: $20,000 (1998-2000) (Fred Singer, Frederick Seitz)

Tech Central Station (Tech Central Science Foundation): $95,000 (Sallie Baliunas, Richard Lindzen, Patrick Michaels, Willie Soon, Roy Spencer)

George C. Marshall Institute: $840,000 (Sallie Baliunas, John Christy, Craig Idso, Sherwood Idso, Richard Lindzen, Patrick Michaels, Frederick Seitz, Willie Soon)

Using Established Scientists

To bolster its claim of a lack of consensus among climate scientists, ExxonMobil supported and publicized the handful of established climate scientists who rejected that consensus. Six of these are Frederick Seitz, Fred Singer, Patrick Michaels, Roy Spencer, John Christy, and Richard Lindzen.

Frederick Seitz: In a *Vanity Fair* article, Mark Hertsgaard described Frederick Seitz as "the highest-ranking scientist among a band of doubters who, beginning in the early 1990s, resolutely disputed suggestions that climate change was a real and present danger." Hertsgaard added:

> He made his case vocally, trashing the integrity of a 1995 I.P.C.C. report on the op-ed page of *The Wall Street Journal,* signing a letter to the Clinton administration accusing it of misrepresenting the science, and authoring a paper which said that global warming and ozone depletion were exaggerated threats devised by environmentalists and unscrupulous scientists pushing a political agenda.[68]

One of Seitz's final acts was his support for the so-called Petition Project, which promoted the most extreme version of the claim about the lack of scientific consensus about climate change. The claim was that over 30,000 climate scientists signed a petition saying: "There is no convincing scientific evidence that the human release of . . . greenhouse gases . . . will, in the foreseeable future, cause . . . disruption of the Earth's climate." By June 2013, the Petition Project's website stated that "31,487 American scientists have signed this petition" – thereby suggesting that climate scientists who disagree with the IPCC's views outnumber those who agree.[69]

This petition was initiated by an organization called the Oregon Institute of Science and Medicine, which sent it to thousands of scientists in 1998. The mailing included (1) an article, formatted to look like one from the *Proceedings of the National Academy of Sciences,* written by a team that included Willie Soon and Sallie Baliunas (two of ExxonMobil's "new faces" to be discussed below), and (2) a covering letter by Seitz, in which he pointed out that he had been the president of the National Academy of Sciences.[70]

The National Academy of Sciences was not amused. As *The New*

York Times' obituary of Seitz pointed out, it "took the extraordinary step of refuting the position of one its former presidents."[71]

Scientific American debunked the claim that the petition was signed by over 30,000 climate scientists. (The criteria for "climate scientists" was extremely permissive, allowing signatories having only a B.S. and/or a degree in one of a wide range of fields, including astronomy, computers, mathematics, mechanical engineering, and general science.[72] Moreover, the signatories merely needed to indicate that they were scientists, and some of the signatories clearly were not – such as novelist John Grisham, one of the Spice Girls, and several crew members of the TV series *M*A*S*H*.[73] Having examined the petition, *Scientific American* "estimated that approximately one percent of the petition signatories might actually have a Ph.D. in a field related to climate science."[74]

Nevertheless, Oreskes and Conway commented, "Fred Seitz is dead, but his letter is alive and well on the Internet." It is also alive in the U.S. Congress. As late as June 2013, Representative David McKinley (R-WV), during an exchange with Energy Secretary Ernest Moniz, disputed Moniz's statement that "98 percent of scientists involved in this area" agree that "a major component [of global warming] is anthropogenic." McKinley replied that "the Petition Project has 32,000 scientists and physicists who've disagreed!"[75]

Fred Singer: Having used the "junk science" claim in debates about acid rain and the ozone layer, Fred Singer used it in ExxonMobil's disinformation campaign on climate change. Although Singer repeatedly denied that he received oil company money, ExxonMobil gave his Science and Environmental Policy Project $20,000 between 1998 and 2000. While under oath in 1993, moreover, Singer admitted that he had often worked as a paid consultant for the Global Climate Coalition and ExxonMobil (as well as Texaco, Arco, Shell, Sun, and Unocal).[76] Singer argued as late as 1998 that "global warming is not happening." But by 2007, he coauthored a book saying that, although it *is* happening, it is due to natural forces and hence unstoppable.[77]

In 2010, Singer served as one of the three lead authors of the Heartland Institute's 400-page report entitled *Climate Change Reconsidered*. Arguing that global warming is "unequivocally good news," it says: "Rising CO_2 levels increase plant growth and make plants more resistant to drought and pests. It is a boon to the world s forests and prairies, as well as to farmers and ranchers." Having quoted part of this statement, a *Rolling Stone* article about the planet's 17 worst "climate killers" included Singer, labeled "The Hack Scientist."[78]

Patrick Michaels: Formerly a professor at the University of Virginia, Patrick

Michaels has published many books and articles with titles such as *Shattered Consensus* (2005), "Global Warming Myth" (2008), and *Climate of Extremes* (2009). He argued: "We know how much the planet is going to warm. It is a small amount, and we can't do anything about it."[79]

Fellow scientists have been brutal about the quality of his work. One critic described Michaels as a "serial deleter of inconvenient data," illustrating this charge by reference to Michaels' critique of James Hansen's 1988 testimony to Congress. Noting that Michaels had deleted two of his three graphs, Hansen said that Michaels was "treading close to scientific fraud." Harvard's John Holdren, who later became Obama's science advisor, said of Michaels: "He has published little if anything of distinction in the professional literature, being noted rather for his shrill op-ed pieces and indiscriminate denunciations of virtually every finding of mainstream climate science."[80]

The funding of Michaels and his "advocacy science consulting firm" (New Hope Environmental Services) has been linked primarily to the coal industry. For example, "A furor was raised," Source Watch reports, "when it was revealed in 2006 that, at customer expense, Patrick Michaels was quietly paid $100,000 by an electric utility, Intermountain Rural Electric Association (IREA), which burns coal, to help confuse the issue of global warming."[81] However, as indicated above, he has also been affiliated with seven of the ExxonMobil-funded organizations named above. At one time, Michaels said: "Most of my funding, the vast majority, comes from taxpayer-supported entities," but he later admitted that perhaps 40 percent of his funding had come from the oil industry.[82]

Roy Spencer: Being a research scientist at Earth System Science Center (ESSC) of the University of Alabama (Huntsville), Roy Spencer has solid credentials. In 2011, however, he co-authored a paper with an ESSC colleague that, although it was well received by *Forbes* and Fox News, was strongly criticized by climate scientists. Kevin Trenberth wrote: "[I]t is evident that this paper did not get an adequate peer review. It should not have been published [because] there is *no* merit whatsoever in this paper." This disaster led the journal's editor to apologize and resign.[83]

In the 1990s, moreover, Spencer and another ESSC colleague, John Christy, had published several essays claiming that the troposphere was not warming in conjunction with surface warming.[84] These essays created one of the most enduring of the denial myths – that the satellite data show no warming. RealClimate wrote: "Spencer and Christy sat by for most of a decade allowing — indeed encouraging — the use of their data set as an icon for global warming skeptics. They committed serial errors in the data analysis, but . . . did little or nothing to root out possible sources of errors, and left it to others to clean up the mess."[85]

Spencer's website claimed that he had "never been asked by any oil company to perform any kind of service. Not even Exxon-Mobil." However, an article entitled "Climate-Science Contrarian Roy Spencer's Oil-Industry Ties" reported that he "doesn't disclose his leadership roles in climate skeptic groups financed by Exxon and other key players in what's been dubbed the 'climate denial machine.'"[86]

Spencer has served as the director of the Marshall Institute, which, as we have seen, received over $840,000 from ExxonMobil. Besides being on the advisory board of the Cornwall Alliance for the Stewardship of Creation – which is closely related to the heavily ExxonMobil-funded Committee for a Constructive Tomorrow (CFACT) - Spencer signed its "Evangelical Declaration on Global Warming," which says: "Earth and its ecosystems – created by God's intelligent design and infinite power and sustained by His faithful providence – are robust, resilient, self-regulating, and self-correcting." In other words, the world is in the hands of a good and omnipotent deity, so we need not worry about global warming.[87]

John Christy: As we have seen, John Christy joined Roy Spencer on several articles that have been strongly criticized by climate scientists. Christy emphasizes the argument from ignorance, saying that we do not know any more about the climate than scientists did in the 1970s. During a U.S. Senate hearing, he said: "The global warming issue is highly overblown. . . . Our ignorance of the climate system is enormous. We cannot predict much at all." To claim we should try to reduce greenhouse gases, he said during a Congressional hearing, would involve "jumping to conclusions" about what is causing climate changes. He does seem to think, nevertheless, that he knows enough to say that climate change can be explained as natural variability.[88]

However, according to testimony he gave under oath in 2007, he admitted to holding the consensus view. In summarizing his testimony, the judge said: "Plaintiffs' own expert, Dr. Christy, agrees with the IPCC's assessment that . . . most of the observed warming over the last fifty years is likely to have been due to the increase in GHG concentrations. . . due to the burning of fossil fuels."[89] Nevertheless Christy has continued to participate in publications supported by ExxonMobil, including the Marshall Institute book Michaels edited, *Shattered Consensus*.[90]

Richard Lindzen: Of all the denialists, Richard Lindzen has the credentials most relevant to discussing climate change. A professor of meteorology at MIT, he helped prepare the IPCC reports of 1995 and 2001 (although he did not help write the "Summary for Policymakers"). A member of the National Academy of Sciences, he served on its 2001 examination of the evidence for global warming. Like Frederick Seitz, Lindzen is recognized as having done first-rate scientific work. One would assume, accordingly, that Lindzen's writings about climate change would be superior to that of other denialists. But it seems that, rather than letting the evidence shape his convictions, Lindzen has let his convictions shape his evaluation of the evidence. This appears to have been similarly the case with regard to cigarettes: Like Frederick Seitz, Lindzen has belittled concerns, saying that they are only weakly connected to lung cancer. Hansen has judged Lindzen's treatment of the health-and-smoking data to be "closely analogous to his view of climate data."[91]

Lindzen's treatment of these data is so flippant that he does not call himself a "climate skeptic," because "to be skeptical assumes there is a strong presumptive case, but you have your doubts. I think . . . there's not a strong presumptive case." Calling his colleagues' warnings about global warming "alarmism," Lindzen says that their expressed concern is "mainly just like little kids locking themselves in dark closets to see how much they can scare each other and themselves."[92]

In addition to ridiculing fellow scientists, Lindzen also charges them with selling out their integrity. Saying that he has no respect for their global warming science, Lindzen added: "Endorsing global warming just makes their lives easier." For example, he said, Wally Broecker "staunchly beats the drums for alarm and is richly rewarded for doing so" (even though Lindzen himself has been "richly rewarded" by fossil-fuel corporations, in spite of his claim about receiving "no funding from energy companies"). Lindzen also charged that "scientists who dissent from the alarmism have seen their grant funds disappear" (even though since 1975 Lindzen himself has received $3.5 million in research grants from the National Science Foundation).[93]

Why is Lindzen so unconcerned about global warming that he assumes his colleagues must be insincere? Because he believes that climate sensitivity is so low that a doubling of CO_2 will not raise the planet's temperature, at least not much. He bases this prediction on confidence that "nature is," as he told a Heartland Institute conference, "dominated by stabilizing negative feedbacks rather than destabilizing positive feedbacks."[94]

Having not yet convinced colleagues of the existence of powerful negative feedbacks, he claimed in a 2009 paper, coauthored with a Korean postdoctoral researcher named Choi, that he had found an example. Utilizing Lindzen's "iris" hypothesis – that as the atmosphere warms, Earth's high clouds will open to let more heat escape – this paper argued that, thanks to clouds, the planet's climate sensitivity will be about 0.5°C, which is extremely low: The IPCC puts the likely range between 2 and 4.5°C and Hansen puts it at the highest part of this range.[95] The Lindzen-Choi paper was severely criticized by several scientists, including Kevin Trenberth, who said that the Lindzen-Choi paper "has nothing to say about climate sensitivity" and does not "stand up to independent testing." When the errors are rectified, Trenberth said, the result is a climate sensitivity of 4.1°C. Lindzen in response admitted that he had made "some stupid mistakes."[96]

In 2011, Lindzen and Choi submitted a revised version of their paper to the *Proceedings of the National Academy of Sciences*. Once again, however, the peer reviewers found errors, and all four of them – including two that Lindzen himself had selected – said that paper should be rejected because of unjustified conclusions. The Lindzen-Choi paper ended up in an obscure Korean journal.[97]

Lindzen said: "If I'm right, we'll have saved money [by avoiding measures to limit emissions]. If I'm wrong, we'll know it in 50 years and can do something." Lindzen's position, however, is circular: His view that the problem could be fixed in 50 years presupposes his view that climate sensitivity is very low. If it becomes obvious in 50 years "that catastrophe looms," points out *New York Times* writer Justin Gillis, "it would most likely be too late."[98]

It is generally agreed among denialists that Richard Lindzen is their intellectual leader, their most credible member. If so, it should be recognized that the denialist movement has no clothes.

Creating New Faces

In order to convince the public of a lack of consensus among climate scientists, Exxon's 2008 Action Plan said that the team should "identify, recruit and train a team of five independent scientists to participate in media outreach. These will be individuals who do not have . . . visibility . . . in the climate change debate. Rather, this team will consist of new faces." The two "new faces" who worked out the best were Willie Soon and Sallie Baliunas, astrophysicists affiliated with the Harvard-Smithsonian Center for Astrophysics, who focused on the influence of solar radiation on the Earth. One means of publicizing Soon and Baliunas was the above-mentioned fact that a report by them was included in the Oregon Institute petition sent out by Seitz in 1998.

Prior to that, Baliunas was commissioned to write several articles for the Marshall Institute suggesting that global warming might be due to solar activity. She and Soon then wrote an article arguing that the climate had not changed significantly over the past 1,000 years, which was accepted for publication in 2003 by *Climate Research*. However, the article was judged by climate scientists to be so bad that they wondered why it was accepted, three of the journal's editors resigned in protest, and 13 scientists who were quoted said that it had seriously misinterpreted their work.[99]

Nevertheless, the Soon-Baliunas paper was trumpeted widely by ExxonMobil-funded organizations and was used by Senator James Inhofe to bolster his claim that global warming is a hoax (see Chapter 13). The paper was widely and strongly criticized by climate scientists, but "[t]he brouhaha in the scientific community had little public impact. The echo chamber had already been set in motion reverberating among the mainstream media." Soon and Baliunas became formally affiliated with several organizations underwritten by ExxonMobil.[100]

The Falsity of Climate Science Denialist Claims

The denialist disinformation campaign has generated many claims. The Skeptical Science website about denialist claims has provided (as of July 2014) 176 such claims, beginning with the most popular ones. A dozen of these are briefly discussed here (further information is provided in notes).

1. The Lack of Consensus: Over 30,000 scientists signed the Petition Project.
　　However, the Petition Project supported by Frederick Seitz was, as shown above, about as far removed from a scientific sampling as could be imagined. By contrast, Naomi Oreskes in 2004, carrying out a scientific test, looked at all the papers regarding "climate change" she had found in refereed journals between 1994 and 2003. Asking how many of these 928 articles argued against the consensus (IPCC) position, she found the number to be *"zero."* She concluded that "there is a scientific consensus on the reality of anthropogenic climate change."[101] This conclusion has been confirmed by later studies:

> A 2009 study found that, when asked whether "human activity is a significant contributing factor in changing mean global temperatures," 97.5% of climatologists who actively publish research on climate change responded "yes."[102]

　　A 2010 survey of 1,372 climate researchers showed that "97–98% of the climate researchers most actively publishing in the field support the tenets of ACC [anthropogenic climate change] outlined by the Intergovernmental Panel on Climate Change."[103]
　　In 2012, James Powell updated Oreskes' 2004 paper. Considering only peer-reviewed articles between 1991 and 2012, he looked at all the articles in the Web of Science with keywords of "global warming" or "global climate change." Having located 13,950 articles, he found that "24 of the 13,950 articles, 0.17 percent or 1 in 581, clearly reject global warming or endorse a cause other than CO_2 emissions for observed warming." In short, 99.8 percent of the scientists who have published peer-reviewed articles say that CO_2-caused global warming is real.[104]

2. Climate Change Reflects Natural Variability: Climate has changed naturally in the past, long before coal-fired power plants, so there is no reason to think humans have caused the current global warming.

Although it is true that climate has changed in the past due to various natural forces, climate always reacts to whatever forces it to change at the time, and humans are now the dominant force. In fact, the climate changes over the past 60 years can be explained by no natural processes, only by human-caused increases in greenhouse gases.[105]

3. The Climate Has Not Changed since 1988: From 1998 to 2005, the temperature did not increase, even though an increasing amount of CO_2 was pumped into the atmosphere.

However, 2005 was hotter than 1998, and 2010 was as hot as 2005. More important are the trends: During the 30 years from 1980 to 2010, the global temperature rose continually, in spite of yearly ups and downs.[106]

4. The Hockey Stick is Broken: Michael Mann's Results Were Due to Errors. A 1998 graph by climate scientist Michael Mann depicting the global temperature during the past 1,000 years, after showing gradual cooling, shows a sharp rise in the 20th century, resulting in a graph that looks somewhat like a hockey stick. In 2005, Stephen McIntyre and Ross McKitrick showed that the graph was based on serious errors, making Mann's conclusions untrustworthy.

Mann's conclusions have been confirmed by several studies. A number of studies involving many different sources – including boreholes, corals, ice cores, stalagmites, and tree rings – have confirmed the conclusion of Mann's 1998 paper: "the 20th century was the warmest in the millennium, and the warming became most dramatic after 1920." Moreover, studies since 1999, using a variety of sources and methodologies, all "find the same result – that the last few decades are the hottest in the last 500 to 2000 years (depending on how far back the reconstruction goes)." These studies were further confirmed in 2013 with the publication of the massive project by PAGES (Past Global Changes), with its 78 researchers from 60 institutions around the world, which confirmed that a 2,000-year cooling trend was radically reversed in the 20th century, which was even warmer than the Medieval Warm Period.[107]

5. The Earth Would Have Warmed Much More if the IPCC Models Were Correct.

This argument by Lindzen depends on ignoring (a) the planet's inertia (due primarily to the ocean), which means that adding greenhouse gases does not raise the temperature until several decades later, and (b) the cooling effects of aerosols, such as the Asian "brown cloud." When calculations are carried out in light of these two factors, "the Earth has warmed almost exactly as much as we would expect."[108]

6. Climategate: There was a top-level conspiracy to lure the global public into believing fraudulent claims of global warming: In what has been represented as one of the biggest scandals in modern science, emails hacked from the Climatic Research Unit at the University of East Anglia were held to suggest that most of the prominent scientists advocating human-caused global warming had been, as blogger Andrew Bolt summarized, guilty of "conspiracy, collusion in exaggerating warming data, possibly illegal destruction of embarrassing information, organized resistance to disclosure, manipulation of data, private admissions of flaws in their public claims and much more."

However, this was a scandal that wasn't. The conclusion that none of the scientists were guilty of any wrongdoing was reached by a large number of investigations, including:

- Pennsylvania State University, where Michael Mann teaches, concluded that "there is no substance to the allegation against Dr. Michael E. Mann."
- The UK's House of Commons Science and Technology Committee concluded that criticisms of the Climate Research Unit (CRU) were misplaced and that CRU's "Professor Jones's actions were in line with common practice in the climate science community."
- The University of East Anglia, in consultation with the Royal Society, found "no evidence of any deliberate scientific malpractice in any of the work of the Climatic Research Unit."
- The US EPA found that the emails simply reflect "a candid discussion of scientists working through issues that arise in compiling and presenting large complex data sets."
- The US National Science Foundation concluded: "Finding no research misconduct. . . , this case is closed."

The reports also indicated that none of the widely quoted statements had the meaning put on them by those who consider global warming a conspiracy. For example, "Mike's [Michael Mann's] Nature Trick" is "nothing more than a statistical method used to bring two or more different kinds of data sets together in a legitimate fashion by a technique that has been reviewed by a broad array of peers in the field." Phil Jones' phrase "hide the decline" referred not to declining temperatures but to "a decline in the reliability of tree rings to reflect temperatures after 1960," which is known as the "divergence problem." And Kevin Trenberth's "travesty" that "we can't account for the lack of warming" referred simply to a 2009 paper by him about the planet's energy budget, in which he lamented the fact that our observation systems cannot track all the energy flow.[109]

Nevertheless, denialists did not stop talking about "climategate." For example, the first four of these reports had been published before August of 2010, but Fox News had a program that month called "The Green Swindle," in which Glenn Beck said that the hacked emails "reveal a plot among the world's top climate scientists to hide the real inconvenient truth that the evidence supporting man-made global warming is far from conclusive."[110]

In response to attacks on his scientific integrity, Mann launched a lawsuit. In 2013, a DC Superior Court found sufficient evidence that the Competitive Enterprise Institute was guilty of "actual malice" to allow Mann's lawsuit to go forward; and in 2014, the court said the same about Mann's suit against Mark Steyn and *National Review* for saying, with a reference to a child molester, that Mann had "molested and tortured data."[111]

7. The Sun Is Responsible: Current climate change is likely due to the sun's activity.

However, insofar there has been any change in the sun's effect on the Earth, it has been in the direction of cooling since 1970, while the planet's atmosphere has continued to warm.[112]

8. Water Vapor Is by Far the Dominant Greenhouse Gas: CO_2 is, therefore, quite unimportant.

Although water vapor is indeed the dominant greenhouse gas, it is also the dominant feedback agent. And, as CO_2 emissions make the temperature go up, evaporation increases, putting more water vapor in the atmosphere, which further increases the temperature. The water vapor feedback doubles the warming that would be caused by rising CO_2 alone. Water vapor largely explains, therefore, why Earth's climate is so sensitive to CO_2 increases.

9. The IPCC Is Alarmist: The IPCC was formed, as Roy Spencer has pointed out, "to build the scientific case for humanity being the primary cause of global warming. Such a goal is fundamentally unscientific, as it is hostile to alternative hypotheses for the causes of climate change."

However, the IPCC predictions, as numerous studies have documented, have underestimated, rather than overestimated, climate changes due to the rise of CO_2. For example, sea-level rise and Arctic sea-ice melting have been greater than the IPCC had predicted.[113]

10. Rather than Melting, Glaciers in Alaska, Canada, New Zealand, Greenland, and Norway Are Growing.

Although a few glaciers have been growing, an examination of long-term trends shows that 90 percent of the glaciers worldwide have been shrinking.[114]

11. The Ice of Much of Antarctica Is Expanding: This fact contradicts the IPCC claim that the polar ice caps are melting.

As discussed in Chapter 5, whereas Antarctica is gaining sea ice, the land ice is declining at an accelerating rate.[115]

12. Global Warming Is Not Dangerous: Warming has always been good for human beings, and it does not threaten plants and animals, because they can adapt to a changing climate, as they have in the past.

As Part I of this book has shown, continued global warming will be much more harmful for human beings than helpful, due to increasing heat waves, droughts, storms, sea-level rise, fresh water shortage, and food short-age.[116] With regard to plants and animals, current climate change is much more rapid than change in the past, so the ways in which species adapted in the past are generally impossible.[117]

Summary: Given the extent to which denialism has contributed to the media and political failures to deal meaningfully with climate change, it is remarkable how weak even the most popular denialist claims are. In acknowledgment of this weakness, Ernest Moniz, in a statement about climate change shortly after becoming the new Energy Secretary, wisely said: "I'm not here to debate what's not debatable."[118]

New Boosts for the Disinformation Campaign

Analyzing a claim that over 900 peer-reviewed articles supported skepticism about human-caused global warming, a recent study concluded that 90 per-cent of the authors had links to ExxonMobil.[119] Although this corporation has obviously not needed any help for its disinformation claim, its efforts have recently been augmented by other interested parties.

Koch Industries

Greenpeace reported in 2010 that since 1997, Koch Industries – the oil, coal, logging, and chemical corporation owned by brothers Charles and David Koch, which is either the largest, or second largest, privately-held company in America[120] – had given over $67 million to climate denialist groups.[121] (This may seem like a lot of money. But the Koch brothers by 2010 were valued at

$35 billion, so $67 million was pocket change.) In 2011, Greenpeace wrote:

> Koch Industries has become a financial kingpin of climate science denial and clean energy opposition. This private, out-of-sight corporation is now a partner to Exxon Mobil, the American Petroleum Institute and other donors that support organizations and front-groups opposing progressive clean energy and climate policy. In fact, Koch has out-spent Exxon Mobil in funding these groups in recent years. From 2005 to 2008, Exxon Mobil spent $8.9 million while the Koch Industries-controlled foundations contributed $24.9 million in funding to organizations of the climate denial machine.[122]

Dark Money Trusts

More recently, however, it is no longer possible to see how much Exxon and Koch are spending, because beginning in 2008, they no longer allowed their contributions to be publicly traceable. This move toward secrecy was part of a more general policy of hiding the funding of climate denial from the public. According to a recent study of "the flood of dark money feeding climate change denial," about 75 percent of the money backing climate-denial efforts is untraceable.[123] Two huge sources of this dark money are Donors Trust and Donors Capital Fund.

Following the 2010 report that Koch Industries was giving more to climate denial groups than ExxonMobil, a 2013 story revealed the existence of an even bigger funder. The *Guardian* reported that two trusts funded by conservative billionaires wanting anonymity, Donors Trust and Donors Capital Fund, doled out $118 million to 102 groups to help "build a vast network of thinktanks and activist groups working to a single purpose: to redefine climate change from neutral scientific fact to a highly polarising 'wedge issue.'" This funding stream "far outstripped the support from more visible opponents of climate action such as the oil industry or the conservative billionaire Koch brothers."[124]

However, given the fact that these trusts do not report their donors, combined with the fact that Whitney Ball, the founder and CEO of these trusts, is closely affiliated with the Kochs, much of the funding for them, for all we know, may have been provided by the Kochs. Indeed, a 2014 *Washington Post* story seemed to suggest that they are simply part of a "Koch-Backed Political Network," which raised over $400 million for right-wing political causes in 2012.[125]

Climate Change Deniers Without Borders

Another type of aid to the denialist disinformation campaign has been provided by the Atlas Economic Research Foundation, "named after Ayn Rand's free-market amorality tale, *Atlas Shrugged*." Funded by ExxonMobil, Koch Industries, and other sources, the Atlas Foundation has "supported more than 30 foreign think tanks that espouse skepticism about the science of climate change."[126]

The Atlas Foundation is, moreover, only one of many organizations, such as the Heartland Institute, that have bankrolled some 500 groups "in dozens of countries that are often bankrolled by American foundations that are, in turn, backed by carbon-spewing American industries." So, although climate denialism originated in the United States, it has now spread to dozens of countries. "With US-backed overseas think tanks parroting denier talking points in dozens of languages, the echo chamber is already up and running."[127]

Note: The final dimension of ExxonMobil's strategy is the use of friendly politicians. This subject is treated in Chapter 13, "Political Failure."

Unprecedented Folly

The denial of climate disruption is foolishness in at least three ways:

There is the folly of those who have been taken in by the denialist claims, including some who have aided the disinformation campaign, not realizing that it was organized by the fossil-fuel corporations. Giving credence to the denialist claims of this disinformation campaign, rather than to the considered conclusions of a vast number of climate scientists, is folly.

There is also the folly of the media and political leaders (to be discussed in the next two chapters) who have allowed their policies to be influenced by the disinformation provided by the fossil-fuel corporations.

Finally, there is the folly of the owners and CEOs of the fossil-fuel corporations, especially ExxonMobil, who engineered this disinformation campaign, along with the Koch brothers and other billionaires. Although these people have become much richer because of this campaign, their grandchildren will be living in an increasingly hellish world. Will they not wonder if their grandparents had no love and concern for them? By slightly modifying a biblical question, we could ask: *What does it profit men to become filthy rich yet lose the respect of their families?*

This threefold folly is unprecedented because it threatens the survival of civilization. The enormity of this threat is unprecedented even in comparison with the threat of nuclear holocaust: Extermination due to nuclear war would result *only if people do something* – if they actually start a nuclear war;

but climate change could bring civilization to an end if people do nothing, except allowing business as usual to continue. If we do allow this, we will have brought about the truth of the final lines of T.S. Eliot's "The Hollow Men":

> *This is the way the world ends*
> *This is the way the world ends*
> *This is the way the world ends*
> *Not with a bang but a whimper.*

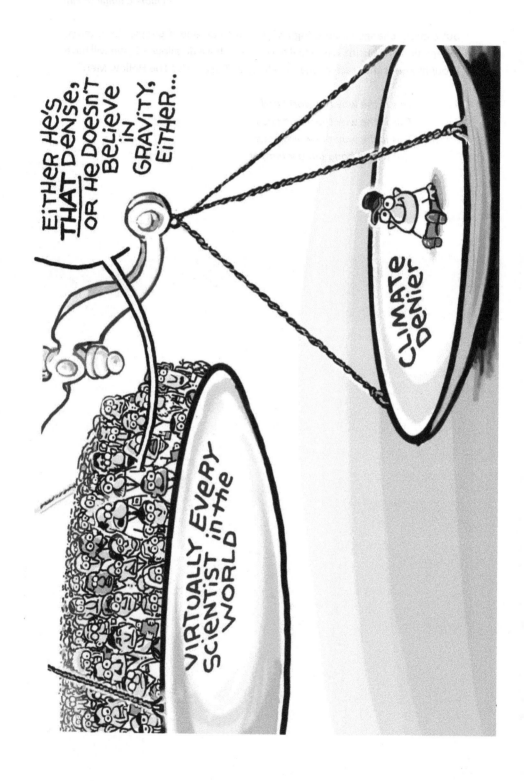

12

MEDIA
FAILURE

*"The entire mainstream media is failing us when it comes to
covering climate change. . . , the story of the century."*
– Thom Hartmann, "The Mainstream Media's
Criminal Climate Coverage," 2014

Why has the U.S. government not acted boldly to respond to the climate crisis? One of the reasons is that – as pointed out by James Hansen, who retired from his day job to spend more time on political efforts and communicating with the public – getting the federal government to act on global warming "likely requires public pressure."[1]

This is, however, an uphill battle: According to a Pew poll in 2013, only 33% of the American public consider global warming a "very serious" problem, and only 28% think that it should be a "top priority" for the politicians in Washington. Of the 21 issues tested, moreover, global warming was at the bottom of the priority list. The *Washington Post*'s headline about the poll was: "Americans Are Less Worried about Climate Change than Almost Anyone Else."[2]

The main problem, Hansen said, is the existence of "a huge gap between the public's understanding of the situation and the scientific understanding." Elaborating on this gap, he said:

> There is remarkable inconsistency between the scientific
> story and public story. The science has become stronger and
> stronger over the past five years while the public perception
> has gone in completely the other direction.

He then added: "That is not an accident. There is a very concerted effort by people who would prefer to see business to continue as usual. They have been winning the public debate with the help of tremendous resources."[3]

Hansen was here speaking about the disinformation campaign discussed in the previous chapter.

The question, however, is why, even with tremendous resources, the small group of climate contrarians, with only a few scientists of stature, could have won the battle against the consensus of the climate scientists. According to this consensus view, global warming is real; it is due to greenhouse gases; and a continuation of business as usual will lead to terrible, even catastrophic, climate disruption. This view is truly a consensus, being shared by at least 97 percent of climate scientists, including – as reported in the previous chapter –– 99.8 percent of climate scientists who have written peer-reviewed articles on the subject.[4]

Given this consensus, the gap between it and the public perception could have occurred only because the media somehow allowed it. Discussing the carbon lobby's "deceptive campaign to put its financial interests ahead of the future of our children and civilization," Mark Hertsgaard wrote: "As a journalist, it shames me that the [carbon] lobby could never have succeeded without the assistance of the media."[5] Why would the media have done this?

A Parable

The failure of the media to resist the carbon lobby's propaganda has been expressed by Eric Pooley, one of America's leading journalists, by means of a parable:

> Suppose our leading scientists discovered that a meteor, hurtling toward the earth, was set to strike later this century; the governments of the world had less than ten years to divert or destroy it. How would news organizations cover this story? Even in an era of financial distress, they would throw teams of reporters at it and give them the resources needed to follow it in extraordinary depth and detail. After all, the race to stop the meteor would be the story of the century.

Having suggested this scenario, Pooley explained that in his parable, carbon-using humanity is the meteor, which is threatening to destroy civilization. This threat is, Pooley said, "the great test, and the great story, of our time. But news organizations have not been treating it that way."[6]

Historic Media Failure

Pooley is only one of several journalists who have spoken of the failure of the media. In 2009, Joe Romm wrote that, although "our scientific understanding of business-as-usual projections for global warming has changed dramatically," the U.S. public has largely "remain[ed] in the dark about just how dire the situation is. Why? Because the U.S. media is largely ignoring the story."[7] Romm and others have tried to capture in a phrase the size of the story the media have missed:

- Saying that 2010 had been "a stunning year in climate science," which revealed that "human civilization is on the precipice," Romm said that the media have been "missing the story of the century, if not the millennium." "The danger posed to the nation and the world by unrestricted emissions of greenhouse gases," Romm also said, "is truly the greatest story never told."

- Pulitzer-prize journalist Ross Gelbspan said that the climate crisis, which "threatens the survival of our civilization," is "undoubtedly the biggest story of this millennium." Indeed, the fact that "the planet is caving in around us," Gelbspan even said, is "the biggest story in our planet's history."

- In 2014, Tom Engelhardt said: "The future of all other stories, of the news and storytelling itself, rests on just how climate change manifests itself over the coming decades or even century. . . . Climate change isn't the news and it isn't a set of news stories. It's the prospective end of all news."[8]

To return to Pooley's parable: We cannot imagine that, if we knew that we had only 10 years to divert or destroy a humanity-destroying meteor heading straight at us, the governments and media would continue with business as usual. Governments, at least those with technological capabilities, would work together day and night to figure out the best approach, then provide all the needed resources – many trillions of dollars, if necessary – to prevent the destruction of human civilization.

The U.S. media would, as they did in World War II, explain the nature of the threat and why citizens will need to make sacrifices – perhaps enormous ones, because no sacrifice would be too great.

In that situation, it is possible that a contrarian movement might emerge, declaring the report about the meteor to be a scientific hoax. But if so, the media would surely not take it seriously – unless at least many of our best scientists agreed. Rather than spreading the contrarian story, the various news organizations would, recognizing that they had the biggest story since the beginning of human civilization, spare no expense in covering it.

However, with regard to climate change, the media – especially the American media – have acted in a very different way. Far from treating the CO_2 threat as the biggest story since the beginning of civilization, they have failed to treat it as the story of the millennium, or the century, or the decade, or even the year.

Dimensions of the Media's Failure

The U.S. media's failure to give the American people an accurate understanding of global warming and climate change has several dimensions.

False Balance

Probably the most pervasive of the reasons for the media's failure involves the journalistic norm of balanced reporting. As one discussion put it: "Balance aims for neutrality. It requires that reporters present the views of legitimate spokespersons of the conflicting sides in any significant dispute, and provide both sides with roughly equal attention."[9]

However, a 2004 article entitled "Balance as Bias," by Maxwell Boykoff and Jules Boykoff, pointed out that "balanced reporting can actually be a form of informational bias. Despite the highly regarded IPCC's consistent assertions . . . , balanced reporting has allowed a small group of global warming skeptics to have their views amplified."[10] To explain why this should not have occurred, Boykoff and Boykoff quoted Ross Gelbspan, who wrote:

> The professional canon of journalistic fairness requires reporters who write about a controversy to present competing points of view. When the issue is of a political or social nature, fairness - presenting the most compelling arguments of both sides with equal weight - is a fundamental check on biased reporting. But this canon causes problems when it is applied to issues of science. It seems to demand that journalists present competing points of views on a scientific question as though they had equal scientific weight, when actually they do not.[11]

With regard to this journalistic norm, according to which balanced reporting about matters of opinion requires giving equal time to "both sides," Naomi Oreskes and Erik Conway added:

> [O]nce a scientific issue is closed, there's only one 'side.' Imagine providing a 'balance' to the issue of whether the Earth orbits the Sun, whether continents move, or whether

DNA carries genetic information. These matters were long ago settled in scientists' minds. Nobody can publish an article in a scientific journal claiming the Sun orbits the Earth.[12]

James Hansen also regards misapplied science to be a major problem in communicating scientific conclusions to the public. He wrote: "The scientific method requires objective analysis of all data, stating evidence pro and con, before reaching conclusions. This works well, indeed is necessary, for achieving success in science. But science is now pitted in public debate against the talk-show method, which consists of selective citation of anecdotal bits that support a predetermined position. Why is the public presented results of the scientific method and the talk-show method as if they deserved equal respect?" Saying that this problem has not always existed, Hansen added:

> A few decades ago that did not happen. In 1981, when I
> wrote a then-controversial paper about the impact of CO_2
> on climate, the science writer Walter Sullivan contacted
> several of the top relevant scientific experts in the world
> for comments. He did not mislead the public by dredging up
> and highlighting contrarian opinion for the sake of a forced
> and unnatural 'balance.' Today most media, even publicly-
> supported media, are pressured to balance every climate
> story with opinions of contrarians, climate change deniers,
> as if they had equal scientific credibility.[13]

In describing global warming as an issue on which the science has been settled, Oreskes and Conway were not exaggerating. As early as 1997, the *Washington Post* published a story entitled "Consensus Emerges Earth Is Warming – Now What?"[14] Recently, however, the media have largely ignored the distinction between disputed opinion and settled fact. As a result, the media have produced bias. Having studied the stories about global warming in the US "prestige press" (*The New York Times,* the *Washington Post*, the *Los Angeles Times,* and the *Wall Street Journal*) between 1988 and 2002, Boykoff and Boykoff reported that a majority of the stories were "balanced" in the sense that "these accounts gave 'roughly equal attention' to the view that humans were contributing to global warming, and the other view that exclusively natural fluctuations could explain the earth's temperature increase."[15]

These stories gave unknowing readers the impression that the scientific community was divided on this issue. This distorted "balance" still continues, especially in Fox News, the *Wall Street Journal,* the *Washington Post,* and recently Reuters. In these publications, false balance is used not in deference to a journalistic ideal but to promote denial. For example, Reuters, once one of the most prolific providers of climate stories, moved Paul Ingrassia, a self-described "climate skeptic," into editorial management. Climate coverage suddenly dropped and, according to former Asia Climate Change reporter John Fogarty, a "climate of fear" about climate change coverage was created and reporters "felt pressure from management to add 'balance' to climate change stories by including the views of global-warming skeptics."[16]

As a result of this perverse type of balance, as the heading of a 2012 Climate Progress story reported, "American Newspapers Are Number One in Climate Denial." Covering a report based on comparing *The New York Times* and *Wall Street Journal* with leading newspapers in Brazil, China, France, India, and the United Kingdom, this story said:

> America is unique when it comes to giving a platform to climate deniers and skeptics. According to a new analysis of data released [in 2011], American newspapers are far more likely to publish uncontested claims from climate deniers, many of whom challenge whether the planet is warming at all.[17]

Unsurprisingly, therefore, a 2014 poll of 20 wealthy countries found that America leads the world in denialism, with 52 percent of the population stating that climate change is a natural phenomenon and denying that we are headed for environmental disaster unless we change our habits quickly.[18]

In any case, for stories to be *truly* balanced, by representing the degree of consensus within the community of climate scientists, contrarian views should be given no more weight than the percentage of these scientists who support them. In May 2014, John Oliver humorously demonstrated on his fake TV news show, "Last Week Tonight," what this would mean in a "Statistically Representative Climate Change Debate." Having described the typical TV debate between a climate scientist and a climate denier, he pointed out that the debate should really be representative of the two positions. So after having two more people join the denier, Oliver brought in 96 more to join the scientist.[19]

Although some have claimed that the problem of false balance with regard to climate change has been overcome in the U.S. media,[20] a July 2014 report showed this not to be true. Fringe scientists who reject the consensus view have still received most of the press coverage, while those who say "greenhouse gases have caused strong global warming" received only 15% of the coverage.[21]

A particularly egregious example of false balance appeared in an otherwise excellent AP story about the then-forthcoming IPCC report, which said that if global warming continues, there will be "severe, pervasive and irreversible impacts for people and ecosystems." The AP then quoted John

Christy as saying: "Humans are clever. We shall adapt to whatever happens." As Joe Romm said, "quoting John Christy on climate change is like quoting Dick Cheney on Iraq."[22]

Insofar as they present climate science within a false-balance framework, they are, in effect, giving misinformation, which can be deadly. Writing in the *Guardian*, Stephan Lewandowsky said: "The media failed to accurately report facts prior to the Iraq War; climate reporting is failing in similar fashion." Afterwards, some of the journalists who had supported the Bush-Cheney administration's claims about weapons of mass destruction felt anguish about having used "'evidence' now known to be bogus" to support the push for war. "The lethal fallout from misinformation a decade ago," wrote Lewandowsky, "primarily affected the people of Iraq." But "the fallout from misinformation about climate change is likely to affect us all."[23]

Loving the Conflict, Loving the Money

Although the misapplication of the journalistic norm of balance has certainly played a central role in the US media's failure with regard to the scientific consensus about climate change, this norm does not by itself explain the attention given to denialism in the American media. After all, the journalists and owners of the prestige press are bright people, and they know that balance is not appropriate for all issues. They do not give equal attention, for example, to the doctrine that the Earth is only a few thousand years old, even though millions of America believe that. It seems, therefore, that an additional factor is needed to explain the American media's receptivity to, even promotion of, denialism.

The scientists who reject the scientific consensus about climate change, Tom Engelhardt has suggested, "provide the 'balance,' the 'two sides,' that the mainstream media adores."[24] The media love these "two sides" because they provide a basis for endless controversy while simultaneously retaining the financial support of polluting corporations (see below). One manifestation of the media's greater concern for provocative stories than accuracy was its treatment of the so-called climategate scandal (discussed in Chapter 11). Hertsgaard wrote:

> As the Copenhagen climate summit began in December 2009, almost every major news organization in the world gave front-page coverage to the deniers' unfounded accusations of widespread fraud on the part of leading climate scientists. . . . The only news organization that took the time to investigate rather than merely echo these charges was the Associated Press. A team of AP reporters

read and analyzed each of the 1,073 stolen e-mails, a total of about 1 million words of text. Bottom line: the AP found zero evidence of fraud, a conclusion later shared by two official investigations by British government bodies.[25]

Not Alienating Fossil-Fuel Advertisers

Another reason why the media do not simply report the truth – that global warming is caused by burning fossil fuels – has been stated by Eric Pooley: "They [the media] don't want to be accused of taking sides, in part because that alienates sources." Most important, perhaps, would be sources of *funding*. Fossil-fuel corporations and automobile companies, by means of buying advertisements, give a lot of money to the various media and hence their owners. Journalist Mark Hertsgaard says that the media, besides continuing "to give platforms to the deniers, generally without challenging their claims," also "gladly accept millions of dollars' worth of advertising from energy companies such as Chevron."[26] Ross Gelbspan told this story:

A few years ago I asked a top editor at CNN why, given the increasing proportion of news budgets dedicated to extreme weather, they did not make [the connection to global warming]. He told me, 'We did. Once.' But it triggered a barrage of complaints from oil companies and automakers who threatened to withdraw all their ads from CNN if the network continued to connect weather extremes to global warming. Basically the industry intimidated CNN into dropping the one connection to [global warming] to which the average viewer could most easily relate.[27]

Explicitly Denialist Journalism

Beyond the implicit denialism involved in false balance, the U.S. media also engage in a lot of explicit denialism.

WSJ and Fox News: The two media giants most guilty of misinformation, both owned by Rupert Murdoch's News Corporation, are the *Wall Street Journal* (WSJ) and Fox News. In September 2012, the Union of Concerned Scientists examined the articles in the opinion section of the WSJ dealing with climate science during the previous year, finding that the "representations of climate science were misleading 81 percent of the time." A study of representations of climate science on Fox News over a six-month period in 2012 found that they "were misleading 93 percent of the time." The misleading representations included "mockery of climate science as a body of knowledge, and the cherry-picking of facts and studies to cast doubt on established climate science."[28]

For example the WSJ in 2013 published an opinion piece entitled "In Defense of Carbon Dioxide," in which the authors said: "[T]he conventional wisdom about carbon dioxide is that it is a dangerous pollutant. That's simply not the case. Contrary to what some would have us believe, increased carbon dioxide in the atmosphere will benefit the increasing population on the planet by increasing agricultural productivity."[29]

The idea that global warming will be minimal and will actually be beneficial had long been advocated by Matt Ridley, who for several years wrote a column for the *Journal*. In 2012, he wrote a piece entitled "Cooling Down the Fears of Climate Change," which was so filled with science and even math errors that Joe Romm asked "how the Journal can possibly maintain its reputation as a credible source of news and financial analysis." Then in September 2014, Ridley wrote an op-ed that asked, "Whatever Happened to Global Warming?" In a critique, Columbia University's Jeffrey Sachs, referring to Ridley as an example of "the crudeness and ignorance of [Rupert] Murdoch's henchmen," explained why Ridley's column was completely wrong. In a response, Ridley claimed that the critique was not actually written by Sachs.[30]

CNBC: Examining CNBC stories that dealt with either "global warming" or "climate change" during the first half of 2013, Media Matters found that 51 percent of the stories "cast doubt on whether manmade climate change existed." The only scientist that CNBC hosted about climate was William Happer, the chairman of the ExxonMobil-funded George C. Marshall Institute, who was one of the authors of the WSJ opinion piece "In Defense of Carbon Dioxide." This treatment of stories fits with the fact that "[s]everal CNBC figures, including host Larry Kudlow, co-anchor Joe Kernen, and contributor Rick Santelli deny manmade climate change."[31]

Washington Post: The editorial pages of the *Post* have long been filled with essays by climate-change deniers. Second to none of these deniers was George Will, whose anti-scientific claims have been debunked year after year by many people – including the secretary general of the World Meteorological Organization and even by fellow writers at the *Post*, who on 2009 showed the falsity of Will's claim that the Arctic ice had not significantly declined since 1979. In 2011, amazingly, the editor of the *Washington Post's* editorial pages, who had allowed Will to publish his nonsense over the years, wrote: "The GOP's climate-change denial may be its most harmful delusion." But then the *Post* continued to publish Will's denialist pieces.[32]

For example, criticizing the President's comments about climate change, including "raging fires," Will asked: "Are fires raging now more than ever? (There were a third fewer U.S. wildfires in 2012 than in 2006.)" Will's rhetorical question was based on the trick of choosing the year 2006, in which the number of U.S. wildfires was far higher than ever before, and then to suggest that, because they had not been so high since then, they were on decline.[33] In addition, Will ignored the fact that, as stated in Chapter 3, the fire season of 2012 ended up "destroy[ing] more acres of forest than in any year on record." In 2014, Will mocked the finding that 97 percent of climate scientists believe that carbon pollution is causing global warming. Asking rhetorically, "who did the poll?" Will suggested that the finding was no more worthy of belief than "100 Authors Against Einstein" produced by a Nazi publishing company.[34]

The *Post*'s Charles Krauthammer has been equally guilty of publishing false claims. He has been in climate denial for so long that in February 2014, Romm described his then-latest essay as "his umpteenth falsehood-fest," which led Michael Mann to say that Krauthammer's "laundry list of shopworn talking points" is so predictable "that one can make a drinking game out of it." In the essay in question, "The Myth of 'Settled Science,'" Krauthammer attacked President Obama for his 2014 State of the Union address, calling him the "propagandist in chief." Quoting two of Obama's statements, "The debate is settled" and "Climate change is a fact," Krauthammer replied: "Really? There is nothing more anti-scientific than the very idea that science is settled, static, impervious to challenge."[35]

Krauthammer was thereby guilty of failing to make an elementary distinction. Although "science" is never settled, because new facts are continually found, some of which require new theories, this does not mean that there are no settled facts. Although plate tectonics was once fiercely debated, it no longer is. Climate science is still evolving, with many remaining questions (such as climate sensitivity). But central issues have been settled, including the fact that increased CO_2 in the atmosphere is raising the planet's average temperature and that this global warming is causing climate disruption.

In general, good newspapers do not publish letters that are based on the denial of basic science. In October 2013, the *Los Angeles Times* enacted this policy with regard to climate science, with letters editor Paul Thornton explaining: "I do my best to keep errors of fact off the letters page. . . . Saying 'there's no sign humans have caused climate change' is not stating an opinion, it's asserting a factual inaccuracy." Writing in his *Guardian* blog, Graham Readfearn said, "Thornton's decision could well leave a few editors wondering if they should follow suit."[36]

In early 2014, Forecast the Facts, hoping to speed up the process, created a petition, saying:

> The *Los Angeles Times* recently announced that they are
> refusing to publish letters that deny climate change. . . .

> Sign the petition below to tell the editors of *The New York Times*, the *Washington Post, USA Today,* and the *Wall Street Journal*: our country's most respected newspapers should refuse to print letters that deny basic science.

A petition aimed at various newspapers around the country was started by CredoMobilize, which said, for example, to *Forbes Magazine*:

> Require James Taylor to follow journalism's ethics. *Forbes* regularly publishes articles by James Taylor which have sensationalized headlines, outrageous misinformation, and deliberate distortions of other's [sic] published works.[37]

After the *Los Angeles Times* made its announcement, Thom Hartmann said:

> It's time for the rest of the media to follow suit. All media outlets, TV, radio, print or otherwise should immediately stop publishing the factual inaccuracies of climate change deniers. . . . It's time for the mainstream media to tell it like it is and stop treating wacko theories like the truth. After all, the future of all life on Earth is at stake.[38]

Perhaps the BBC paid attention: Its governing body has announced that, to eliminate false balance, its programs will henceforth give denialists only the amount of coverage their prominence merits.[39]

Reduction of Coverage

Although the U.S. media's coverage of climate change has never been high, its coverage went up in 2009, the year of the "climategate" allegations and the climate conference in Copenhagen - which had been widely discussed as the world's last chance to prevent catastrophic climate change. But although there were lots of "climategate" stories, "only a few of the major U.S. news outlets," reported the *Energy Daily*, "published accounts of the Copenhagen gathering, which received heavy coverage by news outlets in Europe and Asia." Since 2009, moreover, the coverage has consistently gone down, in spite of the increasingly extreme weather and ever-faster melting of glaciers. Whereas in 2006, there were 2,286 articles mentioning global warming, by 2013 there were only 1,353.[40]

NYT Eliminates Climate Desk: The most important of the reductions in coverage happened at *The New York Times* in 2013. At the beginning of that year, the

Times eliminated its climate desk, which consisted of seven reporters and two editors. Describing the changes as merely "structural," the paper's executive editor, Jill Abramson, declared: "We will continue to cover these areas of national and international life just as aggressively." But, as venerable journalist Dan Froomkin asked, "How is that possible?" Margaret Sullivan, the *Times'* public editor, also expressed skepticism, saying that preventing the coverage of the environment from suffering "will be a particular challenge."[41]

The warnings by Froomkin and Sullivan were not misplaced. Near the end of 2013, Sullivan reviewed how the *Times'* environmental coverage had fared since its "structural changes." Between April and September of 2012, she reported, there had been 362 print articles that featured climate change prominently, whereas in 2013 during those same months this number dropped to 247. Even more strikingly, the number of front-page stories slipped from nine to three. David Sassoon, founder and publisher of InsideClimate News, said that this is "exactly what you'd expect when you eliminate the position of environment editor and deputy environment editor from the newsroom."[42]

When the results for the entire year came in, the number of *NYT* stories mentioning either "global warming" or "climate change" had plummeted more than 40 percent. According to the University of Colorado, which tracks such changes, this drop was bigger than that of any other newspaper. This was a radical change from 2012, when the *Times* "had the biggest increase in coverage among the five largest U.S. daily papers," and when Glenn Kramon, assistant managing editor of the *Times*, had said: "Climate change is one of the few subjects so important that we need to be oblivious to cycles and just cover it as hard as we can all the time."[43]

NYT Eliminates Environmental Blog: As if the *Times'* elimination of its climate desk at the beginning of 2013 were not bad enough, two months later it canceled its Green blog, which had a dozen contributors in addition to its two editors. The background of this development went back to 2008, when the *Times* created the Green Inc. blog. Focusing on the intersection of business and the environment, the blog's mission statement said that it existed to keep readers up to date on "the high-stakes pursuit of a greener globe." Then in 2010, "taking things up a notch," the *Times* introduced a "more ambitious online effort, broadening our lens to include . . . politics and policy, environmental science and consumer choices." This was timely, the paper's editors explained, because the *Wall Street Journal* had shut down its green blog, "Environmental capital."

The blog's editor, Tom Zeller, spoke expansively of the broadened mission, saying:

> We'll be reporting from the halls of Congress, from the
> streets of New Delhi, from green homes and green kitchens,

from the Mojave Desert, the Everglades and the Gowanus
Canal, from communities across the country where green
experiments are unfolding.

To emphasize the expanded coverage, the name "Green Inc." was changed simply to "Green." Zeller concluded: "Better informed citizens are crucial to building a better, greener civilization."[44]

But three years later, the paper's editors wrote: "The *Times* is discontinuing the Green blog, which was created to track environmental and energy news and to foster lively discussion of developments in both areas." This surprise announcement was not well received. Curtis Brainard, the editor of the *Columbia Journalism Review,* wrote:

> The Green blog was a crucial platform for stories that didn't
> fit into the print edition's already shrunken news hole. . . ,
> and it was a place where reporters could add valuable . . .
> context and information to pieces that did make the paper.

The editors who made this decision, continued Brainard,

> should be ashamed of themselves. They've made a horrible
> decision that ensures the deterioration of the *Times*'s
> environmental coverage at a time when debates about
> climate change, energy, natural resources, and sustainability
> have never been more important to public welfare.[45]

Similarly, Drexel University's Robert Brulle, who according to the *Times* is "an expert on environmental communications," told Romm: "The NY Times coverage of the environment has continued its journey from bad to worse. It continues to abrogate its responsibility to inform the public about critical issues." More sardonically, *Slate* entitled its response: "The *Times* Kills Its Environmental Blog to Focus on Horse Racing and Awards Shows."[46]

It did not take long for the *Times'* reduced coverage to be noticed. In August 2013, for example, *The New York Times* failed to cover the NOAA's 258-page State of the Climate report, which is used to set U.S. climate policy. This failure, said Media Matters, "calls into doubt the extent to which the paper can be trusted to maintain strong attention to environmental issues in the face of recent organizational changes."[47]

Why Did the NYT Cancel the Desk and the Blog? Having called the announcement of the Green blog's cancelation "terrible news," Curtis Brainard continued:

> When the *Times* announced in January that it was dismantling
> its three-year-old environment pod and reassigning its
> editors and reporters to other desks, managing editor Dean
> Baquet insisted that the outlet remained as committed as
> ever to covering the environment. Obviously, that was an
> outright lie.[48]

Why did the *Times* cancel both its climate desk and its environmental blog? The paper does not say (aside from lipstick-on-a-pig attempts to claim that these changes will actually help). Part of the reason for the house-cleaning was carried out for money-saving reasons. But part of the reason may have been suggested in a statement by John Horgan of the Stevens Institute of Technology. In 2010, he wrote:

> Two sources at the Science Times section of the *New York
> Times* have told me that a majority of the section's editorial
> staff doubts that human-induced global warming represents
> a serious threat to humanity.[49]

If those sources were correct, this could explain why the *Times* took its money-saving hatchet to the environment instead of to some less fateful issue.

Washington Post Does Likewise: The same weekend that the *Times* canceled its Green blog, the *Washington Post* reassigned its top environmental reporter – who was a bright spot on a paper blighted by climate deniers such as George Will and Charles Krauthammer. Making its own lipstick-on-a-pig announcement, the editors said:

> We're very excited to announce the latest evolution of our
> political team – an online strike force that will help lead our
> journalism during the day. Juliet Eilperin will return to the
> world of politics to cover the White House. Juliet has had a
> terrific run on the environment beat, becoming one of the
> country's leading reporters on climate change.

Said Romm, "Yes, no point in keeping one of the country's leading reporters on climate change on the story of the century. She had a good run, but that climate story is so five minutes ago."[50]

Then the following year, the *Post* dropped star blogger Ezra Klein – one of their only consistent sources of science-based coverage of climate change – and replaced him with a website called the "Volokh Conspiracy." This website was aptly named, pointed out a writer at Grist, because many of its bloggers promoted the idea that global warming is a conspiracy, a hoax. It is alarming, said Romm, that "[new owner] Jeff Bezos of the *Washington Post* would think such uninformed conspiracy mongering belongs at the *Post*."[51]

Television's Inadequate Coverage

In addition to reducing its coverage, the media commonly gives woefully inadequate coverage to important events, sometimes ignoring them completely. Saying that "the TV news is a disgrace," media critic Todd Gitlin wrote,

> Despite the record temperatures of 2012, the intensifying storms, droughts, wildfires, and other wild weather events, the disappearing Arctic ice cap, and the greatest meltdown of the Greenland ice shield in recorded history, their news divisions went dumb and mute.

Moreover, Gitlin said, "The Sunday talk shows, which supposedly offer long chews and not just sound bites. . . , were otherwise occupied." Illustrating this point, he said:

> The Sunday shows spent less than 8 minutes on climate change. . . . ABC's *This Week* covered it the most, at just over 5 minutes. . . . NBC's *Meet the Press* covered it the least, in just one 6 second mention. . . . Most of the politicians quoted were Republican presidential candidates, including Rick Santorum, who went unchallenged when he called global warming 'junk science' on ABC's *This Week*. More than half of climate mentions on the Sunday shows were Republicans criticizing those who support efforts to address climate change. . . . In four years, Sunday shows have not quoted a single scientist on climate change.[52]

In June 2013, President Obama gave a major speech, laying out his plan to cut carbon pollution. But except for MSNBC's Melissa Harris-Perry, the Sunday morning news shows, which supposedly deal with the big stories of the week, ignored it. Except for MSNBC, those who relied on TV for their news had to rely on Jay Leno, David Letterman, and Jon Stewart.[53]

In 2014, the IPCC's massive fifth assessment report, on which it had been working for several years, was published. MSNBC appropriately devoted almost 20 minutes to it, laying out the risks detailed by the report along with the ineffective attempts to cut carbon. But the coverage by both Fox News and CNN was pathetic.

Fox News did what one would expect: It spent only five minutes on it, most of which was devoted to attacking the idea of climate change, with Bill O'Reilly accusing the climate scientists of wanting to destroy the economy with their "phantom global warming theory." While CNN did not attack the IPCC report, it virtually ignored it, devoting only one minute and eight seconds to it. CNN's Jack Tapper did acknowledge that "all of human civilization could be at risk," but CNN considered this point deserving of only 48 seconds.[54]

Ignoring Climate Change while Discussing Extreme Weather

Given the increasingly extreme weather of the last several years, the media were virtually forced to discuss it. But they usually have not felt compelled to connect the extreme weather with climate change. This was even true in 2013, which was "a big year for climate," especially "the increase in ferocity of our weather." The extreme weather events of that year included "deadly flooding in Colorado, the string of major wildfires across the American West, and bouts of unseasonable temperatures across the country." But according to Fairness and Accuracy in Reporting, a study of 450 stories in the nightly news showed that "96 percent of extreme weather stories never discussed the human impact on the climate."[55]

Media Matters reported essentially the same facts, referring to the Midwest floods in the spring of 2013. Whereas ABC, CBS, NBC, and CNN had devoted a total of 74 segments to the flooding, not one mentioned climate change (CBS came the closest, mentioning that heavy downpours have increased). Media Matters found the newspaper stories hardly better. In a total of 35 articles about the floods, only one by *USA Today* mentioned climate change. The Associated Press, *Los Angeles Times*, *New York Times*, Reuters, and *Wall Street Journal* stories remained silent about it.[56]

Even NPR is guilty of this failure. In 2013, it aired a story about "a "plant in the Canadian Arctic that started growing again after being buried under a glacier for 400 years." As more glaciers around the world recede, concluded the story, "we are likely to see more bryophytes appearing and starting to grow again." However, commented Romm, "apparently we won't be hearing more about why more glaciers are receding or speeding up – or what it all really means for humanity, like say, that whole sea level rise thing."[57]

In 2014, one host for a CNN TV show, reflecting on what it would take to change the thinking and actions of average Americans, wrote:

> Here's what is missing from our national conversation about climate change: an emotional charge that hits you in the gut. .
> . . We need in-your-face cause and effect. Every day, it seems,

a new extreme weather catastrophe happens somewhere in America and the media's all over it, profiling the ordinary folks wiped out by forest fires, droughts, floods, massive sinkholes, tornadoes. But do reporters covering the who, what, when, where and how, ever talk about the real why? . . . . No. It's still considered inappropriate to talk about the big elephant in the field, namely what we have long accepted as an act of God is increasingly becoming an act of man.[58]

As for what a good story would be like, an example was provided by reporter Clayton Sandell of ABC News. In a segment headed "Extreme Weather from Mother Nature," Sandell said:

Scientists say human-caused climate change is already helping shift the planet's natural balance. Creating more heat waves, drought, and intense downpours. A stormy and expensive reality, that's already on our doorsteps.

In addition, a writer for *The New Yorker* has explained how slight changes in typical presentations could help people connect extreme weather with climate change. Whereas exceptionally cold weather generally weakens Americans' belief in climate change, in the UK it strengthens it. The reason for the difference, concluded researchers at Cardiff University, is that the UK media "had framed the weather within the context of climate change, emphasizing that it was unnatural, rather than simply cold. Perhaps," said the writer, "if people here were told that it's not just brutal out there, it's *unnaturally* brutal, they, too, might jump to a different conclusion."[59]

An Alternative to Conflict-Driven Media

As many have argued, American democracy would be much healthier if the media, at least the news departments, were dedicated to the common good, rather than the bank accounts of their owners. That battle was lost long ago, of course,[60] but there are still ways in which the media could do a much better job with regard to the climate crisis.

"There Is No Planet B"

One way would be to employ the slogan "There is No Planet B," which now appears on T-shirts and bumper stickers. As the implications of this slogan sink in widely, the media will not need any fabricated "two sides" controversy to create interest. What could be more riveting than learning about and aiding the movement to save the viability of the Earth, which is, as far as we know, the only planet that can support intelligent life?

The lack of a Planet B means that, if the fossil-fuel corporations and politicians succeed in changing our planet so radically that human life is no longer possible, there will come a time when our children, or our grandchildren, or our great-grandchildren will belong to the last generation of human beings. There are some people, to be sure, who will be unmoved by this prospect. But this will not be true of most people.

A Different Type of "Two Sides"

Insofar as the media feel a need for debates between two sides, there will be plenty of debates once the media embrace the truth of human-caused climate disruption and move on to questions about what to do about it. Having fully absorbed the implications of "There is No Planet B," a lot of people would agree with the most famous line in President Kennedy's 1961 inaugural address, slightly modified to read: "We shall pay any price, bear any burden, meet any hardship, oppose any foe, in order to assure the survival of [civilization]."

However, even after we have accepted this willingness, there will still be many issues that will stimulate strong debates – for example, whether to pay to mitigate climate disruption now or to adapt to it later, whether to eliminate coal-produced electricity completely, and whether to engage in geoengineering to bring the atmospheric CO_2 level down. The owners of the media, therefore, need not fear that no longer taking denialism seriously will mean the end of ferocious debates about climate change.

Failed Media Coverage: An Unprecedented Crime

Georgia Congressman John L. Lewis, one of the great civil rights leaders, said: "Without the press, the civil rights movement would have been like a bird without wings."[61] Thus far, the save-our-climate movement has been unable to take off, because it has been like a bird without wings.

Even though the threat of global warming to human civilization should be recognized as the biggest story of the century – even of the millennium, even of civilization itself – the media have allowed, indeed promoted, a gap between the scientific facts and the public perception. The media did this in spite of knowing of the virtually complete consensus among climate scientists.

Human civilization has progressed to the point of having global media, which can bring stories and information to virtually all people on the planet. These media could have been used to inform people around the planet about the climate crisis and to drive home the point that human civilization is facing an unprecedented challenge. The media could have made central the point that if this challenge is not met, our children will inherit an unpleasant planet, our grandchildren a hellish one, and our great-grandchildren a planet with ecosystem collapse. The media could also have driven home the fact that the climate crisis could even bring civilization itself to an end.

At the same time, the media could have emphasized the fact that the reason for this unprecedented crisis is the unprecedented burning of fossil fuels over the past two centuries. Then, having provided this information, the media could have devoted much time to discussions of what steps need to be taken by our governments to prevent climate disruption from destroying us.

However, far from treating the climate crisis as the biggest story of civilization, the media have treated climate change as simply one story among others, not even the most important one. Having the technology to help the world solve the climate crisis, the media have used it – insofar as they have spoken of it at all – for their own and corporate purposes.

Thom Hartmann, in "The Mainstream Media's Criminal Climate Coverage," says that the "mainstream media is failing us when it comes to covering the story of the century." Likewise, Wen Stephenson, who had worked at NPR, PBS, the *Atlantic,* and the *Boston Globe*, wrote an open letter to his former journalism colleagues, saying:

> [Y]ou are failing. Your so-called "objectivity," your bloodless impartiality, are nothing but a convenient excuse for what amounts to an inexcusable failure to tell the most urgent truth we've ever faced. What's needed now is crisis-level coverage. . . . In a crisis, the criteria for top news is markedly altered, as long as a story sheds light on the crisis topic. In crisis coverage, there's an assumption that readers want and deserve to know as much as possible. In crisis coverage, you "flood the zone." The climate crisis is the biggest story of this, or any, generation — so why the hell aren't you flooding the climate "zone," putting it on the front pages and leading newscasts with it every day?[62]

The failures make the media, by aiding and abetting the destruction of civilization, guilty of an unprecedented crime.

13

POLITICAL
FAILURE

"The response to climate change . . . is the greatest political failure the
world has ever seen." – George Monbiot, 2010

"The key challenge is the unprecedented degree of political polarization
that has paralyzed both houses of Congress." – Rob Stavins, March 2013

British journalist George Monbiot's statement, quoted above, was a response
to economist Nicholas Stern's well-known statement, "Climate change is a
result of the greatest market failure the world has seen."[1] In Chapter 11, we
looked at the folly of the fossil-fuel corporations, especially ExxonMobil and
Koch Industries, in preventing climate legislation by launching an enormous
disinformation campaign. In Chapter 12, we documented some of the media's
folly in aiding this campaign. Of course, as also emphasized in Chapter 12,
the foolish activities of the fossil-fuel corporations and media have also been
criminal – unprecedentedly so.

The present chapter, building on William Marsden's *Fools Rule:
Inside the Failed Politics of Climate Change*, looks at some examples of how
"the greatest political failure the world has ever seen" has resulted from the
fact that "fools rule" in the global politics of climate change – fools who are
responsible for the greatest crime ever.[2]

The Global Record: Warnings and Responses

Science, says Marsden, tells us that climate change is "the defining challenge
of our time." This description reflects U.N. Secretary-General Ban Ki-Moon's
2007 statement at the climate conference in Bali, "Climate change is the
defining challenge of our age."[3] However, the political world has not risen to
this challenge.

In 2012, Bill McKibben, pointing out that scientists have said for
30 years that continuing business as usual will lead to catastrophe, wrote:

"[S]uch calls have had little effect. We're in the same position we've been in for a quarter-century: scientific warning followed by political inaction."[4] This warning-followed-by-inaction history illustrates just how great the political failure has been:

- In 1988, the year the IPCC was formed, a Toronto conference said that there needed to be a 20 percent reduction in CO_2 emissions by 2005.

- In 1989, that year's edition of *State of the World* said: "One of these years we would like to be able to write an upbeat *State of the World*, one in which we can report that the trends undermining the human prospect have been reversed. It now seems that if we cannot write such a report in the nineties, we may not be able to write it at all. [Therefore,] the nineties needs to be a 'turnaround decade.'"[5]

- Also in 1989, many of the governments of industrialized countries were ready, at a ministerial conference in the Netherlands, to commit themselves to stabilizing their CO_2 emissions by 2000, but the USA and Japan refused to make any specific commitments, so the Declaration spoke only of a general aim of limiting emissions.[6]

- On Earth Day 1990, Denis Hayes, who had been the chairman of the first Earth Day, said: "Twenty years after Earth Day, those of us who set out to change the world are poised on the threshold of utter failure. Measured on virtually any scale, the world is in worse shape today than it was twenty years ago. . . . Time is running out. We have, at most, ten years to embark on some undertakings if we are to avoid crossing some dire environmental thresholds."[7]

- Also in 1990, the IPCC, predicting that a business-as-usual approach could lead to a temperature rise of 3°C by 2100, said that stabilizing CO_2 at 1990 levels would require a 60-to-80 percent reduction in carbon emissions. At the World Meteorological Organization's second World Climate Conference, some governments were ready to commit industrialized countries to stabilize CO_2 emissions at 1990 levels by 2000 – although the Alliance of Small Island States argued this target was too modest. But "US resistance again resulted in vague language on targets and national strategies."[8]

- Deciding to try another approach, the UN General Assembly established an Intergovernmental Negotiating Committee mandated to produce a convention to be signed at the 1992 Earth Summit at Rio de Janeiro. The objective of the resulting U.N. Framework Convention on Climate Change was to stabilize atmospheric greenhouse gas concentrations at levels that would prevent dangerous changes in the global climate system within "a time frame sufficient to allow ecosystems to adapt naturally." But the Framework Convention signed in Rio contained no specific targets or deadlines.[9]

- These targets were to be provided at a 1995 conference in Berlin. The draft, which stated that developed countries would need to reduce their CO_2 emissions to 20 percent below 1990 levels by 2005, was endorsed by developing countries, including China. But most of the developed countries –- especially the oil-producing states and the JUSCANZ group (Japan, USA, Canada, Australia, and New Zealand), preferred to talk about the need for *developing* countries to adopt commitments, so the resulting Berlin "Mandate" merely recognized the inadequacy of the Framework Convention's commitments. But it did reaffirm the Rio principle that the developed nations need to reduce emissions first.[10]

- Those countries then agreed to have a conference in 1997, where the Kyoto Protocol, to be legally binding, was to be signed. However, the United States would not accept the 20 percent reduction suggested by many other countries. So the Protocol stipulated the creation of a market regime to allow corporations to buy and sell the right to pollute. Although this weak Protocol was signed by President Clinton, it was rejected preemptively by the United States in the form of a 95-0 vote for a "sense of the Senate" resolution that America should not ratify any emissions agreement unless developing countries were equally covered.[11]

- In 2007, more than 200 of the world's leading climate scientists, indicating that their community was "essentially fed up," sent a petition to the government leaders at the Bali conference, urging them to take radical action. But the conference can be summarized by the titles of two stories: "American Bummer in Bali" (Reuters) and "US Rejects Stiff 2020 Greenhouse Goals in Bali" (Salon.com). IPCC chief Rajendra Pachauri said: "If there's no action before 2012, that's too late. What we do in the next two to three years will determine our future. This is the defining moment."[12]

- In 2008, James Hansen and nine colleagues stated that the safe level for CO_2, rather than being 450 ppm as previously thought, is actually "350 ppm or less." Hansen also said: "This Is the Last Chance."[13]

- The 2009 conference in Copenhagen was, in fact, billed as the world's last chance to prevent catastrophic climate change. Britain's Sir Nicholas Stern called it "most important gathering since the Second World War, given what is at stake."[14] However, headlines again tell the story: "Copenhagen – Historic Failure that Will Live in Infamy" (*Independent*); "Copenhagen –The Munich of Our Times?" (*BBC News*); "As the World Burns," which said: "The world once again missed an opportunity to avert disaster" (*Rolling Stone*).

- With regard to the 2010 meeting in Cancun, Mexico, the "most significant result," said Suzanne Goldenberg of the *Guardian*, "was putting off the tough decisions until next year." William Marsden, with reference to the luxurious hotel that housed the conference, said: "The delegates were playing the maracas while world burned."[15]

- The 2011 meeting in Durban, South Africa, was more consequential, agreeing to "develop [by 2015] a new protocol . . . with legal force." The Union of Concerned Scientists had a good news-bad news evaluation: "The good news is we avoided a train wreck. The bad news is that we did very little here to affect the emissions curve."[16]

- In 2012, the United Nations, 20 years after the Earth Summit, organized another conference in Rio. "The Rio+20 Summit," said Fred Pearce, "produced a largely meaningless document that failed to address the daunting environmental challenges the world faces." Referring to the text as "283 paragraphs of fluff," George Monbiot wrote that "190 governments have spent 20 years bracing themselves to 'acknowledge,' 'recognise' and express 'deep concern' about the world's environmental crises, but not to do anything about them."[17]

- Later in 2012, a summit in Doha, Qatar, involved almost 200 nations and lasted two weeks. But the accomplishments were indicated by the heading of the Reuters story, "Climate Summit Ends with a Whimper." This meeting did succeed in reauthorizing the Kyoto Protocol for another seven years, but this would have little effect (other than "keeping Kyoto alive"), because Canada, Russia, New Zealand, and even Japan had opted out, leaving the remaining backers accounting for only 15 percent of world greenhouse gas emissions.[18]

- In May 2013, a week of negotiations involving mid-level bureaucrats ended with no progress.[19]

- By 2014, the new IPCC report showed that top global scientists were "at their wits' end on how to make world leaders realize that the Earth is on the brink of a climate catastrophe if they do not cooperate in cutting down their gas emissions," and NOAA's 2014 report, "State of the Climate 2013," showed that the planet is "changing more rapidly . . . than in any time of modern civilization."[20]

Explaining the Political Failure

As this brief history shows, the failures of governments were not due to their being misinformed. "Our collective failure to take action against global warming," pointed out Mark Hertsgaard, "had been a conscious decision, a result of countless official debates where the case for reducing greenhouse gas emissions was exhaustively considered and deliberately rejected."[21]

Given the repeated warnings by experts over the past three decades, we can wonder how governments, especially the U.S. government, could have made this conscious decision. Recall Elizabeth Kolbert's famous observation: "It may seem impossible to imagine that a technologically advanced society could choose, in essence, to destroy itself, but that is what we are now in the process of doing."[22]

Granting that we cannot *fully* imagine how human beings – most of whom have children and grandchildren they love – could have made choices that could contribute to the destruction of civilization, we can perhaps name some factors that could provide a partial explanation. Perhaps the most important question is how political leaders, especially American political leaders, could have ignored so many science-based warnings. While doing research for his book, Marsden learned of "the utter desperation of scientists as they pile proof upon proof only to see it disappear into the smoke of denial or crash against the excuse of political and economic expediency."[23]

As quoted earlier, Nobel Prize-winning scientist Sherwood Rowland asked, "What's the use of having developed a science well enough to make predictions if, in the end, all we're willing to do is stand around and wait for them to come true?"[24] Why, given the stakes, could politicians still simply be waiting for the predictions of climate scientists to become true?

Simply Foolish

One factor is surely that human beings, including political leaders, often do very foolish things. The centrality of this factor is suggested by Marsden's decision to call his book (on "the failed politics of climate change") *Fools Rule*. What Marsden considers especially foolish is the continuation of business as usual, even after the dangers had become apparent.[25] But how can such reckless foolishness be explained?

Bertrand Russell's statement quoted at the outset of Chapter 11 —"man has never refrained from any folly of which he was capable" – could be used to suggest that human beings have always been equally foolish, and that civilization-ending folly differs from former follies only because humanity now has technological capacities that did not previously exist. However, we now have the technological capacity to drive automobiles so dangerously fast as to threaten ourselves and our families, but most of us do not do this. Kolbert's puzzlement cannot simply be explained in terms of a tendency to foolishness combined with modern technology.

Science Overruled by Politics

A more specific factor is that people in the political world, followed by much of the media, evidently fail to appreciate a key difference between science and politics. Politics has been famously defined as the "art of the possible," and doing what is politically possible often means compromises. But science is different. As Hertsgaard put it, "the laws of physics and chemistry, unlike those of humans, do not compromise."[26]

Marsden made a similar point, saying that too many people "act as if these [climate] negotiations are about politics as usual." In this connection, he quoted Obama's former climate negotiator, Jonathan Pershing, as saying: "The politics of the negotiations does not speak in any way to what *has* to be done." Marsden raised this issue with Michael Martin, Canada's chief negotiator, asking: "How can you say you believe in the science and at the same time campaign against what the science proves is necessary to reduce the risk of runaway climate change?" Martin replied: "That's what these negotiations are for. It's all about what is possible." Marsden asked: "What about what is necessary?" Martin replied: "That's up for negotiation too." However, Marsden said: "Melting glaciers, ice sheets and ice caps as well as rising sea levels, dying coral reefs and altering weather patterns do not respond to the art of the politically possible."[27]

Recognizing that science's laws do not compromise, George Monbiot wrote: "Nature won't wait for us." Pointing out that nature did not wait for us, Gelbspan said: "We have failed to meet nature's deadline," so "it's too late to stop climate change."[28]

However, it is perhaps not too late for us to prevent the unpleasantness from turning into hell and then into complete collapse. But the failures of the political process continue: In spite of the dramatic changes of the past decade, with developments that were not expected for 100 years, the governments are still refusing to do anything significant.

A Failure to Grasp the Stakes

The rich industrialized West, suggests Mardsen, "is actively in denial as to what the stakes are." Although many economists seem to think that the value of nature can be evaluated in solely economic terms, Sir Nicholas Stern does not, saying: "The first thing that struck me as an economist when I began looking at climate change was the magnitude of the risks and the potentially devastating effects on the lives of people across the world. We were gambling the planet."[29]

Hertsgaard, reminding us that the continuation of business as usual will soon lead to a temperature rise of 4°C beyond preindustrial times, said that "a 4°C temperature rise would create planetary conditions all but certain to end civilization as we know it."[30] The stakes could not be higher.

Science Trumped by Materialism

Perhaps Greek mythology could help. In Aeschylus' *Agamemnon,* Apollo had attempted to seduce Cassandra, the "second most beautiful woman in the world." When she rebuffed his advances, he became furious and placed a curse on her: She would correctly prophesy the future but never be believed, a fate that would drive her mad.

In a 2009 essay, Paul Krugman said that "climate scientists have, en masse, become Cassandras — gifted with the ability to prophesy future disasters, but cursed with the inability to get anyone to believe them."[31] In 2012, Richard Falk used the myth more fully, saying:

> The sad story of Cassandra is suggestive of the dilemma confronting the climate change scientific community. In modern civilization, interpreting scientific evidence and projecting trends is as close to trustworthy prophesy as this civilization is likely to get. . . . The culture is supposed to place its highest trust in the scientific community as the voice of reason. . . . Why is the strong consensus of the scientific community so ineffectual on this issue? Why are its dire warnings substantially ignored? The full story is complicated and controversial.

However, Falk continued, the myth of Apollo's curse on Cassandra is relevant:

> By making the political process in a world of sovereign states primarily responsive to the siren call of *money*, the guidance

of science is marginalized. More explicitly, when money in large quantities does not want something to happen, and there is absent countervailing monetary resources to offset the pressures being exerted, knowledge will be subordinated. We have become, maybe long have been, a materialistic civilization more than a scientific civilization.[32]

This characterization fits with Marsden's perspective. Saying that "we have no technological solution [to global warming] other than abstinence from the burning of fossil fuels," Marsden adds that "we don't seem to be keen on even a small amount of that. Society remains unflagging in its almost pathological pursuit of material self-interest."[33]

Fear, Greed, and Self-Interest

Closely related, Marsden said that "most of the problem comes down to the basic human weaknesses of fear, greed, and self-interest." This explanation can certainly account for much of the problem. With regard to fear, Alden Mayer of the Union of Concerned Scientists said in 2013:

> The main barrier to confronting the climate crisis isn't lack of knowledge about the problem, nor is it the lack of cost-effective solutions. It's the lack of political will by most world leaders to confront the special interests that have worked long and hard to block the path to a sustainable low-carbon future.[34]

With regard to greedy self-interest, it is now necessary, Marsden points out, for governments to "face up to the realities of our time by preparing for a post-fossil fuel future." However, "this is not happening. Instead we march ahead in total denial, licking our lips at the fossil fuel reservoirs buried in the melting Arctic." Likewise, "Too many American lawmakers appeared almost giddy with delight at the failure of Copenhagen."[35]

This short-sighted self-interest is, of course, far from being limited to the United States. For example, Marsden quoted the Indian environment minister as saying: "I went to Copenhagen not to save the world. I went to Copenhagen to protect India's national interests, and my mandate was to protect India's right to foster economic growth."[36]

The charge of greedy self-interest applies preeminently to fossil-fuel corporations. For example, ExxonMobil, the most successful corporation ever, has been making a profit of some $40 billion annually, with the CEO receiving over $30 million a year, and yet this corporation still battles to retain a lower tax rate than average Americans, as if ExxonMobil needed tax breaks to stay in business. Although it might seem as if the first part of Mardsen's "fear, greed, and self-interest" does not apply to ExxonMobil, its disinformation campaign has been motivated by the fear that climate legislation would significantly affect its profits. This fear trumps any fear of climate disruption because, as Hertsgaard has said, ExxonMobil has "put its immediate economic interests ahead of humanity's future well-being."[37]

As we saw in the previous chapter, the greedy self-interest of media corporations has led them to color their reporting in ways favorable to fossil-fuel interests and to continue accepting fossil-fuel ads, even though fossil fuels are now known to be as dangerous to our collective health as cigarettes are to our individual health.

A petition for disallowing polluters from participation in climate negotiations has been based on a precedent involving tobacco lobbyists. Believe it or not, oil industry lobbyists are allowed to be present while climate negotiations are going on. Lobbyists used to be allowed in negotiations about tobacco, but in 2005, the U.N.'s Framework Convention on Tobacco Control, which protected policymakers from those with "commercial and vested interests of the tobacco industry," was ratified by 178 countries. There is now an attempt to use this type of "firewall strategy" with regard to climate negotiations: In the words of Environmental Action's Drew Hudson, "lying, destructive, polluting haters should not be allowed to sit at the table while the grown ups are trying to solve problems." In September 2014, Corporate Accountability International called on U.N. Secretary-General Ban Ki-moon and Christiana Figueres, the executive secretary of the Framework Convention on Climate Change, to "keep big energy out of these [climate] talks and create meaningful global policies free from corporate influence."[38]

Industry-Friendly Politicians in the U.S. Senate

As described in Chapter 11, ExxonMobil's disinformation campaign – which has been joined by Koch Industries and Donors Trust - included "using friendly politicians" – a topic that was saved for the present chapter. There have been several members of the U.S. Senate, almost entirely Republicans, who have supported the interests of the fossil-fuel industry come Hell or high water.

Senator James Inhofe (R-OK)

The most important, in terms of seniority and statements, has been Senator James Inhofe, who for a time was the chair of the Senate Environment and Public Works Committee. In 2003, Inhofe declared: "I have offered compelling evidence that catastrophic global warming is a hoax. That conclusion is supported by the painstaking work of the nation's top climate scientists." In 2010, Inhofe used "Climategate" allegations to try to get 17 climate scientists – including Michael Mann, Michael Oppenheimer, Susan Solomon, and Kevin Trenberth – prosecuted. When asked by Rachel Maddow in 2012 about the "97 percent of scientists who agree that global warming is real," Inhofe said: "It's not true. . . . This 97 percent, that doesn't mean anything. I've named literally thousands of scientists on the floor."[39]

In 2012, Inhofe published a book entitled *The Greatest Hoax: How the Global Warming Conspiracy Threatens Your Future*. Learning that he was a target of a documentary about the fossil-fuel industry's disinformation campaign entitled "Greedy Lying Bastards," Inhofe said that he was "proud" to be featured. Inhofe also says that he is proud to be from Oklahoma. He does not, however, trumpet the fact that he is one of the Senate's biggest recipients of oil and gas money, reportedly over $1.3 million by 2012.[40]

Likely Presidential Candidates

Ted Cruz (R-TX): Appearing very much to be planning to run for president, Ted Cruz, a Tea Party Republican (see below), has been doing various things that have made him popular with the Republican base, including things that demonstrate his rejection of concern about global warming. Calling climate change "controversial," Cruz insisted on the deletion, in a Senate resolution on International Women's Day, of a statement saying that women in developing countries "are disproportionately affected by changes in climate because of their need to secure water, food and fuel for their livelihood." A spokesperson for Cruz explained: "A provision expressing the Senate's views on such a controversial topic as 'climate change' has no place in a supposedly noncontroversial resolution requiring consent of all 100 U.S. senators."[41]

Marco Rubio (R-FL): When he was the speaker of the House in Florida, Marco Rubio had supported market-based solutions to climate change. But in 2013, while still agreeing that the climate is changing, he said: "The question is if man-made activity is what's contributing the most to it. I know people said there's a significant scientific consensus on that issue, but I've actually seen reasonable debate." He added: "We can pass a bunch of laws that will destroy our economy, but it isn't going to change the weather." In 2014, he went further, saying, "I do not believe that human activity is causing these dramatic changes to our climate the way these scientists are portraying it." It appears that Rubio changed his public stance for purely political reasons – especially because when asked what sources he relied on to make this judgment, he was unable to name any.[42]

Other Friendly Senators

Senator Orrin Hatch (R-UT): "There is some disagreement among scientists as to whether global warming – regardless of its cause – would result in a net benefit or detriment to life on earth," Hatch wrote in 2010. In any case, he added: "Scientific studies demonstrate overwhelmingly that humans tend to fare better during warming spells than periods of cooling."[43]

Senator Ron Johnson (R-WI): While running for the Senate in 2010, Johnson said: "I absolutely do not believe in the science of man-caused climate change. It's not proven by any stretch of the imagination."[44]

Senator Roger Wicker (R-Miss): In 2009, Wicker wrote:

> Science shows that there is an increase of carbon dioxide in Earth's atmosphere. But it has not been compellingly proven that mankind is responsible for the rise in atmospheric CO_2, nor is it clear what impact CO_2 has on Earth's temperatures.[45]

Industry-Friendly Politicians in the U.S. House of Representatives

Many members of the House support the position taken by ExxonMobil. Here are some of them:

Rep. Joe Barton (R-TX): In 2007, responding to Al Gore's 2007 statement to Congress that carbon dioxide emissions cause global temperatures to rise, Barton said: "You're not just off a little, you're totally wrong."[46]

Rep. Dan Benishek (R-MI): Named one of the "Flat Earth Five" by the League of Conservation voters, Benishek has said that climate change is "unproven science stuff" and "all baloney."[47]

Rep. John Boehner (R-OH): While being interviewed by George Stephanopoulos, Boehner – who in 2009 was the House Minority Leader – said: "George, the idea that carbon dioxide is a carcinogen that is harmful to our environment is almost comical. Every time we exhale," he explained, "we exhale carbon dioxide. Every cow in the world, you know, when they do what they do, you've got more carbon dioxide."[48]

Rep. Duncan Hunter (R-CA): Ridiculing concern for global warming, Hunter said: "Thousands of people die every year of cold, so if we had global warming it would save lives."[49]

Rep. James Sensenbrenner (R-WI): In 2009 hearings on the "Climategate" allegations, Sensenbrenner, the ranking Republican on the House Select Committee for Energy Independence and Global Warming, said that the stolen e-mails "show a pattern of suppression, manipulation and secrecy that was inspired by ideology, condescension and profit. They read more like scientific fascism than the scientific process."[50]

Rep. John Shimkus (R-IL): Being a member of the House Committee on Energy and Commerce, which oversees legislation dealing with air quality and environmental health, Shimkus has opposed legislation to limit CO_2 emissions with one of the stock denialist points – that CO_2 is "plant food," so that decreasing it would be "taking away plant food from the atmosphere."[51]

Rep. James Bridenstine (R-OK): In 2014, two days after the new IPCC report warned of increased extreme weather because of unmitigated greenhouse gases, and one month before the NOAA was to issue its new National Climate Assessment, which gave the same warning, the House voted in favor of a dismissive bill. If it were to be accepted by the Senate, the bill would tell NOAA to give priority to predicting storms, rather than studying climate change, with the intent that this would "protect lives and property." Ironically, Bridenstine represents Oklahoma, which was ravaged by tornadoes the previous year, as he noted – perhaps unaware of new studies (reported in Chapter 4) that climate change likely affects both the frequency and the ferocity of tornadoes.[52]

The Republican Stampede Toward Absolutist Denial

In 2011, highly-respected journalist Ronald Brownstein wrote: "Republicans in this country are coalescing around a uniquely dismissive position on climate change. The GOP is stampeding," he added, "toward an absolutist rejection of climate science that appears unmatched among major political parties around the globe."[53] For example:

- "Since 2011, Senate Republicans have voted seven times for pro-Big Oil interests and against clean energy three times."[54]

- In 2005, Senator John McCain co-sponsored a cap-and-trade bill. But in 2011, after Senator Lindsey Graham had worked on bipartisan cap-and-trade legislation, he could not attract a single Republican co-sponsor, not even John McCain.

- During the 2012 Republican presidential primary, all the candidates – except for Jon Huntsman, who had no chance – denied concern about global warming.

- The 2012 Republican Party platform, criticizing Obama for including climate risk in national security planning, said: "The strategy subordinates our national security interests to environmental, energy and international health issues, and elevates 'climate change' to the level of a 'severe threat' equivalent to foreign aggression."

- Republican presidential candidate Mitt Romney mocked the statement — "We will be able to look back and tell our children that this was the moment . . . when the rise of the oceans began to slow and our planet began to heal" — made in 2008 by then candidate Barack Obama. In Romney's 2012 convention speech, he said: "President Obama promised to begin to slow the rise of the oceans [pausing for the audience to laugh] and to heal the planet. *My* promise . . . is to help you and your family."[55]

- By 2013, more than 65 percent of the Republican members of the new (113th) Congress denied climate science, with 90 percent of the leadership positions filled by climate science deniers.[56]

- Another 2013 study suggested a strong "climate disconnect" between the voting records of GOP House members and the climate-related experiences of the constituents: "Republican representatives from the districts hardest hit by higher temperatures took the anti-climate position on those votes 96 percent of the time."[57]

- In 2014, the League of Conservation Voters found that the House Republicans had taken an almost completely anti-environmental stance by 2013, voting in favor of environmental interests only 5 percent of the time — down from 10 percent in 2012 and 17 percent in 2008.[58]

- By 2014, the Republicans in the Senate had become so anti-environmental that they would block bills with which they otherwise agreed, if they contained something that would have helped clean energy or energy efficiency.[59]

In addition, House Republican leaders have been putting denialists in charge of committees:

- *Rep. Lamar Smith (R-TX):* In 2010, Smith, who refers to those who warn about global warming as "alarmists," charged the major TV networks with bias for failing to air enough "dissenting opinions." In 2013, he wrote: "Contrary to the claims of those who want to strictly regulate carbon dioxide emissions. . . , there is a great amount of uncertainty associated with climate science." As these statements show, there is nothing remarkable about Smith – except that in 2012 he was made the chairman of the House Committee on Science, Space, and Technology. In 2014, after the National Climate Assessment was released, Smith dismissed it as "a political document intended to frighten Americans."[60]

- *Rep. Chris Stewart (R-UT):* In 2013, the House Science, Space and Technology Committee made Stewart the chairman of the subcommittee dealing with climate change. Saying that climate change is "probably not as immediate as some people [think]" and doubting that the idea of human-caused climate change is based on "sound science," Stewart warned against making "any long-lasting policy decisions that could negatively affect our economy."[61]

The Greedy Koch Brothers and the Party of Denial

Although ExxonMobil had long been considered the greediest corporation on the planet, its first-place position has been wrested away by the Koch Industries. And the massive spending by the Koch brothers, mentioned in Chapter 11, has been central to the Republican "stampede" toward an absolutist denial, which was aided by the rise of the Tea Party.

The Tea Party, which hit the headlines in 2009, was generally portrayed in the press as if it were a spontaneous grassroots movement. However, it was an example of "astroturfing" (from Astroturf, the name of a synthetic carpet designed to look like natural grass), in which seemingly grassroots campaigns have been manufactured to mask the sponsor's identity. In this case, the Tea Party was created by the libertarian Koch brothers (whose father had been one of the founders of the John Birch Society).

The Kochs had been carrying out activities to implant their views on the political process for many years, reported Jane Mayer in a 2010 *New Yorker* article. For example, they provided the money for the Cato Institute, the first libertarian think tank (which in 2008 took out full-page ads in *The New York Times* to dispute candidate Barack Obama's statement that the science of global warming is "beyond dispute"), and the Mercatus Center (which provided 14 of the 23 regulations on Bush's "hit list" to be killed or modified).[62]

But then the Koch brothers, in Mayer's words, "concluded that think tanks alone were not enough to effect change. They needed a mechanism to deliver those ideas to the street, and to attract the public's support." In 1984, they created a seemingly grassroots organization called Citizens for a Sound Economy. Having been given many millions of dollars of Koch money, the group soon had "fifty paid field workers, in twenty-six states, to rally voters behind the Kochs' agenda." In 1993, for example, it led the successful assault on Clinton's proposed BTU tax.[63]

In 2004, Citizens for a Sound Economy divided into two organizations: Freedom Works, led by Dick Armey, and Americans for Prosperity, led by David Koch. These two organizations then created and guided the Tea Party movement. Although Americans for Prosperity has claimed to be a grassroots organization, and although David Koch has tried to deny responsibility for the Tea Party, the evidence shows it to be largely his creation, as indicated by the title of Mayer's *New Yorker* article, "Covert Operations," and by a *New York Magazine* article entitled "The Billionaire's Party."[64]

The covert operations of this billionaire's party are carried out on behalf of causes that support Koch interests, which generally are not the interests of the people who have joined the Tea Party. In an essay entitled "The Tea Party Movement: Deluded and Inspired by Billionaires," George Monbiot said that it is "mostly composed of passionate, well-meaning people who think they are fighting elite power, unaware that they have been organised by the very interests they believe they are confronting."[65]

Central to the Koch brothers' self-interests is the aim of preventing climate legislation. In a *New York Times* article in 2010 headed "Climate Change Doubt Is Tea Party Article of Faith," John Broder reported that according to a NYT/CBS poll, "only 14 percent of Tea Party supporters said that global warming is an environmental problem that is having an effect now."[66]

The emergence of the Tea Party has, therefore, provided shock troops for the Koch-ExxonMobil efforts to block climate legislation. Reporting that Republicans in Congress began attacking Obama's climate protection efforts in 2011 from many directions at once, the *Guardian*'s Suzanne Goldenberg wrote: "Much of the momentum for the anti-environment agenda was provided by the success of extremist Tea Party candidates in [the 2010] elections."[67]

David Koch has even more directly influenced Congressional climate denial. In 2008 – after the Supreme Court said that the EPA could regulate greenhouse gases as pollutants - Americans for Prosperity devised a "No Climate Tax" pledge. Signatories include, Jane Mayer reported in 2013,

> the entire Republican leadership in the House of Representatives, a third of the members of the House of Representatives as a whole, and a quarter of U.S. senators. . . . Of the eighty-five freshmen Republican congressmen elected to the House of Representatives in 2010, seventy-six had signed the No Climate Tax pledge.[68]

As Frank Rich said in a 2010 article, "the Koch agenda is morphing into the G.O.P. agenda, as articulated by current Republican members of Congress." So, although the term "party of denial" applied originally to the Tea Party, it now increasingly applies to the Republican Party as a whole. In 2013, Gail Collins said that, although there was a time when "the Republican Party was a hotbed of environmental worrywarts," to be a Republican politician now is, with few exceptions, to vote against climate legislation and to endorse denialism – a fact illustrated earlier in this chapter.[69]

Unlike rich liberal George Soros, who "supports causes that are unrelated to his business interests and that, if anything, raise his taxes," wrote Rich, "This is hardly true of the Kochs," who want to abolish "any government enterprise that would either inhibit [their] business profits or increase [their] taxes." Charles Lewis, the executive editor of the Investigative Reporting Workshop, said: "There is no other corporation in the U.S. today, in my view, that is as unabashedly, bare-knuckle aggressive across the board about its own self-interest." In 2012, InsideClimate News' David Sassoon published an article about the Kochs' investment in Canadian tar sands, documenting the ways in which their activism is wholly in pursuit of its financial interests. The same view of the Kochs has been expressed in the title of a more recent article: "America's Greediest." And Thom Hartmann has compared the Kochs to William A. Clark, who, besides having become "public enemy number 1" in the early 1900s, was said by Mark Twain to be "as rotten a human being as can be found anywhere under the flag" and "a shame to the American nation."[70]

The Kochs are also not shy about buying the media to advance their interests. At about the same time that it became known that the Kochs wanted to buy eight newspapers, including the *Chicago Tribune* and the *Los Angeles Times*, David Koch persuaded PBS – which Koch had given $23 million - not to run a critical documentary entitled "Citizen Koch." (This event symbolizes the fact that America no longer has *public* television – a fact expressed by the title of Mayer's story about this event, "A Word from Our Sponsor.")[71]

The Kochs have been especially aggressive about the stories by Mayer, who is, suggests a 2013 *Washington Post* article, their "Public Enemy No. 1 in the media." To rebut all of the negative media stories that have appeared in recent years since Mayer's 2010 article, the Kochs have established a website called KochFacts. Besides having attacks on all of Mayer's articles about them, they even wrote to the American Society of Magazine Editors to explain why her 2010 article, which had been nominated for the National Magazine Award for reporting, should not be given this award.[72]

In any case, having pointed out that the agendas of the Kochs often run counter to "the interests of those who serve as spear carriers in the political pageants hawked on Fox News," Frank Rich added: "The Koch brothers must be laughing all the way to the bank knowing that working Americans are aiding and abetting their selfish interests." And the Koch brothers do, incidentally, keep going to the bank. Having been valued at $35 billion in 2010, their wealth by 2013 had been brought up to $68 billion.[73]

In preparing for the 2014 elections, the Democrats decided to use the Kochs' money and increasing unpopularity against them. For example, under the slogan "The G.O.P. is addicted to Koch," the Democratic Senatorial Campaign Committee strategy was to tie various Republican candidates to the policies of the Koch brothers.[74]

To conclude by returning to the theme of folly: David Koch, who got married only late in life, has three young children.[75] By 2075, these children will be in their 70s, presumably being concerned about their own children and grandchildren. Will these children, grandchildren, and great-grandchildren, suffering from the greater heat, drought, wildfires, flooding, and other effects of global warming, wonder whether Grandpa Koch had had no love and concern for them – or whether he was simply very greedy or very foolish.

Climate Decisions of U.S. Presidents

A large part of the U.S. failure on climate change has been due to failures of the recent presidents. Here is a very selective summary of statements and decisions made by presidents from Johnson to Obama.

Lyndon Johnson

Having received a report by the Environmental Pollution Board of the President's Science Advisory Committee, Johnson, in a special message to Congress in February 1965, said: "This generation has altered the composition of the atmosphere on a global scale through . . . a steady increase in carbon dioxide from the burning of fossil fuels."[76]

Richard Nixon

Three of the most important tools for combating pollution were created in 1970 during Nixon's presidency: a greatly expanded version of the Clean Air Act; the National Environmental Policy Act; and the Environmental Protection Agency. These tools were created with no reference to global warming – it had not become a public issue, and CO_2 was not considered a pollutant.[77]

Jimmy Carter

Carter was the first "green" president, fighting throughout his presidency for clean energy by providing incentives for people and businesses to install it. Most famously, Carter had 32 solar panels installed on the White House roof, saying:

> A generation from now, this solar heater can either be a curiosity, a museum piece, an example of a road not taken, or it can be a small part of one of the greatest and most exciting adventures ever undertaken by the American people; harnessing the power of the sun to enrich our lives as we move away from our crippling dependence on foreign oil.[78]

Ronald Reagan

Perhaps the most important event of Reagan's presidency for climate change was symbolic: During his second term, the panels came down. In terms of policy, Reagan, as we saw in Chapter 11, was committed to reducing federal regulations. Providing a template for more recent Republican politicians, Reagan dismissed pressure to deal with acid rain by charging proponents with "alarmism," claiming present knowledge was insufficient to justify government controls, which, in any case, would cost too much.

George H. W. Bush

In 1988, America suffered its worst heat wave ever and Hansen made his statement to Congress. Running for the presidency, Bush said: "Those who think we're powerless to do anything about the 'greenhouse effect' are forgetting about the 'White House effect.' As president, I intend to do something about it." He also said: "In my first year in office, I will convene a global conference on the environment at the White House . . . . We will talk about global warming . . . And we will act." However, said *The New York Times* a year later, "Mr. Bush hasn't met, talked or acted."[79]

In 1990, the IPCC issued its first report, which urged major cuts in CO_2 emissions in light of the increase in the global temperature over the past century. But at a global warming meeting, Bush spoke of "scientific uncertainty" about climate change.[80]

In 1992, although there was still no "White House effect," Bush did sign the U.N. Framework Convention on Climate Change, thereby committing America to preventing "dangerous anthropogenic interference with the climate system." In recognizing that America and its allies – Australia, Canada, Europe, and Japan – were largely responsible for the problem, the pact set a special standard for them, with America taking "the lead in combating climate change and the adverse effects thereof" (a principle that would central to the 1995 Berlin Mandate, which laid the groundwork for the Kyoto Protocol). In signing the document, Bush even, noting the special responsibilities of the developed nations, said they "must go further" than the others, offering detailed "programs and measures they will undertake to limit greenhouse emissions." By the time he left office, however, Bush had started no initiatives to provide such leadership.[81]

Bill Clinton

"Under Bill Clinton," said Elizabeth Kolbert, "the U.S. took no meaningful action to reduce its emissions."[82] This verdict, to the extent that it is justified, was not entirely his fault. In 1993, Clinton tried to get a BTU (British Thermal Unit) tax, which would reduce emissions while raising revenue to eliminate the deficit. But Congress rejected it, thanks in part to a campaign run by David Koch's Citizens for a Sound Economy.[83]

Clinton also announced a Climate Change Action Plan with 50 initiatives to bring U.S. emissions back to 1990 levels by 2000. Having had his BTU tax fail, his initiatives were to be voluntary. But Congress would not provide funding – especially after the midterm elections of 1994, which brought Republican control of both houses.

In 1995, Clinton reaffirmed the Berlin Mandate's principle that "developed countries go first." In 1996, he gave the first public support by the United States for a legally binding agreement and actually began leading the climate change policy-making process.

In 1997, Clinton supported the idea of a treaty conference in Kyoto, saying: "[We] know that the Industrial Age has dramatically increased greenhouse gases in the atmosphere, where they take a century or more to dissipate; and that the process must be slowed, then stopped, then reduced if we want to continue our economic progress and preserve the quality of life in the United States and throughout our planet." At Kyoto, the U.S. agreed to accept a 5-percent reduction in its greenhouse emissions.[84]

But success was blocked by four developments. One was the Senate's 95-0 vote for the Byrd-Hagel Resolution, which contradicted the Berlin Mandate by insisting that any treaty had to impose equal restrictions on developing countries. Second, although Clinton worked for participation by China, India, and other developing countries, he had little success. Third, there were claims, supported by fossil-fuel industries, that the proposals would be too costly. Then the news in January 1998 of Clinton's affair with Monica Lewinsky made it difficult to move forward with any policies.[85]

In Clinton's 1999 State of the Union address, he called global warming "our most fateful new challenge." In his 2000 address, he called it "the greatest environmental challenge of the new century" and put $2.4 billion in his budget to fight climate change. However, Congress would not agree. Clinton was criticized by greens and Europeans for making unacceptable compromises and having signed the Kyoto Protocol, for not sending it to the Senate for ratification. But even with all of his compromises, Congress did not support him, and the Byrd-Hagel Resolution put ratification out of the question.[86]

In spite of his efforts, "the United States ended the decade [of Clinton's presidency] failing to meet its voluntary commitment . . . to reduce emissions by 2000 to 1990 levels."[87]

George W. Bush

In the first month of the younger Bush's presidency, just after the release of the IPCC's 2001 report – which stated that global warming was definitely caused by human activity – Bush accepted ExxonMobil's suggestion that he get the IPCC chief, Robert Watson, replaced.[88]

At the same time, ExxonMobil asked Bush to appoint Harlan Watson (no relation) – who had been President George H.W. Bush's climate negotiator at Rio and who worked closely with members of Congress opposing action on global warming – appointed as the new climate negotiator. Revelations about this request led Greenpeace to ask, "Who can now doubt that US policy is being steered by the world's largest oil company?"[89]

Another fateful appointment by the Bush-Cheney team was that of oil industry lobbyist Philip Cooney to be the White House Council on Environmental Quality's chief of staff. Being a lawyer with no scientific credentials, Cooney used his role to censor and even distort government reports "so as to exaggerate scientific uncertainty about global warming" – behavior that led Rick Piltz, a Senior Associate in the Climate Change Science Program, to resign in protest.[90]

During his battle with Al Gore for the presidency, Bush pledged to control CO_2 emissions, saying: "We will require all power plants to meet clean-air standards in order to reduce emissions of carbon dioxide within a reasonable period of time." But two months after entering the Oval Office, Bush said he would not regulate CO_2 emissions, because regulation would impose rising costs upon Americans, combined with the "incomplete state of scientific knowledge of the causes of . . . global climate change." The pressure to change Bush's position, wrote *The New York Times*, "came in part from lobbyists for coal companies and utilities dependent on coal and from the conservative wing of the Republican Party, which saw any move to regulate carbon dioxide as an implicit endorsement of the goals of the Kyoto Protocol."[91]

Although ExxonMobil claimed in 2003 that it had not "campaigned with the United States government or any other government to take any sort of position over Kyoto," Under-Secretary of State Paula Dobriansky told the Global Climate Coalition (GCC), to which Exxon still belonged: "POTUS [the

President of the United States] rejected Kyoto, in part, based on input from you."[92]

The GCC, incidentally, had bragged that the White House had received "a lot of communications" from it. In 2002, the GCC disbanded, saying that, because of the Bush administration's new policies, it was no longer needed.[93]

These new policies were evidently discussed in Vice President Cheney's meetings early in 2001 with members of his energy task force, the names of whom were kept secret. Especially in light of the fact that Cheney and Bush had been oil men, environmentalists had long suspected that oil corporations were involved in the task force. In 2005, the CEOs of five oil companies were asked by Congress if they had been. Shell and BP said they were uncertain, but ExxonMobil, Chevron, and ConocoPhillips said No. Shortly afterwards, however, a document revealed that these denials were false.[94]

At the end of 2008, a survey of over 100 historians showed that almost two thirds of them ranked Bush as the worst U.S. president ever. Still more serious was the judgment of Saleem Huq of the International Institute for Environment and Development – one of the authors of the IPCC's 2007 report – that Bush was possibly the president "who has doomed the planet."[95]

Barack Obama

In 2009, Elizabeth Kolbert wrote: "The election of Barack Obama seemed [with respect to climate change] to offer a fresh start. A few weeks after his victory, Obama vowed to open a 'new chapter' on climate change. And yet, almost a year later, the United States was again - or, really, still - stuck in the same old pattern. We keep saying that we want to be marching at the front of the parade, and then hanging back with the tubas." Obama had certainly said that he meant to lead the parade, stating, for example, at the 2009 climate conference at U.N. Headquarters:

> We risk consigning future generations to an irreversible
> catastrophe. . . . The developed nations that caused much
> of the damage to our climate over the last century still have
> a responsibility to lead.

Kolbert then asked: "What would it take for the United States actually to show leadership, instead of just talking about it?[96]

This complaint about Obama – that his behavior often did not match his statements – became a pattern, leading Bill McKibben to write about "Obama's Two Faces on Climate Change" and Joe Romm to use the names "Jekyll and Hyde" to describe "the two sides of Obama's energy strategy."[97]

- In 2008, Obama said that "generations from now, we will be able to look back and tell our children that this was the moment when . . . the rise of the oceans began to slow and our planet began to heal."[98] But by 2012, he was bragging that his administration had "added enough new oil and gas pipeline to encircle the Earth."[99]

- In Obama's 2009 State of the Union Message, he spoke about the need to "save our planet from the ravages of climate change." But at the end of that year, stories about the Copenhagen climate conference, which had been billed as the final chance to save the planet, had headlines such as "Obama Undermines the U.N. Climate Conference" (Jeffrey Sachs) and "Copenhagen's Failure belongs to Obama" (Naomi Klein).[100]

- In 2010, wrote McKibben, "Just days before the BP explosion, the White House opened much of the offshore U.S. to new oil drilling," justifying this decision by saying, "Oil rigs today generally don't cause spills."[101]

- In his 2011 State of the Union address, Obama made no reference whatsoever to climate change, global warming, or even the environment. Later that year, former Vice President Al Gore wrote: "President Obama has never presented to the American people the magnitude of the climate crisis. He has simply not made the case for action. He has not defended the science against the ongoing, withering and dishonest attacks. Nor has he provided a presidential venue for the scientific community – including our own National Academy – to bring the reality of the science before the public."[102]

- In 2012, "with the greatest Arctic melt on record under way," wrote McKibben, "his administration gave Shell Oil the green light to drill in Alaska's Beaufort Sea," with Obama explaining: "Our pioneering spirit is naturally drawn to this region, for the economic opportunities it presents."[103]

- In Obama's victory speech after winning the election in 2012, he said: "We want our children to live in an America that isn't threatened by the destructive power of a warming planet." But in his first post-election press conference, he spoke on both sides of the issue. On the one hand, he said, "change is real" and "we've got an obligation to future generations to do something about it." On the other hand, he said, it would be wrong to "ignore jobs and growth simply to address climate change."[104]

- In 2013, in his second inaugural, Obama said: "We will respond to the threat of climate change, knowing that the failure to do so would betray our children and future generations. . . . The path towards sustainable energy sources will be long and sometimes difficult. But America cannot resist this transition; we must lead it. We cannot cede to other nations the technology that will power new jobs and new industries – we must claim its promise. . . . That is how we will preserve our planet, commanded to our care by God." That same week, however, Obama officials let it be known that they "have no intention of proposing a carbon tax," even though most informed people — including economists, even William Nordhaus – have declared this to be the single most important legislation that could be passed.[105]

- The following month, in his State of the Union speech, Obama said "we must do more to combat climate change" and urged "Congress to pursue a bipartisan, market-based solution to climate change," and then declared: "But if Congress won't act soon to protect future generations, I will. I will direct my Cabinet to come up with executive actions we can take." However, near the end of that year, Obama said: "Over the last three years, I've directed my administration to open up millions of acres for gas and oil exploration across 23 different states. We're opening up more than 75 percent of our potential oil resources offshore.[106]

- In June 2013, speaking at Georgetown University, Obama said: "[The question now is whether we will have the courage to act before it's too late. And how we answer will have a profound impact on the world that we leave behind not just to you, but to your children and to your grandchildren." McKibben, however, has not been impressed by Obama's courage. He acknowledges that he has taken some important steps: "Obama used the stimulus money to promote green technology, and he won agreement from Detroit for higher automobile mileage standards; in his second term, he's fighting for EPA regulations on new coal-fired power plants." However, McKibben added, "these steps illustrate the kind of fights the Obama administration has been willing to take on: ones where the other side is weak. The increased mileage standards came at a moment when D.C. owned Detroit – they were essentially a condition of the auto bailouts. And the battle against new coal-fired power plants was really fought and won by environmentalists." With regard to Obama's goal of reducing America's carbon emissions by 17 percent by 2020, McKibben pointed out that "climate scientists have long since decided these targets are too timid."[107]

- An example of a courageous decision by Obama would have been to oppose natural gas fracking. As pointed out in Chapter 17, natural gas, especially when it is fracked, puts more carbon – with its combination of CO_2 and methane – into the atmosphere than coal; and yet, McKibben points out, "Obama has backed fracking to the hilt," even bragging that America has become the "Saudi Arabia of Natural Gas." Opposing natural gas fracking in this situation would be courageous. Instead, however, Obama, who normally presents himself as endorsing the views of our top climate scientists, contradicted their views as late as 2014 in order to present natural gas, even when fracked, as "the bridge fuel that can power our economy with less of the carbon pollution that causes climate change." While Obama thereby displeased climate scientists, environmentalists, and communities exposed to fracking, Obama pleased the oil and gas companies, including Exxon Mobil, which crowed that Obama called fracking safe.[108]

- Another decision that would be courageous, given the recent increase in the U.S. exports of coal to other countries, would be to ban such exports, so the coal not used in this country would simply be left in the ground. But although Obama has suggested that his EPA's new rules will reduce pollution from coal, it does not; it simply changes the location of where some of it will be emitted. During the Obama administration, "there has been *no decline* in the amount of carbon the US is taking out of the ground." In fact, "'American carbon' is flowing into the global economy and atmosphere faster than ever."[109]

- In Obama's 2014 State of the Union Message, he said:

    "Climate change is a fact. And when our children's children look us in the eye and ask if we did all we could to leave them a safer, more stable world, with new sources of energy, I want us to be able to say yes, we did." During an interview with Thomas Friedman for the TV series "Years of Living Dangerously," Friedman quoted that statement and then asked the President, "How are you doing with your girls?" Obama replied: "Every day I think about what

I'm leaving behind for them. . . . The truth is we're not yet doing all that we need to do. Now, the good news is that America has actually made significant progress over the last five years." However, as McKibben pointed out, although America during those five years greatly increased its clean energy, "All this new carbon drilling, digging and burning the White House has approved will add up to enough to negate the administration's actual achievements."[110]

What can be described as Obama's two-faced position – with his Dr. Jekyll being committed to "cutting carbon pollution and fighting climate change" while his Mr. Hyde is equally committed to "expansion of domestic fossil fuel production" – is reflected in his "all of the above" strategy. Touted on Obama's Organizing for Action website, this is a "strategy to . . . reduce our dependence on foreign oil – an all-of-the-above approach to developing all our energy resources." In January 2014, this strategy was criticized in two major reports:

- A letter to President Obama from 18 major environmental organizations, including Environment America, the Environmental Defense Fund, the Natural Resources Defense Council, and the Sierra Club, began by praising him for his commitment "to take bold action to reduce carbon pollution" and "lead the world in a coordinated assault on climate change." However, the letter said,

  > We believe that continued reliance on an "all of the above" energy strategy would be fundamentally at odds with your goal of cutting carbon pollution and would undermine our nation's capacity to respond to the threat of climate disruption. . . . America's energy policies must reduce our dependence on fossil fuels, not simply reduce our dependence on foreign oil.[111]

- The Center for the New Energy Economy, headed by former Colorado Governor Bill Ritter, said that federal support for energy resources should be directed "to the 'best of the above' rather than 'all of the above.'"[112]

Jeff Goodell, writing in *Rolling Stone,* said that when Obama took office, he named climate change as one the four tasks for his presidency; but of these four tasks, said Goodell, Obama had done the least about climate change, often treating "the greatest challenge human civilization has ever faced as if it were no more urgent than reforming teachers' unions." How can this be explained? A clue may be provided by a statement that Obama made while he was being interviewed by *The New Yorker*'s David Remnick. "I think we are fortunate at the moment," Obama said, "that we do not face a crisis of the scale and scope that Lincoln or F.D.R. faced. So I think it's unrealistic to suggest that I can narrow my focus the way those two Presidents did."[113]

How could Obama say this? In his 2013 State of the Union, he declared that we should accept "the overwhelming judgment of science – and act before it's too late." And as this book has made clear, it is the overwhelming judgment of the top climate scientists that climate change is an existential threat. "The stakes, for all life on the planet," said James Hansen and fellow scientists in 2008, "surpass those of any previous crisis." Lonnie Thompson said, "virtually all of us [climatologists) are now convinced that global warming poses a clear and present danger to civilization." And 20 previous winners of the Blue Planet Prize said that "society has no choice but to take dramatic action to avert a collapse of civilization."[114] As great as the crises faced by Lincoln and FDR were, they do not compare with the threat to the very continuation of civilization.

In May 2014, the National Climate Assessment, which is issued every four years, appeared. Based on over 300 scientists, consisting of over 1,000 pages, and reviewed by the National Academy of Sciences, it was, in Romm's words, "the definitive statement of current and future impacts of carbon pollution on the United States," and the report did not paint a pretty picture. Justin Gillis of *The New York Times* gave this summary:

> The effects of human-induced climate change are being felt in every corner of the United States, scientists reported Tuesday, with water growing scarcer in dry regions, torrential rains increasing in wet regions, heat waves becoming more common and more severe, wildfires growing worse, and forests dying under assault from heat-loving insects.

Motherboard magazine called its story "The White House's Outline of How Climate Change Is Breaking Down Civilization."[115]

Continuing the greater attention Obama started giving climate change in 2014, the White House devoted an unusual amount of time to the report. Instead of simply giving the Rose Garden speech, Obama gave interviews to prominent meteorologists around the nation. Suggesting that the message came through as to the seriousness of the continuation of business as usual, NBC entitled its coverage "American Doomsday: White House Warns of Climate Catastrophe."[116]

However, not only did Obama's two faces continue, the climate-concerned Obama became increasingly subordinate to the all-of-the-above Obama. In September 2014, Michael Klare published an essay entitled, "Oil Is Back!" In spite of all the warnings and policies to reduce oil usage, Klare wrote, Americans are "driving *more* miles every day, not fewer, filling ever more fuel tanks with ever more gasoline, and evidently feeling ever less bad about it. . . . [N]early one out of three vehicles sold today is an SUV." Part of the explanation, Klare said, was "Obama's turnaround on oil."

> While President Obama once spoke of the necessity of eliminating our reliance on petroleum as a major source of energy, he now brags about rising U.S. oil output and touts his efforts to further boost production. . . . [H]e told a cheering Congress in January, "more oil [was] produced at home than we buy from the rest of the world – the first time that's happened in nearly twenty years."

Being aware that the continued use of oil will lead to global catastrophe while retaining our use of oil and gasoline without worrying much about consequences, America's behavior can be described, said Klare, as a "collective version of schizophrenia" – a condition that is present at the top: "We have a global warming president presiding over a massive expansion of fossil fuel production.[117]

In sum, although Obama's climate record during his first six years has been better than that of his predecessors, it was not nearly enough better.

Unprecedented Political Failure

The failure of political leaders to rise to the challenge of climate change, George Monbiot rightly said, is "the greatest political failure the world has ever seen." It is the greatest failure because it is failure with regard to, in McKibben's words, "the greatest challenge humans have ever faced."[118] In a speech in 2013 entitled "Time to Wake Up," Senator Sheldon Whitehouse said:

> We need to face up to the fact that there is only one leg on which climate denial stands: money. The polluters give and spend money to create false doubt [and] to buy political influence. . . . That's it. Not truth, not science, not economics, not safety, not policy, and certainly not religion, nor morality. Nothing supports climate denial. Nothing except money. But in Congress, in this temple, money rules. . . . In our arrogance, we here in Congress think that we can somehow ignore or trump Earth's natural laws . . . with our own political lawmaking, with our own political influence. But we're fools to think that.[119]

We must hope that the rule of fools will soon be over.

14

MORAL CHALLENGE

*"Climate change is a moral issue of unprecedented scope,
a matter of intergenerational injustice, as today's adults
obtain benefits of fossil fuel use, while consequences are felt
mainly by young people and future generations."*
— James Hansen, 2012

*"Reducing our carbon footprint is . . .
the human rights challenge of our time."*
— Bishop Desmond Tutu, 2014

Fossil-fuel corporations, aided and abetted by political leaders and the major media, especially in the United States, have already put sufficient CO_2 into the atmosphere and ocean to guarantee that coming generations will live on a much less pleasant planet. The crucial question now is whether the political world, with continued inaction, will inflict on coming generations a planet that is not merely unpleasant but hellish – a hellish world that, with still more inaction, will lead to the destruction of civilization. Or will the political world finally rally, acting fast and decisively enough to save a tolerable planet for our descendants? This is an unprecedented moral challenge.

The basic statement of the National Climate Ethics Campaign, which was started in 2011, says:

> The U.S. has failed to take aggressive action on climate change in large part because the issue has been framed around economic self-interest: opponents of action claim that the costs to jobs and the economy are too high; proponents of action claim emission reductions will create jobs and be good for the economy. Missing from this debate is the deeply disturbing moral and ethical implications of climate change.[1]

This challenge, as Bill McKibben has said, is "the greatest challenge humans have ever faced."[2] To have a chance of meeting this challenge, the human race will need to give *primary* attention to this task for at least the next three decades. During this period, the human race will need to operate out of a moral stance that, far from belittling the importance of this task, provides motivation to make whatever sacrifices and tough decisions will prove to be necessary. Decisions need to be made, in other words, on the basis of climate morality.

Climate Morality

An adequate treatment of the issues involved in climate morality would be long and complex, but some of the main issues can be mentioned.

A Global Ethic

Although it is sometimes claimed that there are no universal moral principles, this is an exaggeration of the truth about cultural relativism. Many commentators have pointed out that there is sufficient commonality in the various traditions to ground a global ethic.[3]

Roman Catholic theologian Hans Küng, in a book entitled *A Global Ethic for Global Politics and Economics*, has pointed out that all, or at least most, religious traditions affirm some version of what Christians have called the golden rule – at least in its negative formulation, sometimes called the "silver rule": Do not do to others what you would not want them to do to you.[4]

Even Michael Walzer, who had previously emphasized cultural relativism, has argued that the various traditions provide "the makings of a thin and universalist morality." Such a morality would be "a set of standards to which all societies can be held – negative injunctions, most likely, rules against murder, deceit, torture, oppression, and tyranny." Within Western civilization, he added, "these standards will probably be expressed in the language of rights," which "is not a bad way of talking about injuries and wrongs that no one should have to endure."[5]

Ten Climate Commandments

This is also not a bad way of talking about morality in relation to global warming. Phrased in terms of negative injunctions and couched in biblical language, we could state ten climate commandments thus:

> Thou shalt not deprive people of clean air.
> Thou shalt not deprive people of clean water.

Thou shalt not destroy people's soil.

Thou shalt not flood people's crops and villages.

Thou shalt not otherwise deprive people of means to live.

Thou shalt not ruin people's seas.

Thou shalt not burn people's trees and homes.

Thou shalt not force people to migrate.

Thou shalt not lie to justify any such acts.

Thou shalt not ruin people's climate and weather.

The fossil-fuel corporations have violated all of these commandments. By failing to protect people from these violations, the US government, along with many other governments, is equally responsible for the violation of these commandments. By way of illustrating the minimal amount of protection that people should be able to expect from the present system of global governance, which is led by the United States (although officially by the United Nations), ethicist Henry Shue used the 1994 Rwanda massacre:

> Any system of global governance [said Shue] is ridiculous if it allows . . . people with machetes [to] move house to house, day by day, hacking unarmed civilians to death until half a million innocents have been murdered and twice that number of people have fled from their homes in panic.[6]

This provides a good analogy for what is going on with climate change. Our system of national and global governance is ridiculous insofar as it allows people owning oil, coal, and natural gas companies to pollute our air and oceans day after day, year after year, decade after decade, getting filthy rich by violating all 10 climate commandments, thereby making the planet increasingly inhospitable. These moral reprobates – both the fossil-fuel corporations and the governments that give them a free hand, even providing them with subsidies and low taxes – have already forced millions of people from their habitats, with many tens of millions to follow. It is long past time for the climate commandments to be enforced.

Basic Human Rights

Although the language of "ten commandments" alludes to a particular tradition, Henry Shue, like Michael Walzer, refers to *universal* rights – rights that belong to humans qua humans. In referring to the Universal Declaration of Human Rights, which was approved by the General Assembly of the United Nations in 1948, James Nickel wrote that it referred to rights that are "universal, to be held by people simply as people."[7]

This idea, which goes back at least to the Stoic philosophers, was articulated in 1789 in the French Declaration of the Rights of Man, which spoke of rights that are "natural" and hence *"imprescriptible."* The same basic idea was expressed in the American Declaration of Independence, which spoke of "unalienable rights." This idea has, of course, had major effects. For example, philosopher Alfred North Whitehead pointed out that the idea of "the essential rights of human beings, arising from their sheer humanity," was a necessary condition for the 19th-century delegitimation and abolition of slavery in the West.[8]

The idea of human rights is equally relevant to the delegitimation and abolition of energy systems based on fossil fuels, which will be necessary if human beings in coming decades and centuries are to enjoy their right to a comfortable climate, a flourishing ocean, and clean air and water.

Building on the idea of human rights, Henry Shue, in a book called *Basic Rights*, distinguished between basic and less basic rights. Some human rights are basic because the "enjoyment of them is essential to the enjoyment of all other rights." One of those basic rights – which is stated at the outset of the Declaration of Independence – is the right to life. This right implies rights regarding everything necessary for life. Although the American government has recently given primary attention to violations of physical security, ethicist John Vincent, agreeing with Shue, has written that "the right to life is as much about providing the wherewithal to sustain life as protecting it against violence."[9]

Shue pointed out, moreover, that John Stuart Mill even gave it priority, saying that security from violence is the "most indispensable of all necessaries, after physical nutriment." This point was also made in the 1980 Presidential Commission on World Hunger, which said: "Whether one speaks of human rights or basic human needs, the right to food is the most basic of all. Unless that right is first fulfilled, the protection of other human rights becomes a mockery."[10]

Food is, of course, not the only basic right implied by the right to life. The right to water to drink and to grow food is equally necessary for life, as is the right to non-toxic air and other necessities. To come to the main implication of the distinction: Basic rights, by virtue of being basic, trump all nonbasic rights. Rights that are essential to life are people's *vital interests* in the most literal sense of the term. The vital interests of people should always take precedence over the non-vital interests of others. Even if these non-vital interests be considered *rights*, they are not *basic* rights and hence can be trumped.

Some people hold that an interest in having an unlimited amount of money gives one a right to make it, along with a right to have all the luxury items one desires. But insofar as a right to such riches and luxuries exists – it is really a desire, not a right – it would be immoral to allow it to trump the vital necessities, and hence basic rights, of others. Shue noted that John Locke, whose writings inspired much in early American thought, "had taken for granted that the right to accumulate private property was limited by a universal right to subsistence."[11]

In light of these moral principles, the "right" of ExxonMobil, Chevron, and the Koch brothers to accumulate more and more money would, in a moral system of national and global governance, be trumped by the basic rights of peoples around the world to have non-toxic air, non-polluted water to drink, adequate water for agriculture, thriving land and marine life, and a sea level that will not force them to move.

Intergenerational Justice

Climate-concerned ethicists and activists generally and rightly focus on intergenerational justice, which means that "today's youth and future generations must have at least the same opportunities to meet their own needs as the generation governing today." For example, Graeme Taylor has said: "Preserving life on earth and protecting our children's futures is not just one task among many – it is the most important ethical and practical issue facing humanity. If we do not take immediate action to reverse climate change, our children and grandchildren will inherit a dying world."[12]

The most famous statement about intergenerational justice is the "Great Binding Law" in the *Constitution of the Iroquois Nations*, which says:

> In all your official acts, self-interest shall be cast into oblivion. . . . Look and listen for the welfare of the whole people and have always in view not only the present but also the coming generations, even . . . the unborn of the future Nation.[13]

How many coming generations? Oren Lyons, chief of the Onondaga Nation (one of the nations of the Iroquois Confederacy), said: "We are looking ahead, as is one of the first mandates given us as chiefs, to make sure and to make every decision that we make relate to the welfare and well-being of the seventh generation to come."[14]

Besides being thus affirmed by this continent's early inhabitants, intergenerational equity is also quintessentially American, having been affirmed by Thomas Jefferson while writing to James Madison about the proposed Bill of Rights. Discussing it as self-evident, Jefferson used the old-fashioned term "usufruct," which means the right to make all the use and profit of a thing that can be made without injuring the substance of the thing itself. What is wrong, Jefferson said, is "eating up the usufruct," which means extinguishing the next generation's ability to share equitably in the benefits of a natural resource. In pointing out that this principle is self-evident, Jefferson said that none of us "consider the preceding generation as having had a right to eat up the whole soil of their country." Therefore, it is self-evidently wrong for our generation to use up our country's top soil – or any other natural resource, including the atmosphere.[15]

Intergenerational justice is the moral principle most enunciated by climate scientists.

- "The basic matter," James Hansen has said, "is not one of economics. It is a matter of morality – a matter of intergenerational justice. The blame, if we fail to stand up and demand a change of course, will fall on us, the current generation of adults."[16]

- "As a father of a six-year-old daughter," Michael Mann wrote in 2012, "I believe we have an ethical responsibility to make sure that she doesn't look back and ask why we left her generation a fundamentally degraded planet relative to the one we started with."[17]

- "Only three generations back," said Thomas Lovejoy, "my great-grandfather chaired the commission that designed the New York subway system. How was he to anticipate the sea-level rise that contributed in part to the impact of Hurricane Sandy? How will things look just two or three generations ahead? Can we avoid the greatest intergenerational environmental injustice of all time?"[18]

- Stanford's Ken Caldeira wrote: "Economists estimate that it might cost something like 2% of our GDP to convert our energy system into one that does not use the atmosphere as a waste dump. When we burn fossil fuels and release the CO_2 into the atmosphere, we are saying 'I am willing to impose tremendous climate risk on future generations living throughout the world, so that I personally can be 2% richer today.' I believe this to be fundamentally immoral."[19]

Caldeira's statement points to the source of the failure to deal with climate change that was discussed in the previous chapter: greed. The failure to think in terms of intergenerational justice is significantly caused by the values inherent in our present political economy. "In the moral calculus of today's capitalism," Noam Chomsky has said, "a bigger bonus tomorrow outweighs the fate of one's grandchildren."[20]

Part of the problem is that the most influential contemporary moral theories provide no basis for affirming objective moral truths, hence no basis for saying that saving the planet for future generations is a moral duty.[21] This issue is discussed in the following chapter.

Climate Responsibility

In discussing intergenerational justice, Hansen wrote that "today's changes of atmospheric composition will be felt most by today's young people and the unborn, in other words, by people who have no possibility of protecting their own rights and their future well-being."[22] In putting it that way, Hansen alluded to another basic principle of climate morality – that the countries and companies that have been most responsible for global warming, and that have benefited most from the burning of fossil fuels – need to accept primary responsibility to pay for mitigation (preventing climate disruption from becoming any worse than is already inevitable) and to help poor countries with adaptation (dealing with the climate disruption that is no longer preventable).

Although none of the rich countries have taken issue with this principle in the abstract, most of them have used various means for avoiding its concrete implications. As the Environmental Justice Foundation pointed out in 2012, "the UN climate negotiations have resulted in a formal acknowledgement from the USA and other developed nations that there will be a bill to pay for the havoc that will come from climate change and they will have to pick up at least some of [the] tab." However, it added, the talks have thus far "failed to create a path from recognizing the causes and costs of climate change to delivering the funds and the action to solve these."[23] The EJF continued:

> [O]ur lifestyle choices have tangible impacts on others. Nothing demonstrates this better than the impacts of climate change. Our industrialization, development and consumerism have a price – but we in the developed world are not paying it.[24]

For example, global warming has already created a great injustice by destroying the lives of millions of people by raising the level of the seas. Discussing this issue from a justice point of view, an article at the Earth Reform website says:

> The irony with climate refugees rests in the fact that those being forced to leave their homes and land have played close to no role in increasing the rate of climate change. The level of greenhouse gases emitted by these developing

> countries is close to nothing in comparison to developed
> countries. So while industrialized nations continue to
> pump out pollutants by the ton and enjoy the luxury that
> is ignorant bliss, the effects are felt millions of miles away
> on villagers in self-sustaining communities, where *people
> are forced to pay the price for the mistakes of developed
> countries.*[25]

But although the rich nations, especially the United States, have continued to increase this injustice by accelerating their burning of fossil fuels for two decades after scientific studies showed that this would wreak havoc for island and coastal communities, these nations have thus far shown little inclination to do what they could do to make amends. At the 2009 climate conference in Copenhagen, the countries were supposed to negotiate the long-awaited climate treaty. But the conference stagnated, wrote Rebecca Solnit, "because the rich countries were unwilling to either reduce their own emissions significantly or pledge meaningful funding to help poor nations transition to greener economies." Furthermore, she said,

> the United States, which just spent nearly a trillion dollars
> bailing out its floundering financial corporations and spends
> about $700 billion annually on the military, offered an
> obscenely inadequate $1.2 billion in aid.[26]

At the 2010 climate meeting in Cancun, the government leaders from over 190 countries belatedly *said* the right thing, agreeing that climate migrants qualify for assistance from the UN Green Climate Fund, which is supposed to be increased annually until 2020 when it will have $100 billion a year to assist such people. But thus far, the US has not even made a first step towards paying its fair share. Indeed, Todd Stern, the U.S. State Department's envoy on climate issues, bluntly said in November 2013 that the richest nations will not be providing large-scale compensation to poorer nations that have been severely hit by climate change (in spite of all the beautiful statements by his boss).[27]

Equity

As we saw in the previous chapter, the United States, beginning with the first President Bush, endorsed the principle that, because the United States and other nations that industrialized early had been primarily responsible for climate change, they should take the lead in combating it. This principle, under the name Berlin Mandate, was the main reason why the Kyoto Protocol was rejected preemptively by a 95-0 vote on a US Senate resolution, which objected to the idea that less developed countries would not be held to the same standard as the United States. This was an explicit rejection of the principle that those who caused the greatest ill and benefited the most should pay the most.

Some Americans argue that it would not be fair for us to pay more, because China and India are increasing their emissions so fast that they are now equally responsible for global warming. However, climate change is not driven primarily by current emissions, but by *cumulative* emissions, and China since 1750 has been responsible for about 10% of the CO_2 emissions, while the USA has been responsible for about 27% – almost three times as much as China. Even if China and India were treated as one country, they together would be responsible for less than 13% of the cumulative emissions, still much less then the USA's 27%.[28]

Also, responsibility and fairness should be measured in terms of *per capita*, not national, emissions (otherwise, one would be saying that China should have no more emissions than Luxembourg). In these terms, the contrast is even greater. The USA and Europe, as the parts of the world that were first industrialized, have a combined population of about 1.05 billion, which is less than either China's 1.35 billion or India's 1.3 billion. But the cumulative USA-plus-Europe emissions are about 58% of the world's total – almost six times greater than China's 10% and some 19 times more than India's 3%.

Moreover, if we compare the USA-plus-Europe total with the China-plus-India total, the contrast is only slightly different: 58% to 13%, although the China-plus-India population is about 2.65 billion. So the per capita cumulative emissions of the people in China-plus-India is tiny in comparison with the per capita emissions of the people in the USA-plus-Europe. Americans and Europeans should not, therefore, seek to rationalize their privilege by claiming that China and India are, or soon will be, equally responsible. Germany's Angela Merkel was the first leader of a G8 nation to endorse the per-capita principle.[29]

Accordingly, all discussion of equity should presuppose two indubitable facts. (1) Global warming is due to *cumulative* greenhouse gas emissions, not current emissions, nor current-plus-projected-future emissions. (2) The cause of climate change – as a result of which glaciers and Arctic ice are melting, seas and temperatures are rising, and weather has become more extreme – is primarily the cumulative emissions of the USA and Europe.

Equity, in terms of paying for the changes that are needed to prevent climate disruption from being much worse, can only be discussed in terms of cumulative and per capita emissions. But thus far Western nations, especially the USA, have refused to accept equity in this sense. According to Naomi Klein: "What has bogged down every round of UN negotiations on climate is the basic principle that the people who are most responsible for creating this crisis should take the lead and bear a heavier burden."[30]

Those countries that have been most responsible for global warming are also those that have benefited the most from it economically. There is, therefore, a twofold basis for judging the fair share of the various countries in paying poorer countries for mitigation and adaptation. However, whereas equity on this twofold principle (responsibility plus benefit) is the main basis for duties to help poor countries with adaptation and mitigation, the actual mobilization to save civilization should be based on the principle that "we are all in this together," with all countries and all people doing the most they can. When a boat is in danger of sinking, the passengers should not be worried about having the best clothes and the best view, but only about preventing the boat from sinking.

Divestment

One way to battle against the destruction of civilization by greenhouse gases is to encourage people and institutions to divest from fossil-fuel companies, basing this encouragement on a moral argument supported by a financial argument.

The Moral Argument

The moral argument says, in Bill McKibben's words, "if it's wrong to wreck the climate, it's wrong to profit from that wreckage." It is time to be "going after the fossil fuel companies," because theirs is a "rogue industry." "Mr. McKibben's goal," said *New York Times* writer Justin Gillis, "is to make owning the stocks of these companies disreputable, in the way that owning tobacco stocks has become disreputable." Another precedent appealed to by McKibben was the movement to divest from apartheid South Africa, which was crucial in bringing that system down. By turning fossil-fuel industries "into pariahs," McKibben argues, their "chokehold on politics" can be weakened.[31]

Indeed, Bishop Desmond Tutu wrote: "Just as we argued in the 1980s that those who conducted business with apartheid South Africa were aiding and abetting an immoral system, we can say that nobody should profit from the rising temperatures, seas and human suffering caused by the burning of fossil fuels."[32]

McKibben's divestment campaign began with colleges and universities, where faculties and students seek to convince their administrations and trustees that they should divest. Although several schools quickly saw that this would be the right thing to do, many did not. At Harvard, 72 percent of the students said that the school should divest, but its president, Drew Faust, said that divestment would be neither warranted nor wise: The task of the administration and trustees is to protect and increase its endowment, which should not be used for social purposes. Her argument was publicly challenged by then-Mayor Mike McGinn of Seattle, which had already divested. He agreed that she needed to make sure that Harvard's endowment would be there for future generations, just as he as mayor had to protect the city's pension system. But, he added, "We also share a greater and overlapping responsibility - one to our planet and to future generations," so they needed to figure out how to do both. He also argued that Harvard has a special responsibility: Having "the largest academic endowment in the world, one that rivals the size of the economies of many countries, Harvard is uniquely positioned to lead on this issue."

Responding to Faust's statement that divestment would mean "using the endowment as an instrument of political and social change," he reminded her that Harvard had done this before, when in 1990 it divested from the tobacco industry. This decision was motivated, then-President Derek Bok had explained, because Harvard did not want to be "associated as a shareholder with companies engaged in significant sales of products that create a substantial and unjustified risk of harm to other human beings."[33]

Although the program to divest has now expanded to all public-interest institutions, especially seminaries and churches – including the World Council of Churches, which represents a half billion people[34] – it was wise for divestment movement to begin with colleges and universities, because just as the anti-Vietnam-war movement was primarily fueled by students, who did not want to die or have their friends die in a immoral war, young people do not want their futures destroyed by climate disruption. One student said: "By the time we're ready to have kids, buy a home – it's already a radically different world if we don't put the brakes on as quickly as possible." Other students, disappointed that their school's board of trustees had rejected their call to divest, said: "When it comes down to it, the members of the board are not the ones who are inheriting the climate problem. We are."[35]

However, the appeal to students is not merely to their self-interest. McKibben tells them, "this is not only the crisis of your lives – it is also the crisis of our species' existence."[36]

The Financial Argument

The financial argument for divestment is that fossil-fuel stocks are becoming increasingly risky, so if individuals and institutions do not delete them from their portfolios, they are liable to lose a lot of money. This argument was stimulated by Carbon Tracker, which pointed out that, because we now know that most of the carbon in the ground must stay there, to prevent runaway global warming, those having portfolios with many fossil fuel stocks are destined to end up with lot of stranded assets, meaning that they will be worthless.[37]

Al Gore, who is now the chairman of an investment firm, has referred to the estimated $7 trillion in carbon assets on the books of multinational energy companies, saying: "The valuation of those companies and their assets is now based on the assumption that all of those carbon assets are going to be sold and burned. And they are not." Although people might believe that Gore's opinion is biased because he is opposed to fossil fuels, this warning has already been made in a study ("Oil and Carbon Revisited: Value At Risk From 'Unburnable' Reserves") prepared by HSBC Global Research.[38]

This case has also been made by Craig Mackenzie's Scottish Widows Investment Partnership, a division of Lloyds Banking Group, which has about $230 billion of assets under management. McKenzie has said that "many have a misinformed view that carbon assets will not be stranded until there is a global treaty establishing a uniform price on carbon." McKenzie's institution has, in fact, already sold all of its carbon stocks.[39] Another misinformed view, says Tom Steyer – who founded a hedge fund and is now a billionaire – is that people can wait to get out just before the bubble bursts. That, says Steyer, is "one of the stupidest things I've ever heard."[40]

The Combined Argument

Whereas some people focus on one or the other of the two arguments, some people combine them. Professors at Cornell University wrote:

> Although some financial sacrifice in pursuit of our institutional responsibility would be justified, we have . . . determined that [divestment] will not only have a negligible impact on growth of the university's endowment, [it] may significantly reduce overall risk in the university's investment portfolio.

Likewise, Daniel Kammen, who teaches energy studies at the University of California, has said:

> UC Berkeley and most institutions are financially invested in destroying our future. Instead of funding the problem, we should be investing in solutions that at once aid the transition to a low-carbon economy and grow our university's bottom line. There is no lack of financially and environmentally sustainable reinvestment opportunities.[41]

Finally, this twofold argument has been made on the occasion of the biggest divestment decision to be made so far by one of the major funds, the Rockefeller Brothers Fund: Just before the UN climate meeting in September 2014 at which the announcement was made, Steven Rockefeller, who is a philosophy professor as well as a trustee of the Fund, said, "We see this as having both a moral and economic dimension."[42]

Abolition

An increasing number of writers have been saying that we need a new abolitionist movement: Just as it was necessary at one time for slavery to be abolished, it is now necessary to abolish the fossil-fuel economy.

The Slavery Analogy

Although modern industry is now a threat to civilization, it was originally a great boon, being crucial for the elimination of slavery – an institution that had long been assumed to be necessary for high civilization.[43]

This assumption was held in both Great Britain and the American South, where slaves were a primary source of energy and wealth. "[S]lavery was the most efficient means," wrote historian John McNeill, "by which the ambitious and powerful could become richer and more powerful. It was the answer to energy shortage." David Brion Davis added that, "what made slavery so appealing and seductive, especially in the long era before self-powered appliances, engines, and other labor-saving devices, was the freedom it brought for slaveholders."[44]

The Moral Problem
But there was a problem: Slavery was immoral. At first, only a few white people, primarily a small group of Christians, felt this way strongly enough to start arguing that slavery should be abolished. But these "abolitionists," arguing forcibly and convincingly, began building a movement. The dominant view, however, was that abolition was neither possible nor necessary. "Slavery," wrote Jean-François Mouhot, "seemed normal and indispensable."[45]

When abolitionists began their work in England, stated Andrew Hoffman, "the response was clear and unequivocal: such a move was out of the question as it would cause the collapse of the British Empire's economy and way of life." In the United States, said Charles Justice, "The entire white population of the South rallied around the cause of slavery." Leah Schade, summarizing two of their arguments, wrote:

[F]or 200 years our economy ran on 'slave-fuel.' It was

powered by subjugated human labor. Not only was it inconceivable for our country's economy to function without slaves, there was also biblical and theological rationalization of the practice.[46]

Even if slavery could be eliminated, the leaders of the Confederacy argued to Lincoln, the change to a different economic system would simply cost too much. The abolitionists fought against all of these arguments with "one trump card: forced labour was morally wrong." And this argument gradually won the day:

> Slowly but surely, the idea of buying and selling human beings, of separating members of slave families, of punishing slaves with whippings and other forms of torture, came to be seen as morally unjustifiable.[47]

A recent article in Salon said: "Once third-rail issues transform into moral imperatives, impossibilities sometimes surrender to new realities." Using the rapid acceptance of equal rights for LGBT persons as an example, it argued that the same could occur with immigration and gun control. On this basis, Joe Romm argued that we should, as President Obama started doing in his second term, emphasize climate change as a moral issue, because of our obligation to future generations. This is right. But there is an important way in which climate change, like slavery, differs from LGBT rights, immigration, and gun control.[48] The moral argument by itself probably would not have been sufficient for the abolition movement to prevail, given all the advantages the slave-system had for the ruling class. A technological advance was necessary.

The Fossil-Fuel Technological Advance

As Lloyd Alter said, it was "not a coincidence that the movement to abolish slavery started in nations that, thanks to the Industrial Revolution, didn't need them anymore." Jean-François Mouhot made a similar point, saying that "slavery came to be challenged and finally abolished when people became aware of an alternative . . . - steam power." Fossil-fuel energy had enormous advantages, because it led to the creation of what Buckminster Fuller called "energy slaves" (machines powered by fossil fuels), which, Fuller said, are "enormously more effective [than human slaves] because they can work under conditions intolerable to man, e.g., 5,000°F."[49]

Thanks to these energy slaves, the human standard of living was elevated "to unprecedented levels." More precisely, energy slaves *democratized* this elevation: "Where [human] slavery allowed a mere fraction of the population to live in opulent luxury, fossil fuels allow much of the world to live as such." Most important, energy slaves were able to "do the work in our homes, fields and factories, which used to be carried out by [human] slaves."[50]

The New Moral Problem

By virtue of freeing the ruling class from the perceived need to enslave fellow human beings, fossil-fuel energy "was of course a great moral improvement," said Mouhot, but this was only "until we came to know the consequences of fossil fuel consumption."[51] As we have seen in the previous chapters, those consequences are many, including the likelihood of the destruction of civilization itself. A very strong case, accordingly, has been made for the abolition of the fossil-fuel economy.

Providing a twofold argument for complete abolition, Craig Altemose wrote: First, "We know from the science of 350 that there's already too much carbon in the atmosphere." Second, pointing out that abolitionists did not call for us to "reduce the number of slaves" or the Civil Rights Movement to have "reduced segregation," Altemose declared:

> When something is wrong, people in the past had the *courage* to . . . say that it was wrong, and that it needed to *stop*. They did not call for there to be less of it, they called for its end, for its abolition. That's what you do when something is wrong.[52]

However, the issue is not the complete abolition of fossil fuels, as if campers' propane burners should be made illegal. Rather, asking "what are we 'abolishing?'" Andrew Winston said: "What we want to abolish is our outmoded, broken economic and energy systems that threaten our survival." Likewise, although Leah Schade entitled her essay "Fossil-Fuel Abolitionists," what she argued was that "the fossil fuel economy needs to be completely abolished."[53]

Similarities of the Two Abolitions

In any case, our society thus far has not accepted the view that the fossil-fuel economy needs to be abolished. The case against the abolition of (or even reduction in) fossil fuels has, of course, been spearheaded by fossil-fuel companies and others who have a vested interest in oil, coal, and natural gas – just as the abolition of slavery was especially fought by slave-traders, plantation owners, and others who would suffer financially from abolition.[54] The reasons for not seriously entertaining fossil-fuel abolitionism have been remarkably similar to the early reasons for not taking the idea of the abolition of slavery seriously:

- "Just as few people saw a moral problem with slavery in the 18th century, few people in the 21st century see a moral problem with the burning of fossil fuels."[55]

- Insofar as they *are* aware of the moral problem, "most in our society simply cannot conceive a way for our economy to be powered by anything other than fossil fuels."[56]

- Just as the Confederacy had argued that, even if possible, abolishing slavery would be too costly, now with regard to "tackling climate change, we hear extreme versions of this objection all the time."[57]

- The great resistance to climate science is no surprise: "Our societies, like slave-owning societies, have a vested interest in ignoring the . . . consensus."[58]

- "US congressmen tend to rationalize fossil fuel use despite climate risks to future generations just as southern congressmen rationalized slavery despite ideals of equality."[59]

- The ease and wealth provided by slaves once gave people an incentive not to act on awareness of the immorality of slavery; today's "energy-slaves" give contemporary society "a powerful incentive not to act on climate change."[60]

These points suggest that, just as the arguments for abolition remained ineffectual so long as there seemed to be no alternative, the moral and scientific arguments for the abolition of fossil-fuel energy will remain ineffectual so long as people believe there to be no viable alternative.

Now There Is a Viable Alternative

A crucial issue for fossil-fuel abolition is, therefore, the need for widespread awareness of the viability of clean energy, which can supply the needed energy without much, if any, increase in cost, as will be shown in Chapter 17. People who already have this awareness have been advocating fossil-fuel abolition. For example:

- In 2004, Jeremy Hoff wrote: "Efficiency will buy us time. Discovering more oil will buy us nothing. Wind power freed slaves from the oar. . . . It will take all the power of the sun to free us from ourselves."[61]

- "With renewable energy achieving economic viability at the same time fossil fuels threaten to wreck the climate," Robert Scribbler has argued, "now is the time for a strong movement to abolish the use of fossil fuels and to hasten transition to sustainable energy."[62]

- "The greatest injustice of continued fossil fuel dominance of energy," wrote James Hansen in 2011, "is the heaping of climate and environmental damages onto the heads of young people and those yet to be born in both developing and developed countries. The tragedy of this situation is that a pathway to a clean energy future is not only possible, but even economically sensible."[63]

- Although "fossil fuels have been core to creating our modern world and bringing billions out of poverty," Andrew Winston has written, "we have alternatives and we know what we have to stop doing."[64]

The most important thing we need to do is to put fossil-fuel corporations out of business as soon as humanly possible. As Charles Justice has said, "There is no justification for putting the human race at risk for the sake of oil company profits." There is no justification, because we now have various types of clean energy, which will, if given the kinds of subsidies and tax breaks that have until now been given to fossil-fuel corporations, soon be able to take care of all our energy needs, and at a cost that will be less expensive than fossil fuels. Indeed, Lloyd Alter has said, "our energy slaves [have] become more expensive to feed."[65]

The argument for fossil-fuel abolitionism will only be completed, therefore, with the discussion of clean energy in Chapter 17. Just as slavery came to be seen as morally abhorrent to large numbers of people only after they became aware of the viability of fossil-fuel energy, the awareness of the viability of clean energy will soon bring the day, wrote Leah Schade, "when the idea of powering our world with fossil fuels will be simply abhorrent."[66]

Conclusion

In the film *Lincoln*, President Abraham Lincoln said – in a statement reportedly based on an actual statement – "Abolishing slavery settles the fate for all coming time, not only of the millions in bondage but of unborn millions to come. . . . We must cure ourselves of slavery." In an essay entitled "Obama's Legacy," Amy Luers has written: "Transitioning the world to a low-carbon economy will settle the fate not only of millions afflicted by air pollution today but also for millions of unborn children from the escalating devastation of climate change."[67]

This is, indeed, an unprecedented moral challenge. Rising to it will involve unprecedented religious and economic challenges.

RELIGIOUS CHALLENGE

"We should not and cannot leave our children's children with a fundamentally different planet. Perhaps we should replace the classic image of a polar bear on a small floating piece of ice, with an image of our great grandchild standing in line for his or her water ration."
— Jim Wallis, 2014

"If we don't limit global warming to two degrees or less we are doomed to a period of unprecedented instability, insecurity and loss of species. . . . [O]ur religious communities [must] speak out on the issue from their various pulpits."
— Bishop Desmond Tutu, 2014

Having discussed what some of our basic moral principles say about the CO_2 threat, this chapter looks at ways in which a religious worldview may relate to these principles, either supporting or undermining them, as well as whether it provides motivation to deal with the greatest challenge our species has ever faced. Because our deepest motivations, beyond concerns for survival, come from moral and religious convictions, we need, to meet this challenge, a worldview that is both moral and religious.

Because the United States is the country that is (a) most responsible for global warming and (b) most filled with climate denialism, this religious worldview needs to be germane to American culture. However, indicating what is "needed" does not mean that, simply because it is needed, a new worldview could be created out of whole cloth. The task, instead, is to lift up and emphasize features of our religious traditions that are especially relevant to the present task.

Religiously, American culture has been overwhelmingly Christian. More generally, it has involved the theism exemplified in Judaism, Islam, and Christianity. Most generally, this theism sees the world as created and guided by a purposive divine reality, usually called "God."

Max Weber famously said that modernity has resulted in the "disenchantment" of the world, because "the ultimate and most sublime values have retreated from public life." More prosaically, Weber meant that the cosmos was no longer believed to provide objective moral norms that could ground a public morality. Jürgen Habermas, the best-known social philosopher of recent times, held this disenchantment to be irreversible, because an enchanted worldview can be provided only by religion, and yet religion has been "deprived [by modernity] of its worldview functions."[1]

Many thinkers, recognizing that modernity disenchants the world, hold that an enchanted world is possible only by returning to (or simply retaining) the premodern worldview, with its supernatural deity. In *Reenchantment without Supernaturalism*, I argued, employing the school of thought known as process philosophy and theology, that this claim is false.[2] But even if it were true, climate morality would be undermined by supernaturalism.

Supernaturalism: A Worldview that Undermines Climate Morality

Although theism can support climate morality, it can equally well undermine it. The central feature of theism that undermines climate morality is supernaturalism, the defining characteristic of which is the *omnipotence* of the God who created the world – the idea that this divine being *can do anything* (except perhaps for things involving logical impossibilities). An example of supernaturalism is provided by Evangelical theologian Millard Erickson, who says that his religious community "operates with a definite supernaturalism - God resides outside the world and intervenes periodically within the natural processes through miracles."[3]

Bringing out the implication of this supernaturalism, Erickson says that nature "is under God's control; and while it ordinarily functions in uniform and predictable ways in obedience to the laws he has structured into it, he can and does also act within it in ways which contravene these normal patterns (miracles)."[4] This supernaturalistic worldview, with its omnipotent deity, can breed various beliefs and attitudes that undermine climate morality.

Climate Complacency

Given this worldview, Christians can be complacent about the problems discussed above in Chapters 1-10. This worldview is especially dangerous when it is held by political leaders. For example, Senator James Inhofe, whose book *The Greatest Hoax* was mentioned in Chapter 13, quoted Genesis 8:22 - "As long as the earth remains there will be seedtime and harvest, cold and heat, winter and summer, day and night." Inhofe then quoted a preacher who, speaking on a bitterly cold morning, said that "more than 3,000 years ago God promised that cold and heat should not cease, so I am strengthened by this weather which emphasizes the sureness of His promises." Inhofe concluded: "This is what a lot of alarmists forget. God is still up there, and He promised to maintain the seasons." Also, after quoting Genesis 8:22 and saying "God's still up there," Inhofe criticized the "arrogance of people [who] think that we, human beings, would be able to change what He is doing in the climate."[5]

This omnipotence-based complacency is shared by many members of the House of Representatives, such as Congressman John Shimkus (also discussed in Chapter 13), who expressed the same lack of concern, saying: "The Earth will end only when God declares it's time to be over. Man will not destroy this Earth."[6] In the same vein, Ralph Hall (R-TX) said in 2011 (when he chaired the House's Science, Space, and Technology Committee), "I don't think we can control what God controls."[7]

This climate complacency is also expressed by Calvin Beisner, the spokesman for the Cornwall Alliance for the Stewardship of Creation (which lay behind the Petition Project discussed in Chapter 11). In light of the omnipotence, omniscience, and faithfulness of God, Beisner said, it would be "an insult to God" to believe that global warming could lead to catastrophe.[8]

Rush Limbaugh has expressed a similar view: Taking issue with Secretary of State John Kerry's statement that climate change is "a challenge to our responsibilities as the guardians . . . of God's creation," Limbaugh said: "If you believe in God, then intellectually you cannot believe in manmade global warming." In Limbaugh's mind, the contradiction arises because believers hold that the world was created by an omnipotent deity, whereas Kerry was implying that "we are so . . . omnipotent that we can . . . destroy the climate."[9]

This view also affects the business world. In 2014, for example, the chairman of the Nestlé corporation said: "Are we God to say the climate, as it is today, is the one we have to keep? That's the way it's going to be? We are not God."[10]

Infallible Scriptures

The arguments by fundamentalist Christians against climate science generally presuppose a view of the Bible as having been infallibly (technically: "inerrantly") inspired, as illustrated by Shimkus and Inhofe.

Quoting the passage in Genesis in which God, after the flood, said that he would never again "destroy all living creatures," Shimkus said: "I believe that's the infallible word of God, and that's the way it's going to be for his creation." The following year, he underlined his certainty about his views, saying: "I do believe in the Bible as the final word of God." Inhofe did "not pretend to be a biblical scholar," but this fact did not lessen his confidence that he could safely use biblical passages, such as Genesis 8:22, to prove the needlessness of concern about global warming.[11]

This way of using scriptural passages has been shown to be untenable by the scientific study of the Bible, which can be said to have begun in earnest in the 17th century by Benedict Spinoza (1632-77).[12] Although the history of this scientific study of the Bible is far too complex to summarize briefly, the basic change in interpreting the Bible that came about froms this approach is that the Bible must be interpreted like any other book, rather than viewed as a divine deposit of truths coming directly from the creator of the universe. To settle truth about global warming by appeal to the Bible, while ignoring the results of the scientific study of this collection of writings, would be analogous to using the writings of René Descartes (1596-1650), along with those of Plato and Aristotle, to explain the truth about physics and cosmology.

The belief in the infallible inspiration of the Bible (or any other writings) is closely related to the belief in an omnipotent deity. As I have written elsewhere:

> The ideas of infallible revelation and inerrant inspiration presuppose that … supernatural interruption has occurred. Why? Because the normal way in which human beings arrive at their beliefs is an extremely fallible process, in which false beliefs can enter in through prejudice, wishful thinking, party spirit, the limited information available at a given time and place, and countless other factors. The belief that the ideas put forth by some particular human beings are infallible and inerrant, guaranteed to be devoid of error, presupposes that in these particular human beings the normal human processes of belief-formation, with their fallibility and tendency to error, have been supernaturally overruled, so that pure, unadulterated truth came forth.[13]

End-Times Belief

Concern for climate disruption is also undermined by the traditional Christian belief in "the Second Coming of Jesus Christ," according to which Jesus will return at the end of the world. A 2013 article published in the *Political Research Quarterly* found that "believers in Christian end-times theology are less likely to support policies designed to curb global warming than are other Americans." Whereas it makes sense that most other Americans "would support preserving the Earth for future generations," the "end-times believers would rationally perceive such efforts to be ultimately futile, and hence ill-advised."[14]

Rejection of Evolution

Besides providing a worldview in which the world could be brought to a quick end, the view of the Bible as infallible also provides an alternative to science's evolutionary worldview, according to which humans and other mammals developed through millions of years of biological evolution, built upon billions of years of cosmic and geological evolution. Supernaturalism, with its omnipotent deity who infallibly inspires scripture, allows people to accept the idea that our world came about only a few thousand years ago. According to a 2013 Pew Research poll, 33 percent of Americans reject evolution, holding instead that "humans and other living things have existed in their present form since the beginning of time."[15]

Evolution has, of course, long been rejected in America by fundamentalist-to-conservative Christians. Recently, Republicans have increasingly been introducing bills in state houses that would rule out, or at least provide alternatives to, both climate science and evolutionary science. This twofold target led to an expansion of the mission of the National Center for Science Education: Having been founded in 1981, it was originally devoted to "defending the teaching of evolution." But since 2012, it has been devoted to "defending the teaching of evolution & climate science."[16]

The fact that climate-science-denial is now combined with evolution-denial shows that the rejection of the consensus among climate scientists is an anti-science position, so that bills with this combination are referred to simply as "anti-science" bills. The fact that Republican politicians have succeeded in joining these two denials at the hip in Republican politics is shown by the fact that, just as the Republican candidates for the presidency in 2012 rejected climate science, none of the likely candidates for 2016 have confessed belief in evolution. The fact that this double denial has become the norm among Republican candidates was driven home by outsider Jon Huntsman's 2011 tweet, "I believe in evolution and trust scientists on global warming. Call me crazy."[17]

The denial of evolution reinforces the anti-science nature of the rejection of the scientific consensus about global warming and climate change, while increasing the tendency toward complacency bred by the belief in divine omnipotence. If our world was created within the past 10,000 years – as 46% of Americans believe, according to a 2012 Gallup poll – then our planet's becoming unfit for human life would not be much of a tragedy, because God could simply create a "new heaven and earth" in a "twinkling of an eye."[18]

In addition, belief in a young Earth destroys the basis for realizing the full seriousness of global warming for civilization – that it is taking us out of the Holocene era (as discussed below).

Extreme Weather as "Acts of God"

End-times believers also generally think of extreme weather events as "acts of God." For example, when end-times preacher John Hagee, who heads a megachurch in San Antonio, was asked whether he believed Hurricane Katrina to be divine punishment for immorality, he replied:

> All hurricanes are acts of God, because God controls the heavens. I believe that New Orleans had a level of sin that was offensive to God. . . . [T]here was to be a homosexual parade there on the Monday that the Katrina came. . . . And I believe that the Hurricane Katrina was, in fact, the judgment of God against the city of New Orleans.[19]

David Crowe, the executive director of Restore America, also spoke to the question of why Hurricane Katrina occurred: "The answer," he explained, "is found in understanding that man is not in control. God is! Everything in the sky, the sea and on earth is subject to His control." Saying that Katrina was "God's judgment on America," Crowe referred to the upcoming "gay, lesbian and transgender 'Southern Decadence' Labor Day gala."[20]

Given this perspective, extra-deadly hurricanes (as well as droughts, floods, tornadoes, and heat waves) are to be explained in terms of divine policies, not in terms of the human burning of fossil fuels. Humans are, to be sure, responsible, but not because of using too many fossil fuels, but because of sexual sins and permissiveness.

Vested interests in the status quo seize upon the belief that the world is in God's hands to promote the complacent assumption that continuing to burn fossil fuels will not destroy civilization, because "God will not allow it." History is, however, filled with examples of peoples who foolishly believed that they were under the mantle of divine protection. The assumption that human civilization as a whole is protected is simply one more example of this folly.

The Defeat of the Pro Climate Evangelicals

Climate morality is clearly undermined by the supernaturalist worldview described above, which can be called *extreme* supernaturalism. But there is a modified form of supernaturalism that does not support this denial. This position is supernaturalist, because it affirms belief in an omnipotent deity –

one that has the power to control all events in the world. But believers in this modified vision hold that God does not actually employ this power to control all events. Rather, they say, God allows freedom, so that the future is open.

This position – which has been called both "free-will theism" and "open theism" – has been growing in Evangelical circles, and it offers Evangelicals a better basis for climate morality than does traditional supernaturalism. The question, of course, is whether the Evangelical world will accept this offering, which has helped a growing number of Evangelicals to agree with moderate and liberal Christians that the churches should help try to lessen fossil-fuel emissions.

Richard Cizik

One of these is Richard Cizik, who was long the vice president for governmental affairs of the National Association of Evangelicals (NAE) – the largest umbrella organization of Evangelicals. Having become convinced of the urgency for governments to deal with global warming, he was primarily responsible for the creation of the Evangelical Climate Initiative (ECI), which, he said, "offer[s] a biblically based moral witness that can help shape public policy in the most powerful nation on earth, and therefore contribute to the well-being of the entire world."[21]

Cizik's modified version of supernaturalism is reflected in the ECI statement that "when God made humanity he commissioned us to exercise stewardship over the earth and its creatures," along with its realistic statement that if climate change intensifies, "Millions of people could die in this century because of climate change, most of them our poorest global neighbors."[22]

The ECI was endorsed by over 80 high-profile Evangelical leaders, including megachurch pastors Joel Hunter and Rick Warren, the head of the Salvation Army, and the presidents of 39 Evangelical colleges.[23] For his work as a "green Evangelical," Cizik was in 2008 named by *Time* magazine one of the top 100 most influential people in the world.[24]

Cizik's hope was that the ECI would lead the Evangelical movement to become a powerful force for dealing with climate change. And it appeared at first that this was going to happen. E.J. Dionne of the *Washington Post* said that "Evangelical Protestantism in the United States is going through a New Reformation." Frances FitzGerald wrote in *The New Yorker* of "The New Evangelicals." Juliet Eilperin of the *Washington Post* said that Cizik, Hunter, and others like them "have begun to reshape the politics around climate change."[25] Even very conservative Evangelicals such as Pat Robertson and Mike Huckabee started speaking out on behalf of environmental issues.[26]

However, by 2011, Molly Redden in the *New Republic* asked, "Whatever Happened to the Evangelical-Environmental Alliance?"[27] The answer was in part that the old Evangelicals had begun a counter-offensive.

In 2006, the Cornwall Alliance for the Stewardship of Creation published "An Evangelical Response to Global Warming," which was a point-by-point critique of the Evangelical Climate Initiative (ECI).

This Cornwall document – written primarily by the previously mentioned Calvin Beisner – especially attacked the ECI statement that the consequences of climate change will "hit the poor the hardest." To the contrary, said Beisner's organization, the attempt to mitigate climate change by cutting fossil fuels will hurt the poor much more than any climate change caused by global warming. The following year, the Cornwell Alliance "urged the NAE to make a clear public statement distancing itself from Rev. Cizik's personal activities."[28]

At the same time, James Dobson (Focus on the Family) and Tony Perkins (Family Research Council) – with the aid of reborn Watergate felon Chuck Colson – persuaded the head of the NAE not to sign the Evangelical Climate Initiative on the grounds that concern about climate change was not a "consensus issue." They also argued that concern for climate change would dilute Evangelical "family values" issues, especially the battles against abortion and same-sex marriage.[29]

Having long wanted to get Cizik fired, they found their opening in 2008 when Cizik, who had long worked against same-sex marriage, stated on NPR that he would accept civil unions, after which the head of NAE then forced Cizik to resign. Although the statement about civil unions was the occasion for the firing, Cizik, Dobson, and Perkins all said that the real reason was what Dobson called Cizik's "relentless campaign" against global warming.[30]

Another element in the answer to Redden's question was the growth of public denialism, which was bolstered by the rise of the Tea Party. Senator Inhofe declared 2009 "The Year of the Skeptic." Because of these factors, Redden said,

> Creationism and a "God is in charge" belief became prominent again, along with a sense that any attempt to take climate change seriously was somehow unfaithful. . . . The mood has shifted so far that GOP candidates must not only renounce any environmentally friendly policies, they must also explain their past support for them.

Joel Hunter told Redden that "his generation probably won't be shaking up the climate change debate like they'd hoped."[31]

Katherine Hayhoe

Cizik was not the only victim of the new hostility to climate change in

Evangelical politics. Another was first-rate climate scientist Katharine Hayhoe, the director of the Climate Center at Texas Tech University and an IPCC reviewer. Her modified supernaturalism is reflected in her statement that most Christians believe that "God was involved in creating the planet, and then gave it to mankind to care for," so that "people actually have a responsibility to protect the planet."[32]

In 2009, she and Andrew Farley – a pastor and her husband – published a book subtitled *Global Warming Facts for Faith-Based Decisions*. Like Cizik, she states the facts clearly and describes the problem as urgent. In 2014, she was included in *Time* magazine's list of the 100 most influential people in the world and was one of the featured participants in Showtime's climate series, "Years of Living Dangerously."[33]

Because of her Evangelical stance plus her expertise about climate change, she was asked to contribute a chapter for a book being edited by Newt Gingrich, who was running for the Republican presidential nomination. But after learning that Rush Limbaugh had criticized him for this plan, Gingrich had the chapter deleted. In an interview in 2012, Hayhoe said: "As a Christian community, we're currently allowing politics to inform our faith, rather than allowing our faith to inform our politics."[34]

Although the Cornwall Alliance was not mentioned in the interview, spokesman Calvin Beisner used Hayhoe's statement as an opportunity to launch a full-out attack on her, saying that her view was disproved by the fact that no politicians had written any of its publications. But in trying to argue that the Cornwall Alliance is driven entirely by theological concerns, Beisner concealed the fact that the Cornwall Alliance is a front for CFACT, which in turn is a front for ExxonMobil.[35] Certainly being a shill for the oil lobby cannot be considered apolitical.

In any case, Beisner then attacked Hayhoe, as he had done with regard to Cizik and the Evangelical Climate Initiative, for stating that concern for the poor provides a reason to reduce the burning of fossil fuels. To the contrary, Beisner argues, this concern provides a reason to increase it. This attack by Beisner and his Cornwall Alliance (along with other individuals and organizations), Redden observed, was ironic, because "concern for poorer nations at risk due to climate change had been one of the main selling points for creation care."[36]

This selling point had been used by the NAE after Cizik's departure in a 2011 publication entitled *Loving the Least of These: Addressing a Changing Environment*. Its lead author, Dorothy Boorse, said that "this booklet serves as a starting point to think about and discuss how climate change affects the poor and what we, as followers of Christ, can do about it." The booklet added:

> Wealthy people and nations may be affected by changes

to the climate, but we have resources to adapt. The poor do not. As followers of Jesus, committed to justice and compassion, we seek to understand the potential threats to the lives and well-being of poor and vulnerable people.[37]

With regard to who is correct – Beisner and the Cornwall Alliance, or Katherine Hayhoe, Dorothy Boorse, the NAE, Richard Cizik, and the Evangelical Climate Alliance – the headline of a 2013 *Guardian* article said: "World's Poorest Will Feel Brunt of Climate Change, Warns World Bank." The World Bank report said:

> No nation will be immune to the impacts of climate change. However, the distribution of impacts is likely to be inherently unequal and tilted against many of the world's poorest regions, which have the least economic, institutional, scientific, and technical capacity to cope and adapt.[38]

As illustrated by the ECI and NAE documents, a modified supernaturalism can support concern and excellent statements about global warming. Although this position failed to revolutionize the climate-change discussion, this failure can be attributed in large part to various external factors, especially the hostile climate created by traditional Evangelicals, the (ExxonMobil-funded) Cornwall Alliance, and the (Koch-funded) Tea Party.

An Internal Problem

However, there is also a problem internal to the new Evangelicals' modified supernaturalism. Insofar as it is still a version of supernaturalism, it holds that divine omnipotence could intervene at any time, an issue that has been much discussed in science-religion debates.[39] Although theologians who hold the free-will version of supernaturalism say that science cannot describe any events as miraculous "acts of God," they also usually add that such events can nevertheless occur.[40]

This position can undermine the seriousness of global warming. For example, the description of Hayhoe's book includes, as one of the questions people ask, "Why should Christians care about global warming when we know the world won't end that way?" The Evangelical Environmental Network declaration, "On the Care of Creation," ends by saying: "We make this declaration knowing that until Christ returns to reconcile all things, we are called to be faithful stewards of God's good garden, our earthly home."[41]

Will not confidence that the world will not be destroyed by global warming, at least for most members of this community, make the task of preventing the destruction of civilization seem less important? Advocates of this position may, to be sure, say that it should not. Joel Hunter said, "I think it's morally wrong to say that 'Well, this is all God's will and he's coming back soon anyhow, so we shouldn't be attending to it.'"[42] This attitude would indeed be wrong, but it is likely to make attending to climate change feel less urgent.

People who accept modified supernaturalism do argue, to be sure, that belief in God does not lessen the urgency of stopping climate change. For example, the NAE's *Loving the Least of These* says:

> It is tempting but unwise to assume that God would prevent us from drastically harming the earth. God is sovereign, yet he allows us to experience the natural outcomes of our own actions. . . . [H]umans have the freedom to make decisions that harm even the basic functions of ecosystems, decisions such as polluting the oceans and deliberately or carelessly setting forest fires. God does not always choose to step in and save us from the consequences of our actions in other areas of our lives, and we should not assume that he will do so when we are unfaithful stewards of the earth.[43]

Many Evangelicals believe, however, that although God has allowed the Jewish and Armenian holocausts and many other unspeakable events, God would certainly intervene to prevent humans from bringing civilization to a premature end. This belief goes far to explain why Evangelicals are, as polls have consistently shown, less likely than Americans in general to be very concerned about global warming. This will probably change only with the spread of a form of Evangelical Christian faith that has left behind the idea of divine interruptions.[44]

A closely related issue is whether the Evangelical view provides the basis not merely to say that reducing global warming would be a good thing, but to say that it is now, from a Christian point of view, a commandment. With reference to *Loving the Least of These*, Richard Cizik was glad that the NAE was now discussing climate change, but he remained "sharply critical of its failure to take a stance on the issue" (the NAE, rather than issuing its document as an "official policy statement," offered it as merely "a conversation piece"). Cizik said:

> To say that you care about the consequences of climate change, but you aren't willing to take a position on legal action to curb it, is like saying in the 1960s well, I appreciate the fact that African Americans want equality, but we're not going to do anything about it.[45]

Conclusion

The modified version of supernaturalism is greatly superior to the traditional version. But if climate morality is to be whole-heartedly supported, something better is needed.

Evolutionary Theism and Climate Morality

There is another worldview, which can be called "evolutionary theism," that can embrace climate morality without equivocation. To speak of evolutionary theism is to indicate that this worldview is both scientific and religious. Given the fact that most Americans accept both evolution and theism, such a worldview should in principle be attractive. However, both terms – "evolution" and "theism" – have been unacceptable to large numbers.

Evolution

The idea that human life came about through a long evolutionary process is rejected by many Americans because they have equated evolution with a *particular theory of evolution*, according to which evolution is an atheistic, meaningless process. Although this worldview is commonly called "Darwinism," this is a misnomer: Darwin himself affirmed theism of a sort, often called "deism," according to which God, after creating the world, no longer influenced it. Darwin combined this deism with evolution by affirming that God had created the world so that it would evolve. The universe could not be conceived, he said, as the result of chance – "that is, without design or purpose." With regard to human beings in particular, Darwin said that it was impossible to conceive "this immense and wonderful universe, including man with his capacity of looking far backwards and far into futurity, as the result of blind chance or necessity." Although Darwin had given up his early theological view, according to which the *details* of the world reflected a divine plan, he continued to affirm that beings with moral and intellectual qualities were intended.[46]

    The view of evolution as an atheistic, meaningless process is that of the 20th-century doctrine called *neo-Darwinism*. According to this view, there is no directivity to the evolutionary process. In place of cosmic directivity, neo-Darwinism holds that the evolutionary process results from nothing but natural selection operating on random variations. Stephen Jay Gould, for example, declared that the idea that evolution is completely "undirected" is "the central [neo]Darwinian notion." William Provine, a historian of neo-Darwinism, has described its upshot thus: "The universe cares nothing for us. . . . Humans are as nothing even in the evolutionary process on earth. . . . There is no ultimate meaning for humans."[47]

255

Insofar as Americans believe that they must choose between neo-Darwinism and supernaturalism, a high percentage will continue to accept the latter. Robert Pennock, a critic of Intelligent Design (ID) – which puts the evolutionary timeline within creationism, so that every detail is determined by an omnipotent Designer – says that the primary motivation of the ID movement is the conviction that accepting evolution leads to meaninglessness.[48]

Although neo-Darwinism has led many people to reject evolution, neo-Darwinism is merely *a particular theory about* evolution, whereas belief in *evolution as such* is simply the view that the present living species came about through "descent with modification," rather than each species' being a separate creation. This doctrine, sometimes called "macroevolution," was Darwin's primary concern, with any ideas about how it occurred being of secondary importance.[49]

There is no reason to reject evolution, therefore, on the grounds that it implies a meaningless universe. That consequence does follow from neo-Darwinism, but there are other, arguably better, theories about how evolution occurs – some of which are theistic.[50]

Evolution and Theism

Most discussions of "theism" are as confused as most discussions about evolution. The main problem is that theism has generally been identified in the West with the Jewish-Christian-Muslim view of God as an omnipotent being who created the world *ex nihilo* (out of nothing). Given this identification, all other views of deity were considered non-theistic and hence atheistic.

It is well-known that theism became discredited in intellectual circles during the 18th-century Enlightenment partly because of the problem of evil, namely, the problem of reconciling belief in an all-good, all-powerful creator with the world's evil (see Voltaire's *Candide*). But it also became commonplace in science-based circles to think that theism conflicts with the scientific view of the world: On the one hand, the scientific worldview says that there can be no interruptions of the normal cause-effect relations. On the other hand, (traditional) theism affirms an omnipotent, *ex nihilo* creator who can occasionally cause miracles (in the sense of events with no natural causes).

For example, a dilemma was stated by Harvard's Richard Lewontin in a review of a book by Carl Sagan. On the one hand, Lewontin said, explanations of phenomena from a materialistic and hence non-theistic standpoint sometimes result in "patent absurdity." On the other hand, this standpoint must be maintained, said Lewontin, because "we cannot allow a Divine Foot in the door. . . . To appeal to an omnipotent deity is to allow that at any moment the regularities of nature may be ruptured, that miracles may happen."[51]

It was largely these two problems created by traditional theism – the problem of evil and the conflict with science – that led to the atheistic, neo-Darwinian view of evolution. But there was no good reason for this development. The acceptance of the evolutionary perspective of the world, according to which our present existence came about through a process taking billions of years, undermines (along with other facts) the belief in divine omnipotence. That is, when people believed that the universe, complete with human beings, was created all at once a few thousand years ago, it made sense to believe that the universe was created by an omnipotent deity. But the discovery that the world was created through a long, slow evolutionary process makes that belief extremely implausible: Assuming that the divine creator wanted a world with (among other things) human-like creatures, with capacities for science, art, morality, and religion, why would the creator, if omnipotent, have left the universe without such creatures for most of its existence? One would need to wonder why this planet has had human beings for less than one millionth of its existence.

The evolutionary perspective implies that any divine creator must have power that is very different from the kind of power attributed to God in traditional theism. It has been the refusal to accept a reformed, up-to-date version of theism that has fed the atheistic view of evolution.

Moral Nihilism and the Fabric of the World

The atheistic view of neo-Darwinism led to the idea that the universe is amoral. Provine said, for example, that evolutionary biology, along with modern science in general, "directly implies that there are no inherent moral or ethical laws." Gould agreed, saying that "there is no 'natural law' waiting to be discovered 'out there.'" In philosophical circles, the neo-Darwinian framing of evolution has, by endorsing atheism, contributed to moral nihilism – which, in the words of Princeton moral philosopher Gilbert Harman, is "the doctrine that there are no moral facts, no moral truths, and no moral knowledge."[52]

Oxford philosopher John Mackie published a book entitled *Ethics*, which was subtitled *Inventing Right and Wrong*. Explaining this subtitle, Mackie said that moral values are not "part of the fabric of the world," so that "[t]here are no objective values." Spelling out the implication, he said that "if someone is writhing in agony before your eyes," there is no objective requirement that you should "do something about it if you can."[53]

Mackie's view that moral values do not belong to the fabric of the universe followed from his conviction that atheism is true. "[I]f the requisite theological doctrine could be defended," Mackie conceded, "a kind of objective ethical prescriptivity could be defended."[54] His argument that it could *not* be defended was given in his earlier book, *The Miracle of Theism*:

Arguments for and against the Existence of God, in which Mackie argued the existence of God to be highly unlikely, primarily because of the problem of evil. But Mackie discussed the existence of God only in terms of traditional theism, according to which one of God's attributes is that of being "able to do everything (i.e. omnipotent)."[55]

Gilbert Harman, besides defining moral nihilism, endorsed it. Holding what he calls "the sensible thesis that *all* facts are facts of nature," he declared: "Our scientific conception of the world has no place for gods" and – speaking of moral norms – "no place for entities of this sort."[56] On this basis, although Harman had indicated that he would avoid "endorsing some form of nihilism," he said that "there are no absolute facts of right or wrong." Instead, Harman said, there are only "relative facts about what is right or wrong," meaning relative to some set of conventions adopted by a particular society. But this is exactly what nihilism holds.[57]

Many people have, to be sure, denied that atheism necessarily leads to nihilism. That denial had been expressed in a 1982 book, *Evolution, Morality, and the Meaning of Life,* by Jeffrie Murphy. Arguing that morality does not depend on belief in God, he regarded Nietzsche's proclamation, "God is dead," as no "big deal." Later, however, Murphy became aware of the growing skepticism about the possibility of a philosophical (secular, non-religious) grounding of morality. Having seen that it is now widely assumed among nontheistic thinkers that there is "no reason to believe in the inherent dignity or sacredness of persons," Murphy asked a wider question (rhetorically): "How can one expect to dump God and a religious vision of the universe and yet retain a strong concept of the *sacredness* of anything?"[58]

The Religious Perspective

Murphy's new view is in line with that of the celebrated anthropologist Clifford Geertz. The traditional ground for moral motivation, said Geertz, was what he called the "religious perspective." This perspective involves "the conviction that the values one holds are grounded in the inherent structure of reality, that between the way one ought to live and the way things really are there is an unbreakable inner connection." It is this feature of the religious perspective that accounts for religion's moral vitality:

> The powerfully coercive 'ought' is felt to grow out of a comprehensive factual 'is.' . . . [The power of sacred symbols] comes from their presumed ability to identify fact with value at the most fundamental level.[59]

To affirm this identity of fact with value is to affirm the reality of something sacred, something holy. Beliefs about the holy generate feelings about how we ought to live, because we naturally want to be in harmony with that which is holy. David Hume famously argued that ought-statements cannot be generated from is-statements. That claim is true within nonreligious discourse. But it is not true within a religious framework, because is-statements about the holy reality do generate ought-statements. It is important, however, to recognize the truth of Hume's position within nonreligious discourse: If reality is understood to be neither holy nor rooted in something holy, then no statement about what we morally ought to do can be generated from a purely factual statement about the nature of reality. Therefore, once ethics is severed from any belief in a holy reality, it would be unable to provide justification and motivation for a moral life. And this is what we find.

For example, Bernard Williams, who taught at Cambridge University, argued that morality "can[not] be justified by philosophy." Given the modern rejection of theism, Williams said, we are forced to the conclusion that moral norms are not "part of the fabric of the world." We cannot say that being moral is important from the point of view of the universe, Williams said, because "to the universe . . . nothing is important."[60]

A similar conclusion about morality was reached by Jürgen Habermas. Given the "disenchantment of the world" brought about by the decline of theism, Habermas argued, philosophy cannot "provide a motivating response to the question of . . . why we should be moral," because we cannot "salvage an unconditional meaning without God." From the point of view of Habermas, therefore, a non-theistic worldview could not give us a moral reason to make any sacrifices for the sake of future generations.[61]

Climate Moral Nihilism

Moral nihilism – according to which there are no objective moral truths and values, hence no moral laws or ethical prescriptions – entails, of course, climate moral nihilism in particular. The philosophers quoted above would not be able to say that we have a duty to reduce our carbon emissions for the sake of preserving a decent climate for future generations. Accordingly, intergenerational justice, the central element of climate morality, is regarded as having no basis.

This moral nihilism has been expressed by some academics explicitly with regard to climate change. For example, in an edited book entitled *Obligations to Future Generations*, the first chapter argued *against* "the belief that we owe certain things to posterity," such as "an adequate supply of natural resources [and] a clean environment."[62]

This rejection of climate morality has also been expressed, of course, in less academic writings. One example appeared in a response to the blog article by Joe Romm entitled "Our Hellish Future" (as reported in Chapter 2), which discussed an NOAA-led warning of possible "scorching 9 to 11°F warming over most of inland U.S. by 2090." A person signed "Born in the 80s" responded:

> Who cares, I'll probably be dead by then. And if I'm still alive at that point, I still wouldn't care. Giving up big cars, McMansions, and meat for a few degrees of temperature difference is not a tradeoff I or many other people are willing to make.[63]

This would seem to be essentially the attitude of the Kochs and the CEOs of ExxonMobil and other fossil-fuel corporations, who apparently live by the motto, "Whoever dies with the most toys, wins."

In sum, just as climate morality is discouraged by supernaturalism, it is also discouraged by nihilistic atheism, according to which there is no objective basis for saying that it would be morally wrong to destroy the conditions for future generations to have satisfactory lives.

A Better Definition of Theism

The claim that atheism leads to moral nihilism has been widely resisted. And it is indeed false if atheism is defined as rejection of traditional Western theism, as it is by Mackie and others. But theism should not be understood in such a narrow way. As Charles Hartshorne and William Reese showed in *Philosophers Speak of God*, there are many conceptions of deity, some of which are quite different from the main kind that developed in Judaism, Christianity, and Islam, and like them, most of these conceptions regard morality as belonging to the fabric of the world.[64]

For example, Confucianism does not think in terms of Western theism, but it certainly holds morality to be rooted in the nature of things. The same is true of Buddhism: Although it has often been called atheistic, the only idea that it necessarily denies – because of its doctrine of the "co-dependent arising" of all things – is the idea that our universe was created *ex nihilo*. Few if any forms of Buddhism deny that religious-moral values belong to the fabric of reality.[65] Similar points can be made about other religions beyond the orbit of Christianity, Judaism, and Islam.

Accordingly, we need more universal definitions of the terms "theism" and "atheism." For one thing, the terms should involve, like the terms themselves, complete opposites. The formation of such definitions could begin with the fact that nihilism is not entailed by the rejection of traditional theism; it is entailed only by the idea that there is nothing beyond the totality of finite entities and processes. It was this idea that resulted in the claim that there is, in Harman's words, "no place" for any divine reality and, therefore, "no place" for moral norms.

This starting point allows us to define "theism" and "atheism" as complete opposites, so that each is the denial of the other: Either there is a "place" in which moral norms exist, or there is not. Atheism in the broadest sense can be defined, accordingly, as the doctrine that *the universe has no place for moral norms to exist,* so that they are not part of the fabric of the world. Theism in the broadest sense would, therefore, be the doctrine that *there is a place in which moral norms exist*. This "place" can be regarded as *theos*, deity, the divine reality – whatever more particular conception is in view. The more particular conception might regard God as a being distinct from the universe, or it might be considered, as Buddhist Jeremy Hayward puts it, "the wholeness of the universe" or "the universe considered in its unity." Likewise, the leading process philosopher after Whitehead, Charles Hartshorne, spoke of God as "the soul of the universe," describing his position as "panentheism" (which differs from both pantheism and traditional theism).[66] The conception can be considered theistic – in the sense of being the rejection of atheism – as long as it regards the universe as having, or being, a place in which moral norms exist.

To summarize: Just as the rejection of neo-Darwinism does not entail a rejection of evolution, a rejection of the omnipotent deity of traditional theism does not entail an atheistic view of the universe and hence moral nihilism.

Theism and Evolution

Just as evolution and climate science tend to be closely associated by certain sectors of Christian supernaturalists, with both being rejected, evolution and climate science are closely related from the perspective of naturalistic theism, but as affirmed, with an evolutionary perspective increasing the importance of morality based on climate science.

Theologian Paul Tillich, who had left Nazi Germany in protest, famously defined religion as "ultimate concern." Given that definition, matters of ultimate concern are by definition religious.[67] From the perspective of people who see the planet as created by an omnipotent deity only a few thousand years ago and that, if destroyed, could easily be replaced, the possibility that global warming might destroy civilization could be regarded as a matter of less than ultimate concern. It is very different from the perspective of evolutionary theism.

The evolutionary process reflects a direction, with the emergence of beings with increased complexity, which makes possible more sophisticated experience. But far from having the kind of omnipotence imagined by traditional theists, according to which God brought about transformations unilaterally, the spirit behind the evolutionary process can bring about transformations only slowly.

The spirit behind the evolutionary process is widely called "God." Many people find that, even after learning of the rejection in recent theology of the traditional notion of God, the word "God" has been ruined beyond repair. But there is no need for this word to stand in the way of affirming a religious view of the universe. One can use some other term, perhaps simply speaking of "the divine." What is important is seeing the evolutionary process that brought forth life and finally human beings as rooted in a divine reality, so that moral norms belong to the fabric of the universe.

The creation of our universe evidently occurred (according to the dominant theory) somewhat over 13 billion years ago. It was then roughly 9 billion years before the Earth was formed. After this formation, which occurred approximately 4.5 bya (billion years ago), the Earth underwent transformations for about a billion years before the most elementary forms of life emerged. After these simple cells appeared (about 3.5 bya), roughly another 1.5 billion years passed before the emergence of the kinds of cells (eukaryotic) from which plant and animal bodies are formed (about 2 billion bya). Almost another billion years passed before the emergence of multicellular organisms (about 1.2 bya), after which roughly a half billion years occurred before most of the modern types of animals appeared during the "Cambrian explosion" about a 500 mya (million years ago).

Mammals did not appear until roughly another 400 million years (100 mya), the first hominids not until about 6 mya, the first members of the genus *Homo* until about 2 mya, and the first anatomically modern humans about 200,000 years ago. Finally, civilization emerged about 10,000 years ago.

The Garden of Eden

As pointed out in the Introduction, a precondition for civilization was the emergence of the Holocene epoch. In biblical terms, it can be thought of as the Garden of Eden, in which the conditions for life were (relatively) ideal.

By making possible the emergence of civilization, with its agriculture and cities, the Holocene allowed for philosophy (as exemplified by Plato, Aristotle, Kant, and Whitehead); for modern science (as exemplified by Newton, Darwin, and Einstein); for modern medicine (as exemplified by Curie, Pasteur, Salk, and Sabin); for the flourishing of the arts (such as the plays of

Aeschylus, Sophocles, Shakespeare, Ibsen, and Arthur Miller; the novels of Austen, Dickens, Eliot, Melville, and Tolstoy); the paintings of Leonardo, Van Gogh, and Monet; the sculptures of Donatello, Bernini, Michelangelo and Rodin; and the music of Vivaldi, Bach, Mozart, Beethoven, and the Beatles). As far as we know, civilization – admittedly depicted here only in terms of Western civilization – could exist only in the global climate of the Holocene.

With regard to banishment from the Garden of Eden, the details of the biblical myth – according to which humanity was banished because of its violation of an arbitrary divine command – cannot be applied to our present crisis. But the general notion applies: We had been given ideal conditions for existence, but now we are in a process of being banished – or rather, banishing ourselves – because we are violating divinely grounded laws of nature that, rather than being arbitrary, are laws we understand: ecological laws that are rooted in laws of physics, chemistry, and biology.

An Unprecedented Religious Challenge

Today's challenge to religious thought and action is unprecedented. We are faced with a problem that had never been addressed by any religious traditions. People had always assumed that the human race would continue indefinitely. Or they have assumed that, if the human race were to disappear, this would be brought about by divine power, so the disappearance would be divinely intended. We had never faced the question of whether the human race would commit suicide.

Although human beings have been pondering the possibility of extinction since the rise of nuclear weapons, the present crisis is fundamentally different. Nuclear extinction would come about only if something extraordinary – starting a nuclear war – were done, whereas global warming will bring about human extinction if nothing extraordinary is done, so that the inertia of "business as usual" continues. For these reasons, the current challenge to religious thought and action is unprecedented.

More immediately, the basic religious challenge is for religious individuals, organizations, and institutions to speak out strongly about the various issues – as when Pope Francis called the destruction of the Amazon rain forest "a sin."[68] A few more examples of religious leadership are mentioned in the discussion of mobilization in Chapter 19.

ECONOMIC CHALLENGE

*"Climate change presents an unprecedented global challenge,
and impacts upon a wide range of human economic activity.*
– Bradly J. Condon and Tapen Sinha, August 2013

*"What is needed is an unprecedented re-channeling of investment
from today's economy into the low-carbon economy of tomorrow."*
– Achim Steiner, Executive Director, UN Environment Program, 2014

Besides being impeded by limited moralities and false religious ideas, society's task of saving civilization from climate disruption has also been impeded by destructive economic ideas, ones that undermine the drive to make the needed transition to an economy that is compatible with the continued existence of civilization. To have a chance of saving civilization, we need an economics very different from the type that has brought us to the brink of suicide. The most needed change is to reshape the planet's economies so as to quit increasing the greenhouse gases in the atmosphere. Put otherwise, the challenge is to make the changes in economic policy that are needed to facilitate a transition from a dirty-energy economy to a clean-energy economy – and to do so in an ethical way.

"Climate economics," in the words of Frank Ackerman and Elizabeth A. Stanton, "is the bridge between science and policy, translating scientific predictions about physical systems into projections about economic growth and human welfare that decision makers can most readily use."[1] The statements by climate economists are of crucial importance, because they make the declarations about climate change that are taken most seriously by policy-makers.

The first section of this chapter provides a little background to the recent discussion. The second section summarizes the radical changes that have occurred in the economics of climate change since 2006, due primarily to the *Stern Review*, which appeared that year. The third and fourth sections deal with the two most important *national* economic policies: instituting a carbon price and eliminating fossil-fuel subsidies. The fifth and sixth sections discuss the two *global* policies that are most needed to eliminate carbon emissions worldwide.

Background

When modern economic thought was developed a few centuries ago, the human economy was tiny in relation to nature, with its vast resources. Economic ideas were developed on the assumption that human industry would never be able to use up the planet's resources or harm its ocean and atmosphere. It was assumed, therefore, that economic growth could continue forever.

This assumption became, in fact, an unchallengeable dogma, as was illustrated by the hypercritical response to a 1972 book, *The Limits to Growth* (which was sponsored by the Club of Rome, founded to "rebel against the suicidal ignorance of the human condition"[2]). In summarizing the book's conclusions, the authors said:

> 1. If the present growth trends in world population, industrialization, pollution, food production, and resource depletion continue unchanged, the limits to growth on this planet will be reached sometime. The most probable result will be a rather sudden and uncontrollable decline in both population and industrial capacity.

> 2. It is possible to alter these growth trends and to establish a condition of ecological and economic stability that is sustainable far into the future. The state of global equilibrium could be designed so that the basic material needs of each person on earth are satisfied and each person has an equal opportunity to realize his individual human potential.[3]

Although the book's warning was only that, unless "global equilibrium" was achieved, sudden decline would occur "within the next one hundred years," the economic community's reaction was vitriolic, condemning the book as "doomsday prophecy." Yale University economist Henry Wallich called the book "irresponsible nonsense," and another Yale economist, William Nordhaus, wrote a review of the book upon which *Limits to Growth* was based, entitling it

"Measurements without Data." Two decades later, when an updated version of *Limits* appeared, Nordhaus wrote a review called "Lethal Model 2," saying that putting the book's recommendations into effect would "send humanity back to the living standards of the Dark Ages" and assuring readers that "an efficiently managed economy need not fear shipwreck on the reefs of resource exhaustion or environmental collapse."[4]

One economist who took the book seriously was Herman Daly, whose 1977 book, *Steady-State Economics,* was subtitled *The Economics of Biophysical Equilibrium and Moral Growth.* A steady-state economy, said Daly (who came to be called the "father of ecological economics"), was an alternative to "growthmania," which follows from regarding economic growth as "both the highest good and a panacea for all problems." Rather than being against growth as such, Daly came to criticize "uneconomic growth," which "impoverishes rather than enriches," because additional GNP "would increase costs more than it increased benefits."[5]

In 2008, Daly asked whether our society might find it possible to "overcome the growth idolatry." The notion of "growth idolatry" had been developed in Daly's 1977 book, *For the Common Good,* coauthored with theologian John B. Cobb, Jr. Following Paul Tillich, who had said that idolatry occurs when "something essentially partial is boosted into universality," Cobb and Daly defined idolatry as "commit[ting] oneself finally to anything less than the whole."[6]

Cobb later, speaking of the primary example of idolatry today, used the term "economism," defined as "the belief that primary devotion should be directed to the expansion of the economy." Since the middle of the 20th century, Cobb said, economism started becoming the dominant religion.[7] From that perspective, we can understand the vitriolic reaction to *Limits to Growth*: It was religious heresy.

From the Nordhaus Era to the Stern Era

Since the 1970s, when he essentially founded the economics of climate change, William Nordhaus had been considered its preeminent authority. According to a fellow economist, the optimal economic policy had for decades been simply "what Bill Nordhaus said." This view had been unquestioned until 2006, when the British government published a new review of climate change, led by Sir Nicholas H. Stern.[8] Stern, a professor at the London School of Economics, had served as the Chief Economist of the World Bank. The review that he led was published as *The Economics of Climate Change: The Stern Review,* usually called simply the *Stern Review*. This publication, which gave the world a radically different view of the economics of climate change, led to a new era in the field – a transition from the Nordhaus era to the Stern era.

This naming of a new era does not mean that everyone agrees. Journalists, at least in the United States, still refer to Nordhaus – as does the dust jacket of his 2013 book (*Climate Casino*) – as "the world's leading economic thinker on climate change." Rather, we can speak of the transition to a Stern era because his work, along with that of other economists inspired by it, has brought about a radical transformation in the field. The most helpful book on the subject, Frank Ackerman and Elizabeth A. Stanton's *Climate Economics,* said in 2011: "Stern opened the way for widespread innovation in climate economics. In the five years since the *Stern Review*, there has been a remarkable flourishing of new economic approaches."[9] The transition from the Nordhaus era to the Stern era can be described in terms of several contrasts.

From Balance to Urgency

Nordhaus preeminently exemplified the balance or cost-benefit approach. Although he called global warming "the major environmental challenge of the modern age," he did not express a sense of urgency about it. In his 2008 book, he said: "Neither extreme – either do nothing or stop global warming in its tracks – is a sensible course of action." Nordhaus thereby illustrated his central concern: balance – as indicated by the title of that book, *A Question of Balance*. The question was: "How to balance costs and benefits."[10]

In discussing the sea-level rise that would be caused by the melting of the Greenland and Antarctic ice sheets, he stated: "Although it is difficult to envision the ecological and societal consequences of the melting of these ice sheets, this situation is clearly highly undesirable and should be avoided unless prevention is ruinously expensive." It is startling to see him suggest that if we find avoiding the melting of these ice sheets "ruinously expensive," we should just let them melt.[11]

Nordhaus's 2013 book expressed a somewhat greater sense of urgency. While here he began with the observation that "policies to slow emissions should be introduced as soon as possible" and closed with "immediate action should be taken to slow and eventually halt emissions of CO_2 and other greenhouse gases," he continued to focus on cost-benefit balance, saying that "good policies must lie somewhere between wrecking the economy and wrecking the world."[12]

Nordhaus's focus on balancing our financial costs against benefits to the planet led him to advise our political leaders that they should pay for climate change mitigation, but only to the point at which "further reductions in damages are not worth the additional abatement costs." The target would be a compromise between the costs and the world: "[S]hort of catastrophic impacts," wrote Nordhaus, "we should look at the price tag before committing to any specific target."[13]

The *Stern Review*, by contrast, found climate change "demands an urgent global response," because "what we do in the next 10 or 20 years can have a profound effect on the climate in the second half of this century and in the next." The *Review*, however, did not reject the cost-effective approach. It simply said, in one of its most quoted statements: "*The [economic] benefits of strong, early action on climate change outweigh the costs.*"[14] While Nordhaus, in line with his lack of urgency, advocated a gradual "climate-policy ramp," in which "efficient or 'optimal' economic policies to slow climate change involve modest rates of emissions reductions in the near term," speeding up only later, Stern called for a "rapid transition to a low-carbon economy," in other words, "an energy-industrial revolution."[15] To stabilize carbon emissions within a few years, the *Stern Review* noted, "would mean immediate, substantial and global action to prepare for this transition." Nordhaus raised objections to Stern's "conclusions about the need for extreme immediate action."[16]

From Dated to Current Science

The analyses of climate change by economists, say Ackerman and Stanton, have "rarely portray[ed] the most recent advances in climate science." Instead, they tend to be "out of date by several years, if not decades." Saying that "[t]his near-universal disconnect between the science and the economics of climate change is nothing less than astounding," they add: "In order to be relevant and useful in policy making, climate economics must catch up with climate science."[17]

To give an example from Nordhaus' 2013 book: After quoting a 2011 *New York Times* article entitled "A Warming Planet Struggles to Feed Itself," Nordhaus spoke about how "scientific evidence contrasts with the popular rhetoric," using as evidence the IPCC's 2007 assessment's prediction of an increase in food production from global warming "over a range of 1-3°C." But the *Times* was correct: Scientists by 2011 said that any further temperature increases, especially more than 2°C, will cause decreases in agriculture, as much as 20 percent and, in some places in Africa, 50 percent. "Even 2 to 3°C of warming in this century would result in devastating losses to agricultural yields in many developing countries."[18]

Fortunately, say Ackerman and Stanton, "the *Stern Review* broke new ground by synthesizing the current knowledge in climate science and setting a new standard for good climate-economics analysis, using up-to-date inputs from climate science."[19]

From Complacency to Risk and Uncertainty

Nordhaus's gradualism and lack of urgency fit with the fact that he has been complacent about climate change, based on optimistic readings of the evidence, perhaps partly because he has employed outdated science.

By contrast, Stern's sense of urgency was fueled by his conviction that "climate change presents very serious global risks." Indeed, the economic analysis needs to "have the economics of risk and uncertainty at center stage." There could be no delay in mitigating climate change, because "actions over the coming few decades could create risks of major disruption to economic and social activity, later in this century and in the next, on a scale similar to those associated with the great wars and the economic depression of the first half of the 20th century." Unlike those two traumas, moreover, "it will be difficult or impossible to reverse these changes."[20]

In response to the claim that there is too much uncertainty about the effects of climate change to take immediate and strong action, Stern countered: "Uncertainty is an argument for a more, not less, demanding goal, because of the size of the adverse climate-change impacts in the worst-case scenarios."[21] But Nordhaus said that, although the common presumption is that "uncertainty would lead to tighter restrictions on carbon emissions," this "is not necessarily correct."[22]

From Risk Denial to Risk Management

Although Nordhaus has not been guilty of science denial – indeed, he has publically debated with deniers[23] – his analysis, Stanton, Ackerman, and Ramon Bueno have written, "could be called *risk denial* – accepting a (very optimistic) picture of the most likely climate outcomes, but paying little or no attention to worst-case risks." This risk denial is dangerous because "[w]hen climate economists – and the policy makers they advise – fail to understand the well-established findings of climate science, the result is likely to be too little emission reduction, too late."[24]

Whereas Nordhaus's 2008 book was full of risk denial, his 2013 book showed signs of taking climate change more seriously: He described global warming as a "major threat"; he spoke of "perilous changes in the climate and earth systems"; he said that we need to expect "nasty" surprises; he described sea-level rise as "unprecedented"; he spoke of the need to "slow the freight train of global warming"; and he put "risk" and "uncertainty" in the book's subtitle.[25]

However, while giving more attention to uncertainty than he had before, he continued to belittle risk. After quoting the *Stern Review*'s statement that "a 1°C increase in global temperature . . . could double annual deaths," Nordhaus said that this "all sounds extremely grave," but "human societies increasingly devote resources to insulate their lives and properties from environmental conditions as their incomes rise."[26]

With regard to sea-level rise, he said that "human societies can adapt to [it] without catastrophic losses." He did admit that sea-level rise is "at present beyond the capability of human efforts to stop." He even admitted that the Greenland and Antarctic ice sheets may melt more rapidly than previously thought. Nevertheless, he suggested that these ice sheets will not raise the sea level very much during the present century, with the Greenland sheet adding only three inches. However, acknowledging that significant melting of these ice sheets would probably be "tipping points," Nordhaus based his estimate on a 2008 paper by Timothy Lenton and colleagues, which estimated that no tipping points would occur until the global temperature had increased by 3°C (which Nordhaus believed would not occur before 2100).[27]

There were two problems with Nordhaus's argument. In the first place, a 2011 *Scientific American* article (mentioned above in Chapter 5) predicted that, with continued global warming, the seas may rise from 3 to 6 feet. In the second place, Lenton in 2013 gave a revised view, saying that, even at increases below 2°C, catastrophe-initiating tipping points "cannot all be ruled out."[28]

In any case, in spite of the growing scientific consensus over the decade that sea-level rise will be catastrophic for people and agriculture, Nordhaus continued to exude optimism, saying that "human societies can adapt to [sea-level rise] without catastrophic losses." Because most poor countries will in the future be much richer, he advised, they "will be able to protect themselves against climatic extremes just as Miami and Rotterdam do today." When that is impractical, people can simply migrate.[29]

Stern's 2013 writings expressed a very different picture of what climate economists should be doing. Although "no important errors have been found" in the 2006 *Review*, he said, it had "understated the risks of climate change." His new writings put even more focus on risk, saying that economists must present climate change as "a problem of risk management on an immense scale," which most economists had not done.[30]

To emphasize this point, Stern put the phrase "gross underestimation" in the title of one of his essays. This gross underestimation has occurred, Stern said, not only because scientific models were inadequate, but also because the economic models come close "to assuming that the impacts and costs will be modest" and "to excluding the possibility of catastrophic outcomes."[31]

Stern's approach – along with that of Ackerman and Stanton – clearly won out in the IPCC's 2014 report. The IPCC's press release said that it considered not only the high-probability outcomes but also "outcomes with much lower probabilities but much, much larger consequences"; and it characterized "climate changes as a challenge in managing risks." To emphasize this focus, the IPCC also provided an accompanying video that began with the statement, "Climate change is a challenge in managing risk."[32]

From Best-Guess to Worst-Case Policy Advice

Nordhaus's problematic treatment of sea-level rise and tipping points illustrates a major point about how economists should *not* deal with uncertainty: They should not give policy makers only what they or climate scientists consider the most likely possibility - their best guess. "[W]e rarely make important decisions based solely on the most likely effects of our actions," say Ackerman and Stanton. "Instead, we include in our consideration unlikely but very serious consequences. Today's projections of climate change impacts include low-probability events that could, with some understatement, be described as world changing."[33] This approach is essential, Ackerman and Stanton say, because the "latest science shows that climate outcomes are intrinsically uncertain" and "the worst-case outcomes from climate change appear to be unbounded, involving arbitrarily large threats to our common future."[34]

From Optimism to the "Dismal Theorem"

In speaking about "unbounded" worst-case outcomes, Ackerman and Stanton alluded to the work on "uncertainty" by Harvard economist Martin Weitzman, focusing on his "argument about unbounded risk arising from irreducible uncertainty." Calling this work "the most important contribution to the field since the *Stern Review*, they said that it has "reshaped climate economics."[35]

Weitzman dubbed his basic idea the "Dismal Theorem," according to which the benefit from reducing greenhouse gas emissions "is literally infinite," because (1) the earth's climate is so uncertain that the range of possible negative outcomes is enormous, and (2) the economic consequences "of extreme outcomes is unbounded," even approaching "the point of endangering the survival of the human race." These scenarios, according to Weitzman, "cannot be ruled out or even ruled sufficiently improbable."[36]

In a 2009 article, Nordhaus rejected this "dismal theorem," saying that the economic consequences of climate change would not be unlimited, because Weitzman unrealistically "implies unlimited willingness to pay to avoid even very small risks to human survival." But Weitzman replied that global stakeholders do not dare to save money by risking catastrophic climate change.[37]

Although Nordhaus has continued to suggest that his estimates about the monetary damages from various levels of global warming are roughly accurate, Weitzman disagrees. Having said in 2009 that Nordhaus's estimates about the economic losses from high-temperature catastrophes are merely "extrapolative guesses," Weitzman more recently repeated this point: "No one can say with any assurance what would be the dollar value of damages from the highly uncertain climate changes that might accompany a planet earth warmed by an average of more than 3°C (5.4 F)." Economists do their best, but their estimates "are mostly wild extrapolations from lower temperatures, or are just plain made up."[38]

Weitzman's criticism has been supported by MIT's Robert Pindyck, saying that the analyses made by economists such as Nordhaus "create a perception of knowledge and precision" that is "illusory and misleading." The estimates about how much economic damage will be caused by a particular temperature, says Pindyck, are "completely made up, with no theoretical or empirical foundation." Even if the estimates about the damages at a 2°C temperature increase are correct, this will "tell us nothing about what to expect if temperature increases are larger" and nothing about "the likelihood and nature of catastrophic outcomes," although "it is just such outcomes that matter most for climate change policy."[39]

In his 2013 book, with "risk" and "uncertainty" in the title, Nordhaus, amazingly, agreed in substance with the critiques of Weitzman and Pindyck. He said:

- "[W]e have no reliable assessment of [tipping points'] likelihood [and] the thresholds at which they might occur. . . . [T]he tipping point [is] here assumed to be 3.5°C" [but] "the exact point at which the tipping point enters is poorly understood."

- "[W]e have no reliable assessment of . . . their economic impacts. . . . I assume the that total damages are about 0.5 percent of income at the threshold, but that is just an assumption and has no empirical basis."

- "Above 3.5°C, tipping-point damages rise rapidly. Damages are 9 percent of the world income at 4°C; they shoot up to 29 percent of world income at 4.25°C; and on upward from there. These assumptions . . . have no solid basis in empirical estimates of damages."

- "[W]e do not know any of these parameters even to a first approximation."[40]

However, while making these admissions, Nordhaus did not use them to provide a new climate-change economics – one that explicitly admits that there is no basis for rejecting the dismal theorem, therefore no basis for confidence that society can safely define the "optimal" level of global warming abatement as less than the maximum.

From Complacency to Concern for the Survival of Civilization

In line with his rejection of the dismal theorem, Nordhaus has been complacent about whether the survival of civilization is at risk. In discussing uncertainties in his 2008 book, he said that he assumed that "there are no genuinely catastrophic outcomes that would wipe out the human species or destroy the fabric of human civilizations."[41] In his 2013 book, Nordhaus still seemed to consider this destruction not to be a real possibility: After discussing "particularly intractable impacts of climate change," he said: "They are not necessarily catastrophic for humans, although they are likely to have grave consequences for other species and precious natural systems." How could the continuation of climate change, which is already causing the "sixth mass extinction," not end up extinguishing us?[42]

By contrast, Nicholas Stern in 2013 said that the *Stern Review* had underestimated the risk. Referring to possible climate-change damages that are portrayed in recent economic models, including the model that had been used in his *Review*, Stern said that they are unhelpful, because of "major disconnects with the science." By way of emphasizing the existential threat to civilization, Stern said: "The history of the collapse of the Mayan civilization is written as one of failing to understand and act on the risks."[43] While at the World Economic Forum in 2013, Stern said that the risk to civilization is "potentially so dangerous that we have to act strongly. Do we want to play Russian roulette with two bullets or one?"[44]

From Discounting Future Welfare to Inter-Generational Ethics

Stern's difference from Nordhaus involved an idea that economists call "discounting": valuing present money or goods more than money expected some time in the future, often because the money can make more money by being invested in it. Economists work out "discount rates" to convert expected future value into its present worth. To say that future possessions will not be worth much to us in several years or decades, economists give them a high discount rate, perhaps 6 to 10 percent a year. But to say that our present possessions will be as much value to us in the future as they are now, the discount rate is zero or close to it.

Stern's approach to climate economics is a return to that pioneered by William R. Cline, who in 1992 published the first American book on the subject — *The Economics of Global Warming* — which favored "an aggressive course of abatement." Aggressive abatement, he said, was "justifiable on economic grounds alone." Nordhaus, he said, had an "excessive total discount rate."[45]

The practice of discounting future benefits makes sense in the market and other financial matters, such as discounting the money you are to receive in 40 years, because if you were to receive the money now, you would be able to make interest on it in the meantime. But is market-based discounting appropriate in relation to the benefits that will accrue to people 50 or 100 years from now?

Those who say that it is hold that, whereas we should spend considerable money to reduce the present effects of climate change, we should spend less to prevent damages 50 years from now and even less for those that would occur in 100 years. How much less? Saying that discounting investments in climate abatement should be "consistent with today's marketplace real interest rates and savings rates," Nordhaus has suggested a discount rate of 3 or 4 percent, which would mean that a climate-projection benefit that would be worth $100 million in 100 years would have for us a value of only a few million dollars.[46]

Cline, by contrast, advocated a much lower rate – one percent or even zero. Because "the benefits of avoided greenhouse damage tend to be realized much later than the costs imposed on the economy from restriction of greenhouse gas emissions," a high discount rate "will tend to bias policy toward inaction." Nordhaus did not disagree with this assessment, saying that with a higher discount rate, "future damages look smaller, and we do less emissions reduction today."[47]

Cline also argued that a significant discount rate is unethical. A positive discount rate means that, in Nordhaus's own words, "the welfare of future generations is reduced or 'discounted' compared to nearer generations." However, Cline said, whereas impatience "may be a legitimate basis for a single individuals' preferring consumption earlier rather than later in his lifetime," there is no justification for calling the welfare of future generations less important than our own. But from Nordhaus's perspective, Cline's extremely low discount rate explained why he (wrongly) proposed "massive investments in tangible, human, and environmental capital."[48]

This contrast between the views of Nordhaus and Cline, called the *descriptive* and *prescriptive*, has been repeated in the contrast between Nordhaus and Stern. The idea that the discount rate should be zero, Stern said, is "derived from the principle of equal treatment of people in similar circumstances." Ethically, we should "treat the lives of different individuals equally and not to discriminate between lives by happenstance of the date of birth at which they began."[49]

Employing a 6% discount rate as an example of one that is much too high, Stern pointed out that in 100 years, a unit of benefit would be valued 339 times lower, meaning we would care 339 times less about people alive 100 years now than we care for the present generation. This comes close to saying we should "forget about issues concerning 100 years or more from now."[50]

Nordhaus insisted that a high discount rate "does not mean indifference to the future" nor "putting different values on people," for two reasons: On the one hand, "capital is productive" and, on the other, societies have "a vast array of productive investments from which to choose." One type of investment, to be sure, is to slow climate change. "But others will also be valuable." Therefore, because capital is scarce, "climate investments should compete with investments in other areas."[51] It is our duty to "improve the quality of life for future generations," but this is done best, Nordhaus said, by making efficient investments. Although a "portfolio of efficient investments would definitely include ones to slow global warming," investments should also be made in "other priority areas - health systems at home, cures for tropical diseases, [and] education around the world."[52]

Putting a "discount rate on welfare" is not unethical, Nordhaus argued, because "continued growth is a good bet," so our children and grandchildren will be richer. Accordingly, although we will, in order to protect our own money, degrade our grandchildren's world, these descendants will be richer, so they will be able to "buy down" the degradation. This growth scenario, moreover, includes the poor as well as middle-income countries, because over the next 50 to 100 years, their per capita GDP is projected to rise by "500 to 1,000 percent."[53]

Stern countered, saying the primary basis for advocating high discount rates is "the unwarranted assumption that future incomes will almost certainly be much higher than now." This assumption "is simply not credible," he argued, in face of temperatures that could lead to the possibility of "large-scale destruction of capital and infrastructure, mass migration, conflict, and so on." Economic modelers need to factor in the possibility that global warming will create "an environment so hostile that physical, social, and organizational capital are destroyed [and] production processes are radically disrupted," so that "future generations will be much poorer."[54]

Stern's prediction is supported by many studies, including a 2013 NOAA study saying that increased heat could cause a 50 percent drop in labor capacity in summer months. Reviewing several reports, Joe Romm said that a negative impact on labor productivity begins at about 26°C (79°F), then "[productivity starts to nose-dive at 90°F and falls off the cliff at 100°F." More generally, Romm said, "a collapse in labor productivity from business-as-usual carbon emissions and warming" will have "a cost to society that may well exceed that of all other costs of climate change combined."[55]

Besides having unrealistic optimism about economic growth under climate change, Nordhaus also, saying that investments in stopping climate change should compete with investments in "other priority areas," was treating the climate risk as simply one risk among others. That approach, Stern noted, is "hopelessly flawed."[56] Surely it is a flaw to put the possible end of human life in the same category as other threats.

From Cost-Benefit Analysis to the Standards-Based Approach

Instead of conceding that his long-affirmed approach does not work, Nordhaus sought to handle unknown risks by simply adding an insurance premium to the estimation of the otherwise likely economic damages. "We need to incorporate a risk premium not only to cover the known uncertainties such as those involving climate sensitivity and health risks but also," said Nordhaus, "uncertainties such as tipping points." However, speaking of an insurance premium is confusing. In purchasing fire insurance for a home, you give the premium to a company, which promises that, if your home burns down, you will receive money to rebuild it. But Nordhaus's "risk premium" is not given to a company that will compensate the world and all future generations. Rather, what Nordhaus calls a "premium" just increases his estimate of the economic damages that climate disruption causes. Adding a "premium" to his cost-benefit analysis provides "insurance" only in the sense of urging politicians to increase the amount of money they should provide for global-warming abatement.[57]

Even aside from this problem, Nordhaus's discussion of the risk premium is not helpful. To be such, he would have needed to give some rough estimate of what sort of "premium" should be added to cover all of the uncertainties: the possible economic damages from ocean acidification, the melting of the ice-sheets, the higher temperatures and greater droughts and wildfires, the reduction in water and food, the climate migration and wars, and the loss of various ecosystems and species. But he did not. "All that can be said with confidence," he said, "is that we should not ignore the risks."[58]

Of course, it would be impossible to provide a realistic estimate. But without such an estimate, he has not provided a cost-benefit analysis. *Nordhaus's 40-year effort to provide a cost-benefit analysis of climate change has self-destructed.*

Stern, who has become focused on "the big picture of risk," says that "there are major risks of temperatures the world has not seen for tens of millions of years, far outside the experience of homo sapiens." Moreover, he says, these changes may rewrite "where big fractions of the world could live, possibly resulting in the migration of hundreds of millions, or billions, possibly risking major conflict and possibly the death of tens or hundreds of millions." Stern then asks: "How should we set about or frame an economic analysis of policy towards that sort of risk?"

The answer to this question could be based on Eric Pooley's question, "How Much Would You Pay to Save the Planet?" His implicit answer was "whatever it takes." This is the only rational answer, because the value of saving civilization is limitless.

Ackerman and Stanton recommend that climate economists should switch from cost-benefit to a "precautionary, or standards-based, approach." This approach sets a "maximum temperature increase or concentration level beyond which expected losses are considered to be unacceptable." For example, it was long held that temperature rise beyond 19th-century levels should be kept below 2°C. But then Hansen in 2011, calling this target a "prescription for long-term disaster," advocated that the target be switched to 1.5°C, along with the needed carbon budget to achieve this target. The standards-based approach would be to set such a limit, then pay whatever is necessary to meet it.[59]

By contrast, Nordhaus has continued to advocate a cost-benefit basis. Saying that science provides "no bright line of targets at 1½°C or 2°C or 3°C," Nordhaus has advised: "The best target will depend on the costs of achieving it. We should aim for a lower temperature target if it is inexpensive, but we might have to live with a higher target if costs are high." One must wonder whether Nordhaus had looked recently to see what scientists are saying about such temperatures. Asking whether those who speak complacently about a 3°C world "understand in any significant way what 3°C really means," David Spratt, coauthor of *Climate Code Red*, said:

> In the Pliocene, three million years ago, temperatures were
> 3°C higher than our pre-industrial levels, so it gives us an
> insight into the 3°C world. The northern hemisphere was
> free of glaciers and ice sheets, beech trees grew in the
> Transantarctic mountains, [and] sea levels were 25 metres
> higher.[60]

With the standards-based approach, economists do not need to use projected costs to determine an optimal level of abatement; rather, they look to scientists to set the standard. But there is still a task for economists: "With a predetermined standard in place," write Ackerman and Stanton, "the economic problem becomes one of cost-effectiveness analysis, seeking to determine the least-cost strategy for meeting the standard." With the switch to the standards-based approach, climate scientists and climate economists will finally be on the same page and economists can be "part of the solution rather than part of the problem."[61]

Finally, the standards-based approach can be understood as a new cost-benefit approach. In light of Stern's conclusion – that "the costs of weak action or inaction are much higher that the costs of action" – the two approaches ultimately coincide. As Ackerman and Stanton put it, "welfare optimization can lead to the same result as precautionary, standards-based policy making."[62] What Stern has said from the beginning has been strongly confirmed by the IPCC's 2014 report on mitigation. According to its calculations, the cost of keeping the planet's temperature increase to 2°C (3.6°F) would presumably cost a 0.06 percent reduction of the global gross product. This would mean, for example, an annual growth of 2.24% instead of 2.30% -- a very tiny difference. However, that calculation refers to taking strong mitigation measures immediately, because delay would "substantially increase the difficulty of the transition to low, longer-term emissions levels."

The same message had been given in 2011 by the International Energy Agency (IEA), which said:

> Delaying action is a false economy: for every $1 of investment in cleaner technology that is avoided in the power sector before 2020, an additional $4.30 would need to be spent after 2020 to compensate for the increased emissions.

The IEA made an even stronger statement in its "Energy Technology Perspective" of 2014, which said that the delays of the previous two years had added $4 trillion to the cost of avoiding catastrophe. Keeping the temperature rise down to 2°C would be expensive, costing about 1% of the global economy, or $44 trillion a year between now and 2050. But this investment would result in a savings of $115 trillion, hence a net savings of $71 trillion.[63]

To be sure, to keep the temperature rise to 1.5°C would cost more now, but not much. In fact, in 2013 a team of scientists and economists, including James Hansen and Jeffrey Sachs, estimated the same amount – 1% of the global economy – to keep the temperature rise down to 1°C. Moreover, a 2014 World Bank report entitled "Climate-Smart Development" said that if the world's largest economies adopted policies for clean transportation and energy efficiency in buildings, the global economy could be boosted by as much as $2.6 trillion a year by 2030.[64]

More reports in 2014 gave similar assessments. The New Climate Economy Project put out a report entitled *Better Growth, Better Climate*. Taking aim at "the idea that we must choose between fighting climate change or growing the world's economy," Felipe Calderón, the former president of Mexico, said: "That is a false dilemma. . . . We are proposing a way to have the same or even more economic growth, and at the same time have environmental responsibility." Summarizing this report, along with a new paper by the International Monetary Fund, Paul Krugman said: "Saving the planet would be cheap; it might even be free." In fact, it may be much better than free, Krugman said, referring to a report that said that, if climate change continues, the costs could be "a staggering $1240 trillion." A 2014 study in *Nature Climate Change* concluded that putting a price on carbon, as with a carbon tax or cap-and-trade system, *would save more than 10 times as much as the system itself would cost.* The lead author said:

> If cost-benefit analyses of climate policies don't include
> the significant health benefits from healthier air, they

dramatically underestimate the benefits of these policies.[65]

Paying for climate mitigation, therefore, would provide more money available for health care, not less.

These reports show how much Nordhaus misled U.S. policymakers. Whereas he told them that they should not pay for full-out climate mitigations, because this would not be cost-effective, the truth is the opposite: The only way to economize is to invest in full-out mitigation immediately.

This conclusion is especially important in the United States, because its political leaders tend not to respond to ethical reasons for reducing carbon emissions. Donald Brown, a professor of environmental ethics and law at Penn State, gave this report about his visit to the Scottish Parliament to discuss a proposed climate-change law:

> Before I spoke, a Scottish Parliamentarian made an argument that I have never heard any US politician make. . . . The Parliamentarian argued that Scotland should adopt this tough new legislation even though it might be expensive because the Scotts had an obligation to the rest of the world to do so. In other words, those countries most responsible for causing climate change have ethical duties to reduce their emissions even if it costs are significant.

By contrast, Brown said,

> there is not the faintest murmur in the US climate-change debate or in the media's coverage of the unfolding US legislative fight about duties and responsibilities that the United States has to the rest of the world to reduce the threat of climate change. . . . [T]he U.S. continues to debate this issue as if the only legitimate consideration is how our economy might be affected.[66]

Because of the limits to the U.S. debate, it is important to publicize the fact that the reduction of emissions is justified on economic as well as ethical grounds.

Conclusion to the Nordhaus-Stern Transition

This 40-year development of climate economics has led to a very simple conclusion. As James Hansen said in 2013, "the science is telling us that policy should be set to reduce emissions as rapidly as possible."[67] Had politicians started addressing the problem in the 1990, or even in 2000, there would have been some choices. But now the carbon budget has been so fully used up that, even if emissions were to be completely eliminated by 2050, we will have inflicted much worse weather, with greater food and water problems, on all future generations, as long as humanity lasts. So the only rational and moral policy now is to eliminate emissions as quickly as possible, thereby inflicting as little additional misery as possible on future generations.

The Market Failure to Reflect True Costs

A widespread idea in conservative circles has been that the price for everything should be settled by the market, because it establishes the proper balance between costs and benefits. But the market does this only insofar as there are no "externalities," meaning costs that are not included in setting the price of products. Insofar as there *are* externalities, so that costs and benefits are not balanced, there is *market failure.* Nordhaus and Stern agreed (along with Cline) on the policy that would be most effective in slowing it down: imposing a price on carbon emissions.

The Need for a Carbon Price

The most important externality in the world is the lack of a carbon price in the United States and most other countries. Due to this lack, the *Stern Review* said,

> those who produce greenhouse-gas emissions are bringing about climate change, thereby imposing costs on the world and on future generations, but they do not face the full consequences of their actions themselves.

"Climate change," said the *Review*, is "the greatest example of market failure we have ever seen." Explaining more fully, Stern said: "The problem of climate change involves a fundamental failure of markets: those who damage others by emitting greenhouse gases generally do not pay."[68] Of course, the expenses must be paid, so they are paid by society - the costs are "socialized." Each fossil-fuel corporation thereby gets a tremendous benefit – getting to dump its waste into the atmosphere for free. And so the pollution continues.

The way to fix this market failure is to internalize the "social cost of carbon," meaning the total costs to society from the burning of fossil fuels. This solution is common to economists, so it is not surprising that Stern and Nordhaus agree on this point. Internalizing the price means putting a price on carbon emissions, thereby making it part of the market. "Putting an appropriate price on carbon," explained Stern, means that people are faced with the full social cost of their actions. This will lead individuals and businesses to switch away from high-carbon goods and services, and to invest in low-carbon alternatives.[69]

Similarly, Nordhaus said that "the single most important market mechanism that is missing today is a high price on CO_2 emissions, or what is called 'carbon prices.'" A price on carbon, he explained, provides "strong incentives to reduce carbon emissions" by making things and services with high carbon content more expensive. All those concerned with climate change can be grateful to Nordhaus for having made this argument for the past four decades. "If we actually did what Bill proposed in the late '70s," said Stanford University's John Weyant, "we'd be so much better now."[70]

This method, in which carbon fuels (such as coal) are charged per unit of carbon, is far more efficient (as well as simpler) than the quantitative method, which was adopted at Kyoto. When this approach "proves ineffective and inefficient," Nordhaus said, policy makers "should consider the fact that price-type approaches like harmonized environmental taxes on carbon are powerful tools for coordinating policies and slowing climate change." Calling global warming "the Goliath of all externalities,"[71] Nordhaus said that "placing a near-universal and harmonized price or tax on carbon is a necessary and perhaps even a sufficient condition for reducing the future threat of global warming."[72] In what are arguably *Climate Casino*'s best chapters (19-21), Nordhaus explained why in three points.

- With a significant price on carbon, all goods and services with high carbon content will be more expensive, thereby encouraging customers to use fewer of them.

- A significant price will also encourage producers, in order to keep their profits up, to switch to materials containing little or no carbon – such as generating electricity from wind and solar energy rather than coal, oil, or natural gas.

- Significant carbon prices "will give market incentives for inventors and innovators to develop and introduce low-carbon products and processes to replace current technologies."[73]

Widespread Support for Carbon Pricing

Although it has hardly been discussed by journalists and politicians in the

United States, the idea of a carbon price is broadly supported both in the United States and around the world.

- A poll taken at the end of 2012 showed that almost two-thirds of American voters would prefer solving the deficit crisis by means of a carbon tax rather than cutting spending – even after being exposed to arguments by opponents of a carbon tax.[74]

- Carbon pricing is also endorsed by World Bank President Jim Yong Kim.[75]

- Although it was long assumed that the business world would be opposed to a carbon price, this is no longer true. Asking for a policy to "underpin the investment needed to deliver substantial greenhouse gas emissions reductions by mid-century," more than 100 international companies, including Shell and Unilever, signed a statement saying: "Putting a clear, transparent and unambiguous price on carbon emissions must be a core policy objective."[76]

- Carbon pricing has also been supported, or at least accepted, by most other major oil companies (beyond Shell), including BP, Chevron, ConocoPhillips ExxonMobil, and Statoil. "Several oil executives have said in private conversations," reported Ross Gelbspan, that they could decarbonize their energy supplies, but that they would "need the governments of the world to regulate the process so all companies can make the transition in lockstep without losing market share to competitors."[77]

- At the end of 2013, moreover, a study revealed that at least 29 major companies operating in the United States are already using an "internal carbon price" in their business strategies. These companies use this price as "a planning tool to help identify revenue opportunities, risks, and as an incentive to drive maximum energy efficiencies to reduce costs and guide capital investment decisions." For example, BP and Shell each assume that it will cost $40 per metric ton by 2030, whereas ExxonMobil uses $60.[78]

- Besides being advocated by liberal think tanks, such as the Brookings Institute and the Center for American Progress, the establishment of a carbon price has also been advocated by writers for a number of conservative organizations, including the American Enterprise Institute, CATO, and the Hudson Institute.[79]

- In fact, President Obama, who long seemed to have dismissed this idea, endorsed it in his interview with Tom Friedman for "Years of Living Dangerously."

The most essential point is that there would be no objection to a carbon price, as long as it is installed around the world, so that companies and countries that have a carbon price will not be at a disadvantage.

A Carbon Tax or Carbon Market?

"Whether someone is serious about tackling the global warming problem can be readily gauged," said Nordhaus, "by listening to what he or she says about the carbon price." But there are two quite different ways of setting a price: A carbon tax fixes the price of carbon emissions and lets the quantity fluctuate. A carbon market, which operates in terms of the method known as *cap and trade*, "fixes the quantity of carbon emissions and lets the price fluctuate."[80]

Each method has its strengths and, therefore, its supporters, both among economists and countries. But the carbon tax is far superior, as explained in recent publications by Martin Weitzman, who argues for an "internationally harmonized but nationally retained carbon tax," which is supported by two Stanford University scholars.[81] They provide many reasons the carbon tax is far better, four of which are:

- Whereas a carbon tax prevents price volatility, a trading system allows for extreme volatility, which weakened Europe's Emissions Trading System (ETS). (By 2012, the ETS had "essentially collapsed"; by 2013, its carbon permits were called "worse than junk bonds"; and by 2014 the market, which put the carbon price at a measly 6 pounds a ton, was called "worse than useless.")[82]

- "The revenues from an internationally harmonized carbon tax are retained internally within each nation," whereas that is not the case with cap-and-trade revenues.[83]

- A "carbon tax is more easily administered and more transparent than a cap-and-trade system," which will be "especially important in a comprehensive international context that would include all major emitting countries."

- A carbon market is a "great temptation for kleptocrats to steal these valuable emissions permits and sell them on the international market," which has occurred: The International Criminal Police

Organization (Interpol) revealed that the $176 billion carbon market has become a magnet for organized crime.[84]

Broad Support for a Carbon Tax

Although one would never know this from the national news in the United States, the idea of putting a price on carbon by means of a carbon tax has wide support.

- As the agreement between the liberal Stern and the conservative Nordhaus illustrates, most economists endorse the idea. A recent poll of 52 economists from seven leading departments of economics were asked whether they agree with this statement: "A tax on the carbon content of fuels would be a less expensive way to reduce carbon-dioxide emissions than would a collection of policies such as 'corporate average fuel economy' requirements for automobiles." While 2% of the economists disagreed, 90% agreed.[85]

- Other economists who support a carbon tax include Reagan economist Arthur Laffer, who finds it strange that "the U.S. allows something we want less of – carbon dioxide pollution – to be emitted without penalty."[86]

- It is supported by some conservative members of Congress, including former Representative Bob Inglis, who calls the idea "bedrock conservatism" and "true-cost conservatism."[87]

- A carbon tax has been suggested by the Senate Finance Committee and the Congressional Research Service, which said that a modest carbon tax ($25 per ton of emissions) could cut the federal budget by more than $1 trillion in 10 years.[88]

- Newspapers endorsing the idea of a carbon tax include the *Washington Post,* which said: "The smartest hedge would be a national carbon tax," which would "marshal the market's power to wring carbon out of the economy, putting decisions about the direction of energy and manufacturing in the hands of consumers and businesses," rather than in those of Congress and lobbyists.[89]

- Even Grover Norquist, who had bound hundreds of national Republican politicians to a no-new-taxes pledge, said that a carbon tax, in exchange for cutting income tax, would be acceptable - until he was whipped back into line by the Koch-funded American Energy Alliance.[90]

The Impact on Taxes, the Economy, and the Poor
Critics of carbon taxes regularly allege that carbon taxes would weaken a country's economy, add to citizens' tax burdens, and hurt its low-income citizens, who already pay a significant percentage of their incomes for transportation and heating. But these consequences do not necessarily result, as illustrated by Sweden and British Columbia.

- C. Fred Bergsten, former director of the Peterson Institute for International Economics, has said: "Sweden has one of the lowest inflation rates in Europe; it runs a budget surplus every year; [and] its corporate tax rates are considerably lower than U.S. rates."[91]

- Five years after installing its carbon tax, British Columbia's GDP has kept pace with the rest of Canada, it developed Canada's lowest income taxes (both personal and corporate), all while reducing fuel consumption 19% relative to the rest of Canada. Also, the Liberal Party that introduced it, rather than being punished by the voters, actually gained seats.[92]

Moreover, a 2014 report stated that an aggressive U.S. carbon tax, starting at $10 per metric ton and then increasing by $10 each year, would help the economy, adding over two million jobs (as well as eliminating one-third of the country's carbon emissions by 2015 and preventing over 10,000 premature deaths).[93]

Although opponents portray a carbon tax as an *additional tax*, most advocates talk about tax-*shifting*. This entails raising the tax burden where it serves to curb environmental malfeasance, while using the revenues derived to lessen taxes of more socially beneficial or needy sectors. As Lester Brown has pointed out, tax-shifting has long been practiced in Europe:

> A four-year plan adopted in Germany in 1999 systematically shifted taxes from labor to energy. . . . Between 2001 and 2006, Sweden shifted an estimated $2 billion of taxes from income to environmentally destructive activities. . . . Environmental tax shifting is becoming commonplace in Europe, where France, Italy, Norway, Spain, and the United Kingdom are also using this policy instrument.[94]

The money from the carbon tax could be used in various ways: to help the country's treasury; to subsidize clean energy; to be returned to citizens; or a combination of these. Most proposals for a carbon tax build in rebates. The Center for American Progress lists three major benefits of such a policy: fighting global warming, reducing the deficit, and protecting low-income Americans.[95]

A poorly designed plan could, to be sure, end up hurting the economy and/or the poor. But if well designed, it can have many benefits. Harvard's conservative economist Gregory Mankiw has written:

> Cutting income taxes while increasing gasoline taxes would lead to more rapid economic growth, less traffic congestion, safer roads, and reduced risk of global warming - all without jeopardizing long-term fiscal solvency. This may be the closest thing to a free lunch that economics has to offer.[96]

All three of the standard objections to a carbon tax are targeted by the Citizens Climate Lobby, which advocates James Hansen's proposal. In response to the common objection that a carbon tax would be a tax increase, which especially harmful to poor people, the plan would be tax-neutral, with all tax monies returned to citizens (with one share going to each adult and half share to each child, up to two children per household). Except for the heaviest carbon burners, most Americans would get back more than the carbon tax has cost them. To the objection that a carbon tax would be a "job killer," a study by Regional Economic Models, Inc., concluded that the tax would add 2.2 million jobs in the first 10 years. So the plan would help with jobs and the economy. With regard to carbon emissions, the tax, which would begin at $10 per ton of CO_2 and then increase by that amount each year, should reduce them 33 percent by 2025 and 52 percent by 2035.[97]

In sum, there is no reason for a carbon tax not to be imposed, except for opposition by Congressional Republicans, some of the energy companies, and the extreme free-enterprise organizations sponsored by David and Charles Koch, as well as some other very selfish individuals, such as their brother Bill Koch, who says that anyone who calls for taxes on CO_2 emissions is "on LSD" – something we did not know about fellow billionaire Bill Gates.[98]

Determining the Size of the Carbon Tax

While Stern and Nordhaus agreed on the need for a carbon price, they had very different views about the social cost of carbon and, therefore, on the appropriate carbon tax (or equivalent). Nordhaus has always given low estimates. In 1992, Nordhaus said that "a carbon tax of $5 to $10 per ton is the maximum that would be justified by a cost-benefit comparison." By 2005, Nordhaus figured the social cost of carbon (SCC) to be about $28 per metric ton of carbon (which would mean $7.40 per ton of CO_2), and calculated the optimal carbon tax to be "$27 per ton of carbon in 2005." *The Stern Review* estimated the current social cost of carbon to be "$350 per ton of carbon in 2005 prices," which Nordhaus called way too high.[99]

But was it? It is true that in 2010 the government's Interagency Working Group on Social Cost of Carbon put the SCC even lower, putting the central value at $24. In 2013, the Group produced an updated version, which raised the central value to $37. Although this higher figure reflected merely the fact that the estimates that had been given in the three assessments used in the 2010 study had gone up, Congressional Republicans, suspicious that President Obama was using a raise in the social cost of carbon as a de facto carbon tax, asked for an investigation by the Government Accountability Office (which found that nothing improper occurred).[100]

But the real problem with the 2013 report by the Interagency Working Group is that, even with the raise in the SCC, the government's estimate is still woefully low. In fact, it is low not only compared with several other economists (see below), but even with the notoriously conservative IPCC. As Laurie Johnson pointed out, the Interagency Working Group ignored a large number of issues the IPCC discussed in its 2013 report, such as extreme weather events, ocean acidification, loss of water for agriculture, large-scale migration, and violence due to resource scarcity.[101]

It is not surprising that the Group's estimate was so low, because it was based in part on Nordhaus's recent estimate. And many scholars, Ackerman and Stanton have pointed out, put the price much higher than the Nordhaus optimal price: Michael Hanemann estimated the actual cost to be four times that much and Martin Weitzman, as mentioned earlier, said that higher temperatures could lead to enormously higher costs.[102]

Like most people who advocate a carbon tax, Nordhaus held that it should begin at a relatively low price, to give individuals and businesses time to reduce their carbon use, and then ramp it up progressively. According to Nordhaus's "optimal trajectory," a carbon tax, having started at $27 per ton, "would rise to $95 per ton of carbon by 2050." According to Ackerman and Stanton, however, the true social cost of carbon in 2010 could have been as high as $893 per ton, then rising to $1,500 in 2050. Citing Weitzman's suggestion that the damages of a ton of emissions might be infinite, they said: "Our estimates are not literally infinite, but they may be close enough to infinity for all practical purposes."[103]

Putting a high price on carbon, thereby making fossil fuels and other carbon products too expensive to be profitable, would largely take care of the need to prevent additional carbon going into the atmosphere (assuming, of course, that there is an alternative, and for that, see Chapter 17).

But as it presently stands, carbon has not only not been taxed, it has even been subsidized. "[H]idden in the tax code," wrote Joseph Stiglitz, "are billions of dollars of subsidies to the oil and gas industries."[104]

Eliminating Fossil-Fuel Industry Subsidies

Putting a price on carbon to discourage carbon products presupposes that carbon products – especially fossil fuels – are not to be subsidized. Nordhaus and Stern agree. There have long been attempts to get rid of fossil-fuel subsidies as no longer necessary. More recently, they have been called "immoral" and the continuation of them a "scandal." But the fossil-fuel industry continues to justify them.

The Justification for Fossil-Fuel Subsidies

Subsidies for fossil fuels have been justified on several grounds:

- In the early decades of industrial civilization, such subsidies were in the public interest.

- When finding and producing coal, oil, and natural gas was risky and rewards modest, subsidies gave incentives.

- Subsidies also provided various types of infrastructure needed for the new civilization.

- Subsidies helped the poor to participate in this new civilization.

But these justifications no longer exist:

- Far from being in the public interest, fossil fuels are now making human life more difficult, even threatening to bring it to an end.

- The fossil-fuel industries have become very rich. As President Obama said in his 2011 State of the Union address: "I don't know if you've noticed, but they're doing just fine on their own."[105]

- An enormous amount of money – one estimate suggests $12 trillion – has been put into direct costs and infrastructure simply for the types of transportation based on fossil fuels.[106]

- According to the International Monetary Fund, only 7 percent of the fossil-fuel subsidies have been benefitting the poorest 20 percent of the people, whereas the richest 20 percent benefit from almost 50 percent of the subsidies.[107]

- Even former oilman and then-President George W. Bush said in 2006, when oil was about half its current cost: "I will tell you with $55 oil we don't need incentives to oil and gas companies to explore. There are plenty of incentives.[108]

Nevertheless, the subsidies have continued, due to the fossil-fuel industries and their lobbies.

Determining the Size of Fossil-Fuel Subsidies

These industries sometimes claim that they receive no subsidies. For example, the president of the American Petroleum Institute – the oil and gas industry's lobbying association - has claimed that "[t]he oil and gas industry gets no subsidies, zero, nothing." He was able to make this claim by defining a subsidy as a direct payment by the government to a company. But Politifact countered, saying that fossil-fuel companies get significant tax breaks and, "While it may not involve the sending of a U.S. Treasury check to a company, a tax break has the same practical impact, allowing a company to hold onto money it might otherwise pay in taxes." Politifact was thereby reflecting the World Trade Organization's definition: "a subsidy is any financial contribution by a government, or agent of a government, that confers a benefit on its recipient."[109]

With regard to taxes, the big oil companies "pay an absurdly low tax rate." Although the American Petroleum Institute claims that the oil industry pays an effective tax rate of 44.3 percent and the statutory corporate tax rate is 35 percent, a 2014 report by Taxpayers for Common Sense reported that the big oil companies, such as Chevron and ExxonMobil, paid 11.7 percent in taxes from 2009 to 2013. "In effect," said the report, "these companies are financing significant parts of their business with interest-free loans from U.S. taxpayers."[110]

Insofar as the fossil-fuel industry admits that it receives subsidies, it claims that it needs to retain them in order to keep a "level playing field" with clean energy, because it receives massive subsidies. But this claim is ridiculously false. According to the International Energy Agency, the subsidies for fossil fuels are 12 times greater than those for clean energy. As the headline of a Bloomberg Business Week article has said, "When It Comes to Government Subsidies, Dirty Energy Still Cleans Up."[111]

In a 2013 report entitled *Energy Subsidy Reform: Lessons and*

Implications, the International Monetary Fund (IMF) stated that the worldwide fossil-fuel subsidies have been even greater. The subsidies given to fossil fuels in 2011, the IMF reported, added up to $1.9 trillion, with $480 billion in direct subsidies. The rest consisted of indirect subsidies, $1.4 trillion of which was due to "mispricing" – meaning, that the price of fossil fuels to customers did not include the costs of the various types of damage they cause.[112]

Moreover, the IMF's figure of $1.4 trillion for mispricing was based on taking the social cost of carbon to be only $25 per metric ton of carbon, which is very low. The UK recently calculated the cost to be $83 per ton, which would make the global fossil-fuel subsidies more like $3.5 trillion. Joe Romm judged the actual social cost of carbon to be at least $135 per ton, which would make the global fossil-fuel subsidies at least $8 trillion. And the Ackerman-Stanton calculation would make the fossil-fuel subsidies still higher.[113]

The Immorality of Fossil-Fuel Subsidies

Paul Hawken has said that "we are stealing the future, selling it in the present, and calling it GDP." David Roberts, having quoted this statement, added:

> I can't think of a better description of these fossil fuel subsidies. And when we use a more realistic cost for carbon damages, we get a better sense of just how *much* we are stealing from our descendants – trillions and trillions of dollars a year. The heedless radicalism and grotesque immorality of it are breathtaking.

As to which country was most guilty of this grotesque immorality, the IMF reported the biggest offender by far to be the United States, providing – at $502 billion of fossil-fuel subsidies – more than twice the amount of the second and third countries, China and Russia.[114]

The WWF has called the maintenance of the fossil-fuel subsidies "a scandal."[115] This scandal has continued because of the prostitution-like relations between Congress and the fossil-fuel industry, which buys lawmakers' continued support. Long-time journalist Dan Froomkin, in an essay entitled "How the Oil Lobby Greases Washington's Wheels," said:

> [O]ne of the many things the industry can do with its fat pocketbook is hire a veritable army of sharp lobbyists and back them up with big wads of cash in the form of campaign donations and spending. The end result is that the industry has a remarkable ability to get its way on Capitol Hill. According to the Center for Responsive Politics' website,

the oil and gas industry has spent more than $1 billion on
lobbying since 1998, including a jaw-dropping $147 million
[in 2010].[116]

The Destructiveness of Fossil-Fuel Subsidies

The Overseas Development Institute said: "If their aim is to avoid dangerous
climate change, governments are shooting themselves in both feet."
Explaining, it continued: "They are subsidizing the very activities that are
pushing the world towards dangerous climate change," thereby encouraging
"investment in carbon-intensive energy." The mirror side of this is that the
subsidies discourage investors from funding clean energy. The IMF said that
if fossil-fuel subsidies were to be eliminated, CO_2 emissions could be reduced
by 13 percent.[117]

These reductions would be even greater if a significant portion of
these subsidies were transferred to clean energy. This transfer would not be
at all exceptional, given the historical norm for subsidies. According to a major
report by Nancy Pfund and Ben Healey of DBL Investors, "federal incentives
for early fossil fuel production and the nascent nuclear industry were much
more robust than the support provided to renewables today." To be precise:
Comparing the first 15 years of the oil and gas subsidies with the first 15 years
of subsidies for clean energy, the subsidies for oil and gas were *five times
greater*.[118]

Given the original purpose of subsidies – to help new industries get
off the ground – it was entirely appropriate for the fossil-fuel industries to
have received subsidies during their early years, especially when the world
had no idea about the negative effects of fossil fuels. But now it is time for
clean energy to receive massive subsidies, to make the needed transition as
rapidly as possible. There is simply no time for the gradual transition that
would be made if clean energy were only slightly less expensive than coal,
oil, and gas.

Conclusion to Discussion about Subsidies

Asking "What's the simplest way to tackle global warming?" *Washington Post*
blogger Brad Plumer wrote: "Make sure that fossil fuels are priced properly
and not subsidized." Likewise, Romm, reflecting on the 99 percent drop in
the cost of solar cells said: "If solar power is seeing this kind of growth strictly
on a cost basis, imagine how fast it would be growing if carbon dioxide had
a price reflecting its actual harm to the environment and human health."[119]

This solution, of course, presupposes that this two-fold treatment
of fossil fuels becomes universal.

Agreeing on a Global Carbon Price

Although a few countries have been working hard to reduce their carbon emissions, global warming can be slowed and eventually stopped only if all countries are involved in the effort. Solving global warming is, accordingly, a problem of international cooperation.

Kyoto Autopsy

As the founders of the Kyoto approach to climate negotiations recognized, achieving this cooperation would mean that the various countries would need to subordinate their self-interest to the common good, and doing this would require a common commitment. After all, the atmosphere is a commons: It is valuable to every country, and every country's emissions degrade it, so all countries need to reduce their emissions to protect the common good. But each country's emissions constitute only a small part of the global emissions, and so from the perspective of individual countries, their reductions would seem big sacrifices for little, if any, benefit. With this as a common logic, the atmosphere will be destroyed. Global warming is the "tragedy of the commons" writ large. Only a common commitment can make each country's sacrifices seem rational.

The previous paragraphs have summarized the explanation by University of Maryland's Peter Cramton and two colleagues in a paper entitled "How to Negotiate Ambitious Global Emissions Abatement." Although the founders of the Kyoto negotiations were right to work for a common commitment, the Kyoto Protocol turned out to be a stunning failure. Besides having goals too weak to do much good, Kyoto now covers only 15 percent of the global emissions. What happened?

The failure was inevitable, they said, once the decision was made to put the common commitment in terms of the quantity of a country's emissions: each country was to reduce its emissions by an agreed-upon percent below its level of emissions in 1990. Given the tremendous differences between countries in terms of their wealth and their historic contributions to global warming, it was impossible to come even close to general agreement.[120] As Stiglitz explained:

> The developing countries ask, why should the developed countries be allowed to pollute more now simply because they polluted more in the past? In fact, because the developed countries have already contributed so much, they should be forced to reduce more. The world seems at an impasse: the United States refuses to go along unless

developing countries are brought into the fold; and the developing countries see no reason why they should not be allowed to pollute as much per capita as the United States or Europe. Indeed, given their poverty and the costs associated with reducing emissions, one might give them even more leeway. But, given their low levels of income, that would imply that no restraints would be imposed on them for decades.[121]

In light of this impossibility, the leaders decided to allow each of the rich countries to name its own target (whereas the poor countries needed no targets whatsoever). In making that decision, the Kyoto leaders gave up the idea of a common commitment. So a problem that requires global cooperation ended up with virtually no cooperation, with most countries more concerned with their own right to emit than with overcoming global emissions.

Achieving a Commitment: By Price or Quantity?

However, Stiglitz said: "There is a way out, and that is through a common (global) environmental tax on emissions. There is a social cost to emissions, and the common environmental tax would simply make everyone pay the social cost."[122] Agreeing with Stiglitz, Cramton and colleagues say:

While a common *quantity* commitment proved infeasible, a common *price* commitment can succeed, because there is near-unanimous agreement that each country should commit to the same price. Such a common commitment makes possible the type of agreement that changes self-interests for the better: "I will commit to the common price if you will."

Switching to a common price would eliminate all the acrimonious arguments about fairness. Rather than poor countries saying that rich countries must go first, while some rich countries refuse to do anything until rising poor countries make similar commitments, the price agreement would say that all countries pay the agreed-upon price for their own emissions. Nothing could be fairer.

That said, some countries are so poor that they would not be able pay a very high carbon price – a price high enough to do much good. But this problem might be handled by the Green Climate Fund, which was set up by the U.N. in 2012 to help poor countries, especially those most at risk from climate change. Perhaps one thing the Fund could do, suggest Cramton and colleagues, would be to help make it possible for such countries to support a commitment to a high price. [123]

In any case, the main point is that the commitment to a common price changes the self-interest of countries dramatically. In the present system, each country's self-interest is in tension with the common good, so most countries agree to only minor reductions. But with a common price, it will be in each country's self-interest to choose a high price, knowing that, the higher the price, the more help they are going to receive in saving their food, water, and economy. Of course, the best way to agree on a carbon price would be to have it start at a moderate level, after which it would increase every year or two. In this way, countries will have a chance to start reducing their use of fossil fuels while the price is still modest, but would know that the price will keep going up, so that it will soon be too expensive to use.

With a common price, self-interest and the common good are no longer in tension. To be sure, some countries will likely want to have a free ride. But this problem can be handled, Cramton and colleagues point out, with trade restrictions, perhaps following the World Trade Organization's precedent.

Determining a Common Carbon Price: By Tax or Market?

A remaining question is whether the common carbon price should involve a tax or a market mechanism. Cramton and colleagues say mandating either approach would probably be needlessly contentious. So although a tax might be simpler, countries or regions that are attached to cap-and-trade should be allowed to keep it. Weitzman, however, points out that a carbon tax is *much* simpler than a market and that getting a common price would be very difficult with two radically different methods. Therefore, especially in light of the above-discussed reasons to prefer a tax, countries should be strongly advised to choose a tax, so that the common commitment to a price would simply be a common commitment to a carbon tax.

Equity and Self-Interest: A Final Element

If agreement is reached on a high carbon price (along with an effective means of enforcing it), and if realistic alternatives to fossil fuels are available (to be discussed in Chapter 17), then it might in principle be possible to begin eliminating fossil fuels fast enough to stay within the carbon budget, thereby preventing climate change from becoming hellish and even terminal. Or at least it would be, with the addition of one more element.

As is well known, most of the countries of the "developed" world have reached that status by means of economic growth based on an increase of fossil fuels. Given the fact that developing countries need economic growth to lift millions of their citizens out of stark poverty, it would be unfair to ask these countries to give up their drive for growth in order to help solve the global warming problem, which has been caused almost entirely by the rich world. Indeed, they simply will not do this. Although they, like rich countries, have an interest in saving civilization, they have an *overriding* interest in helping their people escape from poverty. And yet, if developing countries continue to increase their fossil-fuel emissions, then staying within the carbon budget will soon become impossible, no matter what the already developed world does.

Once it is recognized that countries will act for the common good only in a framework in which doing so is not in tension with their immediate interests, the question is whether such a framework is possible. This issue, although central to UN climate conferences, has thus far not been central to the writings of most economists. Although intergenerational ethics has been discussed, global equity is equally important: "Climate policies can be judged in terms of their fairness not only to future generations," point out Ackerman and Stanton along with Ramon Bueno, "but also among different world regions and income groups today."[124]

Global Equity: An Appeal to Fairness

Global equity involves a threefold issue of fairness: First, the island and other poor nations have contributed very little to global climate change. Second, they are the ones that are most threatened by climate change. Third, the countries that have been primarily responsible for global warming are the only ones with the money needed for mitigation and abatement, largely because of activities that have caused the warming. It is obvious, therefore, that the rich world should – morally should - be providing massive funding for mitigation and abatement in the poor countries.

The Green Climate Fund, as mentioned above, was set up by the UN to do just that. Half of the funds are to be used for mitigation, half for abatement.[125] How much will be needed? As the chapters in this book show, the needs for abatement in poor countries are enormous – to deal with rising sea levels in island and coastal nations, with increasing water shortage in countries that have relied on glaciers and snowpack, and with devastating storms and increasing heat, drought and food shortages in many places around the world.

The financial needs for mitigation will be at least equally enormous, for grants and upfront investments for various forms of green (clean) energy, such as massive wind and solar farms. Only thus will low-income countries be able to make the needed transition away from fossil-fuel energy without halting their drive to overcome poverty.

As for what this means in monetary terms, Stern has suggested that "a trillion dollars a year around climate orientated investments" will be needed.[126] How much will actually be provided? Thus far, the record of the rich countries has not been impressive.

At the 2009 Copenhagen conference, the wealthy countries pledged $30 billion in "fast start" funds over the coming three years, with funding increasing to $100 billion annually by 2020. Moreover, besides the fact that $10 billion a year for three years would have been a very slow "fast start," Oxfam concluded that much of the aid was not "new and additional," as the nations had promised, but foreign aid already in the books that was simply repackaged as climate change assistance. As for the United States in particular, it in 2013 said: "International assistance for climate change continues to be a major priority for the United States." And yet the U.S. is reported to have provided (only) $7.45 billion funding for that year.[127]

Even if this were all "new and additional funding," this would be a paltry amount for the world's richest nation, which is also the nation that has contributed the most to global warming. But rather than pledging to do more in the future, U.S. chief climate diplomat Todd Stern indicated that the annual $100 billion is unlikely to appear anytime soon. "The fiscal reality of the United States and other developed countries is not going to allow it," said Stern, due to our obligations for "aging populations and other pressing needs for infrastructure, education, health care and the like."[128]

So, although Nicholas Stern said that $1 trillion annually is needed to deal with mitigation and abatement needs of the low-income countries, Todd Stern indicated that the wealthy nations were not intending to provide even one-tenth of that amount.

In 2011, the World Bank had given a much smaller estimate, $100 billion a year. In 2014, the IPCC mentioned this figure in its 2,500-page report, but it was edited out of the "48-page executive summary to be read by the world's top political leaders," reported *The New York Times'* Justin Gillis. "The edit came after several rich countries, including the United States, raised questions about the language." The language was contentious, Gillis explained, "because poor countries are expected to renew their demand for aid this September in New York at a summit meeting of world leaders," whereas "[m]any rich countries argue that $100 billion a year is an unrealistic demand," because "it would essentially require them to double their budgets for foreign aid, at a time of economic distress at home."

As would be expected, "That argument has fed a rising sense of outrage among the leaders of poor countries, who feel their people are paying the price for decades of profligate Western consumption."[129]

Global Equity: An Appeal to Rich Nations' Self-Interest

It seems that U.S. and most of the other rich nations are not prepared to provide much help to the non-rich nations on the basis of fairness. But perhaps this would be to expect too much. If most of the poor countries will work to reduce global warming only if this does not conflict with their own interests, this is equally true of wealthy nations. The question, therefore, is whether they might see that they need to provide massive funding for mitigation and abatement in the poor world out of self-interest.

Having pointed out that "developing countries are unlikely to direct all of their resources to emission reduction at the expense of poverty reduction," Stanton, Ackerman, and Bueno point out that it is in the rich world's own interests to help these countries increase their standards of living. On the assumption that the rich world is interested in leaving their grandchildren with a decent world, this will be virtually impossible unless the wealthy nations provide massive funding to help the developing nations.

Their case is made in terms of a "policy gap": Even with the most rigorous attempt to reduce CO_2 emissions below the business-as-usual scenario, there will still be a gap of over 100 gigatons in the CO_2 reductions needed to allow us to remain within the carbon budget.[130] The case can be made in terms of a four-step argument:

1. Unless the global temperature is kept down to a minor increase – preferably 1°C, or at least down to 1.5°C, and absolutely not above 2°C – then people over the coming decades will live in an increasingly hellish world.

2. The planet will not be able to stabilize itself at any of these temperature increases, even of 2°C, unless, while the developed world is bringing its own carbon emissions down to practically zero, the rest of the world continues its development without increasing its overall emissions and, in fact, brings them down to near zero.

3. The developing countries will be willing and able to do this only with massive funding from the developed world – funding for abatement, mitigation, and overcoming poverty.

4. Therefore, if the citizens of wealthy countries wish to protect the climate for their grandchildren and, as a bonus, save civilization, they and their governments need to provide many trillions of dollars to help the developing countries.

How many trillion? Eric Pooley asked, "How Much Would You Pay to Save the

Planet?" The only defensible answer is: Whatever it takes. And yet, although the U.S. Federal Reserve committed $7.7 trillion to rescue U.S. banks, the United States government has indicated that it and the other wealthy nations are not prepared to commit $1 trillion, or even $100 billion, to rescue the climate and hence civilization.

The Opposite: The Global Ponzi Scheme

As the father of modern economics, Adam Smith, emphasized, the economy should embody moral principles. Climate morality, as Chapter 14 discussed, emphasizes intergenerational justice, according to which the present generation is careful to ensure that future generations do not have reduced natural capital. We should be concerned at the least with the next seven generations.

A Ponzi scheme in the normal sense of the term – named for Charles Ponzi, who in the 1920s operated a version of it - is an investment operation that promises high rates of return to investors without generating any new money. The scheme works by giving returns to the original investors with money provided by new investors. Then these new investors are paid with money received from still newer investors, and so on.

The operation is fraudulent because, rather than paying investors from profits, it pays them from their own money and that of subsequent investors. Because it can continue only by attracting ever greater numbers of investors, the Ponzi operation cannot continue forever: At some point, many of the investors will lose all of their investments. Bernard Madoff, who ran the biggest Ponzi scheme ever, reportedly bilked investors out of $65 billion.

In the global economy, current generations of human beings are living off the wealth of future generations. Far from increasing the planet's wealth or even preserving it, the current generation is depleting it, more rapidly every decade. Members of the current urrent generation are paying themselves by taking nonrenewable resources from future generations. In Joe Romm's words:

> To perpetuate the high returns the rich countries in particular have been achieving in recent decades, we have been taking an ever greater fraction of nonrenewable energy resources (especially hydrocarbons) and natural capital (fresh water, arable land, forests, fisheries), and, the most important nonrenewable natural capital of all — a livable climate.

This is a Ponzi scheme because we are paying ourselves with wealth taken from future generations, taking advantage of victims who may not have even been born yet. Only later will they realize that we have robbed them. Rather than preserving the world for at least the next seven generations, we are *robbing* the next seven generations – assuming that the human race manages to continue for that long.

"Madoff is reviled as a monster," Romm adds, "for targeting charities. We are targeting our own children and grandchildren and on and on. What does that make us?" Far from taking care to preserve a human-friendly biosphere for future generations, the global economy is operated as if intent on destroying the climate as fast as possible, with present profits being the only concern. To repeat Noam Chomsky's observation: "In the moral calculus of today's capitalism, a bigger bonus tomorrow . . . ." [131]

Running Ponzi schemes is criminal. Having destroyed the savings of thousands of people, Madoff was sentenced to 150 years in prison. But the crime being committed by the present generation is incomparably worse, being on a trajectory that, if continued, will destroy the natural wealth that would rightly belong to billions of people (and other species) in future generations. This generation, Romm says, "has made Madoff look like a penny-ante criminal." Talking to the *New York Times'* Thomas Friedman in 2009, Romm said:

> We created a way of raising standards of living that we can't possibly pass on to our children. . . . You can get this burst of wealth that we have created from this rapacious behavior. . . . But it has to collapse, unless adults stand up and say, 'This is a Ponzi scheme. We have not generated real wealth, and we are destroying a livable climate.

Romm added in 2014 that Naomi Klein's book, *This Changes Everything: Capitalism Vs. the Climate*, makes in different terms the same core argument – that "unchecked capitalism will lead to catastrophe." [132]

Conclusion

As this chapter shows, climate economics in the United States, led by William Nordhaus, encouraged policy-makers to embrace economism, thereby valuing continued economic growth above mitigating climate change.

- In dismissing the *Limits to Growth* as heretical nonsense, U.S. climate economics ignored the warning by that book and Herman Daly that the limits to economic growth have been passed – the truth of which is shown by the fact that today it would take a planet and a half to provide our resources and absorb our wastes each year. [133]

- U.S. economics thereby rejected the Club of Rome's urging to "rebel against the suicidal ignorance of the human condition" – a rebellion shown to be necessary by the increasing number of economists, scientists, and other thoughtful people who have warned that we are committing suicide.

- Most U.S. economists, led by Nordhaus, continued to ignore the warnings by the *Limits to Growth* that, if business as usual continues, the global economy will eventually experience a rapid decline – a warning proven prescient by Weitzman's "dismal theorem," according to which the economic costs of climate change could now be unbounded.

- U.S. economists also ignored Daly's warning that economic growth has already become "uneconomic growth," which impoverishes more than it enriches – demonstrated to be accurate by the enormous costs already caused by climate change, with many more – perhaps infinite - costs to come.

- U.S. economists have likewise ignored the warning by Daly and Cobb that economics has become economism, an idolatrous religion, which teaches that primary devotion should be directed toward continued economic growth – a description illustrated by our government's belief that its continued economic growth is more important then the survival of civilization.

What is most needed now is a sudden rejection of this idolatry, along with a replacement of Nordhaus' climate economics with that grounded in economists such as Cline, Daly, Stern, Weitzman, and Ackerman-Stanton.

PART III

WHAT IS TO BE DONE

PART III

WHAT IS TO BE DONE

17

THE TRANSITION TO CLEAN ENERGY

*"The great energy transition from fossil fuels to
renewable sources of energy is under way."*
– Lester Brown, "The Great Transition, Part I," 2012

*"Germany's energy transition is indeed unprecedented. . . .
The last time when an energy supply was changed was
the industrial revolution."*
– Planet Editor, 2014

Chapter 14 argued that there is a strong moral case for the abolition of the fossil-fuel economy, but that, unless there is a viable alternative, the burning of fossil fuels will probably continue indefinitely. This situation raises two questions: Could fossil fuels be replaced by *clean energy* producing virtually no greenhouse gas? Has clean energy become affordable – no longer too expensive for the poor and likely to weaken the economy?

The term "clean energy" is sometimes called "green energy"; these terms can be used interchangeably. "Renewable energy" is also often used interchangeably with these two terms, but it should not be. Energy is renewable if it is not diminished by use, or is diminished only very slowly, so that it will last forever, at least for all practical purposes – the sun, the primary source of renewable energy, will not run out of fuel for billions of years. But "clean" and "renewable" have different meanings, and some types of renewable energy may not be clean. For example, if oil were replenished underground so quickly that we would never run out it, oil energy would still be dirty. Nevertheless, it is true that most forms of renewable energy are clean, and most forms of clean energy are renewable, so using them interchangeably is understandable. Either term can, therefore, usually be understood to mean "clean and renewable." But in some cases, the distinction between them is crucial (see especially the section on biomass).

It has widely been thought, thanks in part to propaganda from the fossil-fuel industry, that clean energy could not possibly supply more than a small percentage of the world's energy needs, at least in the near future – that fossil-fuel energy will be needed until some revolutionary type of clean energy has been created. But a growing number of scientists and engineers have argued otherwise. As early as 2004, for example, two science professors at Princeton University explained how by 2050 America's energy needs could be provided by various types of clean energy, using only technologies already available.[1]

This chapter looks at various types of clean energy, concluding with a discussion of how 100% clean energy could be realized by 2050. Chapter 18 will then discuss various types of dirty energy and their promoters.

Energy Efficiency: The "Hidden Fuel"

Energy efficiency is generally seen as one of the major ways to reduce fossil-fuel use, in addition to clean or renewable energy. For example, the Obama administration has an Office of Energy Efficiency and Renewable Energy. However, energy efficiency can also fit in the category of clean energy. Joe Romm has argued, in fact, that energy efficiency is the most important type of clean energy.[2]

He is not alone. The World Wildlife Fund, calling energy efficiency "the first and finest 'fuel,'" said that it is the "single most important element" in moving towards a clean-energy system.[3] Maria van der Hoeven, the executive director of the International Energy Agency, has referred to energy efficiency as the "hidden fuel," noting that it is also the "biggest resource," the "cheapest," and the "fastest to deploy."[4]

The great savings that can be achieved by efficiency were documented in a 2009 report, "Unlocking Energy Efficiency in the U.S. Economy," prepared by the prestigious global management consulting firm, McKinsey and Company. If executed at scale, the report said, "a holistic approach would yield gross energy savings worth more than $1.2 trillion, . . . potentially abating up to 1.1 gigatons of greenhouse gases annually."[5]

Although energy efficiency is clean, it has not widely been considered *renewable*, because it has widely been assumed that, once the low-hanging fruit have been picked, there will be few more gains. But Romm, arguing that energy efficiency is actually inexhaustible, has illustrated this in terms of Louisiana's division of Dow Chemical. The energy manager there, Ken Nelson, had a contest in 1982 to choose the best energy-saving plans. The 27 winning plans, which cost a total of $1.7 million to fund, earned a 173 percent return. The investments the second year brought a 340% return. By 1989, the rate of return was 470%, as the 64 projects, which cost $75 million, saved the company $37 million for that year and every year thereafter.[6]

Romm also spoke from his own experience at the Department of Energy. Serving as the executive director for a program of Waste Minimization and Pollution Prevention, he hired Ken Nelson (who had retired from Dow) to train DOE staff around the country to run such contests. The results were similar to the Dow contests, with one project bringing a 1,300% rate on investment.[7]

On being the *least expensive* type of energy, Romm said that "cost of efficiency programs has averaged 2-3¢ per kW – which is about one fifth the cost of electricity generated from new nuclear, coal and natural gas-fired plants." As an illustration, California in the mid-1970s began imposing strict efficiency requirements and, as a result, California's per capita energy consumption has remained virtually flat, while the national consumption has doubled. And the costs have kept coming down. By 2004, the California Energy Commission reported that "the average cost of the efficiency programs had dropped in half, to under 1.4 cents per kilowatt hour, cheaper than any form of new power supply in this country."[8]

However, although California has excelled in efficiency, the country as a whole has not. Indeed, the *Los Angeles Times* reported in 2012 that the United States was worse than China. Obviously, an enormous amount could be done to exploit the "hidden fuel." Fortunately, during the 2013 IPCC meetings in Poland, the United States and other members of the Major Economies Forum on Energy and Climate (MEF) – which has 17 members, including China, the U.S., and the European Union, who account for 75% of the world's greenhouse gas emissions – agreed to launch a major initiative on improving building efficiency.[9]

To give an idea of what a difference can be made: Denmark (which is a not a member of the MEF) has not increased its energy consumption since 1980, even though its economy grew by 80 percent, whereas during that same period U.S. consumption increased by about 70 percent. Moreover, Denmark has passed legislation requiring it to reduce its consumption by another 12 percent by 2020.[10]

Late in 2014, a publication appeared that should inspire the United States to become more like Denmark. A major report by the International Energy Agency, entitled *Capturing the Multiple Benefits of Energy Efficiency*, stated that the main value of energy efficiency had always been assumed to lie in its energy savings. However, the study concluded: "The value of the productivity and operational benefits derived can be up to 2.5 times (250%) the value of energy savings." Indeed, energy efficiency investments have "the potential to boost cumulative economic output through 2035 by USD 18 trillion," which is, commented Joe Romm, "larger than the current size of the U.S. economy!"[11]

Solar Energy

With regard to fuel in the normal sense of the term, the most important question is whether, after gains from efficiency have been achieved, sufficient electricity could be provided by clean energy alone. Aside from hydroelectric power, the best-known type of clean energy is solar. Could it provide a major portion of the planet's clean energy? There have been three arguments that it could not:

- Solar power will never be able to provide much of the power needed for electrification.

- Although solar energy can supplement fossil-fuel electrification, it could never replace it, because it is intermittent: It provides energy only when the sun is shining. It cannot provide 'baseload' power (the minimum amount that a utility must supply to meet demand).

- Electricity's heavy dependence on solar energy will make it too expensive, especially for the poor.

Not long ago, this threefold argument would have been correct. But it no longer is, for several reasons.

Improved Photovoltaics

The technology of solar cells continues to improve. In 2013, Oxford PV announced that it had created a new kind of cell, called "perovskite." Besides replacing lead (which is toxic) with tin, it was over 15 percent efficient (meaning it converts over 15 percent of the light energy into electricity), which was a 400 percent improvement in five years. Although it was expensive, another scientist in 2014 created a perovskite cell that is inexpensive and has an efficiency of 16 percent, and it may get as high as 50 percent.[12]

That same year, a solar company in Silicon Valley created ultra-thin solar cells, with an efficiency of almost 31 percent, German researchers announced a new cell that is 44.7 percent efficient, and MIT researchers published a paper describing the possibility of a still thinner cell using nanotechnology. "Pound for pound the new solar cells" — if they work out, said one of the authors — "produce up to 1,000 times more power than conventional photovoltaics." Accordingly, the same number of PV panels will be able to provide much more electricity.[13]

Late in 2014, Oxford PV announced that its thin-film perovskite solar cell technology can be added to conventional solar cells, increasing their efficiency from 5 to 20 percent.[14]

Improved Storage

Technology has been developed for the energy to be stored for many hours, so it will be available when the sun is not shining. Although great advances had been made before 2014, that year Harvard scientists announced a new kind of battery, which would be qualitatively superior. In distinction from the well-known types of batteries, which employ chemical solids, there are also "flow batteries," which store the charge in liquids. As a result, there is no limit to how much electricity the batteries can hold. The only problem with the first generation flow batteries was that they needed high-cost metals, such as platinum. But the Harvard researchers invented a type that requires no metals. If it tests out, this new battery could completely change the storage issue.[15]

Nano-Technology

Nano-technology working with germanium sulfide (GeS) has created "nano-flowers," which should result in a new generation of solar cells and storage devices. Having extremely thin petals, these nano-flowers provide "a huge surface area in a small amount of space."[16]

Concentrated Solar Power (CSP)

Solar photovoltaics provide only one of the types of solar energy. There is also *concentrated* (also called "concentrating") solar power, which one physicist has called the "technology that will save humanity." In this technology – abbreviated CSP – mirrors create concentrated solar power by aiming sunlight at seawater so as to turn it into steam, which then drives turbines to create electricity. Unlike solar photovoltaic technology, concentrated solar

> stores heat rather than electricity, making storage using CSP technology potentially much cheaper. . . . This storage capacity allows CSP power plants to generate baseload power. . . . Since concentrating solar power can support the nation's electricity grid during all hours of the day, it is able to compete on par with natural gas and other traditional fossil-fuel sources of energy, without the need for expensive battery systems.

In 2011, for example, a CSP plant in Spain showed that it was able to produce electricity for 24 hours straight.[17]

Also, CSP can generate three times more power per acre than solar plants using PV technology, and CSP technology does not require any scarce and hence expensive materials: "CSP plants are made from low-cost and durable materials such as steel and glass."[18]

Perhaps the greatest advantage of CSP plants is their ability to provide "dispatchable energy," meaning "power that can be turned on or off on demand." Accordingly, they can be turned on when the demand for electricity is the greatest. "Current CSP plants can store thermal energy for up to 16 hours, which means that their production profile can match the demand profile (just like a conventional power plant)."[19]

CSP is mainly used in large (utility-scale) solar energy generating systems (SEGS). The largest one in the world is the Ivanpah plant in California's Mojave Desert. Consisting of nine solar plants, it produces 354 megawatts. (A megawatt, abbreviated MW, is 1,000 kilowatts, or a million watts.) Having been around since the 1980s, CSP was dormant for 30 years but is now experiencing a resurgence, which began in Spain. For several years, Spain was the CSP leader, but because of a political change in Spain, combined with the building of enormous CSP facilities in Arizona and Southern California, leadership has shifted to the U.S.[20]

There are also large CSP plants in operation, or in development, in other parts of the world, such as one in India's Gujarat Solar Park and a huge facility in oil-rich Abu Dhabi. By 2013, CSP plants were producing a total of 2.5 gigawatts (GW) worldwide (a gigawatt is 1,000 megawatts, hence a billion watts), and many additional plants were in the pipeline. Greenpeace has predicted that CSP could meet 7 percent of the world's projected power needs by 2030, rising to 25 percent by 2050.[21]

Large Photovoltaic (PV) Plants

The main advantage of PV power – besides requiring less sunlight and water – is that it can provide electricity in kilowatts (rather than megawatts) and hence to individual residences and businesses. However, PV can also be employed in large solar generating systems. After Spain began building large PV systems in 2008, still bigger PV projects have been developed. In 2013, the world's largest PV project was developed in California's Antelope Valley, producing 230 MW, followed by one in California's San Luis Obispo County. But in 2014, leadership shifted to China, where a 329 MW solar plant in Qinghai province, connected to a 1.28 GW hydroelectric dam, was connected to the grid.[22]

Large PV plants have, or are being, built in other countries, including Ukraine's Crimea, Canada, Greece, Mexico, China, and India, which, even before the 2014 election of the new pro-solar prime minister, was planning to add new plants every year.[23]

The Price of Solar Power

At one time, producing electricity from solar energy was more expensive than electricity based on coal (assuming that we continue to subsidize coal and ignore its health and other costs). But the cost of generating electricity from solar energy has been coming down dramatically.

- Whereas a single PV cell in the U.S. cost almost $77 per watt in 1977, by 2013 it had fallen to about $0.65 per watt.[24]

- The cost of installed solar energy systems in the U.S. came down 20 percent between 2009 and 2011, another 27 percent in 2012, and by 2013, it reached grid parity with electricity from new coal plants. In fact, solar and electrical companies in El Paso cooperated in selling electricity at even less than the going price for coal-based electricity.[25]

- In 2013, there was an especially dramatic sign of the new situation: Coal India, the world's largest coal company, installed PV panels in its facilities throughout India – to bring down its utility bills.[26]

- Natural gas has also been marketed on the idea that it is much less expensive than solar. But in 2013, an article entitled, "New ERCOT Report Shows that Texas Wind and Solar Are Highly Competitive with Natural Gas,"[27] countered that contention.

- In 2014, PV with storage was projected to reach parity with electricity from the grid in Germany by the end of the year; the same report led the CSP Today website to publish an article warning of "the threat of electrical storage to CSP."[28]

- In 2013 and 2014, stories started appearing reporting that electricity from solar energy was now less expensive than that from natural gas. Palo Alto, California, signed an agreement to buy solar energy for 7¢ per kilowatt-hour, compared with the 28 to 65¢/kWh estimated by the California Energy Commission for energy from natural gas plants. Austin Energy signed a contract with Recurrent Energy for 25 years for the lowest price yet – less than 5 cents kWh. In Minnesota, an administrative-law judge ruled that solar-based electricity would be less expensive for customers.[29]

Due to the fact that PV electricity is as cheap as and, in some cases, cheaper than coal-based electricity, some of the fossil-fuel-fired utilities are, as one writer put it, "terrified of solar." David Roberts published an article entitled "Solar Panels Could Destroy U.S. Utilities, according to U.S. Utilities." In response, fossil-fuel interests have begun introducing legislation to raise the price of solar electricity. In Arizona, the utility, aided by outside groups including the Kochs, got the state to add a monthly $5 fee (although this was much less than the utility wanted).[30]

If most legislatures, believing that the survival of fossil-fuel companies is less important than that of civilization, follow California in rejecting solar-killing fees, solar electricity in United States as a whole could join many other countries – including Australia, Chile, Germany, Greece, Israel, Italy, Japan, South Africa, and South Korea – in reaching parity with coal-based electricity, so that price will no longer be considered a barrier to a complete transition from fossil-fuel to solar energy to produce electricity.[31]

Of course, if the government would quit subsidizing fossil-fuel energy and/or if it would institute a serious carbon tax, the battle would be over, because solar power would be far less expensive than every type of dirty energy.

Worldwide Solar Energy

The installation of new solar power has been increasing around the world every year. Some 15 countries, led by Bulgaria, Germany, Italy, Belgium and the Czech Republic, have been doing very well in terms of the most important measure, solar capacity per capita.[32] Unfortunately, however, none of the five countries most responsible for CO_2 emissions – the USA, China, India, Russia, and Japan – are in the top 15. That's the bad news. However, four of these countries – all except Russia – have been adding solar power rapidly.

The growth of China's deployment of solar energy, actual and planned, in the past decade has been phenomenal. By 2003, China's installed solar capacity was only 42 MW (0.042 GW), but by 2011, China had installed 7 GW and was planning to add 5 more GW by 2015. Then, having added more than that amount in 2012 alone, China increased its 2015 goal to 15 GW, then raised it again to 40 GW by 2015 and 50 GW by 2020. In seeking to meet this goal, China in 2013 set a world record for solar installations, adding an amazing 12 GW (which is the total amount of the U.S. installed solar power since the beginning).[33]

China will hence probably soon surpass all other countries combined in the total amount of solar power installed – although its population is so huge that the percentage of its electricity generated from solar is still very small.

A government that wants to promote a type of clean energy provides a "feed-in tariff," which covers the difference between the present market price of electricity and what it would cost generating electricity with that form of clean energy. In 2012, Japan provided an especially generous feed-in tariff for solar energy, helping the country increase its solar installation greatly. As a result, during 2013 Japan invested more in solar energy installation than any other country. Whereas China and Japan by 2010 had contributed only 10 percent of the deployment of global solar power, by the end of 2013 they accounted for 45 percent.[34]

India, after getting off to a slow start, authorized a National Solar Mission in 2010 and by 2013 it had added 1 gigawatt of solar power, then announced that it plans to install 10 GW by 2017 and 20 GW by 2020. In 2014 the BJP won the national election, making the new prime minster Narendra Modi – formerly the chief minister of the state of Gujarat, which had built two-thirds of India's solar power. After his election, Modi pledged to increase India's clean energy, especially solar, enough for every home in the country to have at least a little electricity by 2019. Shortly thereafter, India's largest integrated solar company helped by pledging to provide interest-fee loans. Later that year, a report said that by 2024, India could install six times what the government now plans.[35]

As for the United States, it has made great strides this century. From 52 megawatts installed in 2002, it rose to 7,200 megawatts by 2012 and then in 2013 became one of only four countries to have installed 10 GW.[36] However, given America's wealth and technology, this figure is not especially impressive, compared with the other three countries, especially relatively small Italy and Germany, which have installed much more.

But the important thing is what the USA does now. "America's solar energy potential," noted a 2013 report by Environment America, "is virtually endless." Why? Because "America has enough solar energy potential to power the nation several times over." In addition, "every one of the 50 states has the technical potential to generate more electricity from the sun than it uses in the average year." In 19 states, "the technical potential for electricity generation from solar photovoltaics exceeds annual electricity consumption by a factor of 100 or more." Moreover, 85% of the solar electricity generated thus far has occurred in only 12 states, dubbed the "dazzling dozen" (and even they have only begun to realize their potential – California, which does the best, has so far fulfilled only 6 percent of it).[37]

By one measurement, the United States has been doing well, increasing its solar power almost 420 percent between 2010 and 2013. But by another measurement, it has hardly begun, accounting for slightly over 1 percent of America's electricity.[38]

Wind Energy

Whereas solar power has great potential for replacing fossil-fuel electricity, wind power arguably has even more – as indicated by Lester Brown's hope that the world will begin "building a wind-centered economy."[39] Wind has, in fact, been on a roll.

Wind Energy on a Roll

After getting off to a slow start in much of the world, including China and the USA, the development of wind energy has in recent years been growing rapidly in many parts of the world.

Europe: The first region of the world to install wind power in a major way, Europe, has remained on course. Denmark is the world leader in terms of per capita wind power, generating 30 percent of its electricity from wind turbines by the end of 2012 (and pledging to boost this share to 50 percent by 2020), and Spain, Portugal, Sweden, Germany, Ireland and the UK obtain from 10 to 25 percent of their electricity from wind. The UK is especially strong in offshore wind energy, which provides about 60 percent of Europe's offshore wind energy – and this was prior to the operation in 2013 of the London Array, the world's largest offshore wind farm. In 2014, the UK continued to advance, starting to install dozens of massive 6 MW and 8 MW wind turbines, which because of their size provide electricity that is more cost-effective.[40]

United States: Although Europe has remained in the leadership position, the United States has moved up to 7th place, due to an enormous expansion of wind power in recent years. In spite of all the hoopla about natural gas, America already in 2012 was adding more capacity from wind power than from natural gas. Because of the recent wind-power surge, several states now have more installed wind capacity than have most *countries*. "The 12,200 megawatts in Texas and the 5,500 megawatts in California, for example, would rank them sixth and eleventh, respectively, on the world wind power list." In 2013, wind power reduced U.S. power sector emissions by over 5 percent.[41]

Part of the reason for the great U.S. boom in wind energy in recent years has been the production tax credit (PTC), which subsidizes electricity generated by turbines for their first ten years. The PTC has been supported by Republican lawmakers in the middle of the country, including Kansas, "the Saudi Arabia of Wind." Even if they have no concern for climate change, these Republicans like wind energy because it is good for jobs and the economy in their states. However, after the tax credit expired in 2012, uncertainty on whether Congress would reauthorize it led to a 90 percent drop in 2013 and 2014 – resulting in the vast majority of wind turbines made in the United States being exported to other countries.[42]

Nevertheless, America will soon also be producing a great amount of offshore wind energy, with the Department of Energy announcing its attention to develop "54 gigawatts of offshore wind capacity by 2030 – more than 10 times the amount currently installed worldwide."[43]

China: The other country most important to be weaned from fossil-fuel energy, China, had moved up to 19th place by 2013,[44] due to phenomenal growth in wind energy during the past few years: In 2012, China increased its wind power by 41 percent, thereby making wind the country's third largest source of electrical power, behind coal and hydro – meaning that wind power surpassed nuclear energy. In 2013, China installed over 16 GW of wind energy, "just under half all new capacity added worldwide!"[45]

India: Also extremely important in this respect is India, which now ranks 5th worldwide in wind energy capacity and is now the 4th largest market.[46] It has grown significantly under the country's Renewable Energy Certificate scheme, which by 2012 had accredited 520 projects in 7 states since its inauguration in 2010. In 2014, India announced a National Wind Energy Mission, and this was even before Narendra Modi had become prime minister, so we can expect even more growth.[47]

Australia: Another big country coming on strong is Australia, especially its state of South Australia, which already has 24 percent of its electricity generated by wind power. The country as a whole, which in 2013 opened the largest wind farm in the southern hemisphere, planned to have 20 percent wind-generated electricity by 2020 – at least before an anti-green government came to power in 2013.[48]

Japan: Although it is currently only 24th in terms of per capita wind power, Japan in 2012 instituted an extremely attractive three-year feed-in tariff (FIT) for wind (as well as solar and geothermal) energy. By 2015, accordingly, Japan is likely to become one of the world's leaders in terms of per capita wind energy – with most of this energy generated from offshore wind, "a resource plentiful enough to meet national electricity needs nearly three times over."[49]

Other Countries: There have also been noteworthy developments in many other countries – including Canada, Mexico, Brazil, Poland, Romania, Turkey, Egypt, and South Africa – but the above examples suffice to show that wind power has been on a roll, with great increases continuing around the world.

Wind Energy Total: Although many people still tend to equate clean energy primarily with solar, wind energy has already outstripped solar. Whereas there were roughly 100 GW of installed solar capacity worldwide by 2012, there were then already about 240 GW of installed wind power.[50]

Although it is now widely recognized that we must quit using coal, it is not widely recognized that it can be replaced with clean energy. A *Guardian* op-ed piece in 2014 said: "Wind clearly generates electricity, which is good, but not much," so "it could never provide enough energy, even in conjunction with solar energy, to make a significant contribution to the planet's electricity needs." But this thinking is out of date. To abolish coal, many think, we must use both wind and nuclear energy. But wind in China has already outstripped nuclear,[51] and this will happen in other countries if they become as dedicated as China.

Other Charges about Wind Energy

In addition to the claim that wind could never provide much energy, there have been other charges.

The Intermittency Charge: It has been claimed that wind energy could never provide baseline power, becomes "sometimes it blows, sometimes it doesn't." But this is becoming a non-problem, for a number of reasons.

- In large countries, the problem can be largely solved by simply having the country saturated with wind turbines. As the *Economist* pointed out, "with enough wind farms sited in enough places, the supply evens out. The wind is always blowing somewhere."[52]

- Assuming that neither solar nor wind energy could supply all of a country's needs by itself, that problem would be largely solved by combining them: "Solar energy is produced when the sun is shining during the day and is complementary to wind energy, which tends to reach its highest production at night." So when a grid is fed by both of them, the energy generally smoothes out.[53]

- It has been discovered that solar-wind hybrid power plants can produce almost twice as much electricity in a given area as either one by itself. Because "the plants generate wind and solar power at different intervals and during complementary seasons," they balance out the overall supply to the grid, so it remains highly stable throughout the year.[54]

- GE Power & Wind, which has become the world's number one supplier of wind turbines, introduced in 2013 a new version of its turbine, called Brilliant. Besides being 25 percent more efficient than previous turbines, it comes equipped with a grid-scale battery storage system. Previously, when the wind was generating more energy than could be used, wind-farm operators had to "spill wind – reduce the amount of wind energy they capture, convert to electricity, and feed into the grid" – resulting in what the general manager of GE's Wind Products likened to "dollars flying by [in the wind]." But with the new turbines, the excess wind energy is "stored in battery banks as electrochemical energy," which can "then be sold and fed into the grid later in the day at a moment's notice." "As more of these turbines hit the grid, the reliability of renewable energy increases, making it a feasible backbone to the electric grid." Lester Brown agrees, saying that "it is wind that is on its way to becoming the foundation of the new energy economy."[55]

The High-Cost Charge: It has long been said that electricity produced by wind energy is much more expensive than fossil-fuel energy. But to whatever extent this was true, it is not now.

- One reason for the supposed low price of fossil-fuel energy is that it has been subsidized. Furthermore, that price has been calculated without including the "true cost of fossil-fuel energy" – the various external costs, such as the medical problems caused by pollution and the increasing financial costs produced by extreme weather and other effects of global warming. Were these priced in, it would be obvious that wind and other forms of clean energy are far less expensive.

- Moreover, even apart from considering these costs, wind energy is now competitive with, or even cheaper than, much fossil-fuel energy. According to a 2013 report by HSBC Bank, wind has reached parity with new-built coal plants. And wind power is actually cheaper than electricity derived from new fossil-fuel plants in some countries, including Kenya, Nicaragua, and Australia. The chief executive of Bloomberg New Energy Finance said in 2013, "The perception that fossil fuels are cheap and renewables are expensive is now out of date."[56]

- The same is also true of some U.S. states. For example, a 2012 analysis by the Michigan Public Service Commission concluded that electricity from wind (along with other renewables) had become cheaper than new coal plants and that, in fact, the gap is widening. In 2012 and 2013, the cost of wind energy became competitive with natural gas in Texas and with both nuclear and coal in several Midwest states. And then in 2014, wind energy had become competitive with – and in some places cheaper than – natural gas.[57]

The Human Health Charge: Some proposed wind farms, especially in Australia, have been blocked because of public concern about the infrasound (inaudible to humans) generated by wind turbines. They have been said to cause a variety of symptoms, such as ear pressure, fatigue, headache, and even nausea. However, a number of scientific studies have shown these claims to be baseless:

- One study found that the symptoms did not start appearing in Australia until anti-wind farm activists started making such claims about infrasound.

- Double-blind experiments showed that, insofar as people had real physical symptoms, they resulted from the "nocebo effect," in which something inherently harmless produces harmful effects (parallel to the "placebo effect," in which an inherently worthless medicine produces positive effects).

- One of these studies was by Australia's National Health and Medical Research Council, which led the Australian Medical Association to conclude that the symptoms were based on misinformation.[58]

The Property Values Charge: Another charge has been that nearby wind farms bring home property values down. But in 2013, after carrying out the most comprehensive study to date, Lawrence Berkeley National Laboratory found "no statistical evidence that operating wind turbines have had any measureable impact on home sales prices."[59]

Advantages of Wind Energy

In addition to the fact that these charges do not stand up to examination, wind energy, Lester Brown has pointed out, has a great number of advantages in addition to its rapidly falling cost:

- Wind-energy is carbon-free, except for the one-time carbon emissions building the turbines (which is paid back within six months).[60]

- It is ubiquitous and abundant (North Dakota, Kansas, and Texas "have enough harnessable wind energy to easily satisfy national electricity needs").

- It is not depletable ("The amount of wind energy used today has no effect on the amount available tomorrow").

- It uses no water (which the growing water shortage makes very important).

- It uses little land. (Although a wind farm can cover many square miles, turbines occupy only 1 percent of that area, so that "ranchers and farmers can, in effect, double-crop their land, simultaneously harvesting electricity while producing cattle, wheat or corn.")

- It can be installed quickly. (The construction time for the typical wind farm is one year, compared with 10 years for a nuclear power plant.)

- It can be brought online quickly.

- It provides money for local economies and land-owners. (Landowners can receive thousands of dollars a year in royalties for each wind turbine on their land, so whereas a few people – such as the third Koch brother, William – say NIMBY ["not in my backyard"], many farmers, ranchers, and communities say PIMBY ["put it in my backyard"].)[61]

The Potential for Meeting Civilization's Need for Electricity

In speaking about the possibility of a wind-centered economy, Lester Brown did not mean that wind-energy by itself could provide all the electricity the world needs. But an examination of plans and studies suggests that it could come closer than has been commonly thought. To summarize:

- Denmark plans to get 30 percentage of its electricity from wind by 2020.[62]

- Scotland, which plans to supply the equivalent of 100 percent of its need for electricity by 2020., was by 2013 obtaining 68% of its clean energy from wind.[63]

- Germany and the UK both have "enough potential wind generating capacity to be 100 percent wind-powered.[64]

- North Dakota, Kansas, and Texas "have enough harnessable wind energy to easily satisfy [U.S.] national electricity needs."[65]

- A study led by Harvard and Beijing professors said: "Wind power alone could provide electricity for all of China if the country overhauls its rural grids and raises the subsidy for wind energy."[66]

Hydropower

Hydropower – also called "hydroelectric power" and "hydroelectricity" – is electricity created from moving water (defined here as excluding ocean energy, discussed later). Having long been used to generate electricity, hydropower presently accounts for roughly 20 percent of the world's generation of electricity. A few countries, such as Canada, Norway, and Brazil, get a majority of their electricity from hydropower, and it provides a significant percentage for many other countries, including the United States, for which it provides about 7 percent. It is by far the largest source of clean energy, providing about 80 percent of America's and 97 percent of the world's.[67]

Since the 1980s, however, big hydroelectric dams have become controversial, due to their environmental, social, and cultural damage. Indeed, "large-scale hydropower developments have been viewed as something of a pariah within the renewable energy sector."[68]

Indeed, because most big dams have had these types of negative effects, many states confusingly do not (unlike the EPA) classify hydroelectric power – at least from large dams – as a type of renewable energy, because of a tendency to equate "renewable" with "good" – along with a desire not to see it as fulfilling renewable energy mandates - and because "there is already so much hydro out there."[69] It would make more sense to reword the mandate to apply to *non-hydro* energy that is clean and renewable.

In any case, like it or not, there is now a resurgence of large-scale hydropower, partly because of the desire to replace coal with a cleaner source of energy. This resurgence is even being supported by the World Bank, which "it had all but abandoned a decade ago but now sees as crucial . . . to the drive to tame carbon use" while also eliminating poverty.[70]

Whereas some large dams in some places need not be very damaging, those in many other places inevitably are. But some countries believe that their need for hydropower outweighs the likely problems, and the new drive to build big dams has led to anti-dam movements in several countries, including Brazil, Chile, China.[71]

These huge hydroelectric projects, by causing one kind of disaster to prevent another, evoke different opinions among people seeking positive outcomes. On the one hand, those who favor them point out that although they are inevitably destructive, the continued use of coal will be even more so. On the other hand, while acknowledging that it would not make sense to tear down most of them, opponents point out that the same amount of energy can be supplied from "smaller, more flexible hydroelectric projects that . . . are more easily adapted to social and environmental concerns," as demonstrated by Norway, which now gets virtually all of its electricity from hydropower.[72]

In the United States, there have been few new hydroelectric power plants since the 1970s because of the environmental movement, which has increased the difficulties of getting licenses. However, while America's present hydroelectric power comes from about 2,500 dams, the country has some 80,000 dams. Realizing that the opposition to hydroelectric dams was because of the dams, not the hydroelectric plants, the government in 2005 passed a law providing a tax credit and a shorter licensing process for hydropower where dams were already in place, leading to a great surge in applications. The Department of Energy judges that about 600 of these already-built dams are suitable for power plants, which together could boost the US hydroelectric power by 15 percent.[73]

In addition, there is an emerging technology called "hydrokinetic power," which employs turbines that can be placed in spillways, water treatment plants, and especially canals, thousands of miles of which are owned and operated by the U.S. Bureau of Reclamation. These turbines are small, of course. But there is also a plan to place larger turbines in the Mississippi and other rivers.[74]

Offering a balanced view about hydropower, the Union of Concern Scientists, having summarized the arguments against big dams, said that "if it's done right, hydropower can be a sustainable and nonpolluting power source that can help decrease our dependence on fossil fuels and reduce the threat of global warming."[75]

Ocean Energy

Sometimes hydroelectric power is grouped together with two types of ocean power: wave energy and tidal energy. Normally, however, these two types of ocean energy are distinguished from hydroelectric power. These two types of power, which employ the ocean to produce electricity, are much less developed. (A third type of ocean energy, called "ocean thermal energy conversion" [OTEC], is ignored here, being only ready to be developed.)[76]

The ocean, which covers 71 percent of the Earth's surface, has the potential to produce an enormous amount of energy that is renewable and clean. And yet it has thus far been largely untapped, even though about 40 percent of the world's population lives within 70 miles (100 kilometers) of the coast.[77]

The question is how to turn this potential into electricity. The two ways of doing this – wave energy and tidal energy – are quite different, although "the general public and press often mistakenly treat 'wave energy' and 'tidal energy' as interchangeable terms." They are very different because they are derived from different energy sources: Wave energy is the conversion of the ocean's surface waves into useful power, whereas tidal energy gets useful power from the changing tides.[78]

1. Wave Energy

"Wave energy is essentially an accumulation of wind energy," but it is much more powerful, because water is 800 times denser than air.[79] Wave energy also has many more virtues. It is clean and inexhaustibly renewable; free, with no fuel needed and no waste produced; inexpensive to operate and maintain; distributed across the globe, so that many countries can benefit from it; predictable, because waves can be anticipated a day or two in advance; and never too weak to generate some electricity.

In addition, wave energy works well with wind energy to smooth out their contributions of electricity to the grid: Although wave energy is derived from wind energy, it has often traveled large distances, so "it is regularly out of phase with the local wind conditions."[80]

The Potential

"The appeal of wave energy is clear: the untapped resource is huge." According to one estimate, it could supply over 2,000 gigawatts. However, rather than megawatts and gigawatts, ocean energy potential is usually given in terawatt hours per year (TWh/yr). A terawatt hour is sizeable; "just 1 TWh/yr of energy will supply around 93,850 average U.S. homes with power annually," and the United States uses about 4,000 TWh of electricity in a year. As for the amount of wave energy available for America, one estimate puts the recoverable resource along the U.S. shelf at about 1/3 of that: 1,170 TWh/yr. As for the Earth as a whole, the U.N. has estimated that there is theoretically a potential for 29,500 TWh/yr – considerably more than the 21,500 TWh of electrical power generated worldwide in 2010 – although not all of this will be useable.[81]

Even though wave energy is still in its infancy, advances have been made. Wave energy was first made commercially operative in 2014 off the coast of Perth, Australia, where giant buoys shoot high-water through pipes to drive onshore generators and turbines. Because the coasts in that part of Australia provide some of the world's best wave energy resources, this type of clean energy should be able to provide the country with a significant percentage of its electricity.[82]

The other country that has advanced most fully is Scotland, which has 10 percent of Europe's wave power potential and is set to construct the world's largest wave-energy farm thus far – as reported in a *Popular Science* story entitled "The Amazing Potential of Wave Energy."[83]

In the United States, projects in Hawaii, Alaska, and Oregon have been developed,[84] but California could end up being the leader, as suggested in a 2013 *Los Angeles Times* opinion piece:

> California could face its biggest power shortages in more than a decade this summer, with San Onofre idled and projections of low hydroelectric output. Yet the state's 1,100-mile coastline is packed with unused sustainable energy potential. Done right, California could be leading instead of following the next wave of energy innovation that will make blue the new green.[85]

Difficulties

But turning that wave power into affordable electricity has proved difficult, mainly because building wave-energy plants is very expensive. One of the reasons for this expense is that, because water is so dense and the ocean is so powerful, it is difficult to produce devices that are efficient and yet "can withstand monster waves and gale-force winds, not to mention corrosive saltwater, seaweed, floating debris and curious marine mammals," wrote Elizabeth Rusch in the *Smithsonian*.[86]

In any case, because of the upfront expense, corporations are reluctant to invest in wave energy, because they will have to wait a long time to get a return. If the "appeal of wave energy" is to lead to widespread electrification of wave energy, so that it can make a major contribution to the abolition of fossil-fuel energy, government action is needed. The executive director of the Oregon Wave Energy Trust said: "In my opinion the biggest issue is the failure to price carbon," because right now "we're playing on an unlevel playing field." If carbon is given a realistic price, or fossil-fuel subsidies are removed, or wave energy is adequately subsidized until it is developed sufficiently for its price to come down, then wave energy could play a huge role in America's becoming 100 percent clean. According to the Department of Energy, wave power could provide more than one quarter of America's electricity use.[87]

Allure

In spite of the difficulties faced by wave energy, Elizabeth Rusch said, the allure is irresistible. A machine that could harness an inexhaustible, nonpolluting source of energy and be deployed economically in sufficient numbers to generate significant amounts of electricity – that would be a feat for the ages.

Especially alluring, because of the growing shortages of fresh water caused by climate change, is the ability of wave energy to feed high-pressure water into desalination plants, so that fresh water can be created without pumps and hence electricity.[88]

2. Tidal Energy

Tidal energy is based, of course, on the tides, which result from the gravitational fields from the sun and the moon, combined with the Earth's rotation around its axis, producing high and low tides. Because the gravitational attraction by the moon is the most important factor, tidal energy could be called – analogously to solar energy – "lunar energy." There are two types of systems for converting tidal energy into electrical energy: tidal barrages and tidal stream (or "tidal current") turbines.

Tidal Barrages

A tidal barrage, which was the first type of tidal energy, is a dam blocking off a tidal bay or estuary. The energy is based on the difference between high and low tides. The difference must be quite large, at least 16 feet (about 5 meters). The operation begins with flood gates ("sluice gates") allowing the incoming tidal waters to fill a reservoir. Once the water reaches its maximum level, the gates are closed and held until the ebb tide creates a sufficient drop in elevation. Water is then released through turbines, which produce electrical energy (just as a hydroelectric power plant does).

The first tidal barrage was constructed in 1966 at La Rance estuary in northern France. But there are only four other commercial-sized tidal barrages operating in the world (in Russia, Nova Scotia, China, and South Korea). There are so few because of a host of problems:

- They cause substantial ecological damage: heavy siltation, erosion, and damage to marine life.

- The upfront cost – for the installation of the plants and underwater wiring and the transmission to a grid – is very high.

- Given the need for a big difference between high and low tides, there are only about 40 potential sites on the planet.[89]

Because tidal barrages were the first type of tidal energy developed, the idea arose that tidal energy plants necessarily cause a great deal of ecological damage and that there are few sites where they could be installed. But there is a second type, to which most of the research on tidal power shifted in recent decades.

Tidal Stream Turbines

This second type involves fixing turbines to the seabeds in tidal streams (or currents), which are places with accelerated flow. These streams result from the movement of masses of water in the ocean caused by the moon's gravitational attraction. A stream turns the generator blades much like wind does with a wind turbine, except that the blades can be mounted back to back, so they can harness the tides whether they are coming in or going out.[90] Being still in the testing phase, these "in-stream turbines" have become operational only at three sites, but big plans lie ahead, because the turbines can be installed in hundreds of places, some of which have enormous potential.

- A turbine placed at one of Scotland's Orkney's islands has passed its test, paving the way for the construction of the world's first major tidal stream power station, consisting of an array of 10 turbines on the seabed of the Sound of Islay, which has a "canyon" with a very strong and reliable tidal stream.[91] Having called Scotland's Pentland Firth "almost certainly the best site for tidal stream power in the world," an Oxford professor of engineering added that "it could potentially generate power equivalent to almost half of Scotland's annual electricity consumption." Near the end of 2014, construction began of the world's largest tidal array, with 269 1.5 MW turbines.[92]

- The UK, which hopes to be the world's leader in tidal stream electrical generation, is estimated to have about 50 percent of Europe's tidal energy resource, which theoretically could provide about 12 percent of the UK's current electricity demand. In 2014, one of the world's first grid-connected tidal sources, a seven-storey tidal generator in Wales, began a 12-month trial period. The UK hopes its tidal and wave power will replace a fifth of its aging coal and gas plants.[93]

- Nova Scotia's Bay of Fundy "pushes over 160 billion tonnes of water on the incoming tide: more than four times the combined flow of every freshwater river in the world," it has an enormous amount of energy to be tapped.[94] (Having sites in Canada as well as Nova Scotia, Canada is likely to challenge the UK for leadership in tidal stream energy.)

- The United States has good sites in Alaska, Washington, Maine, New York, Massachusetts, and especially Alaska: Although False Pass, an Alaskan town in the Aleutians, was "legendary for its high current velocities," expectations about it were "blown out of the water" by a 2013 study.[95]

According to the International Energy Agency, the world's potential tidal power is 2200 TWh and, according to another source, about 700 TWh a year could be *realistically* used.[96] Accordingly, besides providing a significant portion of the world's electricity, tidal power in certain areas "could play an important role in providing baseload renewable energy generation, in much the same way that concentrating solar thermal and geothermal power might do in other places."[97]

Tidal Energy: Pros and Cons

Besides being capable of providing a lot of energy (an in-stream turbine can produce up to 2 MW of power, and many of them can be installed at any one location), tidal energy is:

- *Renewable*, lasting as long as the sun, moon, and oceans endure.

- *Clean*, requiring no fuel and creating no greenhouse-gas emissions.

- *Efficient*, turning 80% of the kinetic energy into electricity (compared with 30% for coal).

- *Predictable*, generating the same amount of energy (for that location), no matter the weather.

- *Inexpensive to operate* (once the turbines have been built and installed).[98]

Right now, electricity from tidal energy, like any new technology, is expensive, so it will need to be subsidized until the costs are brought down (unless fossil-fuel subsidies are eliminated). In any case, although in-stream turbine energy does not have the problems that plagued tidal barrages, it does have – in addition to the initial costs – a few disadvantages:

- *Distance from Grid:* Most sites are far from a grid, making connections expensive.

- *Possible Need for Repairs*, because of damage from strong storms and salt-water corrosion.

- *Potential conflict with shipping or recreation.*

But these are problems that could be handled.

Conclusion

Although the implementation of both forms of ocean energy will create some problems, these problems are quite minor in comparison with the great benefits that can come from wave and tidal energy, especially the benefit of helping us reduce and finally abolish fossil-fuel energy, with its enormous problems. The U.S. Department of Energy says that wave and tidal energy could provide 15 percent of the country's electricity by 2030, whereas the UK government says that ocean energy could potentially provide as much as 75 percent of its electricity.[99]

Geothermal Energy

As we have seen, all the electricity needed by America and China in particular, and the world in general, could be provided by energy efficiency in combination with solar, wind, and ocean energy. But some experts believe that geothermal energy might turn out to be as important as any of these. According to one scientist in 2012, geothermal energy is "begging to be used." And yet in most countries, it has largely gone begging: Although the "United States is the world leader in installed geothermal capacity," this resource "remains virtually untapped in the U.S." China, likewise, has hardly begun to use geothermal energy to produce electricity.[100] Geothermal energy is exactly what the name says: heat of the Earth. The heat sources are bodies of molten rock, called *magma*, that exist at depth, in some places associated with surface volcanic activity:

> Most of the time magma stays beneath the surface, heating surrounding rocks and the water that has become trapped within those rocks. Sometimes that water escapes through cracks in the Earth to form pools of hot water (hot springs) or bursts of hot water and steam (geysers). The rest of the

heated water remains in pools under the Earth's surface, called geothermal reservoirs.[101]

Whereas hot springs have been used to provide heat for thousands of years, the use of modern piping to heat buildings began at the end of the 19th century, and the first geothermal plant was created in the first decade of the 20th century. There are different types of these plants, but they all use steam to turn turbines to create electricity.[102]

Geothermal Energy as Clean and Renewable

Geothermal energy is clean because it can be generated without burning fossil fuels, and a plant's operations produce near-zero greenhouse gas emissions. Geothermal energy is renewable, because the magmas at depth are inexhaustible heat sources on human timescales, and as long as a site is given time to restore its heat, it can last indefinitely.[103]

Traditional and Enhanced

There are two types of geothermal technologies: traditional and enhanced. Traditional geothermal generation employs water from naturally occurring reservoirs at relatively shallow depths, whereas enhanced geothermal systems (EGS) produce geothermal reservoirs artificially by fracturing very hot rocks at much greater depth, after which fluid is pumped into the newly porous system. The heated fluid is then used to drive a turbine.[104]

Whereas the traditional systems have been commercially available for over 100 years, EGS is in its infancy, at present having only research and pilot projects.[105] EGS can potentially provide much more energy because it can be employed anywhere that magma bodies are present, not only where there are natural geothermal reservoirs. But there are two major obstacles to its development.

Obstacles

Earthquakes: One problem is that EGS can produce earthquakes. Usually, the tremors are not noticeable to the public, but in a few cases, they have caused serious problems. In 2009, two EGS projects – one in Basel, Switzerland, and one at the Geysers in California – were permanently halted by government actions. As a result, governments have imposed safeguards to avoid the problems: EGS projects should not be developed near to fault lines and human settlements, and care needs to be taken not to put too much water, and too quickly, into the artificial fractures.[106]

More recent studies have indicated that the dangers may be even more serious than originally thought, and studies are presently being carried out to decide when EGS can be employed without unacceptable damage.[107]

In France, controversy has arisen because the EGS "stimulation" of rock fissures has similarities to the hydraulic fracturing, or "fracking," used to extract oil and gas from shale (see the section on natural gas in the following chapter). Fracking has now been banned in France, and the oil and gas lobbies have argued that, given the government's endorsement of EGS, it should lift the ban on fracking. Defenders of EGS argue that, although superficially similar, they really are not: Although EGS originally used hydraulic fracking techniques, it no longer does, but merely uses existing fissures.[108]

Costs: The other major obstacle is "the initial test drilling phase for geothermal projects, which is expensive and risky."[109] Although geothermal electricity will over the life of the vehicle be less expensive than most other types, the upfront costs, combined with the risk that the exploration drilling will end in failure, have prevented most of the countries with the geological potential to develop it from doing so.

In 2013, however, solutions were offered. Bloomberg New Energy Finance has proposed a Geothermal Exploration Drilling Fund, which would spread the financial risks. And the World Bank is now devoting 10% of its renewable energy lending to a Global Geothermal Development Plan, which "will identify promising sites and leverage financing for exploratory drilling, to develop commercially viable projects."[110]

Geothermal Electricity: Actual and Potential

On the potential for geothermal energy, a Worldwatch article said: "If the world were able to tap just a small portion of the Earth's heat, we could provide everyone with clean and safe energy for centuries." The geothermal potential has thus far been developed most fully by the "top ten" countries,[111] which are here listed in the order of their present installed capacity.

- *The United States:* Although it has more installed geothermal energy than any other country, the United States by 2013 had only 3.4 gigawatts (340,000 MW) of installed geothermal energy – compared with more than 50 GW of wind energy. In 2009, the Union of Concerned Scientists, saying that the "amount of heat within 10,000 meters (about 33,000 feet) of Earth's surface contains 50,000 times more energy than all the oil and natural gas resources in the world," declared that geothermal energy "could one day supply nearly all of today's U.S. electricity needs." This judgment was supported by a U.S. Geological Survey estimate that America's "untapped thermal resource is between 100 and 500 gigawatts" – which is a lot, given the fact that the U.S. needs only about 100 GW to keep its grid reliable.[112]

- *The Philippines:* Having the second greatest amount of geothermal power in the world, the Philippines, which is part of the famous "Ring of Fire," hopes that it will become the world's largest producer of geothermal energy.[113]

- *Indonesia:* Indonesia, also part of the Ring of Fire, has 40 percent of the world's geothermal resources, so it, like the Philippines, hopes to become the world's leading producer of geothermal power (which may happen if it can overcome some obstacles).[114]

- *Mexico:* Having installed the first geothermal power plant in the Western Hemisphere in 1959, Mexico is today the fourth largest geothermal producer in the world.[115]

- *Italy:* The first geothermal plant to generate electricity was built in 1911 in Italy, which is today the fifth leading geothermal country in the world.[116]

- *New Zealand:* Being New Zealand's fastest-growing source of electricity, geothermal energy is projected to provide 20 percent of its electricity by 2020.[117]

- *Iceland:* Being "basically one big volcano," Iceland uses geothermal energy for 80 percent of its electricity and 90 percent of its hot water and heat.[118]

- *Japan:* Since its nuclear disaster in 2011, Japan, having more geothermal reserves than any country except the United States and Indonesia, has been making a big push to develop geothermal, planning to triple it by 2020.[119]

- *El Salvador:* Known as the "land of volcanoes," El Salvador obtains 24 percent of its electricity from geothermal.[120]

- *Kenya:* Although hydropower has long provided most of the country's energy, Kenya has been suffering blackouts because of rain shortages, so it is developing its geothermal potential, which is vast: Because of volcanic activity in its Great Rift, Kenya "has more than enough power to light up the entire nation, and then some." Like Indonesia and the Philippines, Kenya hopes to become the world's leader.[121]

- Although by the end of 2013 China was not in the top ten, this will probably change soon, as it has plans to develop a great amount of geothermal power by 2020.[122]

In sum: Geothermal energy can provide a great boost in the drive to become 100 percent fossil free – especially if EGS geothermal works out.

Biomass and Biofuels

"Biomass is," as the EPA says, "a fancy name for material from plants and animals."[123] More precisely, biomass refers to anything – whether plants, animals, or algae – that was recently living (as distinct from oil and coal, which came from organisms that died eons ago).

One of the uses of biomass is to make biofuels, which can be used in various kinds of transportation, including automobiles, trucks, and jet planes. However, the term "biomass" is usually used to mean *non-biofuel biomass*. For example, a 2013 article was entitled "Will the Draft European Biomass Policy Repeat Biofuel Mistakes?"[124] The first part of this section deals with biomass in this non-biofuel sense; the second part with biofuels.

1. Biomass

Among rural populations in many less developed countries, biomass has provided most of the people's energy. There are many kinds of biomass, such as charcoal, straw, manure, crop residues, garbage, sawdust, wood chips, bark, tree branches, and complete trees. The traditional uses of biomass, usually being inefficient, contributed to the degradation of forests and contributed "on the order of 5% of total global warming derived from human activities." However, biomass could now "play a significant role in minimizing net emissions of carbon dioxide to the atmosphere." For example, the UK, wanting to "meet its energy needs while cutting carbon," wants biomass by 2020 to provide 11 percent of its primary energy (meaning energy that is raw, prior to being transformed into a useable form).[125]

Biomass is certainly capable, even in some highly developed countries, of providing much of their primary energy. For example, biomass accounts for 15 percent of Sweden's primary energy and 19 percent of

Finland's.[126] However, as shown by the traditional ways in which biomass was used, it cannot simply be assumed to be *clean* and hence to help reduce greenhouse emissions, and there have been arguments in Europe about using it to meet carbon emissions targets. These arguments have been aided by the fact that the targets have been stated in terms of "renewable energy," rather than "clean energy," implicitly assuming these terms to be identical.

Woody Biomass

The European Union's quest to reduce greenhouse emissions led to ambitious targets for the percentage of Europe's total energy to be provided by renewable energy: 20 percent by 2020 and 95% by 2050. To meet these targets, the EU decided that about half of the renewable energy would be provided by biomass, most of which would be provided by wood, rated as "carbon neutral."

Carbon Neutral? The burning of woody biomass could be carbon neutral but usually it is not, because it takes energy to grow the trees, to cut and transport the logs, to turn the logs into usable wood (such as pellets to burn). Further, cutting trees down removes them as "carbon sinks." In fact, argued a well-known article, woody biomass can be "dirtier than coal." Woody biomass differs from fossil fuels only in the sense that trees can replace themselves, and new trees can absorb the carbon that was emitted by the first trees. But in the meantime, by producing more carbon emissions than would fossil fuels, the burning of trees creates a "carbon debt." Eventually, to be sure, the process could end up with a "carbon dividend."[127] But how long does the debt remain?

According to Princeton University's Tim Searching, burning trees increases carbon emissions "by 79% over 20 years and 49% over 40 years; there is no carbon reduction until 100 years have passed, when the replacement trees have grown up." This causes a problem, because "we're trying to cut carbon now," said Tom Brookes of the European Climate Foundation, "not in 100 years' time." In other words, the EU's goal is to reduce carbon emissions by 95 percent by 2050, but burning trees will leave us deep in debt in 2050, with no hope of getting out until sometime in the next century.[128]

This is no minor problem, given the fact that Europe committed itself to fulfill about half of its renewable energy commitment from biomass, with most of this consisting of wood. In other words, biomass is to provide as much energy as wind, solar, hydroelectric, tidal and geothermal energy combined. This is especially a problem because, as the European Environment Agency said, some biomass programs could end up emitting more carbon than the fossil fuels they are being subsidized to replace. Indeed, insofar as the biomass consists of whole trees, the burning of biomass will definitely emit more carbon than fossil fuels by 2050.

How did Europe get itself into this "environmental lunacy," as the *Economist* calls it?[129] It began with the convention of using the term "renewable," instead of "clean" or "green," for the kind of energy that is needed to replace fossil-fuels. This was a disastrous mistake, because the goal is to replace dirty with clean energy, and yet not all types of renewable energy are clean – with the burning of woody biomass being the most important example.

Having settled on "renewable energy," the policy made woody biomass eligible for subsidies, feed-in tariffs, and other benefits – which led to what has been called the "dash for biomass" and the "biomass gold rush." This effect of the mistake plus the incentives led to various problems, the *Economist* pointed out:

> European firms are scouring the Earth for wood. . . . Prices are going through the roof. . . . . Europe does not produce enough timber to meet that extra demand. So a hefty chunk of it will come from imports [which take energy]. . . . [Wood may be] in short supply in many places before long.[130]

But the most important problem is simply that Europe committed itself to a policy that does little if anything to reduce carbon emissions and may even increase them.

Lumping biomass together with types of renewable energy that are clean, such as solar, wind, and geothermal, led to confusion with regard to the goal of reducing GHG emissions. The fact that wood is good in the sense of being *renewable* led many EU members to assume that it is good in the sense of being *carbon neutral*. Speaking of biomass "insanity," one insider said:

> We're paying people to cut their forests down in the name of reducing greenhouse gas emissions, and yet we are actually increasing them. No-one is apparently bothering to do any analysis about this. They're just sleepwalking into this insanity. [131]

Regarding this insanity, the *Economist* said: "Europe's wood subsidies show the folly of focusing green policy on 'renewables.'" The desired goal is, of course, to bring down carbon emissions, but "those who pursue renewable energy as an end in itself," added the *Economist*, "fail to see the wood for the trees."[132]

The mistake made in the wording of the European Union's "Renewables Direction," which was passed in 2009, has cost several years of wasted time. But now recognizing the mistake, the European Union, along with the world in general, should change the terminology, no longer referring to "renewable" when "clean" energy is sought. Moreover, this entire fiasco could have been avoided if the politicians had taken the *Economist*'s advice on another matter: "set a carbon tax and let the market decide the cheapest, cleanest answer."[133]

Indirect land usage change: The EU's "biomass gold rush" also involved a failure to prevent unwanted "indirect land use change" (ILUC). This problem arises when a policy encourages countries to use land to grow energy crops at the expense of food crops – which is a very serious matter, given the fact that the people in many countries already do not have enough to eat. ILUC can also involve the increase of biomass for energy in ways that remove "carbon sinks," such as wetlands and rain forests. The European regulations did not, at least until 2013, guarantee against ILUC.

Problems Fixed? In August 2013, the draft of an EU proposal to correct such problems appeared. This draft specified that trees would only be taken from sustainably managed forests and in ways that would not reduce biodiversity. It also said that biomass production "should not cause land use change" and that it needed a greenhouse-gas saving of at least 60 percent compared with fossil fuel. But critics of the previous policy did not find the problems adequately addressed by the new proposed policy:

- It gave no specific requirements that developers need to follow to avoid ILUC.

- It ignored the problem of "carbon debt."

- It ignored the carbon emitted when biomass is burned (leading one critic to call the 60-percent criterion a "sham" because it ignores "the 800 pound gorilla in the room").[134]

So no, the problems were not fixed.

Energy from Waste

Whereas the EU's policy on woody biomass has arguably caused as many problems as it has solved, environmentalists are much less ambivalent about using garbage for biomass. Indeed, an "Energy from Waste" (EfW) movement has been gaining momentum. It began with the European Environmental

Agency's waste sector, which brought about a 34 percent reduction in greenhouse emissions from 1990 to 2007 by using EfW, along with recycling and other strategies. Within the United States, this approach has been largely ignored thus far: There are only 86 EfW plants in the entire country. In 2013, however, then-New York Mayor Michael Bloomberg announced a plan to construct a composting facility that will turn 100,000 tons of food waste a year into biogas, to reduce the city's electric bill, which may inspire other cities to do likewise.[135] Getting energy from waste has many benefits.

- Energy from waste is renewable – we could add garbage to "death and taxes" to make a trio of things that will always be with us.

- "According to the EPA, for every ton of garbage processed at an EfW facility, approximately one ton of emitted carbon-dioxide equivalent in the atmosphere is prevented. This is because the trash burned at an EfW facility doesn't generate methane."[136]

- Turning trash into energy also drastically cuts the amount of money and diesel used to transport trash to landfills, often hundreds of miles away.[137]

- Using garbage to produce energy, rather than sending it to the landfill, has three more benefits. Besides producing electricity without using fossil fuels, it can solve much of the landfill problem, and it can also solve a significant portion of the methane problem, because "landfills are the third-largest contributor of anthropogenic methane emissions in the U.S.," exceeded "only by the natural gas and agricultural sectors."[138]

Energy from Sewage

Washington D.C., like a few other cities, has begun to use sewage to generate electricity. Instead of sending the solid waste to surrounding farms for fertilizer, the city now puts it into an "anaerobic digester," along with a special mix of bacteria, which devour it, thereby producing methane, which is then used to power turbines. D.C. Water figures that this procedure will, besides reducing carbon emissions, save $10 million a year. This process is being employed in some other cities, including Ithaca, Oakland, Philadelphia, and Sheboygan.[139]

Conclusion

Biomass has great potential for reducing greenhouse gases. But because it is a type of renewable energy that is not inherently clean, it must be used wisely if it is to be helpful. This is especially important with regard to woody biomass, so that it ends up with a carbon benefit rather than a debt. But many kinds of biomass, especially garbage and sewage, can help toward the goal of making the world's energy 80% green by 2035 and 100% by 2050.

2. Biofuels

Biofuels are fuels made from various kinds of biomass, such as corn, seed oil, animal fats, trees, agricultural residues, and algae. Biofuels come in three forms: Liquid, solid, and gas. Transportation, of course, largely uses liquid fuels, with ethanol being by far the most important kind. When added to gasoline, the resulting blend reduces the use of petroleum and thereby greenhouse-gas emissions (as well as reducing dependence on foreign oil).

In 2007, the United States established the Renewable Fuel Standard (RFS), which mandated that gasoline must be blended with a certain percentage of ethanol. In practice, this meant 10 percent ethanol (E10), which was at that time regarded as the most that cars built before 2001 could use without danger of engine damage.[140]

Food Security and Environmental Problems

Thus far, ethanol has been made primarily from sugarcane, wheat, rapeseed, and especially corn. However, as one writer put it, "the corn ethanol project has been a disaster." In 2008, the UN's special rapporteur on the right to food even called the biofuel program "a crime against humanity."[141] This program has been adjudged so negatively for two reasons.

First, it has resulted in a large percentage of the planet's food — especially corn and wheat — being used to make fuel. In the United States, this turned out to be an incredible 40 percent of the country's corn. Shortly after 2007, reported the World Bank, food prices around the world had increased overall by 75% (partly because the rise in corn prices caused prices of beef, pork, chicken, eggs, and milk, among other commodities, to rise). This was indeed a disaster, given the fact that malnutrition, which affects close to 4 billion people, is the leading cause of death in the world. For example, roughly 50% of Guatemala's children are chronically malnourished and "the average Guatemalan is now hungrier because of biofuel development." After most families were already spending two thirds of their income on food, the US biofuel policy caused the price of corn tortillas to double and that of eggs to triple.[142]

Second, although one of the reasons for blending gasoline with ethanol has been to reduce fossil-fuel emissions, the scientific consensus is that, when ILUC and other factors are taken into account, the ethanol does not help and has even hurt – with a report for the European Commission saying that ethanol and other biofuels are sometimes twice as polluting as fossil fuels. Such problems led the European Union in 2012 to cut in half the allowable amount of crop-based biofuels.[143]

Advanced Biofuels

The problems created by crop-based biofuels have led scientists to create "advanced" (or "second-generation") biofuels made from "cellulosic" biomass (such as grasses, trees, seaweed, and agricultural residues). "Because cellulosic ethanol is the leading candidate for replacing a large portion of U.S. petroleum use, it is the focus of DOE's Biomass Program." The National Renewable Energy Laboratory, a DOE research facility, works on it (along with several other cellulosic fuels, including "green gasoline" and algae-based "green diesel").[144]

If crop-based ethanol is completely replaced by cellulosic ethanol, the conflict between food and fuel will be overcome. With that in mind, the RFS was modified in 2009 to stipulate that a certain percent of ethanol had to be cellulosic. However, difficulties with making cellulosic ethanol commercial forced the EPA to reduce it, finally bringing it down to zero in 2012.[145]

But in the meantime, the mandate has been rising again, because research to create new kinds of cellulosic fuel has been fruitful. One method is to make the fuel from corn plants – the stalks and leaves - while saving the kernels for food. A cellulosic ethanol plant using this method opened for business in Iowa in September 2014, with another plant in Iowa and one in Kansas right behind it.

Ethanol can also be made from other types of biomass, such as switchgrass and forestry waste. One way to do this involves the creation of ethanol by employing an enzyme isolated from the fungus used by cutter ants to break leaves down.[146]

Evidence that cellulosic ethanol is now viable is provided by the fact that three major corporations, including Dupont Industrial BioSciences, are constructing processing plants for producing millions of gallons of it in the next few years. Also, cellulosic ethanol is already being produced by plants in Florida and other states and by a much bigger plant in Italy.[147]

Oil companies and their front groups had long been pressuring Congress to rescind the biofuel mandate. Although they argued their case in terms of some distorted facts, there were real problems with the legislation, which put the required amount of ethanol in terms of the gallons of ethanol blended with the gasoline, rather than the percentage. Then, because the legislation also said that the amount of ethanol had to be raised every year, the refineries were approaching the "blend wall" – meaning the point at which the percent of ethanol would be harmful to engines. Unfortunately, Congress dealt with the problem by reducing the biofuel mandate, rather than simply rewriting the legislation in terms of a percentage.[148]

In any case, better cellulosic biofuels have been created. A fungus with E. coli produces isobutanol. This new biofuel may turn out to be revolutionary, because it provides 82% of gasoline's energy – much more than traditional ethanol. Also, the residue from whisky production can be used to create biobutanol, which is also as powerful as gasoline. And fungus has been used to create biodiesel, which is especially significant, given the fact that biodiesel has been the most used biofuel in Europe.[149]

Perhaps most important, cellulosic biofuel made from a type of plants called halophytes is, in the estimation of Zachary Shahan of Clean Technica, the biggest biofuel breakthrough thus far. For one thing, the halophytes solve two of the main problems with previous cellulosic biofuels: that they require a tremendous amount of both fresh water and arable land, but halophytes can be grown in the desert and irrigated with seawater. This new biofuel was created by the Sustainable Bioenergy Research Consortium, which was founded in Abu Dhabi by Boeing, along with some partners, after learning that most of today's oil, made from shale oil and tar sands oil (see Chapter 18), damages airplane engines. Another advantage of halophytes results from the increasing use of aquaculture (in response to declining fish stock in open waters), which produces a tremendous waste stream. Halophytes can use this waste as a feedstock.

For these reasons, biofuels from halophytes should be inexpensive. The creators hope to have this biofuel commercially available before 2020.[150]

Conclusion

Advanced biofuels could turn out, as Jeff Spross has said, to be a "game-changer." Explaining the potential of the cellulosic technology for producing isobutanol, one of the scientists involved said: "The U.S. has the potential to sustainably produce 1 billion tons or more of biomass annually, enough to produce biofuels that could displace 30 percent or more of our current petroleum production."[151]

Electric Vehicles

The previous sections of this chapter have shown that by 2050 all of the world's need for energy could be provided by clean energy. Now we turn to the contribution possible through advances in transportation, which globally is responsible for about 25 percent of the greenhouse gases. On-road transportation by automobiles, buses, and trucks worldwide, moreover, has been the greatest contributor to global warming.[152]

Of these modes of transportation, automobiles have been paramount, and the number of them has been increasing dramatically. In 1950, the world contained 50 million automobiles; by 1997, the number had increased to 580 million; and today, there are about one billion automobiles. By 2050, furthermore, the number is projected to be 2.3 billion.[153]

With regard to the United States, which produces about 18 percent of the world's energy-related CO2, transportation causes over one third of America's CO_2 emissions, over 60 percent of which are due to autos, SUVs, and light trucks, so they cause over 20% of the US greenhouse gases.[154] (*Note:* For simplicity's sake, SUVs and light trucks are regarded as types of automobiles.)

One of the most important dimensions of the transition to a fossil-free economy will, accordingly, be a complete switch to clean automobiles, which will require the total replacement of gasoline, diesel, and hybrid vehicles with all-electric vehicles (EVs), powered entirely by clean energy. Although EVs have generally been powered by batteries, there are also EVs that are powered by hydrogen fuel cells. In discussing whether a complete switch to EVs is possible, therefore, it is necessary, to distinguish between battery electric vehicles (BEVs) and fuel-cell electric vehicles (FCVs).

Battery Electric Vehicles (BEVs)

EVs have thus far been largely equated with BEVs, also called plug-in automobiles. These currently account for less than 1 percent of America's autos. Gas-electric hybrids have been selling better, but they account for only about 3 percent of U.S. auto sales.[155]

The fact that hybrids and BEVs have thus far captured only a tiny portion of the market can be explained partly by the fact that they have been more expensive than gasoline-powered autos. Although they will, in the long run, turn out to be less expensive, most people are concerned primarily with the immediate purchase price.[156]

Even if people can afford to wait several years for the savings, the tiny percent of the U.S. market captured by hybrids and BEVs can also be partly explained in terms of inertia: the tendency of most people to stay with what is tried-and-true, rather than switching to innovative technologies. As sociologists have documented, innovative technologies are at first adopted by only a tiny portion of the population, referred to as "early adopters." If their experience shows the new technology to be superior to the old one, it is then adopted by a much larger portion, called the "early majority" – after which come the "late majority" and finally the "laggards."[157]

But if this phenomenon can account for the slowness with which both

BEVs and hybrids have been adopted, there needs to be an explanation for the fact that hybrids have been purchased by three times as many Americans as BEVs. There are several explanations: (1) BEVs were at first only able to travel a short distance (perhaps 50 miles) before needing recharging, and then (2) the recharging took many hours. The original BEVs were useful, therefore, only for driving around town or taking very short trips. Even if the potential purchasers need cars only for short trips, many of them are dissuaded by "range anxiety" – fear of running out of power before getting home or to a recharging station. A third reason to shun BEVs was their high purchase price and a fourth that they were not "good to drive."

Recently, however, BEVs have started to outsell plug-in hybrids (PHEVs),[158] which is probably because all four reasons for preferring either hybrids or gas-powered autos to BEVs are beginning to be overcome:

- Many of the recent BEVs have disproved the notion that they are not good to drive, with Tesla doing so most dramatically. In 2013, it was named Car of the Year by *Motor Trend Magazine,* and *Consumer Reports* asked whether it was "the best car ever."[159]

- The car companies are providing rapid chargers, which can recharge a BEV in 20 or 30 minutes, and rechargers are being installed around the country, so that in many places drivers can take trips without anxiety. Tesla even makes its "superchargers" free to Tesla drivers. Tesla also signed an agreement with China Unicom to build charging stations in 120 Chinese cities.[160]

- The United Kingdom is leading the way in having an "electric highway," a network of fast-chargers that would connect every part of a country. In the UK, the plan was that the network, built by Nissan and Ecotricity, would be in all motorway services by the beginning of 2015.[161]

- Improved batteries are increasing the number of miles they can go without recharging. Tesla's Model 3 sedan, scheduled to be released in 2014, will travel 200 miles with one charge, and Tesla projected that its 2-seat roadster would have a battery that would last for 400 miles.[162]

- The up-front cost of BEVs has been going down dramatically. Even Tesla, whose Model S cost about $70,000, planned to sell its Model 3 for about $35,000.

- Tesla and Panasonic, which produces Tesla's batteries, have predicted that they will soon have a battery that is 30% to 50% less expensive than previous batteries, which will be made in Tesla's Gigafactory. The new plant, covering land the size of 174 football fields, is intended to produce 500,000 batteries per year after it opens in 2017.[163]

It is likely, therefore, that the BEV "early adopters" will quickly create an "early majority" in the United States as well as in other countries. With regard to adoption around the world, the Electric Vehicles Initiative, supported by 15 governments, has a goal of at least 20 million passenger EVs by 2020. The Indian government by itself plans to stimulate the sale of 6 to 7 million EVs in its country by 2020. In Europe and the United States, there was already significant growth in the first half of 2014, with sales of BEVs and PHEVs being about 75 percent higher than the first six months of 2013. During that same period, China's sales in BEVs increased 700 percent, and they are likely to increase much faster, because China has made a big push by means of various new policies, such as eliminating the standard heavy taxes on new vehicles.[164]

There is little doubt that electric motorcycles and scooters will become very popular. According to a 2014 report from Navigant Research, sales of these vehicles worldwide will exceed 55 million by 2023.[165]

Electrics trucks are also starting to be made. For example, Chicago is starting to change its fleet of garbage trucks to all-electric trucks.[166]

There are good financial reasons to believe that EVs will soon replace oil-powered cars. According to the French investment bank Kepler Chevreux, "$100 billion invested in either wind energy or solar energy – and deployed as energy for light and commercial vehicles – will produce significantly more energy than that same $100 billion invested in oil." Charging EVs with onshore wind or solar, for example, already provides almost four times as much energy. Accordingly, said analysis Mark Lewis, "the balance of competitive advantage will shift decisively in favour of EVs over oil-powered cars over the next two decades."[167]

Fuel-Cell Electric Vehicles (FCVs)

Instead of drawing electricity from the grid, fuel-cell electric vehicles (FCVs, also called FCEVs) produce their own electricity by means of fuel cells, which combine hydrogen stored in the vehicle with oxygen from the atmosphere. Although it seems that most Americans have not yet heard of them, wrote a NYT blogger, "Many researchers regard fuel cells as more promising than batteries as an electricity source for vehicles." The reason for this is that, while emitting no greenhouse gases, an FCV is like a gas-powered auto in two important respects: An FCV can go 400 miles before needing refueling, and the refueling takes only a few minutes.[168]

Problems

However, these benefits have been neutralized by a set of problems, which have resulted in a long-running joke: that FCVs "are the technology of the future – and always will be."[169] The problems are four:

- *Price:* When first invented, FCVs would have cost $1 million dollars each and, even after coming down drastically, they have still been priced at about $100,000.

- *Refueling Stations:* As late as 2013, AutoCar said: "The fundamental issue with hydrogen-powered cars is still the chronic lack of the infrastructure required to refuel them."

- *Platinum:* Fuel cells produce electricity by means of a catalytic reaction that requires platinum, but platinum is "less common and more costly than gold." The use of platinum, therefore, threatens to make FCVs permanently expensive.

- *Natural Gas:* Although hydrogen is the most common element in the universe, it is never found by itself. Pure hydrogen has been created by "reforming" natural gas. So, although hydrogen-based FCVs do not emit any greenhouses gases, the process of creating hydrogen does, so the FCVs are not "clean" (just as BEVs will not be clean until the electricity on the grid is created without the use of fossil fuels). MIT's John Heywood, said: "If the hydrogen does not come from renewable sources, then it is simply not worth doing." (Worse yet, if the natural gas is produced by "fracking," it is arguably worse than creating hydrogen from oil or coal – as will be discussed in the following chapter.)[170]

Possible Solutions

Although researchers had been creating experimental FCVs in the 1990s, most people, because of such problems, had lost interest in them by the mid-2000s.[171] In recent years, however, possible solutions have reportedly been found for these problems.

- *Price:* According to an article in *Scientific American,* "Department of Energy research has helped drive down the cost of automotive fuel cells by 80 percent."[172]

- *Refueling Stations:* The various car-makers are also collaborating to encourage further development of infrastructure and, in the United States, with the Department of Energy in cooperation with hydrogen and fuel-cell industries, to deal with infrastructure challenges and to bring FCV costs down.[173]

- *Platinum:* In 2013, a University of Copenhagen press release said that chemists at the school had reported finding that, by packing the particles of platinum more tightly, they could generate the same amount of electricity with a fifth of the amount of platinum traditionally used.[174]

- *Natural Gas:* Discussions of the creation of hydrogen often imply that it can only be done by reforming natural gas. But, promoters of FCVs say, there are many fossil-fuel-free ways to produce hydrogen. Researchers at the National Renewable Energy Laboratory have reportedly developed six ways, the best known of which is renewable electrolysis, in which hydrogen is created from water. Why, then, has reforming natural gas become the standard process? The Bush administration, in alliance with oil and gas companies, made sure that "the process would benefit traditional energy industries."[175] Given the systems that have been built up since the creation of this fateful process, it would be difficult to shift to a different process, but it would not be impossible.

It might appear, therefore, that all of the previously identified problems could be solved in the foreseeable future. However, each of these "solutions" is problematic: The price is still very high (although new technology may bring it down further[176]); refueling stations beyond the metropolitan areas will be slow coming; a fifth of today's platinum would still be a lot of platinum if the FCVs were mass produced; and changing to electrolysis would be *extremely* difficult.

Negative Verdicts on FCEVs

Moreover, both Julian Cox of CleanTechnica and Joe Romm have said that the current hype for FCEVs by Honda, Hyundai, and Toyota, with support from the EPA, is entirely misleading.

When Romm was in the DOE's Office of Energy Efficiency and Renewable Energy in the 1990s, he was a "big supporter of hydrogen and transportation fuel cell vehicle (FCV) programs." However, finding that the research "did not pan out as expected," he did research, which ended up as his 2004 book, *The Hype about Hydrogen: Fact and Fiction in the*

Race to Save the Climate. In 2009, he added, President Obama and Energy Secretary Steven Chu wanted to kill the DOE's program, saying: "Hydrogen fuel cell cars are a dead end from a technological, practical, and climate perspective."[177]

Then in 2014, Cox wrote a report with essentially the same message. Addressing primarily the first and fourth of the above points, he said that there are no "environmental benefits attributable to hydrogen either now or in any foreseeable future economic reality." Moreover, "Hydrogen is locked by the force of economics to natural gas and natural gas is increasingly locked by the same force to the practice of on-shore hydraulic fracturing of shales."[178]

Summarizing the moral of Cox's report, Romm said: "Fuel cell cars running on hydrogen simply won't be greener than the Prius running on gasoline (!) – or even as practical as a mass-market vehicle – for a long, long time, if ever." Indeed, Romm added, "It would take several miracles to overcome all of those problems simultaneously in the coming decades."[179]

Railroads

The challenge to improve railroads – by making them 100% electric and more attractive for most trips than automobiles, trucks, buses, and airplanes – is one of the most important, and most difficult, challenges faced by the movement to abolish fossil-fuel energy. This is especially true of the United States. The most important element needed to make railroads attractive, for transporting both passengers and goods, is a network of clean-energy high-speed rail in every country. This is, again, especially true of the United States.

As stated above, automobiles – understood here as including SUVs and light trucks – are responsible for over 20% of America's CO_2 emissions. Trains are about nine times more energy-efficient than cars and trucks. So getting much more transportation handled by rail will be especially important as long as passenger vehicles and trucks are still using fossil fuels.

It will even continue to be important after we move to all-electric vehicles. Besides reducing congestion, high-speed rail can make travel *more* attractive than air travel for mid-distance trips, as they already have in many other countries. Airplanes are now the fastest-growing contributor to global warming. If rail travel could take people from Los Angeles to downtown San Francisco, or from San Francisco to Portland, in two hours or less, most people would probably take the train.

Why Doesn't America Have High-Speed Rail?

There is no technological reason why America could not have a network of high-speed rail (HSR), at least in its five largest megaregions (the Northeast, the Chicago Hub Cities, the Pacific Northwest, Florida, and California). Japan's high-speed trains – called "bullet trains" – began operating in 1964. France began operating HSR in 1967 and Germany in 1991. China – which we old-timers had always known to be a poor, backward country – now has the longest HSR network in the world.[180]

Since World War II, the United States has been the richest country in the world. Hence the common question: "Europe and Asia have [bullet trains], so why doesn't America?" The answer goes back to the end of World War II, at which time "passenger rail became the orphan child of a transportation system increasingly transformed by the automobile and commercial aviation."[181] President Lyndon Johnson tried to change this. Shortly after Japan had unveiled its Shinkansen "bullet train," Johnson signed the High-Speed Ground Transportation Act of 1965, saying:

> We have airplanes which fly three times faster than sound.
> We have television cameras that are orbiting Mars. But we
> have the same tired and inadequate mass transportation
> between our towns and cities that we had 30 years ago.
> . . . The same science and technology which gave us our
> airplanes and our space probes, I believe, could also give
> us better and faster and more economical transportation
> on the ground. And a lot of us need it more on the ground
> than we need it orbiting the earth.[182]

This idea came to nought, and two decades later, President Clinton and Congress passed the Amtrak Reform and Accountability Act of 1997. However, there was no chance for Amtrak to have anything close to high-speed lines, for three reasons.

- Congress gave Amtrak very little money: By 2001, the government was spending only $500 million on Amtrak – while spending $12 billion on aviation and $33 billion on highways.

- Amtrak had to employ 19th-century technology, which "limit[ed] trains to an effective average speed of 48 miles per hour."

- Amtrak had to share tracks with freight trains, which often causes delays.[183]

At a hearing in 2001, a member of the House of Representatives spoke of France's HSR, saying, "It goes fast, it is smooth, they put a lot of money into it, and we just don't." As a result, "What was once the envy of the world is now an international embarrassment."[184]

Hoping – as New York Times journalist David Carr put it – "to make the leap into the 21st century after largely bypassing the 20th," Amtrak was eventually able to spend $1.7 billion to create a somewhat high-speed rail called the "Acela Express," which opened in 2001. Acela is capable of going over 150 miles an hour. But unlike the Japanese and French, which have new, dedicated, and mostly straight HSR tracks, the Acela train from Boston to New York gets up to speed for only a few minutes.[185]

Although Acela is the fastest train in America, completing the trip from Boston to New York in 2 hours and 46 minutes, Justin Lin, the World Bank's top economist, was not impressed, saying that in China a high-speed train would make the trip in an hour. In short, America still does not have a single high-speed line.[186]

The question of why America does not have HSR is made even more pressing by the fact that, in addition to Japan, France, and China, HSR is also operational in England, Italy, Spain, Russia, Sweden, Turkey, and South Korea, while several other countries, including Argentina, Brazil, Turkey, and Morocco, are planning it.[187] Referring to such developments, a 2011 Reuters article was entitled "U.S. High-Speed Rail: Time to Hop Aboard or Be Left Behind."[188]

In 2009, President Obama began trying to do something about this. In his first State of the Union Address, he said, "There is no reason why other countries can build high-speed rail lines and we can't," after which he and his (Republican) Secretary of Transportation, Ray LaHood, called for the creation of a nation-wide HSR. As part of the American Recovery and Reinvestment Act (generally called the "stimulus"), Obama provided $8 billion to jump-start such a program.[189]

The first HSR line was to be in Florida, which Obama and LaHood wanted completed by 2015 to be "a showpiece that would sell the rest of the nation on high-speed rail." This was extremely important, said LaHood in an editorial, because "High-speed-rail Will Be Our Generation's Legacy."[190]

However, although the previous governor, Republican Charlie Crist, had wanted the HSR line, new Republican governor Rick Scott rejected the money for HSR, claiming that it would cost the state too much money – even though the federal government was to pay $2.4 billion of the projected cost of $2.6 billion. Scott probably expressed the real reason when he admitted that he made his decision on the basis of "documents provided by the libertarian Reason Foundation and the Heritage Foundation."[191]

These two foundations, along with the Cato Institute, had long been the three right-wing think tanks leading the ideological war against HSR. The reality of this war, the Economist in 2010 said, is that "high-speed rail has become an ideological issue, supported by Democrats and opposed by Republicans with little reference to the specifics of any given project." The ideological opposition became especially strong in 2009 after Obama announced his vision for a nation-wide HSR. The Republican response to his State of the Union address was given by Louisiana's Governor Bobby Jindal, who included HSR in his list of "wasteful spending." From then on, the GOP, at least at the national level, systematically opposed the idea.[192]

Then in 2010, two new Republican governors rejected funding. John Kasich of Ohio turned back $385 million for a line linking the three big "C's" (Cincinnati, Columbus and Cleveland), and Scott Walker of Wisconsin rejected $810 million for a train from Milwaukee to Madison, claiming that it was would have been "too costly to taxpayers" – even though "a state-sponsored ridership study," pointed out a *New York Times* writer, "concluded that the proposed line would actually have been a money-maker from the start." This writer added, "The rest of the world calls them bullet trains because they go so fast. But in the United States, the nickname is apt for a different reason: They keep getting shot down."[193]

In a 2011 *National Review* article, "The Death of a High-Speed-Rail Program," the author gave "analysts at Cato, Reason, and Heritage" credit for shooting down Obama's plan. "[M]ost journalists and commentators have overlooked," he gloated, "the decisive role a handful of pro-market think tanks and Tea Party activists played in putting these projects in the morgue." This gloating was accurate, because a "small group of critics [of HSR] have organized themselves into a well-oiled campaign." The term "well-oiled" was apt, because these three "pro-market think tanks" are funded by the Koch brothers, ExxonMobil, and other oil companies. With regard to the Reason Foundation, which is the least well-known, a *San Francisco Chronicle* article in 2011 reported that it is "funded by Chevron, ExxonMobil, Shell Oil, the American Petroleum Institute, Delta Airlines, the National Air Transportation Association and, of course, the Koch Family Foundation."[194]

Besides being explained in part by this campaign, the anti-HSR stance of Republicans has also reflected their desire to make Obama's presidency a failure. "[S]ome Republicans in Washington," said a *New York Times* story, "worried privately that the [HSR] project might prove too popular." The anti-HSR coalition's victory dance was even more jubilant later in the year: After Obama had requested $53 billion over six years for HSR, Congress axed it.[195]

However, Obama's dream, while greatly diminished, was not dead, due to three developments in 2012. First, "Congressional hatchets did not touch most of the $10 billion allotted, under the 2009 economic stimulus act, for high-speed rail." Second, Amtrak announced a $150 billion upgrade for the Northeast Corridor, with true HSR as its centerpiece. Third, California lawmakers approved $5.8 billion to begin the HSR line from San Francisco to San Diego.[196]

The anti-HSR animus then focused on California, with efforts fueled, as before, by the oil industry, which does not want rail travel to cut significantly into transportation by autos and trucks, and the airline industry, which does not want HSR to threaten its virtual monopoly on mid-distance trips. As one writer put it, HSR "would compete directly with California's lucrative but highly polluting short-route intercity air carrier market, one of the largest in the United States, and would directly impact the economic fortunes of the aircraft industry."[197] This has already happened in other countries:

- In South Korea, "airports can't compete with the new high-speed rail network," wrote *Business Insider* in 2011. "Eleven of the 14 airports managed by the Korean Airports Corporation lost money in 2009 and 2008. Several are ghost airports with no regular flights."

- In China, "more than 50 percent of flights less than 500 km [310 miles] in length will become unprofitable due to competition from high-speed trains"; even "nearly 70 percent of flights less than 600 km [372 miles] in length [from Wuhan] have been canceled."[198]

By 2014, Acela, in spite of its very modest speed, had led some airlines to cancel routes.[199]

HSR: Critiques and Rebuttals

The fact that certain arguments serve the interests of wealthy industries does not necessarily mean that the arguments are bad, so they need to be examined. What follows are some prevalent claims, followed by facts that contradict them:

Claim: There is no reason to expect HSR to work in the United States, as the Cato Institute said in 2009, because HSR "doesn't work in Europe or in Asia either."[200]

Fact: After sometimes initially having low ridership, HSR has become very successful in both Europe and Asia. Since Japan's bullet train began in 1964, it has been Japan Railway's "cash cow." On the 284-mile trip from Paris to Lyon, 80% of the travelers use HSR. Of those who travel between Madrid and Seville by either air or rail, 80% of them go by rail. China's HSR is carrying nearly twice as many passengers as the country's domestic airlines. After Taiwan's HSR opened, "half of the air routes between Taipei and the country's western cities [were] discontinued."[201]

Claim: Whatever may be true about Europe and Asia, HSR will never be popular in the United States.[202]

Fact: America thus far has only one HSR line, the Acela Express, which goes from Boston to NYC and Philadelphia and then to Washington DC. Prior to its introduction in 2000, Amtrak had only about 20 percent of the business from Boston to NYC, but now, although it is slower than the Asian and European HSR lines – because it does not have fully dedicated tracks - the Acela Express has 54% of the travelers. Before HSR, Amtrak had only 33% of the business from New York to Washington but now it has 75%.[203]

Claim: "Among intercity transportation modes, only Amtrak is materially subsidized. User fees pay virtually all of the costs of airlines and airports."[204]

Fact: Although this criticism of HSR is the most prevalent one, it has the facts almost exactly backwards.

- Not just railroads require subsidies; *all* forms of travel require subsidies.[205]

- Automobile travel in America is subsidized via public expenditure on roads. As the Tax Foundation pointed out in 2013, "every state finances most of its road spending though general taxes (like property taxes, sales taxes, and general funds)."[206]

- Contrary to the claim that auto travel requires fewer subsidies than rail travel - because highways are funded by user-fees – a 2009 Pew study showed that "user fees financed 51 percent of highway construction and maintenance costs," leaving the remaining 49% to be paid by tax-payers. Moreover, the government spent $360 billion on highways and only $2.4 billion on passenger rail in the last ten years, so the government was "spending over 150 times more public money on highways than railroads."[207]

- Contrary to the claim that rail travel requires more subsidies than air travel, government funding for air travel is 63 times higher than for Amtrak. Most of the subsidies for air travel have been for infrastructure, which was estimated to be $1 trillion. In addition, air travel needs a subsidy of $3 billion every year to maintain the system of air traffic towers and controllers. In a discussion of "The Great, the Good and the Gruesome," Warren Buffett put airlines in the category of the gruesome.[208]

Claim: "High-speed rail has proven a drain on government coffers. Every HSR line in the world requires some sort of government subsidy.... No high-speed rail in the U.S. will ever pay its operating, much less capital costs."[209]

Fact: HSR, unlike air and road travel, does not need ongoing subsidies for operating expenses. In addition, some HSR lines have even made a profit, such as the Paris-Lyon HSR line and Amtrak's Acela Express.[210]

The Cost of HSR

Sarah Palin has called HSR "a bullet train to bankruptcy," a charge that reflects the general anti-rail view that HSR would cost far more than it would be worth. But although the cost should be considered, it is equally essential to ask, with one recent article, "What is the Cost of *Not* Investing in High-Speed Rail?" which said that "failing to invest in high-speed rail in our rapidly-growing megaregions will prove very costly as time goes on."[211]

Justin Lin, the World Bank's top economist, has said the United States would profit from following the lead of China, which "averaged 9.6 percent economic growth from 1979 to 2002, as it quintupled the size of the country's highway system to 25,000 kilometers (15,000 miles)." As for the future, "the Chinese are spending $100 billion and have so far built over 8,358 km (about 5,193 miles) of high-speed rail lines."[212]

While the anti-rail writers have continued to fight against California's HSR – although projections say that it "will cost less than half the amount of expanding freeways and airports to meet future intercity travel demand" – "China is committed to opening a dozen HSR lines equal in size and complexity to the California project."[213]

And China is not alone: Spain is "investing $170 billion to extend its acclaimed high-speed rail system," and Japan is planning to spend $64 billion to build a maglev (magnetic levitation) line, which will cut the 320-mile (515-kilometer) trip from Tokyo to Osaka from 138 minutes on the fastest bullet train to 67 minutes. Perhaps the leaders of these countries know something that Sarah Palin does not.[214]

HSR and the Environment

For the present book, the most important thing about HSR is its contribution to the battle against global warming. Besides the fact that train travel uses much less energy per capita than auto and air travel, "electrified high-speed trains traveling on their own right of way are about 9 times more energy-efficient per passenger mile than private automobiles or domestic jet travel (and hence emit about one-ninth as much pollution as air and auto)." Electric trains can be even more frugal when equipped with regenerative braking, which feeds 8% to 17% of the electricity back into the grid.[215]

The maglev trains will be still more frugal, because the trains (once they get moving) are levitated and moved forward with magnets. Because they glide through the air, there is no friction from wheels, so they can travel twice as fast as ordinary HSR trains and use far less electricity.[216]

In any case, the 9-to-1 contrast refers only to the present system, in which the grid's electricity comes from fossil-fuel energy. Once the grid is totally powered by clean energy, HSR will require no fossil-fuel energy whatsoever. When that grid transformation occurs and both automobiles and trains are completely powered by clean energy, only air travel will require fossil-fuel energy.

Immediately, moreover, California's HSR is intended to be completely carbon-free from the beginning, using only electricity generated in California from clean energy. Better yet, HSR could generate its own electricity. Moves in this direction have already been made:

- The UK's DB Schenker Rail is developing "carbon free" rail services by building its own turbines.

- Germany's Deutsche Bahn already gets 20% of its energy from solar, wind, and hydro power. In 2011, it reported its intention to increase that to 28% by 2014 and 100% by 2050.

- In Antwerp, on the railroad from Paris to Amsterdam, there is a two-mile solar-powered train tunnel – called the Solar Tunnel. Originally built to protect trains from falling trees, this tunnel has been covered with 16,000 solar panels, which provide energy for trains as well as Antwerp's central station.[217]

There would seem to be no limit to how much one or more of these strategies could be used around the world.

Conclusion to Discussion of HSR

Developing the plan of the US High Speed Rail Association – perhaps employing maglev trains rather than conventional HSR – would be one of the most important ways in which America's energy system can become fossil free. Just as this book was being readied for press, the *Baltimore Sun* reported that the Japan Bank for International Cooperation has offered $5 billion in financing for a maglev train from Baltimore to Washington, which should cut the travel time to 15 minutes. In addition, the Central Japan Railway Company has agreed to waive licensing fees for using maglev technology. Japan's motive is to use the Northeast Corridor as a showcase for its maglev trains to American and other audiences. The American investor group hopes that the $5 billion from Japan will encourage other investors, so that the project can be completed and also extended to New York City.[218]

Airplanes

A central reason to develop HSR is that it would get people to take short trips – under 600 or even 1,000 miles – by train instead of air, so that passenger airplanes will be used only for really long trips.

Importance: Overcoming an Environmental Sin

Cutting down air trips is important because airplanes are responsible for three percent of the greenhouse emissions in the world. The enormity of this percentage has been dramatized by pointing out that aviation "would be the 7th largest emitter in the world if it were a country."[219]

Moreover, "Air travel is now the fastest-growing contributor to global warming." How fast? The WWF says that it has been "rising 3 to 4% per year." With regard to the future, airplane emissions, left unregulated, are "expected to skyrocket by mid-century" – likely to almost triple, said the International Civil Aviation Organization (ICA0).[220]

Moreover, emissions from jet planes are even more damaging than those figures would indicate. "Airliners emit their CO_2 directly into the upper atmosphere" and "CO_2 emitted by jets can survive in the atmosphere for upwards of 100 years." In addition, the planes have other emissions, including ozone and nitrous oxide. Accordingly, "the overall impact on global warming of aircraft could be between two and four times that of their CO_2 emissions alone."[221]

To put this issue in terms of the global warming produced by individuals: For many Americans, wrote Elisabeth Rosenthal in a *New York Times* article, "air travel is their most serious environmental sin." George Monbiot, writing in the *Guardian*, said that "flying dwarfs any other environmental impact a single person can exert." It has rightfully been said that "if we don't get a handle on airplane emissions, our other carbon footprint reduction efforts could be for naught." This is especially important for the United States, because it is "responsible for nearly half of the worldwide CO_2 emissions from aircraft."[222]

Why Such a Problem

Part of the reason air travel has become such as problem is that after WW II, "member governments of ICAO agreed that airlines should be free of fuel taxes," perhaps "to boost the fledgling airline industry emerging from the fighting." In the remainder of the 20th century, no regulations whatsoever were placed on airplanes, but regulations are needed.[223]

Regulations

At Kyoto in 1997, the governments ducked the issue of regulating aviation emissions by giving the task to ICAO. But it did nothing, so the task was given back to governments. After they also failed to come up with an international plan, the European Union decided that its 27 countries would include airline emissions in its market-based Emissions Trading System (ETS), according to which it will cost any country that goes beyond the allowable tons of carbon. Passed in 2008, the law was scheduled to go into effect at the end of 2012. However, the ETS scheme would include non-EU flights entering or leaving Europe, and various countries (including the U.S.) and various airlines argued that the scheme infringed on national sovereignty and hence violated international law, but the European Court of Justice declared a cap on airline emissions to be entirely legal.[224]

Nevertheless, when the deadline for its application to non-EU planes was approaching, "airlines and governments in the United States, India and China went ballistic," wrote Elisabeth Rosenthal, "filing lawsuits, threatening trade actions and prompting legislation." The US Congress even passed, and the President signed, a bill prohibiting any US airlines from participating in the EU's ETS.[225]

In response, the EU put the program on hold for a year and offered to delay the implementation of its policy, on the understanding that the ICAO would work toward reaching a global deal by 2016, which would come into effect in 2020. In any case, as John Kerry said in 2012 (before he became the secretary of state), "We've got to have an international agreement." If the effort to get international regulations fails, or if the regulations turn out to be too weak, strong emissions regulations for the United States, which has been an obstacle, could probably be imposed by the EPA, under the Clean Air Act.[226]

Within the United States, environmental groups started in 2007 petitioning to the EPA to make a finding on whether airplane emissions likely endanger public health. In 2011, a U.S. District Court declared that the EPA had a duty to make an endangerment finding. But the EPA did not do this, so in August 2014, Friends of the Earth and the Center for Biological Diversity notified the EPA of their intention to sue, because of the "unreasonable delay." Finally, in September 2014, the EPA promised to issue an endangerment finding by April 2015. Assuming that the finding is positive, the EPA will then need to issue regulations, which will likely lead to international regulations, because of the need for uniformity. Unfortunately, if the ICAO establishes an international standard, it is not scheduled to go into effect until 2020.[227]

Fuel Efficiency

One benefit of international regulations would be stimulating airlines to make their planes more fuel-efficient. Some steps have already been made, due to the increasing cost of fuel, but the means are available to do much more. The ICAO has estimated that improvements made in fuel efficiency, along with other technological advances, could reduce aviation's use of fuel by (only) as much as 30% by 2020 and 35% by 2030.[228] In the meantime, however, there have been advances in fuel efficiency.

NASA has funded programs to make airlines much more ecofriendly by reducing their fuel consumption. One program, called "N+3," is to make such airliners within three generations, i.e., between 2030 and 2035. Another program, called "N+2," wants planes ready between 2020 to 2025. The subsonic program, known as SUGAR (Subsonic Ultra Green Aircraft Research), is for airliners using 70% less fuel than current planes (as well as emitting 75% less nitrous oxide). The N+2 subsonic program is for airliners with 50 percent reductions. In 2010, awards were given for N+3 designs by MIT, GE Aviation, Northrop Grumman, and Boeing for either the subsonic or supersonic programs, or both. For example, the Boeing subsonic design, called SUGAR Volt, was a hybrid airplane intended to reduce fuel consumption by 70 to 90 percent. The MIT design, dubbed the "double-bubble," was for a 180-passenger airplane intended to replace the Boeing 735, and MIT also submitted a design for a plane carrying 350 passengers. In 2011, the go-ahead was given under the N+2 program to Boeing, Northrop Grumman, and Lockheed Martin.[229]

Use of Biofuels

When such airliners become operational, they will make great reductions in fuel consumption. But more will be required for the complete elimination of fossil fuels. Essential for this task is the use of biofuels. It has generally been assumed that biofuels will not go far towards that goal. The ICAO estimation that technological advances could at most reduce fuel consumption 35% by 2030, for example, presupposes its view that one should not assume that biofuels "could account for more than 10% of global aviation fuel by 2050."[230] However, this statement, published in 2010, was made without the benefit of the great strides in biofuel research in the past few years. For one thing, it had been assumed that biofuels would be crop-based, so that the percentage of biofuels in auto and airline fuels needed to be limited. In recent years, however, cellulosic biofuels have been developed, some of which could be used in airplanes.

For example, well-known gene scientist Craig Venter has worked, in partnership (believe it or not) with ExxonMobil, on developing algae-based fuel that can be used by airplanes without the need for any engine modifications.[231] Given this development, it is important that the airlines use only "biofuels that are certified as sustainable," says the Natural Resources Defense Council (NRDC), because aviation's "massive purchasing power has the potential to reshape the supply chain," for good or for ill.

For this reason, NRDC in 2013 generated an Aviation Biofuel Sustainability Survey, which was sent to the 22 U.S. airlines that "have used, or are making public claims of plans to use, biofuels in their operations," 12 of which responded to NRDC's questionnaire. According to the main results: Only two airlines have committed to using only certified biofuels, and only two reported that they assessed the potential indirect land use change risks of their biofuels. NRDC reported the results anonymously this first year, but in future years it "intend[s] to publish airline names and their progress toward sourcing certified sustainable biofuels."[232]

Electric Aircraft

The use of cellulosic biofuels opens the possibility of totally green airplanes, and some have already been developed. NASA sponsored a Green Flight Challenge, for which designers were to build an electric airplane with two specifications: They were to fly at least 200 miles (322 km) in under two hours and to use less than a gallon (3.8 liters) of fuel. The first-place prize ($1.35 million) went to a Slovenian four-passenger plane, Taurus G4. This team and the second-place winner both fulfilled the requirements, even using only half a gallon of fuel. The winning inventor said: "Two years ago the thought of flying 200 miles at 100 mph in an electric aircraft was pure science fiction. Now, we are all looking forward to the future of electric aviation." He plans to invest his winnings in the development of a 100% electric supersonic plane, similar to the ZEHST (below).[233]

Zero Emission Hypersonic Transportation

Airbus's parent company, EADS, unveiled the most exciting airplane in the 2011 Paris Air Show, ZEHST: Zero Emission Hypersonic Transportation. ZEHST is considered the heir to the Concorde, except that it produces no sonic boom, requires no fossil fuel, and flies faster: Whereas the Concorde went from London to New York in 3.5 hours, the ZEHST, which will carry 50-100 passengers, will require (theoretically) only 1.5 to 2.5 hours. The plane will cruise using ordinary jet engines running on biofuels made from seaweed or algae (while using rockets and ramjets to reach Mach 4). The hope is to have this plane commercially available by 2050, perhaps by 2040.[234]

VoltAir: Zero-Emissions Airplane for Ordinary Travelers

EADS also unveiled at the 2011 Paris Air Show a more conventional all-electric concept airplane named VoltAir. It would be propelled by two highly efficient superconducting electric motors, which would turn two propellers. Although it does not fly nearly as fast as ZEHST, VoltAir has a good turnaround time, because its batteries are simply swapped out at an airport. The plane will be largely ready to fly as soon as the needed batteries are created – hence perhaps in 20 or 25 years.[235]

Conclusion to Discussion of Airplanes

A few years ago, it probably seemed self-evident to most people that our energy could never be 100% fossil free, because green airliners would be impossible, at least in the present century. Recent developments, however, have shown the possibility that even airliners could have zero fossil-fuel emissions.

100% Clean Energy

A few countries already use clean energy for all or most of their electricity – or at least could, if they did not export much of their electricity to other countries – namely: Iceland 100%; Bhutan 100% (but exports most); Lesotho 98; Norway 98% (but exports all but 24%); Paraguay 90%; Albania 85; Mozambique, high amount (but exports much); Austria 75% (most of these countries get much of their energy from hydro and/or geothermal power.) The other leading countries are: Denmark 45%; Scotland 40; Germany 31%; Portugal 25%; Spain, 22%; China 17%; United States 13%.[236]

These figures show that, as the world moves toward 100% clean energy, the world's countries are at very different places, which in a few cases are because of unusual natural resources, but in most cases are because of policies. They show in particular that the two countries that emit the most greenhouses gases, China and the United States, have a very long way to go.

Various studies and reports have indicated that the United States and the world as a whole could have electricity that is 100% clean by 2050, if not earlier. However, to guarantee that each country has enough energy to provide all of the needed electricity all of the time, a country's electric grid should – according to a study carried out at the University of Delaware – have almost three times (290%) of the power needed for peak times, in order to keep the cost and the need for storage back-ups to a minimum.[237]

Redundant capacity is not only good for each country; it is also good for the world as a whole, because types of available clean energy vary greatly from country to country. For example, some countries have a lot of solar energy, others have a lot of wind energy, and still others have a lot of ocean, hydro, or geothermal power. So, although a given country may have little sun, or little wind, it can still get sufficient clean energy from other sources to provide its electrical grid with 290% of the power needed for peak times. Also, if some countries have even more than 290% of the power needed for their own grids, they can sell it to neighboring countries without enough.

United States

Studies showing the clean energy potential for the United States include:

- As mentioned at the outset of this chapter, two Princeton professors laid out a plan whereby America's energy needs could be fulfilled by clean energy, using technologies already available.[238]

- Environment Ohio, with input by Environment America, said that "America has enough solar energy potential to power the nation several times over."[239]

- The Worldwatch Institute added that "seven states in the Southwest alone have the potential to provide 10 times the current electric generating capacity through solar power."[240]

- A study by the National Renewable Energy Laboratory said that "renewable electricity generation from technologies that are commercially available today . . . is more than adequate to supply 80% [and perhaps 90%] of total U.S. electricity generation in 2050." Because the NREL's study did "not explore the full portfolio of clean technologies that could contribute to future electricity supply" (such as offshore wind, enhanced geothermal, and wave and tidal, energy its study *with* the full portfolio would have probably declared the resources adequate to provide at least 100%.[241]

- "Resources in the contiguous US," said a study by Harvard professors, "could accommodate as much as 16 times total current demand for electricity in the US."

China

A 2014 WWF report entitled "China's Future Generation" stated: "By embracing conservation measures and renewable energy, China can transition to an 80% renewable electric power system by 2050 at far less cost than continuing to rely on coal."[242]

The World as a Whole

The most important issue, of course, is whether the world as a whole could be powered by clean energy anytime soon. Several reports have focused on this issue:

- *Energy Strategy Reviews* published a study by three scientists showing in detail how clean technologies, using only presently available technologies – but all of them – could provide 95% of the world's energy needs by 2050.[243]

- Dealing with energy of every type (not simply electricity), a report by the World Wildlife Fund (WWF) and Ecofys argued that it "is technically feasible to supply everyone on the planet in 2050 with the energy they need, with 95 percent of this energy coming from renewable sources." This 95 percent includes transport, which is to be electrified; electricity for all other purposes; and building heat. With regard to electricity alone, the WWF says that solar energy alone could electrify the world and that this would take less than 1% of the total land mass.[244]

- Focusing on Europe, the WWF showed how it could have a 100% clean energy system by 2050, if not earlier.[245]

- Professors at the University of Delaware and Delaware technical College laid out a scenario in which humanity's electric systems could be powered 99.9% of the time by wind and solar energy combined with electrochemical storage. The other 0.1% of the time requires a backup, which could be provided by hydropower (or nuclear or fossil energy).[246]

Contributions from Types of Clean Energy

Another way to estimate the clean energy available to the world is to summarize the estimates for the various types of clean energy discussed above:

- *Energy Efficiency:* Called the "single most important element" by the WWF/Ecofys study, it was said by Cambridge University scientists to be capable of saving "73% of global energy."[247]

- *Solar Energy:* According to the WWF, solar energy by itself could electrify the world.

- *Wind Energy:* Scientists at Lawrence Livermore and Stanford reported out that the current global demand for power is about 18 trillion watts (TW), while wind turbines could in principle provide 428 TW (more than 23 times the current demand). According to a study by Harvard professors, "Resources in the contiguous US . . . could supply more than 40 times current worldwide consumption of electricity."[248]

- *Hydropower:* The total "technically exploitable" potential for hydropower, according to U.N. estimates, is 15,090 terawatt-hours per year, which is equal to half of projected global electricity use in 2030.[249]

- *Geothermal:* According to the U.S. Geological Survey, America's geothermal energy could produce 50% of the country's current capacity to generate electricity, so geothermal combined with some other forms of energy could provide the country's needs many times over. According to Bloomberg New Energy Finance, the world has "113 GW of untapped potential," which is "located in 39 developing countries."[250]

- *Ocean Energy:* The United Nations has estimated that wave energy alone has the potential to provide more electrical power than is presently generated worldwide. If tidal energy is added, ocean energy could in principle provide *many times more* electricity than is presently used. According to one estimate, in fact, 0.1% of the energy in ocean waves could be capable of supplying the entire world's energy requirements five times over.[251]

- *Biomass* and *Biofuels:* Insofar as they are problematic for using food and for ILUC, they cannot be counted. But the potential for the cellulosic type is great, especially for halophytes.

As these reports show, there is far more clean energy potential than civilization will ever need. Some very bright and moral people believe that to power civilization without energy from coal, oil, and natural gas, we need to continue using, and even increase the use of, nuclear energy. But the summary in this chapter seems to suggest otherwise.

A Grid for Transmitting Clean Energy

Besides having sufficient sources for 100% clean energy, there needs to be a grid that is capable of distributing it. "The 'grid' amounts to the networks that carry electricity from the plants where it is generated to consumers. The grid includes wires, substations, transformers, switches and much more."[252]

The grid is woefully inadequate in many countries, including China and the United States. Although China has developed an amazing amount of wind and solar energy in the last few years, "China's grid hasn't expanded fast enough to deliver all the power that these projects can generate." After waiting months to get connected, developers are often forced to shut down part of their turbines to balance energy with demand. "In Eastern Mongolia, for example, some wind farms ran at only about 50 percent capacity in 2012."[253]

Likewise, the United States – to which the ensuing discussion will be limited, is being held back less by available energy than by its inadequate, out-of-date electric grid.

The Electric Grid: Modernization and Transformation

People who favor clean energy have sometimes argued in favor of "getting off the grid" by generating clean energy locally, perhaps by means of roof-top solar photovoltaics and private wind turbines. This is great for those who can do it. But many people in America and around the world cannot; they must get their electricity from the electric grid. The only question, then, is whether the grid is green. (There are people who call themselves "green gridders."[254])

The grid is now not very green, and unless it becomes greener, the switch to electric vehicles will not do much for clean energy: It will simply trade oil-based emissions for coal-based emissions. Beginning to make the grid much greener will require a new grid with at least four elements:

1. *A Grid with Transmission Lines to Clean Energy Sources:* "[I]f you place the map of regions with the best wind and solar energy on top of a map of our current transmission system," has written Bill White of Americans for Clean Transmission, "you won't find too much overlap."[255]

The problem is that the grid was designed a century ago for a system based on fossil fuels, primarily coal. But now we need transmission lines that run to radically different places. "The most cost-effective wind farms," wrote Elisabeth Rosenthal, "are in desolate areas where the wind howls and land is cheap, meaning they are the farthest from users." What is needed is "next generation" energy transport with "high-voltage transmission lines that connect large-scale wind and solar farms to population centers."[256]

2. A Smart, Resilient Grid: Another problem is that the grid is old and fragile: "70% of transmission lines and power transformers are 25 years or older, while 60% of circuit breakers are more than 30 years old," said a 2011 report by the American Society of Civil Engineers (ASCE).[257]

    As a result, hot weather, which leads people to turn up air conditioners and thereby to overstress the lines, are likely to cause outages, which may then lead to cascading blackouts – such as the September 2011 blackout in southern California, which cost the public over $100 million in losses.[258]

    More generally, the President's Council of Economic Advisers, in conjunction with the Department of Energy, said that weather-related power outages now cost between $18 and $33 billion per year, while spiking to $75 billion in 2008 (when Hurricane Ike occurred) and $52 billion in 2012 (the year of Sandy).[259] In efforts to prevent blackouts, grid operators now sometimes engineer brownouts, which can cause great inconvenience.

    The grid operators' other method is simply to take sources of electricity – typically clean energy sources – offline, or at least order them to run at partial speed, making it difficult for the investors to recoup their investments. An Associated Press story reported that over a billion dollars have been spent on wind turbines in Maine, New Hampshire, and Vermont, resulting in the region's now having 700 megawatts of capacity, but "getting it to market remains a challenge."[260]

    In "A Policy Framework for the 21st Century Grid," President Obama in 2011 laid out a policy to deal with such problems. His central concept was that of a "smart grid," the main feature of which is "microgrids," which have already being developed by Denmark and the Pentagon. In the developing world, the spread of microgrids in remote locations is now "outpacing that of conventional utilities." In the United States, many businesses are expected to install microgrids in the coming years, the value of which was demonstrated by the businesses that were able to keep their lights on during Hurricane Sandy.[261] The smart grid also includes many other new technologies, including the capacity to deal automatically with power outage and "smart meters," which track a home's real-time energy usage, so that modifications can be made. By 2014, investments in smart grid technologies had exploded, with a Navigant Research report entitled "Smart Grid Technologies" predicting that almost $600 billion will be spent on them between 2014 and 2023.[262]

3. A Competitive Market-Based Grid: The grid also needs to be based on a competitive market, in which the least expensive sources of electricity are employed first – rather than the sources that make the most money for the owners.[263]

A *New York Times* story, reporting about Green Mountain Power of Vermont, said that during the heat wave of July 2013, Green Mountain was told by the grid operator to turn its wind turbines way down – in favor of "diesel-fired units that are very expensive and dirty," complained the CEO. Besides costing both the environment and the public, this policy makes it difficult for clean energy investors to get their money back. "My gosh," said the CEO, "so we'll build all this stuff that we'll be running half the time?"[264] If market principles were employed, then if it provides the cheapest electricity, Green Mountain – along with dozens of other wind and solar farms – would likely be generating at full capacity all the time.

In 2011, the Federal Energy Regulatory Commission (FERC) announced Order 1000, which would change the U.S. grid so that it would get more of its electricity from clean energy. This order was challenged by utilities and others with vested interests in the status quo, but in 2014, the D.C. Circuit Court rejected their arguments and Order 1000 became law. This law has a number of provisions that will level the playing field, so that as clean energy becomes increasingly less expensive, grid operators will choose it over fossil-fuel generated electricity.[265]

The main argument for sticking largely with fossil-fuel energy is that a grid based heavily on clean energy will be unreliable, leading to frequent blackouts. However, Germany's grid, with its high quota of clean energy, has proved to be more reliable than the grids of any of other European country or (of course) the USA. In September 2014, moreover, one portion of Germany is now, thanks to batteries, 100% green, so the grid operators no longer need to keep coal plants fired to provide back-up energy.[266]

4. *A Coordinated Grid:* The national grid is organized regionally. But most of these regions are not coordinated. "Almost all planning is done within those regions, as if they were islands. . . . Federal officials say there is not even a regulatory mechanism for planning a line that does more than connect two regions," wrote Matthew Wald of the *New York Times*. The current grid is usually described as "balkanized." However, said a former member of the Federal Energy Regulatory Commission, "To call the U.S. grid balkanized would insult the Macedonians."[267]

"Our interconnected grid system can no longer be regulated as it was a century ago," Ryan Fitzpatrick has noted. "To manage a regional system, we're going to need regional coordination and authority that, in limited situations, supersedes that of the states." A planning process for redesigning the grid, for which President Obama had called, concluded that building the needed kind of grid, which would integrate clean energy on a large scale, would cost about $115 billion. Although this might sound like a lot of money, it would pay for itself in many ways, such as by stopping most of the "line loss" of the present grid. In 2010, it lost 6.6% of the electricity generated – which was "$25.7 billion worth of electrons, lost into thin air." A savings of $25 billion a year from this improvement alone would cover the $115 billion investment in five years.[268]

The aforementioned ASCE report *Failure to Act* estimated the cost of the investment in the grid to be even higher. But the costs incurred by failing to invest in a resilient grid will be, said this report, "higher than the investment itself." This failure to act would cost households $354 billion and businesses $641 billion by 2040, in addition to costing the economy $33 billion annually by that year.[269]

Summary of the Grid Discussion

The creation of a smart, modern, resilient grid will be essential to keeping climate change (which with the continuation of business as usual will cost trillions of dollars) to the lowest level now possible. Such a grid will make it possible to realize the ideal suggested in 2014 by the International Energy Agency: Rather than adding solar, wind, and other forms of clean energy to the present system, change the system, so that it is based on clean energy from the ground up – a change that will make everything much more cost-effective.[270]

Conclusion

The various sections of this chapter have shown that the world could be powering itself with clean energy by 2050. Whether this will actually occur will depend on many things, not least of which will be whether the United States, along with other countries, creates a "green grid." But the twofold point of this chapter is that the world needs to make an unprecedented transition, and that this is possible, because there is far more than enough potential clean energy in every country to make this transition.

At the head of this chapter is a quotation speaking of Germany's energy transition as unprecedented. It has been showing other countries what is possible. During the first half of 2014, Germany was already getting almost 1/3 of its power from clean energy, even though Germany does not have much sunshine.[271]

Nicholas Stern said, "a transition to a low-carbon economy looks not only feasible at reasonable cost, but also attractive."[272] It is attractive because it will free us from the fossil-fuel industry, which is terribly *unattractive* in its behavior, as well as its products – as discussed in the following chapter.

18

THE ABOLITION
OF DIRTY ENERGY

"We now know that fossil fuels cause climate change
of unprecedented destructive potential."
– Harvard Faculty for Divestment, 2014

The foregoing chapters have argued that:

- The need to abolish the fossil-fuel economy gives our generation an unprecedented moral challenge, analogous to the challenge to abolish slavery (Ch. 14).

- The human race seems to be behaving like lemmings rushing to the sea to self-destruction, adhering to practices that destroy nature, human lives, and civilization (Ch. 15).

- Economics has become an idolatrous religion, with economic growth understood to be the highest good. This religion is especially destructive insofar as economic growth is based on fossil-fuel energy and influential economists treat continued growth as more important than mitigating climate change (Ch. 16).

- The rise of clean energy shows that most of modern society's way of life could continue without a fossil-fuel economy, just as the rise of fossil-fuel energy showed that, without slavery, society's way of life otherwise continued (Chs. 14 & 17).

But society's present way of life will not continue very long unless the fossil-fuel economy, based on dirty energy, is replaced by a clean-energy economy, and quickly. As pointed out in the Introduction, scientists' calculation of the "carbon budget" shows that, to have a chance of avoiding truly terrible disruption and even collapse, civilization can put no more than roughly 565 more gigatons of carbon dioxide into the atmosphere by midcentury, and yet, "at the present rate," in McKibben's words, "we'll blow through our 565-gigaton allowance in 16 years."[1]

Addressing this climate emergency requires a radical change in the projections of the fossil-fuel industries. Whereas they have been planning business as usual, meaning increased profits every year, their sales must start being cut almost immediately and be cut virtually to zero by 2050.

In this situation, some people may consider this unfair, thinking that insofar as the coal, gas, and oil companies have been providing us with energy for electricity and transportation for over a century, we should feel bad about putting them out of business. But the practices of the coal, natural gas, and oil industries show that there should be no regrets. We also need not fear that the abolition of the fossil-fuel industry will lead to increased unemployment, as the burgeoning clean energy industry will employ more people than were employed by dirty energy.

The Fossil-Fuel Industry: Fighting, not Switching

The fossil-fuel corporations, who with their dirty energy have been responsible for almost two-thirds of greenhouse emissions since the beginning of the industrial age,[2] have shown themselves to be very bad citizens in at least four ways.

- Although the world does not dare burn more than 565 gigatons of carbon, the world presently has fossil-fuel reserves of five times that amount: 2,795 gigatons. For civilization to have a chance of staying within the carbon budget, it will need to keep four-fifths of the carbon reserves in the ground. And yet the dirty-energy companies have indicated that they have no intention on doing this. The reason is simple: "[A]t today's market value, those 2,795 gigatons of carbon emissions are worth about $27 trillion."[3] They see present profits as more important than the possibility of destroying civilization.

- U.S. fossil-fuel companies have been awarded an atypical special status: With regard to oil and gas, "the United States [is] the only one of the 62 petroleum-producing nations that allows private entities to control large amounts of oil and gas reserves."[4] This singular U.S. policy has allowed these corporations, especially the five companies constituting Big Oil — (BP, Chevron, ConocoPhillips, ExxonMobil, and Shell) — to earn enormous profits. But instead of using their extraordinary riches to join in the battle against global warming, these corporations have been spending a significant portion of their profits for propaganda to prevent the world from dealing successfully with this crisis (as discussed in Chapters 11 and 13).

- The fossil-fuel companies use part of their profits to keep their taxes low.[5] In 2011, Big Oil spent $65.7 million for lobbying, "successfully persuading their congressional friends to retain tax breaks." The lobbyists, in Dan Froomkin's words, are backed up "with big wads of cash in the form of campaign donations and spending." Big Oil's investments paid off handsomely: "For every $1 the big five spent on lobbying in D.C. last year, they effectively received $30 in subsidies disguised as tax breaks." Big Oil's annual subsidies (in the form of tax breaks), according to Taxpayers for Common Sense, come to $10.5 billion a year ($5.5 billion in general business tax breaks, plus $5 billion in tax breaks exclusive to oil and gas). As a result, although the standard tax rate for corporations is 35%, the 20 largest U.S. oil and gas companies paid an average of only 11.7% between 2009 and 2013.[6]

- Besides fighting to protect its own tax-break subsidies, the fossil-fuel industries attempt to eliminate clean energy's modest subsidies, partly by implying that these are larger than its own (Ch. 16).

Should we not, as Tom Engelhardt suggests, begin calling the conscious act of destroying the planet "terracide," and those who commit it, "terrarists"? The fossil-fuel companies are guilty of the ultimate crime, Engelhardt said, because they are earning their "profits directly off melting the planet, knowing that their extremely profitable acts are destroying the very habitat, the very temperature range that for so long made life comfortable for humanity." Pointing out how the tobacco companies, while aware of the deadly effects of their products, "went right on producing and selling while others suffered and died," he said:

> [Imagine that] everyone on Earth was forced to smoke several packs of [cigarettes] a day. If that isn't a terrorist – or terrarist – attack of an almost unimaginable sort, what is? If the oil execs aren't terrarists, then who is?

The national security state has put a lot of attention on protecting us from terrorists, but should it not also "safeguard us from terrarists and terracide as well as terrorists and their destructive plots?"[7]

Eliminating Coal

In addition to the bad-citizen characteristics exemplified by all of the fossil-fuel industries, there are at least five additional reasons why we should have a "no-regrets" attitude about the elimination of coal-based energy:

- Coal-based power plants are second to none as threats to the planet's climate.

- Coal-based power plants cause an extreme amount of human illness and death.

- So-called "clean coal" will not solve the problem of global warming.

- Coal is a much more expensive source of energy than has been generally recognized.

- The U.S. coal industry has long prevented regulations to reduce coal's deleterious effects on health and climate.

Coal as a Major Threat to the Planet's Climate

After referring to some changes in the climate that may be "approaching the point of becoming irreversible," James Hansen in 2008 said: "In the face of such threats it is madness to propose a new generation of power plants based on burning coal, which is the dirtiest and most polluting of all the fossil fuels."[8]

Alluding to the dirtiness of power plants, President Obama said in his June 2013 remarks on climate change: "Power plants can still dump unlimited amounts of carbon pollution into the air for free." This is insane because, as pointed out by the Center for Climate and Energy Solutions, "coal use accounts for 43.1 percent of global CO_2 emissions."[9]

While Obama did something about this – in June 2014, his EPA proposed new rules for power plants to ensure a reduction of CO_2 emissions by 30 percent from 2005 levels by 2030 – that is too little and too slow. David Hawkins of the Natural Resources Defense Council said, "We'll be pushing for 2020 reductions of at least 35 percent below 2005 levels, ramping up to more ambitious targets later in the decade." But perhaps Obama aimed at a 30 percent reduction by 2030 to get the conversation with China and India started.[10]

Doing so is essential, according to a study by Fergus Green and Nicholas Stern, because unless China can curb its carbon emissions, the goal of preventing terrible climate disruption will be "almost impossible."

In any case, coal-based power plants now threaten to become an even bigger threat. In an essay entitled "The Road to Climate Disaster Is Paved with Coal," Stephen Lacey points out that there are plans for 1,200 new coal plants around the world. "If all these plants were built," Lacey added, "they would amount to generation capacity four times greater than the [present] entire U.S. coal fleet." In 2014, fortunately, China started taking some steps toward reducing its use of coal.[11]

The coal industry, unfortunately, evidently has no concern about the preservation of civilization: Although the building of even half of these plants would quickly break our civilization's carbon budget, the coal industry is working for at least most of these plants to be constructed. America's use of coal has been going down and so, as a 2013 *New York Times* article header indicated, "Coal Industry Pins Hopes on Exports as U.S. Market Shrinks." These hopes have led coal mining companies to plan to build six export terminals in Oregon and Washington and a dozen in Gulf Coast states to ship coal to China and India. Thanks to resistance from environmental groups and local communities, some of these terminals have been terminated.[12]

Nevertheless, "the U.S. is still exporting a massive amount of coal." Being the world's fourth leading exporter of coal (behind Australia, Indonesia, and Russia), the United States has in recent years increased its exports greatly. As a result, as quoted in Chapter 13, "'American carbon' is flowing into the global economy and atmosphere faster than ever."[13]

Australia too has been planning even greater increases in exports of coal to Asia. Back in 2007, its booming export of coal was referred to as "Australia's dirty little secret": Coal exports had tripled in the previous 25 years, "and coal corporations want to double that figure." In 2012, the Australian Coal Association proudly announced: "Over the past 10 years black coal exports have increased by more than 50%." Moreover, Australia, whose coal reserves by themselves could burn up 75 percent of the remaining climate budget, elected climate denier Tony Abbott as its prime minister, so its mining of coal is sure to rise — even though Australia began the 2014 year with a record-breaking heat wave and has been devastated by wildfires that ravaged towns and farmlands, killing significant numbers of people. Australia likes to say that it contributes only 1.5% of the global total of greenhouse gases. However, by including its coal exports, Australia is responsible for 4.8% of the greenhouse gas emissions and is the sixth largest emitter of CO_2.[14]

If it ends up that civilization commits suicide, coal will likely be one of the primary instruments.

Coal as a Threat to Human Health

Besides being deadly for the climate, coal-burning is also deadly for human beings. Entitled "Coal Isn't Just Dirty, Outdated Energy – It's Also Making Us Sick," a Sierra Club report said that coal-caused sickness leads to over 10,000 deaths in America every year.[15]

In 2011, Congressman Joe Barton suggested that air pollution causes no health problems and that science provides no support for the EPA's claim that there would be great benefits from cleaning up coal-fired plants. In response, the American Lung Association and six other medical societies sent him a letter, which said that even short-term exposure to the particulate matter created by coal causes death from various respiratory and cardiovascular causes, including strokes, heart attacks, and congestive heart failure.[16]

Robert Murray, the founder and CEO of Murray Energy, said that, if the EPA's policies are carried out, "Grandma is going to be cold and in the dark."[17] The real effect, however, will be that Grandma will be healthier and live longer.

Coal, of course, also carries out its killing ways in other parts of the world. In Europe, coal pollution causes 22,000 premature deaths annually. In China, cancer is now the leading cause of death, due primarily to coal-fired factories, which have spawned hundreds of nearby "cancer villages," in which "an unusually high number of residents are struck by the same types of cancer." According to a Greenpeace study, these plants in 2011 caused 9,900 premature deaths, most of which occurred in Hebei, which has 75% of the coal plants. According to a 2013 Greenpeace report entitled "Coal Kills," coal has been killing 80,000 to 115,000 Indians a year.[18]

Could "Clean Coal" Save the Coal Industry?

In light of the harm that coal causes to the environment and human health, the coal industry can be saved, it is widely thought, by making coal "clean." The industry has, in fact, long been advertising its coal as clean, referring to the fact that U.S. power plant smokestacks, due to a 1990 clean-air law, are now fitted with filters and scrubbers to remove pollutants that cause illness and acid rain. However, although this technology is partially effective, it does nothing about the CO_2, so coal remains the number 1 cause of global warming (unless natural gas is surpassing it; see below). Appropriately, therefore, the U.K.'s Advertising Standards Authority told Peabody Energy to take down any ad that could be read by customers as implying that its coal does not emit CO_2.[19]

The technology to save coal by making it truly clean is known as "carbon capture and storage" (CCS), which would extract the carbon from coal and store it underground. In 2013, a group of 27 scientists stated: "New Unabated Coal Is Not Compatible with Keeping Global Warming below 2°C."[20] The Energy Department tried during the Bush and Obama administrations to find a technology that will make coal both clean and affordable, but questions remain:

- *Will CCS Technology Work?* Although the technology can work, as demonstrated by a coal plant in Mississippi, "the technology for capturing carbon has not been proved to work on a commercial basis." However, even if CCS can work on a commercial basis – as a project in Saskatchewan intends to show[21] – other questions remain.

- *Could the CO_2 Be Stored without Leaking?* Vaclav Smil wrote:

> Sequestering a mere 1/10 of today's global CO_2 emissions [would] call for putting in place an industry that would have to force underground every year the volume of compressed gas . . . equal to the volume of crude oil extracted globally by [the] petroleum industry.

  Nobel Prize-winning physicist Burton Richter said that, although large quantities could be stored in deep saline aquifers, "no one knows if these can contain carbon dioxide for centuries without leaking."[22]

- *Would CCS Produce Leak-Causing Earthquakes?* In late 2013, seismologists reported that 93 earthquakes in a Texas oil field in 2009-10, some of which exceeded Magnitude 3, correlated closely with large-scale CO_2 injections. Quoting an expert who said "carbon dioxide injection under high enough pressures and with high enough volume could induce seismicity just like any other fluid at high enough pressures and with high enough volume," Joe Romm pointed out that CCS would require "a staggering amount of CO_2 injection to make a difference as a climate solution." Accordingly, earthquake-induced leaks would "undercut the climate value of CCS."[23]

- *Would CCS Provide Affordable Energy?* Although the Global CCS Institute claimed that CCS coal will generate electricity more cheaply than wind or solar, studies quoted by the Congressional Budget Office indicated that the electricity generated by CCS plants will be 75% more expensive than ordinary coal plants.[24]

Accordingly, as far as we know, commercial CCS may never be available.

Coal: Not Cheap

It has long been assumed that coal is the cheapest type of energy, which is a primary reason why it has provided 40% of the world's electricity (45% in America; 75% in Australia).[25] Many people would be surprised to learn that it is far more expensive than clean energy.

Coal has seemed to be cheap because of the reasons discussed in Chapter 16: Besides not taxing coal for its carbon content, the United States and other governments have even been subsidizing it. In a 2011 study, William Nordhaus and two colleagues set out to "include environmental externalities into a system of national accounts," saying that "emissions should be valued by the damage they cause." Recognizing that the "largest industrial contributor to external costs is coal-fired electric generation," they calculated coal's external damages by using an extremely low estimate. But even so, the team concluded that "if the external costs were fully internalized, prices would change."[26]

The same year, Harvard Medical School's Paul Epstein and 11 other academics wrote: "Each stage in the life cycle of coal – extraction, transport, processing, and combustion – generates a waste stream and carries multiple hazards for health and the environment." Whereas Nordhaus estimated the social cost of coal to be 3 cents per kWh, Epstein and his colleagues put it at 18 cents per kWh, so if the costs were paid by the coal industry, the price of coal would be (at least) tripled, which would make clean energy much cheaper than coal.[27] Moreover, as mentioned in Chapter 16, Ackerman and Stanton estimated the social cost of carbon to be at least 40 times higher than Nordhaus' estimate.

The Coal Industry Has Long Prevented Meaningful Regulations

Lobbyists for the coal industry have said that the EPA rules requiring CCS on all new coal-fired plants were unfair: Because CCS is not now commercially available, the rule could mean an indefinite ban on new American plants. Bloomberg replied that "ruining the atmosphere is too high a price for protecting one type of power when others are available."[28]

At one time, few editors or politicians would have given such a reply. Coral Davenport, writing in the *National Journal*, said:

> For a century, coal dominated America's energy landscape.
> . . . King Coal also enjoyed almost unrivaled influence in Washington. On Capitol Hill, the muscular coal lobby routinely rolled its opponents. In particular, the clout of the coal lobby - and the money it doled out - was a major reason Congress has never enacted a serious climate-change law.[29]

The coal industry has continued using these tactics – for example, claiming that the EPA rules would cost "millions of jobs," although there are only 84,000 Americans working in coal mining – but coal's claims have become less influential. Although it launched a $35 million ad campaign during the 2012 presidential election, accusing Obama of launching "a war on coal," it was "a total failure."[30]

Although the coal industry no longer has its old clout in the United States, the fact remains that its responsibility for the threat to civilization posed by climate change is still second to none. It is necessary, said Epstein, "to phase out coal rapidly."[31] We should have no regrets about replacing it quickly with various kinds of clean energy, now that they are available.

Indeed, it appears that traditional power plants are already on the way out in Europe. Investment bank UBS has advised people that because of the increasingly lower costs of clean energy and battery storage in Europe, energy from coal and natural gas power plants will soon be relatively too expensive: "Large-scale power stations could be on a path to extinction."[32]

If so, it should be just a matter of time until this becomes true in the rest of the world. However, the urgency of reducing carbon emissions is so great that it is essential for governments to eliminate fossil-fuel subsidies in order to speed up the process.

Natural Gas

In 1988, the American Gas Association, stating that natural gas emits far less greenhouse gas than coal, started promoting it as "a bridge fuel" – as the least harmful fossil fuel "while the world looks for other, longer-lasting solutions to the 'greenhouse' effect."[33] Today, because of the natural gas boom starting in about 2009, one can find hundreds of books and articles about this idea.

A Bridge Fuel?

This boom occurred after a period in which both oil and gas production had seemed to have "peaked," so that there would be increasingly fewer new projects: There was still a lot of oil and gas in the ground, but the drillers could not get to them. However, the impending shortages raised prices so much that the oil and gas companies were motivated to develop a new technology: horizontal drilling plus "fracking" (which is short for hydraulic fracturing). Here, after the hole is drilled vertically for thousands of feet, it is drilled horizontally, which yields a higher recovery than a vertical well. During that drilling, water, sand, and chemicals are injected into the well under high pressure so as to help the fracturing, thereby releasing the oil or gas from the shale formation in which it had been locked.[34]

As a result, there was suddenly an abundance of gas (oil is discussed in the next section), at which point natural gas as a "bridge" became heavily marketed. The basic idea is that it is much cleaner than coal, because it emits far less CO_2, so it can be used to reduce coal usage until there is time for wind, solar, and other clean energies to be more fully developed. This program got its biggest boost in 2012, when the International Energy Agency (IEA) published a report saying that "natural gas is poised to enter a golden age," which will help improve things if the industry only follows – as the title puts it – "Golden Rules for a Golden Age of Gas."[35]

But although the idea of natural gas as a bridge was endorsed at the highest levels, including the Obama White House, "Gas is cleaner only at the point of combustion," said McKibben. "If you calculate the greenhouse gas pollution emitted at every stage of the production process – drilling, piping, compression – it's essentially just coal by another name."[36] There are several problems with natural gas that make it no better than coal.

Methane Leakage

One problem is that natural gas, which is primarily methane (CH_4),[37] tends to leak. It can leak at every stage of the production of natural gas: drilling, well-completion, processing, and transporting. This leakage has become a serious problem for two reasons.

First, scientists have learned that methane has much more global-warming potential than previously thought: The IPCC now says that it is 34 times, rather than 25 times, more powerful than CO_2 during the first 100 years and a whopping 86 times during the first 20 years.[38]

Second, scientists have determined that natural gas is worse for the climate than coal if the leakage is 3.2% or more. The leakage was long assumed to be no more than 1%,[39] but recent studies indicate the leakage to be much higher.

- A 2012 examination of a natural gas field near Denver showed the methane leakage to be as much as 4%.

- A 2013 study of a Utah site suggested leakage of "an eye-popping 9% of the total production."

- Then in 2014, a study published by the *Proceedings of the National Academy of Sciences* said that various sites in Pennsylvania's Marcellus formation "released methane into the atmosphere at rates that were 100 to 1,000 times [!] greater than federal regulators had estimated." Moreover, "the wells leaking the most methane were in the drilling phase, a period that has not been known for high emissions."[40]

On the basis of the 2013 report of methane leakage of about 9%, Robert Howarth stated that natural gas "will speed climate change, not help stave it off"; Romm said that "natural gas may be more of gangplank than a bridge";

and George Birchard called methane emissions "the road to climate Hell." The 2014 report, which reports extraordinarily high leakage, arguably should by itself put an end to fracking.[41]

These negative views of the benefits of natural gas were supported by another 2013 report, which said that the decrease in U.S. emissions in 2012 was based mainly on "demand reduction primarily due to the economy-wide energy efficiency and conservation measures," combined with the year's mild winter.[42]

Extravagant Water Use

A second problem with the idea of natural gas as relatively "green" is that the current drilling of new natural gas wells uses up vast quantities of fresh water. This is because drilling new wells now consists largely of fracking, and each such well uses 2-9 million gallons of water, for an average of five million. And yet many of the fracking wells are drilled in places, such as Texas, Colorado, and New Mexico, that are already short on drinking and agricultural water, "driving up the price of water and burdening already depleted aquifers and rivers." In Texas, where in 2013 about 30 communities were in danger of running out of water, one of them did, apparently "because the water was being extracted for shale gas fracking."[43]

This high usage is especially important because, unlike water used for other purposes, most of the fracking water becomes so toxic that it is permanently lost to the water cycle. As Nancy Sorrells, who works to ensure that the people of Shenandoah Valley have a supply of safe water, has asked: "Water is the foundation for everything. Why would we sacrifice that?"[44]

Negative Health Impacts

The third problem with natural gas as a bridge is that fracking causes unacceptable health problems. The natural gas industry, to be sure, claims that fracking causes no problems. But it can make this claim, as *The New York Times* pointed out, by means of defining fracking as only the process in which rocks deep underground are fractured. As Environment America says, this narrow definition "obscures the broad changes to environmental, health and community conditions that result from the use of fracking in oil and gas extraction." Rather, fracking needs to be conceived more broadly, namely,

> impacts resulting from all of the activities needed to bring
> a shale gas or oil well into production using high-volume
> hydraulic fracturing . . . , to operate that well, and to deliver
> the gas or oil produced from that well to market.[45]

Methane Pollution: Many of the health problems caused by fracking result from the pollution of air and water by methane. Given the gas industry's preferred meaning of "fracking," these health problems are not caused by fracking, because "methane contamination is not caused by injecting chemicals down the well."[46] However, given the ordinary understanding of what fracking entails, the methane pollution of air and water (and hence soil and food) is probably the best-known way in which fracking causes problems. It became widely known primarily thanks to Steve Lipsky of Texas.

Having felt fatigued and nauseated for several months, Lipsky one day accidentally set the water from his well on fire. He also learned that his submersible pump had quit working because the water contained too much gas. Lipsky's flammable water was made famous by the 2010 film *Gasland* (which was nominated for an Oscar for best documentary).[47]

Realizing that all of the strange phenomena began after two horizontal gas wells beneath his home had been fracked by Range Resources (a natural gas company), Lipsky sued. Range tried to discredit Lipsky's account and even counter-sued him for defamation. But then stories similar to his appeared elsewhere.[48]

Range claimed that its measurements showed the methane levels of the water in the houses in question to be comfortably below the level of concern, but Duke University scientists found the methane to be far *above* that level.[49] They also found that fourth-fifths of the wells over the Marcellus shale in Pennsylvania within one kilometer of natural gas operations had high percentages of methane. Then in 2014, a study of people living in the heart of the Marcellus Shale, led by a former professor at the Yale School of Medicine, found that people living close to a natural gas well were far more likely to develop health upper respiratory and skin problems than people living farther away.[50]

Wastewater Chemicals: Studies have shown people near these drilling operations have the kinds of ailments reported in *Gasland*.[51] Most of the ailments evidently result not from the drilling itself, but from leakage from wastewater wells. Reporting that over 30 trillion gallons of toxic liquid have been used for fracking, ProPublica wrote in 2012 that "wells drilled to bury this waste deep beneath the ground have repeatedly leaked, sending dangerous chemicals and waste gurgling to the surface or, on occasion, seeping into shallow aquifers that store a significant portion of the nation's drinking water."[52]

This wastewater, most scarily, contains substances that are carcinogenic – famous scientist Theo Colborn showed wastewater to contain 353 harmful chemicals, 25% of which can cause cancer[53] – and radioactive, which can get into drinking water.[54] This is no small problem, as fracking creates billions of gallons of this waste every year – 280 billion gallons in 2012.[55] By

2014, the Associated Press reported, "hundreds of complaints have been made about well-water contamination from oil or gas drilling, and pollution was confirmed in a number of them, according to a review that casts doubt on industry suggestions that such problems rarely happen."[56]

Air Pollution: "[D]espite the proclivity of PA water to catch fire," said a professional report, "the vast majority of reported health effects were related to exposure to air." "Air pollution from fracking," Environment America says, "contributes to the formation of ozone 'smog,' which reduces lung function among healthy people, triggers asthma attacks, and has been linked to . . . cancer and other serious health effects."[57]

The air pollution can be fierce in surprising places, as indicated by the startling title of a 2011 article, "Wyoming Air Pollution Worse than Los Angeles Due to Gas Drilling." Equally bad air is found in Utah's Uintah basin, where "scientists found far more methane than anyone had anticipated."[58]

Gagging: People naturally want to learn which ingredients have caused their ailments, but this has been made difficult by gas industry lobbyists. Besides convincing the federal government to exclude fracking from laws about revealing ingredients, they convinced some state governments to keep the ingredients in the fracking chemicals secret, even making it illegal for doctors – if they are told the identity of the chemicals that have made their patients ill – to inform anyone, including the suffering patients.[59]

Animal Deaths: Ranchers can provide additional incriminating information. Two Cornell University researchers learned, for example, that on one ranch, 60 head of cattle drank water from a creek that had been polluted by wastewater, while 36 did not. The 36 had no health problems, whereas 21 of the 60 that had drunk the polluted water died and another 16 failed to produce calves.[60]

Conclusion: In a 2012 article asking whether wastewater wells are "poisoning the ground beneath our feet," *Scientific American* quoted a former engineering expert for the EPA's underground injection program as saying: "In 10 to 100 years we are going to find out that most of our groundwater is polluted," adding: "A lot of people are going to get sick, and a lot of people may die."[61]

Pennsylvania's Department of Environmental Protection has been especially bad about revealing health effects from fracking. For years, news outlets and others have filed Freedom of Information Act requests for information. In April, a Superior Court case claimed that the DEP's procedures made it impossible for citizens to know what processes may be damaging their health. Finally in September 2014, Pennsylvania revealed 243 cases of fracking-caused pollution of private water wells.[62]

Also in 2014, over 1,000 doctors and other health care professionals signed a letter to President Obama asking him to regulate fracking more seriously and to reverse the law making it exempt from the Clean Water Act and Clean Air Act.[63]

Frackquakes

A fourth problem with fracking is that it causes earthquakes – sometimes called "frackquakes" – including fairly big ones. Although some of the quakes may be triggered by fracking itself, most of them seem to be caused by the subsequent injection of wastewater into the ground. The industry and some government geologists initially said they were unconvinced, but indisputable evidence has appeared.[64]

- Prior to 2011, Youngstown, Ohio, had never had earthquakes. But the injection of wastewater into a well was followed by a series of over 100 earthquakes, 12 of which, including a 3.9 quake, were humanly detectable. After the well was closed down, the quakes tapered off quickly.[65]

- A 2012 USGS report dealt with seismicity in the Raton Basin of Colorado and New Mexico, which increased significantly after fracking operations began there in 2001. In the 30 years from 1970 to 2001, there had been only five earthquakes of magnitude 3 or more in that basin, but in the 10 years from 2001 to 2011, the basin had 95 earthquakes of that size, most of which occurred within 5 kilometers of disposal wells into which exceptionally high volumes of wastewater had been injected.[66]

- Fracking also induced such earthquake swarms in Oklahoma: Having had only a few earthquakes a year before drilling began in 2008, there were a dozen quakes that year, 50 in 2009, and then over 1,000 in 2010.[67]

- A USGS article in 2013 said: "The number of earthquakes has increased dramatically over the past few years within the central and eastern United States. More than 300 earthquakes above a magnitude 3.0 occurred in the three years from 2010-2012, compared with an average rate of 21 events per year observed from 1967-2000."[68]

- By the beginning of 2014, the north Texas town of Azle, which had not had any earthquakes for 100 years, experienced over 30 small earthquakes within three months – which led residents to appeal to the Railroad Commission to halt the use of injection wells. Although at first the Commission denied the request, the appointment of a new seismologist led the Commission to propose stiffer regulations.[69]

Besides inducing earthquakes, including swarms, where they had never been before, fracking sometimes induces rather large ones. The 95 earthquakes that occurred in the Raton Basin included a magnitude 5.3 earthquake in Trinidad, Colorado, and the swarm in Prague, Oklahoma, included a magnitude 5.7 quake. In 2014, reflection on these large quakes led seismologists at their annual meeting to say that the frackquakes may well become stronger.[70] The natural gas industry claims that fracking hardly ever causes quakes that can be felt. But it can make this claim only by means of its restricted definition of fracking that excludes wastewater disposal. This is deceptive, because the disposal of toxic fluids – which appears to be the immediate cause of big earthquakes – is an essential part of the process used to produce natural gas from shale.[71]

Calculating the Social Costs

A fifth reason why natural gas cannot be a bridge is that, in spite of claims that it is inexpensive, it actually costs too much. Thus far, most of these costs have been paid by society. But the market price of natural gas should include its social costs:

- The health problems caused by fracking will cost billions.

- Cleaning up water contamination is very costly.

- Fracking in many places has greatly increased the price of water.

- When water wells and aquifers are exhausted, the costs to communities are extreme.

- The truck traffic in fracking towns wears out their roads quickly.

- Fracking in a community can greatly reduce the value of its homes.

- Due to its water-usage and pollution, fracking can be especially damaging to farms, sometimes leading to large livestock losses.

- If natural gas helps cause climate disruption, the costs will be incalculable.[72]

If these costs of natural gas were factored into the market price, the cost of natural gas would be far more expensive than clean energy.

Would Fracking Changes Solve the Problems?

In recent years, some gas companies have started reducing the amount of chemicals used for fracking and recycling the water. They have thereby addressed some of the criticisms of fracking.[73] But would these changes mean that natural gas could be rightfully regarded as a bridge?

Having all of the water of each well recycled would certainly reduce the amount of fresh water required. But although a company in Pennsylvania claimed that it was recycling 90% of its water, a *New York Times* article reported, records showed it to be more like 65%. Moreover, a 2013 article about recycling in Texas said that "only about 5 percent" was recycled. Also, even with recycling and fewer chemicals, the wastewater after many uses becomes ever more carcinogenic and radioactive, and there appears to be no way of preventing these materials from getting into the air, land, and water.[74]

Finally, although getting close to 100% recycling should mean fewer earthquakes, there would still be the methane leakage, the other causes of sickness, and the other social costs.

Banning Fracking

Earth America's senior attorney has said: "The numbers on fracking add up to an environmental nightmare." Because of this nightmare, wrote Ellen Cantarow, "an astonishing grassroots resistance has arisen." Even Pope Francis has publicly supported activists.[75] This resistance to fracking around the world has led to various public protests – with posters saying "Leave Our Communities the Frack Alone!" and the like – and to bans, or at least moratoria, by towns and cities, counties, states or provinces, and countries.[76]

Even those CEOs who inflict fracking on communities do not want fracking near their own homes. ExxonMobil is the greatest producer of natural gas in America, and its CEO, Rex Tillerson, has criticized opponents of fracking, saying: "This type of dysfunctional regulation is holding back the American economic recovery, growth, and global competitiveness." However, Tillerson joined a lawsuit to prevent the construction near his home of a water tower for carrying water to a drilling site, saying that it would cause too much noise and traffic.[77]

While CEOs do not want fracking near their own homes, the oil lobby spends enormous sums to prevent ordinary people from banning fracking – as it did in 2014 with regard to a bill for a moratorium in California while the issue is studied.[78]

Back to the "Golden Age"

The IEA report that helped create the recent excitement about natural gas was misleading. It argued that fracking could be made safe rather inexpensively, if only the "golden rules" were followed, which many commentators took to mean that natural gas was safe for the environment. But such commentators missed the fact that, buried deeper in the report, the IEA said that relying on natural gas would lead to a 3.5°C (6°F) temperature increase – at which point, as a *Guardian* article noted, "global warming could run out of control, deserts would take over in southern Africa, Australia and the western US, and sea level rises could engulf small island states."[79] Hardly safe.

Conclusion: Good News, Bad News, and Hope

The good news about natural gas is that the fracking boom is evidently a bubble, which will burst in the next few years. This is the main point of Richard Heinberg's *Snake Oil*: Just as shysters had used false claims to sell worthless snake oil, today the oil and gas industry has been making false claims about fracking – that thanks to it, the United States will have abundant oil and gas for 100 years and hence energy independence. Considering the hype about fracking as a Ponzi scheme, Heinberg says that the U.S. production of gas (as well as oil) will probably decline by 2020.[80]

The bad news about fracking is that it could continue the insane consumption of gas (as well as oil) long enough to ensure that the world will go beyond the guardrail. The hope is that the world, especially America, will come to see "natural gas as a bridge to a clean energy future" to be a bad joke.

Oil

Just as easily accessible natural gas has been disappearing, the same has been happening to "easy oil," leaving the petroleum industry with what Michael Klare calls "a tough-oil world."[81] In this world, most new sources of oil are difficult and expensive to bring to market. But a lot of oil is still flowing from the era of easy oil. Also, after it seemed that we had reached "peak oil," after which the availability of oil would decline, new techniques for getting at tough oil, especially fracking, turned this around dramatically.

Before looking at three examples of tough oil – deepwater oil, tar sands oil, and oil shale oil - I will summarize crucial facts about two of the giants who were created during the easy-oil era, showing that they have been bad U.S. and global citizens.

ExxonMobil

Once again, here are examples of the bad citizenship of ExxonMobil (henceforth Exxon):

- After the Global Climate Coalition (GCC) was told by its advisory committee that the "scientific basis for the Greenhouse Effect. . . cannot be denied," Exxon continued to deny it.

- When in 1997 most of the other important oil corporations dropped out of the GCC, Exxon remained.

- Exxon has spent many millions of dollars to fund some 100 organizations to engage in climate change denial.

- Exxon has used money to get scientists to spread disinformation.

- Exxon has also bought numerous politicians.

- Although Exxon is the most profitable business in the world, it has been unwilling to pay its fair share of taxes, using lobbyists to get a lower tax rate than most Americans.

- Exxon helped President Bush to reject the Kyoto Protocol.

- Exxon lied about not being part of Vice-President Cheney's 2001 energy task force.

- After it became widely accepted that four-fifths of the known oil and gas reserves must remain in the ground if civilization is to survive, Exxon CEO Rex Tillerson said he had no intention of halting exploration, instead saying that his company plans to spend $37 billion a year to find more oil and gas.

- As Mark Hertsgaard has said, Exxon has "put its immediate economic interests ahead of humanity's future well-being."

Exxon demonstrated its bad citizenship in 1989, when the *Exxon Valdez* spilled over 11 million gallons of crude oil, seriously damaging the ecosystem: As of 2013, Exxon had still not paid the $92 million it owes to Alaska and the Department of Justice.[82] It did so again in 2010, after Exxon's subsidiary XTO Energy dumped thousands of gallons of fracking waste in Pennsylvania. When criminal charges were filed, XTO fought them, saying there was "no lasting environmental impact."[83]

Chevron

Chevron also has a very long history of bad behavior. "Like the other oil giants," Bill McKibben wrote, "Chevron shows the same casual disregard for people around the world."[84] Here are three examples:

Richmond Explosion: In August 2012, there was an explosion at Chevron's refinery in Richmond, California, resulting in a big fire and toxic release, which sent 15,000 people to the hospital. Failing to get adequate compensation from Chevron, Richmond filed a lawsuit in 2013, charging it with "disregard of public safety," reflecting "years of neglect, lax oversight and corporate indifference to necessary safety inspection and repairs." According to Reuters, the U.S. Chemical Safety Board said:

> Chevron did not act upon six recommendations over 10 years to increase inspection and replace the line. . . . During the 10 years before the August 6 blast, refinery officials saw signs the pipeline's walls were thinning due to corrosion.[85]

California Carbon Emissions: Although Chevron has from the beginning been aware of California's 2007 order to develop a cellulosic biofuel replacement for gasoline, in 2013 it declared that it has "not come up with a solution to be able to comply," because the task is "not achievable." Chevron's assessment, however, is likely due to the fact that it "quietly shelved most of its biofuels work in 2010." As we have seen, the effort to create cellulosic biofuel for vehicles has made tremendous progress in the past few years. But far from continuing to test the breakthroughs, "Chevron is leading a lobbying and public relations campaign to undercut the California mandate." As for Chevron's real reason for declaring the mandate unachievable, a man who left Chevron in 2010 said: "You can make money today making advanced biofuels, you just won't make as much money as the oil companies would like."[86]

Amazon Pollution – Refusal to Compensate: Another example of Chevron's bad citizenship has been its refusal to pay for "the worst oil-related environmental disaster on the planet." Although much of the pollution was actually caused by Texaco, which operated oil fields in Ecuador from 1964 to 1990, Chevron absorbed Texaco in 2001, thereby assuming all of its liabilities as well as its assets.[87]

An Amazonian website says: "Texaco's operations were systematically drilling and dumping 24/7 for almost three decades." Because of its destruction of the habitat of Ecuadorean Indian tribes who lived near the wells, members of the tribes sued Texaco in a New York court in 1993 with the guidance of attorney Steven Donziger, who has given much of his life to defending Ecuadoreans. According to the suit:

> Texaco dumped more than 18 billion gallons of toxic waste into Amazon waterways, abandoned more than 900 waste pits, burned millions of cubic meters of gases with no controls and spilled more than 17 million gallons of oil due to pipeline ruptures.[88]

After absorbing Texaco and hence its liabilities, Chevron asked a New York appeals court to transfer the case to Ecuador. The court agreed, with the stipulation that Chevron would need to abide by the Ecuadorian court's decision. In 2011, the Ecuadorian court found Chevron guilty and ordered it to pay damages of $8.6 billion, but after Chevron failed to make the public apology ordered by the court, the fine was raised to $19 billion. A month later, this Ecuadorian court order was blocked by federal judge Lewis A. Kaplan in Manhattan. However, an appeals court reversed Kaplan's order, telling him that he had no authority "to dictate to the entire world which judgments are entitled to respect and which countries' courts are to be treated as international pariahs." Chevron then appealed to the U.S. Supreme Court, asking it to override this decision, but the Court refused.[89]

Still not willing to pay the fine, Chevron decided on a three-fold plan: (1) To arrange a retaliatory trial, arguing that Ecuador's victory over Chevron had been based on a fraudulent conspiracy. (2) To rely on Judge Kaplan to support Chevron. (3) To carry out, in the words of a Chevron press operative, an "L-T [long-term] strategy . . . to demonize Donziger."[90]

In the retaliatory trial, Chevron attacked Donziger under the RICO statute (Racketeer Influenced and Corrupt Organizations Act), which is generally used to prosecute big crime bosses. Although Chevron's counter-suit began as a jury trial with the goal of winning $60 billion in damages, Chevron dropped the claim for damages, which meant that no jury was necessary, so that the verdict could be reached by Kaplan alone. Chevron then asked Kaplan to bar scientific evidence about damage to the environment and human health – which were the bases on which the Ecuadorian court had convicted Chevron.[91] Chevron also asked for many kinds of evidence to be barred, including:

- Contacts with high-level government officials in Ecuador to try to illegally quash the case;

- Videos showing company technical experts in Ecuador laughing at the pollution while discussing ways to hide it from the court;

- The attempt to orchestrate a fake bribery scandal to derail the trial;

- The existence of dummy companies to hide Chevron's control of a supposedly independent laboratory.

Kaplan acceded, and with all of this evidence hidden, Chevron's lawyer was able to charge that Donziger "'masterminded and orchestrated' a scheme that involved multiple acts of wire and mail fraud, extortion, bribery, witness tampering and money laundering."[92]

However, reported *Rolling Stone,* "The oil company's sole witness to its central charge of bribery was a corrupt Ecuadorean ex-judge named Alberto Guerra, whose entire family has been naturalized and relocated on Chevron's dime." Not surprisingly, Kaplan accepted Chevron's three-point argument and the truthfulness of this corrupt judge, charging Donziger with fraud, witness tampering, and bribery, and on this basis blocked the ruling from being enforced in the United States. Donziger, saying that he had made mistakes but engaged in no fraud, witness tampering, or bribery, planned to appeal.[93]

Since absorbing Texaco, Chevron has become the second-largest and most profitable oil company in America. But Chevron has refused to pay the fines for Texaco's crimes, although Chevron had accepted Texaco's liabilities and also agreed to abide by the Ecuadorian court's verdict. As one commentator said, if Chevron would pay the fine, "the money would fund a cleanup of the contamination and provide clean drinking water and health care services for people living in Chevron's former concession area."[94] Chevron is indeed a bad U.S. and global citizen.

Deepwater Oil and BP

Until recently, offshore oil was drilled in shallow waters. But now, oil companies have turned to deepwater drilling, which occurs in depths exceeding 1,000 feet, and which is therefore much more expensive: "It requires specialized, sophisticated, and immensely costly drilling platforms that can run into the billions of dollars to produce." Because of the depth, the operations, being under immense pressure, are also very dangerous.[95]

In spite of these dangers, BP (previously known as British Petroleum) is known to take risks and be "an unapologetic polluter."[96] In 2010, having leased a mobile drilling rig named *Deepwater Horizon,* BP drilled a well in the Gulf of Mexico, 50 miles off the Louisiana coastline. Due to haste as it was finishing up, BP caused "the worst environmental disaster in American history," which had several terrible consequences:

- The blowout, which it took 3 months to cap, resulted in the escape of almost 210 million gallons (almost 5 million barrels) of oil, according to government estimates.

- The explosion killed 11 workers and 17 others.

- Hundreds more came down with symptoms similar to the Gulf War syndrome: muscle spasms twisting arms into claws; short-term memory loss; excruciating pain; incredibly itchy skin; and pulmonary problems.[97]

- The 170,000 thousand workers hired to clean up were exposed not only to the toxic oil – which includes the carcinogen benzene – but also 2 million gallons of dangerous dispersants. In September 2013, a study in the *American Journal of Medicine* reported that these workers are at an increased risk of cancer, leukemia, kidney and liver damage, asthma, and many other illnesses.

- As of 2013, baby dolphins were dying at record rates; oysters, crab, shrimp, and fish populations have been decimated and afflicted with tumors and deformities; mangroves that used to be habitats for brown pelicans, terns and roseate spoonbills still have not recovered. And although BP dropped its search for tar early in 2013, tar balls continued to wash up, a 4000-pound tar mat was found, and "over 3 million pounds of 'oily material were cleaned up on [the coastline of] Louisiana in 2013, this being a 20-fold increase in the oil collected in 2012."[98]

In spite of being responsible for such death, illness, and destruction, BP has continued to behave badly, as shown by stories from 2013 and 2014.

- Louisiana, following a state law requiring the removal of navigation obstructions, ordered BP to remove thousands of metal anchors used to hold down oil spill booms, which BP left in the water when it removed the booms. But BP sued the state, saying it should not need to remove them, because they were part of the federally-directed response.

- Finding that the bill to compensate business claimants was getting higher than it had expected, BP told a court in July that a claims administrator had misinterpreted the terms of the settlement reached in 2012 – even though BP had negotiated and signed the settlement.

- In seeking to bring costs down, BP also claimed that it was being required to pay hundreds of millions of dollars to businesses that had exaggerated or invented losses. BP even placed full-page ads in newspapers accusing coastal businesses of widespread fraud. Even Republican governor Bobby Jindal said that BP officials "are spending more money on television commercials than they have on actually restoring the natural resources they impacted." In 2014, a U.S. appeals court said that BP must pay the claims.[99]

- In a further attempt to bring down its costs, BP argued that 10 percent of the spilled oil dissolved, so that it should not be included in the fine. BP also claimed that only 2.45 million barrels entered the water (rather than the 4.9 million calculated by the government) – which is important, because the Clean Water Act says that the polluter must pay $1,100 per barrel – or $4,300 per barrel if, as plaintiffs allege, the polluter was criminally negligent.

- BP also sued the EPA to reopen its gas and oil leases, saying that temporarily banning BP from federal contracts showed a "lack of business integrity." This suit was filed, pointed out ProPublica, by the same company that had previously been criminally convicted in several cases.

- In spite of all the harm it caused, it had "a still larger fleet of drilling rigs" in the Gulf by 2013.

- Two weeks after the U.S. government had lifted its ban on seeking new oil leases in the Gulf, a BP refinery in Indiana leaked over 1,500 gallons of oil into Lake Michigan.

- In 2014, many of the wildlife species were still struggling, with large numbers of dolphins and turtles continuing to die and oyster reproduction still low – and yet BP was telling the public that the Gulf had been healed.[100]

The only bright spot in this litany of BP stories is that, in September 2014, a district court judge found BP guilty of "reckless" and "grossly negligent" conduct which was "primarily driven by a desire to save time and money." Whereas BP argued that Halliburton and Transocean were chiefly responsible and hence should pay most of the penalties, the judge rejected this contention, assigning 67 percent of the blame to BP – a ruling that could result in civil penalties of as much as $18 billion.[101]

Tar Sands Oil

The other best-known type of tough oil is from Alberta's tar sands (sometimes misleadingly called "oil sands"), "a colossal deposit of sand and clay mixed with petroleum-rich bitumen." It is tough, because it must be "mined like a mineral ore, or heated underground in order to make it fluid. Either approach is expensive." Tar sands oil is destructive to people and the planet for several reasons:

- It "burns up tremendous amounts of energy, and involves multiple environmental risks."

- The open-pit mining "requires cutting down vast forests of virgin pine and spruce and scraping aside the topsoil," turning parts of Alberta "into a blackened moonscape, with enormous man-made craters sitting alongside vast piles of discarded rock and pools of poisonous wastewater."

- When the bitumen deposits are deeper, steam is injected, turning the buried tar sands into liquid, which can be pumped to the surface. This process requires enormous quantities of water, which after being polluted by chemical solvents must be stored indefinitely in tailings ponds, which can leak. One local resident said: "The land is dead: There are no moose, no rabbits, no squirrels anymore."

- In addition, "Oil Sands Mining Uses Up Almost as Much Energy as It Produces," says the title of an article, which reports that, whereas 1 unit of conventional crude oil produces 25 units of energy, the ratio for tar sands retrieved from surface mining is 1 to 5, and that retrieved from steam injection results in a 1:3 ratio.[102]

- With regard to global warming, greenhouse gas emissions from tar sands oil are as much as 20% higher than conventional oil, with a Stanford University professor finding them to be 23% higher. Moreover, in 2013 it was discovered that, for some reason, the emissions per barrel have in recent years grown by an astounding 21%.

- The Alberta tar sands, according to researchers, "contain 360 to 510 billion tons of carbon – more than double that of all oil burned in human history."[103]

Major Oil Company Involvement: In any case, given the multiple threats posed by tar sands oil, it is no surprise to learn that three of the biggest exploiters are BP, Chevron, and Exxon.[104] It is also no surprise to learn that the Koch brothers are heavily invested in it. They had long denied this, telling a U.S. Congressional committee that the proposed Keystone XL oil sands pipeline, intended to transport this oil from Canada to the Gulf Coast (see below), had "nothing to do with any of our businesses." But it was discovered in 2011 that this was not true, because a Koch Industries subsidiary had declared its "substantial interest" in the pipeline. The following year, David Sassoon of InsideClimate News wrote an exposé, saying:

> Koch Industries has touched virtually every aspect of the tar sands industry since the company established a toehold in Canada more than 50 years ago. It has been involved in mining bitumen . . . ; in pipeline systems to collect and transport Canadian crude; in exporting the heavy oils to the U.S.; in refining the sulfurous, low-grade feedstock; and in the subsequent distribution and sale of a variety of finished products . . . . The company has also created or collaborated with other companies that have become leading players in the development of Alberta's oil resources.[105]

This was confirmed in 2014, when a *Washington Post* story reported that the largest non-Canadian lease holder in Canada's oil sands was a subsidiary of Koch Industries.[106]

Dilbit Disaster: For bitumen to be sent through pipes, it must be diluted with liquid chemicals. This diluted bitumen is generally called "dilbit." Pipelines carrying dilbit are extremely controversial because, in addition to bitumen's problems listed above, dilbit "doesn't behave like conventional crude oil when it spills into water."

In Michigan in 2010, a ruptured pipeline built by Enbridge energy company (of Alberta) spewed over a million gallons of dilbit into the Kalamazoo River. The bitumen sank to the bottom, "leaving a mess unlike anything regulators and emergency responders had seen before." The cleanup, which was still not completed by 2014, has already cost $800 million, "making it the most expensive oil pipeline spill in U.S. history."[107]

In 2013, an Exxon pipeline ruptured in Mayflower, Arkansas, releasing over 200,000 gallons into this little town, which ruined many lives, giving people nausea, nosebleeds, hemorrhoids, rashes, unbearable headaches, cancer, and debilitating weakness. Also, although Exxon claimed that none of the bitumen got into nearby Lake Conway, it did, causing a stench and ruining fishing in places.[108]

Keystone XL Pipeline: Because of all of these factors, the most controversial environmental issue in recent years was the Keystone XL Pipeline, proposed by the Canadian pipeline company TransCanada, through which dilbit would flow from Alberta to refineries in Louisiana and Texas. After President Obama was lobbied by TransCanada, the oil industry, and Republicans, he said that the pipeline should be approved "only if this project does not significantly exacerbate the problem of carbon pollution."[109]

The State Department (while it was still under Hillary Clinton) declared that the pipeline would have little environmental effect, because if the pipeline were not built, the dilbit would reach the refineries by rail.[110] But this evaluation was disputed by many, including major environmental organizations, the Sierra Club, 29 major climate scientists (who declared the report to be "without merit in many critical areas"), and Reuters.[111]

Also, the State Department report was in tension with a Congressional Research Service report, which noted that tar sands oil emits up to 20% more greenhouse gases than conventional oil and that the pipeline could raise U.S. greenhouse gas emissions by as much as 21 million metric tons a year.[112]

In addition, evidence suggests that the pipeline was "built to spill." Although TransCanada advertised its pipelines as the safest, the record suggests that they are the *least* safe. In TransCanada's Keystone 1 pipeline's first year, it suffered 12 spills, the largest number in U.S. history, which is especially important in light of the plan to have the pipeline cross over the Ogallala Aquifer, which, underlying eight states, provides 30 percent of the country's groundwater.[113]

In 2011, McKibben's 350.org organized a number of protests in front of the White House, after which Obama delayed his decision about the pipeline, saying that the deadline imposed by Congress did not leave time for an adequate review. Then in 2013, when Obama's decision was expected, 350.org held the then-largest climate rally ever, with tens of thousands of people, to urge him to reject the pipeline. Writing in advance about this rally, Michael Klare said that Obama's decision could determine the "future well-being of the planet."[114]

But the Canadian government, concerned about its own short-term economic well-being, engaged in high-level lobbying. Besides launching a multi-million-dollar ad campaign, it sent its natural resources minister to Europe, while Prime Minister Stephen Harper came to New York, arguing that "all the facts are overwhelmingly on the side of approval." Elizabeth Kolbert said that, if Obama approves the pipeline, it will be "another step on the march to disaster.[115]

In 2014, oil started flowing through the Keystone XL pipeline's Southern Leg, which runs from Oklahoma to the Gulf Coast. Because this leg did not cross an international boundary, it did not require State Department permission. But such permission will be needed for the proposed northern leg.[116]

Oil Shale

Extracting oil from tar sands is somewhat similar to extracting it from oil shale (not to be confused with shale oil, which requires fracking). But getting the oil from oil shale is even more difficult, because the oil-containing substance, rather than being mixed with sand, is locked into sedimentary rocks. Accordingly, whereas extraction from oil shale and tar sands share many of the same destructive effects, oil shale extraction can in some respects be worse.[117]

One of the shared destructive effects is that both processes require an enormous amount of water. While the amount of water used for tar sands has been well known, the same was not true with regard to oil shale. Various agencies and organizations, including the U.S. Bureau of Land Management, Government Accountability Office, and the RAND Corporation, had long stated that this process must be very water intensive. The oil companies, including Chevron, long denied this. But in 2014, Western Resource Advocates challenged Chevron in court with regard to its oil shale in Colorado, and Chevron had to admit that the critics were right. To produce its desired amount of oil, Chevron said, would require the use of 120,000 acre-feet (almost 40 billion gallons) of water per year – an enormous amount of water to draw from the already-stressed Colorado River.

Commenting on the victory, a policy advisor to Western Resource Advocates said: "Now the debate for decision makers is whether allowing oil shale development to use enormous quantities of water in a strained Colorado River Basin is acceptable." Besides providing more evidence that the various types of tough oil and gas should be outlawed, this court case also showed that Chevron had lied for many years about its destructive activities in order to protect its profits.[118] In a review entitled "Oil Madness," Osha Gray Davidson, the author of *Clean Break*, wrote: "In our obsession to wring every last drop of oil from the earth – whatever the costs – we've polluted the air, fouled the ocean, sacrificed workers' lives, and altered the climate."[119] Why would we as a society continue this madness, given the fact that oil, which is used almost entirely for transportation, is no longer economical: "Wind-generated electricity to operate cars," said Lester Brown in 2012, "could cost the equivalent of 80-cent-per gallon gasoline."[120]

Fracking Shale Oil

Although fracking was discussed above in terms of natural gas, the use of it on shale formations liberates oil as well as natural gas. Because essentially the same process is used for both fuels, there is no need for a separate discussion of fracking for oil. The point to be made here is that fracking completely turned the oil industry around.

U.S. oil production had declined "from a peak of 9.6 million barrels per day in 1970 to a low of 5 million barrels in 2008," reported Michael Klare. But with the introduction of fracking, "U.S. crude output jumped from 5.7 million barrels per day in 2011 to 7.5 million in 2013," with 2014 projected to rise to 8.5 million barrels per day. In fact, wrote Klare, "America's demand for oil grew more than China's in 2013, the first time that's happened since 1999."[121]

In 2012, a paper delivered at the meeting of the America Geophysical Union asked, "Is Earth F**ked?"[122] If it is, no small part of this fate will be due to the fact that the Earth is fracked.

But there are other reasons for the disastrous growth of U.S. oil production, one of which is a policy switch by the Obama administration. This change helped the figures for the oil growth in 2014 to be greater than that of 2013, and more new White House policies will help it grow even more in 2015:

- The Bureau of Ocean Energy Management has decided to reopen the waters off the Eastern seaboard from Florida to Delaware to new oil and natural gas exploration.

- The Bureau of Land Management has increased the sales of leases for oil and gas drilling on federal lands.

- An additional 59 million acres for oil and gas drilling in the Gulf of Mexico, where the disastrous BP oil spill occurred – has been approved.

"In other words," Klare said, "global warming be damned!"[123]

Conclusion

The fossil-fuel industry has products that, if it is allowed to continue producing them, will destroy civilization. Although this in itself would be a sufficient reason to shut it down without regrets, the leading fossil-fuel companies have also been very bad citizens. As Bill McKibben has said, "The fossil fuel industry has behaved so recklessly that they should lose their social license."[124] Not only should we have no regrets about abolishing fossil-fuel energy, we are morally required to do so.

19

MOBILIZATION

"In the face of an absolutely unprecedented emergency, society has no choice but to take dramatic action to avert a collapse of civilization."
– Blue Planet Laureates, 2012

"We are facing issues of near-overwhelming complexity and unprecedented urgency."
– Lester Brown, *Plan B 4.0*, 2009

Lester Brown's *Plan B* is subtitled *Mobilizing to Save Civilization*.[1] To save civilization, he explained, would mean moving its energy basis from fossil fuels to clean energy. In another book, Brown said that this effort "will take a massive mobilization – at wartime speed."[2] What would this mean?

Americans are most naturally led by this language to think of the mobilization for World War II. Joe Romm, speaking of the need for industry to switch to clean energy, wrote: "This national (and global) re-industrialization effort would be on the scale of what we did during World War II, except it would last far longer." How much longer? Although many writers suggest that this transition would take 50 or even 100 years, Romm said:

> If humanity gets truly serious about emissions reduction – and by serious I mean "World War II serious" in both scale and urgency – we could go to near-zero global emissions in, say, 2 decades and then quickly go carbon negative.[3]

"[W]e need to mobilize like the WW II mobilization," added Ross Gelbspan, "but worldwide and even more thorough." The mobilization must be unprecedented, Brown agrees, "because the entire world has never before been so threatened."[4]

It could be said that carrying out a worldwide transformation in a few decades is unreasonable; such a major transformation should be carried out incrementally, in a less hurried way. That was once correct. But now, the transformation must be very rapid because the international community, led by the United States, failed to start on it earlier.

Evidence that CO_2 emissions will cause global warming began appearing in the 1980s; by 1988, scientists were sufficiently certain to form the IPCC; and in 1990, the IPCC said that to avoid an intolerable increase in the planet's temperature, CO_2 levels needed to be stabilized at 1990 levels. This statement should have put politicians into action, because they, like military leaders, usually operate on the "precautionary principle," according to which, in matters in which carelessness could lead to disaster, we should choose to err on the side of caution. After the nations of the world failed to begin reducing CO_2 emissions in 1995, they clearly should have done so in 1998, when the IPCC stated that it had detected a human "fingerprint." However, rather than following the precautionary principle, the political world did the opposite: Instead of working to stabilize the planet's CO_2 level, it began increasing it more rapidly.

Because of this fundamentally irrational and potentially suicidal behavior, the world now needs to reduce its emissions with extreme rapidity. In the words of IPCC chief Rajendra Pachauri, "We have five minutes before midnight." This is why the United States, China, and the rest of the world must now act with unreasonable haste, working together as if – to use Peter Goldmark's analogy – "some huge rocky projectile, big enough to destroy most forms of life, was hurtling towards the earth, and it seemed that deep international co-operation offered the only hope of deflecting the lethal object."[5]

Although it will not produce its effects as suddenly as a giant asteroid, unabated global warming will be equally deadly. Worldwide mobilization is necessary, and if such mobilization is to succeed, the United States, China, and other countries will need to provide leadership. However, the discussion of leadership in this chapter is carried out almost entirely in terms of the United States.

For America to mobilize with sufficient speed and thoroughness, leadership will be needed by people and institutions of various levels. The two levels that are most crucial are the presidency and the media, so they will be treated first. The other levels will be discussed in alphabetical order.

Presidential Leadership

There is no other single individual who is more important to the success of the needed mobilization than the president of the United States. Indeed, if the American president fails in this regard, global warming will continue to rise and we will be headed toward the destruction of civilization. So we must hope that our president acts with the needed wisdom, courage, and energy. There are many things that our current president could and should do. But we must bear in mind the crucial reality that the president can lead only if he or she is strongly supported (and even led) by the American people and our other institutions. With such support, there are many things that the president could do

Declaring a National Emergency

In an article saying that a climate emergency exists, John J. Berger wrote: "An emergency has two basic components: it presents a grave threat to life, liberty, property, or the environment, and the situation requires immediate action." When the situation warrants it, an American president has the power to declare a national emergency, as President Franklin D. Roosevelt did in 1941.[6]

"We have a planetary emergency," said James Hansen, pointing out that it could destroy civilization. Because the destruction of civilization would involve the destruction of the United States, the planetary emergency is obviously a national emergency. It would seem self-evident, therefore, that the American president should declare the climate emergency to be a national emergency and then act accordingly. In the words of Ban Ki-moon, "This is an emergency and for emergency situations we need emergency action."[7]

American presidents only have authority to declare emergencies for the United States. And yet the mobilization of this county will not be able to prevent the destruction of civilization apart from the mobilization of other countries. Accordingly, in 2011, Bill McKibben and a large number of other environmental leaders, including Paul Hawken and Lester Brown, wrote a letter to the presidents of the United States and China – the two countries that "dominate world carbon emissions" – saying:

> It is time to publicly acknowledge that the continued burning of fossil fuels threatens the survival of civilization. . . . It is with a deepening sense of dread over the fate of future generations that we call on you to acknowledge the severity of the global climate emergency.[8]

A growing number of individuals and organizations have called for the public recognition of this fact. For example:

- Bob Doppelt, executive director of the Resource Innovation Group, wrote an article headed, "President Obama Should Issue Emergency Declaration Now to Address Climate Crises."

- "Today we face a real and rising risk of catastrophic runaway global heating and this constitutes a global climate emergency," say Canadians for Emergency Action on Climate Change. "At this point in the crisis nothing less than an all out global emergency response can save humanity."

- The Campaign against Climate Change says: "The Climate Emergency should be the overriding priority of every politician and to which all available human and material resources should be immediately directed."[9]

When U.S. presidents formally declare a national emergency, they have extensive authority to respond to the emergency. Because the climate emergency has been caused by excessive emissions of CO_2 and other greenhouse gases, emergency action would be to go full out – at World War II speed – to eliminate such emissions. As one article about this emergency says:

> If we do not act now we could push the climate beyond tipping points, where the situation spirals out of our control. . . . Instead of stepping on or easing off the accelerator, we need to be slamming on the brakes.[10]

A Clear and Present Danger

The President should explain to the Congress and the American people that the declaration of a national emergency is necessary because climate disruption caused by global warming constitutes *a clear and present* danger not just to America but to the world.

A Clear Danger: If the temperature of the planet continues to rise, our children, grandchildren, and great-grandchildren will inherit from us an increasingly difficult, even hellish, world. The president should point out some or all of the following:

- The weather will become more extreme: Summers will become increasingly hot, with more intense heat waves and temperatures in places exceeding livable limits and making farming impossible; drought in the American Southwest will become what Australians call the "permanent dry"; and wildfires will become more intense and occur more often.

- Storms will become worse. Extreme rainfall, followed by

extreme flooding, will occur more often and in more places. The "Snowpocalypse" of 2009 and the "Snowmageddon" of 2010 will become commonplace – at least until it becomes too warm for snow to form. And deadly hurricanes and tornadoes will become even deadlier.

- The sea-level rise will inundate land along America's coasts and do the same in China and many other countries, ruining much of their best agricultural land.

- Because of drought and the loss of snowpack, much of the American Southwest and Midwest will have increasingly less water for drinking and farming, and because of the melting of glaciers in various parts of the world, billions of people will lose their primary sources of water.

- Food shortages will become increasingly severe because of climate disruption and ocean acidification, which will eventually lead to the death of sea life.

- The rising sea level and other types of climate change will create hundreds of thousands and then millions of climate refugees, all demanding to be allowed into luckier countries.

- As our militaries have started warning us, climate change has already contributed to warfare and will increasingly bring about climate wars, especially because of shortages of food and water.

- Most frighteningly, climate change will increasingly bring about the collapse of ecosystems, ultimately the *global* ecosystem, and thereby the destruction of civilization and perhaps even the extinction of human beings altogether. The main threat to global collapse is the melting of the Arctic's permafrost, which will release great amounts of methane, a greenhouse gas much stronger than CO_2.

Climate scientists agree that if global warming continues, it will bring about the destruction of civilization. They only disagree about how quickly this will occur. Although most scientists believe that we still have time to save civilization, they say that we will need to act very quickly and decisively. Besides being a clear danger, the threat to civilization is also a present danger.

A Present Danger: Since the rise of the industrial revolution, with its increasing use of fossil fuels, the president should also point out, the planet's average temperature has risen approximately 1.4 degrees Fahrenheit (which is 0.8 degrees Celsius). Some have said that the climate will not become unacceptably bad if the global temperature stays below a rise of 3.6°F (2°C). However, seas are already rising and glaciers – including the giant ice sheets of Greenland and Antarctica – are melting. There is already too much CO_2 in the atmosphere.

Throughout civilization, CO_2 constituted about 275 parts per million (ppm) of the atmosphere. But with the industrial revolution, it started rising, and by 1988 – the year that scientists said that they had clearly detected the human influence on global warming – the CO_2 had risen to about 350 ppm. In recent years, during which our weather has clearly become more extreme, CO_2 was approaching, and then exceeding, 400 ppm.

But if we act quickly, we could quit adding more CO_2 and then bring the concentration back down to 350. This number is far more important than the numbers indicating where the stock market is. So we need to make this number – the current percent of CO_2 in the atmosphere – publicly visible, so that people can see where we are every day.

Another number we need to keep track of involves what scientists call the "carbon budget." If we are to prevent a threat to civilization, they have determined, we must keep the total CO_2 emissions since the industrial age to about 750 billion tons (750 gigatons). Although this may suggest that we have a very big budget to spend, about 500 gigatons of CO_2 have already been put into the atmosphere. Accordingly, we can afford to emit only 250 gigatons more, and if business as usual continues, this budget will be used up within 20 years.

Presidential Announcement of New Policies

After explaining the need for the emergency proclamation, the President should announce the new policies most needed to deal with the emergency:

- All fossil-fuel subsidies will be turned into subsidies for the various types of clean energy.

- In line with what virtually all economists have recommended, a price will be put on carbon, with the price beginning low (perhaps $10 per ton of CO_2) and then increasing by that amount every year. (Some method, such as a rebate or a dividend, will be used to prevent the carbon fee from raising overall costs to poor and middle-class citizens.)" [11]

- These first two policies will largely take care of a third: To remain within the carbon budget, the energy policy of "all of the above," designed to reduce dependence on foreign energy, is to be replaced with "best of the above," designed to reduce and finally eliminate fossil fuels.

- The electric grid will be radically upgraded to facilitate the distribution of the various types of clean energy.

- The government will help accelerate the installation of various types of clean energy, so that soon the electric grid will be based entirely on clean energy.

- At the same time that the grid is becoming green, electric vehicles – motorcycles, autos, SUVs, vans, trucks – will be improved, so that people can travel everywhere as easily as they had with gasoline and diesel.

- High-speed rail, of the types pioneered in Europe, Japan, and China, will be quickly developed, for both passengers and freight. Besides cutting down congestion, high-speed rail will eliminate the need to use airplanes for trips of only a few hundred miles.

- The government will help speed up the development of airplanes using fossil-free fuel.

During World War II, much of the country was mobilized. The Manhattan Project alone employed 130,000 scientists. In addition:

> [T]he president set staggering goals for the nation's factories: 60,000 aircraft in 1942 and 125,000 in 1943; 120,000 tanks in the same time period and 55,000 antiaircraft guns. In an attempt to coordinate government war agencies Roosevelt created the War Production Board in 1942 and later in 1943 the Office of War Mobilization.... War production profoundly changed American industry. Companies already engaged in defense work expanded. Others, like the automobile industry, were transformed completely. . . . Chrysler made fuselages. General Motors made airplane engines, guns, trucks and tanks. Packard made Rolls-Royce engines for the British air force.... The Ford Motor plant [built long-range bombers].[12]

Carrying out the new policies needed for the present emergency will require an even greater mobilization, because it requires a complete change in the energy system. Fortunately, it has progressed far enough that we know it is possible. A big part of the American president's job is to motivate Americans, and leaders of other countries, to take on this most-difficult-of-all-times task.

Implementation

In order to lead in this task, the presidency brings with it a number of tools that could be used.

Executive Agreements: It has become customary for presidents to work out binding agreements with leaders of other countries, without the need for Congressional consent; indeed, such agreements are now more common than treaties. The president could, for example, work out an agreement with China about the speed at which both countries make the transition to 100 percent clean energy. This could be crucial: As former U.S. Senator Tim Worth said, "[Secretary] Kerry understands that the best way to unlock the stalemate in Washington is through Beijing," because "that kills the whole argument that cutting carbon in the US would give China an economic advantage."

A first step in this direction was taken during the G-20 meeting in July 2013, when President Obama and Chinese President Xi Jinping agreed to use the Montreal Protocol to work to reduce their HFCs. As one observer remarked, "This high-level agreement during the G-20 in St. Petersburg shows how effective climate policy can be when it's done at the leader level."[13] The agreement, moreover, could be broadened, with perhaps Japan, India, and the European Union included. Indeed, such executive agreements might prove to be a swifter and more effective substitute for the U.N. attempt to achieve agreement on a global treaty.

In fact, after this chapter was first written news came that President Obama was working out some such agreement. The idea was that, although it could not be *legally binding* for the USA (because there was virtually no chance that the Senate would ratify such a treaty), negotiators could work out an agreement that would be "politically binding." At the UN meeting in September 2014, moreover, Obama challenged China to join the United States in an agreement, saying that their two countries, as the biggest polluters on the planet, had a "special responsibility to lead."[14]

Powers as Commander-in-Chief of the Armed Forces: By virtue of being the commander of America's armed forces, the president has enormous powers with regard to energy, partly because the military is the major user of it. The president's powers could be exercised here in many ways, in the context of recognition that the major security threat to the country is climate change, rather than other countries or terrorists (as many military leaders have said). As a result:

- A much larger part of the Defense Department budget could be allocated to this threat.

- Part of the DoD budget could be used to increase energy efficiency within the military and to provide technologies that can then be used in the economy.

- DARPA (the Defense Advance Research Projects Agency) could be tasked with speeding up the development of the various types of clean energy.

- The military could share its efficiency and clean energy expertise with other countries, thereby making friends (rather than enemies) and demonstrating that it regards the primary enemy today as global warming.

Special Sessions with Congress: In special sessions, whether open or closed, the president can explain to Congress the need for the new policies and respond to objections. These sessions, along with meetings with small groups of members of both Houses, should be held before votes on any of the policies. In all of these discussions, the president needs to remind members that preventing civilization from being destroyed by climate change is not simply one more optional policy, for which they might let their votes be determined by money provided by fossil-fuel lobbyists.

Bully Pulpit: By means of the bully pulpit that comes with the office, the president can inform, educate, and persuade both Congress and the American people of the need for full-out mobilization to save civilization. It is likely, of course, that many members of Congress will regard their own welfare, such as reelection, as more important than saving civilization for future generations. So the president needs to solicit the enthusiastic support of the American people in order to persuade Congress to cooperate. The president can also explain to people the possibility and importance of energy efficiency, which is a way in which all citizens can participate – in the context of broader policies addressing the pollution and energy efficiency of larger corporate and government actors.

Fireside Chats: One way to employ the bully pulpit would be frank talks by the president similar to FDR's "fireside chats," in which he explained his policies, quelled false rumors, and motivated and encouraged people. Since the time of Ronald Reagan, presidents have had weekly radio addresses. But today, most people get their news from television, and it is always used for important events, so the president should arrange with one of the cable networks for weekly televised discussions with the public – perhaps sometimes talking with a guest.

Climate Corps: By using the bully pulpit, the president could create a "climate corps," consisting of millions of citizen volunteers ready to help. The Climate Corps could involve a large number of activities:

- It could work to get the president's agenda through Congress.

- Insofar as members Congress continue to resist the president's policies, even after hearing the reasons, the Corps could target them for the next election, explaining to the voters why it is important to replace these members.

- The Corps could arrange for teach-ins in communities around the country, led by educators, doctors, scientists, economists, engineers, and others.

- It could also, modeled on the Peace Corp, send capable people to other countries where people need help with various things, such as energy efficiency and small-scale solar energy.

Convening Power: The president can bring various parties together, through which understandings and agreements may be reached, such as::

- Governors and the mayors of major cities in various regions of the country to discuss how they can work together.

- The owners and program directors of the major television networks, so the president can explain how their role is vital to the attempt to respond adequately to the climate emergency.

Executive Powers: The president could ask Congress for executive powers to expedite the U.S. response to the emergency, similar to FDR's War Production Board and his Controlled Material Plan. If the Congress refuses, the president could use the Clean Air Act, which has already been supported by the courts for dealing with greenhouse gases, to reduce them much more fully than before.

Conclusion: By means of such policies and tools, America could be put in position to do what President Obama said he wanted to do – "to take bold action to reduce carbon pollution" and "lead the world in a coordinated assault on climate change."[15]

Media Leadership

Recognizing the extent to which the media have been guilty of aiding and abetting companies that use deceitful propaganda in order to promote their own short-term benefits, even at the risk of destroying civilization, the media could determine that it will no longer:

- Suggest that climate scientists are divided on the reality and cause of climate change.

- Frame reports by climate scientists within "two-sides" segments in which the views of denialists are given credence.

- Publish editorials expressing skepticism about climate science.

- Ignore or tone down reports for the sake of not alienating advertisers.

- Accept false climate advertisements from fossil-fuel corporations.

- Exclude climate change from television's Sunday morning talk shows, but instead make it central.

- Ignore the connection to climate change while reporting extreme weather events.

Positively, the media could commit to doing everything it can to inform people of the reality of the climate emergency.

- The media could treat the climate threat to the continuation of civilization as the overwhelmingly most important story of our time – just as U.S. newspapers and films did all they could to mobilize America to address the threat of the Axis Powers.

- The media could report on the various attempts to prevent a climate-caused catastrophe as seriously as it would treat attempts to prevent a meteor-caused devastation of the planet's life.

- If some newspapers or networks persist in supporting climate denial, responsible newspapers and networks could criticize them, explaining why their behavior is irresponsible – similar to supporting fascist propaganda during WW II.

Beyond correcting the defects in their previous treatments of the climate threat, the media could develop programs to educate people about climate change and inspire them to do what they can. For example, there could be:

- High-quality series (such as Showtime's "Years of Living Dangerously") provided for the entire viewing public.

- A talk show in which an informed host (such as Chris Hayes) talks with the world's leading climate scientists, along with politicians, economists, and others dealing with climate change, explaining, among other things, how the President's policies will get us started towards a solution.

- A series, perhaps entitled "Climate Denial Exposé," which explains how climate denialism has been orchestrated by the Koch brothers and the fossil-fuel companies; how they fund front groups, so the denials appear to come from ordinary citizens; and how much money they have funneled to members of Congress who support denialism.

- An ongoing entertainment show featuring some comedian, such as Jon Stewart, Stephen Colbert, or John Oliver, in which climate denial is lampooned.

- Just as newspapers and TV news programs keep people informed about the stock market, they will keep people apprised of the atmosphere's CO_2 concentration and the number of gigatons left in the planet's carbon budget.

Leadership in Other Sectors

If America is to deal with its share of responsibility for the climate crisis – which will be the precondition for it to provide an example for other big countries, such as China, India, and Brazil - America must be mobilized throughout. The media could do much to help the president lead this mobilization. But if the mobilization is to succeed, leaders of every profession and skill must also provide climate leadership. Here are some examples of the kinds of leadership needed.

Academic Leadership

Along with scientists, college, university, and graduate-school professors provide much of the intellectual leadership for dealing with climate change. Most of them do this by means of writing books and articles, many of which have been mentioned in previous chapters; by teaching their regular courses or creating new ones; and by creating new centers – such as Vanderbilt's Climate Change Research Network – to give more attention to climate change.

Some professors, moreover, have moved beyond these normal roles to provide more direct leadership.

- David Orr, professor of environmental studies and politics at Oberlin, has led both the university and the town to become the greenest town-and-gown community in the country.[16]

- Some professors lead by speaking out publically, such as philosophy professor Lawrence Torcello of the Rochester Institute of Technology, who wrote a blog post arguing that those behind well-funded efforts to deny global warming should be held criminally responsible.[17]

- Other professors encourage their institutions to divest from fossil-fuel stocks, such as Daniel Kammen, an energy studies professor at the University of California, who was mentioned in Chapter 14.

- Still others create educational non-profits, such as the Alliance for Climate Education, which intends to reach 20 million high-school students by 2020 with its program inspiring students to take action on climate change.[18]

Activist Leadership

To get the country seriously mobilized, much of the leadership will have to come from activists – including people who engage in civil protest and disobedience to try to change the present state of affairs.

- The best-known climate activist, at least in America, is author and environmentalist Bill McKibben, who started 350.org, the first global grassroots movement focused on climate change, as well as campaigns for divestment and against the Keystone XL pipeline. Many activists have been inspired by him.

- Probably the other best-known activist is scientist James Hansen, who has been arrested several times for civil disobedience in front of the White House. Giving special attention to motivating young people, he hopes that they will fight for carbon fee-with-dividend legislation.

- Some activists launch organizations, such as the Sierra Club and Greenpeace. In 2013, the Sierra Club became more active than it traditionally had been, engaging for the first time in civil disobedience (about the KXL pipeline). "For civil disobedience to be justified," said Executive Director Michael Brune, "something must be so wrong that it compels the strongest defensible protest."

- By contrast, Greenpeace members have been arrested for civil disobedience many times. Saying that "civil disobedience and direct action are at the heart of what we do," Greenpeace argues that when people have justice on their side but little power, civil disobedience is the only way to bring about change.

Most activism does not, of course, involve civil disobedience. However, an increasing number of concerned citizens and organizations will probably follow the logic of Greenpeace and the Sierra Club's Brune, who said, "time is running out, and there is so much more to do." Getting America reoriented to clean energy will likely require millions of activists; it is impossible to anticipate, let alone enumerate, the unique and creative measures they will bring to bear to save the planet.

Agricultural and Forestry Leadership

To do America's share of saving civilization, there is nothing more important – aside from eliminating fossil-fuel energy – than improved agricultural and forestry practices. According to the calculations of James Hansen and colleagues, reforestation worldwide could extract about 100 gigatons of carbon from the atmosphere. The United States needs to play a big role stopping its own deforestation and helping other countries, especially those in Amazonia, reforest. Also, improved practices could convert agriculture from a source of carbon into a carbon sink – whereas present-day agriculture is responsible for about one-third of the country's greenhouse gas emissions – especially serious are methane and nitrous oxide, which are, respectively, roughly 50 and 300 times more potent than CO_2.[19]

However, although there has been an amazing growth of climate-friendly agriculture in recent decades, there has been little change in American agriculture, which is monocultural, energy-intensive, and heavily dependent on chemical fertilizers and pesticides. Although the IPCC has discussed the issue, it has continued officially to ignore it, partly because of the resistance to any change by American agribusiness, and partly, evidently, because of the fears of China, India, and other developing companies that the rich nations would restrict their farming by imposing restrictions on carbon emissions.[20]

In spite of the failure to change agricultural practices in the big countries, there have been many examples of how agriculture could be made better for the climate (as well as for taste, health, and soil sustainability). For example:

- Wes Jackson's *Land Institute* has been writing about and demonstrating the need for and workability of an agricultural polyculture of perennial crops.

- Fetzer Vineyards has become a leader in economically and ecologically sustainable organic wine-making. Besides employing efficient and clean energy, the winery builds the soil, sequesters carbon, and conserves biodiversity. Its Bonterra vineyard is the largest seller of organic wines in the country.

- For instances of how to replace conventional agricultural practices, we can look to Costa Rica, which intends to become "the world's first carbon-neutral nation by 2021 – transportation, energy, everything – including agriculture, which represents a whopping 37 percent of Costa Rica's emissions."[21]

At the 2014 World Economic Forum at Davos, the report by the U.N. Environmental Program concluded by stating that "agriculture in the 21st century must and can reinvent itself."[22] These examples are just three of many models that U.S. agribusiness could use to reinvent itself.

Business Leadership

At one time, it was commonly thought that care for the environment and business profits were in conflict. But, except for fossil-fuel companies, this is no longer the case. In 2013, the Business Council for Sustainable Energy, having stated that "the window to prevent catastrophic climate change is rapidly closing," told President Obama that investing in clean energy will not only stimulate the tech industry and address climate change but might also pull the American economy out of the hole.[23] Moreover, a growing number of businesses are enthusiastically working towards being 100 percent green. For example:

- Apple Inc., reporting that it has almost reached its goal of powering all of its operations by 100 percent clean energy, is working towards that goal by building for its new headquarters the largest solar array in America dedicated to a single corporate campus. Apple's CEO, aware that remaining silent about global warming could cost the company sales, has told skeptics that if they do not like Apple's backing for clean energy, they should sell their shares. Apple's commitment was symbolized by its hiring former EPA administrator Lisa Jackson as its vice president for environmental initiative.

- Although by 2014, Google's data centers around the world were only 33 percent powered by clean energy, it is aiming to change this to 100 percent, as illustrated by its investment in 2013 of $155 million in solar facilities and its 10-year contract with a Swedish windfarm.

- IKEA, which by 2013 was producing 37 of its own energy by means of solar and wind power, has committed to increase this to 100 percent by 2020.[24]

Congressional Leadership

If the Congress were working in the way it should be and previously did, Congress could lead America on climate issues as strongly as, or even more strongly than, the president. Indeed, there are many members of the Senate who have supported controls on carbon much more fully than President Obama. For example, Senate Majority Leader Harry Reid in 2014 said, "Climate change is the worst problem facing the world today." Barbara Boxer and Bernie Sanders wrote a climate bill that included a carbon tax. Boxer and Sheldon Whitehouse created a Climate Action Task Force. And the new senator from Hawaii organized 30 Senators to stay up all night making speeches to draw attention to the need for climate action.[25]

However, the House of Representatives is as opposed to seriously dealing with climate change as most Democrats are for it – hence the deadlock that forced the President to work around Congress to get anything accomplished. But the fact that the Senate is unable to get any climate bills passed does not mean that members of Congress should give up, thereby letting all of their informed passion for the issue go to waste. Their effective speakers should appeal to the public, explaining why the country needs to mobilize as fully as present conditions allow.

Leadership by Economists

One of the main arguments against cutting carbon emissions radically has been economic – that it would undermine both the global economy and individual businesses. However, recent economic studies, as discussed in Chapter 16, have shown the opposite to be the case – that it is *not* treating climate change, rather than treating it, that is too expensive, because spending money now for mitigation is far less expensive than paying later for extreme weather events and abatement.

But most people, including a lot of media writers and lawmakers, do not know this. Just as some climate scientists have started speaking out directly to the public and the press, no longer counting on dissemination of the results of their academic studies, economists such as Robert Pindyck, Martin Weitzman, Frank Ackerman, and Elizabeth Stanton need to do the same, as Nicholas Stern has done in the UK, using TV and radio interviews and op-ed pages to get the true picture out, thereby showing that Paul Krugman is far from alone. Again, the media should allow for and even encourage such opportunities.

Economists also need to flood the media with the fact that virtually all economists, even William Nordhaus, advocate a significant price on carbon as the single most important thing – along with eliminating subsidies – that could be done, as former Bush Treasury Secretary Henry Paulson stated very visibly in 2014.[26]

Entertainment Leadership

The entertainment world could play a very important role. Humor in particular can help make it possible for people to talk about climate change and thereby become ready to deal with it constructively, just as TV sit-coms featuring gay people helped many people overcome their prejudice and thereby their support for laws forbidding gay marriage. Humor most obviously has the power to undermine the effectiveness of climate denialists by ridiculing them, as Andy Borowitz, Stephen Colbert, John Oliver, Jon Stewart, and the Onion have done. One of the helpful things the media could do would be to make their spoofs, along with those of other comedians – such as Will Ferrell, Sacha Baron Cohen, and Yoram Bauman (the "the world's first and only stand-up economist") – much more widely known.[27]

Also, serious drama could be used more effectively than it has thus far to help people understand the issues and become motivated to stop global warming. Hollywood and TV studios could put the word out that they are looking for good scripts.

Financial Leadership

Wall Street, as the financial capital of the world, has generally been regarded as hostile to attempts to regulate emissions, as indicated by the discussion in

Chapter 12 of the *Wall Street Journal*, CNBC, and *Forbes*. If asked how many finance-based billionaires use their money to stop global warming, most people would have been able to name only George Soros. If this were the full truth about wealthy financiers, it would be very unfortunate for two reasons: Money from "green billionaires" is needed to counteract the enormous sums of money spent for anti-climate activities provided by the Kochs and the fossil-fuel companies, and the less developed world needs enormous sums of money to switch to efficiency and clean energy – money that the rich nations have not been willing to provide.

However, this situation has changed, due in large part to former hedge fund founder Tom Steyer, who was influenced by Bill Gates and Warren Buffett to take the pledge to give half of his money to charity, and by Bill McKibben to give much of this money to deal with climate change. Steyer decided, among other things, to provide $100 million to an organization called NextGen Climate, which will work to defeat political candidates who deny climate change or oppose reductions in carbon emissions.[28]

In addition, Steyer and fellow billionaire Michael Bloomberg, along with Henry Paulson, put out a major report entitled "Risky Business." Besides providing an assessment of the economic risk exposure that various industries have to global warming, the study was meant to persuade the financial community to reject anti-scientific claims made by Murdoch's media outlets and the Kochs, and even to change the culture of the financial sector.[29]

As is obvious, people in the financial sector, partly by giving information that contradicts long-standing myths and partly by using their wealth, can make very important contributions to the task of saving civilization. Readers might be surprised to learn that well over 100 billionaires have already made the Gates-Buffett pledge. But this represents only 5% of billionaires as yet.[30] If a significant percentage of these people follow Steyer in using their money to help deal with climate change, the financial world can make even greater contributions.

Gubernatorial Leadership

Governors have great power to determine whether their states will do their share to prevent continued climate change or will block efforts to do so. For example, Governor Mary Fallin of drought-stricken Oklahoma, who has told people that relief would come from praying more, has fought against the EPA's attempt to regulate the oil and gas industry and passed legislation to discourage solar energy.[31]

At the opposite end of the spectrum, California's Jerry Brown has led his state to be by far the greenest state in America. To name of few of his accomplishments:

- Brown raised the state's mandate for zero-emission vehicles to 15 percent by 2025.

- He worked out an eight-state pact on electric cars.

- He led the creation of a $120 billion green stimulus package, about $20 billion annually through 2020.

- His policies have created lots of green jobs – more in 2012, for example, than the other top four states combined.

- Brown created a program to make clean energy available for the 75 percent of California's households living in places where it is impossible to install solar energy.

- He continued the policy of his predecessor to reduce greenhouse emissions to 1990 levels by 2020 and 80 percent below that level by 2050.

- In 2013, he opened the first state-wide cap-and-trade program in the nation, the second largest carbon trading system in the world.

- Brown then supported the creation in Shenzhen of the first of China's seven carbon market pilot programs, after which California and Shenzhen formed a partnership.

- Brown also formed a compact with Oregon, Washington, and British Columbia, intending to promote clean-energy jobs and zero-emissions vehicles and to harmonize their energy-efficiency standards, their fee for carbon pollution, and their carbon reductions by 2050 – hoping thereby to provide a model to be adopted by other states and regions and eventually the entire country.

- In 2014, Brown signed a climate agreement with Mexico – the world's 11th largest carbon emitter – to reduce carbon emissions, with the hope of future collaboration on carbon pricing.[32]

Although California under Brown's leadership has not been perfect (such as on fracking), Matt Kasper of the Center for American Progress has called it "a shining example of state-based leadership on climate."[33]

One example of things governors could do is to encourage the K-12 schools in their states to install solar energy systems on their roofs. A recent report said that school roofs have the potential to provide the country 5.4 gigawatts of solar energy.[34]

Legal Leadership

"When it comes to saving civilization," says Mary Christina Wood of the University of Oregon law school, "law should have a role to play." She is part of a movement advocating the public trust doctrine (PTD), which holds that all vital resources essential for the continuation of civilization are to be held in perpetual trust for all citizens, present and future. This doctrine came down from Roman law and was influential in U.S. law at the end of the 19th and beginning of the 20th century. After falling into disuse for a few decades, it was revitalized in the 1970s and '80s by Joseph Sax of the University of California, Davis, and then given full treatment in *The Planetary Trust* by Georgetown University's Edith Brown Weiss.[35]

In Wood's 2014 book, *Nature's Trust*, she gives special attention to Atmospheric Trust Litigation (ATL), which is aimed at "divesting the world's political leaders of their assumed prerogative to take action only according to their political objectives." ATL consists of suits filed against governments, asking the judicial branch of government to find the executive branch and some of its agencies guilty of a breach of trust with regard to their responsibility to safeguard the atmosphere, and to force them to stop the breach-causing behavior. Stating that the "failure to safeguard it amounts to generational theft," ATL lawyers argue that politicians have gotten away with this theft because children and future generations do not vote, so they require the courts to protect their property rights.[36]

If the various objections that have blocked ATL can be overcome, law could become a means by which the moral and economic principles discussed in previous chapters could be made efficacious, and through which the trajectory toward the extinction of human civilization might be overcome.

Mayoral Leadership

Mayors can be as important as governors, because most people now live in urban areas, which produce about 80 percent of America's carbon emissions. Partly because of the slowness of national governments and the apparent futility of international discussions, cities have decided to take a central role. When Michael Bloomberg was the mayor of New York City, he declared: "Cities are on the frontline because federal, national and international organizations aren't doing anything."

Be that as it may, mayors have formed organizations to deal with global warming. There is a worldwide organization of the world's megacities that is taking action to address climate. Although named "C40 Cities," it now has 68 members. Its mission statement says:

While international negotiations continue to make incremental progress, C40 Cities are forging ahead. Collectively they have taken more than 5,000 actions to tackle climate change, and the will to do more is stronger than ever. As innovators and practitioners, our cities are at the forefront of this issue – arguably the greatest challenge of our time.

In September 2014, the C40's leadership group put out a report saying that city governments could by themselves cut GHG emissions 8 billion tons by 2050. The work to stop climate change, said Philadelphia Mayor Michael Nutter, "will be done mostly by mayors. And then we will drive our respective nations' national agendas around these issues."[37]

Within America, over 1,000 mayors belong to the U.S. Conference of Mayors, which is open to cities with populations of at least 30,000. Having previously created "The U.S. Conference of Mayor's Climate Protection Agreement," in 2014 it issued a resolution on the need for emergency action, saying:

> The U.S. Conference of Mayors calls on the Administration and Congress to enact an Emergency Climate Protection law that provides a framework and funding for the implementation, in conjunction with state and local government and the private sector, of a comprehensive national plan to dramatically reduce GHG emissions to avoid catastrophic impacts of climate change on the planet.[38]

Mayors have responded to the need for local action in various ways:

- In 2007, Mayor Bloomberg, wanting to make New York the country's first sustainable city, oversaw the creation of PlaNYC, which calls for 30 percent reductions in greenhouse gases by 2030 and 80 percent by 2050.

- In 2009, Cleveland inaugurated an initiative to transform its community into a "Green City on a Blue Lake" within ten years. Called Sustainable Cleveland 2019, its action plan also pledges to reduce emissions 80 percent by 2050.

- Seattle mayors have developed a Climate Action Plan to make the city carbon neutral by 2050 by making its buildings more energy efficient, making it easier to avoid using automobiles, and eliminating the use of coal.

- In 2014, the Conference of U.S. Mayors gave its Climate Protection Award to Las Vegas Mayor Carolyn Goodman, who was recognized for her progress in seeking to make Las Vegas the first major city to achieve net zero carbon emissions.

- Under the leadership of Mayor Miro Weinberger, Burlington, which is Vermont's largest city, purchased a hydroelectric facility, thereby enabling it to become the first city of any size to get 100% of its electricity from clean energy.[39]

- At the 2014 UN Climate Summit in New York, the city's new mayor, Bill De Blasio, pledged that NYC by 2050 would reduce greenhouse gas emissions by 80 percent (from 2005 levels), by means of improving the energy efficiency of buildings.[40]

- Rex Parris, the Republican mayor of Lancaster, California, wants to make it the solar capital of the world, saying: "We want to be the first city that produces more electricity from solar energy than we consume on a daily basis." When asked by *The New York Times* whether he considered global warming a threat, he said, "I may be a Republican. I'm not an idiot."[41]

Military Leadership

Congressional Republicans have worked to prevent money being given to the Pentagon to make the U.S. military less dependent on fossil fuels, claiming that such expenses lessen the available resources for national security, but many military leaders have spoken out to the contrary. In addition to the statements quoted in Chapter 9, here are a few more:

- Brig. General Steven Anderson, a former chief of logistics and self-described conservative Republican, said: "Our oil addiction, I believe, is our greatest threat to our national security. Not just foreign oil but oil in general."

- General Gordon Sullivan, former chief of staff of the Army, said: "Climate change is a national security issue. We found that climate instability will lead to instability in geopolitics and impact American military operations around the world."

- Vice Admiral Dennis McGinn (ret.) has said: "The Department of Defense and national intelligence communities recognize [the] clear link between climate change, national security, and instability and have begun strategic plans and programs to both mitigate and adapt to the most likely and serious effects."[42]

Although there are some issues that are inappropriate for military leaders to address, it is certainly appropriate for them to argue that continued climate change is going to make their tasks more difficult, and that the military's shift to clean energy will aid national security. It is also appropriate for them to state that, just as the U.S. military was able to play a major role in the WW II battle against fascism only because the country had fully mobilized, another kind of full mobilization is now necessary for the fight to save civilization.

Religious and Moral Leadership

Second to none in importance in mobilizing the country are those who are in position to address climate issues from a moral and religious perspective. As James Hansen said, although economic issues are important, the basic issue "is a matter of morality – a matter of intergenerational justice." If one overrides this moral issue by continuing to spew CO_2 into the atmosphere, one is saying, as Ken Caldeira put it: "I am willing to impose tremendous climate risk on future generations living throughout the world, so that I personally can be 2% richer today."[43] Moral and religious leaders should focus attention on this issue.

People who are by profession involved with religious and moral issues have already done much in various ways, such as writing books and articles, holding conferences, providing declarations to be endorsed, and forming organizations. One of the biggest of these organizations is Interfaith Power & Light, whose missions is to "protect the earth's ecosystem" by being "faithful stewards of Creation by responding to global warming through the promotion of energy conservation, energy efficiency, and renewable energy." With branches in 40 states, this organization provides occasions for talking to people about these matters, such as the four-day bike trip taken by seven Penn State faculty members "to raise awareness about the ethical dimensions of climate change."

In addition, pastors, priests, ethicists, scientists – in fact, everyone who is capable of doing so – should flood the newspapers, the Internet, Twitter, and TV and radio programs with statements about the moral and religious importance of stopping global warming, so that the country is constantly aware of the need to win this battle, just as Americans were always aware during WW II of the need to defeat fascism. It is, of course, especially helpful when admired national and world figures speak out, as when Pope Francis posed for a photograph with a no-fracking t-shirt and said that destroying the rain forest is a sin.[44]

Republican Leadership

Strong leadership is also needed by sensible Republicans to turn around their party, especially the Congress, so that it will not continue to thwart the kinds of bold changes needed in the generation of energy. At least one Republican, former South Carolina Congressman Bob Inglis, has made an attempt by launching in 2012 an "Energy and Enterprise" initiative to encourage "conservative solutions to America's energy and climate challenges" – one of these solutions being a carbon tax. The call for a carbon tax has also been supported by other Republicans who have been involved in national politics:

- Art Laffer, a conservative economist who was a senior adviser to President Reagan.

- George Shultz, Reagan's secretary of State.

- Douglas Holtz-Eakin, former head of Bush's Council of Economic Advisers and later economic adviser to John McCain's 2008 presidential campaign.

- Gregory Mankiw, who was the chief economist of President George W. Bush's Council of Economic Advisors and later economic advisor to the Mitt Romney presidential campaign.

- More recently, as discussed earlier, Hank Paulson, treasury secretary in George W. Bush's administration, wrote a *New York Times* editorial in favor of a carbon tax.

Additional prominent Republicans include four former EPA heads, who in 2014 told a Senate Committee that there is no doubt about the reality and cause of climate change and that the EPA has the authority to regulate greenhouse gases.

Three additional sensible Republicans are former California governor Arnold Schwarzenegger, Maine Senator Susan Collins, and former presidential candidate Jon Huntsman, who wrote a *New York Times* op-ed saying: "Our approach as a party should be one of neither denial nor extremism. Science must guide sensible policy discussions that will lead to well-informed choices, which may mean considering unexpected alternatives."[45]

Bob Inglis, referring to Congress, said that there are several conservatives in "foxholes on this hill" who accept the scientific consensus but remain silent to avoid being targeted by the Tea Party.[46] If there is a chance that Congress will help save the planet, many of the Republicans will need to come out their foxholes.

Scientific Leadership

At one time, as Lonnie Thompson has pointed out, climate scientists used to assume that all they had to do was to report their findings, after which the press would report them and then the political world would respond appropriately. However, as Thompson and many other scientists, such as James Hansen and Michael Mann, came to realize, the traditional way of disseminating scientific information was not working, so scientists need to go directly to the politicians and the public – as Hansen did by giving a TED Talk, "Why I Must Speak Out about Climate Change" (2012).

A related issue is the way in which scientists report their findings. Far from being guilty of alarmism, as critics allege, they have had a bias toward "erring on the side of least drama," by regularly giving predictions about various matters, such as sea-level rise and Arctic ice-melt, that tend to underestimate the likely developments. UK hedge fund manager Jeremy Grantham has spoken out on this issue, saying:

> Scientists are understandably protective of the dignity of science and are horrified by publicity and overstatement. . . . Overstatement may generally be dangerous in science (it certainly is for careers) but for climate change, uniquely, understatement is even riskier and therefore, arguably, unethical. It is crucial that scientists take more career risks and sound a more realistic, more desperate, note on the global-warming problem. . . . This is not only the crisis of your lives – it is also the crisis of our species' existence. I implore you to be brave.

Another helpful thing scientists can do is to encourage journalists to avoid resorting to false balance. For example, astrophysicist Neil deGrasse Tyson, the host of "Cosmos," said during an interview, "you don't talk about the spherical Earth with NASA, and then say 'now let's give equal time to the flat Earthers.'"

Another good piece of advice to fellow scientists came from NASA's Gavin Schmidt, who said: "It's important for people who know things not to give up the public sphere to people who don't know things." In a *New York Times* op-ed, Michael Mann talked about his own change of view on this issue. Whereas he at one time insisted on speaking in public only about scientific facts, he now says:

> [T]here is nothing inappropriate at all about drawing on
> our scientific knowledge to speak out about the very real
> implications of our research. . . . If scientists choose not
> to engage in the public debate, we leave a vacuum that
> will be filled by those whose agenda is one of short-term
> self-interest. There is a great cost to society if scientists fail
> to participate in the larger conversation – if we do not do
> all we can to ensure that the policy debate is informed by
> an honest assessment of the risks. In fact, it would be an
> abrogation of our responsibility to society if we remained
> quiet in the face of such a grave threat.[47]

As Schmidt pointed out, many scientists, especially younger ones, are already doing this, discussing the reality and implications of climate change on Facebook, Twitter, and so on, as well as by more traditional means. In such ways, scientists can, beyond their scientific work, contribute to the mobilization of the country to deal with civilization's most serious challenge ever.

Technological Leadership

Technology is closely related to science; indeed, technology is nowadays defined as the practical application of scientific knowledge to make useful products. In any case, this book has mentioned dozens of technological developments that help reduce global warming. Most of these developments have involved the major cause of global warming, fossil fuels. But another example of technological leadership involves cement. The most common form of cement, called "Portland" (because of its similarity to building stone quarried on England's Isle of Portland), has accounted for 5 to 10 percent of the emissions of CO_2.

Until recently, so-called green technology had been able to reduce the CO_2 produced by cement manufacturing by only 20 percent, a reduction that was more than balanced by the great increase in the use of concrete for buildings around the world, especially China. So cement has been contributing ever-increasing amounts of CO_2 emissions. But newer technological developments promise to cut the production of these emissions dramatically.

One development is the creation of a new blend by Swiss and Indian researchers that reduces the CO_2 emissions by 30 percent. Another discovery, which reduces the percentage of calcium in the cement, can reduce CO_2 emissions by as much as 60 percent while making the resulting concrete stronger. Still another approach is to replace Portland cement with Geopolymer Cement, which can reduce the CO_2 emissions by as much as 90 percent. Another approach proposes to use the fumes from power plants to make cement, thereby sequestering 90 percent of the CO_2.[48]

If one of these developments becomes widely accepted, especially if it can reduce CO_2 by 90 percent, one of the major causes of global warming will be greatly reduced.

Women's Leadership

In 2013, 100 global women leaders participated in the first International Women's Earth and Climate Summit. Their statements illustrated the fact that women's leadership is essential, because they often bring distinctive perspectives. For example:

- Nobel Peace Laureate Jody Williams announced that women are putting the world on notice that women will "raise our voices followed by serious actions," pointing to the possibility that they will boycott corporations, such as Monsanto, that are contributing to climate change escalation.

- Mary Robinson, the former president of Ireland and UN High Commissioner for Human Rights, said: "Women on the forefront are . . . coping with the impacts of climate change in communities worldwide. . . . Women must insist on transformative leadership worldwide. . . . We must have climate justice by having sustainable goals in all countries of the world."

- Scientist and activist Vandana Shiva of India said: "Our challenge is to put forth a new paradigm about the Earth, and create a new leadership in the world. The Earth is not dead; she's a living Earth. We want the 7th generation thought of. In India, we have the same thought as First Nations here about always considering the 7th generation. Uncivilized people rape Earth for today."

- Sally Ranney, one of the directors of the summit, said: "Women are not going to be silent. We are 51% of the world's population, and we are demanding to be heard. Our lives are immediately depending on solutions to the climate change crisis."

- Osprey Lakes, the other co-director, proclaimed: "Nature is not waiting while politicians debate. We need a deep overall analysis about climate change right now. Enough is enough."

This summit also drew many other prominent women leaders, including Maude Barlow, Sylvia Earle, and Jane Goodall.[49]

Youth Leadership

Young people can play a major role in mobilizing the country, by drawing public attention to the fact that it is they among the living who face the actual prospect of being the future victims of climate disruption. There are many organizations to teach young people about what looms ahead and how to take steps to avert it. Some of these organizations have been started by young people themselves.

For example, an organization called Plant-for-the-Planet was inspired by a nine-year-old. Focused on planting trees, this initiative seeks to raise the awareness of adults as well as children about climate change and global justice. Some children belonging to this organization, James Hansen reported, held meetings with staff for two Washington state senators, during which the children put forward these astonishingly well-informed requests:

- Stop speaking of a warming increase of 2°C as the target, because 2°C is catastrophic for 10-year-olds.

- Spell out the plan to keep warming close to 1.2°C in speeches.

- Pledge "No New Carbon Pollution" to oppose more dirty energy infrastructure, exports, and exploration.

- Put a price on carbon pollution.

- Introduce a resolution for protecting our children with 6% annual reductions and our fair share of 1 Trillion Trees.

- Plant trees!

Hansen's response: "Wow – that from kids." Here, more briefly, are descriptions of other organizations:

- *Alliance for Climate Education* is dedicated to educating America's high school students about the science behind climate change and inspiring them to do something about it. Motivated students are then given leadership training.

- *C2C Fellows* is a national network for college undergraduates and recent graduates aspiring to sustainability leadership in politics and business. Upon graduation from the workshops, students join the C2C Fellows Network.

- *Climate Education in an Age of Media*, directed at high school students and teachers as well as university students, focuses on bringing student media production into climate change education

- *Earth Guardians* is a Colorado-based network of students and adults trying to leave a better world for future generations, especially by getting fracking banned.

- *Energy Action Coalition* involves 50 youth-led environmental and social justice groups focused on winning local elections.

- *Kids vs. Global Warming,* which was started by Alec Loorz after he, then 12 years old, saw Al Gore's "An Inconvenient Truth," seeks to inform and mobilize kids to take action. After Julia Olson, a young environmental lawyer in Eugene, was introduced to Loorz by James Hansen, she began *Our Children's Trust,* which helped members of Kids vs. Global Warming use the courts to protect the planet. A typical member is Glori Dei Filippone of Iowa, who in 2012 wrote:

  > I am 14 years old. I am sick of global warming. I'm sick of wondering if our world will last much longer, of not knowing if my children will grow up in a healthy, stable world. The best way to not worry is to fix the problem. . . . This is a revolution, and it won't be easy. Revolutions never are. They take time, effort, and dedication. Sometimes change seems to be out of reach. But change leads to wonderful things. . . . Please contact your Iowa legislators and President Obama on behalf of your kids and grandkids. Ask them to side with the children of this country rather than the fossil-fuel lobbyists.

- *Focus the Nation* is an organization reaching some 300,000 young people each year, inspiring them to confront clean energy challenges.

- *Interfaith Youth for Climate Justice* is a program for students active in local congregations in the Washington, DC area. Students from different faith traditions spend a year gaining the knowledge, skills and experience needed to become leaders for climate justice.

- *National Wildlife Federation's Campus Ecology Fellows* help to educate and engage campus communities – about a thousand campuses each year – about global warming impacts and solutions. Founded in 1989, its student outreach programs, campus consulting, climate action competitions, and educational events and resources reach about 1,000 campuses each year.

- *The Will Steger Foundation* seeks to empower youth leaders on climate change solutions across the Midwest through access to decision-makers, funding resources, and training and leadership opportunities.[50]

Once the U.S. president calls for national mobilization to deal with the climate change emergency, these and other organizations will provide millions of young people to serve in the cause.

CONCLUSION

> *"Climate change is happening faster, more intensely and,*
> *in many cases, at an unprecedented rate of change*
> *. . . . This demands action."*
> – World Wildlife Fund, 2013

There are amazing numbers of scientists, organizations, and networks focused on global warming and climate change, explaining what will happen if business as usual continues. But thus far these efforts, while making great progress scientifically, have done little to slow global warming. We must again ask Sherwood Rowland's question, "What's the use of having developed a science well enough to make predictions if, in the end, all we're willing to do is stand around and wait for them to come true?"[1]

Speaking of the generation that defeated the Nazi-Fascist alliance in World War II, journalist Tom Brokaw called it "the greatest generation." Speaking of the world's response to the ecological crisis thus far, George Monbiot has called it "the greatest political failure the world has ever seen."[2] If we do not decisively take action to prevent a hellish climate, our children, grandchildren, and great-grandchildren will rightly refer to us as *the pathetic generation*.

Given our refusal to cut emissions over the past 30 years, it is already too late to save the kind of world that has been hospitable to human beings since the rise of civilization. But as Bill McKibben says: "We *may*, with commitment and luck, yet be able to maintain a planet that will sustain *some kind* of civilization."[3]

We need to mobilize as fast and thoroughly as possible to win the battle of life against death – the battle with what Chris Hedges calls "the drive by corporations to extract the last remaining natural resources from the earth, even if it kills us all."[4]

In many battles, the war is against an enemy no more evil than one's own side; it may simply be competing for the same prize. But in the present battle, this is not the case. To repeat Tom Engelhardt's statement:

> To destroy our planet with malice aforethought, with only
> the most immediate profits on the brain, with only your own
> comfort and wellbeing (and those of your shareholders) in
> mind: Isn't that the ultimate crime?[5]

In conventional wars, traitors to their countries are not dealt with tolerantly. Treason is a crime, and the traitors are not allowed to continue their criminal activities. Why should we be more tolerant with traitors to humanity as a whole and life itself? Not only should we treat them as pariahs, as McKibben has recommended, and divest from their criminal enterprises; we need to put them out of business – and quickly.

We are thus far the pathetic generation because there is no mystery about what we need to do but have not done. Besides reforming agriculture and helping the world reforest, our government simply needs to (1) eliminate fossil-fuel subsidies, (2) impose an escalating tax on carbon, and (3) do everything possible to accelerate, both nationally and globally, the transition to a 100 percent green economy. The third of these three steps will, to be sure, be more demanding than the World War II mobilization. But whereas that mobilization involved the Manhattan Project to build an atom bomb before the Nazis did, the technology needed now is already available. And once clean energy, because of the first two steps, becomes much less expensive than fossil-fuel energy, clean-energy technology will be advanced and employed with unprecedented rapidity. The "race for what's left" of the world's coal, oil, and natural gas will be transformed into a race to replace them.

But this new race has yet to begin in earnest.

POSTSCRIPT

After this book was ready to be published, a development occurred of such importance that I got permission from Clarity Press to add a couple of pages.

This development may change the final observation above – that the race to replace fossil fuels had not begun in earnest. The agreement on carbon emissions reached by China and the United States, announced on 11 November 2014, may have marked the beginning of that race.

In the chapter "Mobilization" above, I had advocated, as had several others, that President Obama make an executive agreement with Chinese President Xi Jinping about carbon emissions. After the two presidents had already agreed to work together to reduce HFCs, Obama in September 2014, at the U.N. meeting in New York, issued his counterpart a challenge about climate change. Then in October, Obama sent his advisor, John Podesta, to China to finalize a deal.[6]

Most observers – except for Congressional Republicans, the *Wall Street Journal*, and Fox News – have described the deal as "historic." According to the agreement, the United States will by 2025 reduce its greenhouse gas emissions by 26-28 percent below 2005 levels, which will mean doubling its annual emission reduction rates (and likely require Obama to reverse his "all of the above" approach).

On China's side, it pledged to peak its carbon emissions no later than 2030 and raise clean energy to 20 percent of the country's energy sources (compared with 9.8 percent in 2013).[7]

Romm called this agreement a "game-changer," because "prior to this deal, neither the U.S. or China were seriously in the game of trying to stave off climate catastrophe. Now both countries are." In addition, said Romm, the deal

> guarantees that the recent explosive growth – and amazing price drops – experienced by renewables like solar and wind will continue for decades to come. And that means the long-predicted ascendance of carbon-free energy has now begun in earnest.[8]

Still more, Obama's agreement with China undercuts what had become the Republicans' main argument for doing nothing about climate change: that U.S. sacrifices will make no difference, because China will not reduce its emissions. For example, Charles Krauthammer said that, given China's emissions, "you could shut down every coal mine in Kentucky [and] it won't make a dime's worth of difference." The one thing that would make a difference, said Krauthammer, would be if "Obama gets an agreement with China, which he won't."[9]

Once Obama did get the agreement, Republicans replied that the deal "requires the Chinese to do nothing at all for 16 years" (this was Senator Mitch McConnell's claim) and that, in any case, it would be foolish to trust China to keep its pledge (Christopher Flavelle of Bloomberg View reported that he got "a flood of e-mails from readers" making this argument, along with the McConnell argument).[10]

However, to keep either pledge, China will need to start right away. Given the enormous amount of clean energy that it will need by 2030 – "an additional 800-1,000 gigawatts of nuclear, wind, solar, and other zero emission generation capacity," which is "close to total current electricity generation capacity in the United States" – China will not be able to wait long before starting. With regard to coal, Frank Jotzo, an Australian professor of climate economics, said:

> [C]oal use in China will have to decline well before the peak date for CO_2. Why is that? Because you've got oil use on an increasing trajectory, because of increasing road transport and increasing aviation. And you've got increasing gas use.

The thing that has to give in that equation is coal. Coal use will have to decline, and probably decline significantly, well ahead of that peak date. It's not something that you can leave to, say, 2025 and then suddenly turn the lever and start declining.[11]

Less than a week later, China showed that it was serious about the pledge, announcing that it would cap its use of coal by 2020. Joe Romm said: "This is a staggering reversal of Chinese energy policy, which for two decades has been centered around building a coal plant or more a week." In a sense, however, this new announcement was not a surprise, because fulfilling the pledge to peak CO_2 in 2030 would, according to analysts, require China's use of coal to peak by (roughly) 2020.[12]

The U.S.-China agreement, which undermined the Republicans' argument, resulted in some humor: Jonathan Chait's New York Magazine headline was, "China Tries to Save Earth; Republicans Furious." Andy Borowitz's satirical piece for the New Yorker, headed "Republicans Demand Return of Passive Obama," reported that House Speaker John Boehner and soon-to-be Senate Majority Leader Mitch McConnell accused Obama of "engaging in a flagrant display of leadership that we find deeply offensive."[13]

In any case, while the U.S.-China agreement is historic and game-changing, it is far from sufficient, as many experts have observed. Bill McKibben wrote: "It is not remotely enough to keep us out of climate trouble." Amory Lovins' Rocky Mountain Institute said that it is "not a panacea," because if the two countries remain content with this agreement, they will likely exhaust the carbon budget all by themselves, so the agreement should be viewed not as an end goal, but as a "momentum-builder." Obama himself probably looked at it this way, and President Xi evidently did too, saying: "A pool begins with many drops of water."[14]

One thing for which the agreement might build momentum is the 2015 U.N. climate conference in Paris, at which it is hoped that a global agreement might finally be reached. This possibility is increased by the fact that in October of 2014, the European Council proposed a law requiring the European Union to reduce greenhouse emissions 40 percent below 1990 levels by 2030. This proposal will become law if the European Commission suggests legislation that the European Parliament then passes. Assuming this will happen, "all three of the world's biggest emitters are now on record with new commitments to get their greenhouse gas emissions under control."[15]

Thanks to these commitments by Europe, China, and the United States, the chance for the survival of civilization is a little better than it was before.

ENDNOTES

Introduction

1   James Hansen et al., "Earth's Energy Imbalance," Goddard Institute for Space Studies, NASA, January 2012.

2   Joe Romm, "Bombshell: Recent Warming Is 'Amazing and Atypical' and Poised to Destroy Stable Climate that Enabled Civilization," Climate Progress, 8 March 2013.

3   Stefan Rahmstorf, "Paleoclimate: The End of the Holocene," Realclimate.org, 22 September 2013; Marcott quoted in Tim McDonnell, "The Scariest Climate Change Graph Just Got Scarier," *Mother Jones*, 7 March 2013.

4   Rahmstorf, "Paleoclimate"; Joe Romm, "New Science Study Confirms 'Hockey Stick': The Rate of Warming Since 1900 Is 50 Times Greater than the Rate of Cooling in Previous 5000 Years!" Climate Progress, 23 April 2013. (Romm's earlier articles were signed "Joseph Romm," but he later switched to "Joe Romm." For the sake of consistency, this latter name is here always used.)

5   Dana Nuccitelli, "CO_2 Lags Temperature - What Does It Mean?" Skeptical Science, 9 April 2012; "Sun & Climate: Moving in Opposite Directions," Skeptical Science, Intermediate Level, 22 February 2014; "Earth's Sensitivity to Climate Change Could Be 'Double' Previous Estimates, Say Geologists," Science Daily, 10 December 2013.

6   Rahmstorf, "Paleoclimate."

7   Elizabeth Kolbert, *The Sixth Extinction: An Unnatural History* (New York: Henry Holt, 2014), 107-10. Coined in the early 1980s by University of Michigan biologist Eugene F. Stoermer, the term "Anthropocene" was popularized in a 2000 article by atmospheric chemist Paul Crutzen and a colleague; see Andrew C. Revkin, "Confronting the 'Anthropocene,'" Dot Earth, *New York Times*, 11 May 2011; Paul J. Crutzen and Christian Schwägerl, "Living in the Anthropocene: Toward a New Global Ethos," Environment 360, Yale University, 24 January 2011.

8   Elizabeth May, "Can Civilization Survive Climate Change?" Killam Lecture, Dalhousie University, Halifax, Nova Scotia, 24 August 2006.

9   Elizabeth Kolbert, *Field Notes from a Catastrophe: Man, Nature, and Climate Change* (Bloomsbury, 2006), 189.

10   Paul J. Crutzen, "The Anthropocene: Are Humans Now Overwhelming the Great Forces of Nature?" *Ambio* 36/8 (December, 2007), 614-21.

11   Lester Brown, *Plan B 4.0: Mobilizing to Save Civilization*, substantially revised edition (New York: W. W. Norton, 2009).

12   Lester Brown, "Could Food Shortages Bring Down Civilization?" *Scientific American*, 22 April 2009.

13   Lonnie G. Thompson, "Climate Change: The Evidence and Our Options," *Behavior Analyst*, 33/2 (Fall 2010), 153–70.

14   Ross Gelbspan, "U.S. Press Coverage of the Climate Crisis: A Damning Betrayal of Public Trust," The Heat is Online, June 2010.

15   Al Gore, "Climate of Denial: Can Science and the Truth withstand the Merchants of Poison?" *Rolling Stone*, June 2011.

16   The Blue Planet Laureates, "Environment and Development Challenges: The Impera-

tive to Act," 20 February 2012.

17   Noam Chomsky and Andre Vitchek, *On Western Terrorism: From Hiroshima to Drone Warfare* (Pluto Press, 2013), 2.

18   Paul R. Ehrlich and Anne H. Ehrlich, "Can a Collapse of Global Civilization Be Avoided?" *Proceedings of the Royal Society B*, 9 January 2013.

19   Tom Engelhardt, "Is Climate Change a Crime against Humanity?" TomDispatch, 22 May 2014; Naomi Oreskes and Erik M. Conway, *The Collapse of Western Civilization: A View from the Future* (Columbia University Press, 2014).

20   Lester R. Brown, "The Geopolitics of Food Scarcity," *Der Spiegel Online*, 11 February 2009.

21   Brown, "Could Food Shortages Bring Down Civilization?"

22   Gore, "Climate of Denial."

23   Graham Wayne, "Global Warming vs. Climate Change," Skeptical Science, 1 August 2013.

24   Gregory Boyce, "The Winter of 2010 vs. Global Warming: God's Sense of Humor?" Examiner, 13 February 2010; Igor Volsky, "Fox News Discusses Climate Change, Insanity Ensures," Climate Progress, 16 February 2014.

25   Andrew Moseman, "Once Again, Cold Weather Doesn't Disprove Global Warming," *Discover Magazine*, 8 January 2010; see also "Does Cold Weather Disprove Global Warming?" Skeptical Science; Steve Connor, "Expect More Extreme Winters Thanks to Global Warming, Say Scientists," *Independent*, 24 December 2010; Stephen Leahy, "Arctic Sea Ice Melt 'May Bring Harsh Winter to Europe,'" *Guardian*, 14 September 2012.

26   "Climate Change," Environment, Community and Local Government.

27   John Abraham and Dana Nuccitelli, "We Haven't Hit the Global Warming Pause Button," *Guardian*, 24 June 2013; Chris Mooney, "Is Global Warming Really Slowing Down?" Skeptical Science, 28 August 2013; Dana Nuccitelli, "New Research Confirms Global Warming Has Accelerated," Skeptical Science, 25 March 2013 (referring to Magdalena A. Balmaseda et al., "Distinctive Climate Signals in Reanalysis of Global Ocean Heat Content," *Geophysical Research Letters*, 10 May 2013); Joe Romm, "Faux Pause: Ocean Warming, Sea Level Rise and Polar Melt Speed Up, Surface Warming to Follow," Climate Progress, 25 September 2013.

28   Joe Romm, "Faux Pause 2: Warmest November on Record, Reports NASA, as New Studies Confirm Warming Trend," Climate Progress, 15 December 2013.

29   George Monbiot, "Time to Change 'Climate Change'," *Guardian*, 12 March 2009; David Malakoff, "Let's Call It 'Climate Disruption,' White House Science Adviser Suggests (Again)," *Science*, 2 May 2014; David W. Orr, *Down to the Wire: Confronting Climate Collapse* (Oxford: Oxford University Press, 2009; reprint 2012).

30   Justin Gillis, "Heat-Trapping Gas Passes Milestone, Raising Fears," *New York Times*, 10 May 2013; "Carbon Dioxide Hits 400 ppm – Does It Matter?" *Discover Magazine*, January-February 2013.

31   David Spratt, "NASA Climate Chief: Labor's Targets a 'Recipe for Disaster,'" Climate Code Red, 27 January 2011.

32   The issue is, to be sure, not simply CO_2, but all the greenhouse gases, with the other most important ones being methane, nitrous oxide, and chlorofluorocarbons (CFCs). It has been customary to refer to the total amount as CO_2e (carbon dioxide equivalent), meaning the amount of CO_2 that would have the same global warming potential as a mixture of all the greenhouse gases. But I will focus on CO_2, which is by far the most important – at least thus far.

33   George Lakoff, "Global Warming Systemically Caused Hurricane Sandy," Salon, 31 October 2012.

34   The lag time of 30 years is merely an estimate. Romm has suggested 20 years (see the next note); other researchers suggest 25-30 years (Daniel Whittingstall, "Projected Effects and Historical Overview of Civilizational Forced Climate Change," Canadians for Emergency Action on Climate Change, 5 March 2013; Alexander Ac, "Paralyzed Warming World," Amsterdam Law Forum, 2010); others suggest 40 years (Alan

Marshall, "Climate Change: The 40 Year Delay Between Cause and Effect," Skeptical Science, 22 September 2010); and James Hansen suggested 25-50 years (Hansen et al., "Earth's Imbalance: Confirmation and Implications," Science Express, 29 April 2005). For simplicity's sake, I simply speak of a 30-year lag.

35   Joe Romm, "Climate Panel Stunner: Avoiding Climate Catastrophe Is Super Cheap – but Only if We Act Now," Climate Progress, 13 April 2014.

36   "Long Time Target of 2°C Now Seen as 'Prescription for Disaster,'" Daily Climate, 6 December 2011.

37   Bill McKibben, "Obama and Climate Change: The Real Story," *Rolling Stone,* 17 December 2013.

38   James Hansen et al., "Target Atmospheric CO_2: Where Should Humanity Aim?" *Open Atmospheric Science Journal* 2 (2008), 217-31.

39   James Hansen et al., "Assessing 'Dangerous Climate Change': Required Reduction of Carbon Emissions to Protect Young People, Future Generations and Nature," PLOS ONE, December 2013; see also the summary of this document in James Hansen and J. Pushker Kharecha, *Popular Science*, 3 December 2013.

40   F. R. Rijsberman and R. J. Swart, ed., "Targets and Indicators of Climate Change," Stockholm Environment Institute, 1990 (http://www.scribd.com/doc/121702780/Responding-to-Climate-Change-Tools-For-Policy-Development-Part-I-of-II); described in Cory Morningstar, "Exposé: The 2º Death Dance – The 1º Cover-up," Part I, 10 December 2010.

41   For more about sensitivity, see the discussion of Richard Lindzen in Chapter 11.

42   H. Damon Matthews et al., "Cumulative Carbon as a Policy Framework for Achieving Climate Stabilization," *Philosophical Transactions of the Royal Society*, 6 August 2012.

43   Myles Allen et al., "The Exit Strategy," *Nature Climate Change*, 30 April 2009. A limit of 750 billion tons may seem extreme (and it is), and yet that goal, climate scientists have estimated, would give us only a 67-percent chance of avoiding a rise of greater than 2°C. We should want better odds than this (just as we would not want to get on a plane with only two chances out of three of not crashing). To have a 75 percent chance of keeping the warming below 2°C, according to these scientists, we would need to lower the total CO_2 to 600 billion tons. (The year 2050 was selected because "most of the requisite emission reductions will need to have been achieved by that date" [Messner et al., "The Budget Approach"].)

44   Messner et al., "The Budget Approach."

45   Quoted in Mark Hertsgaard, "Climate Roulette," The Nation, 26 October 2009; Justin Gillis, "U.N. Climate Panel Endorses Ceiling on Global Emissions," New York Times, 27 September 2013.

46   See e.g., "Whitehead's Contributions to a Theology of Nature," *Bucknell Review* 20 (Winter, 1972), and "Whitehead's Deeply Ecological Worldview," in Mary Evelyn Tucker and John Grim, eds., *Worldviews and Ecology: Religion, Philosophy, and the Environment* (Maryknoll: Orbis Books, 1994).

47   Brown, *Plan B 4.0: Mobilizing to Save Civilization.*

48   Lester Brown, *World on the Edge: How to Prevent Environmental and Economic Collapse* (Earth Policy Institute, 2011), 117.

49   "Met Office's Bleak Forecast on Climate Change," *Guardian*, 30 September 2008.

50   Bill McKibben, *Eaarth: Making a Life on a Tough New Planet* (New York: Times Books, 2010); Joe Romm, *Hell and High Water: The Global Warming Solution* (New York: Harper, 2007), 2.

51   Clive Hamilton, *Requiem for a Species: Why We Resist the Truth about Climate Change* (Routledge, 2010).

52   Verner E. Suomi, foreword to Jule Charney et al., *Carbon Dioxide and Climate: A Scientific Assessment: Report to the Climate Research Board*, National Research Council (Washington, D.C.: National Academies Press, 1979).

53   Mason Inman, "Carbon Is Forever," *Nature Reports Climate Change*, 20 November 2008.

54   William Marsden, *Fool's Rule: Inside the Failed Politics of Climate Change* (Alfred A.

Knopf Canada, 2011), 242-43.

55   Quoted in Mark Hertsgaard, *Hot: Living Through the Next Fifty Years on Earth* (New York: Houghton Mifflin Harcourt, 2011), 46.

Chapter 1: Extreme Weather

1   Joe Romm, "Climate Story of the Year: Extreme Weather from Superstorms to Drought Emerges as Political, Scientific Gamechanger," Climate Progress, 21 December 2012.

2   Bill McKibben, "Weather Extremes," *Sierra Atlantic*, Spring 2011; Curt Stager, "The 'New Normal' Weather," Fast Company, 6 June 2011.

3   Andrew Cuomo, "We Will Lead on Climate Change," *New York Daily News*, 15 November 2012; Seth Borenstein, "2012 Extreme Weather Sets Records, Fits Climate Change Forecasts," Huffington Post, 20 December 2012.

4   Jane Velez-Mitchell, "Let's Tell the Truth about Extreme Weather," CNN, 16 May 2014.

5   Joe Romm, "Jet Stream Changes Driving Extreme Weather Linked again to Global Warming, Arctic Ice Loss," Climate Progress, 19 August 2014.

6   John M. Broder, "Scientists See More Deadly Weather, but Dispute the Cause," *New York Times*, 15 June 2011; James Hansen et al., "Perception of Climate Change," *Proceedings of the National Academy of Sciences*, 30 July 2012. Hansen has also put it this way: "I don't want people to be confused by natural variability — the natural changes in weather from day to day and year to year. We now know that the chances these extreme weather events would have happened naturally — without climate change — is negligible."

7   Hansen et al., "Perception of Climate Change"; Andrew Freedman, "Hansen Study: Extreme Weather Tied to Climate Change," 6 August 2012.

8   Jeff Masters used this analogy while being interviewed in "How 2011 Became a 'Mind-Boggling' Year of Extreme Weather," PBS Newshour, 28 December 2011.

9   Graham Wayne, "What is the Link between Hurricanes and Global Warming?" Skeptical Science, 1 August 2013.

10   Quoted in Joe Romm, "The Year of Living Dangerously," Climate Progress, 23 December 2010.

11   IPCC, "Summary for Policy Makers," *Special Report on Managing the Risks of Extreme Events and Disasters to Advance Climate Change Adaptation*, 2011. Fields is quoted in Seth Borenstein, "This US Summer Is 'What Global Warming Looks Like,'" Associated Press, 3 July 2010.

12   Jeff Masters, "Summer in March, 2002, Draws to a Close," WunderBlog, 23 March 2012.

13   Ibid.

14   John Vidal, "2013 in Review: A Year of Increasing Extreme Weather Events," *Guardian*, 18 December 2013.

15   John Vidal, "World Begins 2014 with Unusual Number of Extreme Weather Events," *Guardian*, 25 February 2014.

16   John Lawrence, "Extreme Weather Watch: April 2014 – Tornadoes, Flash Floods Pound US," *San Diego Free Press*, 6 May 2014.

17   *Fox & Friends*, Fox News, 27 September 2011; Chris Mooney, "Dear Donald Trump: Winter Does Not Disprove Global Warming," *Mother Jones*, 2 January 2014.

18   "Does Record Snowfall Disprove Global Warming?" Skeptical Science, 7 March 2010.

19   Suzanne Goldenberg, "Extreme Weather More Persuasive on Climate Change than Scientists," *Guardian*, 15 December 2012.

20   Bill McKibben, "Sandy Forces Climate Change on US Election," *Guardian*, 1 November 2012.

21   Justin Gillis, "In Weather Chaos, a Case for Global Warming," *New York Times*, 14 August 2010; President Dmitri Medvedev, "Speech at Expanded Security Council Meeting on Fire Safety Measures for Strategic Facilities," 4 August 2010.

22   Ibid.

23   Christopher Burt, "2012 a Record Warm Year for Continental U.S.," Weather Underground, 2 January 2013.

24   Joe Romm, "2012 Saw 362 All-Time Record High Temperatures in U.S. but Zero All-Time Record Lows," Climate Progress, 5 January 2013.

25   Personal letter of Hoeppe to Joe Romm, quoted in the latter's "The Year of Living Dangerously," Climate Progress, 23 December 2010.

26   "'Unprecedented,' 'Amazing,' 'Goliath': Scientists Describe Arctic Sea Ice Melt," Common Dreams, 7 September 2012; Andrew Freedman, "'Astonishing' Ice Melt May Lead to More Extreme Winters," Climate Central, 12 September 2012.

27   Seymour W. Laxon et al., "CryoSat-2 Estimates of Arctic Sea Ice Thickness and Volume," *Geophysical Research Letters*, 2 February 2013; Hannah Hickey, "European Satellite Confirms UW Numbers: Arctic Ocean Is on Thin Ice," University of Washington (Press Release), 13 February 2013; quoted in Joe Romm, "Arctic Death Spiral Bombshell: CryoSat-2 Confirms Sea Ice Volume Has Collapsed," Climate Progress, 14 2013.

28   Jennifer A. Francis and Stephen J. Vavrus, "Evidence Linking Arctic Amplification to Extreme Weather in Mid-Latitudes," *Geophysical Research Letters*, Vol. 39 (2012): Abstract; Joe Romm, "Arctic Sea Ice: The Death Spiral Continues," 11 April 2013. (The term "Arctic amplification" refers to the fact that global warming increases the temperature in the Arctic more rapidly than that in lower latitudes, thereby reducing the contrast; see John Cook, "What Causes Arctic Amplification?" Skeptical Science, 2 May 2010.)

29   Eric Roston, "Why Is It So Cold? The Polar Vortex, Explained," Bloomberg Business-Week, 7 January 2014; "How Frigid 'Polar Vortex' Could Be Result of Global Warming," *Christian Science Monitor*, 6 January 2014.

30   Bryan Walsh, "Climate Change Might Just Be Driving the Historic Cold Snap," *Time*, 6 January 2014.

31   Ryan Koronowski, "Hot Alaska, Cold Georgia: How the Shifted Polar Vortex Turned Winter Upside-Down," Climate Progress, 8 February 2014.

32   "Unusual July Temperatures," NASA Earth Observatory, August 2014; quoted in Dahr Jamail, "Peak Water, Methane Blowholes and Ice-Free Arctic Cruises: The Climate Crisis Deepens," Truthout, 18 August 2014.

33   John Galvin, "How the Dual Jet Stream Sparks This Weird Summer Weather," *Popular Mechanics*, 27 June 2013; Romm, "Jet Stream Changes Driving Extreme Weather."

34   Fiona Harvey, "Extreme Weather Will Strike as Climate Change Takes Hold, IPCC Warns," *Guardian*, 18 November 2011.

35   Bill McKibben, "Sandy's Real Name," EcoWatch, 30 November 2012.

Chapter 2: Heatwaves

1   Jeff Masters, "U.S. on Track for Warmest Year on Record," Wunderblog, 10 November 2012.

2   Philip Shabecoff, "Global Warming Has Begun, Expert Tells Senate," *New York Times*, 24 June 1988.

3   Terrell Johnson, "13 of 14 Hottest Years on Record All Occurred in 21st Century," Weather Channel, 24 March 2014.

4   "Shadi Rahimi, "Deadly Heat Wave Sends Temperatures Above 100°," *New York Times*, 26 2005; "Sweltering Temperatures Dominated Weather Maps Across the United States in July 2005," Earth Observatory, 26 July 2005.

5   Joe Romm, "NBC Meterologist on Record Heat Wave: 'If We Did Not Have Global Warming, We Wouldn't See This," Climate Progress, June 30, 2012.

6   "Heat Wave 2011: Records Broken Across the U.S.," Huffington Post, 10 January 2011; "July Heat Becomes Historic," Oklahoma Climatological Survey, 1 August 2011.

7   Justin Gillis, "Not Even Close: 2012 Was Hottest Year Ever in U.S.," *New York Times*, 9 January 2013.

8   "California Temperatures Could Reach 130F as Heat Wave Hit Western US," *Guardian*, 29 June 2013; "With Rising Temperatures, Infrastructure Falters," NPR, 5 July 2013; Fernanda Santos, "Deadly Heat Wave in the West Brings Fires and Travel Delays," *New York Times*, 30 June 2013; Jason Samenow, "Death Valley Hit Hottest U.S. June Temperature ever Recorded," *Washington Post*, 1 July 2013; "Death Valley Officials

Ask Tourists Stop Trying to Fry Eggs during National Park's Heat Wave," Associated Press, 14 July 2013; Joe Romm, "Northern Over-Exposure: Record Heat Wave Envelops Alaska," Climate Progress, 19 June 2013; Benjamin Mueller, "'Heat Dome' Grips Two-Thirds of the U.S.," Los Angeles Times, 18 July 2013.

9   Joseph Serna, "California Breaks Heat Record Since Measurements Began in 1895," Los Angeles Times, 12 September 2014; Joe Romm, "NASA: Hottest August Globally Since Records Began in 1880," Climate Progress, 15 September 2014; SAPA, "The Heat Is On: August Hottest Month," IOL, 19 September 2014.

10   Jean-Marie Robin et al., "Death Toll Exceeded 70,000 During the Summer of 2003," National Center for Biotechnology Information, 31 December 2007; "Sizzling Temperatures Break UK Record," BBC News, 11 August 2003.

11   "Record-breaking 2010 Eastern European/Russian Heatwave," Science Daily, 18 March 2011; Jeff Masters, "Extreme Heat Wave Hits the Middle East and Africa," WunderBlog, 24 June 2010; "High temp Recorded at Lowest Spot on Earth: The Dead Sea," CCTV.com, 25 October 2012.

12   Jeff Masters, "Historic Heat Wave Brings Australia Its Hottest Average Temperature on Record," WunderBlog, 8 January 2013; "Australia's Climate 'On Steroids' after Record-Breaking Summer," Telegraph, 4 March 2013; Emily Atkin, "'Climate Change Is Here': Australia Experiences Hottest Two Years Ever Recorded," Climate Progress, 2 June 2014.

13   Andrew Breiner, "Siberia, the Newest Hot Spot," Climate Progress, 6 April 2013; Justin Grieser, "Austria Sets New All-Time Temperature as European Heat Wave Hits Peak," Washington Post, 9 August 2013; Nick Wiltgen, "Shanghai Still Broiling as Deadly, Relentless Heat Wave Grips China," Weather Channel, 14 August 2013.

14   Joanna M. Foster, "Record-Breaking Heat Grips India, Causing Blackouts And Riots," Climate Progress, 10 June 2014; Eric Holthaus, "Earth Just Finished Its Warmest Quarter-Year Ever," Slate, 15 July 2014.

15   Joe Romm, "Mother Nature Is Just Getting Warmed Up: June 2011 Heat Records Crushing Cold Records by 13 to 1," Climate Progress, 11 June 2011.

16   "New Research Finds that Most Monthly Heat Records Today are Due to Global Warming," Skeptical Science, 30 January 2013; Joe Romm, "Nature Stunner: As Climate Change Speeds Up, the Number of Extremely Hot Days Is Soaring," 26 February 2014, referring to Sonia I. Seneviratne et al., "No Pause in the Increase of Hot Temperatures," Nature Climate Change, 26 February 2014.

17   NOAA National Weather Service, Office of Climate, Water, and Weather Services, 2012.

18   "Droughts and Heat Waves," Infoplease; Katie Valentine, "Extreme Heat Is Proving Deadly in Sweden," Climate Progress, 23 October 2013.

19   Shaoni Bhattacharya, "European Heatwave Caused 35,000 Deaths," New Scientist, 10 October 2003; Jean-Marie Robin et al., "Death Toll Exceeded 70,000 During the Summer of 2003," Comptes Rendus Bilogies, February 2008.

20   Jeff Masters, "Over 15,000 Likely Dead in Russian Heat Wave," Dr. Jeff Masters' WunderBlog, 9 August 2010; Ricardo Machado Trigo, "The 2010 Russian Heat Wave," April 2012.

21   Alexander White, "The Blackouts during Australia's Heatwave Didn't Happen by Accident," Guardian, 27 January 2014.

22   Robert Scribbler, "China Falls under Suspicion of Covering Up Deaths as Ocean Heat Dome Expands to Blanket Korea and Japan," WordPress.com, 13 August 2013.

23   Tom Bawden, "Heatwave Death Toll: Up to 760 Killed and Total May Double as Temperatures above 30C Set to Continue," Independent, 18 July 2013; Ryan Koronowski, "Intense Heat Wave in India Brings Sunstroke Deaths, Electric Grid Meltdown, and Spoiled Fruit," Climate Progress, 29 May 2013.

24   Joanna M. Foster, "Deaths from Heat Waves May Increase Ten Times by Mid-Century," Climate Progress, 8 November 2013; citing Jianyong Wu et al., "Estimation and Uncertainty Analysis of Impacts of Future Heat Waves on Mortality in the Eastern United States," Environmental Health Perspectives, January 2014.

25   Mex Cooper, "Death Toll Soared during Victoria's Heatwave," *The Age*, 6 April 2009; Sarah Perkins, "It's a Scorcher: New Site Tracks Heatwaves across Australia," *The Conversation*, 19 December 2013; Katie Valentine, "Heat-Related Deaths in Australia Are Set to Quadruple by 2050," Climate Progress, 1 August 2013.

26   Katie Valentine, "Globally, Last Month Was the Fourth Hottest July on Record," Climate Progress, 18 August 2014; Christopher C. Burt, "July 2014 Global Weather Extremes Summary," Wunderground, 19 August 2014.

27   Joe Romm, "Must-Read IEA Report Explains What Must Be Done to Avoid 6 Degrees C Warming," Grist, 14 November 2008; David Chandler, "Climate Change Odds Much Worse Than Thought," MIT News Office, 19 May 2009; Joe Romm, "Science Stunner: Observations Support Predictions of Extreme Warming and Worse Droughts This Century," Climate Progress, 9 November 2012.

28   Thomas R. Karl et al., "Global Climate Change Impacts in the United States," *Global Change Research Program* (Cambridge: Cambridge University Press, 2009); Joe Romm, "Our Hellish Future: Definitive NOAA-led Report on U.S. Climate Impacts Warns of Scorching 9 to 111°F Warming Over Most of Inland U.S. by 2090," Climate Progress, 15 June 2009.

29   "Global Warming: Future Temperatures Could Exceed Livable Limits, Researchers Find," Science Daily, 4 May 2010.

30   Andrea Germanos, "2047: The Year the World Hits 'Climate Departure,'" Common Dreams, 9 October 2013.

31   Kevin Anderson, "Climate Change Beyond Dangerous – Brutal Numbers and Tenuous Hope," in Niclas Hällström, ed., *What Next? Volume III: Climate, Development and Equity*, September 2012: 16-40 (online book).

32   World Bank, *Turn Down the Heat: Why a 4°C World Must Be Avoided*," November 2012.

33   Bill McKibben, "We're Hot as Hell and We're Not Going to Take It Any More," Tom-Dispatch, 4 August 2010.

Chapter 3: Droughts and Wildfires

1   Joe Romm, "U.S. Southwest Could See a 60-Year Drought Like that of 12th Century – only Hotter – This Century," Climate Progress, 14 December 2010.

2   Kevin Trenberth quoted in Andrew Freedman, "Causes of Midwest Drought: La Nina and Global Warming Thought to Contribute to Dry Weather," Climate Central, 21 July 2012.

3   Aiguo Dai, "Drought Under Global Warming: A Review," *Wiley Interdisciplinary Reviews: Climate Change* 2 (2011).

4   Stephen Lacey, "Climate Change: How the Wet Will Get Wetter and the Dry Will Get Drier," Climate Progress, 5 September 2012.

5   Matt Kasper, "When It Rains, It Pours," Climate Progress, 31 July 2012.

6   David D. Breshears et al., "Regional Vegetation Die-Off in Response to Global-Change-Type Drought," *Proceedings of the National Academy of Sciences,* 2005; Joe Romm, "Must-Have PPT: The 'Global-Change-Type Drought and the Future of Extreme Weather," Climate Progress, 11 March 2009.

7   "World Water Day," UN Water, 22 March 2012; Joe Romm, "*Nature* Publishes My Piece on Dust-Bowlification and the Grave Threat It Poses to Food Security," Climate Progress, 26 October 2011.

8   Max Frankel, "Intensifying Midwestern Drought Threatens Farmers, Water Supplies," Climate Progress, 6 July 2012; Jeff Wilson, "U.S. Corn Growers Farming in Hell as Midwest Heat Spreads," Bloomberg, 9 July 2012.

9   Dashiell Bennett, "U.S. Declares the Largest Natural Disaster Area Ever Due to Drought," *Atlantic Wire*, 12 July 2012; Lisa Baertlein, "U.S. Food Banks Raise Alarm as Drought Dents Government Supplies," Reuters, 21 November 2012.

10   Joe Romm, "Desertification: The New Dust Bowl," *Nature*, 26 October 2011; Helmut Geist, *The Causes and Progression of Desertification* (Ashgate, 2005), 2; Joe Romm, "USGS on Dust-Bowlification: Drier Conditions Projected to Accelerate Dust Storms in

the U.S. Southwest," Climate Progress, 7 April 2011; Romm, "Dust Bowlification Hits Eastern Australia – Next Stop the U.S. Southwest," Climate Progress, 24 September 2009.

11   James West, "How Climate Change Makes Wildfires Worse," *Mother Jones*, 13 June 2013.

12   Amanda Staudt, "Connecting the Dots: How Climate Change Is Fueling Western Wildfires," National Wildlife Federation, 20 June 2012.

13   Joe Romm, "NBC: 'Scientists . . . Said Climate Change Plays a Factor in What's Become a Deadly and Historic Fire Season," Climate Progress, 18 July 2013.

14   Joe Romm, "U.S. Sees Hottest 12 Months and Hottest Half Year on Record," Climate Progress, 9 July 2012; Stephen Lacey, "2012 U.S. Wildfire Activity Moves Past Ten-Year Average," Climate Progress, 5 December 2012; "America's War on Wildfires," *The Week*, 14 September 2012; Ari Phillips, "Wildfires in West Increasing Burn Area at Nearly One Denver Per Year, Study Finds," Climate Progress, 22 April 2014; Rebecca Leber, "Dry Conditions Fuel an Alaska Wildfire That's Bigger than Chicago," Climate Progress, 26 May 2014.

15   "Western Bark Beetles," U.S. Forest Service; Stephen R. Clarke and J. T. Nowak, "Southern Pine Beetle," Forest Insect & Disease Leaflet 49, USDA, April 2009.

16   Katie Valentine, "Bear-Human Encounters Are Expected to Rise Thanks to Climate Change," Climate Progress, 13 September 2013; Justin Gillis, "In New Jersey Pines, Trouble Arrives on Six Legs," *New York Times*, 1 December 2013.

17   Jeff Spross, "Climate Change Keeps Expanding Canada's Unprecedented Epidemic of Forest-Destroying Beetles," Climate Progress, 11 April 2013; Katie Valentine, "Pine Beetles Are Decimating New Jersey's Pine Barrens as Winters Get Warmer," Climate Progress 2 December 2013; Michael D. Lemonick, "Why Bark Beetles are Chewing Through U.S. Forests," Climate Central, 7 January 2013; James West, "Colorado Is Burning Even Worse Than Last Year," *Mother Jones*, 13 June 2013.

18   Seth Borenstein, "2007 a Year of Weather Records in US," Associated Press, 29 September 2007; Joe Romm, "2007: A Record-Setting U.S. Drought Year," Climate Progress, 16 October 2007.

19   Carey Gillam, "Drought Deepens in South; Texas Driest in Century," Reuters, 11 August 2011.

20   Andrew Freedman, "2012 Drought Will Probably Last through Winter in the Midwest, Says U.S. Monitor," Climate Central, 29 November 2012; "State of the Climate Drought September 2012," National Climatic Data Center, NOAA, 15 October 2012.

21   Jeff Spross, "A Dry Spring: Drought Expands in Texas and Florida," Climate Progress, 11 March 2013; Daniel Yawitz, "U.S. Drought Intensifies in Texas and Florida," Climate Central, 7 March 2013.

22   R. Leigh Coleman, "Global Warming: Now Real to Most Americans," *Christian Post*, 16 July 2011; Christopher R. Schwalm et al., "Scientists: Widespread Annual Drought Set to Become the 'New Normal,'" *New York Times*, 11 August 2012.

23   Kiley Kroh, "California Gripped by Driest Year Ever – with No Relief in Sight," Climate Progress, 27 December 2013; Steven Heimoff, "How Bad is California's Drought?" 17 June 2013; Paul Rogers, "California Drought: Feds Say Farmers Won't Get Any Central Valley Project Water this Year," *San Jose Mercury News*, 21 February 2014; Sharon Bernstein, "Rain Soaks California Causing Floods, but Won't End Drought," Reuters, 1 March 2014; "Federal Water Allocation for Drought-Stricken California Farms Cut to Zero," Reuters, 21 February 2014.

24   Emily Atkin, "California Is Now Experiencing Its Most Severe Drought Ever Recorded," Climate Progress, 1 August 2014.

25   Jacob O. Sewall and Lisa Cirbus Sloan, *Geophysical Research Letters*, 2 March 2004; Joe Romm, "Leading Scientists Explain How Climate Change Is Worsening California's Epic Drought," Climate Progress, 31 January 2014; Sherwood Rowland, Nobel Prize acceptance speech, 1995.

26   "Raging California Wildfire Threatens More of Yosemite," NBC News, 25 August 2013; Katie Valentine, "'Mother Nature Turned Off the Spigot': California Wildfires Fueled

by 'Remarkable' Dry Weather Conditions," Climate Progress, 3 May 2013; Joanna M. Foster, "California 2013 Wildfire Season Goes Out with a Blaze," Climate Progress, 17 December 2013.

27   Ari Phillips, "More Than 20,000 Evacuated as California Spring Turns to Summer of Fire," Climate Progress, 15 May 2014; Eric Holthaus, "Get Used to the Flames: California's 'Fire Season' Is Basically Year-Round Now," Slate, 24 April 2014; Rong-Gong Lin II, Los Angeles Times, 2 August 2014; Katie Orr, "California Dealing with Unprecedented Fire Season," Capitol Public Radio, 15 September 2014.

28   Michael Castellon, "Texas Wildfires," Fiscal Notes, Window on State Government, 2013; Marty Toohey, "Water Official: Drought Is Worst Central Texas Has Experienced," American-Statesman, 3 October 2013; "Texas Wildfires: 2011 Officially Worst Season in State's History," HuffPost Green, 19 January 2012.

29   Mark Peters, "Drinking Water Runs Low as Dry Conditions Drag On," Washington Post, 7 June 2013; "Tremendously Dry Start to 2014 Intensifies Drought," ICRA, 2014.

30   Andrew Freedman, "The Climate Context behind the Deadly Arizona Wildfire," Climate Central, 1 July 2013.

31   Tom Kenworthy, "Déjà Vu Fire Season Off to a Roaring Start in Colorado," Climate Progress, 12 June 2013; West, "Colorado Is Burning Even Worse."

32   Andrew Satter, "Oregon's Massive Wildfires, as Seen through Google Glass," Climate Progress, 11 September 2013; Lynne Terry, "Oregon Department of Forestry Experiences Record-Breaking Wildfire Season," Oregonian, 27 January 2014.

33   Joanna M. Foster, "Idaho Wildfire Rages On as Media Avoids Mentioning Climate Change," 19 August 2013; "Firefighters Move Out as Beaver Creek Fire Dies Down," Idaho Press-Tribune, 26 August 2013; "Idaho Residents Flee From Encroaching Blazes," Associated Press, 16 August 2012.

34   Emily Atkin, "In Washington State, the 20114 Wildfire Season Has Been 6 Times Worse than Normal," Climate Progress, 12 September 2014.

35   "The Extended Reach of Australian Drought," Nature, 1 March 2012; "Australia's Dry Horrors 'Worst for 1000 Years,'" New Zealand Herald, 8 November 2008; Rachel Nowak, "Australia – the Continent that Ran Dry," New Scientist, 13 June 2007; Rachel Kleinman, "No More Drought: It's a 'Permanent Dry,'" The Age, 7 September 2007.

36   Asa Wahlquist, "Melbourne Suffers as Drought in Southern Australia Declared Worst on Record," The Australian, 10 October 2008; Andy Coghlan, "Australia's Decade-Long Drought Ends," New Scientist, 1 May 2012; Jeff Spross, "'Sprawling Heat Wave of Historical Proportions' Brings 'Horrendous' Wildfires to Australia," Climate Progress, 8 January 2013.

37   Joanna M. Foster, "UN Officials Speak Out on Climate Change as Australian Drought Deepens," 9 March 2014; Blair Trewin, "Drought Conditions Return to Australia's Eastern States," The Conversation, 5 December 2013; Ari Phillips, "Australia Becomes First Country To Repeal Carbon Price — Too Bad It Was Working," Climate Progress, 17 July 2014.

38   Reese Ewing, "Brazil's Coffee Belt Grapples with Rare Threat: Dry Heat," Reuters, 12 February 2014; Kenneth Rapoza, "Brazil Loses Billions as Crops Reduced by Wacky Weather," Forbes, 3 March 2014; "More than 140 Brazilian Cities Ration Water," Associated Press, 15 February 2014; Emily Atkin, "Amid Epic Drought, South America's Largest City Is Running Out of Water," 7 February 2014; Katie Valentine, "Amazonian Smokestack? The Rainforest's Dry Season Is Three Weeks Longer Now than It Was 30 Years Ago," Climate Progress, 22 October 2013; Maryum Fahran, "Will the 2014 FIFA World Cup End in a Blackout?" Damage Assessment, 23 June 2014.

39   Katie Valentine, "Amazonian Smokestack?" Climate Progress, 22 October 2013; "Study Finds Severe Climate Jeopardizing Amazon Forest," NASA Jet Propulsion Laboratory, 17 January 2013; Becky Oskin, "Global Warming Forecast for Amazon Rain Forest: Dry and Dying," LiveScience, 21 October 2013.

40   Andrea Germanos, "Canada's Harper, Australia's Abbott Forge 'Climate Deniers Club,'" Common Dreams, 10 June 2014.

41   Jeff Spross, "Historic Wildfires Burn Through Canada as Sub-Arctic Forests Heat Up,"

Climate Progress, 25 August 2014; Andrew Freedman, "Arctic's Boreal Forests Burning at 'Unprecedented' Rate," Climate Central, 22 July 2013; "State of Emergency in Siberia's Permafrost Region due to Wildfires," Daily Kos, 15 July 2014.

42   "China Drought 2012: Three-Year-Long Dry Spell Continues in Southwest," *International Business Times*, 6 April 2012; Eric Baculinao, "Chinese Expert: Drought Is a 'Warming Signal,'" NBC News, 31 May 2011.

43   "Central, North China Hurt by Drought," English News, 31 July 2014.

44   Mamta Badkar, "Droughts: Bad for the US, Catastrophic for India," Business Insider, 16 August 2012; Vandana Shiva, "Climate Change, Drought and India's Looming Food and Water Crisis," *Current*, 14 August 2009.

45   Rajendra Jadhav, "As Drought Looms in India, Fear for Its Cattle," *Reuters*, 12 August 2012; Kathy Daigle, "India Frets Over Delayed Monsoon Damaging Crops," Associated Press, 24 July 2012 ; "Drought in Maharashtra," Act Alliance, 10 April 2013.

46   Michael McCarthy, "The Century of Drought," *Independent*, 4 October 2006.

47   Aiguo Dai, "Drought Under Global Warming: A Review," *Wiley Interdisciplinary Reviews: Climate Change* 2 (2011): 45-65, at 60.

48   Clay Dillow, "The 2000-2004 North American Drought Was the Worst in 800 Years," POPSCI, 7 September 2012.

49   Joe Romm, "NOAA Stunner: Climate Change 'Largely Irreversible for 1000 Years,'" Climate Progress, 26 January 2009.

50   Joe Romm, "New Study Puts the 'Hell' in Hell and High Water," Climate Progress, 20 October 2010.

51   Rachel Warren, "The Role of Interactions in a World Implementing Adaptation and Mitigation Solutions to Climate Change," in Mark New et al., "Four Degrees and Beyond: The Potential for a Global Temperature Increase of Four Degrees and Its Implications," *Philosophical Transactions of the Royal Society*, 369/1934 (November 2011), 217-41.

52   Damian Carrington, "Climate Change Scientists Warn of 4C Global Temperature Rise," *Guardian*, 28 November 2010.

53   Joe Romm, "Science on the Risks of Climate Engineering," Climate Progress, 29 August 2009. For his statement about 0.1 percent of our GDP, see Romm, "McKinsey 2008 Research in Review: Stabilizing at 450 ppm Has a Cost Near Zero," Climate Progress, 29 December 2008.

Chapter 4: Storms

1   "Study: Global Warming Could Explain Why Northeast Is Seeing More, and Fiercer, Rainstorms," Associated Press, 5 April 2010.

2   Justin Gillis, "Study Indicates a Greater Threat of Extreme Weather," *New York Times*, 26 April 2012; Michael D. Lemonick, "Climate Change Has Intensified the Global Water Cycle," Climate Central, 26 April 2012.

3   Joe Romm, "AP: Calling Deadly Tennessee Superstorm an 'Unprecedented Rain Event' Did 'Not Capture the Magnitude,'" Climate Progress, 3 May 2010.

4   Joe Romm, "Exclusive Interview: NCAR's Trenberth on the Link between Global Warming and Extreme Deluges," Climate Progress, 14 June 2010.

5   Brenda Goodman, "Drought-Stricken South Facing Tough Choices," *New York Times*, 16 October 2007; Joe Romm, "Hell and High Water Hits Georgia," Climate Progress, 23 September 2009; Robbie Brown, "Georgians Grappling with Flood Damage," *New York Times*, 24 September 2009.

6   Jeff Goodell, "Climate Change and the End of Australia," *Rolling Stone*, 13 October 2011.

7   Adam Vaughan, "UK's Year of Drought and Flooding Unprecedented, Experts Say," *Guardian*, 18 October 2012.

8   John Eligon, "After Drought, Rains Plaguing Midwest Farms," *New York Times*, 9 June 2013; Ryan Koronowski, "'Biblical' Amounts of Rainfall Slam Colorado, Causing Death, Destruction, and Massive Flooding," Climate Progress, 13 September 2013; Kiley Kroh, "After the Flood: How Climate Change Changed One Colorado Community Forever,"

Climate Progress, 10 October 2013.

9   "Line of Deadly Storms Moves through the South," Associated Press, 3 May 2010; Jeff Masters, "Flooding from Record Rains Kills 11 in Tennessee," WunderBlog, 3 May 2010; Peter Miller, "Weather Gone Wild," *National Geographic*, September 2012; Joe Romm, "Stunning NOAA Map of Tennessee's 1000-Year Deluge," Climate Progress, 26 May 2010.

10 Juan Cole, "The Great Pakistani Deluge Never Happened. Don't Tune In, It's Not Important," TomDispatch, 9 September 2010; "UN Chief Ban Ki-Moon: Pakistan Floods Are Worst Disaster I've Ever Seen," Associated Press, 15 August 2010.

11 "California Rain Shatters Records, and More Is Coming," Associated Press, 21 December 2010.

12 "Extreme Weather Endangers Food Security: 2010-11: A Grim Foretaste of Future Suffering and Hunger?" Oxfam Media Briefing, 28 November 2011.

13 Jason Samenow, "National Weather Service: Ft. Belvoir Rain Was More than 1 in 1,000 Year Event, 'Off the Charts,'" Capital Weather Gang, *Washington Post*, 9 December 2011.

14 "Flooding Kills 150 People in South Russia," Moscow, CNN.com, 7 July 2012.

15 Christopher C. Burt, "Extreme Rainfall Event in Western Australia," Weather Underground, 17 December 2012.

16 Palko Karasz and Melissa Eddy, "Danube Crests Near Record Level in Budapest," *New York Times*, 10 June 2013; Kiley Kroh, "Thousands Flees as Record Floods Inundate Central Europe," Climate Progress, 4 June 2013; "Worst Flood in Decade Causes Havoc in NE China," Xinhua, 20 August 2013; Ryan Koronowski, "You Can See the Historic Flooding on the Chinese-Russian Border from Space," Climate Progress, 10 September 2013.

17 Katie Valentine, "While the West Dries Up, the East Is Drenched," Climate Progress, 1 May 2014; Sean Breslin and Jon Erdman, "Louisiana, Texas Flooding: Caskets Wash Away as Water Level Rises; EF1 Tornado Confirmed," Weather.com, 29 May 2014.

18 Dennis Hoey, "Record Rainstorm Causes 'Life Threatening' Flooding, Road Closures in Southern Maine," *Portland Press Herald*, 14 August 2014; Katie Valentine, "The Midwest Receives Two Months of Rainfall in One Week," Climate Progress, 23 June 2014; Pete Spotts, "Heavy Rain and Floods: The 'New Normal' with Climate Change?" *Christian Science Monitor*, 14 August 2014; Joel Kurth, "A Vortex of Weird Weather: 2014 Starts Cold and Snowy, but Gives Way to Deluges of Rain," *Detroit News*, 13 August 2014; Matt Daniel, "Unusual Precipitation Patterns in the U.S.," EarthSky Blog, 20 August 2014; Katie Valentine, "Flooding in Arizona Prompts Dramatic Rescues," Climate Progress, 19 August 2014.

19 Melissa Turtinen, "Slow-Moving Storms Head East after Dumping Heavy Rain in Western Minnesota," Bring Me the News, 17 August 2014; "Cleanup Begins after Storms Dump Heavy Rain on Parts of Arizona; Phoenix Cactus Farm Hit Hard," Associated Press, 20 August 2014.

20 Joanna M. Foster, "'Most Exceptional Period of Rainfall in 248 Years' in the U. K. Is 'Consistent with Climate Change,'" Climate Progress, 10 February 2014; Joanna M. Foster, "Years of Drought Exacerbate Deadly Floods in Afghanistan," Climate Progress, 29 April 2014; Andrea Thompson, "The Climate Context for 'Unprecedented' Balkans Flooding," Climate Central, 20 May 2014; Ari Phillips, "More than One Million Suffer Worst Flooding in Over a Century," Climate Progress, 18 May 2014; Robert Scribbler, "Climate Change and a Mangled Jet Stream: Historic May Deluge for Bosnia and Serbia," robertscribbler.wordpress.com, 15 May 2014.

21 "Flooding of Europe Continues," Mail Online, 22 August 2014.

22 Kurth, "A Vortex of Weird Weather."

23 Joe Romm, "Jet Stream Changes Driving Extreme Weather Linked Again to Global Warming, Arctic Ice Loss," Climate Progress, 19 August 2014.

24 "Climate Study: Extreme Rain Storms in Midwest Have Doubled in Last 50 Years, Often Leading to Worsened Flooding," Natural Resources Defense Council, 16 May 2012.

25 "Extreme Downpours Up 30 Percent: Scientists Link Trend to Global Warming," Envi-

ronment America, 31 July 2012.

26   Peter Miller, "Weather Gone Wild," *National Geographic*, September 2012.

27   "Increases in Extreme Rainfall Linked to Global Warming," University of Adelaide, 1 February 2013; Seth Westra et al., "Global Increasing Trends in Annual Maximum Daily Precipitation," *Journal of Climate*, 2012; University of Adelaide, "Après Nous, Le Déluge: Extreme Rainfall Rises with Global Temperatures," Climate Progress, 17 February 2013.

28   Joe Romm, "AP: Calling Deadly Tennessee Superstorm an 'Unprecedented Rain Event' Did 'Not Capture the Magnitude," Climate Progress, 3 May 2010.

29   Masters, quoted in Bradford Plumer, "What The Snowpocalypse Tells Us About Global Warming," *New Republic*, 10 February 2010.

30   Kathryn Prociv, "Three Year Anniversary: Snowpocalypse of December 18-19, 2009," *Washington Post*, 19 December 2012; "'Snowmageddon': Obama Names Blizzard," Huffington Post, 6 February 2010; Jeff Masters, "Top U.S. Weather Event of 2010: Snowmageddon," Jeff Masters' WunderBlog, 5 January 2011.

31   "Alaska Town Digging Its Way Out after Record 18 Feet of Snow," CNN, 9 January 2012.

32   "Snow Blankets Iran," NASA Earth Observatory, 6 February 2014.

33   James B. Eisner et al., "The Increasing Intensity of the Strongest Tropical Cyclones," *Nature*, 4 September 2008: 92-95; Joe Romm, "Why Global Warming Means Killer Storms Worse than Katrina and Gustav, Part 1," Climate Progress, 31 August 2008; Erin Overbey, "Sandy and the Rise of Extreme Weather," *New Yorker*, 1 November 2012.

34   "What is the Link between Hurricanes and Global Warming?"; Quirin Schiermeier, "Hurricanes Are Getting Fiercer: Global Warming Blamed for Growth in Storm Intensity," *Nature*, 3 September 2008.

35   Robert Leben et al., "CU-Boulder Researchers Chart Katrina's Growth in Gulf of Mexico," University of Colorado at Boulder, 1 March 2009; Romm, "Why Global Warming Means Killer Storms Worse than Katrina and Gustav."

36   "Facts about Katrina: Surviving Katrina," Discovery Channel, 2008; Dan D. Swenson and Bob Marshall, "Flash Flood: Hurricane Katrina's Inundation of New Orleans," *Times-Picayune*, 14 May 2005; Joe Romm, "100 Katrinas and the Launch of Climate Progress," 29 August 2006.

37   Tropical cyclones (also called hurricanes and typhoons) have a warm core, while extratropical cyclones have a cold core. Cold-core cyclones can be very destructive and can have their destructiveness increased by global warming, as can be illustrated by the Great Midwest Cyclone of 2010: In October 2010, the US Midwest's strongest cyclone – complete with hail, torrential rains, near-hurricane force winds, snow, and over 60 tornadoes – struck Minnesota and Wisconsin ("Strong Extratropical Cyclone Over the US Midwest," Earth Observatory, 29 October 2010; "Strongest Storm Ever Recorded in the Midwest Smashes All-Time Pressured Records," Dr. Jeff Masters' WunderBlog, 27 October 2010). A Minnesota meteorologist said, "Welcome to the Land of 10,000 Weather Extremes" (quoted in Joe Romm, "'Weather Bomb' Hits Midwest with Power of Major Hurricane," 27 October 2010). This storm was special in having, in Masters' words, "the lowest barometric pressure readings ever recorded in the continental United States, except for from hurricanes and nor'easters affecting the Atlantic seaboard" (Masters, "Strongest Storm"). In addition, this storm was huge: While the area of low pressure was centered over the Upper Midwest, "the storm reached from the Gulf of Mexico into Canada, and from the Rocky Mountains to the Atlantic Ocean" ("Strong Extratropical Cyclone").

38   "Cyclone Nargis," *New York Times*, 30 April 2009; Steve Scolnik, "Super Cyclone Giri Strongest on Record to Hit Myanmar," Climate Central, 22 October 2010; "Cyclone Nargis Embodied the 'Perfect Storm,'" Associated Press, 8 May 2008.

39   Scolnik, "Super Cyclone Giri Strongest on Record"; Lisa Schlein, "Burma Devastated by Cyclone Giri," Voice of America, 1 November 2010.

40   Meraiah Foley, "Australians Take Cover as Cyclone Lashes Coast," 3 February 2011; "Cyclone Damage to Great Barrier Reef," *Australian Geographic*, 8 March 2011.

41   Bill McKibben, "Global Warming's Terrifying New Math," *Rolling Stone*, 19 June 2012.

42   Suzanne Goldenberg, "Superstorm Sandy," *Guardian*, 21 December 2012.

43   Bryan Norcross, "The Sandy Paradox," Wunderground.com, 26 October 2012.

44   Bill McKibben, "Sandy's Real Name," EcoWatch, 30 November 2012; "Sandy Is the Largest Hurricane to Ever Form in the Atlantic Basin (INFOGRAPHIC)," Huffington Post, 30 October 2012, quoting the National Hurricane Center.

45   Seth Borenstein, "Forecasters Warn East Coast about 'Frankenstorm,'" Associated Press, 25 October 2012; "CNN Bans 'Frankenstorm' from Hurricane Sandy Coverage," Huffington Post, 26 October 2012.

46   Joe Romm, "CNN Bans Term 'Frankenstorm,' But It's a Good Metaphor," Climate Progress, 28 October 2012.

47   Bill McKibben, "'Frankenstorm' Is Just Right for Hurricane Sandy," Daily Beast, 30 October 12.

48   Dan Satterfield, "What Those Who Understand Atmospheric Physics Are Talking about after Sandy," Dan's Wild Wild Science Journal, 1 November 2012.

49   This is Fiona Harvey's paraphrase in her "Extreme Weather Will Strike as Climate Change Takes Hold, IPCC Warns," *Guardian*, 18 November 2011.

50   Bill McKibben, "Sandy's Real Name," EcoWatch, 30 November 2012; Joe Romm, "NOAA: Warming-Driven Sea Level Rise to Make Sandy-Type Storm Surges the Norm on East Coast," Climate Progress, 5 September 2013.

51   Jeff Spross, "Super Typhoon Haiyan Death Toll Tops 5,200, Rebuilding Cost Could Approach $6 Billion," Climate Progress, 22 November 2013; Ari Phillips, "What Typhoon Haiyan Means for Climate Change – and the UN's Ongoing Climate Talks," Climate Progress, 12 November 2013; Andrew Freedman, "Typhoon Haiyan's Deadly Surge Noted in Warsaw Talks," Climate Central, 11 November 2013.

52   Emily Atkin, "Tropical Cyclone Hits Australia as 'One of the Most Powerful Storms' in 'Living Memory,'" Climate Progress, 11 April 2014; Jeff Masters, "Amanda Peaks as Strongest May Eastern Pacific Hurricane on Record: 155 mph Winds," Weather Underground, 27 May 2014.

53   "Hawaii Braces for 'Unprecedented Double Whammy' of Two Major Storms within a Few Days," Associated Press, ABC News, 6 August 2014.

54   Jeff Masters, "2011: Year of the Tornado," WunderBlog, 27 December 2011.

55   Jeff Masters, "Top Ten U.S. Weather Events of 2012," WunderBlog, 21 December 2012; "Heavy Snow and Largest Christmas Tornado Outbreak on Record Slam U.S.," Wunderblog, 26 December 2012.

56   Brendan O'Brien, "Oklahoma Tornado Was Widest Ever Measured in U.S. – NWS," Reuters, 4 June 2013.

57   Jeff Masters, "Violent Tornado Devastates Moore, Oklahoma," WunderBlog, 21 May 2013; Masters, "Moore Tornado Likely to be One of the Five Most Damaging Tornadoes in History," 21 May 2013; "Midwest Tornado Outbreak Recap: Map of the Trail of Destruction," Weather Channel, 28 November 2013.

58   Jon Erdman, "Plains, South Tornado Outbreak Recap: April 27-29, 2014," Weather Channel, 7 May 2014; Michael Avok, "Deadly Tornado All but Wipes Nebraska Village Off the Map," Reuters, 17 June 2014.

59   David A. Fahrenthold, "More Tornadoes, or Just Better Tracking?" *Washington Post*, 21 May 2008; Chris Mooney, "Is Global Warming Causing More Tornadoes? Not So Fast, Says Harold Brooks," DeSmogBlog, 26 May 2011; Mark Landsbaum, "Global Warming Causes Tornadoes? Oops. Not Exactly," *Orange County Register*, 6 April 2011.

60   Andrea Thompson, "NASA: Global Warming to Cause More Severe Tornadoes, Storms," Live Science, 4 September 2007.

61   *Science News*, 2007; Paul Epstein, "An Era of Tornadoes: How Global Warming Causes Wild Winds," *Atlantic*, 8 July 2011; Trenberth quoted in Joe Romm, "Update: Tornadoes, Extreme Weather and Climate Change, Revisited," Climate Progress, 4 March 2012; Becky Oskin, "Stronger Tornadoes May Be Menacing US," LiveScience, 11 December 2013; Jill Elish, "Researchers Develop Models to Correct Tornado Record," *Florida State University*, 5 September 2013; Kathleen Haughney, "New Research Links

Tornado Strength, Frequency to Climate Change," Florida State 24/7, 6 August 2014.

62   Joe Romm, "100 Katrinas and the Launch of Climate Progress," 29 August 2006.

63   Joe Romm, "Climate Panel Stunner: Avoiding Climate Catastrophe Is Super Cheap – but Only if We Act Now," Climate Progress, 13 April 2014. (Romm wrote "a couple decades ago," but I am using the estimate of 30 years; see n. 34 of the Introduction.)

Chapter 5: Sea-Level Rise

1   Orrin H. Pilkey and Rob Young, *The Rising Sea* (Shearwater, 2009).

2   James Hansen, "Cowards in Our Democracies: Part 1," Climate Progress, 27 January 2012.

3   A major study published in 2014 put the rise from unmitigated warming in the range of 0.7 to 1.2 meters by 2100, hence higher than the IPCC's 2013 estimate; Benjamin P. Horton, Stefan Rahmstorf, et al., "Expert Assessment of Sea-Level Rise by AD 2100 and AD 2300," *Quaternary Science Review*, 15 January 2014.

4   Stefan Rahmstorf, "Sea Level in the 5th IPCC Report," Real Climate, 15 October 2013. In a 2012 study, Rahmstorf had shown that the sea levels were rising 60 percent faster than the IPCC had projected (Joe Romm, "Study: Sea Levels Rising 60% Faster Than Projected, Planet Keeps Warming As Expected," Climate Progress, 28 November 2012).

5   Rob Young and Orrin Pilkey, "How High Will Seas Rise? Get Ready for Seven Feet," Environment 360, 14 January 2010; Lauren Morello and ClimateWire, "Polar Ice Sheets Melting Faster than Predicted," *Scientific American*, 9 March 2011.

6   Michael McCarthy, "Rising Sea Level Threatens 'Hundreds' of Caribbean Resorts, Says UN Report," *Independent*, 1 December 2010; "Rising Sea Levels Threaten Island Nations," Voice of America, 25 May 2011.

7   Joanna I. Lewis, "China," in Daniel Moran, ed., *Climate Change and National Security: A Country-Level Analysis* (Washington DC: Georgetown University Press, 2010): 9-16, at 11.

8   "Sea Levels Rising Fast on U.S. East Coast," *National Geographic News*, 25 June 2012; Michael D. Lemonick, "The Secret of Sea Level Rise: It Will Vary Greatly by Region," Yale Environment 360, 22 March 2010; Mark Hertsgaard, *Hot: Living Through the Next Fifty Years on Earth* (New York: Houghton Mifflin Harcourt, 2011), 42; Paul Brown, "Ice Caps Melting Fast: Say Goodbye to the Big Apple?" AlterNet , 9 October 2007.

9   Emily Badger, "These Scary Maps Explain What Sea Level Rise Will Mean in Boston," *Atlantic Cities*, 5 February 2013.

10   Baden Copeland et al., "What Could Disappear," *New York Times*, 24 November 2012. Other cities on the list are: Newport News 8%, Savannah 8%, Norfolk 9%, Boston 9%, Tacoma 10%, Wilmington 11%, Tampa Bay 18%, Charleston 19%, Jersey City 20%, Virginia Beach 21%, Cambridge 26%, Huntington Beach 27%, St. Petersburg 32%, Atlantic City 62%, Galveston 68%, and New Orleans 88%.

11   Jeff Goodell, "Goodbye, Miami," *Rolling Stone*, 20 June 2013.

12   Lester Brown, "Raging Storms, Rising Seas Swell Ranks of Climate Refugees," Grist, 16 August 2011.

13   Pilkey and Young, "How High?"

14   J. L. Chen, "Contribution of Ice Sheet and Mountain Glacier Melt to Recent Sea Level Rise," *Nature Geoscience*, 2 June 2013; "Ice Caps," All about Glaciers, National Snow & Ice Data Center. (Ice caps are also called "miniature ice sheets," but they can be pretty big: By definition, an "ice cap" can be up to 50,000 square kilometers. For example, the mass of ice on Iceland is an ice cap.) Orrin Pilkey, "Sea Level Rise and the World's Beaches," Coastal Care, 2011.

15   "Melting Glaciers Raise Sea Level," Science Daily, 14 November 2012; E. Rignot et al., "Acceleration of the Contribution of the Greenland and Antarctic Ice Sheets to Sea Level Rise," *Geophysical Research Letters*, 4 March 2011.

16   "Are Glaciers Growing or Retreating?" Skeptical Science, 17 December 2011.

17   Robin McKie, "Rate of Arctic Summer Sea Ice Loss is 50% Higher than Predicted," *Observer*, 11 August 2012; Neven Acropolis with Kevin McKinney, "Why the Arctic Sea Ice Death Spiral Matters," Climate Progress, 2012.

18   Simon Butler, "Arctic Melting: Is Global Warming Going into Overdrive?" Green Left Weekly, 23 August 2012; Seth Borenstein , "Ominous Arctic Melt Worries Experts ," Associated Press, 11 December 2007; Josefino C. Comiso et al., "Accelerated Decline in the Arctic Sea Ice Cover," *Geophysical Research Letters*, Vol. 35 (2007).

19   Acropolis with McKinney, "Why the Arctic Sea Ice Death Spiral Matters; Michael Lemonick, "Arctic Has Lost Enough Ice to Cover Canada and Alaska," Climate Central, 12 September 2012; John Vidal, "Arctic Expert Predicts Final Collapse of Sea Ice within Four Years," *Guardian*, 17 September 2012.

20   Damian Carrington, "Polar Bears: Politics Trumps Precaution Every Time," *Guardian*, 7 March 2013. The polar bear was "the first species added to the endangered and threatened species list solely because of threats from global warming" ("Obama Administration Again Proposes Polar Bear Extinction Plan," *Living Green Magazine*, April 20, 2012). Because the sea-ice, on which the bears depend, is rapidly disappearing, "They're drowning and starving" (Kim Murphy, "Polar Bear's Long Swim Illustrates Ice Melt," *Los Angeles Times*, January 29, 2011).

21   Ibid. See also Justin Gillis, "As Permafrost Thaws, Scientists Study the Risks," *New York Times*, 16 December 2011, and a film, "Arctic Methane: Why the Sea Ice Matters," featuring interviews with James Hansen and others.

22   Doug Struck,, "At the Poles, Melting Occurring at Alarming Rate," *Washington Post*, 22 October 2007.

23   Alan Buis, "Is a Sleeping Climate Giant Stirring in the Arctic?" NASA, 10 June 2013; Joe Romm, "The Hockey Stick Lives: Canadian Arctic Warming Unprecedented in 120,000 Years," Climate Progress, 27 January 2014.

24   Acropolis with McKinney, "Why the Arctic Sea Ice Death Spiral Matters"; Bill McKibben, "The Arctic Ice Crisis," *Rolling Stone*, 30 August 2012; Andrew Freedman, "Study: Greenland Melting Is More Pervasive, Adding to Sea Level Fears," Mashable, 16 March 2014.

25   Paul Brown, "Ice Caps Melting Fast: Say Goodbye to the Big Apple?" AlterNet , 9 October 2007.

26   The Greenland ice sheet covers an area of 708,000 square miles (1.83 million sq. km), while the Antarctic ice sheet covers 5.4 million sq. miles (14 million sq. km). See "Greenland Ice Sheet," Britannica Online Encyclopedia; "Quick Facts on Ice Sheets," National Snow & Ice Data Center.

27   "Greenland Rose Faster as 100 Billion Tons of Ice Melted Away," MSNBC, 13 December 2011; "Extreme Melting on Greenland Ice Sheet, Reports CCNY Team," City College of New York, 13 October 2011.

28   Joe Romm, "JPL Bombshell: Polar Ice Sheet Mass Loss Is Speeding Up, on Pace for 1 Foot Sea Level Rise by 2050," Climate Progress, 10 March 2011; Suzanne Goldenberg, "Speed of Greenland Melt Shocks Scientists," *Guardian*, 24 July 2012; Michael D. Lemonick, "Widespread Greenland Melting to Become the Norm in the Next Two Decades," Climate Central, 21 May 2013; Joe Romm, "Greenland and Antarctica 'May Be Vulnerable to Rapid Ice Loss through Catastrophic Disintegration,'" Climate Progress, 30 July 2013.

29   Joe Romm, "Greenland Ice Sheet 'Could Undergo a Self-Amplifying Cycle of Melting and Warming – Difficult to Halt,' Scientists Find," Climate Progress, 24 October 2011; Jason Box, "Greenland Ice Sheet Getting Darker," Meltfactor.org., 29 December 2011; Amy Hubbard, "Loss of Greenland Could Become Irreversible, Scientists Say," *Los Angeles Times*, 12 March 2012; Alexander Robinson et al., "Multistability and Critical Thresholds of the Greenland Ice Sheet," *Nature Climate Change*, 11 March 2012. Box is speaking about a permanent change, not the rapid but brief melting that happened in June 2012, which, scientists said, "occurs about every 150 years"; see Suzanne Goldenberg, "Speed of Greenland Melt Shocks Scientists," *Guardian,* 24 July 2012."

30   Joe Romm, "Science Stunner: Greenland Ice Melt Up Nearly Five-Fold Since Mid-1990s, Antarctica's Ice Loss Up 50% in Past Decade," Climate Progress, 30 November 2012; "Like Butter: Study Explains Surprising Acceleration of Greenland's Inland Ice," CIRES, 16 July 2013.

31   Joe Romm, "Redefining 'Glacial Pace.'"Joe Romm and Jeff Spross, "See Levels to Rise More than Expected Due to Warming-Driven Surge in Greenland Ice Loss," Climate Progress, 17 March 2014.

32   Joe Romm, "Redefining 'Glacial Pace': Greenland's Fastest-Moving Glacier Sets New Speed Record of 150 Feet a Day," 6 February 2014.

33   Steven Connor, "Fears of Faster Rising Global Sea Levels as 'Stable' Greenland Ice Sheet Starts to Melt," *Independent,* 16 March 2014; Stefano Salustri, "Greenland Ice Sheet Is Melting More Rapidly," Liberty Voice, 16 March 2014.

34   Becky Oskin, "Greenland Ice Sheet Loses Its Grip," CBS News, 17 March 2014.

35   Naomi Oreskes and Erik M. Conway, *Merchants of Doubt: How a Handful of Scientists Obscured the Truth of Issues from Tobacco Smoke to Global Warming* (New York: Bloomsbury, 2010), 265; James Hansen and Makiko Sato, "Update of Greenland Ice Sheet Mass Loss: Exponential?" 26 December 2012.

36   Quoted in McKibben, "The Arctic Ice Crisis," *Rolling Stone,* 30 August 2012.

37   Jeff Masters, "The Heat Is on in Greenland: Support the Dark Snow Project," 25 June 2014; Joe Romm, "Greenland and West Antarctic Ice Sheet Loss More than Doubled in Last Five Years," Climate Progress, 22 August 2014.

38   Joe Romm, "The Antarctic Ice Sheet Hits the Fan," Climate Progress, 14 January 2008; Romm, "Large Antarctic Glacier Thinning 4 Times faster than It Was 10 Years Ago," Climate Progress, 13 August 2009; Peter N. Spotts, "Little Time to Avoid Big Thaw, Scientists Warn," *Christian Science Monitor,* 24 March 2006.

39   Erik Conway, " Is Antarctica Melting?" NASA, *Jet Propulsion Laboratory,* 2010; Joe Romm, "Deep Ocean Heat Is Rapidly Melting Antarctic Ice," Climate Progress, 15 December 2010.

40   Conway, " Is Antarctica Melting?"

41   Michael Reilly, "First Signs of Melting Seen in East Antarctica," *Discovery News,* 23 November 2009; Ian Sample, "World's Largest Ice Sheet Melting Faster than Expected," *Guardian,* 22 November 2009; Conway, "Is Antarctica Melting?"

42   Romm, "Large Antarctic Glacier Thinning 4 Times Faster"; "West Antarctica Warming Three Times Faster than Global Average, Threatening to Destabilize this Unstable Ice Sheet," Climate Progress, 17 December 2012.

43   "Quick Facts on Ice Shelves," National Snow & Ice Data Center; R. Lindsey, "Collapse of the Larsen-B Ice Shelf," NASA Earth Observatory; "Antarctic Ice Shelf Disappears, Arctic Melting Rapidly," Environment News Service, 3 April 2009.

44   "West Antarctica Warming More than Expected," Atmos News, 23 December 2012; Denise Chow, "Warm Water under Antarctic Glacier Spurs Astonishing Rate of Melting," *NBC News,* 12 September 2013.

45   Ari Phillips, "Massive Antarctic Glacier Has Entered Irreversible Melt, Could Add Up to 1 Centimeter to Sea Level," Climate Progress, 13 January 2014; Laura Poppick, "Massive Antarctic Glacier Uncontrollably Retreating, Study Suggests," LiveScience, 16 January 2014.

46   Matt King, "Is Antarctica Losing or Gaining Ice?" Skeptical Science, 10 July 2013.

47   James Taylor, "Antarctic Sea Ice Sets Another Record," *Forbes,* 19 September 2012; Michael D. Lemonick, "Why Antarctic Sea Ice Is Growing," Weather Underground, 24 September 2013; Mark Robison, "Does Record Antarctic Sea Ice Refute Global Warming?" Fact Checker, RJM.com, 6 October 2012.

48   Rebecca Jacobson, "The Antarctic's Ice Paradox," PBS, 1 May 2013; "Accelerated Warming of the Southern Ocean and Its Impacts on the Hydrological Cycle and Sea Ice," *Proceedings of the National Academy of Sciences,* 16 August 2010; repeated in Judith Curry, "Why Is There So Much Antarctic Sea Ice?" Climate Etc., 3 February 2014.

49   Romm, "Greenland and West Antarctic Ice Sheet Loss More than Doubled"; King, "Is Antarctica Losing or Gaining Ice?"

50   "The Word: Sink or Swim," Colbert Report, 4 June 2012.

51   Joe Romm, "An Illustrated Guide to the Science of Global Warming Impacts: How We Know Inaction Is the Gravest Threat Humanity Faces," Climate Progress, 28 September 2011; "JPL Bombshell: Polar Ice Sheet Mass Loss Is Speeding Up, on Pace for 1 Foot

Sea Level Rise by 2050," Climate Progress, 10 March 2011; Brown, "Raging Storms, Rising Seas."

52   Andrew Breiner, "In Washington D.C., Record-breaking Floods Could Happen Every Year," 17 September 2014.

53   Hertsgaard, *Hot,* 35.

Chapter 6: Fresh Water Shortage

1   Fen Montaigne, "Water Pressure," *National Geographic*, September 2002; Justin Gillis, "Water Supply in a Warming World," Green Blog, *New York Times*, 12 November 2012; Quirin Schiermeier, "Water Risk as World Warms," *Nature*, 31 December 2013.

2   Maude Barlow and Tony Clark, *Blue Gold: The Fight to Stop the Corporate Theft of the World's Water* (New Press, 2002); Kimberly Dozier, "Global Trends 2030 Predicts Water Struggles and Climate Change Challenges," Associated Press, 10 December 2012; Juliette Jowit, "Water 'More Important than Oil' Businesses Told," *Guardian*, 26 February 2009.

3   Lester R. Brown, "Peak Water: What Happens when the Wells Go Dry?" Earth Policy Institute, 9 July 2013; Jeff Spross, "Study: Climate Change May Dry Up Important U.S. Reservoirs Like Lake Powell and Lake Mead," Climate Progress, 25 February 2013.

4   Lester Brown, "Melting Glaciers Mean Double Trouble for Water Supplies," *National Geographic*, 20 December 2011; Jon Gertner, "The Future Is Drying Up," *New York Times Magazine*, 21 October 2007.

5   As explained in Chapter 5, ice sheets are continental glaciers, but here "glaciers" (without an adjective) is used to refer only to smaller glaciers.

6   Mike Diferdinando, "Global Warming Threatens the Availability of Fresh Water around the Globe," Medill Reports, 11 October 2011; Lester Brown, *Plan B. 4.0: Mobilizing to Save Civilization*, Chapter 3, "Climate Change and Energy Transition: Melting Glaciers, Shrinking Harvests"; Brown, "Melting Glaciers Mean Double Trouble"; Ari Phillips, "Humans Overtake Ice Ages as Main Driver of Glacier Melt," Climate Progress, 15 August 2014.

7   Jessica Ellis, "Montana's Melting Glaciers: The Poster-Child for Climate Change," CNN, 6 October 2010; Anne Minard, "No More Glaciers in Glacier National Park by 2020?" *National Geographic News*, March 2, 2009; Joshua Frank, "Glacier National Park May Need a Name Change Soon," AlterNet, 20 January 2010. (Glaciers by definition require at least 25 acres of ice.)

8   Ellis, "Montana's Melting Glaciers."

9   Brown, "Melting Glaciers Mean Double Trouble."

10   Kirk Johnson, "Alaska Looks for Answers in Glacier's Summer Flood Surges," *New York Times*, 22 July 2013; Laura Poppick, "Melting Mendenhall Glacier Reveals Ancient Forest," HuffPost Green, 23 September 2013; Katie Moritz, "Climate Change Coming . . . to Glacier Center," *Juneau Empire*, 1 April 2014.

11   Carolyn Kormann, "Retreat of Andean Glaciers Foretells Global Water Woes," Yale Environment 360, 9 April 2009; "Patagonian Glaciers Melting in a Hurry," *Scientific American*, 6 September 2012; "Andean Glaciers Melting at 'Unprecedented' Rates," Reuters, 23 January 2013.

12   "Largest Tropical Glacier Retreating at 200 Feet Per Year in Peru," Mongabay, 19 February 2007; "Receding Glaciers Erase Records of Climate History," *Science News*, 14 February 2009; Justin Gillis, "In Sign of Warming, 1,600 Years of Ice in Andes Melted in 25 Years," *New York Times*, 4 April 2013; Gillis, "Study Links Temperature to a Peruvian Glacier's Growth and Retreat," *New York Times*, 25 February 2014, referring to Justin S. Stroup, Meredith A. Kelly, et al., "Late Holocene Fluctuations of Qori Kalis Outlet Glacier, Quelccaya Ice Cap, Peruvian Andes," *Geology*, 24 February 2014.

13   Kormann, "Retreat of Andean Glaciers"; Joe Romm, "Bolivia's 18,000 Year-old Chacaltaya Glacier Is Gone," Grist, 8 May 2009; Elisabeth Rosenthal, "In Bolivia, Water and Ice Tell of Climate Change," *New York Times*, 13 December 2009; Kormann, "Retreat of Andean Glaciers ."

14   "Patagonian Glaciers Melting in a Hurry," *Scientific American*, 6 September 2012.

15   Juliette Jowit, "Many Glaciers Will Disappear by Middle of Century and Add to Rising Sea Levels, Expert Warns," *Guardian*, 8 January 2009.

16   "Regional Climate Change and Adaptation: The Alps Facing the Challenge of Changing Water Resources," European Environment Agency, 2009: 32; Bob Berwyn, "As Glaciers Melt in the European Alps, a Famed Austrian Peak Is Nearly Ice-Free," Climate Progress, 10 September 2012.

17   Berwyn, "As Glaciers Melt in the European Alps."

18   "Alps: The Impacts of Climate Change in Europe Today," European Environment Agency, 22 March 2010.

19   "The Alps: People and Pressures in the Mountains: The Facts at a Glance," Permanent Secretariat of the Alpine Convention, 2010.

20   Giles Tremlett, "Climate Change Lays Waste to Spain's Glaciers," *Guardian*, 23 February 2009.

21   John Roach, "Kilimanjaro's Snows Gone by 2022?" *National Geographic News*, 1 November 2009.

22   The sublimation theory is contradicted by at least three facts. First, even if the drier conditions could explain the retreat of Kilimanjaro's glaciers in the late 19th century, it cannot explain the continuation of this retreat to the point of virtual disappearance. Second, the warming theory of Kilimanjaro's retreat fits with the fact that warming has caused glaciers all around the world to retreat. Third, the 11,000-thousand-year-old Kilimanjaro glaciers had survived many precipitation fluctuations, including a 300-year drought some 4,000 years ago. The glaciers of Kilimanjaro have been disappearing at the same time that many other climate indicators - such as hotter weather, disappearing sea ice, and more extreme weather - show the effects of human influence. The idea that in this situation the disappearance of the glaciers of Kilimanjaro has occurred without human influence is quite implausible.

23   Brown, *Plan B 4.0*, 56.

24   "Rwenzori Mountains: 'Africa's Alps' Melting Away," *New Vision* (Uganda), 16 March 2014; John Vidal, "Race to Map Africa's Forgotten Glaciers before They Melt Away," *Observer*, 2 June 2012.

25   Robin Mcdowell, "Indonesia's Last Glacier Will Melt within Years," Associated Press, 1 July 2010.

26   "Climate Change in the Himalayas," Navdanya.

27   Jane Qiu, "Glaciologists to Target Third Pole," *Nature*, 2 April 2012; "The Tibetan Plateau, the 'Water Tower of Asia,'" Tibet 3rd Pole.

28   Quirin Schiermeier, "Glacier Estimate Is on Thin Ice," *Nature*, 21 January 2010; Geoffrey Lean, "Himalayan Glaciers Are Melting Rapidly after All, Say Scientists," *Science*, 27 July 2012.

29   Tenzin Norbu, "Tibet: The Third Pole & the Himalayas," Tibet.net.

30   Tandong Yao, Lonnie Thompson et al., "Different Glacier Status with Atmospheric Circulations in Tibetan Plateau and Surroundings," *Nature Climate Change*, 15 July 2012.

31   Jane Qiu, "Tibetan Glaciers Shrinking Rapidly," *Nature*, 15 July 2012.

32   Schiermeier, "Glacier Estimate Is on Thin Ice"; Moynihan, "Climate Change in Tibet: Asia's Rivers at Risk."

33   Quoted in Schiermeier, "Glacier Estimate Is on Thin Ice."

34   See John Cook, "Himalayan Glaciers: How the IPCC Erred and What the Science Says," Skeptical Science, 17 September 2010; Fred Pearce, "Debate Heats Up Over IPCC Melting Glaciers Claim," *New Scientist*, 11 January 2010; Rich Trzupek, "Global Warming Dogma Melts in Glaciergate," Frontpagemag.com, 27 January 2010; "Brrrrrrr! Earth's Glaciers Are Growing, Not Shrinking!" Astute Blog, 12 March 2010; Wesley J. Smith, "Global Warming Hysteria: Himalayan Glaciers Growing, Not Shrinking!" *National Review*, 28 January 2011.

35   Cook, "Himalayan Glaciers: How the IPCC Erred and What the Science Says," Skeptical Science, 2010; Schiermeier, "Glacier Estimate Is on Thin Ice."

36   Jack Phillips, "Himalayan Glacier Melt Accelerating, Says Study," *Epoch Times*, 22 July

2012; Jane Qiu, ""The Third Pole," *Nature,* 24 July 2008.

37   Qiu, "Tibetan Glaciers Shrinking Rapidly"; Tandong Yao, Lonnie Thompson, et al., "Different Glacier Status with Atmospheric Circulations in Tibetan Plateau and Surroundings," *Nature Climate Change,* 15 July 2012.

38   Jane Qiu, "Tibetan Glaciers Shrinking Rapidly"; Brown, *Plan B 4.0,* 68.

39   Javaid Laghari, "Climate Change: Melting Glaciers Bring Energy Uncertainty," *Nature,* 15 November 2013.

40   Jon Gertner, "The Future Is Drying Up," *New York Times Magazine,* 21 October 2007; Rob Jordan, "Study: Climate Threatens Snowpack, Freshwater Source for Billions," Stanford Woods Institute for the Environment, 11 November 2012.

41   Jordan, "Study: Climate Threatens Snowpack"; Joe Romm, "USGS: Global Warming Drives Rockies Snowpack Loss Unrivaled in 800 Years, Threatens Western Water Supply," 13 June 2011.

42   "California Farms, Vineyards in Period from Warming, U.S. Energy Secretary Warns," *Los Angeles Times,* 4 February 2009; "Has Pacific Northwest Snowpack Declined? Yes," Real Climate, 20 March 2007.

43   Gregory Pederson et al., "The Unusual Nature of Recent Snowpack Declines in the North American Cordillera," *Science,* 15 July 2011.

44   Richard A. Lovett, "Global Warming Burning Lakes?" *National Geographic News,* 2 December 2010.

45   "Introduction: The Great Lakes," Great Lakes, U.S. Environmental Protection Agency.

46   "2 Great Lakes Hit Lowest Water Level on Record," Associated Press, 5 February 2013.

47   Matt Kasper, "How Climate Is Damaging the Great Lakes, with Implications for the Environment and the Economy," Climate Progress, 18 January 2013; "2 Great Lakes Hit Lowest Water Level on Record."

48   Michael Wines, "Colorado River Drought Forces a Painful Reckoning for States," *New York Times,* 5 January 2014.

49   Ibid.; Tom Kenworthy, "How Two Reservoirs Have become Billboards for What Climate Change Is Doing to the American West," Climate Progress, 12 August 2013.

50   Wines, "Colorado River Drought"; Ian Lovett, "Parched, California Cuts Off Tap to Agencies," *New York Times,* 31 January 2014; Ken Clark, "Lake Mead Reaches a Record Low Level," AccuWeather.com, 11 July 2014.

51   Wines, "Colorado River Drought"; Joe Romm, "Dust Bowlification Hits Eastern Australia – Next Stop the U.S. Southwest," Climate Progress, 24 September 2009.

52   Mike Stark, "Study: Shortage Likely on Colorado River by 2050," Associated Press, 21 April 2009.

53   Richard G. Taylor et al., "Ground Water and Climate Change," *Nature Climate Change* 3, December 2012; "Groundwater Depletion Linked to Climate Change," Science Daily, 25 January 2013; Robert Pore, "Overuse, Climate Threaten Ogallala Aquifer," Morris News Service, 6 August 2006; "Water at a Crossroads," *Nature Climate Change,* 25 November 2012; "Climate Change Threatens Drinking Water, As Rising Sea Penetrates Coastal Aquifers," *Science Daily,* 7 November 2007; "Groundwater Depletion Linked to Climate Change."

54   Jane Dale Owen, "Long-Term Costs of Fracking Are Staggering," Climate Progress, 19 March 2013; Joe Romm, "Drought-Stricken New Mexico Farmers Drain Aquifer to Sell Water for Fracking," Climate Progress, 5 August 2013; Suzanne Goldenberg, "Fracking Is Depleting Water in America's Driest Areas, Report Shows," *Guardian,* 5 February 2014.

55   "Satellite Study Reveals Parched American West Using Up Underground Water," NASA, 25 July 2014.

56   Fred Pearce, "Grabbing Water from Future Generations," *National Geographic News,* 30 November 2012; Michael Wines, "Wells Dry, Fertile Plains Turn to Dust," *New York Times,* 19 May 2013.

57   Pearce, "Grabbing Water."

58   Brown, *Full Planet, Empty Plates,* 18.

59   "A World without Water," *Financial Times,* 14 July 2014.

60   Quirin Schiermeier, "Water Risk as World Warms," *Nature*, 31 December 2013; Jeff Spross, "It Doesn't Take Much Global Warming to Drive Global Water Scarcity Way Up," Climate Progress, 17 December 2013.

Chapter 7: Food Shortage

1   Lester Brown, "Could Food Shortages Bring Down Civilization?" *Scientific American*, 22 April 2009; Ian Sample, "World Faces 'Perfect Storm' of Problems by 2030, Chief Scientist to Warn," *Guardian*, 18 March 2009.

2   "Annan: Climate Impacts Are Devastating World Food Supplies," Associated Press, 10 November 2011; Adam Gorlick, "At Stanford, Kofi Annan Warns of Worldwide Hunger, Political Unrest if Climate Change Persists," Stanford Report, 11 November 2011; "Climate Change vs. Food Security: A Bleak Future for the Poor," Oxfam International, 5 September 2012.

3   Lester R. Brown, *Full Planet, Empty Plates: The New Geopolitics of Food Scarcity* (New York: W.W. Norton, 2012), 1-5.

4   Nafeez Ahmed, "Peak Soil: Industrial Civilization Is on the Verge of Eating Itself," Earthsight Blog, *Guardian*, 7 June 2013; "Creating a Sustainable Food Future I: The Great Balancing Act," World Resources Institute, 2013.

5   Katie Valentine, "Eating More with Less: Leaked IPCC Report Confirms Climate Change Will Shrink World's Food Supply," 4 November 2013; Joe Romm, "Conservative Climate Panel Warns World Faces 'Breakdown of Food Systems' and More Violent Conflict," Climate Progress, 30 March 2014.

6   John D. Podesta and Jake Caldwell, "The Coming Food Crisis," *Foreign Policy*, 26 August 2010.

7   "Extreme Weather Endangers Food Security: 2010-11: A Grim Foretaste of Future Suffering and Hunger?" Oxfam Media Briefing, 28 November 2011; Joe Romm, "Climate Story of the Year: Warming-Driven Drought and Extreme Weather Emerge as Key Threat to Global Food Security," Climate Progress, 21 December 2011.

8   George Monbiot, "If Extreme Weather becomes the Norm, Starvation Awaits," *Guardian*, 15 October 2012; Damian Carrington, "NFU Claims Extreme Weather Poses Biggest Threat to British Farming," *Guardian*, 28 July 2013.

9   Brian K. Sullivan et al., "Extreme Weather Wreaking Havoc on Food as Farmers Suffer," Bloomberg, 17 January 2014.

10   David S. Battisti and Rosamond L. Naylor, "Historical Warnings of Future Food Insecurity with Unprecedented Seasonal Heat," *Science*, 9 January 2009; "Tropics Face Food Crisis by 2100," Stanford News, 8 January 2009.

11   Battisti and Naylor, "Historical Warnings of Future Food Insecurity."

12   "Extreme Weather Endangers Food Security," Oxfam.

13   Lester R. Brown, "Rising Temperatures Melting Away Global Food Security," Inter Press Service, 6 July 2011.

14   Fiona Harvey, "World's Poorest Will Feel Brunt of Climate Change, Warns World Bank," *Guardian*, 19 June 2013; Jeff Spross, "Just One Degree of Warming Could Cut One-Fifth of Kansas's Wheat Production," Climate Progress, 5 September 2013.

15   Gerson Freitas Jr., "Brazilian Cattle Price Surges to Record as Heat Chars Pastures," *Bloomberg*, 4 February 2014.

16   "Climate Change Threatens Extinction for 82 Percent of California Native Fish," Science Daily, 30 May 2013; Joanna M. Foster, "The 2014 Shrimp Season in the Gulf of Maine Has Been Canceled," 4 December 2013; Katie Valentine, "Salmon Are Dying in the Salmon River because the Water's Too Warm," Climate Progress, 28 July 2014.

17   Joe Romm, "*Nature* Publishes My Piece on Dust-Bowlification and the Grave Threat It Poses to Food Security," Climate Progress, 26 October 2011; "Extreme Weather Endangers Food Security," Oxfam.

18   "Study: Food Crisis Imminent within Next Decade if No Change to Climate Policy," Phys.Org., 12 September 2012.

19   Hugh Bronstein, "Analysis – Argentine Corn Crop Slammed by Drought; Harvest Estimates Wither," Reuters, 14 January 2014.

20   "World Water Day," UN Water, 22 March 2012; "Globally Almost 870 Million Chronically Undernourished – New Hunger Report," Food and Agricultural Organization, 9 October 2012; Dashiell Bennett, "U.S. Declares the Largest Natural Disaster Area Ever Due to Drought," *Atlantic Wire*, 12 July 2012.

21   Juan Cole, "The Great Pakistani Deluge Never Happened: Don't Tune In, It's Not Important," TomDispatch, 9 September 2010; "UN Chief Ban Ki-Moon: Pakistan Floods Are Worst Disaster I've Ever Seen," Associated Press, 15 August 2010; Omar Waraich, "Pakistan's Floods Threaten Economy and President," *Time*, 17 August 2010.

22   "Extreme Weather Endangers Food Security," Oxfam; Jeff Masters, "Thailand Flood Is Most Expensive in History," WunderBlog, 14 October 2011; Suttinee Yuvejwattana and Supunnabul Suwannakij, "Thailand Flood 'Crisis' May Spread to Bangkok, Kittiratt Says," Bloomberg News, 11 October 2011.

23   "Hurricane Mitch: The Damage and Destruction Report," National Climatic Data Center, National Oceanic and Atmospheric Administration; "Cyclone Nargis," *New York Times*, 30 April 2009; Janet McConnaughey, "Hurricane Isaac Crop Damage Estimates Reach $100 Million for Louisiana," Associated Press, 9 November 2012; Donna Bowater, "Battered Haiti Facing Food Shortages after Sandy Destroyed Crops," *Telegraph*, 31 October 2012; "Hurricane Sandy Destroys Crops in Caribbean," Farm Chemicals International, 31 October 2012.

24   "Bangladesh: Rising Sea Levels Threaten Agriculture," UN Office for the Coordination of Humanitarian Affairs, IRIN (Integrated Regional Information Networks), 1 November 2007; "Ganges-Brahmaputra Delta, Bangladesh," Climate Hot Spot, Union of Concerned Scientists.

25   Sonja Butzengeiger and Britta Horstmann, "Sea-Level Rise in Bangladesh and the Netherlands: One Phenomenon, Many Consequences," Germanwatch, 2004.

26   Rob Young and Orrin Pilkey, "How High Will Seas Rise? Get Ready for Seven Feet," Environment 360, 14 January 2010; Tom Narins et al., "Where Are Rising Sea Levels Threatening Human and Natural Environments?" Association of American Geographers, 2010.

27   Kit Gillet, "Vietnam's Rice Bowl Threatened by Rising Seas," *Guardian*, 21 August 2011; Marwaan Macan-Markar, "Sea Level Rise Threatens Mekong Rice," Inter Press Service, 17 April 2012.

28   Jonathan Spollen, "Rising Sea Threatens Millions in Egypt," *The National*, 20 November 2008.

29   Lester R. Brown, "The Geopolitics of Food Scarcity," *Der Spiegel* Online, 11 February 2009.

30   Ibid.; "Everyone Eats There," Mark Bittman, *New York Times Magazine*, 10 October 2010.

31   Brown, "Peak Water."

32   Ibid.

33   Kathleen McAuliffe, "Ocean Acidification: A Global Case of Osteoporosis," *Discover*, July 2008; Scott C. Doney et al., "Ocean Acidification: The Other CO_2 Problem," *Annual Review of Marine Science*, January 2009: 169-92; Elizabeth Kolbert, "NOAA's New Chief on Restoring Science to U.S. Climate Policy," Environment 360, 9 July 2009; "Ocean Acidification: Global Warming's Evil Twin," Skeptical Science, 2012.

34   Shauna Theel, "Study: Kardashians Get 40 Times More News Coverage than Ocean Acidification," Media Matters, 27 June 2012; McAuliffe, "Ocean Acidification"; Julian Siddle, "Marine Life Faces 'Acid Threat,'" BBC News, 25 November 2008.

35   McAuliffe, "Ocean Acidification"; Alex Morales, "Oceans Acidifying Fastest in 300 Million Years Due to Emissions," Bloomberg News, 2 March 2012.

36   "Ocean Acidification: Global Warming's Evil Twin," Skeptical Science, 2012; "Acid Oceans Warning," ARC Center of Excellence for Coral Reef Studies, October 2007.

37   Seth Borenstein, "Plankton, Base of Ocean Food Web, in Big Decline," Associated Press, 28 July 2010; Steve Connor, "The Dead Sea: Global Warming Blamed for 40 Per Cent Decline in the Ocean's Phytoplankton," *Independent*, 29 July 2010.

38   Daniel G. Boyce et al., "Global Phytoplankton Decline over the Past Century," *Nature*,

29 July 2010; Connor, "The Dead Sea"; Joe Romm, "Nature Stunner: 'Global Warming Blamed for 40% Decline in the Ocean's Phytoplankton,'" Climate Progress, 19 July 2010.

39   "Has Climate Change Caused a Drop-Off in a Food Source Crucial to Ocean Creatures?" Associated Press, 25 November 2013.

40   Susan Solomon et al. *Climate Stabilization Targets: Emissions, Concentrations, and Impacts of Decades to Millennia*, National Academies Press, 2011; F. M. M. Morel et al., *Ocean Acidification: A National Strategy to Meet the Challenges of a Changing Ocean*, National Academies Press, 2010.

41   "When corals are stressed by changes in conditions such as temperature, light, or nutrients, they expel the symbiotic algae living in their tissues, causing them to turn completely white," National Ocean Services, National Oceanic and Atmospheric Administration, "What Is Coral Bleaching?" Jeff Goodell, "Climate Change and the End of Australia," *Rolling Stone*, 13 October 2011.

42   "Evidence Highlights Threat to Caribbean Coral Reef Growth," University of Queensland, 4 February 2013; see also Doug Bostrom, "Climate Myth: Coral Atolls Grow as Sea Levels Rise," Skeptical Science, 12 March 2013.

43   Nancy Baron, "Hot, Sour, and Breathless," CompassBlogs, 27 September, 2012.

44   Julian Siddle, "Marine Life Faces 'Acid Threat,'" BBC News, 25 November 25, 2008; "Acid Oceans Warning," ARC Center of Excellence for Coral Reef Studies, October 2007; see also Joe Romm, "Imagine a World without Fish: Deadly Ocean Acidification – Hard to Deny, Harder to Geoengineer," Climate Progress, 2 September 2009.

45   Tom Lewis, "Billions of Shellfish Die as Ocean Turns to Acid," Daily Impact, 24 March 2014; Randy Shore, "Acidic Water Blamed for BC's 10-Million Scallop Die-Off," Green Man Blog, *Vancouver Sun*, 26 February 2014.

46   Tom Lewis, "West Coast Marine Ecosystem May Be Crashing," Daily Impact, 8 May 2014; *A Sea Change: Imagine a World without Fish*.

47   "Oceans," Rio+20: The Future We Want, United Nations; Save the Sea.

48   "Acid Oceans Warning," ARC Center of Excellence for Coral Reef Studies, October 2007.

49   Joe Romm, "Nature Geoscience Study: Oceans Are Acidifying 10 Times Faster Today than 55 Million Years Ago when a Mass Extinction of Marine Species Occurred," Climate Progress, 18 February 2010; Katie Valentine, "NOAA Lists 20 Coral Species as Threatened Due to Climate Change, Fishing and Pollution," Climate Progress, 28 August 2014.

50   Brown, *Full Planet, Empty Plates*, 122.

51   See "Sensitivity of Ocean Acidification to Geoengineered Climate Stabilization," which says: "The results of this paper support the view that climate engineering will not resolve the problem of ocean acidification," H. Damon Matthews et al., *Geophysical Research Letters*, May 2009. See also Joe Romm, "Imagine a World without Fish: Deadly Ocean Acidification – Hard to Deny, Harder to Geoengineer, but Not Hard to Stop – Is Subject of Documentary," Climate Progress, 2 September 2009. In addition, some academies of science – including those of China and the United States – have declared, "Ocean acidification is irreversible on timescales of at least tens of thousands of years," "IAP Statement on Ocean Acidification," Interacademy Panel on International Issues, June 2009.

Chapter 8: Climate Refugees

1   *Climate Refugees* (2010), directed by Michael Nash, featuring Lester Brown and others; *Sun Come Up* (2011), directed by Jennifer Redfearn; *The Island President*, directed by Jon Shenk.

2   Lester R. Brown et al., "Twenty-Two Dimensions of the Population Problem," Worldwatch Paper, 1976; Jodi L. Jacobson "Environmental Refugees: A Yardstick of Habitability," Worldwatch Paper, 1988.

3   "Climate Change Displacement Has Begun – But Hardly Anyone Has Noticed," *Guardian*, George Monbiot's Blog, 8 May 2009. Some articles have given a lower figure, sometimes 1,700. But Jennifer Redfearn, who made *Sun Come Up*, said "2,000 to

3,000" (Brian Clark Howard, "*Sun Come Up*: An Intimate Look at the World's First Climate Refugees," *Daily Green,* 8 July 2009); Neil MacFarquhar, "Refugees Join List of Climate-Change Issues," *New York Times,* 29 May 2009.

4   Howard, "*Sun Come Up.*"

5   "PNG Attitude," Keith Jackson & Friends, 18 August 2011.

6   "Papua New Guinea: The World's First Climate Change 'Refugees,'" IRIN, 8 June 2008.

7   "Papua New Guinea"; Neil MacFarquhar, "Refugees Join List of Climate-Change Issues," *New York Times,* 29 May 2009.

8   Maureen Nandini Mitra, "A Leader's Struggle to Save his People from Turning Into Climate Refugees" [Film Review: *The Island President*], *Earth Island Journal,* 2 March 2012; Simon Denyer, "Deposed Maldives President Says Coup Has Fueled Radical Islam," *Washington Post,* 19 April 2012; "Maldives President: Australia Should Prepare for Climate Refugees," Responding to Climate Change, 13 February 2012.

9   "Maldives Government Highlights the Impact of Climate Change . . . By Meeting Underwater," *Daily Mail,* 20 October 2009; Mitra, "A Leader's Struggle"; "Maldives Cabinet Goes Underwater for Official Meeting," 350.org, 17 October 2009; "Maldives President: Australia Should Prepare for Climate Refugees," Responding to Climate Change, 13 February 2012.

10   Mitra, "A Leader's Struggle"; Denyer, "Deposed Maldives President."

11   "Nasheed Fears 'Suicide Pact' at Copenhagen," *Agence France-Presse,* 9 November 2009; John Vidal and Allegra Stratton, "Low Targets, Goals Dropped: Copenhagen Ends in Failure," *Guardian,* 18 December 2009; Joss Garman, "Copenhagen - Historic Failure that Will Live in Infamy," *Independent,* 18 December 2009; George Monbiot, "Climate Change Enlightenment Was Fun While It Lasted. But Now It Is Dead," *Guardian,* September 20, 2010; Mitra, "A Leader's Struggle"; Charles Morris, "The Island President: Real Consequences to Climate Change," *National Catholic Reporter,* 7 June 2012.

12   "Maldives Government Highlights the Impact"; Mat McDermott, "Maldives President Mohamed Nasheed Is an Eco-Rock Star - Brings Down the House in Copenhagen," TreeHugger, 14 December 2009; "The Climate Vulnerable Forum was founded at the initiative of Maldives government in late 2009. Eleven governments met near Maldives capital of Malé in November 2009 and signed the Malé Declaration," which "expressed alarm at the rate of changes and danger witnessed around the planet due to the effects of human-induced global warming and called for most urgent international cooperation to tackle the challenge" ("Climate Vulnerable Forum," DARA).

13   "Nasheed Fears 'Suicide Pact' at Copenhagen," *Agence France-Presse,* 9 November 2009; "Maldives Government Highlights the Impact."

14   C. Bryson Hull, "Ousted at Gunpoint, Ex-President of Maldives Takes to Streets," Reuters, 8 February 2012; Olivia Lang, "Dramatic Fall for Maldives' Democratic Crusader," BBC News, 8 February 2012; Elizabeth Flock, "Mohamed Nasheed: Arrest Warrant Issued for Deposed Maldives President," *Washington Post,* 9 February 2012; "Maldives Crisis: Commonwealth Urges Early Elections," BBC News, 22 February 2012.

15   Stephen Zunes reported that the election commission declared that an amazing 88 percent of the eligible votes had cast votes (the media had said 70 percent), and some voting districts where Yameen was popular reported between 10 percent to 300 percent more votes than the number of eligible voters ("Apparent Fraud in Maldivian Elections Threatens Prospects for Democracy," Open Democracy, 16 September 2013); "Yameen Wins Maldives Presidential Run-Off," Al Jazeera, 16 November 2013.

16   Bahar Dutt, "Locals in Sunderbans Turn Climate Refugees, CNN-IBN, 17 October 2007.

17   "World's First Climate Change Refugees," *South-Asian Life & Times,* April-June 2009; Takver, "Mangrove Forests Threatened by Climate Change in the Sundarbans of Bangladesh and India," Climate Inc., 12 January 2013.

18   Dan McDougall, "The World's First Environmental Refugees," *Ecologist,* 30 January 2009.

19   Achintyarup Ray, "Lohachara Rises from Waters Again," *Times of India,* 3 April, 2009. The title of this story refers to the fact that, as is not unusual, a portion of the island

now appears above the sea-level. This does not mean, however, that people would be able to reoccupy the island.

20   McDougall, "The World's First Environmental Refugees"; "World's First Climate Change Refugees."

21   Jayanta Basu and Zeeshan Jawed, "Sea Change," *Telegraph* (Calcutta), 14 June 2009.

22   "Tuvalu – Climate Displacement," Displacement Solutions; Dana Nuccitelli, "What's Happening to Tuvalu Sea Level," Skeptical Science, 27 November 2011.

23   Lester Brown, "Raging Storms, Rising Seas Swell Ranks of Climate Refugees," Grist, 16 August 2011.

24   Al Gore, "Rising Seas from Antarctica to Bangladesh: The Story of Rising Seas," Climate Reality Project, 31 January 2012.

25   John Vidal, "Bangladesh's Climate Refugees: 'It's a Question of Life,'" *Guardian*, 29 January 2013; Vidal, "Sea Change: The Bay of Bengal's Vanishing Islands," *Guardian*, 29 January 2013.

26   "Bangladesh's Disappearing Island," You Tube, 18 December 2009.

27   Emily Wax, "In Flood-Prone Bangladesh, a Future That Floats," *Washington Post*, 27 September 2007.

28   Pinaki Roy, "Climate Refugees of the Future," Climate Change Media Partnership, 31 May 2009.

29   John Vidal, "Sea Change: The Bay of Bengal's Vanishing Islands," *Guardian*, 29 January 2013.

30   Simit Bhagat, "What about 30 Million Climate Refugees?" *Times of India*, 15 December 2009.

31   "Mozambique: Climate Change Adaptation Can't Wait," IRIN, 28 May 2009.

32   Ibid.

33   Ibid.

34   Davina Wadley, "There's No Such Thing as a 'Climate Refugee,'" Refugees International Blog, 24 January 2013.

35   Brook Meakins, "Kiribati Man Wanting 'Climate Change Refugee' Status Denied by New Zealand Immigration," Huffington Post, 5 September 2012; Emily Atkin, "Rejecting Man's Bid for Refugee Status, Court Rules Climate Change Is Not 'Persecution,'" Climate Progress, 26 November 2013.

36   Frank Biermann and Ingrid Boas, "Protecting Climate Refugees: The Case for a Global Protocol," *Environment Magazine,* November-December 2008; Fiona Harvey, "More than 30 Million Climate Migrants in Asia in 2010, Report Finds," *Guardian,* 19 September 2011.

37   Ibid.

38   Ibid.

39   Michael B. Gerrard and Andrew Sabin, *Threatened Island Nations* (Cambridge University Press, 2013).

40   Anam Sultan, "Mass Migration: The Untold Crisis of Climate Refugees," Earth Reform, 4 August 2012.

41   Biermann and Boas, "Protecting Climate Refugees."

42   Rick Noack, "Has the Era of the 'Climate Change Refugee' Begun?" *Washington Post*, 7 August 2014.

43   Biermann and Boas, "Protecting Climate Refugees."

44   "Maldives President: Australia Should Prepare for Climate Refugees," Responding to Climate Change, 13 February 2012.

45   *Climate Refugees: People Displaced by Climate Change and the Role of the Churches* (World Council of Churches, 2013).

46   "New Analysis Shows Global Exposure to Sea Level Rise," Climate Central, 23 September 2014.

47   Steve Trent, "Climate Change: It's Not Just an Environmental Issue; It's a Human Rights Issue Too," Environment Justice Foundation, 11 December 2012.

Chapter 9: Climate Wars

1   Daniel Moran, ed., *Climate Change and National Security: A Country-Level Analysis* (Washington DC: Georgetown University Press, 2010); Gwynne Dyer, *Climate Wars: The Fight for Survival as the World Overheats* (Oxford, Oneworld, 2010).

2   Joe Romm, "Syria Today Is a Preview of Veterans Day, 2030," Climate Progress, 11 November 2013.

3   Secretary of State John Kerry, "Remarks With Swedish Prime Minister Fredrik Reinfeldt," U.S. Department of State, 14 May 2013.

4   Bryan Bender, "Chief of US Pacific Forces Calls Climate Biggest Worry," *Boston Globe*, 9 March 2013.

5   CIA Opens Center on Climate Change and National Security, CIA, 25 September 2009.

6   Francesco Femia and Caitlin E. Werrell, "Climate and Security 101: Why the U.S. National Security Establishment Takes Climate Change Seriously," Center for Climate & Security, 26 February 2014.

7   Seth Borenstein, "UN Report: Global Warming Worsens Security Woes," Associated Press, 30 March 2014; Nafeez Ahmed, "UN - Climate 'Perfect Storm' Is Already Here. Time to Slay Zombie Big Oil," Earth Insight, *Guardian*, 3 April 2014.

8   Peter Schwartz and Doug Randall, "An Abrupt Climate Change Scenario and Its Implications for United States National Security."

9   Mark Hertsgaard, "Weathering the Crisis," *The Nation*, 24 February 2004.

10   David Stipp, "The Pentagon's Weather Nightmare," *Fortune*, 9 February 2004.

11   Mark Townsend and Paul Harris, "Now the Pentagon Tells Bush: Climate Change Will Destroy Us," *Guardian/Observer*, 21 February 2004,

12   Ibid., quoting Rob Gueterbock of Greenpeace.

13   *Stern Review: The Economics of Climate Change*, Executive Summary (2006).

14   Ibid.

15   "To the Reader," *National Security and the Threat of Climate Change*, CNA Corporation, 2007; emphasis added.

16   Gen. Gordon R. Sullivan, "On Risk," *National Security and the Threat of Climate Change*, CNA Corporation, 2007.

17   Ibid.

18   Kurt M. Campbell et al., *The Age of Consequences: The Foreign Policy and National Security Implications of Global Climate Change*, Executive Summary, Center for Strategic and International Studies/Center for a New American Society, November 2007.

19   Brad Johnson, "Pentagon: 'Climate Change, Energy Security, and Economic Stability Are Inextricably Linked,'" Climate Progress, 1 February 2010.

20   John M. Broder, "Climate Change Report Outlines Perils for U.S. Military," *New York Times*, 9 November 2012; "New Report Highlights Link Between Climate Change, National Security," Voice of America, 9 November 2012.

21   Steve Horn, "Pentagon Calls Climate Change Impacts 'Threat Multipliers,' Could Enable Terrorism," DeSmogBlog.com, 5 March 2014.

22   "Climate Change: Beyond the Hype of 'Climate Wars,'" IRIN (Integrated Regional Information Networks), 29 October 2012.

23   Ibid.

24   "Environmental Degradation Triggering Tensions and Conflict in Sudan," UNEP, 22 June 2007; "Climate Change: Beyond the Hype; "Sudan: Climate Change – Only One Cause among Many for Darfur Conflict," IRIN, 28 June 2007.

25   Joanna I. Lewis, "China," in Daniel Moran, ed., *Climate Change and National Security: A Country-Level Analysis* (Washington DC: Georgetown University Press, 2010): 9-16, at 12-13; Ros Donald, "Threat Multiplier: An Interview with Climate Conflict Expert Ian Shields," Climate Progress, 16 August 2012. On the coinage of the term, see Francesco Femia and Caitlin E. Werrell, "Climate and Security 101: Why the U.S. National Security Establishment Takes Climate Change Seriously," 26 February 2014.

26   Bruno Tertrais, "The Climate Wars Myth," *Washington Quarterly*, Summer 2011.

27   Ibid.

28   Andrew Freedman, "Climate & Conflict: Warmer World May Be More Violent," Climate Central, 1 August 2013.

29   Quoted in Monte Morin, "Violence Will Rise as Climate Changes, Scientists Predict," *Los Angeles Times*, 1 August 2013.

30   Dan Smith and Janani Vivekananda, *A Climate of Conflict: The Links between Climate Change, Peace and War* (Stockholm: Swedish International Development Cooperation Agency, 2008), 7.

31   Gwynne Dyer, *Climate Wars: The Fight for Survival as the World Overheats* (Oxford: Oneworld, 2010), xii, xi.

32   "Sudan May Be the First Site of Violence Induced by Climate Change," SNHDR [Sudan National Human Development Report]," Sudan Vision, 8 May 2014.

33   Jeffrey D. Sachs, "Ecology and Political Upheaval," *Scientific American*, 26 June 2006.

34   Julian Borger, "Darfur Conflict Heralds Era of Wars Triggered by Climate Change, UN Report Warns," *Guardian*, 22 June 2007.

35   "Sudan: Climate Change – Only One Cause among Many for Darfur Conflict."

36   Gen. Anthony C. Zinni, USMC (ret.), "On Climate Change, Instability and Terrorism," *National Security and the Threat of Climate Change*, CNA Corporation, 2007.

37   Martin Hoerling et al., "On the Increased Frequency of Mediterranean Drought," *Journal of Climate*, March 2011; discussed in Joe Romm, "NOAA Bombshell: Human-Caused Climate Change Already a Major Factor in More Frequent Mediterranean Droughts," Climate Progress, 27 October 2011.

38   Thomas L. Friedman, "Without Water, Revolution," *New York Times*, 18 May 2013.

39   William R. Polk, "Your Labor Day Syria Reader, Part 2: William Polk," *Atlantic*, 2 September 2013.

40   David Arnold, "Drought Called a Factor in Syria's Uprising," Voice of America, 20 August 2013.

41   Francesco Femia and Caitlin E. Werrell, "Syria: Climate Change, Drought and Social Unrest," Center for Climate and Security, 29 February 2012.

42   Ibid.; Friedman, "Without Water"; Joe Romm, "Arab Summer: Warming-Fueled Drought Helped Spark Syria's Civil War," Climate Progress, 8 September 2013; David Arnold, "Drought Called a Factor in Syria's Uprising," Voice of America, 20 August 2013.

43   Brian Merchant, "How Climate Change Warmed Syria Up for War," Motherboard, 4 September 2013; Brian Merchant, "Climate Change-Fueled Droughts Are about to Make Syria Even More Hellish," Motherboard, 9 April 2014.

44   Dyer, *Climate Wars*, 20.

45   Lewis, "China," in Moran, ed., *Climate Change and National Security*, at 17.

46   Ibid., 19-20.

47   Brahma Chellaney, *Water: Asia's New Battleground* (Georgetown University Press, 2011). The quoted statement is under "From the Author" in the Editorial Reviews available at Amazon.com.

48   Ayesha Siddiqi, "Kashmir: The Forgotten Conflict," Al Jazeera, 1 August 2011; Lydia Polgreen and Sabrina Tavernise, "Water Dispute Increases India-Pakistan Tension," *New York Times*, 20 July 2010.

49   Siddiqi, "Kashmir: The Forgotten Conflict."

50   Rathnam Indurthy, "Kashmir between India and Pakistan: An Intractable Conflict, 1947 to Present," February 2012; Niharika Mandhana, "Water Wars: Why India and Pakistan Are Squaring Off over Their Rivers," *Time*, 16 April 2012.

51   Sankar Ray, "Blood in Kashmir's Water," *Asia Sentinel*, 18 June 2008.

52   Mandhana, "Water Wars."

53   Ibid.; Polgreen and Tavernise, "Water Dispute Increases India-Pakistan Tension."

54   Khaled Ahmed, "'Water War', Pakistani Style," *Friday Times*, 30 November – 6 December 2012. Besides reporting that Jamaat Ali Shah said Pakistan was getting less water because there has been less rain, Khaled Ahmed quoted Brahma Chellaney's report that Shah Mahmood Qureshi said in 2010: "Is India stealing that water from you? No, it is not. Please do not fool yourself and do not misguide the nation. We are mismanaging that water," (Chellaney, *Water: Asia's New Battleground*, 223).

55   Athar Parvaiz, "India/Pakistan: Reduced Himalayan Snowfall Could Spark Water War,"

Inter Press Service, 18 January 2010; Parvaiz, "Kashmir's Melting Glaciers May Cut Ice With Sceptics," Inter Press Service, 31 August 2012.

56   "Black Carbon Driving Himalayan Melt," *Space Daily,* 8 February 2010.

57   Stephan Faris, "The Last Straw," *Foreign Policy,* 22 June 2009.

58   James Lamont, "Pakistan Steps Up Water Dispute," *Financial Times,* 29 March 2010; Parvaiz, "India/Pakistan"; Ayesha Siddiqi, "Kashmir: The Forgotten Conflict," *Al Jazeera,* 1 August 2011; Mandhana, "Water Wars."

Chapter 10: Ecosystem Collapse and Extinction

1   Charles J. Krebs, (2009). *Ecology: The Experimental Analysis of Distribution and Abundance,* 6th ed. (San Francisco: Benjamin Cummings), 572.

2   Chris D. Thomas et al., "Extinction Risk from Climate Change," *Nature,* 8 January 2004. It is unusual to include topsoil among the *species.* The authors defend their usage thus: "While topsoil is not a living organism, it is the foundation of the Earth's terrestrial ecosystems and is loosely analogous to plankton. Topsoil refers to far more than just dirt: it is actually a very complex micro ecosystem made up of numerous different forms of life. One teaspoon of topsoil contains 5 billion bacteria and 20 million fungi. . . . It can take centuries for just an inch of topsoil to form naturally. . . . Without healthy topsoil, food production is virtually impossible."

3   "Global Warming – Ecosystem Collapse – An Unnatural Disaster," *Anaspides,* 8 January 2004.

4   Paul Alois and Victoria Cheng, "Keystone Species Extinction Overview," Arlington Institute, July 2007. On the disappearance of topsoil, the authors cite Sara J. Scherr, "Soil Degradation: A Threat to Developing-Country Food Security by 2020?" International Food Policy Research Institute, 1999.

5   Johan Rockström, "Planetary Boundaries: Exploring the Safe Operating Space for Humanity," *Ecology and Society* 14/2 (2009).

6   Ibid.

7   For evidence, the paper cites T. P. Hughes et al., "Phase Shifts, Herbivory, and the Resilience of Coral Reefs," *Current Biology,* 20 February 2007; Marten Scheffer et al., "Catastrophic Shifts in Ecosystems," *Nature,* 11 October 2001.

8   Rockström, "Planetary Boundaries."

9   The other six boundaries involve ocean acidification, stratospheric ozone, phosphorus inflow to the ocean, global freshwater use, chemical pollution, and atmospheric aerosol loading.

10   Rockström, "Planetary Boundaries."

11   Anthony D. Barnosky et al., "Approaching a State Shift in Earth's Biosphere," *Nature,* 7 June 2012; "Environmental Collapse Now a Serious Threat: Scientists," *Agence France-Presse,* 6 June 2012; Brian Merchant, "Scientists Fear Global Ecological Collapse Once 50% of the Natural Landscape Is Gone," Treehugger, 6 June 2012.

12   David P. Bell, "Earth on Brink of 'Irreversible' Collapse of Global Ecosystem, New SFU Study Warns," *Vancouver Observer,* 6 June 2012.

13   "Environmental Collapse Now a Serious Threat;" Bell, "Earth on Brink."

14   "Study Says Earth on Brink of Mass Extinction," Reuters, 18 June 2014.

15   Jenny Fyall, "Tyndall Center: Global Warming Will Kill 90% of the Earth's Population," Real Science, 29 November 2009.

16   Joe Romm, "Nature Bombshell: Climate Experts Warn Thawing Permafrost Could Cause 2.5 Times the Warming of Deforestation!" Climate Progress, 1 December 2011.

17   Alan Buis, "Is a Sleeping Climate Giant Stirring in the Arctic?" NASA, 10 June 2013.

18   Ibid.; Justin Gillis, "As Permafrost Thaws, Scientists Study the Risks," *New York Times,* 16 December 2011.

19   Natalia Shakhova et al., "Anomalies of Methane in the Atmosphere over the East Siberian Shelf: Is There Any Sign of Methane Leakage from Shallow Shelf Hydrates?" *Geophysical Research Abstracts,* 2008; Shakhova et al., "Extensive Methane Venting to the Atmosphere from Sediments of the East Siberian Arctic Shelf," *Science,* 5 March 2010; "Methane Releases from Arctic Shelf May Be Much Larger and Faster

than Anticipated," National Science Foundation, Press Release, 4 March 2010.

20   Joe Romm, "Science Stunner: Vast East Siberian Arctic Shelf Methane Stores Desta-bilizing and Venting," Climate Progress, 4 March 2010.

21   Kevin Schaefer et al., "Amount and Time of Permafrost Carbon Release in Response to Climate Warming," Tellus B, 15 February 2011.

22   Edward A. G. Schuur and Benjamin Abbott, "Climate Change: High Risk of Permafrost Thaw," Nature, 1 December 2011.

23   Andy Skuce, "Carbon Feedback from Thawing Permafrost Will Likely Add 0.4°F – 1.5°F to Total Global Warming by 2100," Skeptical Science, 4 October 2012.

24   "Stable" Antarctic Permafrost Melting Faster than Expected, Researchers Say," Nature World News, 24 July 2013.

25   Anton Vaks et al., "Speleothems Reveal 500,000-Year History of Siberian Permafrost," Science, 12 April 2013; discussed in Michael Marshall, "Major Methane Release Is Almost Inevitable," New Scientist, 21 February 2013.

26   Andrew Glikson, "Methane and the Risk of Runaway Global Warming," The Conversa-tion, 26 July 2013.

27   Gail Whiteman, Chris Hope, and Peter Wadhams, "Climate Science: Vast Costs of Arctic Change," Nature, 24 July 2013; "Cost of Arctic Methane Release Could Be 'Size of Global Economy,' Experts Warn," Science Daily, 24 July 2013.

28   Ibid.

29   Dahr Jamail, "Are We Falling Off the Climate Precipice? Scientists Consider Extinction," Tom Dispatch, 17 December 2013, summarizing the views of atmospheric and marine scientist Ira Leifer; see also Thom Hartmann, "Mass Extinction: Let's Not," Climate State, 28 September 2013 (video); James Hansen, Storms of My Grandchildren, 150.

30   Joe Romm, "Doubling of CO2 Levels in End-Triassic Extinction Killed Off Three Quarters of Land and Sea Species," Climate Progress, 24 March 2013.

31   Niles Eldredge, "The Sixth Extinction," ActionBioScience.org, June 2001.

32   John Cook, "Do Volcanoes Emit More CO2 than Humans?" Skeptical Science, 10 Au-gust 2012; Anne E. Magurran and Maria Dornelas, "Biological Diversity in a Changing World," Philosophical Transactions of the Royal Society, 27 October 2010.

33   Jeremy Jackson, "The Future of the Oceans Past," Philosophical Transactions of the Royal Society, 27 October 2010. This and the previous article are summarized in Joe Romm, "Royal Society: 'There Are Very Strong Indications that the Current Rate of Species Extinctions Far Exceeds Anything in the Fossil Record,'" Climate Progress, 15 November 2010.

34   Elizabeth Kolbert, The Sixth Extinction: An Unnatural History (New York: Henry Holt, 2014), 267-68. A good introduction to the thinking of some scientists about the methane threat is provided by a 2013 video called "Mass Extinction: Let's Not," which was narrated and co-authored by Thom Hartmann.

35   Jenny Fyall, "Tyndall Center: Global Warming Will Kill 90% of the Earth's Population," Scotsman, 29 November 2009.

36   Jamail, "Are We Falling Off the Climate Precipice?"

37   Stephanie Rogers, "Human Could Go Extinct within 100 Years, Says Renowned Scien-tist," Mother Nature Network, 25 June 2010; referring to Cheryl Jones, "Frank Fenner Sees No Hope for Humans," The Australian, 16 June 2010.

38   Thom Hartmann, "Mass Extinction: Let's Not," Climate State, 28 September 2013 (video).

39   Guy R. McPherson, "Three Paths to Near-term Human Extinction," Canadians for Emergency Action on Climate Change, 9 November 2011; "19 Ways Climate Change Is Now Feeding Itself," Transition Voice, 19 August 2013; Going Dark (Baltimore: PublishAmerica, 2013).

40   Malcolm Light, "Global Extinction within One Human Lifetime as a Result of a Spread-ing Atmospheric Arctic Methane Heat Wave and Surface Firestorm," Arctic News, 6 March 2012.

41   Aaron Strong et al., "Ocean Fertilization: Time to Move On," Nature, 17 September 2009.

42   Clive Hamilton, *Earthmasters: The Dawn of the Age of Climate Engineering* (New Haven: Yale University Press, 2013).

43   John Vidal, "Geo-Engineering: Green versus Greed in the Race to Cool the Planet," *Observer*, 10 July 2011; quoted *Earthmasters*, 17

44   Hamilton, *Earthmasters*, 1.

45   Fred C. Ikle and Lowell Wood, "Thinking Big on Global Warming," *Wall Street Journal*, 15 October 2007.

46   Joe Romm, "Exclusive: Dysfunctional, Lop-Sided Geoengineering Panel Tries to Launch Greenwashing Euphemism, 'Climate Remediation,'" Climate Progress, 6 October 2011.

47   All of these problems are listed in Hamilton's book (52-55), except the second, which is discussed in Joe Romm, "Key 'Geoengineering' Strategy May Yield Warming, Not Cooling," Climate Progress, 10 April 2011.

48   Hamilton, *Earthmasters*, 59.

49   These points are discussed in Hamilton's book (57-68), except for the third, which is discussed in Tim Radford, "Geoengineering Could Trigger Disaster in Parts of Africa," Climatecentral.org, 7 April 2013.

50   David P. Keller et al., "Potential Climate Engineering Effectiveness and Side Effects during a High Carbon Dioxide-Emission Scenario," *Nature Communications*, 25 February 2014.

51   Hamilton, *Earthmasters*, 20.

52   Alex Kirby, "Volcano 'Did Little to Lower CO_2,'" Climate News Network, 21 March 2013; Eric P. Achterberg et al., "Natural Iron Fertilization by the Eyjafjallajökull Volcanic Eruption," *Geophysical Research Letters*, 16 March 2013.

53   Martin Lukacs, "World's Biggest Geoengineering Experiment 'Violates' UN Rules," *Guardian*, 15 October 2012.

54   Keller et al., "Potential Climate Engineering Effectiveness and Side Effects."

55   Hamilton, *Earthmasters*, 35.

56   Keller et al., "Potential Climate Engineering Effectiveness and Side Effects."

57   Hamilton, *Earthmasters*, 29, 33, 34.

58   Keller et al., "Potential Climate Engineering Effectiveness and Side Effects."

59   Joe Romm, "Martin Bunzl on 'the Definitive Killer Objection to Geoengineering as even a Temporary Fix,'" Climate Progress, 27 September 2010; Joe Romm, "Caldeira Calls Lomborg's Vision 'a Dystopic World Out of a Science Fiction Story,'" Climate Progress, 15 November 2010.

60   Clive Hamilton, "Geoengineering: Our Last Hope, or a False Promise?" *New York Times*, 26 May 2013.

61   "Richard S. Courtney on Geo-Engineering," BigCityLib Strikes Back, 12 August 2009; quoted in Romm, "British Coal Industry Flack Pushes Geo-Engineering 'Ploy,'" Climate Progress, 12 August 2009.

62   Hamilton, "Geoengineering: Our Last Hope?"

63   Clive Hamilton, *Requiem for a Species: Why We Resist the Truth about Climate Change* (Routledge, 2010).

Chapter 11: Climate Change Denial

1   Bertrand Russell, *History of the World in Epitome (For Use in Martian Infant Schools)*.

2   Mark Hoofnagle, "Don't Take Denialism for Debate," Denialism Blog.

3   Mark Hertsgaard, *Hot: Living Through the Next Fifty Years on Earth* (New York: Houghton Mifflin Harcourt, 2011), 264.

4   Naomi Oreskes and Erik M. Conway, *Merchants of Doubt: How a Handful of Scientists Obscured the Truth of Issues from Tobacco Smoke to Global Warming* (New York: Bloomsbury, 2010). (A Robert Kenner film of this title was scheduled to be released at the end of 2014; see Peter Sinclair, "Heads Up: 'Merchants of Doubt' Movie to Hit Theaters Soon," Skeptical Science, 25 September 2014.)

5   Ibid., 7.

6   Ibid., 34 (citing *Smoking and Health Proposal*, Legacy Tobacco Documents Library, 1969).

7   Ibid., 15.

8   Mark Parascandola, "Public Health Service Then and Now: Cigarettes and the US Public Health Service in the 1950s," *American Journal of Public Health* 91/2 (February 2001): 196-205.

9   Mark Parascandola, "Two Approaches to Etiology: The Debate over Smoking and Lung Cancer in the 1950s," *Endeavour* 28/2 (June 1008): 81-86, at 85.

10   Leonard M. Schuman, "The Origins of the Report of the Advisory Committee on Smoking and Health to the Surgeon General," *Journal of Public Health Policy* 2/1 (March 1981): 19-27.

11   See "Nicotine and Cigarettes," Frontline, PBS, 14 April 1994, or "The Seven Dwarves: I believe that Nicotine Is Not Addictive," You Tube, 26 November 2006.

12   Stanton A. Glantz et al., *The Cigarette Papers* (Berkeley: University of California Press, 1996), 15, 18.

13   "Brown & Williamson Company Statement on Smoking and Health," 12 May 1967.

14   David Michaels and Celeste Monforton, "Manufacturing Uncertainty: Contested Science and the Protection of the Public's Health and Environment," *American Journal of Public Health*, 1 September 2005).

15   Oreskes and Conway, *Merchants of Doubt*, 5.

16   Mark Hertsgaard, "While Washington Slept," *Vanity Fair*, May 2006; cited in James Lawrence Powell, *The Inquisition of Climate Science* (New York: Columbia University Press, 2011), 61.

17   Oreskes and Conway, *Merchants of Doubt*, 14.

18   Glantz et al., *The Cigarette Papers*, Ch. 10.

19   Oreskes and Conway, *Merchants of Doubt*, 414.

20   Ibid., 138.

21   *The Health Consequences of Involuntary Smoking* (U.S. Department of Health and Human Services, 1986); Oreskes and Conway, *Merchants of Doubt*, 139.

22   Oreskes and Conway, *Merchants of Doubt*, 139.

23   Ibid., quoting *Ellen Merlo, Vendor Conference Draft*, December 1993.

24   Ibid. At about the same time, Stallone, having smoked heavily from a young age, reportedly decided to quit, because, he said to himself: "This is going to bring an early death." In addition, he decided that "cigarettes looked somewhat silly on adults." See "Play It Again," Tobacco Control, 1988.

25   *Deposition Transcript of Martin J. Cline*, Legacy Tobacco Documents Library, 46; cited in Oreskes and Conway, *Merchants of Doubt*, 30-31.

26   Ibid., 14.

27   Ibid., 236.

28   *Smoke, Mirrors & Hot Air: How ExxonMobil Uses Big Tobacco's Tactics to Manufacture Uncertainty on Climate Science* (Union of Concerned Scientists, January 2007), 17-18.

29   Powell, *The Inquisition of Climate Science*, 97-98.

30   *Respiratory Health Effects of Passive Smoking: Lung Cancer and Other Disorders*, Environmental Protection Agency, 1992.

31   Oreskes and Conway, *Merchants of Doubt*, 142, citing EPA's "Fact Sheet: Respiratory Effects of Passive Smoking," 1-6.

32   Ibid., 143-44.

33   Ibid., 154-55.

34   Ibid., 159.

35   Ibid., 67-71.

36   Ibid., 71-72, citing Jerome O. Nriagu and Robert D. Coker, "Isotopic Composition of Sulphur in Atmospheric Precipitation around Sudbury, Ontario," *Nature*, 31 August 1978.

37   Ibid., 72 citing Gene E. Likens et al., "Acid Rain," *Scientific American*, October 1979: 43-51.

38   Gus Speth, "The Sisyphus Syndrome: Air Pollution, Acid Rain and Public Responsibility," *Proceedings of the Action Seminar on Acid Precipitation*, November 2-3, 1979 (Canada: A.S.A.P. Organizing Committee, 1979), 170.

39   Ibid., citing J. N. B. Bell, "Acid Precipitation – a New Study from Norway," *Nature*, 16 July 1981: 199-200.

40   David W. Schindler (chair), *Atmosphere-Biosphere Interaction: Toward a Better Understanding of the Ecological Consequences of Fossil Fuel Combustion*, Committee on the Atmosphere and Biosphere, National Research Council (Washington, D.C.: National Academy of Sciences, 1981).

41   Jack Calvert (chair), *Acid Deposition: Atmospheric Processes in Eastern North America: A Review of Current Scientific Understanding*, Committee on Atmospheric Transport and Chemical Transformation in Acid Precipitation, National Research Council (Washington, D.C.: National Academies Press, 1983).

42   Oreskes and Conway, *Merchants of Doubt*, 77, attributing this assessment to Richard Ayers, who at the time was the chairman of the National Clean Air Coalition.

43   Ibid., 38, 78-79.

44   Ibid., 81-82, 86.

45   Ibid., 87-88, 95-100.

46   Ibid., 91-94.

47   Ibid., 94, 101.

48   *Acid Deposition in North America: A Review of Documents Prepared under the Memorandum of Intent between Canada and the United states of America*, Royal Society of Canada, Technical Report, May 1983.

49   William M. Brown, "Maybe Acid Rain Isn't the Villain," *Fortune*. 28 May 1984: 170-74.

50   Magda Havas et al., "Red Herrings in Acid Rain Research," *Environmental Science and Technology* 18/6 (1984): 176A-186A.

51   Oreskes and Conway, *Merchants of Doubt*, 103.

52   Ibid., 107-11.

53   Mario F. S. Molina and F. S. Rowland, "Stratospheric Sink for Chlorofluoromethanes: Chlorine Atom Catalyzed Destruction of Ozone," *Nature*, 28 June 1974: 810-12.

54   Oreskes and Conway, *Merchants of Doubt*, 113.

55   Ibid., 114.

56   Lydia Dotto and Harold Schiff, *The Ozone War* (Garden City: Doubleday, 1978), 225; Oreskes and Conway, *Merchants of Doubt*, 115.

57   Oreskes and Conway, *Merchants of Doubt*, 117, 125.

58   Ibid., 126-29.

59   Ibid., 133.

60   Ibid., 134.

61   Eric Pooley, *The Climate War: True Believers, Power Brokers, and the Fight to Save the Earth* (New York: Hyperion, 2010), 36.

62   Andrew C. Revkin, "Industry Ignored Its Scientists on Climate," *New York Times*, 24 April 2009.

63   Ibid.

64   Joe Walker, "Global Climate Science Communications Action Plan," American Petroleum Institute, April 1998; Oliver Burkeman, "Memo Exposes Bush's New Green Strategy," *Guardian*, 3 March 2003.

65   In 2001, a new scientific report led to many more drop outs. In 2002, GCC disbanded, saying - with a reference to the new Bush administration's policies – that it was no longer needed ("Global Climate Coalition," Source Watch).

66   "Smoke, Mirrors & Hot Air: How ExxonMobil Uses Big Tobacco's Tactics to Manufacture Uncertainty on Climate Science," Union of Concerned Scientists, January 2007.

67   "Greenpeace Presents ExxonSecrets.org," see especially "Organizations in ExxonMobil's Data Base"; *Smoke, Mirrors, and Hot Air*, 1.

68   Mark Hertsgaard, "While Washington Slept," *Vanity Fair*, May 2006.

69   "Global Warming Petition" (http://www.petitionproject.org).

70   Oreskes and Conway, *Merchants of Doubt*, 244-45.

71   Dennis Hevesi, "Frederick Seitz, Physicist Who Led Skeptics of Global Warming, Dies at 96," *New York Times*, 6 March 2008.

72   Brian Angliss, "Scrutinizing the 31,000 Scientists in the OISM Petition Project," Skepti-

cal Science, 11 March 2010.

73   Powell, The Inquisition of Climate Science, 22-23.

74   George Musser, "Climate of Uncertainty," Scientific American, 16 October 2001, 14–15.

75   Oreskes and Conway, Merchants of Doubt, 244-45.

76   S. Fred Singer, "My Salad Days," Letter to the Editor, Washington Post, 12 February 2001; ExxonSecrets.org, Science and Environmental Policy Project; "In the Matter of S. Fred Singer vs. Justin Lancaster," 24 September 1993.

77   Response to Kevin Trenberth, "Global Warming: It's Happening," NaturalScience, 29 January 1998; Fred Singer and Dennis T. Avery, Unstoppable Global Warming: Every 1,500 Years, updated and expanded ed. (Rowman & Littlefield, 2007).

78   Craig D. Idso et al., Climate Change Reconsidered: The Report of the Nongovernmental International Panel on Climate Change, Vol. 1 (Heartland Institute, 2009); Tim Dickenson, "The Climate Killers," Rolling Stone, 6 January 2010.

79   John Carey with Sarah R. Shapiro, "Global Warming," Bloomberg Businessweek Magazine, 15 August 2004.

80   Dana Nuccitelli, "Patrick Michaels: Serial Deleter of Inconvenient Data," Climate Progress, 17 January 2012; quoting James Hansen, "Michael Crichton's 'Scientific Method,'" 27 September 2004; Comments by John P. Holdren on "The Shaky Science behind the Climate Change Sense of the Congress Resolution," 9 June 2003.

81   "Patrick J. Michaels – Funding," SourceWatch.

82   Marc Fisher, "Virginia's Heated Battle over Global Warming," Washington Post, 8 August 2006; Brad Johnson, "Cato's Pat Michaels Admits 40 Percent of Funding Comes from Big Oil," Climate Progress, 16 August 2010.

83   Roy W. Spencer and William D. Braswell, "On the Misdiagnosis of Surface Temperature Feedbacks from Variations in Earth's Radiant Energy Balance," Remote Sensing, 15 July 2011; Sue Sturgis, "Climate-Science Contrarian Roy Spencer's Oil-Industry Ties," Institute of Southern Studies, 7 September 2011.

84   For example, Roy W. Spencer and John R. Christy, "Precision and Radiosonde Validation of Satellite Gridpoint Temperature Anomalies, Part II: A Tropospheric Retrieval and Trends during 1979–90," Journal of Climate 5 (1992): 858–66.

85   Joe Romm, "Should You Believe Anything John Christy and Roy Spencer Say?" Climate Progress, 22 May 2008; Ray Pierrehumbert, "How to Cook a Graph in Three Easy Lessons," RealClimate, 21 May 2008.

86   Sturgis, "Climate-science Contrarian Roy Spencer's Oil-Industry Ties."

87   George C. Marshall Institute, Organizations, Exxonsecrets.org.

88   Dana Nuccitelli, "Christy Crock #1: 1970s Cooling," Skeptical Science, 8 April 2011; "Liveblogging the Senate Hearing, Quark Soup by David Appell, 1 August 2012; Kerry A. Emanuel, "Christy Crock #2: Jumping to Conclusions?" Sceptical Science, 10 April 2011; Nuccitelli, "Christy Crock #3: Internal Variability," Skeptical Science, 14 April 2011.

89   William K. Sessions, Chief Judge of the United States District Court for the District of Vermont. September 12, 2007: 44–45.

90   Smoke, Mirrors, and Hot Air; Factsheet: John Christy; Romm, "Should You Believe Anything John Christy and Roy Spencer Say?"

91   Fred Guterl, "The Truth about Global Warming," Newsweek, 22 July 2001; Romm, "Should You Believe Anything John Christy and Roy Spencer Say?"

92   Interview with BBC World Service, One Planet, 3 October 2010; "Could Global Warming Kill Us?" Larry King Live, CNN, 31 January 2007.

93   Lindzen, "Climate Alarm"; Sourcewatch.org on Richard S. Lindzen; Lindzen, "Climate of Fear: Global Warming Alarmists Intimidate Dissenting Scientists into Silence," Global Research: Opinion Journal of the WSJ, 12 April 2006; Powell, The Inquisition of Climate Science, 64.

94   Richard S. Lindzen and Yong-Sang Choi, "On the Observational Determination of Climate Sensitivity and Its Implications," Asia-Pacific Journal of Atmospheric Science, 47/4 (2011); Lindzen "Climate Alarm: What We Are Up Against, and What to Do," Heartland Institute, 8 March 2009.

95   Richard S. Lindzen and Yong-Sang Choi, "On the Determination of Climate Feedbacks from ERBE Data," *Geophysical Research Letters* 36/16 (August 2009); Joe Romm, "Hansen Study: Climate Sensitivity Is High, Burning All Fossil Fuels Would Make Most of Planet 'Uninhabitable,'" Climate Progress, 17 September 2013, referring to James Hansen et al., "Climate Sensitivity, Sea Level and Atmospheric Carbon Dioxide," *Philosophical Transactions of the Royal Society*, 28 October 2013.

96   Dana Nuccitelli, "Working out Climate Sensitivity from Satellite Measurements," Skeptical Science, 6 July 2012; Andrew C. Revkin, "A Rebuttal to a Cool Climate Report," *New York Times*, 8 January 2010; Justin Gillis, "Clouds' Effect on Climate Change Is Last Bastion for Dissenters," *New York Times*, 30 April 2012.

97   "Working out Climate Sensitivity"; Richard S. Lindzen and Yong-Sang Choi, "On the Observational Determination of Climate Sensitivity and Its Implications," *Asia-Pacific Journal of Atmospheric Science*, 47/4 (2011).

98   Gillis, "Clouds' Effect on Climate Change."

99   Willie Soon and Sallie Baliunas, "Proxy Climatic and Environmental Changes of the Past 1,0000 Years," *Climate Research*, 31 January 2003; *Smoke, Mirrors, and Hot Air*, 15.

100   Ibid., citing Senator James M. Inhofe, "The Science of Climate Change," U.S. Senate, 28 July 2003.

101   Naomi Oreskes, "Beyond the Ivory Tower: The Scientific Consensus on Climate Change," *Science*, 3 December 2004. Benny Peiser claimed that Oreskes' list actually contained 34 articles that "reject or doubt" the consensus; but after considerable back-and-forth, he admitted that there was only one such article – which was merely a statement by a committee of the American Association of Petroleum Geologists; see "What Does Naomi Oreskes' study on Consensus Show?" Skeptical Science.

102   Peter T. Doran and Maggie Kendall Zimmerman, "Examining the Scientific Consensus on Climate Change," *Earth and Environmental Sciences* 90/20 (20 January 2009).

103   William R. L. Anderegg et al., "Expert Credibility in Climate Change," *Proceedings of the National Academy of Sciences*, 21 June 2010.

104   James Powell, "The State of Climate Science: A Thorough Review of the Scientific Literature on Global Warming," *Science Progress*, 15 November 2012. For more on this issues, see Graham Wayne, "Is There a Scientific Consensus on Global Warming," Skeptical Science.

105   Stephen Leahy, "It's a Natural Cycle," Skeptical Science.

106   Dana Nuccitelli, "What Has Global Warming Done Since 1998?" Skeptical Science.

107   John Cook, "What Evidences Is There for the Hockey Stick?" Skeptical Science; "Major PAGES 2k Network Paper Confirms the Hockey Stick," Skeptical Science, 22 April 2013.

108   Dana Nuccitelli, "Has Earth Warmed as Much as Expected?" Skeptical Science.

109   For references, see "What Do the Climategate' Hacked CRU Emails Tell Us?" Skeptical Science, 18 March 2012.

110   William Marsden, *Fool's Rule: Inside the Failed Politics of Climate Change* (Alfred A. Knopf Canada, 2011), 216.

111   Joe Romm, "DC Court Bluntly Affirms Michael Mann's Right to Proceed in Defamation Lawsuit against National Review and CEI," Climate Progress, 29 July 2013; Andrew Breiner, "Could a Climate Scientist's Defamation Suit Shut Down the Nation's Leading Conservative Magazine?" Climate Progress, 3 February 2014.

112   Stephen Leahy, "Solar Activity & Climate: Is the Sun Causing Global Warming?" Skeptical Science, intermediate level.

113   Dana Nuccitelli, "Climate Scientists Erring on the Side of Least Drama," Skeptical Science, 30 January 2013; Glenn Scherer, "Special Report: IPCC, Assessing Climate Risks, Consistently Underestimates," Daily Climate, 6 December 2012.

114   Dana Nuccitelli, "Are Glaciers Growing or Retreating?" Skeptical Science, 17 December 2011.

115   John Cook, "Is Antarctica Losing or Gaining Ice?" Skeptical Science, 4 May 2012.

116   Graham Wayne, "Positives and Negatives of Global Warming," Skeptical Science, 17 August 2010, intermediate level.

117   Daniel Bailey, "Can Animals and Plants Adapt to Global Warming?" Skeptical Science, 22 December 2011.

118   "White House Leadership Summit on Women, Climate and Energy," Energy.gov, 31 May 2013; "DOE Head Ernest Moniz Delivers First Major Policy Address," GreenTech-Media," 26 August 2013.

119   Analyzing the '900 Papers Supporting Climate Scepticism': 9 out of Top 10 authors Linked to ExxonMobil," Carbon Brief, 15 April 2011; Mihai Andrei, "9 out of 10 Top Climate Change Deniers Linked with Exxon Mobil," ZME Science, 10 May 2011.

120   Daniel Fisher, "Mr. Big," *Forbes*, 13 March 2006; Jane Mayer, "Covert Operations," *New Yorker*, 30 August 2010.

121   "Koch Industries: Still Fueling Climate Denial," Greenpeace, 2011.

122   Ibid. Political activities of the Kochs are discussed in Chapter 13.

123   Robert J. Bruelle, "New Study Exposes Flood of Dark Money Feeding Climate Change Denial," Drexel University, 23 December 2013; George Zornick, "The Dark Money in Climate Change," *Washington Post*, 17 December 2013.

124   Suzanne Goldenberg, "Secret Funding Helped Build Vast Network of Climate Denial Thinktanks," *Guardian*, 14 February 2013.

125   Andy Kroll, "Exposed: The Dark-Money ATM of the Conservative Movement," *Mother Jones*, 5 February 2013; Matea Gold, "Koch-Backed Political Network, Designed to Shield Donors, Raised $400 Million in 2012," *Washington Post*, 5 January 2014.

126   Josh Harkinson, "Climate Change Deniers without Borders," *Mother Jones*, 22 December 2009.

127   Ibid.

Chapter 12: Media Failure

1   Justin Gillis, "Climate Maverick to Retire from NASA," *New York Times*, 1 April 2013; Juliet Eilperin, "The Public's Interest in Climate Change Is Waning," *Washington Post*, 2 April 2013.

2   Gregory Giroux, "Bloomberg by the Numbers: 33," Bloomberg, 22 April 2013; "Climate Change: Key Data Points from Pew Research," Pew Research Center, 2 April 2013; Max Fisher, "Americans Are Less Worried about Climate Change than Almost Anyone Else," *Washington Post*, 27 September 2013.

3   Richard Gray, "Climate Scientists Are Losing the Public Debate on Global Warming," *Telegraph*, 8 April 2012.

4   James Powell, "The State of Climate Science: A Thorough Review of the Scientific Literature on Global Warming," *Science Progress*, 15 November 2012.

5   Mark Hertsgaard, *Hot: Living Through the Next Fifty Years on Earth* (New York: Houghton Mifflin Harcourt, 2011), 263.

6   Eric Pooley, "How Much Would You Pay to Save the Planet? American Press and the Economics of Climate Change," Joan Shorenstein Center on the Press, Politics and Public Policy, John F. Kennedy School of Government, January 2009. He first encountered this image of humanity as a meteor, Pooley said, in Eric Roston, *The Carbon Age* (New York: Walker and Company, 2008).

7   Joe Romm, "Media Largely Ignores Latest Warning from Climate Scientists," Climate Progress, 19 March 2009.

8   Romm, "A Stunning Year in Climate Science Reveals that Human Civilization Is on the Precipice," Climate Progress, 15 November 2010; Romm, "Silence of the Lambs: Media Herd's Coverage of Climate Change 'Fell Off the Map' in 2010," Climate Progress, 3 January 2011; Ross Gelbspan, "U.S. Press Coverage of the Climate Crisis: A Damning Betrayal of Public Trust," The Heat is Online, June 2010; Ross Gelbspan, *Boiling Point*, with a new preface by the author (New York: Basic Books, 2004), xv, xvii; Tom Engelhardt, "Ending the World the Human Way: Climate Change as the Anti-News," TomDispatch, 2 February 2014.

9   Robert M. Entman, *Democracy Without Citizens: Media and the Decay of American Democracy* (New York and Oxford: Oxford University Press, 1989), 30.

10   Maxwell T. Boykoff and Jules M. Boykoff, "Balance as Bias: Global Warming and the

US Prestige Press," *Global Environmental Change* 14 (2004), 125–136.

11   Ross Gelbspan, *The Heat Is On: The Climate Crisis, the Cover-Up, the Prescription* (Perseus Press: Cambridge, 1998), 57-58.

12   Naomi Oreskes and Erik M. Conway, *Merchants of Doubt* (New York: Bloomsbury, 2010), 214.

13   "Climatologist James Hansen on 'Cowards in Our Democracies: Part 1,'" Climate Progress, 27 January 2012.

14   Joby Warrick, "Consensus Emerges Earth Is Warming – Now What?" *Washington Post*, 11 November 1997.

15   Boykoff and Boykoff, "Balance as Bias."

16   Denise Roberts, "Reuters' Climate Coverage Continues to Decline under 'Skeptic' Editor," Media Matters, 26 February 2014; Alexis Sobel Fitts, "Reuters's Global Warming About-Face," *Columbia Journalism Review,* 26 July 2013.

17   Stephen Lacey, "American Newspapers Are Number One in Climate Denial," Climate Progress, 14 October 2012.

18   Joanna B. Foster, "Poll: U.S. Leads the World . . . in Climate Denial," Climate Progress, 22 July 2014.

19   Joe Romm, "The 97 Percent: Watch John Oliver's Hilarious 'Statistically Representative Climate Change Debate,'" Climate Progress, 12 May 2014.

20   Joe Romm, "Killing a False Narrative before It Takes Hold," Nieman Watchdog, 18 April 2011.

21   John Abraham and Dana Nuccitelli, "New Study Finds Fringe Global Warming Contrarians Get Disproportionate Media Attention," *Guardian*, 11 August 2014; discussing Bart Verheggen et al., "Scientists' Views about Attribution of Global Warming," *Environmental Science and Technology*, 22 July 2014.

22   Joe Romm, "Climate Scientists Spell Out Stark Danger and Immorality of Inaction in New Leaked Report," Climate Progress, 27 August 2014; referring to Seth Borenstein, "Draft Of Upcoming IPCC Report Presents Stark View of the Future As Climate Change Rages On," Associated Press, 26 August 2014.

23   Stephan Lewandowsky, "Media Failure on Iraq War Repeated in Climate Change Coverage," *Guardian,* 6 December 2013.

24   Tom Engelhardt, "Why It's So Tough to Get Your Head Around Climate Change," Tom Dispatch, 4 March 2013.

25   Hertsgaard, *Hot*, 262.

26   Pooley, "How Much Would You Pay?" Hertsgaard, *Hot*, 266.

27   Gelbspan, "U.S. Press Coverage of the Climate Crisis."

28   "Science Group Calls on News Corp. to Improve Climate Science Content," Union of Concerned Scientists, 21 September 2012.

29   Harrison H. Schmitt and William Happer, "In Defense of Carbon Dioxide," *Wall Street Journal*, 9 May 2013.

30   Jeffrey Sachs, "The 'Wall Street Journal' Parade of Climate Lies," Huffington Post, 7 September 2014; "Matt Ridley Replies to His Climate-Change Criticism," *Wall Street Journal*, 9 September 2014; Joe Romm, "Matt Ridley Returns with Error-riddled Articles, As Wall Street Journal Discredits Itself," Climate Progress, 10 September 2014.

31   Shauna Theel, "CNBC's Climate Denial Is Bad For Business," Media Matters, 18 June 2013.

32   Joe Romm, "Washington Post Publishes Two Strong Debunkings of George Will's Double Dose of Disinformation," Climate Progress, 21 March 2009; Joe Romm, "Washington Post Reporters Take Unprecedented Step of Contradicting Columnist George Will in a News Article," Climate Progress, 7 April 2009.

33   Joe Romm, "Shameless Flameout: *Washington Post* Once Again Publishes George Will's Anti-Scientific Nonsense," Climate Progress, 17 January 2013.

34   Joe Romm, "Paging Jeff Bezos: George Will Compares Climate Scientists to Nazis," Climate Progress, 28 February 2014.

35   Romm, "Shameless Flameout"; Lindsay Abrams, "Debunking Charles Krauthammer's Climate Lies: A Drinking Game," *Salon*, 25 February 2014.

36   Paul Thornton, "On Letters from Climate-Change Deniers," *Los Angeles Times*, 8 October 2013; Graham Readfearn, "Should Newspapers Ban Letters from Climate Science Deniers?" Planet Oz, *Guardian*, 16 October 2013.

37   Brian Young, "Tell the Washington Post and New York Times: Don't Promote Climate Change Denial," CredoMobilize, February 2014; "Forbes: Stop Promoting Climate Change Denial," CredoMobilize.

38   Thom Hartmann, "The Mainstream Media's Criminal Climate Coverage," 26 February 2014.

39   Emily Atkin, "To Improve Accuracy, BBC Tells Its Reporters to Stop Giving Air Time to Climate Deniers," Climate Progress, 7 July 2014.

40   Quoted in Joe Romm, *Straight Up: America's Fiercest Climate Blogger Takes on the Status Quo Media, Politicians, and Clean Energy Solutions* (Island Press, 2010), 58; Douglas Fischer, "Climate Coverage Down Again in 2011," Daily Climate, 17 January 2012; Jack Shafer, "Why We're So Blasé about Global Warming," Reuters, 30 August 2014.

41   Margaret Sullivan, "Keeping Environmental Reporting Strong Won't Be Easy," *New York Times*, 11 January 2013.

42   Joanna M. Foster, "Climate Coverage Drops at the *New York Times* after Paper Closed Its Environmental Desk," Climate Progress, 25 November 2013.

43   Joe Romm, "Silence of the Lambs: Climate Coverage Drops at Major U.S. Newspapers, Flatlines on TV," Climate Progress, 14 January 2014; Douglas Fischer, "Climate Coverage, Dominated by Weird Weather, Falls Further in 2012," *Daily Climate,* 2 January 2013.

44   Tom Zeller, Jr., "Green: A New Name, a Broader Mission," *New York Times*, 21 April 2010.

45   Curtis Brainard, "NYT Cancels Green blog," *Columbia Journalism Review*, 1 March 2013.

46   Joe Romm, "In Epic Blunder, NY Times and Washington Post All but Abandon Specialized Climate Science Coverage," Climate Progress, 4 March 2013.

47   Max Greenberg, "Two Big Climate Stories You Didn't Read About in *The New York Times: Times* Skips Stories Soon after Closing Environmental Desk and Green Blog," Media Matters, 7 August 2013.

48   Brainard, "NYT Cancels Green blog."

49   "Science Times Stunner: '. . . a Majority of the Section's Editorial Staff Doubts that Human-Induced Global Warming Represents a Serious Threat to Humanity,'" Climate Progress, 13 August 2013.

50   Joe Romm, "In Epic Blunder, NY Times and Washington Post."

51   Joe Romm, "Washington Post Drops Climate Hawk Ezra Klein, Adds Climate Confusionist Blog Volokh Conspiracy," Climate Progress, 23 January 2014.

52   Todd Gitlin, "Is the Press Too Big to Fail? It's Dumb Journalism, Stupid," in "The Tinsel Age of Journalism," Tomgram, 25 April 2013.

53   Joe Romm and Andrew Breiner, "Sunday News Shows Ignored Obama's Climate Plan but Late-Night Comics Picked Up the Slack," Climate Progress, 1 July 2013.

54   Andrew Breiner, "CNN Ignores Major Climate Report, But Fox News Does Something Even Worse," Climate Progress, 2 April 2014.

55   Emily Atkin, "96 Percent of Network Nightly News' Coverage of Extreme Weather Doesn't Mention Climate Change," Climate Progress, 19 December 2013.

56   Jill Fitzsimmons and Shauna Theel, "Media Ignore Climate Context of Midwest Floods," Media Matters, 7 May 2013.

57   Joe Romm, "NPR Airs Story on Melting Glaciers without Explaining Why They Are Melting," Climate Progress, 30 May 2013.

58   Jane Velez-Mitchell, "Let's Tell the Truth about Extreme Weather," CNN, 16 May 2014.

59   Clayton Sandell, "Extreme Weather from Mother Nature," ABC News, 24 June 2013; Maria Konnikova, "Hot Heads in Cold Weather," *New Yorker,* 7 February 2014.

60   See, e.g., Robert W. McChesney, *The Problem of the Media: U.S. Communication Politics in the Twenty-First Century* (Monthly Review, 2004).

61 Rep. John Lewis, Theodore H. White Lecture on Press and Politics, Joan Shorenstein Center, John F. Kennedy School of Government, Harvard University, 20 November 2008; quoted in Pooley, "How Much Would You Pay?"

62 Thom Hartmann, "The Mainstream Media's Criminal Climate Coverage," 26 February 2014; Wen Stephenson, "A Convenient Excuse," *The Phoenix*, 5 November 2012.

Chapter 13: Political Failure

1 Alison Benjamin, "Stern: Climate Change a 'Market Failure,'" *Guardian*, 29 November 2007; George Monbiot, "The Process Is Dead," *Guardian*, September 21, 2010.

2 William Marsden, *Fools Rule: Inside the Failed Politics of Climate Change* (Alfred A. Knopf Canada, 2011), especially 255.

3 Ibid., 3; "'Crunch Time' for Climate Change," BBC, 12 December 2007.

4 Bill McKibben, "Global Warming's Terrifying New Math," *Rolling Stone*, 19 July 2012.

5 *State of the World 1989*, xiv, xvi.

6 Lorraine Elliott, *The Global Politics of the Environment* (Washington Square: New York University Press, 1998), 67.

7 Dennis Hayes, "Earth Day 1990: Threshold of the Green Decade," 8 November 1989.

8 Elliott, *The Global Politics of the Environment*, 67.

9 Ibid., 69.

10 Ibid., 71; Christopher Flavin, "Facing Up to the Risks of Climate Change," in Lester Brown et al., *State of the World 1996* (New York & London: W. W. Norton, 1996), 33-35; "Report of the Conference of the Parties on Its First Session, Held at Berlin from 28 March to 7 April 1995," Framework Convention on Climate Change, 6 June 1995.

11 "Byrd-Hagel Resolution," U.S. Senate, 25 July 1997.

12 Seth Borenstein, "Scientists Beg for Climate Action," Associated Press, 5 December 2007; Elisabeth Rosenthal, "U.N. Report Describes Risks of Inaction on Climate Change," *New York Times*, 17 November 2007.

13 James Hansen et al., "Target Atmospheric CO_2: Where Should Humanity Aim?" *Open Atmospheric Science Journal* 2 (2008); Seth Borenstein, "NASA Scientist's Global Warming Warning: 'This Is The Last Chance,'" Associated Press, 23 June 2008.

14 Patrick Wintour, "Copenhagen Climate Talks Are Last Chance, Says Gordon Brown," *Guardian*, 18 October 2009; Louise Gray, "Copenhagen Summit Is Last Chance to Save the Planet, Lord Stern," *Telegraph*, 2 December 2009.

15 Suzanne Goldenberg, "Cancún Agreement Rescues UN Credibility but Falls Short of Saving Planet," *Guardian*, 12 December 2010; Marsden, *Fools Rule*, 255.

16 "Climate Conference," Associated Press.

17 Fred Pearce, "Beyond Rio's Disappointment: Finding a Path to the Future," Yale Environment 360, 28 June 2012; George Monbiot, "Rio+20 Draft of Text is 283 Paragraphs of Fluff," *Guardian*, 22 June 2012.

18 "Climate Summit Ends with a Whimper," Reuters, 9 December 2012; Andrew Light et al., "Doha Climate Summit Ends, Marking Start of a Long March to 2015," Climate Progress, 10 December 2012.

19 Stephen Leahy, "Climate Talks End Inconclusively, Again," Al Jazeera, 7 May 2013.

20 Desiree Q. Sison, "Scientists Warn of Catastrophic Climate Change by 2050," China Topix, 14 April 2014; Joe Romm, "NOAA State of the Climate in 2013: 'Our Planet Is Becoming a Warmer Place,'" Climate Progress, 18 July 2014.

21 Mark Hertsgaard, *Hot: Living Through the Next Fifty Years on Earth* (New York: Houghton Mifflin Harcourt, 2011), 12.

22 Elizabeth Kolbert, *Field Notes from a Catastrophe: Man, Nature, and Climate Change* (Bloomsbury, 2006).

23 Marsden, *Fools Rule*, 3.

24 Sherwood Rowland in his 1995 Nobel Prize acceptance speech.

25 Ibid., 255.

26 Hertsgaard, *Hot*, 285.

27 Marsden, *Fools Rule*, 5, 67.

28 George Monbiot, "The Process Is Dead," *Guardian*, September 21, 2010; Ross Gelb-

span, "It's Too late to Stop Climate Change, Argues Ross Gelbspan — So What Do We Do Now?" *Grist*, 11 December 2007.

29   Marsden, *Fools Rule*, 4; Nicholas Stern, *The Global Deal: Climate Change and the Creation of a New Era of Progress and Prosperity* (New York: Public Affairs [Perseus] 2009), 2.

30   Hertsgaard, *Hot*, 252.

31   Paul Krugman, "Cassandras of Climate," *New York Times*, 28 September 2009.

32   Richard Falk, "Apollo's Curse and Climate Change," richardfalk.wordpress.com, 29 September 2012.

33   Mardsen, *Fools Rule*, 163.

34   Ibid., 17; Stephen Leahy, "Climate Talks End Inconclusively, Again," *Al Jazeera*, 7 May 2013.

35   Mardsen, *Fools Rule*, 7, 241.

36   Ibid., 80.

37   Chris Isidore, "Exxon Mobil Profit Is Just Short of Record," CNN Money, 1 February 2013; Valeri Vasquex, "Exxon Mobil Dodges the Tax Man," Center for American Progress, 11 May 2011; Hertsgaard, *Hot*, 13.

38   Alexis Goldstein, "Can a 'Firewall Strategy' Keep Big Energy Out of Climate Talks? It Worked for Fighting Tobacco," *Yes Magazine*, 19 September 2014.

39   Sen. Inhofe Delivers Major Speech on the Science of Climate Change,"Catastrophic Global Warming Alarmism Not Based on Objective Science," Part 2: 2003; James M. Inhofe, U.S. Senator, Oklahoma; John Gizzi, "Inhofe Was First to Declare Global Warming 'the Greatest Hoax,'" Human Events, 6 August 2012; Rick Piltz, "Sen. Inhofe Inquisition Seeking Ways to Criminalize and Prosecute 17 Leading Climate Scientists," Climate Progress, 25 February 2010; Rebecca Leber, "Inhofe on the 97% of Scientists Who Agree Global Warming Is Real: 'That Doesn't Mean Anything,'" Climate Progress, 16 March 2012.

40   Washington, WND Books, 2012; "The Greatest Hoax," Voice of Christian America, 7 March 2012; Lucia Graves, "James Inhofe 'Proud' to Be a Target in Climate Change Documentary," Huffington Post, 29 March 2013; Rebecca Leber, "Senators Who Voted to Protect Oil Tax Breaks Received $23,582,500 from Big Oil," Climate Progress, 29 March 2012; Brad Johnson, "Inhofe: God Says Global Warming Is a Hoax," Climate Progress, 9 March 2012.

41   Collins, "Cooling on Warming."

42   Adam Peck, "GOP 'Savior' Marco Rubio Mocks Climate Change," Climate Progress, 13 February 2013; Annie-Rose Strasser, "Rubio Can't Name a Single Source behind His Climate Denialism," Climate Progress, 13 May 2014.

43   United States Senator Orrin G. Hatch, Issues & Legislation, 2010.

44   Steve Benen, "Political Animal," *Washington Monthly*, 17 August 2010.

45   "Wicker: U.S. Should Not Sign Climate Pact Amid Economic Risks, Scientific Doubts," U.S. Senator Roger Wicker, 14 December 2009.

46   "Gore Takes Warming Warning to Congress," MSNBC, 21 March 2007.

47   Dan Benishek, Michigan, League of Conservation Voters, 24 July 2012.

48   "Transcript: Rahm Emanuel and Rep. John Boehner," This Week with George Stephanopoulos, ABC News, 19 April 2009.

49   Miriam Raftery, "Politics in Paradise: Filner, Hunter Clash on Healthcare, Budget, Climate Change & More," *East County Magazine*, 10 June 2013.

50   Rick Piltz, "Rep. Sensenbrenner Projects 'Fascism' and 'Fraud' onto Scientists, Is Rebutted at Hearing," Climate Science Watch, 8 December 2009; "Sensenbrenner to Tell Copenhagen: No Climate Laws Until 'Scientific Fascism' Ends," Fox News, 9 December 2009.

51   "Shimkus: Capping CO_2 Emissions Will 'Take Away Plant Food,'" Progress Illinois, 27 March 2009.

52   Emily Atkin, "House Passes Bill Requiring Agencies to Put Climate Change on the Back Burner," Climate Progress, 2 April 2014.

53   Ronald Brownstein, "GOP Gives Climate Science a Cold Shoulder," *National Journal*,

16 February 2011.

54   Rebecca Leber, "Senators Who Voted to Protect Oil Tax Breaks Received $23,582,500 from Big Oil," Climate Progress, 29 March 2012.

55   Joanna Zelman, "Mitt Romney Slams Obama on Climate Change in Convention Speech," Huffington Post, 31 August 2012.

56   Tiffany Germain et al., "The Anti-Science Climate Denier Caucus: 113th Congress Edition," Climate Progress, 26 June 2013.

57   Jeff Spross, "New Report Shows Remarkable 'Climate Disconnect' in House GOP Voting Record," Climate Progress, 9 July 2013, discussing a report by Rep. Henry Waxman (D-CA).

58   Katie Valentine, "House Republicans Voted against Environmental Interests 95 Percent of the Time in 2013," Climate Progress, 11 February 2014.

59   Emily Atkin, "Senate Blocks $85 Billion Tax Cut Bill because It Would Have Helped Wind Energy," Climate Progress, 16 May 2014.

60   Amanda Terkel, "Lamar Smith, Global Warming Skeptic, Set to Chair House Science Committee," *Huffington Post*, 27 November 2012; Stephen Lacey, "Rep. Lamar Smith, Who Criticized 'the Idea of Human-Made Global Warming,' Set to Chair House Science Panel," Climate Progress, 28 November 2012; Lamar Smith, "Overheated Rhetoric on Climate Change Doesn't Make for Good Policies," 19 May 2013; Frank Rich, "Why the GOP Still Denies Climate Change," New York Magazine, 10 May 2014.

61   Rebecca Leber, "Climate Science Denier Leads House Science Subcommittee," Climate Progress, 20 March 2013.

62   Jane Mayer, "Covert Operations," New Yorker, 30 August 2010.

63   Ibid.

64   Ibid.; Andrew Goldman, "The Billionaire's Party," New York Magazine, 25 July 2010.

65   George Monbiot, "The Tea Party Movement: Deluded and Inspired by Billionaires," Guardian, 25 October 2010.

66   John M. Broder, "Climate Change Doubt Is Tea Party Article of Faith," New York Times, 20 October 2010.

67   Suzanne Goldenberg, "Republicans Attack Obama's Environmental Protection from All Sides," Guardian, 4 March 2011.

68   Jane Mayer, "Koch Pledge Tied to Congressional Climate Inaction," New Yorker, 1 July 2013.

69   Frank Rich, "The Billionaires Bankrolling the Tea Party," New York Times, 28 August 2010; Gail Collins, "Cooling on Warming," New York Times, 27 March 2013.

70   Rich, "The Billionaires Bankrolling"; Lewis quoted in Mayer, "Koch Pledge Tied to Congressional Climate Inaction"; David Sassoon, "Koch Brothers' Political Activism Protects Their 50-Year Stake in Canadian Heavy Oils," InsideClimate News, 10 May 2012; Jason Sattler, "America's Greediest: Koch Brothers, 'Libertarians' Who Hate the Free Market," National Memo, 28 December 2013; Thom Hartmann, "Are the Koch Brothers the New 'Copper Kings'?" Thom Hartmann Show, 22 October 2013.

71   Jane Mayer, "A Word from Our Sponsor," New Yorker, 27 May 2013.

72   Paul Farhi, "Billionaire Koch Brothers Use Web to Take on Media Reports They Dispute," Washington Post, 14 July 2013.

73   Rich, "The Billionaires Bankrolling the Tea Party"; Pam Martens, "Koch Brothers' Wealth Grew by $33 Billion in 3 Years as America's Schools Report 1 Million Homeless Kids," Wall Street on Parade, 24 April 2013.

74   Ashley Parker, "New Democratic Strategy Goes after Koch Brothers," New York Times, 5 March 2014.

75   Goldman, "The Billionaire's Party."

76   Naomi Oreskes, "The Long Consensus on Climate Change," Washington Post, 1 February 2007.

77   "Six Good Things Richard Nixon Did for the Environment," Mother Nature Network; Alexis C. Madrigal, "Gallery: Why Nixon Created the EPA," Atlantic, 2 December 2010.

78   John Wihbey, "Jimmy Carter's Solar Panels: A Lost History that Haunts Today," Yale Forum on Climate Change and the Media," 11 November 2008; Tom Murse, "A Brief

History of White House Solar Panels," About.com: US Government Info.

79 Murse, "A Brief History of White House Solar Panels"; David Biello, "Where Did the Carter White House's Solar Panels Go?" *Scientific American*, 6 August 2010; "Hot Air and the White House Effect," *New York Times*, 24 November 1989.

80 A. C. Thompson, "Timeline: The Science and Politics of Global Warming," Frontline, 24 April 2007.

81 Elizabeth Kolbert, "Leading Causes," *New Yorker*, 5 October 2009.

82 Ibid.

83 Jane Mayer, "Covert Operations."

84 Amy Royden, "U.S. Climate Change Policy under President Clinton: A Look Back," *Golden Gate University Law Review* 32/4 (2002). This section as a whole is based on Royden's article.

85 Ibid.

86 Ibid.

87 Ibid.

88 Memo to John Howard, White House Council on Environmental Quality, from Exxon-Mobil Lobbyist Arthur G. "Randy" Randol, 6 February 2001; Andrew Lawler, "Battle over IPCC Chair Renews Debate on U.S. Climate Policy," *Science*, 12 April 2002.

89 Charles Clover, "US Climate Talks Chief 'Recommended by Oil Company,'" *Telegraph*, 15 May 2002.

90 "Smoke, Mirrors & Hot Air: How ExxonMobil Uses Big Tobacco's Tactics to Manufacture Uncertainty on Climate Science," Union of Concerned Scientists, January 2007; citing Rick Piltz, "On Issues of Concern about the Governance and Direction of the Climate Change Science Program," memo to agency principals, 1 June 2005.

91 Ibid.; Douglas Jehl with Andrew C. Revkin, "Bush Reverses Vow to Curb Gas Tied to Global Warming," *New York Times*, 14 March 2001.

92 John Vidal, "Revealed: How Oil Giant Influenced Bush," *Guardian*, 8 June 2005.

93 Jehl and Revkin, "Bush Reverses Vow"; Global Climate Coalition, Source Watch.

94 Dana Milbank and Justin Blum, "Document Says Oil Chiefs Met With Cheney Task Force," *Washington Post*, 16 November 2005.

95 Joe Romm, "Bush Will Go Down in History as Possibly a Person Who Has Doomed the Planet," Climate Progress, 13 December 2008.

96 Elizabeth Kolbert, "Leading Causes," *New Yorker*, 5 October 2009.

97 Bill McKibben, "Obama's Two Faces on Climate Change," Sojourners, February 2014; Joe Romm, "Jekyll and Hyde: The Two Sides of Obama's Energy Strategy," Climate Progress, 28 January 2014.

98 Obama speech in St. Paul, 3 June 2008.

99 "Remarks by the President on American-Made Energy," Cushing Pipe Yard, Cushing, Oklahoma, 22 March 2012.

100 Jeffrey Sachs, "Obama Undermines the U.N. Climate Conference," Project Syndicate, 20 December 2009; Naomi Klein, "Copenhagen's Failure belongs to Obama," *Guardian*, 21 December 2009.

101 Bill McKibben, "Obama and Climate Change: The Real Story," *Rolling Stone*, 17 December 2013.

102 Suzanne Goldenberg, "Climate Change: Barack Obama Less Interested than Bush, Analysis Reveals," *Guardian*, 26 January 2011; "Al Gore Blasts Obama on Climate Change for Failing to Take 'Bold Action,'" Associated Press, 22 June 2011; Al Gore, "Climate of Denial: Can Science and Truth withstand the Merchants of Poison," *Rolling Stone*, 22 June 2011.

103 McKibben, "Obama and Climate Change."

104 "Remarks by the President on Election Night," White House, 7 November 2012; John M. Broder, "Obama on Climate Policy: Not Just Now, Thanks," Green Blog, *New York Times*, 16 November 2012.

105 "Inaugural Address by President Barack Obama," White House, 21 January 2013; Neil Munro, "Carney Rejects Carbon Tax," *Daily Caller*, 23 January 2013; Thomas L. Friedman, "It's Lose-Lose vs. Win-Win-Win-Win-Win," *New York Times*, 16 March 2013;

William D. Nordhaus, *The Climate Casino,* 221 ("the single most important market mechanism that is missing today is a high price on CO_2 emissions").

106   "Obama's 2013 State of the Union Address," *New York Times,* 12 February 2013; "Remarks by the President on American-Made Energy."

107   "Remarks by the President on Climate Change," Georgetown University, 25 June 2013; McKibben, "Obama and Climate Change."

108   McKibben, "Obama and Climate Change"; Jason Koebler, "Obama: U.S. 'Saudi Arabia of Natural Gas,'" *U.S. News,* 26 January 2012; "President Obama Acknowledges Climate Change While Fully Supporting Fracking in SOTU," EcoWatch, 28 January 2014; "Obama's Support for Natural Gas Drilling 'A Painful Moment' for Communities Exposed to Fracking," Democracy Now! 2 February 2012; Kevin Begos, "Obama Fracking Support in Climate Speech Worries Environmental Groups," Huffington Post, 27 June 2013; Ken Cohen, "Fracking Safe, Says Obama Administration," ExxonMobil Perspectives, 22 November 2013.

109   Kroh, "The Declining Value of Coal"; Duncan Clark, "The Rise and Rise of American Carbon," *Guardian,* 5 August 2013.

110   President Barack Obama's State of the Union Address, White House, 28 January 2014; Joe Romm, "Daddy, Could We Have Our Planet Back Now?" Climate Progress, 15 June 2014; McKibben, "Obama and Climate Change."

111   "Environmentalists to President: Embrace Climate Action over 'All of the Above,'" Sierra Club, 16 January 2014.

112   "Powering Forward: Presidential and Executive Agency Actions to Drive Clean Energy in America," Center for the New Energy Economy, January 2014.

113   Jeff Goodell, "Obama's Last Shot," *Rolling Stone,* 23 April 2014; David Remnick, "Going the Distance: On and Off the Road with Barack Obama," *New Yorker,* 27 January 2014.

114   James Hansen et al., "Target Atmospheric CO_2: Where Should Humanity Aim?" *Open Atmospheric Science Journal* 2 (2008); Lonnie G. Thompson, "Climate Change: The Evidence and Our Options," *Behavior Analyst,* 33/2 (Fall 2010), 153–170; The Blue Planet Laureates, "Environment and Development Challenges: The Imperative to Act," February 20, 2012.

115   *Motherboard,* 6 May 2014.

116   Matthew Delucca, NBC News, 6 May 2014.

117   Michael Klare, "Oil Is Back! A Global Warming President Presides over a Drill-Baby-Drill United States," TomDispatch, 4 September 2014.

118   George Monbiot, "The Process Is Dead," *Guardian,* September 21, 2010; Bill McKibben, "Global Warming's Terrifying New Math," *Rolling Stone,* 19 July 2012.

119   Sen. Sheldon Whitehouse (D-RI), "Time to Wake Up: Magical Thinking on Climate Change," May, 2013.

Chapter 14: Moral Challenge

1   "Statement of Our Nation's Moral Obligation to Address Climate Change," National Climate Ethics Campaign, 30 November 2011.

2   Bill McKibben, "Global Warming's Terrifying New Math," *Rolling Stone,* 19 July 2012.

3   Gene Outka and John P. Reeder, Jr., eds., *Prospects for a Common Morality* (Princeton: Princeton University Press, 1992); Henry Shue, *Basic Rights: Subsistence, Affluence, and U.S. Foreign Policy,* 2nd edition (Princeton: Princeton University Press, 1996); Hans Küng, *A Global Ethic for Global Politics and Economics* (New York: Oxford University Press, 1998); David Ray Griffin, "Ethics and the Fabric of the Universe," *Whitehead and Ethics in the Contemporary World: For Sustainability and the Common Good,* ed. Haruo Murata (The Japan Society for Process Studies, 2010), 7-17.

4   Küng, *A Global Ethic,* 98-99.

5   Michael Walzer, *Thick and Thin: Moral Argument at Home and Abroad* (Notre Dame: University of Notre Dame Press, 1994), xi, 10. See also David Ray Griffin, "Is a Global Ethic Possible?" in Luis Cabrera, ed., *Global Governance, Global Government: Institutional Visions for an Evolving World System* (Albany: State University of New York Press, 2011), 101-26.

6   Henry Shue, "Let Whatever is Smouldering Erupt? Conditional Sovereignty, Reviewable Intervention and Rwanda 1994," in Albert J. Paolini et al., ed., *Between Sovereignty and Global Governance: The United Nations, the State, and Civil Society* (New York: St. Martin's Press, 1993), 60-84, at 60-61.

7   James Nickel, *Making Sense of Human Rights: Philosophical Reflections on the Universal Declaration of Human Rights* (Berkeley: University of California Press, 1987), 3.

8   Biancamaria Fontana, "Democracy and the French Revolution," in John Dunn, ed., *Democracy: The Unfinished Journey, 508 BC to AD 1993* (Oxford: Oxford University Press, 1992), 107-24, at 115; Alfred North Whitehead, *Adventures of Ideas* (1933; New York: Free Press, 1967), 13-28.

9   Henry Shue, *Basic Rights: Subsistence, Affluence, and U.S. Foreign Policy*, 2nd edition (Princeton: Princeton University Press, 1996), 19; R. J. Vincent, *Human Rights and International Relations* (Cambridge: Cambridge University Press, 1986), 90.

10   Shue, *Basic Rights*, 188n16, quoting John Stuart Mill, *Utilitarianism* (Indianapolis: Bobbs-Merrill, 1957), 67; Philip Alston, "International Law and the Right to Food," in Asbjorn Eide et al., ed., *Food as a Human Right* (Tokyo: The United Nations University, 1984), 162-74, at 162.

11   Shue, *Basic Rights*, 153, referring to John Locke, *Two Treatises of Government*, Book II, Ch. V.

12   Graeme Taylor, "Humanity at the Crossroads: A Time for Commitment and Action," *Tikkun*, 2009.

13   The Constitution of the Iroquois Nations: The Great Binding Law.

14   "An Iroquois Perspective," in Christopher Vecsey and Robert W. Venables, ed., *American Indian Environments: Ecological Issues in Native American History* (Syracuse University Press, 1994).

15   Joe Romm, "The Declaration of Interdependence and Jefferson's 'Brilliant Statement of Intergenerational Equity Principles,'" Climate Progress, 4 July 2013.

16   James Hansen et al., "The Case for Young People and Nature: A Path to a Healthy, Natural, Prosperous Future," From James Hansen (Blog), 5 May 2011. Hansen has further said: "The situation we're creating for young people and future generations is that we're handing them a climate system which is potentially out of their control"; Severin Carrell, "NASA Scientist: Climate Change Is a Moral Issue on a Par with Slavery," *Guardian*, 6 April 2012.

17   Michael Mann, "The Danger of Climate Change Denial," Climate Progress, 23 April 2012.

18   Thomas E. Lovejoy, "The Climate Change Endgame," *New York Times*, 21 January 2013.

19   Ken Caldeira, "The Only Ethical Path Is to Stop Using the Atmosphere as a Waste Dump for Greenhouse Gas Pollution," Climate Progress, 15 April 2012. In speaking of a "2% cost," Caldeira is, of course, referring to the Gross National Product or the Gross World Product. These "gross" numbers are high abstractions, which tell us little about the costs of climate disruption or abatement for different cities, communities, and individuals. But because he is speaking about abatement costs, the 2% is a rough estimate of the national and global costs for serious abatement. His statement serves to make the point, therefore, that abatement costs will be very low. Moreover, as stated in the Chapter 16 and elsewhere, the costs of rigorous abatement to national and global economies are projected to be even less, with some studies showing that it will actually help the national and global economies.

20   Noam Chomsky, "The Dimming Prospects for Human Survival," Alternet, 1 April 2014.

21   See Mark Vernon, "Without Belief in Moral Truths, How Can We Care about Climate Change," *Guardian*, 25 May 2011.

22   Hansen, "The Case for Young People and Nature."

23   Steve Trent, "Climate Change: It's Not Just an Environmental Issue; It's a Human Rights Issue Too," Environment Justice Foundation, 11 December 2012.

24   Ibid.

25   Anam Sultan, "Mass Migration: The Untold Crisis of Climate Refugees," Earth Reform, 4 August 2012.

26 Rebecca Solnit, "Terminator 2009: Judgment Days in Copenhagen ," in "Tomgram: Rebecca Solnit, Earth, Too Big to Fail?" TomDispatch, 20 December 2009.

27 Marwaan Macan-Markar, "Will Climate Refugees Get Promised Aid?" Inter Press Service, 8 April 2012; Steven Lee Myers and Nicholas Kulish, "Growing Clamor About Inequities of Climate Crisis," *New York Times*, 16 November 2013.

28 See James Hansen, "A New Age of Risk," 22 September 2012.

29 Mark Hertsgaard, "A Scary New Climate Study Will Have you Saying 'Oh, Shit!'" 14 October 2009.

30 Naomi Klein, quoted in Wen Stephenson, "I'd Rather Fight Like Hell': Naomi Klein's Fierce New Resolve to Fight for Climate Justice," *The Phoenix*, 14 December 2012.

31 Bill McKibben, "The Case for Fossil-Fuel Divestment," *Rolling Stone*, 22 February 2013; Stephen Lacey, "Do the Math: Mr. McKibben Goes to Washington," Climate Progress, 19 November 2012; Justin Gillis, "To Stop Climate Change, Students Aim at College Portfolios," *New York Times*, 4 December 2012.

32 Desmond Tutu, "We Fought Apartheid. Now Climate Change Is Our Global Enemy," *Observer*, 20 September 2014.

33 Mike McGinn, "Let's Prevent This Crisis: A Letter to Harvard's President Faust," Office of the Mayor, City of Seattle, 17 October 2013.

34 Antonio Blumberg, "Union Theological Seminary in NYC Unanimously Votes to Divest from Fossil Fuels," Huffington Post, 10 June 2014; Paul Brandeis Rauschenbusch, "Fossil Fuel Divestment Strategy Passes at United Church of Christ Convention (UCC)," Huffington Post, 2 July 2013; Emily Atkin, "Group Representing Half a Billion Christians Says It Will No Longer Support Fossil Fuels," Climate Progress, 11 July 2014.

35 McKibben, "The Case"; Gillis, "To Stop Climate Change."

36 McKibben, "The Case."

37 "Unburnable Carbon 2013: Wasted Capital and Stranded Assets," Carbon Tracker, 2013.

38 Aaron Task, "Al Gore: 'Carbon Bubble' Is Going to Burst – Avoid Oil Stocks," Daily Ticker, 18 October 2013; "Climate Action Could Halve Energy Firms' Worth – Bank," Dailyclimate.org, 4 February 2013.

39 Tom Randall, "Oil's Future Draws Blood and Gore in Investment Portfolios," Bloomberg, 18 November 2013.

40 McKibben, "The Case for Fossil-Fuel Divestment."

41 Ilaria Bertini, "US Academics: Fossil Fuel Divestment Reduces Long-Term Financial Risks," Blue and Green Tomorrow, 5 December 2013.

42 John Schwartz, "Rockefellers, Heirs to an Oil Fortune, Will Divest Charity of Fossil Fuels," 21 September 2014.

43 In *Bury the Chains: Prophets and Rebels in the Fight to Free an Empire's Slaves* (New York: Houghton Mifflin Harcourt, 2006), Adam Hochschild estimated that prior to the Industrial Revolution, some 75 per cent of the world's population was in bondage, either slavery or serfdom.

44 Andrew J. Hoffman, "By Invitation: Climate Change: Calling the Fossil Fuel Abolitionists," Ethical Corporation, 28 March 2008; Charles Justice, "Slavery and Fossil Fuels," Earthjustice.blogspot.com, January 2008; John R. McNeill, *Something New Under the Sun: An Environmental History of the Twentieth-Century World* (New York: W. W. Norton, 2000); David Brion Davis, *Inhuman Bondage: The Rise and Fall of Slavery in the New World* (New York: Oxford University Press, 2006), 179.

45 Jean-Francois Mouhot, "We Are Like Slave-Owners," *Ecologist*, 29 December, 2010.

46 Hoffman, "By Invitation"; Justice, "Slavery and Fossil Fuels"; Leah D. Schade, "Fossil Fuel Abolitionists," Ecopreacher, 9 November 2012.

47 Andrew Winston, "The Climate Change Abolitionists," *Guardian*, 27 February 2013; Justice, "Slavery and Fossil Fuels."

48 Kerry Eleveld, "Making Gun Control Inevitable," Salon, 13 February 2013; Joe Romm, "Moral Majority: Team Obama Finally Embraces the Winning Argument for Climate Action," 27 June 2013.

49 Lloyd Alter, "Energy Slaves Growing Too Expensive to Feed," Corporate Knights, 11

March, 2013; Jean-François Mouhot, "Once, Men Abused Slaves, Now We Abuse Fossil Fuels," *Guardian*, 3 February 2012; R. Buckminster Fuller et al., "Document 1: Inventory of World Resources, Human Trends and Needs," in *World Design Science Decade 1965–1975* (Carbondale: Southern Illinois University, 1965–1967), 29–30.

50   Jeremy Hoff, "Prioritizing Externalities: The Combustion of Slavery and Abolition of Fossil Fuels," Vermont Law School, 2004; Mouhot, "We Are Like Slave-Owners."

51   Mouhot, "Once, Men Abused Slaves."

52   Craig Altemose, "Why 'Reducing Emissions' Is Killing Us (Literally): An Argument for Abolition," It's Getting Hot in Here, 7 July 2010.

53   Schade, "Fossil Fuel Abolitionists."

54   "The Case Against Abolition," Bristol and Transatlantic Slavery.

55   Hoffman, "By Invitation."

56   Schade, "Fossil Fuel Abolitionists."

57   Winston, "The Climate Change Abolitionists."

58   Mouhot, "Once, Men Abused Slaves."

59   Ibid.

60   Mouhot, "We Are Like Slave-Owners."

61   Jeremy Hoff, "Prioritizing Externalities: The Combustion of Slavery and Abolition of Fossil Fuels," Vermont Law School, 2004.

62   Scribbler, "When Burning Is No Longer Moral."

63   James Hansen et al., "The Case for Young People and Nature: A Path to a Healthy, Natural, Prosperous Future," From James Hansen (Blog), 5 May 2011.

64   Winston, "The Climate Change Abolitionists."

65   Justice, "Slavery and Fossil Fuels"; Alter, "Energy Slaves Growing Too Expensive to Feed."

66   Schade, "Fossil Fuel Abolitionists."

67   These words of Lincoln were written by *Lincoln* screenwriter Tony Kushner on the basis of an account provided at the time by Massachusetts Congressman John B. Alley, when he was trying to get a 2/3 vote in the House in favor of the 13th Amendment. See "Lincoln: Images of History," Socialist Action, 11 January 2013; Amy Luers, "Obama's Legacy: Curing the World of Its Fossil Fuel Addiction?" Take Part, 26 November 2012.

Chapter 15: Religious Challenge

1   Max Weber, *From Max Weber*, H. H. Gerth and C. Wright Mills, eds. (New York: Oxford University Press, 1958), 122, 155; Jürgen Habermas, "A Reply to My Critics," in John B. Thompson and David Held, eds., *Habermas: Critical Debates* (Cambridge: MIT Press, 1982), 219-83, at 248; Habermas, *Postmetaphysical Thinking: Philosophical Essays*, trans. William Mark Hohengarten (Cambridge: MIT Press), 51.

2   David Ray Griffin, *Reenchantment without Supernaturalism: A Process Philosophy of Religion* (Ithaca: Cornell University Press, 2001). Process philosophy is based primarily on the later thought of Alfred North Whitehead, who came from England in the 1920s to teach philosophy at Harvard University. He spent his early career on mathematics and logic (he and his former student Bertrand Russell collaborated on *Principia Mathematica*) and then on natural philosophy (he wrote, for example, an alternative to Einstein's theory of relativity). But after coming to Harvard University, he developed a philosophical system integrating science and logic with morality, aesthetics, and religion. Only after working on philosophy did he give up his atheism, or at least agnosticism, for (a non-traditional form of) theism.

3   Millard J. Erickson, *Christian Theology* (Grand Rapids: Baker Book House, 1985), 304.

4   Ibid., 54.

5   Senator James Inhofe, *The Greatest Hoax: How the Global Warming Conspiracy Threatens Your Future* (Washington, WND Books, 2012), 70-71.

6   Brian Tashman, "James Inhofe Says the Bible Refutes Climate Change," Right Wing Watch, 3 August 2012; "God Won't Allow Global Warming, Congressman Seeking to Head Energy Committee Says," Raw Story, 11 November 2010.

7   Jeffrey Mervis, "Ralph Hall Speaks Out on Climate Change," *National Journal*, 14

December 2011.

8   Meredith Bennett-Smith, "Calvin Beisner, Evangelical Christian, Claims Environmentalism Great Threat to Civilization," Huffington Post, 21 March 2013.

9   David Edwards, "Limbaugh: Christians 'Cannot Believe in Manmade Global Warming,'" *Raw Story*, 14 August 2013.

10 Jo Confino, "Nestlé Chairman Warns against Playing God over Climate Change," *Guardian*, 31 January 2014.

11 "God Won't Allow Global Warming"; Darren Samuelsohn, "John Shimkus Cites Genesis on Climate Change," Politico, 10 November 2010.

12 See Mark S. Gignilliat, *A Brief History of Old Testament Criticism: From Benedict Spinoza to Brevard Childs* (Zondervan, 2012).

13 David Ray Griffin, *Two Great Truths: A New Synthesis of Scientific Naturalism and Christian Faith* (Louisville: Westminster John Knox Press, 2004), 64.

14 David C. Barker and David H. Bearce, "End-Times Theology, the Shadow of the Future, and Public Resistance to Addressing Global Climate Change," *Political Research Quarterly*, June 2013.

15 "Public's Views on Human Evolution," Pew Research, 30 December 2013.

16 Stephen D. Foster Jr., "Oklahoma GOP Introduces Bill that Attacks Evolution and Climate Change," Addicting Info, 22 January 2012; Katherine Stewart, "The New Anti-Science Assault on US Schools," *Guardian*, 12 February 2012; "Anti-Evolution and Anti-Climate Science Legislation Scorecard: 2013," National Center for Science Education, 20 May 2013; "Frequently Asked Questions about NCSE," National Center for Science Education.

17 Stewart, "The New Anti-Science Assault"; Jenny McCarthy, "AntiEvolution Legislation Update – Nine Out of Ten States Have Killed Anti-Science Bills," Skeptical Raptor, 28 May 2013; "AIBS State News on Teaching Evolution," American Institute of Biological Sciences, 2013; Pema Levy and Evan McMorris-Santoro, "Creationism Controversies: The Norm among Potential Republican 2016 Contenders," Talking Points Memo, 20 November 2012; Justin Sink, "Huntsman: 'Call Me Crazy,' I Believe in Evolution, Global Warming," E2 Wire, The Hill, 18 August 2011.

18 Frank Newport, "In U.S., 46% Hold Creationist View of Human Origins," Gallup, 1 June 2012; Revelation 21:1; 1 Corinthians 15:52.

19 K.C. Boyd, "The End-Times Politics of Pastor John Hagee," AlterNet, 29 January 2013; Ryan Chiachiere and Kathleen Henehan, "Will MSNBC Devote as Much Coverage to McCain's Embrace of Hagee's Support as It Did to Obama's Rejection of Farrakhan?" *Media Matters*, 28 February 2008.

20 David Crowe, "Katrina: God's Judgment on America," Beliefnet, September 2005.

21 "Climate Change: An Evangelical Call to Action," Evangelical Climate Initiative, 2006.

22 Ibid. For more on Cizik, see Paul Rogat Loeb, *Soul of a Citizen: Living with Conviction in Challenging Times* (St. Martin's Griffin, 2nd ed., 2010), and Loeb, "Soul of a Citizen: Jesus and Climate Change - The Journey of Rich Cizik," paulloeb.org.

23 J. Lester Feder, "The Floral Majority," New Republic, 30 December 2008.

24 Napp Nazworth, "Evangelicals and Climate Change," Christian Post, 3 Parts, June 2012.

25 E. J. Dionne Jr., "Christians Who Won't Toe the Line," *Washington Post*, 16 March 2007; Frances FitzGerald, "The New Evangelicals," New Yorker, 30 June 2008; Juliet Eilperin, "Warming Draws Evangelicals into Environmentalist Fold," *Washington Post*, 8 August 2007.

26 Molly Redden, "Whatever Happened to the Evangelical-Environmental Alliance?" New Republic, 3 November 2011.

27 Ibid.

28 E. Calvin Beisner et al., "A Call to Truth, Prudence, and Protection of the Poor: An Evangelical Response to Global Warming," Cornwall Alliance for the Stewardship of Creation, 2006; "Contrary to Media Reports, National Association of Evangelicals Has Not Endorsed Latest Statement on Global Warming," Cornwall Alliance for the Stewardship of Creation, 2007.

29 Adelle M. Banks, "Dobson, Others Seek Ouster of NAE Vice President," *Christianity*

Today, 2 March 2007; J. Lester Feder, "The Floral Majority," *New Republic*, 30 December 2008.

30   Feder, "The Floral Majority"; Richard Cizik, "My Journey Toward the 'New Evangelical-ism,'" *Religion and Politics*, 13 September 2012; Cizik, "My Journey"; Banks, "Dobson, Others Seek Ouster."

31   "Inhofe Calls 2009 'The Year of the Skeptic'" (Press Release), U.S. Senate Committee on Environment and Public Works, 18 November 2009; Redden, "Whatever Happened to the Evangelical-Environmental Alliance?"

32   Ashley Portero, "What Do Christians Have Against Climate Science?" *International Business Times*, 14 February 2012. (There were not quotation marks around her statement, but it seemed to be a direct quotation.)

33   Katherine Hayhoe and Andrew Farley, *A Climate for Change: Global Warming Facts for Faith-Based Decisions* (FaithWorks, 2009); Joe Romm, "Dr. Katharine Hayhoe, Star of Showtime Climate Series, Makes TIME 100 Most Influential People List," Climate Progress, 24 April 2014.

34   Kate Sheppard, "Newt Dumps Christian Climate Scientist," *Mother Jones*, 6 Friday 2012; Marc Morano, "Hayhoe Gets the Heave-Ho! Gingrich Boots Warmist Professor from New Book after Limbaugh Reads Climate Report on Radio – Newt Kills Chapter on Climate," Climate Depot, 30 December 2011; Portero, "What Do Christians Have Against Climate Science?"

35   E. Calvin Beisner, "Are Evangelical Critics of Global Warming Driven by Politics?" Cornwall Alliance, 28 February 2012; Lee Fang, "Exclusive: The Oil Operators behind the Religious Climate Changed Denial Front Group, Cornwall," Climate Progress, 15 June 2010. (CFACT's relation to ExxonMobil was mentioned in Chapter 12.)

36   Beisner, "Are Evangelical Critics?" Redden, "Whatever Happened to the Evangelical-Environmental Alliance?"

37   Dorothy Boorse, *Loving the Least of These: Addressing a Changing Environment*, National Association of Evangelicals, 2011.

38   Fiona Harvey, "World's Poorest Will Feel Brunt of Climate Change, Warns World Bank," *Guardian*, 19 June 2013; *Turn Down the Heat: Why a 4°C Warmer World Must be Avoided*, World Bank, November 2012.

39   See David Ray Griffin, "Process Theology and the Christian Good News: A Response to Classical Free Will Theism," in John B. Cobb, Jr., and Clark H. Pinnock, eds., *Searching for an Adequate God: A Dialogue between Process and Free Will Theists* (Grand Rapids: Eerdmans, 2000), 1-38, at 12-16.

40   See David Ray Griffin, *Religion and Scientific Naturalism: Overcoming the Conflicts* (Albany: State University of New York Press, 2000), 55-61. On the basis of that discussion, incidentally, well-known evangelical theologian Howard Van Till gave up supernaturalism in favor of a form of theism that allows for no interruptions; see Howard J. Van Till, foreword to Griffin, *Two Great Truths*.

41   "On the Care of Creation," Evangelical Environmental Network, 2011. Two recent examples of books by traditional theologians who take climate change seriously are Michael S. Northcott, *A Political Theology of Climate Change* (Eerdmans, 2013), and Michael S. Northcott and Peter M. Scott, eds., *Systematic Theology and Climate Change: Ecumenical Perspectives* (Routledge, 2014).

42   James Carlson, "What Would Jesus Do about Global Warming?" *Orlando Weekly*, 13 April 2006.

43   Boorse, *Loving the Least of These*, section entitled "A Biblical Basis for Christian En-gagement."

44   "Evangelicals Support Some Climate Change Policies," *Conservation Magazine*, June 2013, referring to Neil Smith and Anthony Leiserowitz, "American Evangelicals and Global Warming," *Global Environmental Change*, 28 May 2013. For another example (beyond Howard Van Till) of Evangelical theology that rejects divine interruptions, see Thomas Jay Oord, *The Nature of Love: A Theology* (St. Louis, Missouri: Chalice, 2010).

45   Leith Anderson (President, National Association of Evangelicals), Foreword to Boorse,

Loving the Least of These; Nazworth, "Evangelicals and Climate Change."

46   Darwin spoke of "the laws impressed on matter by the Creator" (*The Origin of Species* [New York: Mentor Books, 1958], 448), and said that "some few organic beings were originally created, which were endowed with a high power of generation, & with the capacity for some slight inheritable variability" (Robert C. Stauffer, ed., *Charles Darwin's Natural Selection: Being the Second Part of His Big Species Book Written from 1856 to 1859* [Cambridge: Cambridge University Press, 1975], 224); Neil C. Gillespie, *Charles Darwin and the Problem of Creation* (Chicago: University of Chicago Press, 1979), 140-45; Charles Darwin, *The Autobiography of Charles Darwin*, ed. Nora Barlow (New York: Norton, 1969), 92; Dov Ospovat, *The Development of Darwin's Theory: Natural History, Natural Theology & Natural Selection 1838-1859* (Cambridge & New York: Cambridge University Press, 1981), 72-73, 226.

47   Stephen Jay Gould, *The Panda's Thumb* (New York: W. W. Norton, 1982), 38; William Provine, "Progress in Evolution and Meaning in Life," in Matthew H. Nitecki, ed., *Evolutionary Progress* (Chicago & London: University of Chicago Press, 1988), 49-74, at 64-66, 70.

48   Robert T. Pennock, *Tower of Babel: The Evidence against the New Creationism* (Cambridge: MIT, 1999). 311-27.

49   Gillespie, *Charles Darwin and the Problem of Creation*, 130.

50   See John B. Cobb, Jr., ed., *Back To Darwin: A Richer Account of Evolution* (Eerdmans, 2008). (This book contains two chapters of mine: "Neo-Darwinism and Its Religious Implications," and "Whitehead's Naturalism and a Non-Darwinian View of Evolution.")

51   Richard Lewontin, "Billions and Billions of Demons," *New York Review of Books*, 9 January 1997: 28-32, at 31.

52   Provine, "Progress in Evolution," 64-66; Stephen Jay Gould, "Impeaching a Self-Appointed Judge" *Scientific American*, July 1992: 118-21, at 118; Gilbert Harman, *The Nature of Morality: An Introduction to Ethics* (New York: Oxford University Press, 1977), 11.

53   John Mackie, *Ethics: Inventing Right and Wrong* (New York: Penguin, 1977), 24, 15, 79-80.

54   Ibid., 48.

55   John Mackie, *The Miracle of Theism: Arguments for and against the Existence of God* (Oxford: Clarendon, 1982), 1. Mackie pointed out that his argument would cause no difficulty for forms of theism that do not think of divine power as omnipotence (ibid., 151), but in making his argument he ignored this alternative idea of deity

56   Gilbert Harman, *The Nature of Morality: An Introduction to Ethics* (New York: Oxford University Press, 1977), 17; Gilbert Harman, "Is There a Single True Morality?" in *Relativism: Interpretation and Confrontation*, ed. Michael Krausz (Notre Dame: University of Notre Dame Press, 1989), 363-86, at 381, 366.

57   Harman, *The Nature of Morality*, 11-13, 131-32.

58   Jeffrie G. Murphy, *Evolution, Morality, and the Meaning of Life* (Totowa, N.J.: Rowman and Littlefield, 1982), 16; Murphy, "Constitutionalism, Moral Skepticism, and Religious Belief," in Alan S. Rosenbaum, ed., *Constitutionalism: The Philosophical Dimension* (New York: Greenwood, 1988), 239-49, at 241, 244.

59   Clifford Geertz, *Islam Observed: Religious Development in Morocco and Indonesia* (New Haven: Yale University Press, 1968), 97; Geertz, *Interpretation of Cultures: Selected Essays* (New York: Basic Books, 1973), 126-27.

60   Bernard Williams, *Ethics and the Limits of Philosophy* (Cambridge: Harvard University Press, 1985), 22; Williams, "Ethics and the Fabric of the World," in *Morality and Objectivity: A Tribute to J. L. Mackie*, ed. Ted Honderich (London: Routledge & Kegan Paul, 1985), 182, 205.

61   Jürgen Habermas, *Justification and Application: Remarks on Discourse Ethics* (Cambridge: Polity, 19937), 71, 146.

62   Thomas Schwartz, "Obligations to Posterity," in R. I. Sikora and Brian Barry, ed., *Obligations to Future Generations* (Philadelphia: Temple University Press, 1978), 3-13.

63   Joe Romm, "Our Hellish Future: Definitive NOAA-led Report on U.S. Climate Impacts

Warns of Scorching 9 to 11°F Warming Over Most of Inland U.S. by 2090," Climate Progress, 15 June 2009. It is not clear whether or not this writer meant this statement ironically.

64   Charles Hartshorne and William L. Reese, eds., *Philosophers Speak of God* (Chicago: University of Chicago Press, 1953).

65   See Tu Wei-Ming, *Centrality and Commonality: An Essay on Confucian Religiousness* (Albany: State University of New York Press, 1989), and E. E. Evans-Pritchard, *Theories of Primitive Religion* (Oxford: Clarendon Press, 1965), who wrote: "Serious distortions may result when it is said that Buddhism and Jainism are atheistic religions" (119). Also Gene Reeves, an expert on the Lotus Sutra (which is the most important scripture for Buddhists in Southern Asia), has pointed out that Buddhism could be called atheistic only by those who insist that this label be applied to any position that rejects the omnipotent deity of traditional theism ("The Lotus Sutra and Process Thought," *Process Studies* 23/2 [Summer 1994]: 98-118).

66   Jeremy W. Hayward, *Perceiving Ordinary Magic: Science and Intuitive Wisdom* (Boulder and London: Shambhala, 1984), 241; Charles Hartshorne, *Omnipotence and Other Theological Mistakes* (Albany: SUNY Press, 1984), 52-62; discussed in Griffin, *Reenchantment without Supernaturalism*, 140. I have explained and defended panentheism in Griffin, *Panentheism and Scientific Naturalism* (Claremont: Century Press, 2014).

67   "Ultimate Concern – Tillich in Dialogue by D. Mackenzie Brown" (religion online).

68   Jack Jenkins, "Pope Francis: Destroying the Rainforest Is a Sin," Climate Progress, 7 July 2014.

Chapter 16: Economic Challenge

1   Frank Ackerman and Elizabeth A. Stanton, *Climate Economics: The State of the Art* (Stockholm Environment Institute, 2011). This book was originally published online, then republished as a hardcopy book in 2013. The 2011 online version has been used here.

2   Christian Parenti, "'The Limits to Growth': A Book That Launched a Movement," *The Nation*, 5 December 2012.

3   "The Limits to Growth: Abstract Established by Eduard Pestel. A Report to The Club of Rome (1972), by Donella H. Meadows, Dennis I. Meadows, Jorgen Randers, William W. Behrens III."

4   Henry Wallich, *Newsweek*, 13 March 1972; William D. Nordhaus, "World Dynamics: Measurements without Data," *Economic Journal* 83/332 (December 1973), 1156-83; William D. Nordhaus, "Lethal Model 2: The Limits to Growth Revisited," Brookings Institute, 1992.

5   Herman E. Daly, "*Steady-State Economics: The Economics of Biophysical Equilibrium and Moral Growth* (Freeman, 1977); Daly, "The Steady-State Economy: Postmodern Alternative to Growthmania," David Ray Griffin, ed., *Spirituality and Society: Postmodern Visions* (Albany: SUNY Press, 1988), 110; Daly, "Uneconomic Growth: Conflicting Paradigms," Acceptance Speech, Right Livelihood Award, 9 December 1996.

6   Daly, "Climate Policy: From 'Know How' to 'Do Now,'" Keynote Address on Federal Climate Policy, American Meteorological Society, 4 September 2008; Paul Tillich, *Systematic Theology*, Vol. 1 (Chicago: University of Chicago Press, 1951), 13; Herman E. Daly and John B. Cobb, Jr., *For the Common Good: Redirecting the Economy toward Community, the Environment, and a Sustainable Future*, updated and expanded ed. ([1977] Boston: Beacon Press, 1994), 389.

7   John B. Cobb, Jr., *The Earthist Challenge to Economism: A Theological Critique of the World Bank* (London: Macmillan, 1999), 13-28.

8   Paul Voosen, "Cool Head on Global Warming," *Chronicle Review*, 4 November 2013.

9   Ackerman and Stanton, *Climate Economics: The State of the Art*.

10   Ibid.; William R. Nordhaus, *A Question of Balance: Weighing the Options on Global Warming Policies* (Yale University Press, 2008), 1-2.

11   Ibid., 144.

12   William D. Nordhaus, *Climate Casino: Risk, Uncertainty, and Economics for a Warming World* (Yale University Press, 2013), 146, 76.

13   Ibid., 6, 325, 198.

14   Nicholas Stern, *The Economics of Climate Change: The Stern Review* (Cambridge University Press, 2007), Executive Summary. (*The Stern Review,* including the Executive Summary, is available online.)

15   Nordhaus, *A Question of Balance,* 165-66; Nicholas Stern, "The Structure of Economic Modeling of the Potential Impacts of Climate Change: Grafting Gross Underestimation of Risk onto Already Narrow Science Models," *Journal of Economic Literature* 51/3 (2013), 838–59.

16   *Stern Review,* 34 (online pagination); Nordhaus, *A Question of Balance,* 191.

17   Ackerman and Stanton, *Climate Economics,* 18, 26, 145; Elizabeth A. Stanton, Frank Ackerman, and Ramon Bueno, "Reason, Empathy, and Fair Play: The Climate Policy Gap," DESA Working Paper, April 2012.

18   Nordhaus, *Climate Casino,* 83; Ackerman and Stanton, *Climate Economics,* 11, 58-63.

19   Ibid., 18.

20   Frank Ackerman, "Debating Climate Economics: The Stern Review vs. Its Critics," July 2007, Global Development and Environment Institute.

21   Executive Summary, *Stern Review.*

22   Nordhaus, *A Question of Balance,* 193.

23   William D. Nordhaus, "Why the Global Warming Skeptics Are Wrong," *New York Review of Books,* 22 March 2012.

24   Stanton et al., "Reason, Empathy, and Fair Play."

25   Nordhaus, *Climate Casino,* 3, 66, 76, 108, 221.

26   Nordhaus, *Climate Casino,* 91, 99.

27   Ibid., 146, 56-57, 60, 61, 66.

28   Timothy M. Lenton and Juan-Carlos Ciscar, "Integrating Tipping Points into Climate Impact Assessments," *Climatic Change,* April 2013.

29   Nordhaus, *Climate Casino,* 103, 112-13, 145, 146.

30   Nicholas Stern, "Ethics, Equity and the Economics of Climate Change: Paper 1, Science and Philosophy," Centre for Climate Change Economics, and Grantham Research Institute on Climate Change and the Environment, November 2013.

31   Nicholas Stern, "The Structure of Economic Modeling of the Potential Impacts of Climate Change.

32   James Painter, "The IPCC's Risky Talk on Climate Change," The Blog, Carbon Brief, 4 April 2014.

33   Stanton et al., "Reason, Empathy, and Fair Play," 37.

34   Ackerman and Stanton, *Climate Economics,* 6.

35   Ibid., 20.

36   This summary of Weitzman's dismal theorem is provided by Ackerman and Stanton (ibid).

37   William D. Nordhaus, "An Analysis of the Dismal Theorem," Cowles Foundation Discussion Paper, Yale University, 16 January 2009; Martin Weitzman, "Revisiting Fat-Tailed Uncertainty in the Economics of Climate Change," Harvard University, 2011.

38   Weitzman, "The Odds of Disaster: An Economist's Warning on Global Warming," PBS, May 2013.

39   Robert S. Pindyck, "Climate Change Policy: What Do the Models Tell Us?" *Journal of Economic Literature* 51/3 (2013).

40   Nordhaus, *Climate Casino,* 213-15.

41   Ibid., 28.

42   Ibid., 134, 122-25.

43   Stern, "The Structure of Economic Modeling of the Potential Impacts of Climate Change."

44   Heather Stewart and Larry Elliott, "Nicholas Stern: 'I Got It Wrong on Climate Change – It's Far, Far Worse,'" *Guardian,* 26 January 2013.

45   William R. Cline, *The Economics of Global Warming* (Institute for International Eco-

nomics, 1992), 307, 311, 256-57.

46   Nordhaus, *A Question of Balance*, 191.

47   Cline, *The Economics of Global Warming*, 235; Nordhaus, *A Question of Balance*, 11.

48   Nordhaus, *A Question of Balance*, 60; Cline, *The Economics of Global Warming*, 249, 256; Nordhaus, "Reflections on the Economics of Climate Change," *Journal of Economic Perspectives* 7/4 (1993), 11-25, at 15.

49   Nicholas Stern, "Ethics, Equity and the Economics of Climate Change: Paper 2: Economics and Politics," Centre for Climate Change Economics, and Grantham Research Institute on Climate Change and the Environment, August 2013.

50   Ibid., 91, 99, 103-04, 145.

51   Ibid., 187, 191, 188, 193.

52   Ibid., 193.

53   Ibid., 189, 91, 99, 103-04, 145.

54   Stern, "The Structure of Economic Modeling." Support for Stern's view was provided in 2014 with a report published about the costs of coastal flooding from sea-level rise in the 21st century. This effect of climate change alone, it predicted, could reduce the global economy by as much as 9.3 percent; Jochen Hinkel et al., "Coastal Flood Damage and Adaptation Costs under 21st Century Sea-Level Rise," *Proceedings of the National Academy of Sciences*, 4 March 2014.

55   "New NOAA Study Estimates Future Loss of Labor Capacity as Climate Warms," National Oceanic and Atmospheric Administration, 25 February 2013; Joe Romm, "Labor Day 2050: Global Warming and the Coming Collapse of Labor Productivity," Climate Progress, 1 September 2014.

56   Stern, "Ethics, Equity."

57   Nordhaus, *Climate Casino*, 142.

58   Ibid., 142-43.

59   Ackerman and Stanton, *Climate Economics*, 7; in 2013, Ackerman was part of a Hansen-led study that advocated an increase of no more than 1°C (1.8°F). See James Hansen et al., "Assessing 'Dangerous Climate Change': Required Reduction of Carbon Emissions to Protect Young People, Future Generations and Nature," PLOS ONE, December 2013; this report is summarized in Hansen and J. Pushker Kharecha, Summary of and Opinions about Hansen et al., "Assessing 'Dangerous Climate Change,'" *Popular Science*, 3 December 2013.

60   Nordhaus, *Climate Casino*, 198; David Spratt, "What Would 3 Degrees Mean," Code Red, 1 September 2010. (*Climate Road Red: The Case for Emergency Action* [Melbourne: Scribe, 2008], was coauthored by David Spratt and Philip Sutton.)

61   Ackerman and Stanton, "Climate Economics," 98, 148.

62   Ibid., 98.

63   Joe Romm, "Climate Panel Stunner: Avoiding Climate Catastrophe Is Super Cheap – but Only If We Act Now," Climate Progress, 13 April 2014; Romm, "The $4 Trillion Mistake: Climate Action Delayed Is Climate Action Denied," Climate Progress, 14 May 2014, referring to *Energy Technology Perspectives 2014*, International Energy Agency, 13 May 2014.

64   Fen Montaigne, "New Paper Offers Sweeping Plan to Decarbonize the Global Economy," Environment 360, 4 December 2013; referring to Hansen et al., "Assessing 'Dangerous Climate Change'"; Joe Romm, "World Bank: Fighting Climate Change Would Boost Global Economy Up to $2.6 Trillion a Year," Climate Progress, 24 June 2014.

65   "Economic Growth and Action on Climate Change Can Now Be Achieved Together, Finds Global Commission," press release for "Better Growth, Better Climate: The New Climate Economy Report," Global Commission on the Economy and Climate, 16 September 2014; Justin Gillis, "Fixing Climate Change May Add No Costs, Report Says," *New York Times*, 16 September 2014; Paul Krugman, "Errors and Emissions: Could Fighting Global Warming Be Cheap and Free?" *New York Times*, 18 September 2014; Audrey Resutek, "Study: Cutting Emissions Pays for Itself," MIT, 24 August 2014; referring to Tammy M. Thompson et al., "A Systems Approach to Evaluating the Air Quality Co-Benefits of US Carbon Policies," *Nature Climate Change*, 24 August 2014.

66   Donald A. Brown in Joe Romm, "The Most Crucial Missing Element in U.S. Media Coverage of Climate Change: The Ethical Duty to Reduce GHG Emissions," *Climate Progress*, 14 August 2009.

67   Hansen et al., "Assessing 'Dangerous Climate Change,'" 21.

68   *Stern Review*, Executive Summary; *Stern Review*, 1; Nicholas Stern, Royal Economic Society lecture, quoted in Alison Benjamin, "Stern: Climate Change a 'Market Failure,'" *Guardian*, 29 November 2007.

69   *Stern Review*, Executive Summary.

70   Nordhaus, *Climate Casino*, 224-25; John P. Weyant, quoted in Paul Voosen, "Cool Head on Global Warming," *Chronicle Review*, 4 November 2013.

71   Nordhaus, *Climate Casino*, 17-18.

72   William D. Nordhaus, "Life After Kyoto: Alternative Approaches to Global Warming Policies," Yale University, 9 December 2005; *Climate Casino*, 17-18; *A Question of Balance*, 29.

73   Ibid., 225.

74   "National Carbon Tax Survey," Friends of the Earth, 16-19 December 2012.

75   "World Bank President Advocates Putting a Price on Carbon," Green Market Oracle, 15 May 2013.

76   Alex Morales, "Shell, Unilever Lead 100 Companies Calling for CO_2 Price," Bloomberg Businessweek, 19 November 2012.

77   Stephen Lacey, "Exxon: Carbon Tax Would 'Play a Significant Role in Addressing Rising Emissions,'" Climate Progress, 15 November 2012; Ryan Koronowski, "A Price Is Right: Carbon Tax Has Very Broad, Bipartisan Support (Outside of Congress)," Climate Progress, 8 May 2013; Jeff Spross, "Big Oil and the White House Agree: Carbon Pollution Will Cost Money," 5 December 2013.

78   "Use of Internal Carbon Price by Companies as Incentive and Strategic Planning Tool," Carbon Disclosure Project, December 2013.

79   Nigel Purvis and Abigail Jones, "Establishing a Global Carbon Market Reserve: A Low Cost Climate Solution with Big Returns," Brookings, 5 December 2013; Richard W. Caperton, "How a Progressive Carbon Tax Will Fight Climate Change and Stimulate the Economy," Climate Progress, 6 December 2012; Ryan Koronowski, "A Price Is Right: Carbon Tax Has Very Broad, Bipartisan Support (Outside of Congress)," Climate Progress, 8 May 2013.

80   *A Question of Balance*, 22; "Carbon Pricing," Climate Group, May 2013.

81   Martin L. Weitzman, "Can Negotiating a Uniform Carbon Price Help to Internalize the Global Warming Externality?" *Harvard University*, 8 January 2014; Lawrence H. Goulder and Andrew R. Schein, "Carbon Taxes vs. Cap and Trade: A Critical Review," Stanford University, August 2013.

82   Fiona Harvey, "Global Carbon Trading System Has 'Essentially Collapsed,'" *Guardian*, 16 September 2012; Tristan Edis, "Carbon Permits Worse than Junk Bonds," Climate Spectator, 17 April 2013; "European Climate Policy: Worse than Useless," *Economist*, 25 January 2014; Weitzman, "Can Negotiating a Uniform Carbon Price Help?" Joshua Hill, "European Carbon Price Set to Rise to €23/t between 2021 and 2030," Clean Technica, 2 September 2014.

83   Weitzman, "Can Negotiating a Uniform Carbon Price Help?"

84   Ibid.; "Interpol Warns of Criminal Focus on $176 Billion Carbon Market," RTCC.org, 7 August 2013. (The Interpol report is "Guide to Carbon Trading Crime," June 2013.)

85   Sita Slavov, "A Carbon Tax Beats a Vacuum Ban," *U.S. News & World Report*, 23 January 2014.

86   Amy Wolf, "Economist Arthur Laffer Proposes Taxing Pollution Instead of Income," Vanderbilt News, 20 February 2012.

87   Koronowski, "A Price Is Right."

88   Jonathan L. Ramseur et al., "Carbon Tax: Deficit Reduction and Other Considerations," CRS Report for Congress, Congressional Research Service, 17 September 2012; Jeff Spross, "A Carbon Tax Would Cut the Deficit by $1 Trillion," Climate Progress, 14 November 2013.

89   "A Sweltering Planet's Agenda," Editors, *Washington Post*, 12 January 2013; see also "Carbon Tax Is Best Option Congress Has," Editors, *Washington Post*, 7 May 2013.

90   Coral Davenport, "Norquist: Carbon-Tax Swap for Income-Tax Cut Wouldn't Violate No-Tax-Hike Pledge," *National Journal*, 12 November 2012; Tanya Snyder, "Grover Norquist Buckles to Pressure from Koch-Backed Group on Carbon Tax," StreetBlogs, 13 November 2012.

91   Ryan Koronowski, "Why Obama Just named Sweden as a Model for Energy Policy," Climate Progress, 4 September 2013; C. Fred Bergsten, "The Swedish Model for Economic Recovery," *Washington Post*, 29 August 2013.

92   Stewart Elgie and Jessica McClay, "BC's Carbon Tax Shift after Five Years: Results: An Environmental (and Economic) Success Story," Sustainable Prosperity, July 2013.

93   Jeff Spross, "Why A National Carbon Tax Would Be Amazing — In Four Charts," Climate Progress, 23 June 2014; referring to *The Economic, Climate, Fiscal, Power, and Demographic Impact of a National Fee-and-Dividend Carbon Tax,* by Regional Economic Models, Inc. and Synapse Energy Economics, Inc., June 2014.

94   Lester R. Brown, "Chapter 10. Can We Mobilize Fast Enough? Shifting Taxes and Subsidies," *Plan B 4.0: Mobilizing to Save Civilization.*

95   Caperton, "The Newly Proposed Carbon Tax Will Fight Global Warming."

96   N. Gregory Mankiw, "Gas Tax Now!" *Fortune*, 24 May 1999.

97   James Hansen, "Game Over for the Climate," *New York Times*, 9 May 2012; "A Climate Solution That's Also Good for the Economy," Citizen Climate Policy, 9 June 2014.

98   Emily Atkin, "Billionaire Koch Brother Says Carbon Tax Supporters Are on Acid," Climate Progress, 8 November 2013. (Gates said: "When we get a carbon tax we should put some of that into innovation.")

99   Nordhaus, *A Question of Balance*, 196, 186.

100   Ryan Koronowski, "The 'Social Cost of Carbon' Is Almost Double what the Government Previously Thought," Climate Progress, 5 June 2013; Jeff Spross, "The Government's Calculations of the Cost of Carbon Are Above Board, Says New Report," Climate Progress, 26 August 2014.

101   Laurie Johnson, "The Social Cost of Carbon: Playing Catch Up to the IPCC," Switchboard, Natural Resources Defense Council, 22 April 2014.

102   Frank Ackerman and Elizabeth A. Stanton, "Climate Risks and Carbon Prices: Revising the Social Cost of Carbon," Economics for Equity and Environment, July 2011; Martin L. Weitzman, "GHG Targets as Insurance Against Catastrophic Climate Damages," Department of Economics, Harvard University, 2010.

103   Nordhaus, *Question of Balance*, 197; Ackerman and Stanton, "Climate Risks and Carbon Prices."

104   Joseph E. Stiglitz, "A Cool Calculus of Global Warming," Project Syndicate, 9 November 2006.

105   Quoted in "The Senate Shills for Big Oil," Editorial, *New York Times*, 3 March 2008.

106   David Roberts, "Direct Subsidiaries to Fossil Fuels Are the Tip of the (Melting) Iceberg," Grist, 27 October 2011.

107   Jeff Spross, "Bombshell IMF Study: United States Is World's Number One Fossil Fuel Subsidizer," Climate Progress, 29 March 2013.

108   "President Addresses American Society of Newspaper Editors Convention," White House, 14 April 2006.

109   Rebecca Leber, "Big Oil Lobby Claims the Industry 'Gets No Subsidies, Zero, Nothing,'" Climate Progress, 9 January 2013; "Bill Johnson Says Subsidies for the Oil Companies that Barack Obama Has Attacked Don't Exist," PolitiFact, 17 April 2012.

110   Joanna Rothkopf, "Big Oil Companies Pay an Absurdly Low Tax Rate," *Salon*, 4 August 2014; discussing "Effective Tax Rates of Oil & Gas Companies: Cashing in on Special Treatment," Taxpayers for Common Sense, 30 July 2014.

111   Jonathan Watts, "Activists Hail Success of Twitter Storm against Fossil Fuel Subsidies," *Guardian*, 18 June 2012; Emily E. Adams, "The Energy Game is Rigged: Fossil Fuel Subsidies Topped $620 Billion in 2011," *Earth Policy Institute*, 27 February 2013; Charles Kenny, "When It Comes to Government Subsidies, Dirty Energy Still Cleans

Up," Bloomberg Business Week, 21 October 2012.

112 Brad Plumer, "IMF: Want to Fight Climate Change? Get Rid of $1.9 Trillion in Energy Subsidies," WonkBlog, *Washington Post*, 27 March 2013.

113 Laurie T. Johnson and Chris Hope, "The Social Cost of Carbon in U.S. Regulatory Impact Analyses: An Introduction and Critique," *Journal of Environmental Science* , 20 August 2012; David Roberts, "IMF Says Global Subsidies to Fossil Fuels Amount to $1.9 Trillion a Year – and That's Probably an Underestimate," Grist, 28 March 2013; Joe Romm, "What's Wrong with Climate Change Economics in One Chart," Climate Progress, 8 March 2012.

114 Roberts, "IMF Says"; Jeff Spross, "Bombshell IMF Study: United States Is World's Number One Fossil Fuel Subsidizer," Climate Progress, 29 March 2013.

115 "Maintenance of Fossil Fuel Subsidies Is a Global Scandal, Supporting IMF Findings," Cool Planet Blog, WWF, 26 September 2013.

116 Frommkin, "How the Oil Lobby Greases Washington's Wheels."

117 Quoted in Emily Atkin, "Fossil Fuels Receive $500 Billion a Year in Government Subsidies Worldwide," Climate Progress, 7 November 2013; Spross, "Bombshell IMF Study."

118 Nancy Pfund and Ben Healey, "What Would Jefferson Do? The Historical Role of Federal Subsidies in Shaping America's Energy Future," DBL Investors, September 2011; Plumer, "IMF: Want to Fight Climate Change?"

119 Plumer, ibid.; Joe Romm, "Must-See Charge: Cost of PV Cells Has Dropped an Amazing 99 percent since 1977, Bringing Solar Power to Grid Parity," 6 October 2013.

120 Peter Cramton et al., "How to Negotiate Ambitious Global Emissions Abatement," 30 May 2013.

121 Joseph E. Stiglitz, "A New Agenda for Global Warming," *The Economists' Voice*, July 2006.

122 Ibid.

123 "Green Climate Fund," UN Framework Convention on Climate Change.

124 Elizabeth A. Stanton, Frank Ackerman, and Ramon Bueno, "Reason, Empathy, and Fair Play: The Climate Policy Gap," DESA Working Paper, April 2012.

125 Megan Rowling, "Green Climate Fund Aims to Allocate Half of Money for Adaption," Reuters, 24 February 2014.

126 "COP19: Lord Nicholas Stern on Why the Costs and Risks of Inaction Will Be Severe," Responding to Climate Change, 19 November 2013.

127 Fiona Harvey, "Green Climate Fund to Discuss $100bn Pledged by Rich Countries," *Guardian*, 23 August 2012; "Climate Crisis Finance: Poor Countries Are Left in the Dark," Countercurrents, 11 November 2013; Brad Plumer, "Wealthy Nations Pledged Billions to Help the Poor Adapt to Climate Change. Where Did It All Go?" WonkBlog, *Washington Post*, 18 November 2013.

128 "Climate Crisis Finance ."

129 Justin Gillis, "Panel's Warning on Climate Risk: Worst Is Yet to Come," *New York Times*, 31 March 2014.

130 Stanton, Ackerman, and Bueno, "Reason, Empathy, and Fair Play."

131 Joe Romm, "Is the Global Economy a Ponzi Scheme?" Climate Change, 9 March 2009; Noam Chomsky, "The Dimming Prospects for Human Survival," Alternet, 1 April 2014.

132 Diana B. Henriques, "Madoff Is Sentenced to 150 Years for Ponzi Scheme," *New York Times*, 29 June 2009; Joe Romm, "This Changes Everything: Naomi Klein Is Right: Unchecked Capitalism Will Destroy Civilization," Climate Change, 16 September 2014; ref. to Naomi Klein, *This Changes Everything: Capitalism Vs. the Climate* (Simon & Schuster, 2014).

133 "World Footprint: Do We Fit on the Planet?" Global Footprint Network.

Chapter 17: The Transition to Clean Energy

1 Stephen Pacala and Robert Socolow, "Stabilization Wedges: Solving the Climate Problem for the Next 50 Years with Current Technologies," *Science*, 13 August 2004; Joe Romm, "Socolow Reaffirms 2004 'Wedges' Paper, Urges Aggressive Low-Carbon

Deployment ASAP," Climate Progress, 18 May 2011.

2 Joe Romm, "Energy Efficiency Is *the* Climate Solution: Part 1: The Biggest Low-Carbon Resource by Far," Climate Progress, 1 June 2011.

3 *The Energy Report: 100% Renewable Energy by 2050*, by WWF (World Wildlife Fund) and Ecofys (2010).

4 Maria van der Hoeven, "We Can Have Safe, Sustainable Energy," *Guardian*, 24 April 2012; "Energy Efficiency Simply Makes Sense," in "Visualizing the 'Hidden' Fuel of Energy Efficiency," *Journal of the International Energy Agency*, Spring 2013. Van der Hoeven, to be sure, uses the term "renewable," saying that efficiency is renewable because "the efficiency potential never runs out." But her discussion focuses primarily on the fact that efficiency is a type of *clean* energy, because it cuts down the use of fossil fuels.

5 "Unlocking Energy Efficiency in the U.S. Economy," McKinsey and Company, 2009, Executive Summary.

6 Joe Romm, "Energy Efficiency is *the* Climate Solution: Part 2: The Limitless Resource," Climate Progress, 15 July 2008.

7 Ibid.

8 Romm, "Efficiency, Part 3: The Only Cheap Power Left," Climate Progress, 27 July 2008; "Efficiency, Part 4: How Does California Do It So Consistently and Cost-Effectively?" Climate Progress, 30 July 2008.

9 Tiffany Hsu, "U.S. Wastes More Energy than Europe, China," *Los Angeles Times*, 12 July 2012; Ben Geman, "White House Seeks Carbon Curbs through Energy Efficiency Gains," The Hill, 18 July 2013.

10 "Denmark Awarded International Energy Efficiency Prize," State of Green, 21 May 2014; Andrew Breiner, "Denmark to Cut Energy Use by 12 Percent, and Power Companies Like It," Climate Progress 10 October 2013.

11 Joe Romm, "$18 Trillion Windfall: Health and Productivity Benefits of Efficiency Top Energy Savings," Climate Progress, 11 September 2014.

12 Joshua S. Hill, "New Class of Solar Cell Reaches New Efficiency Breakthrough," Clean Technica, 11 June 2013; Jeff Spross, "Get the Lead Out: How a New Super-Efficient Solar Cell Technology Just Got Better," Climate Progress, 5 May 2014; Bernie Bulkin, "Perovskites: The Future of Solar Power?" Guardian Professional, 7 March 2014.

13 Jeff Spross, "New Ultra-Thin Solar Cell Could Massively Boost Battery Life of Personal Mobile Devices," Climate Progress, 24 March 2013; Katie Valentine, "Researchers Just Hit a New World Record in Solar Cell Efficiency," Climate Progress, 26 September 2013; James Ayre, "Are Super-Thin Solar Cells the Future? New Solar Cells Developed that Are Pound for Pound up to 1000 Times More Powerful than Conventional Photovoltaics," Solar Love, 28 June 2013.

14 Tina Casey, "'Turbo Boost' for Silicon Solar Cells Could Seal Doom for Diesel," Clean Technica, 12 September 2014.

15 Jeff Spross, "Now a New Rhubarb-Based Battery Could Massively Increase Renewable Energy Use," Climate Progress, 13 January 2014.

16 "Researchers Create 'Nanoflowers' for Energy Storage, Solar Cells," NC State University, 11 November 2012; James Ayre, "Nano-Flowers Could Help Create Next-Gen Energy Storage & Solar Cells," Clean Technica, 12 October 2012.

17 Kristopher Kettle, "Energy Storage Study Predicts Boom Through 2022," Energy Collective, 21 March 2013; Stephen Lacey, "Solar Can Be Baseload: Spanish CSP Plant with Storage Produces Electricity for 24 Hours Straight," Climate Progress, 5 July 2011.

18 Sean Pool and John Dos Passos Coggin, "Fulfilling the Promise of Concentrating Solar Power: Low-Cost Incentives Can Spur Innovation in the Solar Market," Center for American Progress, June 2013.

19 "NREL Quantifies Significant Value in Concentrating Solar Power CSP," National Clean Energy Laboratory, 24 April 2013; Romeu Gaspar, "How Solar PV Is Winning over CSP," Clean Energy World.com, 12 March 2013.

20 "Spain's Government 'Devastates' the CSP Sector," CSP Today, 4 February 2013; Zachary Shahan, "Top 10 Solar Power Stories Of 2012," Clean Technica, 31 December 2012;

Beatriz Gonzalez, "2013: An Important Year for CSP in the United States," *CSP Today,* 28 January 2013. In 2014, stories appeared – some inflammatory – stating that the plant, with its very high towers, was incinerating birds flying over, with the estimated number ranging from 1,000 to 28,000 to 100,000 ("BrightSource Solar Plant Sets Birds on Fire as They Fly Overhead," Associated Press, 18 August 2014; Sebastian Anthony, "California's New Solar Power Plant Is Actually a Death Ray That's Incinerating Birds Mid-Flight," ExtremeTech, 20 August 2014). However, besides the fact that the higher estimates were based on no evidence (BrightSource contends that the true number is even lower than 1,000), they did not put their figures in context, such as the estimate that power lines kill as many as 175 million birds a year and the fact that millions die from fossil-fuel exploration and burning (Jake Richardson, "Bird Deaths from Solar Plant Exaggerated by Some Media Sources," Clean Technica, 22 August 2014). Because of the controversy, *U.S. News and World Report* compiled data on how many bird deaths are caused by the various energy industries, finding that studies estimate that solar power kills between 1,000 and 28,000 birds a year; wind power kills between 140,000 and 328,000; nuclear power kills 330,000; oil and gas kill between 500,000 and 1,000,000; and coal kills 7,900,000 birds a year. (Emily Atkin, "Chart: How Many Birds Are Killed by Wind, Solar, Oil, and Coal?" Climate Progress, 25 August 2014.)

21 Shahan, "Top 10 Solar Power Stories Of 2012"; "Largest CSP Project in the World Inaugurated in Abu Dhabi," Greenpeace, 18 March 2013; Belén Gallego, "2013 Update: The State of the Concentrated Solar Power Industry," *CSP Today,* 2013; "Global Concentrating Solar Power Outlook 2009," Greenpeace, 25 May 2009.

22 Pete Danko, "World's Biggest Solar PV Projects Underway in SoCal," EarthTechling, 29 April 2013; "World's Largest Solar-Hydro Power Station Getting Connected to the Grid," PowerChina, 2 January 2014.

23 Andrew Burger, "Active Solar Commissions 100-Plus MW Perovo Solar PV Station in Ukraine's Crimea," Clean Technica, 29 December 2011; "Top 10 World's Largest Solar PV Power Plants," Solar Plaza, 2011; Zachary Shahan, "Largest Solar Photovoltaic Facility in World Built in Canada," Clean Technica, 11 October 2010; "Qinghai Leads in Photovoltaic Power," *China Daily,* 2 March 2012; "Project Helios: Revitalizing the Greek Economy with Solar Power," Green Energy Solutions Center, 2013; Ari Phillips, "Mexico Building Latin America's Largest Solar Farm to Replace Old, Dirty Oil-Power Plant," Climate Progress, 25 February 2014.

24 Kiley Kroh and Jeff Spross, "13 Major Clean Energy Breakthroughs of 2013," Climate Progress, 18 December 2013.

25 Tony Dutzik and Robert Sargent, *Lighting the Way: What We Can Learn from America's Top 12 Solar States,* Environment America, July 2013; Kroh and Spross, "13 Major Clean Energy Breakthroughs"; Tina Casey, "Solar Power Cheaper than Coal Foreseen by German Solar CEO," Clean Technica, 10 July 2013.

26 Ryan Koronowski, "The World's Biggest Coal Company Is Turning to Solar Energy to Lower Its Utility Bill," Climate Progress, 6 June 2013.

27 Collin Meehan, "New ERCOT Report Shows that Texas Wind and Solar Are Highly Competitive with Natural Gas," Climate Progress, 29 January 2013.

28 Zachary Shahan, "Solar PV + Storage Likely = Retail Electricity in Germany This Year," Clean Technica, 11 August 2014.

29 John Farrell, "Utility Agrees: (Their) Solar Should Supplant Natural Gas," Clean Technica, 16 September 2013; Cynthia Shahan, "Austin's Super Cheap Solar Agreement (5¢/kWh) Goes To Recurrent Energy, Not SunEdison," Clean Technica, 21 May 2014; Zachary Shahan, "Judge Rules Solar Power a Better Deal for Minnesota than Natural Gas," Clean Technica, 2 January 2014.

30 Giles Parkinson, "Why Generators Are Terrified of Solar," Renew Economy, 26 March 2012; David Roberts, "Solar Panels Could Destroy U.S. Utilities, According to U.S. Utilities," Grist, 10 April 2013; Lenny Bernstein, "Utilities and Solar Advocates Square Off over the Future," *Washington Post,* 9 June, 2013; Chris Meehan, "Solar's Momentum Faces Opposition from Fossil Fueled Legislation," Clean Energy, 19 March 2013; Ryan Randazzo, "APS Seeks Higher Bills for New Solar Customers," *The Republic,* 12

July 2013; Evan Halper, 'Koch Brothers, Big Utilities Attack Solar, Green Energy Policies," *Los Angeles Times*, 19 April 2014; Kiley Kroh, "U.S. Residential Solar Just Beat Commercial Installations for the First Time," Climate Progress, 31 May 2014; Katie Valentine, "Africa Will Add More Renewable Energy in 2014 than in the Last 14 Years Combined," Climate Progress, 21 August 2014.

31   Jeff Spross, "California Regulators Decide Utilities Can't Charge Solar-Killing Fees," Climate Progress, 17 April 2014; Spross, "Solar Power Is Now Just as Cheap as Conventional Electricity in Italy and Germany," Climate Progress, 24 March 2014; Jeff Spross, "The Massive Demand for Solar in Asia Shows Us Where the Industry Is Headed," 9 August 2013.

32   Zachary Shahan, "Top Solar Power Countries Per Capita & Per GDP," Clean Technica, 26 June 2013"; "Solar Power Breaks World Record in Q1, IHS Raises 2014 Forecast to 45,000 MW," Clean Technica, 8 April 2014.

33   Adam Johnston, "China Targeting 10 GW of New Solar Capacity in 2013," Clean Technica, 16 January 2013; Zachary Shahan, "China's New Solar Target: 40 GW By 2015 (8 Times More Than Its Initial 5 GW Target)," Clean Technica, 13 December 2012; Emily Atkin, "New 1,000 Megawatt Solar Project in China Marks 'Significant Shift' for Global Market," 2 January 2014; Brad Plumer, "China Installed Record Amounts of Solar Power in 2013. But Coal Is still Winning," Wonk Blog, *Washington Post*, 30 January 2014.

34   Susan Kraemer, "Japan Creates Potential $9.6 Billion Solar Boom with FITs," Clean Technica, 21 June 2012; Rudolf ten Hoedt, "Solar Power Booming in Japan," Clean Technica, 17 May 2014; "Explosive Growth in Japan and China to Drive Annual Solar Photovoltaic Demand above 35 Gigawatts," NPD Solarbuzz, 2 July 2013.

35   Ari Phillips, "India almost Doubled Its Solar Power in 2013 with Big Plans for More," 21 January 2014; Ari Phillips, "Massive Interest-Free Loan Program Announced For Solar Users In India," Climate Progress, 17 July 2014; Sophie Varrath, "Australian Coal Prospects Dim as Modi Turns Spotlight on Solar," ReNew Economy, 20 May 2014; Eileen Shim, "India Has a Radical Plan to Power Every One of Its Homes by 2019," PolicyMic, 22 May 2014; Mridul Chadha, "India Can Add 145 GW Solar Power Capacity by 2024: Report," Clean Technica, 4 September 2014.

36   Silvio Marcacci, "US Passes 10 GW Installed Solar PV Capacity Milestone," Clean Technica, 9 July 2013.

37   Dutzik and Sargent, *Lighting the Way*; Jeff Spross, "The Birthplace of Big Oil Is about to Get Its Biggest Solar Plant Yet," Climate Progress, 17 May 2014.

38   Kiley Kroh, "U.S. Solar Capacity Grew 418 Percent in the Last Four Years," Climate Progress, 24 April 2014.

39   Brown, "The Great Transition, Part II."

40   Zachary Shahan, "Top Wind Power Countries Per Capita," Clean Technica, 20 June 2013; J. Matthew Roney, "Denmark, Portugal, and Spain Leading the World in Wind Power," Earth Policy Institute, 28 May 2014; "Kenneth Matthews: Nothing Quixotic about Wind Energy Industry," *Irish Independent*, 27 March 2013; James Montgomery, "Wind Power Peaks in the UK, Denmark, US," Clean Energy World, 25 March 2013; Joshua S. Hill, "Commissioning of Final Turbine Completes World's Largest Offshore Wind Farm," Clean Technica, 9 April 2013; Hill, "UK Installs First 6 MW Wind Turbine In North Sea," 18 August 2014; Hill, "Siemens to Provide 67 Turbines for UK Offshore Wind Farm," 22 August 2014; Hill, "Vestas Registers Net Profit, Set to Provide Biggest Offshore Turbines," Clean Technica, 22 August 2014.

41   Shahan, "Top Wind Power Countries Per Capita"; Adam Johnson, "Wind Generation Outpacing Natural Gas in US in 2012," Clean Technica, 24 December 2012; J. Matthew Roney, "After Record 2012, World Wind Power Set to Top 300,000 Megawatts in 2013," Earth Policy Institute, 2 April 2013; Katie Valentine, "Wind Energy in 2013 Was Equivalent to Taking 20 Million Cars Off the Road," Climate Progress, 27 May 2014.

42   Dana Nuccitelli, "Low Emissions Are No Justification for Kansas Scaling Back Cleans," *Guardian*, 21 February 2013; "Blown Away," *Economist*, 8 June 2013; Silvio Marcacci, "2013 Wind Energy Installations Stall in US, Surge in China," Clean Technica, 6 February 2014; Emily Atkin, "More U.S.-Made Wind Turbines Are Being Sold Overseas as

Congress Fails to Support Wind Power," Climate Progress, 18 August 2014.

43 Michael Conathan, "Making the Economic Case for Offshore Wind," Center for American Progress, 28 February 2013.

44 Shahan, "Top Wind Power Countries Per Capita."

45 "China Approaches 2015 Target with 41% Wind Power Growth," Climate Group, 9 April 2013; Andrew Burger, "Wind Energy Surpasses Nuclear as China's 3rd Largest Source Of Electrical Power," Clean Technica, 29 January 2013; J. Matthew Roney, "Wind Surpasses Nuclear in China," Earth Policy Institute, 19 February 2013; Marcacci, "2013 Wind Energy Installations Stall in US, Surge in China."

46 Roney, "After Record 2012, World Wind Power Set to Top 300,000 Megawatts in 2013"; Ryan Koronowski, "We're Number One: U.S. Installed Most Wind Power in 2012, U.S. Company GE Wind Is #1 Supplier," Climate Progress, 27 March 2013.

47 "Share of Wind Energy in REC Increases by 22% in 2012, Total Capacity Crosses 2,000 MW," Climate Connect News, 31 October 2012; J. Matthew Roney, "World Wind Power Poised to Bounce Back after Slowing in 2013," Earth Policy Institute, 10 April 2014.

48 Ronald Brakels, "Largest Wind Farm in Southern Hemisphere Opens Down Under," Clean Technica, 15 April 2013; Roney, "After Record 2012, World Wind Power Set to Top 300,000 Megawatts in 2013."

49 Jake Richardson, "24.9 GW of Clean Energy Capacity for Japan by 2016?" Clean Technica, 2 October 2012; Ryan Koronowski, "U.S. Offshore Wind Lease Auction Set as Grid-Connected Test Turbine Is Installed in Maine," Climate Progress, 10 June 2013.

50 Brown, "The Great Transition, Part II." Brown said that the world had about 70 GW of solar installed solar capacity, but he spoke about "solar panels," evidently failing to mention CSP. I have hence changed his 70 to about 100 GW of installed solar capacity.

51 Simon Jenkins, "Renewable Energy Won't Rid Us of the Horrors of Coal," *Guardian*, 15 May 2014; J. Matthew Roney, "Generation Gap: Wind Opens Big Lead over Nuclear in China," Earth Policy Institute, 4 March 2014.

52 "Blown Away," *Economist*, 8 June 2013.

53 "Wind and Solar," Clean Line Energy Partners.

54 Tim Tyler, "Solar–Wind Hybrid Power Plants Approximately Twice as Efficient," Solar Love, 1 May 2013.

55 Andrew Deple, "GE's Brilliant Wind Turbine — Wind Power Cheaper than Coal or Natural Gas (Part 1)," Clean Technica, 29 June 2013; Ryan Koronowski, "Gamechanger: Next Generation Wind Turbines with Storage Are Cheap, Reliable and Brilliant," Climate Progress, 14 July 2013; Brown, "The Great Transition, Part I: From Fossil Fuels to Clean Energy," *Earth Policy Institute*, 25 October 2012.

56 Sophie Vorrath, "Wind at Parity with New Coal in India, Solar to Join by 2018: HSBC," RenewEconomy, 11 July 2013, referring to "India Cleans: Good Bye Winter, Hello Spring," HSBC Bank, 20 April 2013; Zachary Shahan, "Wind Cheapest Form of Energy in Kenya and Nicaragua," Clean Technica, 13 May 2012; "Clean Energy Now Cheaper than New Fossil Fuels in Australia," Bloomberg New Energy Finance, 7 February 2013.

57 Silvio Marcacci, "Cleans Now Cheaper than Coal in Michigan, Could Be $5-Billion Industry," Clean Technica, 28 February 2012; Jeff Spross, "Wind Reaches Its Highest Generation Level Ever in Texas, Heralding a Challenge to Natural Gas," Climate Progress, 31 March 2014; Conway Irwin, "Midwest Wind Cost-Competitive with Gas and Coal," Breaking Energy, 7 December 2013; Ari Phillips, "Californians Could Save $750 Million on Energy Bills Thanks to Huge Wind Farm in Wyoming," Climate Progress, 11 February 2014; Tina Casey, "How Low Can Wind Energy Go? 2.5¢ Per Kilowatt-Hour Is Just the Beginning," Clean Technica, 23 August 2014.

58 Graham Readfearn, "Research Finds Wind Farm Health Concerns Probably Caused by Anti-Wind Scare Campaigns," DeSmogBlog, 14 March 2013; Fiona Chrichton, "How the Power of Suggestion Generates Wind Farm Symptoms," *The Conversation*, 15 March 2013; Oliver Milman, "AMA Gives Wind Farms Clean Bill of Health and Attacks 'Misinformation,'" *Guardian*, 17 March 2014.

59 Allan Chen, "No Evidence of Residential Property Value Impacts Near U.S. Wind Turbines, a New Berkeley Lab Study Finds," Berkeley Lab, 27 August 2013.

60   Joe Romm, "A New Turbine Generates Back the Energy It Takes to Build It in Just 6 Months," Climate Progress, 27 June 2014.

61   Brown, "The Great Transition, Part II."

62   Matthew Roney, "After Record 2012, World Wind Power Set to Top 300,000 Megawatts in 2013," Earth Policy Institute, 2 April 2013.

63   Ryan Koronowski, "Wind Power in the UK and Ireland: Growing, Reliable and Making Donald Trump's Hair Stand Up," Climate Progress, 28 March 2013; Catherine Brahic, "Scotland: Wind Will Power the Scots' Green Ambitions," *New Scientist*, 30 May 2014; "Scotland's Renewable Energy Sector in Numbers," Scottish Renewables, 2013.

64   Roney, "Denmark, Portugal, and Spain Leading the World in Wind Power."

65   Brown, "The Great Transition, Part II."

66   Xi Lu et al., "Global Potential for Wind-Generated Electricity," *Proceedings of the National Academy of Sciences*, 29 July 2013.

67   "Hydropower," *Renewable Electricity Generation and Storage Technologies*, National Renewable Energy Laboratory, 2012; Hydroelectricity, EPA; "Why Hydro?" National Hydropower Association; "Hydroelectric Power," Alternative Energy.

68   David Appleyard, "Hydropower 2014 Outlook: Hydro Industry to Expand Its Global Reach," Renewable Energy World, 28 January 2014.

69   Elizabeth Daigneau, "Is Hydropower a Renewable Energy or Not?" Governing.com, September 2013.

70   Howard Schneider, "World Bank Rethinks Stance on Large-Scale Hydropower Projects," Guardian Weekly, 14 May 2013; Ian Talley, "World Bank to Invest in African Hydro-electric Project," Real Time Economics Blog, *Wall Street Journal*, 6 August 2013.

71   Charles Lyons, "The Dam Boom in the Amazon," *New York Times*, 30 June 2012; Steven Bodzin, "Chileans Protest Government Approval of Five Patagonia Dams," *Christian Science Monitor*, 10 May 2011; Diego Cupolo, "Tough Questions for Chile as Ongoing Protests Stall Patagonian Dam Project," Upside Down World, 20 February 2013; Andrew Jabobs, "Plans to Harness Chinese River's Power Threaten a Region," *New York Times*, 4 May 2013; Yoolim Lee, "China Hydropower Dams in Mekong River Give Shocks to 60 Million," Bloomberg, 26 October 2010; Rachel Nuwer, "Hobbled on Energy, India Ponders a Multitude of Dams," Green Blog, *New York Times*, 7 January 2013.

72   Bent Flyvbjerg and Atif Ansar, "Hydroelectric Dams Are Doing More Harm than Good to Emerging Economies," Guardian Professional, 7 April 2014.

73   David Pitt, "Hydroelectric Power Makes a Big Comeback at U.S. Dams," Associated Press, 15 September 2013.

74   John Upton, "The New New Hydropower: Small-Scale Turbines Have Big Potential," Grist, 4 June 2012.

75   "How Hydroelectric Energy Works," Clean Energy, Union of Concerned Scientists, 2006.

76   The first operating OTEC plant was an experimental one in Japan built in 1980 ("Brief History of our OTEC Study," Institute of Ocean Energy, Saga University, Japan). A commercial plant is to be built by Lockheed Martin off the coast China's Hainan Island (Daniel Cusick and ClimateWire, "Ocean Thermal Power Will Debut off China's Coast," *Scientific American*, 1 May 2013).

77   Eric Stoutenburg, "Combining Offshore Wind and Wave Energy Farms to Facilitate Grid Integration of Variable Renewables," Stanford University, 2012.

78   Felicity Jones and Robert Rawlinson-Smith, "Wave and Tidal Energy Need Different Policies," Renewable Energy World, 10 June 2013; John Davenport, "New Wave and Tidal Energy Technologies Review," Daily Fusion, 10 July 2013.

79   Kirk Johnson, "Project Aims to Harness the Power of Waves," *New York Times*, 3 September 2012; Erik Sofge, "The Energy Fix: Engineering Triumphs over Wave and Tidal Forces," *Popular Science*, 12 June 2013.

80   Stoutenburg, "Combining Offshore Wind and Wave Energy Farms to Facilitate Grid Integration of Variable Renewables."

81   Jones and Rawlinson-Smith, "Wave and Tidal Energy Need Different Policies"; "Ocean Wave Energy," Bureau of Ocean Energy Management.

82   Oliver Milman, "Western Australia Wave Energy Project on the Brink of Commercialization," *Guardian*, 9 April 2014.

83   "The Amazing"; "World's Largest Ocean Energy Site Approved in Scotland," Daily Fusion, 27 May 2013.

84   David Ferris, "Oregon Races to Catch Up to Europe in Wave Energy," Green Tech Blog, *Forbes*, 3 October 2012; Kirk Johnson, "Project Aims to Harness the Power of Waves," *New York Times*, 3 September 2012; Pete Danko, "OPT Oregon Wave Energy Project Delayed Again," EarthTechling, 28 March 2013.

85   David Helvarg, "California, Catch the Next Big Energy Wave," *Los Angeles Times*, 13 July 2013.

86   Elizabeth Rusch, "Catching a Wave, Powering an Electrical Grid?" *Smithsonian*, July 2009.

87   "America's Premiere Wave Power Farm Sets Sail," Alternative Energy, 14 March 2010; Dave Levitan, "Why Wave Power Has Lagged Far behind as an Energy Source," Guardian Environment Network, 28 April 2014; Tina Casey, "US Taps into 1400 Terawatt Hours of Clean Ocean Power," Clean Technica, 30 August 2013.

88   Rusch, "Catching a Wave?"; Jeff Spross, "How the Power of Ocean Waves Could Yield Freshwater with Zero Carbon Emissions," Climate Progress, 30 August 2013; Milman, "Western Australia Wave Energy Project."

89   Arthur Caldicott, "Ocean Energy in BC," *Watershed Sentinel*," June/July 2008; see also "Tidal Energy," *National Geographic*; "Tidal Energy," U.S. Department of Energy; Andy Goldman, "Tidal Energy (Tidal Power) Pros and Cons," Renewable Green Energy Power, 27 January 2013.

90   "Tidal Energy Systems," Tribal Energy and Environmental Information.

91   Severin Carrell, "10MW Tidal Power Station Gets Scottish Government's Approval," *Guardian*, 17 March 2011.

92   Damian Carrington, "Tidal Power from Pentland Firth 'Could Provide Half of Scotland's Electricity,'" *Guardian*, 10 July 2013; James Ayre, "Scotland Could Receive Roughly 50% of Its Electricity from Tidal Energy, Research Finds," Clean Technica, 25 July 2013; Katie Valentine, "Scotland Is Building the World's Largest Tidal Array," Climate Progress, 25 August 2014.

93   "Wave and Tidal Energy: Part of the UK's Energy Mix," UK Department of Energy & Climate Change; Ari Phillips, "Major Milestone in Tidal Power Emerges with 'Spirit of the Sea,'" Climate Progress, 7 August 2014; Valentine, "Scotland Is Building."

94   "Tidal Energy in Nova Scotia," Nova Scotia Department of Energy; "Fundy Ocean Research Centre for Energy (FORCE)," Natural Resources Canada; "Acadia University Launches Tidal Energy Institute," Acadia University, 1 September 2011.

95   "First Tidal Power Delivered to US Grid off Maine," *CBS MoneyWatch*, 14 September 2012; Brian Wingfield, "Energy Turbines May Be Spinning in New York's East River by 2013," Bloomberg, 24 January 2012; "Washington Leads Way in Harnessing Tidal Power, but Challenges Persist," *Tri-City Herald*, 7 August 2011; Jon Chesto, "This Big Step Forward for Tidal Energy Could Bode Well for Similar Massachusetts Projects," Mass. Market, 29 January 2012; Hannah Heimbruch, "Tidal Energy in Aleutians Blows Expectations out of Water," *Alaska Dispatch*, 5 May 2013.

96   L. D. Danny Harvey, "Tidal Energy," *Energy and the New Reality* (Earthscan 2010); Mathias Aarre Maehlum, "Tidal Energy Pros and Cons," Energy Informative, 5 May 2013.

97   Alisdair Cameron, "Nova Scotia Joins Surge on Tidal Power," Renewable Energy World, 15 March 2011.

98   "Tidal Energy Systems," Tribal Energy and Environmental Information.

99   Ken Silverstein, "Ocean Energy Has Vast Potential but Many Waves to Skirt," EnergyBiz, 3 September 2013; Levitan, "Why Wave Power Has Lagged Far behind as an Energy Source."

100   Po Keung Cheung, "Geothermal Energy Is Begging to Be Used," *Deutsche Welle*, 29 January 2012; "Climate Change Update: Baseload Geothermal is One of the Lowest Emitting Energy Technologies," Geothermal Technologies Office, U.S. Department

of Energy, 26 June 2013; Shaopeng Huang, "Geothermal Energy in China," *Nature Climate Change*, August 2012.

101   Stephanie Watson, "How Geothermal Energy Works," How Stuff Works, 2009.

102   Watson, "How Geothermal Energy Works"; "Geothermal Electricity," *Center for Climate and Energy Solutions*, 2013.

103   Watson, "How Geothermal Energy Works"; "Geothermal Electricity," Center for Climate and Energy Solutions, 2013; Po Keung Cheung, "Geothermal Energy Is Begging."

104   Christopher Mims, "Iceland's Geothermal Bailout," *Popular Science*, 19 June 2009.

105   "Enhanced Geothermal Systems," *Center for Climate and Energy Solutions*, 2012.

106   James Glanz, "Deep in Bedrock, Clean Energy and Quake Fears," *New York Times*, 24 June 2009; Rebecca Boyle, "Two Major Geothermal Projects Abandoned Due to Induced Quake Risk," *Popular Science*, 14 December 2009; Elizabeth Svoboda, "Does Geothermal Power Cause Earthquakes?" *Popular Science*, 23 March 2010; James Glanz, "Geothermal Drilling Safeguards Imposed," *New York Times*, 15 January 2010.

107   Natalie Starkey, "Pumping Water Underground Could Trigger Major Earthquake, Say Scientists," *Guardian*, 11 July 2013; Emily E. Brodsky and Lia J. Lajoie, "Anthropogenic Seismicity Rates and Operational Parameters at the Salton Sea Geothermal Field," *Science*, 2 August 2013.

108   Tara Pate, "Le Fracking for Geothermal Heat Drawing Ire of French Oil," *Bloomberg*, 5 April 2013; Jen Alic, "France's Geothermal 'Fracking' Conundrum," Energy Voices, *Christian Science Monitor*, 11 April 2013.

109   "World Bank Calls for Global Initiative to Scale Up Geothermal Energy in Developing Countries," 6 March 2013.

110   Ibid.; "A Global Fund to De-Risk Exploration Drilling: Possibility or Pipe Dream?" Bloomberg New Energy Finance, 23 May 2013.

111   Sean Ahearn, "El Salvador Prioritizes Geothermal Energy Development," Worldwatch Institute, 11 January 2013; John Shimkus, "Top Ten: Geothermal Energy Locations," Energy Digital, 8 April 2011.

112   "Geothermal Electricity," *Center for Climate and Energy Solutions*, 2013; "How Geothermal Energy Works," Union of Concerned Scientists, 16 December 2009; "Energy Department Announces $10 Million to Speed Enhanced Geothermal Systems into the Market," Department of Energy, 20 February 2014; "How Much Electric Supply Capacity Is Needed to Keep U.S. Electricity Grids Reliable?" U.S. Energy Information Administration, 23 January 2013.

113   Alena Mae S. Flores, "Philippines Geothermal Output to Rise 75% by 2030," *Manila Standard Today*, 3 July 2013; Leslie Blodgett, "Philippines Government Pushes Geothermal, Strong 2013 Outlook," Geothermal Energy Association, 4 January 2013.

114   Amahl S. Azwar, "Protests Freeze out Lampung Geothermal Power Plant," *Jakarta Post*, 20 June 2013; L. X. Richter, "The Need for an All or Nothing Approach in Indonesia," Think Geo Energy, 12 July 2013.

115   Andrew Burger, "Mexico Geothermal Energy Off to Good 2012 Start with 50-MW Los Humeros II," Clean Technica, 12 January 2012; "New Geothermal Power Plant to be Built in Mexico," *Mexico Today*, 16 October 2012; L. X. Richter, "Mexico Depending on IPCC for Geothermal Growth," Think Geo Energy, 12 June 2013.

116   "First Geothermal Power Station Built in 1911 in Tuscany, Italy," Green Prospects Asia, 29 July 2012; Alessandra Migliaccio, "Geothermal Beating Coal Lures Enel from Tuscan Geysers," Bloomberg, 18 July 2013.

117   Grant Bradley, "Underground Resources Ready to be Tapped," *New Zealand Herald*, 9 August 2011.

118   Christopher Mims, "Iceland's Geothermal Bailout," *Popular Science*, 19 June 2009; "Geothermal Electricity," *Center for Climate and Energy Solutions*, 2013.

119   Yuriko Nagano, "Geothermal Power Tests Tradition in Japan," *New York Times*, 1 October 2012; "Storm in a Hot Tub: Clean Bodies versus Clean Energy," *Economist*, 7 April 2012; Jake Richardson, "20 GW of Geothermal Power Potential in Japan," Clean Technica, 3 October 2012.

120   Ahearn, "El Salvador Prioritizes Geothermal Energy Development."

121   "Kenya's Untapped Geothermal Energy More than Enough to Power Entire Nation," Catholic Online, 30 July 2013; Jessica Hatcher, "Kenya's Energy Revolution: Full Steam Ahead for Geothermal Power," *Guardian*, 22 November 2013.

122   Shaopeng Huang, "Geothermal Energy in China," *Nature Climate Change*, August 2012; "China Aiming High with Geothermal Energy," Proactive Investors (Australia), 19 February 2013.

123   "Biomass Energy," Environmental Protection Agency, Student's Guide to Climate Change.

124   Tildy Bayar, "Will the Draft European Biomass Policy Repeat Biofuel Mistakes?" Renewable Energy World, 22 August 2013.

125   "Traditional Use of Biomass," Climate Change Mitigation, UNEP; "Biomass," David Suzuki Foundation; Janet Cushman et al., "Biomass Fuels, Energy, Carbon, and Global Climate Change," Oak Ridge National Laboratory; Mat Hope, "New Report Hopes to Bring Clarity to Biomass Debate," Carbon Brief, 17 May 2013.

126   "Biomass," David Suzuki Foundation.

127   Mat Hope, "New Government Research Adds to Biomass Emissions Controversy," Carbon Brief, 13 March 2013; "Study Analyzes 'Carbon Debt' of Woody Biomass," Sustainable Business, 14 June 2010.

128   "The Fuel of the Future: Environmental Lunacy in Europe," *Economist*, 6 April 2013.

129   "Bonfire of the Subsidies," *Economist,* 6 April 2013; "The Fuel of the Future: Environmental Lunacy in Europe."

130   "The Risk of Assuming that Biomass Is Sustainable," Birdlife, 11 February 2013; "The Fuel of the Future"; "Bonfire of the Subsidies."

131   "Biomass 'Insanity' May Threaten EU Carbon Targets," EurActiv, 2 April 2012.

132   "Bonfire of the Subsidies."

133   Ibid.

134   Bayar, "Will the Draft European Biomass Policy Repeat Biofuel Mistakes?"; Barbara Lewis "Woody Biomass Draft Rules Too Weak – Campaigners," Reuters, 19 August 2013; Dave Keating, "Commission Floats 'Weak' Criteria for Biomass," European Voice, 13 August 2013.

135   Matt Kasper, "Energy from Trash: How to Curb Carbon Pollution with Junk," Climate Progress, April 2013; Annie-Rose Strasser, "New York's 'Food Recycling' Program Could Be the Future of Waste and Energy," Climate Progress, 17 June 2013.

136   Kasper, "Energy from Trash."

137   Ibid.

138   Matt Kasper, "Throw It Out and It Powers Your Home: Puerto Rico Turns to Garbage for Renewable Energy," Climate Progress, 13 June 2013.

139   Joanna M. Foster, "How D.C.'s Sewage Will Soon Generate Electricity," Climate Progress, 15 January 2014.

140   Sadhbh Walshe, "Big Oil Attacks Ethanol Industry with Misleading Claims," *Guardian*, 14 August 2013; Jeff Spross, "Untangling the Political and Policy Knot around America's Biofuel Mandate," Climate Progress, 26 July 2013.

141   David Pimentel, "Biofuel Food Disasters and Cellulosic Ethanol Problems," Bulletin of Science, Technology & Society 29/3 (June 2009), 205-12; Julian Borger, "UN Chief Calls for Review of Biofuels Policy," *Guardian*, 4 April 2008.

142   Colin A. Carter and Henry L. Miller, "Corn for Food, Not Fuel," *New York Times*, 30 July 2012; Pimentel, "Biofuel Food Disasters." On wheat, see Fiona Harvey, "Biofuels Plant to Become UK's Biggest Buyer of Wheat," *Guardian*, 8 July 2013; Elisabeth Rosenthal, "As Biofuel Demand Grows, So Do Guatemala's Hunger Pangs," *New York Times*, 5 January 2013.

143   "EU Parliament Vote Significantly Reduces Target for Use of Food-Based Biofuels by 2020," *Associated Press*, 11 September 2013; EU Research Adds to Evidence Biofuels Pollute More: Draft," Business Spectator, 11 July 2013; Richard van Noorden, "European Parliament Votes to Limit Crop-Based Biofuels," Nature News Blog, 11 September 2013; EU Parliament Vote Significantly Reduces Target for Use of Food-based Biofuels

by 2020," Associated Press, 11 September 2013.

144   "From Biomass to Biofuels: NREL Leads the Way," National Renewable Energy Laboratory, August 2006.

145   Steven Mufson, "Why Hasn't Cellulosic Ethanol Taken Over, Like It Was Supposed to?" *Washington Post*, 8 November 2013.

146   Tim McDonnell, "Are Fungus-Farming Ants the Key to Better Biofuel?" *Mother Jones*, 18 June 2013; Jeff Spross, "America's First Cellulosic Biofuel Plant to Use Corn Waste Is Open in Iowa," Climate Progress, 4 September 2014; Jeff Spross, "A Possible Biofuel Breakthrough, Via the Leafcutter Ant," Climate Progress, 19 June 2013;

147   Sadhbh Walshe, "Big Oil Attacks Ethanol Industry with Misleading Claims," *Guardian*, 14 August 2013; "USDA and DuPont Collaborate to Promote Sustainable Harvesting of Biobased Feedstocks for Cellulosic Ethanol," DuPont Biofuel Solutions, 3 April 2013; Jeff Spross, "How a 75-Million-Gallon Plant in Italy Heralds the Rise of a More Efficient Kind of Biofuel," Climate Progress, 17 October 2013.

148   Jeff Spross, "Why the EPA Cut Down the Biofuel Standard for the First Time Ever," Climate Progress, 18 November 2013.

149   Jeff Spross, "The Latest Clean Energy Cocktail: Bacteria and Fungus," Climate Progress, 23 August 2013; Jeff Spross, "How Whisky Makers Could Soon Be Providing a Superior Biofuel," Climate Progress, 15 November 2013; "Fungus Among Us Could Become Non-Food Source for Biodiesel Production," *Science Daily*, 17 September 2010; referring to Gemma Vicente et al., "Direct Transformation of Fungal Biomass from Submerged Cultures into Biodiesel," *Energy & Fuels*, 2 April 2010.

150   Zachary Shahan, "Boeing Biofuel Breakthrough — This Is a BIG Deal," Clean Technica, 27 January 2014; Shahan, "Breakthrough Halophyte Biofuel & the Failure of Tar Sands Oil," Clean Technica, 24 July 2014.

151   Spross, "The Latest Clean Energy Cocktail."

152   "Reducing Transport Greenhouse Gas Emissions: Trends & Data," International Transport Forum, 7; "Road Transportation Emerges as Key Driver of Warming," Goddard Institute for Space Studies, NASA, 18 February 2010; referring to Naomi Unger et al., "Attribution of Climate Forcing to Economic Sectors," *Proceedings of the National Academies of Sci*ence, 2010.

153   "Transport: More Cars, More Trade, More CO_2."

154   "What Are Greenhouse Gas Emissions? How Much Does the US Emit?" U.S. Energy Information Administration, 26 June 2012.

155   Brian Thevenot, "Electric Cars Are Getting as Cheap as Gasoline Rivals," *Los Angeles Times*, 1 June 2013; Julia Pyper, "Hybrid-Electrics Race for Mainstream and High-End Buyers," ClimateWire, 11 March 2013.

156   Leslie Hayward, "New Tools Show How Much EVs Really Cost," GreenBiz, 18 June 2013.

157   Everett M. Rogers, *Diffusion of Innovations* (Glencoe, Free Press, 1962), 150. These categories have been employed in Catherine Green, "Toyota Steps up Hydrogen Fuel Cell Development," *Los Angeles Times*, 26 June 2013.

158   Zachary Shahan, "EV Sales Beating PHEV Sales in US," EV Obsession, 17 July 2013; Jeff Spross, "Electric Vehicles Sales Near 9,000 for June 2013 – One of Their Best Months Ever," Climate Progress, 29 July 2013.

159   *Forbes* asked, "The Price of Electric Vehicles Is Falling; Is It Time To Buy?" and a *Los Angeles Times* story was headed: "Electric Cars Are Getting as Cheap as Gasoline Rivals"; Jeff Spross, "Battery Innovation Is Doubling Core Performance for Electric Cars Every Decade," Climate Progress, 11 February 2013; Julia Pyper, "Nissan's Leaf: Iconic Car or Risky Bet on Emissions-free Mobility?" ClimateWire, 23 July 2013; "Elon Musk Says Fourth Tesla Will Be Small SUV Costing about $35,000," *Los Angeles Times*, 31 May 2013; "Video: The Tesla Model S Is Our Top-Scoring Car," Consumer Reports News, 9 May 2013. Angus MacKenzie, "2013 Motor Trend Car of the Year: Tesla Model S," *Motor Trend*, January 2013.

160   Ken Green Burridge, "Tesla Superchargers – Latest Superhero Feats," EV.com, 19 July 2014; "Tesla, Unicom to Build Charging Stations," *China Weekly*, English News, 29

August 2014.

161   Christopher DeMorro, "Britain's Electric Highway Serves 1 Million Electric Miles," Clean Technica, 11 September 2014.

162   "Selling SIIIX: Tesla's Model 3," *Economist*, 26 July 2014; Luis Gonzalez, "Tesla Roadster Targets 400-Mile Range With Battery Pack Upgrade," Clean Technica, 6 August 2014.

163   Emily Atkin, "We Are on the Verge of an Electric Car Battery Breakthrough," Climate Progress, 31 August 2014; Ari Phillips, "Nevada Hits Electric Car Jackpot, Gets $5 Billion Tesla 'Gigafactory' That Will Employ 6,500," Climate Progress, 4 September 2014.

164   Rebecca Lefton, "First Ever Global Electric Vehicle Outlook Released at Clean Energy Ministerial in New Delhi," Climate Progress, 18 April 2013; Jeff Spross, "Electric Car Sale Are up over 70 Percent in Europe and the United States," Climate Progress, 8 August 2014; "China's New Energy Car Output Surges," *China Weekly*, English News, 17 August 2014; Christopher DeMorro, "Chinese Automakers Get More EV Incentives," Clean Technica, 4 September 2014.

165   James Ayre, "55 Million Electric Motorcycles & Scooters by 2023," Clean Technica, 31 August 2014; discussing "Electric Motorcycles and Scooters," Navigant Research.

166   Tina Casey, "Bet Your EV Can't Do This: Electric Garbage Truck Hauls 9 Tons of Trash," Clean Technica, 16 September 2014.

167   Impact Lab, "$100B in Wind or Solar Will Now Produce More Energy Than the Same Investment in Oil," Reader Supported News, 20 September 2014.

168   Lindsay Brooke, "G. M. and Honda to Collaborate on Fuel-Cell Development," Wheels Blog, *New York Times*, 2 July 2013.

169   Martin LaMonica, "Ford, Daimler, and Nissan Commit to Fuel Cells," *MIT Technology Review*, 28 January 2013.

170   "Hyundai ix35 PHEV," AutoCar, 2013; "Hydrogen Cars Quickened by Copenhagen Chemists," Eureka Alert, University of Copenhagen Press Release, 21 July 2013; Barry C. Lynn, "Hydrogen's Dirty Secret," *Mother Jones*, 1 May 2003.

171   Peter Fairley, "Hydrogen Cars: A Dream That Won't Die," *MIT Technology Review*, 8 October 2012.

172   Julia Pyper and ClimateWire, "Will Cheap Natural Gas Resurrect the Hydrogen Car?" *Scientific American*, 26 September 2012.

173   Brooke, "G. M. and Honda to Collaborate"; "Collaboration May Lead to World's First Affordable Fuel Cell EV," Electric Vehicle Research, 30 January 2013; "U.S. Musters Fuel Cell Electric Vehicle Partners," *Environment News Service*, 20 May 2013.

174   "Hydrogen Cars Quickened by Copenhagen Chemists," Eureka Alert, University of Copenhagen Press Release, 21 July 2013.

175   "Hydrogen and Fuel Cell Research," National Renewable Energy Laboratory; Lynn, "Hydrogen's Dirty Secret."

176   Tina Casey, "Toyota Could Be Wrong about the High Cost of Hydrogen," Clean Technica, 22 August 2014.

177   Joe Romm, "Tesla Trumps Toyota: Why Hydrogen Cars Can't Compete with Pure Electric Cars," Climate Progress, 5 August 2014.

178   Julian Cox, "Time To Come Clean About Hydrogen Fuel Cell Vehicles," Clean Technica, 4 June 2014.

179   Romm, "Tesla Trumps Toyota Part II: The Big Problem with Hydrogen Fuel," Climate Progress, 13 August 2014.

180   Dan Schned, "What is the Cost of *Not* Investing in High-Speed Rail?" American 2050, 10 July 2012; "High-Speed Rail," Wikipedia.

181   Ben Coxworth, "California to Get America's Fastest High-Speed Rail Line," 31 July 2013; "An Inventory of the Criticisms of High-Speed Rail: With Suggested Responses and Counterpoints," American Public Transportation Association, January 2012.

182   Michael Byrne, "Farewell Ray LaHood, and Thanks for All the Trains," Motherboard, June 2013.

183   David Carr, "Slower Than a Speeding Bullet," *Washington Monthly*, October 2001; "An Inventory of the Criticisms of High-Speed Rail.".

184   Mathew L. Wald, "Auditors Doubt Amtrak Will Meet Profit Mandate," *New York Times*,

26 July 2001; "An Inventory of Criticisms."

185   Carr, "Slower Than a Speeding Bullet."

186   "An Inventory of Criticisms."

187   "High-Speed Trains: Where India Stands?" Rail News, 3 September 2013; Andy Kunz, "U.S. High-Speed Rail: Time to Hop Aboard or Be Left Behind," Reuters, 11 March 2011.

188   Ibid.

189   "Remarks by the President in State of the Union Address," White House, 27 January 2009; Yonah Freemark, "Will They or Won't They? The Romance Between Obama & High-Speed Rail," Next City, 26 February 2013.

190   Michael Cooper, "How Flaws Undid Obama's Hope for High-Speed Rail in Florida," New York Times, 11 March 2011; Ray LaHood, "High-Speed-Rail Will Be Our Generation's Legacy," Orlando Sentinel, 19 December 2010.

191   Cooper, "How Flaws Undid Obama's Hope"; "An Inventory of the Criticisms."

192   "High-Speed Trains: Running Out of Steam," Economist, 9 December 2010; Freemark, "Will They or Won't They?"

193   David Dayen, "LaHood Revokes Wisconsin, Ohio High Speed Rail Money, Gives to Other States," FireDogLake, 9 December 2010; Cooper, "How Flaws Undid Obama's Hope."

194   "Ronald D. Utt, "The Death of a High-Speed-Rail Program," National Review, 11 April 2011; "Organizations in ExxonMobil's Data Base" (Greenpeace); Roger Christensen, "The Great High-Speed Rail Lie," San Francisco Chronicle, 3 August 2011.

195   Michael Winter, "Congress Kills Funding for Obama's High-Speed Rail," USA Today, 17 November 2011.

196   Mark Clayton, "Obama Plan for High-Speed Rail, after Hitting a Bump, Chugs Forward Again," Christian Science Monitor, 21 August 2012.

197   Alex Lennartz, "Airlines & Oil Barons in Fear of High Speed Rail: The South Central Corridor," Clean Techies, 6 July 2009; Tanya Snyder, "Can High-Speed Rail Reduce Air Travel and Highway Expansion?" DC.StreetsBlog.org, 9 June 2011; James P. Repass, "Researcher Discrediting High Speed Rail Had Bias," The Day, 19 August 2012.

198   Gus Lubin, "High Speed Rail Has Basically Killed a Dozen Airports in South Korea," Business Insider, 15 February 2011; "China's High-Speed Rail Threatens Domestic Airlines," China Weekly, English News, 8 April 2011. In 2013, Keith Bradsher in "Speedy Trains Transform China" (New York Times, 23 September 2013) said: "Airlines have largely halted service on routes of less than 300 miles when high-speed rail links open."

199   Sandy Dechert, "Amtrak Expands Fast East Coast Acela Fleet," Clean Technica, 6 August 2014; Ron Nixon, "$11 Billion Later, High-Speed Rail Is Inching Along," New York Times, 6 August 2014.

200   Randall O'Toole, "High-Speed Fail," Cato Institute, 24 August 2009.

201   Chris Cooper and Kiyotaka Matsuda, "World's Fastest Train Resumes Trials as Japan Plans Maglev Line," Bloomberg, 29 August 2013; Daniel Ferry, "While Buses Play a Valuable Role, They are No Replacement for High-Speed Rail," America 2050, 27 July 2011; Bradsher, "Speedy Trains Transform China"; "Taiwan High Speed Rail," Wikipedia.

202   "Less than 1 percent will ride." – Cato Institute, July 2009.

203   Ron Nixon, "Frustrations of Air Travel Push Passengers to Amtrak," New York Times, 16 August 2012; "Amtrak Kicks Ass, Republicans Kick Amtrak," The Stranger, 15 August 2012.

204   Wendell Cox, "High-Speed Rail, Budget Buster," National Review, 31 January 2011.

205   Robert Cruickshank, "Kevin McCarthy's New Attempt to Block HSR," California High Speed Rail Blog, 3 October 2011; Ferry, "While Buses Play a Valuable Role"; America 2050, 27 July 2011; "America's Long History of Subsidizing Transportation," Trainweb. org.

206   Joseph Henchman, "Road Spending by State Funded by User Taxes and Fees, Including Federal Gas Tax Revenues," Tax Foundation, 17 January 2013.

207   Pew Analysis Finds Highways Increasingly Paid for by 'Non-User' Funding Sources," Pew, 24 November 2009; Ferry, "While Buses Play a Valuable Role"; Tanya Snyder,

"Transit's Not Bleeding the Taxpayer Dry — Roads Are," DC.StreetsBlog, 12 December 2011.

208 "America's Long History of Subsidizing Transportation," Trainweb.org; Kevin A. Carson, "The Distorting Effects of Transportation Subsidies," *Freeman*, 22 October 2010; Warren Buffett, "To the Shareholders of Berkshire Hathaway Inc.," 2007.

209 Quoted in Robert Cruickshank, "Kevin McCarthy's New Attempt to Block HSR," California High Speed Rail Blog, 3 October 2011; *Cato Institute, July 2009*

210 "Facts Vs. Fiction on HSR; Ferry, "While Buses Play a Valuable Role."

211 Sarah Palin, Facebook, 2011 (quoted in Cooper, "How Flaws Undid Obama's Hope"); Dan Schned, "What Is the Cost of *Not* Investing in High-Speed Rail?" American 2050, 10 July 2012.

212 Quoted in "An Inventory of the Criticisms."

213 Ibid.

214 "The Future of Train Travel: Life in Hyper-Speed," Arch Daily, 2013; "Maglev Trains Could Cut Tokyo-Osaka Trip to 67 Minutes," *Japan Times*, 14 October 2009.

215 "Fact vs. Fiction on HSR," Midwest High Speed Rail Associat ion, 2009; "Regenerative Braking in Trains," ClimateTechWiki; George Berka, "Op-Ed: How Electric Freight Trains Can Help Save Us," Inside EVs, 9 August 2013.

216 Kevin Sonsor, "How Maglev Trains Work," How Stuff Works; "Maglev Trains: On Track with Superconductivity," Magnet Lab.

217 Charlie Osborne, "UK Rail Service Introduces 'Carbon Free' Trains," Smart Planet, 14 February 2012; Erik Kirschbaum, "Analysis: German Rail to Run on Sun, Wind to Keep Clients Happy," Reuters, 22 August 2011; Amar Toor, "Europe's First Solar Powered Train Tunnel Goes Live on Belgian High-Speed Line (Video)," Endgadget, 7 June 2011; Nino Marchetti, "High Speed Rail Goes Solar in Europe," Earth Techling, 6 June 2011.

218 Kevin Rector, "Backers of High-Speed 'Maglev' Train to Washington Claim $5 billion in Funding," *Baltimore Sun*, 4 September 2014.

219 Elisabeth Rosenthal, "Your Biggest Carbon Sin May Be Air Travel," *New York Times*, 26 January 2013; Jake Schmidt, "Secretary Kerry: Secure a Global Agreement to Reduce Aviation's Carbon Pollution," Huffington Post, 20 March 2013.

220 "CO_2 Emissions & Global Warming: Trains versus Planes"; Jake Schmidt, "Aviation Global Warming Pollution Will Rise Without New Action: Study Details," Switchboard, 5 March 2013; referring to "ICAO, Aviation's Contribution to Climate Change," Chap. 1 of *ICAO Environment Report 2010*.

221 "CO_2 Emissions and Global Warming: Trains versus Planes," The Man in Seat 61; Roddy Scheer and Doug Moss, "Airplane Exhaust," EarthTalk, 20 January 2013; "The Sky's the Limit," *Economist*, 8 June 2006.

222 Rosenthal, "Your Biggest Carbon Sin"; George Monbiot, "On the Flight Path to Global Meltdown," *Guardian*, 20 September 2006; "Airplane Exhaust," EarthTalk; "Airplane Emissions 11% of Total Transportation CO_2 Emissions," *Curacao Tribune*, 13 May 2013.

223 "The Sky's the Limit," *Economist*, 8 June 2006.

224 Jake Schmidt, "How the European Program to Reduce Carbon Pollution from Aviation Works," Jake Schmidt's Blog, Switchboard, 4 January 2012; "U.S. Airlines Take EU To Court Over Emissions Cap," Associated Press, 5 July 2011; Rebecca Lefton, "EU High Court Upholds Law Limiting Global Warming Pollution from Aviation," Center for American Progress, 7 October 2011.

225 Rosenthal, "Your Biggest Carbon Sin"; Aaron Kart, "Obama Signs Bill Enabling US Airlines to Skirt EU ETS," ATW Plus, 27 November 2012.

226 Roddy Scheer and Doug Moss, "Airplane Exhaust," EarthTalk, 20 January 2013; Dave Keating, "EU Offers Retreat on Aviation Emissions," European Voice, 5 September 2013; Nicholas Rock et al., "Aviation Emissions: The ICAO Outcome and Its Impact on the EU Aviation Emissions Trading Scheme," Read Smith, 7 January 2014; Schmidt, "Secretary Kerry: Secure a Global Agreement"; "Quick Action Needed from Obama Administration to Limit Airplane Emissions," Environmental Defense Fund, 14 March 2012.

227 Rick Piltz, "Pushing EPA to Regulate Aviation Greenhouse Gas Emissions," Climate

Science Watch, 8 August 2014; Lindsay Abrams, "The EPA Is (Finally) Taking on Air Travel," *Salon*, 5 September 2014; Dan Rutherford, "Airline Efficiency: Waiting for ICAO?" International Council on Clean Transportation, 5 May 2014.

228   "Quick Action Needed."

229   Adam Marcus, "NASA Puts the 'Green' in Its Other Mission: Developing Revolutionary, Energy-Efficient Airplanes," *Scientific American*, 26 July 2010; Daryl Stephenson,"Envisioning Tomorrow's Aircraft," Boeing, June 2010; Britt Liggett, "Boeing Team's SUGAR Volt Aircraft Concept Burns 70% Less Fuel," Inhabitat, 3 August 2012; Stephen Trimble, "NASA Reveals Three Visions for a Future Airliner," Flightglobal, 18 January 2011.

230   "ICAO, Aviation's Contribution to Climate Change."

231   Alok Jha, "Gene Scientist to Create Algae Biofuel with Exxon Mobil," *Guardian*, 14 July 2009.

232   Debbie Hamel, "Aviation Biofuel Sustainability Survey," NRDC Issue Brief, National Resources Defense Council, 21 March 2013.

233   "Green Flight Challenge: Towards Zero-Emission Planes?" Sustainable Mobility, 13 November 2011; Ben Cosworth "Pipistrel Takes US$1.35 Million First Prize in NASA Green Flight Challenge," GizMag, 5 October 2011.

234   Matt Burns, The ZEHST Is the 3,000 MW, Zero Emissions Airplane of 2050," 20 June 2011; "Changes in the Air," *Economist*, 3 September 2011.

235   Kit Eaton, "VoltAir: The Electric Passenger Jet of the Future," NBC News, 28 June 2011; Ben Coxworth, "EADS VoltAir All-Electric Aircraft Concept Unveiled in Paris," Gizmag, 21 June 2011.

236   See Daryl Elliott, "Renewable Energy Momentum Has Passed The Tipping Point," Clean Technica, 25 August 2014; "Countries with 100% Renewable Energy," Make Wealth History, 2012.

237   Cory Budischak et al., "Cost-Minimized Combinations of Wind Power, Solar Power and Electrochemical Storage, Powering the Grid Up to 99.9% of the Time," *Journal of Power Sources*, 11 October 2012.

238   Pacala and Socolow, "Stabilization Wedges."

239   Judee Burr et al., "Shining Cities: At the Forefront of America's Solar Energy Revolution," Environment Ohio, April 2014.

240   "United States Has Vast Renewable Energy Potential, Says Report," Worldwatch Institute, 18 September 2006.

241   Pacala and Socolow, "Stabilization Wedges"; Romm, "Socolow Reaffirms 2004 'Wedges' Paper"; "United States Has Vast Renewable Energy Potential, Says Report," Worldwatch Institute, 18 September 2006.

242   "China's Future Generation: Assessing the Maximum Potential for Renewable Power Sources in China to 2050," WWF, 18 February 2014.

243   Yvonne Y. Deng, Komelis Blok, Kees van der Leun, "Transition to a Fully Sustainable Global Energy System," *Energy Strategy Reviews*, September 2012.

244   "WWF Report Finds Solar Land Use Doesn't Conflict With Conservation Goals," *The Energy Report: 100% Renewable Energy by 2050*, Clean Technica, 17 January 2013.

245   Adam White and Jason Anderson, "Putting the EU on Track for 100% Renewable Energy," WWF 2013.

246   Budischak et al., "Cost-Minimized Combinations of Wind Power, Solar Power and Electrochemical Storage."

247   *The Energy Report: 100% Renewable Energy by 2050*;; Jonathan M Cullen, Julian M. Allwood, and Edward H. Borgstein, "Reducing Energy Demand: What Are the Practical Limits?" *Environment, Science, and Technology*, 12 January 2011.

248   Kate Marvel et al., "Geophysical Limits to Global Wind Power," *Nature Climate Change*, 9 September 2012; Xi Lu et al., "Global Potential for Wind-Generated Electricity."

249   *Our Planet: The Magazine of the United Nations Environment Programme*, United Nations Environment Programme (UNEP), 16/4.

250   "Enhanced Geothermal Systems," *Center for Climate and Energy Solutions*, 2012; "A Global Fund to De-Risk Exploration Drilling: Possibility or Pipe Dream?" Bloomberg

New Energy Finance, 23 May 2013.

251   John Huckerby et al., "Ocean Energy Systems: An International Vision for Ocean Energy," Ocean Energy Systems, October 2011; R. F. Nicholls-Lee and S.R. Turnock, "Tidal Energy Extraction: Renewable, Sustainable and Predictable," *Science Progress*, 91/1 (2008): 81-111; "Ocean Energy," Research and Innovation, European Commission.

252   Smart Grid, Energy.gov.

253   Hal Bernton, "Renewable-Energy Surge Slow to Wean China Off Coal," *Seattle Times*, 6 May 2014.

254   Bill White, "The Five Most Important Names in Renewable Energy that You've Never Heard of," Americans for Clean Energy Blog, 29 July 2013.

255   Ibid.

256   Elisabeth Rosenthal, "Drawing the Line at Power Lines," *New York Times*, 18 February 2012.

257   *Failure to Act: The Economic Impact of Current Investment Trends in Electricity Infrastructure*, Economic Development Research Group, American Society of Civil Engineers, 2011.

258   Bryan Walsh, "The Power Grid: From Rickety to Resilient," *Time*, 17 July 2012; Bill White, "California Blackout: What It Tells Us about Our Grid," Americans for Clean Transmission, 27 September 2011.

259   Jeff Spross, "America's Electric Grid Is Far Too Vulnerable to Extreme Weather, and Needs an Update," Climate Progress, 12 August 2013.

260   Wilson Ring and David Sharp, "Wind Power Systems Hit Hurdles," Associated Press, 9 August 2013.

261   Amory Lovins, "How to End Blackouts Forever," *Time*, 15 November 2012; Joanna M. Foster, "Independence through Microgrids: When the Power Goes Out, Some Are Just Going Off the Grid," Climate Progress, 21 October 2013.

262   Joshua S. Hill, "Smart Grid Spending Expected to Total Nearly $600 Billion By 2023," Clean Technica, 22 August 2014.

263   Dustin Thaler, "Taming the Wild West of Energy," Americans for Clean Transmission, 1 July 2013.

264   Diane Cardwell, "Intermittent Nature of Green Power Is Challenge for Utilities," *New York Times*, 15 August 2013.

265   Ari Phillips, "Major Court Ruling Clears the way to Let Renewables into the Grid," Climate Progress, 19 August 2014.

266   Jeff Spross, "Germany Added a Lot of Wind and Solar Power, and Its Electric Grid Became More Reliable," Climate Progress, 12 August 2014; Roy L. Hales, "The First 100% Green Grid Is Online, Figuratively Speaking," Clean Technica, 16 September 2014.

267   Matthew L. Wald, "Ideas to Bolster Power Grid Run Up Against the System's Many Owners," *New York Times*, 12 July 2013.

268   Ryan Fitzpatrick, "Investing in the Grid: When the Going Gets Tough, the Tough Get . . . Creative," Americans for Clean Transportation, 20 August 2012.

269   *Failure to Act*, Executive Summary.

270   "The Power of Transformation: Wind, Sun and the Economics of Flexible Power Systems," Press Conference, International Energy Agency, 26 February 2014.

271   Kiley Kroh, "Renewable Energy Provided One-Third of Germany's Power in the First Half of 2014," Climate Progress, 8 July 2014. See also Osha Gray Davidson, *Clean Break: The Story of Germany's Energy Transformation and What Americans Can Learn from It* (Kindle Edition, 2012).

272   Nicholas Stern, "Ethics, Equity and the Economics of Climate Change: Paper 1, Science and Philosophy," Centre for Climate Change Economics, and Grantham Research Institute on Climate Change and the Environment, November 2013.

Chapter 18: The Abolition of Dirty Energy

1   Bill McKibben, "Global Warming's Terrifying New Math," *Rolling Stone*, 19 June 2012.

2   Suzanne Goldenberg, "Just 90 Companies Caused Two-Thirds of Man-Made Global Warming Emissions," *Guardian*, 20 November 2013.

3   Ibid.

4   Charles C. Mann, "What If We Never Run Out of Oil?" *The Atlantic*, 24 April 2013.

5   This cyclical feedback is described by Joe Romm thus: "Rake in billions from consumers, use the money to buy influence to maintain tax breaks" ("Conoco Phillips Rakes in $3.4 Billion in Profits from High Oil Prices, Buys More Influence to Keep Billion-Dollar Tax Breaks," Climate Progress, 27 July 2011).

6   Daniel J. Weiss et al., "Big Oil's Banner Year," Center for American Progress, 7 February 2012; Dan Froomkin, "How the Oil Lobby Greases Washington's Wheels," Huffington Post, 6 June 2011; Seth Hanlon, "Big Oil's Misbegotten Tax Gusher: Why They Don't Need $70 Billion from Taxpayers Amid Record Profits," Center for American Progress, 5 May 2011; Jordan Weissmann, "America's Most Obvious Tax Reform Idea: Kill the Oil and Gas Subsidies," *Atlantic*, 19 March 2013; "Bill Johnson Says Subsidies for the Oil Companies that Barack Obama Has Attacked Don't Exist," PolitiFact, 17 April 2012; Rebecca Leber, "Big Oil Lobby Claims the Industry 'Gets No Subsides, Zero, Nothing,'" Climate Progress, 9 January 2013; Emily E. Adams, "The Energy Game Is Rigged: Fossil Fuel Subsidies Topped $620 Billion in 2011," *Earth Policy Institute*, 27 February 2013; "Effective Tax Rates of Oil & Gas Companies: Cashing in on Special Treatment," Taxpayers for Common Sense, 30 July 2014.

7   Tom Engelhardt, "Terracide and the Terrarists: Destroying the Planet for Record Profits," TomDispatch, 23 May 2013.

8   Quoted in Jonathan Leake, "Climate Scientist They Could Not Silence," *Sunday Times*, 10 February 2008.

9   "Coal," Center for Climate and Energy Solutions.

10   Ben Adler, "Obama's Proposed Power Plant Rules Fall Slightly Short of Environmentalists' Hopes," Grist, 1 June 2014; David Remnick, "The Obama Tapes," *New Yorker*, 23 January 2014.

11   Fergus Green and Nicholas Stern, "An Innovative and Sustainable Growth Path for China: A Critical Decade," Center for Climate Change Economics and Policy, Grantham Research Institute on Climate Change and Environment, May 2014; Stephen Lacey, "The Road to Climate Disaster Is Paved with Coal: 1,200 New Coal Plants Planned around the World," Climate Progress, 20 November 2012; Joshua S. Hill, "China Continues War Against Coal," Clean Technica, 17 September 2014.

12   "Coal Industry Pins Hopes on Exports as U.S. Market Shrinks," *New York Times*, 14 June 2013; Kiley Kroh, "The Declining Value of Coal Just Killed Another Export Terminal," Climate Progress, 20 August 2013.

13   Kroh, "The Declining Value of Coal"; Duncan Clark, "The Rise and Rise of American Carbon," *Guardian*, 5 August 2013.

14   Seth Borenstein, "Ominous Arctic Melt Worries Experts," Associated Press, 11 December 2007; "Black Coal Is Australia's Second-Highest Export Commodity and Australia Is the World's Leading Coal Exporter," Australian Coal Association, 2012; Jeff Spross, "Australia's Coal Reserves Alone Could Take Up 75 Percent of What We Can Still Risk Burning," Climate Progress, 29 April 2013; Ari Phillips, "Australia Rings in the New Year with Record-Breaking Heat Wave," Climate Progress, 2 January 2014; Brett Parris, "Expanding Coal Exports Is Bad News for Australia and the World," The Conversation, 12 September 2013.

15   "The Health Costs of Coal: Coal Isn't Just Dirty, Outdated Energy – It's also Making Us Sick," Sierra Club, 2012.

16   American Lung Association et al., to The Honorable Joe Barton, Chairman, 10 May 2011.

17   Emily Atkin, "Murray CEO Says EPA Has Permanently Destroyed Coal: 'Grandma Is Going to be Cold," Climate Progress, 23 September 2014.

18   John Vidal, "European Coal Pollution Causes 22,300 Premature Deaths a Year, Study Shows," *Guardian*, 12 June 2013; Janet Larsen, "Cancer Now Leading Cause of Death in China," Earth Policy Institute, 25 May 2011; "Pollution from Coal Power Plants in

the Beijing-Tianjin-Hebei Region Causes Nearly 10,000 Premature Deaths," Greenpeace, 17 June 2013; Lisa Friedman and ClimateWire, "Coal-Fired Power in India May Cause More Than 100,000 Premature Deaths Annually," *Scientific American,* 11 March 2013; John Vidal, "Indian Coal Plants Kill 120,000 People a Year, Says Greenpeace," *Guardian,* 10 March 2013; referring to Debi Goenka and Sarath Guttikunda, "Coal Kills: An Assessment of Death and Disease Caused by India's Dirtiest Energy Source," Greenpeace, 12 March 2013.

19   Coral Davenport, "The Coal Lobby's Fight for Survival," *National Journal,* 29 June 2013; Joe Romm, "U.K. Ad Council Rules 'Clean Coal' Isn't Clean, Bars Peabody Energy from 'Misleading' Public," Climate Progress, 20 August 2014.

20   "Coal without CCS Is Not an Option," Bellona Environmental CCS Team, 21 November 2013.

21   "Don't Believe the Coal Industry's Warnings," Bloomberg, 12 September 2013; Matthew Wald, "Despite Climate Concern," Global Study Finds Fewer Carbon Capture Projects," *New York Times,* 10 October 2013; Yadullah Hussain, "SaskPower to Roll Out World's First Carbon Capture-Embedded Power Plant," *Financial Post,* 14 February 2014.

22   Vaclav Smil, "Energy at the Crossroads," quoted in Joe Romm, "Carbon Capture and Storage: One Step Forward, One Step Back," Climate Progress, 10 October 2013; Burton Richter, "New Clean Air Rules Would Do Little," *New York Times,* 23 October 2013.

23   Joe Romm, "Carbon Capture and Storage Can Cause Earthquakes, Making It 'a Risky and Likely Unsuccessful Strategy,'" Climate Progress, 5 November 2013.

24   Joe Romm, "Goldman Sachs Finds 'Window for Profitable Investment in Coal Mining Closing, Ditto for Coal Exports,'" Climate Progress, 8 August 2013.

25   Dana Nuccitelli, "The True Cost of Coal Power," Skeptical Science, 18 March 2011; "Australia's Electricity: Appendix to Australian Uranium Paper," World Nuclear Association, August 2012.

26   Nicholas Z. Muller, Robert Mendelsohn, and William Nordhaus, "Environmental Accounting for Pollution in the United States Economy," *American Economic Review* (August 2011).

27   Paul R. Epstein et al., "Full Cost Accounting for the Life Cycle of Coal," *Annals of the New York Academy of Sciences,* 2011; Nuccitelli, "The True Cost of Coal Power."

28   Mark Drajem, "Obama Said to Ban New Coal Plants without Carbon Controls," Bloomberg, 11 September 2013; Bloomberg, "Don't Believe the Coal Industry's Warnings."

29   Coral Davenport, "The Coal Lobby's Fight for Survival," *National Journal,* 29 June 2013.

30   Ibid.

31   Brian Merchant, "Coal Costs US Public Up to $500 Billion Annually: Harvard Study," Treehugger, 16 February 2011.

32   Giles Parkinson, "UBS: Time to Join the Solar, EV, Storage Revolution," Renew Economy, 21 August 2014.

33   Quoted in Joe Romm, "Natural Gas Is a Bridge to Nowhere – Absent a Serious Price for Global Warming Pollution," Climate Progress, 24 January 2012.

34   Richard Heinberg, *Snake Oil: How Fracking's False Promise of Plenty Imperil Our Future* (Santa Rosa: Post Carbon Institute, 2013).

35   Alex Trembath et al. "Coal Killer: How Natural Gas Fuels the Clean Energy Revolution," Breakthrough Institute, June 2013; World Energy Outlook 2012 – Special Report: "Golden Rules for a Golden Age of Gas," International Energy Agency," May 2012.

36   Bill McKibben and Mike Tidwell, "A Big Fracking Lie," Politico, 21 January 2014.

37   Joe Romm, "Natural Gas Is Mostly Methane," Climate Progress, 13 April 2011.

38   Joe Romm, "More Bad News for Fracking: IPCC Warns Methane Traps Much More Heat than We Thought," Climate Progress, 2 October 2013. In "Fracking Good for the Climate? What a Load of Hot Air" (*New York Daily News,* 29 November 2012), Robert Howarth said: "The methane that is inevitably emitted from natural gas wells and pipelines is more than 100 times more powerful than CO_2 as a greenhouse gas during the first two decades after emission."

39   Ramón A. Alvarez et al., "Greater Focus Needed on Methane Leakage from Natural Gas Infrastructure," *Proceedings of the National Academy of Sciences*, 11 March 2013; Tom M. L. Wigley, "Coal to Gas: The Influence of Methane Leakage," *Climatic Change*, October 2011, quoted in Joe Romm, "Natural Gas Bombshell: Switching from Coal to Gas Increases Warming for Decades, Has Minimal Benefit Even in 2100," Climate Progress, 9 September 2011.

40   Anna Karion et al., "Methane Emissions Estimate from Airborne Measurements over a Western United States Natural Gas Field," *Geophysical Research Letters*, 27 August 2013; Jeff Tollefson, "Methane Leaks Erode Green Credentials of Natural Gas," *Nature*, 2 January 2013; Neela Banerjee, "EPA Drastically Underestimates Methane Released at Drilling Sites," *Los Angeles Times*, 14 April 2014; referring to Dana R. Caulton et al., "Toward a Better Understanding and Quantification of Methane Emissions from Shale Gas Development," *Proceedings of the National Academy of Sciences*, 14 April 2014.

41   Robert W. Howarth et al., "Methane and the Greenhouse-Gas Footprint of Natural Gas from Shale Formations," *Climatic Change*, June 2011; Howarth, "Fracking Good for the Climate?"; Joe Romm, "Bridge or Gangplank? Study Finds Methane Leakage from Gas Fields High Enough to Gut Climate Benefit," Climate Progress, 7 August 2013; George Birchard "NOAA Investigation Finds Massive Methane Emissions from Utah Fracking: 6% to 12% Lost to Atmosphere," Daily Kos, 7 August 2013.

42   Shakeb Afsah and Kendyl Salcito, "Demand Reduction Slashes US CO_2 Emissions in 2012," CO_2 Scoreboard, 1 May 2013.

43   Felicity Barringer, "Hydrofracking Could Strain Western Water Resources, Study Finds," *New York Times*, 2 May 2013; Mindy Lubber, "Escalating Water Strains in Fracking Regions," Green Tech, 28 May 2013; "Fracking Fuels Water Battles ," Associated Press, 16 June 2013; Suzanne Goldenberg, "A Texan Tragedy: Ample Oil, No Water," *Guardian*, 11 August 2013.

44   Jessica Goad, "The Oil and Gas Industry Wants to Start Fracking at the Source of D.C.'s Water Supply," Climate Progress, 21 October 2013.

45   "Baffled About Fracking? You're Not Alone," *New York Times*, 13 May 2011; Environment America, "Fracking by the Numbers."

46   Ibid.

47   Brantley Hargrove, "How One Man's Flaming Water Fired Up a Battle between Texas and the EPA," *Dallas Observer*, 26 April 2012.

48   Julie Dermansky, "Fracking Victim Steve Lipsky's Flaming Water Is No Joke," DeSmogBlog, 6 November 2013; Rebecca Leber, "Texas Homeowner Battles $3 Million Defamation Lawsuit for Exposing Fracking Company's Pollution," Climate Progress, 8 November 2013; Sharon Wilson, "More Flammable Water Near Range Resources' Parker County Fracking Well," Blue Daze, 11 July 2013.

49   Dermansky, "Fracking Victim Steve Lipsky's Flaming Water"; Mike Soraghan, "Barnett Shale: Homeowners Renew Complaints about Water Near Range Wells," EnergyWire, 18 September 2013.

50   Robert B. Jackson et al., "Increased Stray Gas Abundance in a Subset of Drinking Water Wells Near Marcellus Shale Gas Extraction," *Proceedings of the National Academy of Sciences*, 19 June 2013; John Roach, "Natural Gas Found in Drinking Water Near Fracked Wells," NBC News, 16 May 2013; Peter M. Rabinowitz et al., "Proximity to Natural Gas Wells and Reported Health Status: Results of a Household Survey in Washington County, Pennsylvania," *Environmental Health Perspectives*, 10 September 2014.

51   See Joanna M. Foster, "More than Flaming Water: New Report Tracks Health Impacts of Fracking on Pennsylvania Residents' Health," Climate Progress, 26 August 2013; Ellen Cantarow, "The Downwinders: Fracking Ourselves to Death in Pennsylvania," TomDispatch, 2 May 2013.

52   Abraham Lustgarten and ProPublica, "Are Fracking Wastewater Wells Poisoning the Ground beneath Our Feet?" *Scientific American*, 21 June 2012.

53   Nathaniel R. Warner et al., "Impacts of Shale Gas Wastewater Disposal on Water

Quality in Western Pennsylvania," *Environmental Science & Technology*, 2 October 2013; Theo Colborn et al., "Natural Gas Operations from a Public Health Perspective," *Human and Ecological Risk Assessment: An International Journal*, 2011.

54   "Report: Fracking's 'Radioactive Wastewater' Discharged Into Drinking Water Supplies," *Environmental Leader*, 1 March 2011; Felicity Carus, "Dangerous Levels of Radioactivity Found at Fracking Waste Site in Pennsylvania," *Guardian*, 2 October 2013; Harrison Jacobs, "Duke Study: Fracking Is Leaving Radioactive Pollution in Pennsylvania Rivers," *Business Insider*, 9 October 2013; Environment America, "Fracking by the Numbers."

55   Katie Valentine, "Report: Fracking Creates Billions of Gallons of Toxic — Sometimes Radioactive — Byproduct," 4 October 2013.

56   "Pennsylvania, Other States Confirm Water Pollution from Natural Gas Drilling," Associated Press, 5 January 2014.

57   Foster, "More than Flaming Water"; Environment America, "Fracking by the Numbers."

58   Mead Gruver, "Wyoming Air Pollution Worse than Los Angeles Due to Gas Drilling," *Huffington Post*, 8 March 2011; George Birchard, "NOAA Investigation Finds Massive Methane Emissions from Utah Fracking: 6% to 12% Lost to Atmosphere," *Daily Kos*, 7 August 2013.

59   Kate Sheppard, "For Pennsylvania's Doctors, a Gag Order on Fracking Chemicals," *Atlantic*, 27 March 2012. Moreover, when people forced to relocate win settlements, companies impose the gag order on the children as well; Andrew Breiner, "'Frack Gag' Bans Children from Talking about Fracking, Forever," Climate Progress, 2 August 2013; Emily Atkin, "Fracking Chemicals in North Caroline Will Remain Secret, Industry-Funded Commission Rules," Climate Progress, 16 January 2014.

60   Michelle Bamberger and Robert E. Oswald, "Impacts of Gas Drilling on Human and Animal Health," *New Solutions*, 2012.

61   Lustgarten, "Are Fracking Wastewater Wells Poisoning?"

62   Katie Valentine, "Pennsylvania Finally Reveals Fracking Has Contaminated Drinking Water Hundreds of Times," Climate Progress, 29 April 2014.

63   Katie Valentine, "Doctors Call on President Obama for More Regulation On Fracking," Climate Progress, 20 February 2014.

64   Joe Romm, "Shale Shocked: Studies Tie Rise of Significant Earthquakes in U.S. Mid-continent to Wastewater Injection," Climate Progress, 4 December 2012.

65   John Upton, "Fracking Triggered More than 100 Earthquakes in Ohio," Grist, 5 September 2013; Bill Chameides, "Fracking Waste Wells Linked to Ohio Earthquakes," Energy Collective, 2 September 2013.

66   Romm, "Shale Shocked."

67   Michael Behar, "Fracking's Latest Scandal? Earthquake Swarms," *Mother Jones*, 28 March 2013.

68   William Ellsworth, et al., "Man-Made Earthquakes Update," U.S. Geological Survey, 12 July 2013.

69   Emily Atkin, "Shaken by 'Frackquakes,' Texans Demand Halt on Wastewater Injection Wells," Climate Progress, 22 January 2014; Atkin, "Texas Proposes Tougher Rules on Fracking Wastewater after Earthquakes Surge," Climate Progress, 27 August 2014.

70   Behar, "Fracking's Latest Scandal?" Renee Lewis, "Fracking-Triggered Earthquakes Could Get Stronger, Seismologists Say," Al Jazeera America, 1 May 2014.

71   "Seismologist: Fracking Does NOT Cause Earthquakes," Marcellus Drilling News, 2013.

72   This list is based on "The Costs of Fracking," Environment America, 20 September 2012.

73   Don Hopey, "Gas Driller Recycling More Water, Using Fewer Chemicals," *Pittsburgh Post-Gazette*, 1 March 2011.

74   Ian Urbina, "Wastewater Recycling No Cure-All in Gas Process," *New York Times*, 1 March 2011; Jim Fuquay, "Recycling of Fracking Water Is Still Rare, but It's Growing," *Fort Worth Star-Telegram*, 27 May 2013.

75   Environment America, "Fracking by the Numbers"; Ellen Cantarow, "New York's New Abolitionists: The Fight to Stop Fracking," EcoWatch, 19 April 2013. Richard Heinberg has said: "Across America, hundreds of grassroots groups with names like New Yorkers

Against Fracking, Save Colorado from Fracking . . . and Ban Michigan Fracking have spring up and formed mutual support Networks" (*Snake Oil*, 92); Kiley Kroh, "Next Up for Pope Francis: Anti- Fracking Activist?" Climate Progress, 14 November 2013.

76   Paul Batistelli, "Three Colorado Cities Ban Fracking," Inhabitat, 13 November 2013; Julie Cart, "New Mexico County First in Nation to Ban Fracking to Safeguard Water," *Los Angeles Times*, 28 May 2013; "Vermont First State to Ban Fracking," CNN, 17 May 2012; Tiffany Germain, "Last-Minute Attempt to Repeal Fracking Moratorium Fails in North Carolina," Climate Progress, 26 July 2013; "France Cements Fracking Ban," *Guardian*, 11 October 2013; "Bulgaria Bans Shale Gas Drilling with 'Fracking' Method," BBC News, 19 January 2012.

77   Rebecca Leber, "Exxon CEO Comes Out against Fracking Project because It Will Affect His Property Values," Climate Progress, 21 February 2014.

78   Emily Atkin, "Oil Lobby Overpowers Votes to Kill Statewide Fracking Ban in California," Climate Progress, 30 May 2014.

79   Andrew C. Revkin, "Energy Agency Finds Safe Gas Drilling Is Cheap," Dot Earth (blog), *New York Times*, 29 May 2012; Brad Plumer, "Why Regulating Gas Fracking Could Be Cheaper than the Alternatives," Wonkblog, *Washington Post*, 29 May 2012; Joe Romm, "IEA's 'Golden Age of Gas Scenario' Leads to More than 6F Warming and Out-of-Control Climate Change," Climate Progress, 7 June 2011; Fiona Harvey, "Natural Gas Is No Climate Change 'Panacea,' Warns IEA," *Guardian*, 6 June 2011; Joe Romm, "International Energy Agency Finds 'Safe' Gas fracking Would Destroy a Livable Climate," Climate Progress, 30 May 2012.

80   Heinberg, *Snake Oil*, 58, 79. See also Tam Hunt, "The Future of Energy, Part II — Natural Gas Revolution May Not Be All It's Cracked Up to Be," Noozhawk, 21 November 2013.

81   Michael Klare, "A Tough-Oil World: Why Twenty-First Century Oil Will Break the Bank - and the Planet," Tomgram, 15 November 2013.

82   Kiley Kroh, "25 Years after Exxon Valdez Oil Spill, Company Still Hasn't Paid for Long-Term Environmental Damage," Climate Progress, 15 July 2013.

83   Rebecca Leber, "Charged with Illegally Dumping Polluted Fracking Fluid, Exxon Claims 'No Lasting Environmental Impact,'" Climate Progress, 11 September 2013.

84   Bill McKibben, "Movements Without Leaders: What to Make of Change on an Over-heating Planet," TomDispatch, 18 August 2013.

85   Jodi Hernandez and Wire Services, "Richmond Files Lawsuit against Chevron for Alleged Negligence in 2012 Refinery Fire," NBC News, 2 August 2013; Braden Reddall and Erwin Seba, "U.S. Board Tells Chevron to Check Refiners for Damage," Reuters, 15 April 2013.

86   Ben Elgin and Peter Waldman, "Chevron Defies California on Carbon Emissions," Bloomberg, 18 April 2013.

87   Lisa Garber, "The Amazon's Chernobyl: Ecuadorian Court Orders Chevron to Pay $19 Billion for Environmental Damages," Activist Post, 31 July 2012; "Smooth Criminal: Chevron Sues Rainforest Communities It Contaminated," Eye on Amazon, 15 October 2013; "Retaliation Trial Opens against Victims of Chevron Contamination in Ecuador," Eye on the Amazon, 15 October 2013.

88   "Smooth Criminal"; "Supreme Court Won't Consider Blocking $18B Judgment against Chevron," CNN, 24 October 2012 (CNN's paraphrase).

89   "Reporters Get Sucked in by Chevron's Spin," Chevron Pit, 24 September 2013; "Smooth Criminal"; "Argentina Freezes Chevron's Assets," SustainableBusiness.com News, 9 November 2012; Garber, "The Amazon's Chernobyl"; Smith and Gullo, "Texaco Toxic Past"; "Judge Hears Arguments in Chevron's Case Against Ecuadorean Judgment," Associated Press, 15 October 2013; "Supreme Court Won't Consider Blocking."

90   "Judge Kaplan Denies Jury Trial for Donziger and Ecuadorians," Chevron Pit, 8 October 2013.

91   Kaplan even questioned their existence, referring to the "so-called Lago Agrio plaintiffs" and referred to their litigation as a "game"; see "U.S. Federal Judge Insults Ecuadorian Indigenous Plaintiffs Who Won $18 Billion Judgment Against Chevron," *Amazon Defense Coalition* , June 2011 (Lago Agrio is the town where Texaco had its

headquarters from 1964 to 1992); "Chevron Continues Abusive Efforts to Rig Trial in Retaliatory RICO Case vs. Donziger and Ecuadorian Villagers," Chevron Pit, 3 October 2013.

92   "Chevron Launches New Effort to Deny Ecuadorians and Donziger a Fair Trial in RICO Case," Gowen Group Law Office, 3 October 2013; "Judge Hears Arguments in Chevron's Case Against Ecuadorean Judgment," Associated Press, 15 October 2013.

93   Clifford Krauss, "Big Victory for Chevron Over Claims in Ecuador," *New York Times*, 4 March 2014; Alexander Zaitchik, "Sludge Match: Inside Chevron's $9 Billion Legal Battle with Ecuadorean Villagers," Rolling Stone, 28 August 2014.

94   Rebecca Leber, "Exxon, Chevron Made $71 Billion Profit in 2012 as Consumers Paid Record Gas Prices," 1 February 2013; Lou Dematteis, "Chevron Says These People Don't Matter," World Blog, Huffington Post, 12 April 2012.

95   Klare, "A Tough-Oil World"; Michael T. Klare, *The Race for What's Left: The Global Scramble for the World's Last Resources* (New York: Metropolitan Books, 2012), 43; Emily Atkin, "BP Wants to Speed Up 'Toxic Soup' Lawsuit, Says Injury Claims Are 'Clogging' the Court," Climate Progress, 22 November 2013.

96   Emily Atkin, "BP Wants to Speed Up 'Toxic Soup' Lawsuit."

97   Ibid.; Mark Hertsgaard, "What BP Doesn't Want You to Know About the 2010 Gulf Spill," *Newsweek*, 12 April 2013.

98   Annie-Rose Strasser, "BP Oil Spill Cleanup Workers Are at Higher Risk of Sickness, Cancer," Climate Progress, 17 September 2013; David Yarnold, "What BP Owes America," Politico, 21 October 2013; Dahr Jamail, "Gulf Ecosystem in Crisis Three Years after BP Spill," Al Jazeera, 20 October 2013; Katie Valentine, "BP Tries to Avoid Payments for Deepwater Horizon by Accusing Gulf Businesses of Fraud," Climate Progress, 17 July 2013; Annie-Rose Strasser, "Coast Guard Discovers a 4,000-Pound Mat of Tar in the Gulf," Climate Progress, 17 October 2013.

99   Mark Schleifstein, "BP Sues Louisiana Officials after Being Ordered to Remove Oil Spill Boom Achors from State Waters," *Times-Picayune*, 19 February 2013; Clifford Krauss and Stanley Reed, "Leaner BP Blanches at Bill for Cleanup," *New York Times*, 11 July 2013; Yarnold, "What BP Owes America"; Jamail, "Gulf Ecosystem in Crisis"; Katie Valentine, "Appeals Court Rules BP Must Pay Gulf Oil Spill Claimants," Climate Progress, 4 March 2014.

100   Valentine, "BP Tries to Avoid Payments"; "BP Looks to Shave More Money Off Gulf Oil Spill Fines Tab," Fuel Fix, 15 July 2013; Rebecca Leber, "Sick of the Deepwater Horizon Disaster, BP Gets Aggressive with Lawsuits," Climate Progress, 14 August 2013; Emily Atkin, "BP Dips Back into the Gulf with Its Largest-Every Oil Fleet," 20 November 2013; Katie Valentine, "Appeals Court Rules BP Must Pay Gulf Oil Spill Claimants," Climate Progress, 4 March 2014; Lacey McCormick, "Report: Four Years after BP Oil Spill, Wildlife Still Struggling: Dolphins and Sea Turtles Still Dying in High Numbers," National Wildlife Federation, 8 April 2014.

101   Campbell Robertson and Clifford Kraus, "BP May Be Fined Up to $18 Billion for Spill in Gulf," *New York Times*, 4 September 2014.

102   Klare, *The Race for What's Left*, 100, 102, 103; Rachel Newer, "Oil Sands Mining Uses Up Almost as Much Energy as It Produces," Inside Climate News, 19 February 2013; Katie Valentine, "The Climate Impact of Canada's Tar Sands Is Growing," Climate Progress, 7 November 2013.

103   Lisa Song, "Exclusive Interview: Why Tar Sands Oil Is More Polluting and Why It Matters," Inside Climate News, 22 May 2012; James Hansen, "Keystone XL: The Pipeline to Disaster," Op-Ed, *Los Angeles Times*, 4 April 2013.

104   Klare, *The Race for What's Left*, 104.

105   Stacy Feldman, "Koch Subsidiary Told Regulators It Has 'Direct and Substantial Interest' in Keystone XL," InsideClimate News, 5 October 2011; David Sassoon, "Koch Brothers' Political Activism Protects Their 50-Year Stake in Canadian Heavy Oils," InsideClimate News, 10 May 2012.

106   Steven Mufson and Juliet Eilperin, "The Biggest Foreign Lease Holder in Canada's Oil Sands Isn't Exxon Mobil or Chevron. It's the Koch Brothers," *Washington Post*, 20

March 2014.

107   Lisa Song, "In 2012, Canada's 'Dilbit' Becomes a Contentious American Issue," Inside Climate News, 27 December 2012. For an extensive examination, see Elizabeth McGowan, Lisa Long, and David Hasemyer, The Dilbit Disaster: Inside the Biggest Oil Spill You've Never Heard Of (InsideClimate News, 2012). The three authors of this report were awarded the Pulitzer in 2013; Peregrine Kate, "#NoKLX: InsideClimate News Wins Pulitzer for Coverage of Kalamazoo River Dilbit Spill in 2010," Daily Kos, 16 April 2013.

108   Jesse Coleman, "New Documents Show Exxon Knew of Contamination from the Mayflower Oil Spill, Still Claimed Lake Was 'Oil-Free,'" Polluterwatch, 21 May 2013; Nora Caplan-Bricker, "This Is What Happens When a Pipeline Bursts in Your Town," New Republic, 18 November 2013; Ben Jervey, "While Exxon Spins on Mayflower Tar Sands Spill Cleanup, Oil Threatens Fishing Lake and Arkansas River," 1 May 2013.

109   Michael D. Shear and Jackie Calmes, "Obama Says He'll Evaluate Pipeline Project Depending on Pollution," New York Times, 27 July 2013.

110   Jeff Spross, "State Department Report: Keystone XL Is Environmentally Sound," 1 March 2013.

111   Michael Brune, "Why Keystone XL Flunks the Climate Test," Sierra Club, 30 August 2013; John H. Cushman Jr.; "Scientists: Key Parts of State Dept Keystone Review Are 'Without Merit,'" InsideClimate News, 4 June 2013; Daniel J. Weiss, "Reuters Debunks State Dept. Claim of Major U.S. Tar Sands Imports by Rail if Keystone Pipeline Scrapped," Climate Progress, 18 April 2013.

112   Song, "Exclusive Interview: Why Tar Sands Oil Is More Polluting," InsideClimate News, 22 May 2012.

113   "Keystone Pipeline Infographic: 'Built To Spill,'" Huffington Post, 29 October 2011; Magnifico, "Revised Keystone XL Still Crosses Vital Ogallala Aquifer, Republicans Pressuring Obama to Give OK," Daily Kos, 20 April 2012.

114   Talia Buford, "Thousands Rally in Washington to Protest Keystone Pipeline," Politico, 17 February 2013; Suzanne Goldenberg, "Keystone XL Protestors Pressure Obama on Climate Change Promise," Guardian, 17 February 2013; Michael T. Klare, "A Presidential Decision That Could Change the World: The Strategic Importance of Keystone XL," in "Tomgram: Michael Klare, Will the Keystone XL Pipeline Go Down?" 10 February 2013.

115   Elizabeth Kolbert, "Lines in the Sand," New Yorker, 27 May 2013.

116   Jeff Spross, "Oil Starts Flowing through the Keystone XL Pipeline's Southern Leg Today," Climate Progress, 22 January 2014.

117   Charles Hall, "Unconventional Oil: Tar Sands and Shale Oil - EROI on the Web, Part 3 of 6"; "Oil Shale and Tar Sands," Center for Biological Diversity; "Why Oil Shale Is a Problem," Western Resource Advocates.

118   "It's Official! Western Resource Advocates Exposes Oil Shale Would Strain Western Water," Western Resource Advocates, 8 July 2014; Tom Kenworthy, "Chevron Admits the Truth: Oil Shale Will Use Huge Amounts of Western Water," Climate Progress, 8 July 2014.

119   Osha Gray Davidson, Amazon.com review of Elizabeth McGowan et al., The Dilbit Disaster. See Osha Gray Davidson, Clean Break: The Story of Germany's Energy Transformation and What Americans Can Learn from It (Kindle Edition, 2012).

120   Lester R. Brown, "The Great Transition, Part I: From Fossil Fuels to Renewable Energy," 25 October, 2012.

121   Michael Klare, "Oil Is Back! A Global Warming President Presides over a Drill-Baby-Drill United States," TomDispatch, 4 September 2014.

122   Joe Romm, "AGU Scientist Asks, 'Is Earth F**ked?' Surprising Answer: Resistance Is Not Futile!" Climate Progress, 9 December 2012.

123   Ibid.

124   Wen Stephenson, "Cue the Math: McKibben's Roadshow Takes Aim at Big Oil," Grist, 18 October 2012.

Chapter 19: Mobilization

1   Lester Brown, *Plan B 4.0: Mobilizing to Save Civilization*, substantially revised edition (New York: W. W. Norton, 2009).

2   *World on the Edge*, 183.

3   Joe Romm, *Hell and High Water: The Global Warming Solution* (New York: Harper, 2007), 235; Romm, "The Ghost of Climate Yet to Come," Climate Progress, 25 December 2012.

4   Ross Gelbspan, "Rewiring the World with Clean Energy," The Heat Is On, 2010; Brown, *The World on Edge*, 96.

5   "U.N. Researchers: Global Warming Clock Is at 'Five Minutes to Midnight,'" Agence France-Presse, 2 September 2013; Peter Goldmark, "Fiddling with Words as the World Melts," *Economist*, 18 December 2008.

6   John J. Berger, "In 2013, a Climate Emergency Exists," *Sante Fe New Mexican*, 1 July 2013.

7   "We Have a Planetary Emergency: Hansen, Leading NASA Climate Scientist, Urges Unions to Act," Cornell University, 23 October 2012; Ban Ki-moon, Juan Jose Lagorio, "UN's Ban Says Global Warming Is 'An Emergency,'" Planet Ark, 12 November 2007.

8   "Presidents Obama, Hu: Declare Global Climate Emergency, say Green Business Leaders, NGOs," Sustainable Business, 19 January 2011; "We Have a Planetary Emergency."

9   Bob Doppelt, "President Obama Should Issue Emergency Declaration Now to Address Climate Crises," Climate Access, 24 July 2012; "Climate EMERGENCY Declaration ," Canadians for Emergency Action on Climate Change; "Climate Emergency," Campaign against Climate Change.

10   James Wight, "Climate Emergency: Time to Slam on the Brakes," Skeptical Science, 8 March 2011.

11   Joe Romm, "'Science Is Science': Obama Embraces Price on Carbon, Leaving Fossil Fuels in the Ground," Climate Progress, 8 June 2014.

12   *The War*, "War Production," PBS.

13   Jeff Goodell, "Obama's Climate Challenge," *Rolling Stone*, 17 January 2013; Juliet Eilperin, "U.S., China Agree to Work on Phasing Out Hydrofluorocarbons," *Washington Post*, 6 September 2013.

14   Coral Davenport, "Obama Pursuing Climate Accord in Lieu of Treaty," *New York Times*, 26 August 2014; Mark Landler and Coral Davenport, "Obama Presses Chinese on Global Warming," *New York Times*, 23 September 2014.

15   Quoted from Chapter 13, above.

16   Scott Carlson, "Oberlin, Ohio: Laboratory for a New Way of Life," *Chronicle of Higher Education*, 6 November 2011.

17   Rachel Barnhart, "RIT Professor Talks about Backlash to Climate Change Blog," Rochester Institute of Technology, 3 April 2014.

18   Pic Walker, "Alliance for Climate Education: A Million Students and the Power of Awesome," Climate Progress, 11 November 2011.

19   "Agriculture," Climate Institute; Sam Eaton, "Carbon-Neutral Lunch: Costa Rica Looks to Lead on Climate-Friendly Ag," Public Radio International, 20 June 2013. James Hansen et al., "The Case for Young People and Nature: A Path to a Healthy, Natural, Prosperous Future," From James Hansen (Blog), 5 May 2011; "Agriculture," Climate Institute; Sam Eaton, "Carbon-Neutral Lunch: Costa Rica Looks to Lead on Climate-Friendly Ag," Public Radio International, 20 June 2013.

20   Tom Laskawy, "Why Does Agriculture Keep Getting a Climate Pass?" Grist, 25 January 2012; Fred Pearce, "UN Negotiators Ditch Climate-Friendly Agriculture," *New Scientist*, 19 November 2013.

21   Dan Allen, "An Agriculture that Stands a Chance: Perennial Polyculture and the Hard Limits of Post-Carbon Farming," Resilience, 13 December 2010; "Case Study: Climate-Friendly Farming: Fetzer Vineyards," California Climate and Agriculture Network; Sam Eaton, "Carbon-Neutral Lunch: Costa Rica Looks to Lead on Climate-Friendly Ag," Public Radio International, 20 June 2013.

22   "Achim Steiner, Executive Director of UNEP, Sees Much Progress, But Davos Is but

One Moment on the Long Road to Change," *Guardian,* 25 January 2014.

23   Julius Fischer, "The Business Council for Sustainable Energy's Ideas to Immediately Address Climate Change," Climate Progress, 5 March 2013.

24   Adam Peck, "Apple's New Corporate Headquarters Will Feature One of the World's Largest Solar Arrays," Climate Progress, 20 November 2013; Adam Vaughan, "Apple: Climate Change Is Real and It's a Real Problem," *Guardian,* 22 April 2014; Katie Valentine, "Google Buys Power from Four Swedish Windfarms in Bid to Be Fueled by 100 Percent Renewable Energy," Climate Progress, 27 January 2014; Kiley Kroh, "IKEA Produces Enough Clean Energy to Match a Third of Its Global Energy Use, and Keeps Going," Climate Progress, 19 November 2013.

25   Kate Sheppard, "Harry Reid: 'Climate Change Is the Worst Problem Facing the World Today,'" Huffington Post, 6 March 2014; Lisa Hymas, "Sanders and Boxer Introduce 'Fee and Dividend' Climate Bill; Greens Tickled Pink," Grist, 15 February 2013; "Senators Pull Off All-Nighter for Climate Action #up4climate," Earth Justice, 11 March 2014.

26   Henry M. Paulson, "The Coming Climate Crash," *New York Times,* 21 June 2014.

27   Nichole Force, "The Hidden Power of Humor, PsychCentral, 2 March 2010; "Climate Change – Is It a Laughing Matter?" Good Energy, 29 May 2014; Graham Readfearn, "Great Climate Change Comedy Moments in Video Clips," *Guardian,* 28 May 2014; "Yoran Bauman, Ph.D., The World's First and Only Stand-Up Economist."

28   John Light, "The Billionaires on Both Sides of Climate Change," Moyers & Company, 19 February 2014; Coral Davenport, "Pushing Climate Change as an Issue this Year, but With an Eye on 2016," *New York Times,* 22 May 2014; Joshua M. Patton, "'Green' Billionaire Turning Citizens United Decision against Republicans on Climate Change," Issue Hawk, 13 June 2014.

29   "Risky Business: The Economic Risks of Climate Change in the United States," Risky Business Project, June 2014; Brad Johnson, "Fox Business Marks Sandy Anniversary with Climate Denial," Climate Progress, 29 October 2013.

30   "Why Only 5% of the World's Billionaires Have Signed the Giving Pledge," Wealth-X Institute, 14 November 2013.

31   Brad Johnson, "Climate Denying Oklahoma Governor Tells Residents to Pray for Rain," Climate Progress, 18 July 2011.

32   Tom Hayden, "California the Focal Point of Green Revolution," Huffington Post, 13 June 2013; Jorge Madrid, "California's Secret to Green Jobs and a Thriving Clean Economy? It's Policy," California Dream 2.0, *Environmental Defense Fund,* 10 April 2013; Kiley Kroh, "Clean Energy for All: California Advances Pioneering Shared Renewables Bill," Climate Progress, 1 July 2013; Emily Reyna, "Four Reasons California Cap and Trade Had an Extraordinary First Year," Reuters, 8 January 2014; Derek Walker, "Hopeful Signs for U.S. and Chinese Cooperation on Climate Change," EDF Voices, 10 July 2013; Michael Wines, "Climate Pact Is Signed by 3 States and a Partner," *New York Times,* 29 October 2013; Ari Phillips, "California and Mexico Sign Climate Pact During Governor Brown's Visit," Climate Progress, 29 July 2014.

33   Matt Kasper, "California to Other 49 States: Can You Match Our Clean Energy Economy," Climate Progress, 17 March 2013.

34   Brighter Future: A Study on Solar in U.S. Schools," Solar Energy Industries Association, 2014; discussed in Cynthia Shahan, "Solar Schools Could Produce a Ton of Solar Electricity," Clean Technica, 19 September 2014.

35   Mary Christina Wood, "Atmospheric Trust Litigation," in *Climate Change: A Reader,* ed. William H. Rodgers Jr. et al. (Carolina Academic Press, 2011); Edith Brown Weiss, "The Planetary Trust: Conservation and Intergenerational Equity," *Ecology Law Quarterly,* 1984); Joseph L. Sax, "The Public Trust Doctrine in Natural Resource Law," *Michigan Law Review,* January, 1970; Sax, "Liberating the Public Trust Doctrine from Its Historical Shackles," *University of California at Davis Law Review,* 1980.

36   Mary Christina Wood, *Nature's Trust* (Cambridge University Press, 2014), 127, 272; Wood, "Atmospheric Trust Litigation," in *Climate Change,* ed. Rodgers Jr., 1034.

37   Jeff Spross, "Cutting Carbon City by City Could Have a Huge Impact on Climate Change," Climate Progress, 25 September 2014.

38   Ari Phillips, "As Mayors Step in on Climate Change, New York City's Air Is at Its Cleanest in Decades," Climate Progress, 27 September 2013; C40 Cities: Climate Leadership Group; "Resolution: Emergency Action Needed to Address Climate Change and Protection," 82nd Annual Meeting, U.S. Conference of Mayors, 2014.

39   Jake Richardson, "100% Renewable Energy for Burlington, VT," Clean Technica, 23 September 2014; "Mayor Miro Weinberger and BED Announce Completion of City Purchase of Winooski One Hydroelectric Facility," Burlington Electric, 4 September 2014.

40   Matt Flegenheimer, "De Blasio Orders a Greener City, Setting Goals for Energy Efficiency of Buildings," *New York Times*, 20 September 2014.

41   "Green Buildings and Energy Efficiency," PlaNYC; Sustainable Cleveland 2019; Mike McGinn, "Let's Prevent This Crisis: A Letter to Harvard's President Faust," Seattle, 17 October 2013; Las Vegas Mayor Carolyn Goodman and Gresham Mayor Shane Bemis Are the Nation's Top Winners in the 2014 Mayors' Climate Protection Awards," 20 June 2014; Felicity Barringer, "With Help From Nature, a Town Aims to Be a Solar Capital," *New York Times*, 8 April 2013.

42   Ari Natter, "Republicans Move to Cut Military's Alternative Fuels," Bloomberg, 29 May 2012; Jill Fitzsimmons, "15 Military Leaders Who Say Climate Change Is a National Security Threat," Media Matters, 20 May 2012.

43   James Hansen et al., "The Case for Young People and Nature;" Ken Caldeira, "The Only Ethical Path Is to Stop Using the Atmosphere as a Waste Dump for Greenhouse Gas Pollution," Climate Progress, 15 April 2012.

44   Interfaith Power & Light: A Religious Response to Global Warming; "Professors to Embark on D.C. Cycling Trip to Raise Climate Change Awarenesses," Penn State University, 28 April 2014; Kiley Kroh, "Next Up for Pope Francis: Anti-Fracking Activist?" Climate Progress, 14 November 2013.

45   Rebecca Leber and Joe Romm, "Republicans Tired of Climate Change Deniers Launch Initiative for Global Warming Action, Carbon Price," 10 July 2012; Chris Adams, "Republican Ex-EPA Chiefs Say It's Time to Act on Climate Change," McClatchy, 18 June 2014; Paulson, "The Coming Climate Crash"; Jon M. Huntsman Jr., "The G.O.P. Can't Ignore Climate Change," New York Times, 6 May 2014.

46   David Roberts, "Hey, Look, a Republican Who Cares about Climate Change!" Grist, 10 July 2012.

47   Dana Nuccitelli, "Climate Scientists Erring on the Side of Least Drama," Skeptical Science, 30 January 2013; Jeremy Grantham, "Be Persuasive. Be Brave. Be Arrested (If Necessary)," *Nature*, 14 November 2012; Katie Valentine, "Neil Degrasse Tyson to Science Deniers: 'Science Is Not There for You to Cherry Pick,'" 10 March 2014; Bruce Lieberman, "Gavin Schmidt ... Speaking Up and Speaking Out," Yale Forum on Climate Change, 12 December 2013; Michael E. Mann, "If You See Something, Say Something," New York Times, 17 January 2014.

48   Elisabeth Rosenthal, "Cement Industry Is at Center of Climate Change Debate," *The New York Times*, 26 October 2007; "How to Make Stronger, 'Greener' Cement: New Formula Could Cut Greenhouse-Gas Emissions," Science Daily, 25 September 2014; "Cement Which Reduces CO2 Emission Developed," Aggregate Research, 24 September 2014; "Geopolymer Cement for Mitigation of Global Warming," Geopolymer Institute, Updated 8 August 2014; David Biello, "Cement from CO2: A Concrete Cure for Global Warming?" Scientific American, 7 August 2008.

49   Jane Ayers, "Women Say 'Enough is Enough' to Climate Changes Worldwide," Nation of Change, 11 October 2013.

50   James Hansen, "Children and Adults on Climate Policy: Evidence that They 'Get It,'" From James Hansen, 1 April 2014; G. Brown, Youth Climate Change Initiatives (2013); Heather Libby, "Partner Spotlight: Alec Loorz, Kids vs. Global Warming and the iMatter Campaign," tcktcktck, 6 May 2011; "Determination and Commitment Keeps Iowa Teen Fighting for Her Future," iMatter Blog, 3 August 2012.

Chapter 20: Conclusion

1   Sherwood Rowland, Nobel Prize acceptance speech, 1995

2   Tom Brokaw, *The Greatest Generation* (Random House, November 30, 1997); George Monbiot, "The Process Is Dead," *Guardian*, September 21, 2010.

3   Bill McKibben, *Eaarth: Making a Life on a Tough New Planet* (New York: Times Books, 2010), 27.

4   Chris Hedges, "The Saboteurs," Truthdig, 1 December 2013.

5   Tom Engelhardt, "Terracide and the Terrarists: Destroying the Planet for Record Profits," TomDispatch, 23 May 2013.

6   Mark Landler, "U.S. and China Reach Climate Accord after Months of Talks," *New York Times*, 11 November 2014.

7   Clay Stranger and Jon Creyts, "What the Joint Climate Policy Announcement from US & China Means," Rocky Mountain Institute, 14 November 2014; Jeff Spross, "We Have a Deal: The U.S. and China Agree to Historic Emission Reduction Targets," Climate Change, 12 November 2014.

8   Joe Romm, "Why the U.S.-China CO_2 Deal Is an Energy, Climate, and Political Gamechanger," Climate Progress, 12 November 2014.

9   For this and similar statements, see: "These Republicans use China as an excuse for climate inaction. What will they say now?" You Tube, 11 November 2014 (https://www.youtube.com/watch?v=NDI8SWckRaM).

10   Ed O'Keefe, "McConnell Sharply Criticizes Obama's Climate Change Deal with China," *Washington Post*, 12 November 2014; Christopher Flavelle, "Don't Just Trust China on Climate," Bloomberg View, 14 November 2014.

11   Romm, "Why the U.S.-China CO_2 Deal Is an Energy, Climate, and Political Gamechanger"; Frank Jotzo quoted in Austin Ramzy and Chris Buckley, Politicians and Climate Experts React to U.S.-China Emissions Pact," *New York Times*, 12 November 2014.

12   Joe Romm, "China to Cap Coal Use by 2020 to Meet Game-Changing Climate, Air Pollution Targets," Climate Progress, 19 November 2014.

13   Jonathan Chait, "China Tries to Save Earth; Republicans Furious," *New York Magazine*, 12 November 2014; Andy Borowitz, "Republicans Demand Return of Passive Obama," *New Yorker*, 19 November 2014.

14   Bill McKibben, "The Big Climate Deal: What It Is, and What It Isn't," Reader Supported News, 12 November 2014; Stranger and Creyts, "What the Joint Climate Policy Announcement from US & China Means"; Landler, "U.S. and China Reach Climate Accord."

15   Arthur Neslen, "EU Leaders Agree to Cut Greenhouse Gas Emissions by 40% by 2030," *Guardian*, 23 October 3014; Spross, "We Have a Deal."

ACKNOWLEDGMENTS

As the endnotes show, this book was dependent upon literally hundreds of people, especially Lester Brown, James Hansen, Bill McKibben, Joe Romm, and Nicholas Stern, whose commitment to truth and the health of our planet was constantly a source of education and inspiration.

The seed for for this book was some lectures I gave at Chinese universities in 2012, which I had been invited to give by Zhihe Wang and Meijun Fan, who founded and run the Institute for Postmodern Development of China. Zhihe and Meijun are leaders in the Chinese movement to create an "ecological civilization."

In the first draft of these acknowledgments, I had written: "I cannot begin to express my gratitude to Tod Fletcher, who, besides being an amazingly good proof-reader, seems to know something about almost everything and has often prevented me from going astray." But shortly after he had helped with my final chapters, Tod died suddenly and self-sacrificially. I miss him terribly. This book is published in his memory.

When I was looking around for a possible publisher of this book, a few colleagues suggested Clarity Press. Knowing that I was interested in a press that would bring the book out quickly, they told me that the editor, Diana Collier, is fast, efficient, and easy to work with. This turned out to be understatement.

As always, my greatest debt is to my wife, Ann Jaqua, sine qua non.

This book is dedicated to our grandsons with the hope that it might help make the world better for them – and *their* grandsons

INDEX

A

abatement, 141, 267, 272, 273-74, 276-77, 292, 295-97, 407, 464n19

Abbott, Prime Minister Tony, 49, 50, 366

abolition: of fossil-fuel economy, 240-43; of slavery, 230, 239-43

Abramson, Jill, 192

Ackerman, Frank, 264, 267-71, 276-77, 287, 290, 295, 297, 300, 369, 407

Acropolis, Neven, 71-72

Ahmed, Nafeez, 150

airplanes, 342, 343, 350-54; biofuels for, 352-53; electric, 353-54

alarmism, 77, 124, 161, 170, 175, 212, 246, 415

Alley, Richard, 75

Altemose, Craig, 241

Alter, Lloyd, 240

Amtrak, 343-44, 345. 347-48; Acela Express, 344, 346, 347, 348

Anderson, Kevin, 39, 138

Anderson, Brig. Gen. Steven, 412

Annan, Secretary-General Kofi, 94

Antarctica, 37, 68, 72, 73, 75-76, 77-78: East, 70, 75-76; West, 34, 70, 75-77

Antarctic ice sheets, 70, 72, 75-76, 78, 79

Antarctic sea ice, 77-78, 176

Anthropocene, 12, 135, 140, 423n7

Apple, 405-06

aquifers, 91-92, 100-01, 127, 129, 372, 373, 376, 387

Arctic amplification, 427n28

Arctic melting, 16, 18, 30-31, 46, 62, 70-72, 138, 139, 140, 149, 175, 189, 195, 207, 221, 235, 415

Arctic sea ice, 30, 46, 62, 70-72, 77, 175

Aristotle, 247

Armey, Dick, 214

Arnold, David, 129

Assad government, 128, 129

atheism and morality, 255-58, 260-61, 470n65

B

Baliunas, Sallie, 165-66, 171-72

Ball, Whitney, 177

bark beetles, 44

Barlow, Maude, 80, 418

Barnosky, Anthony D., 137, 148

Barton, Rep. Joe, 210, 367

Bast, Joseph L., 157

Battisti, David, 96

Bauman, Yoram, 407

Beisner, Calvin, 246

Benishek, Rep. Dan, 210

Bergsten, C. Fred, 285

Berlin Mandate, 217, 218, 234

Bernstein, Leonard S., 163

Bezos, Jeff, 195

Biermann, Frank, 113-16

biofuels, 329, 334, 336; cellulosic (advanced), 335-36; food as, 334-35; halophytes, 336, 357

biomass, 303, 329-34; sewage as, 333; waste as, 332-33; woody, 330-32

Bloomberg, Mayor Michael, 333, 408, 410, 411

Boas, Ingrid, 113-16

Boehner, Rep. John, 210, 424

Bok, Derek, 237

Boorse, Dorothy, 252-53
Borenstein, Seth, 119
Borowitz, Andy, 407, 424
Box, Jason, 73-74, 437n29
Boxer, Senator Barbara, 406
Boyce, Daniel, 102
Boykoff, Maxwell and Jules, 184-85
BP: bad behavior of, 220, 382, 383, 385; caused America's worst environmental disaster, 382-83; Governor Bobby Jindal on, 384; enormous profits of, 363; lies about damage, 383-84
Brainard, Curtis, 193-94
Bridenstine, Rep. James, 211
Broder, John M., 214
Broecker, Wally, 170
Brokaw, Tom, 421
Brookes, Tim, 330
Brown and Williamson, 153, 155
Brown, Donald, 279
Brown, James, 137, 149
Brown, Governor Jerry, 408-09
Brown, Lester, 13, 14-15, 21, 69, 73, 81, 85, 88, 92, 94, 96, 100, 104, 106, 110-11, 285, 303, 311, 315, 316, 317, 389, 391, 393
Brown, Paul, 72, 135
Brown, Tom, 81
Brownstein, Ronald, 211
Brulle, Robert, 193
Brune, Michael, 404
Buddhism, 260, 261, 470n65
budget approach, 19. *See also* carbon budget
Bueno, Ramon, 269, 295, 297
Buffett, Warren, 347, 408
Burt, Christopher, 29
Bush, George H.W., 164, 217-18, 234
Bush, George W., 60, 120, 128, 187, 213, 219-20, 289, 341, 367, 379
Byrd-Hagel Resolution, 218-19

C

Caldeira, Ken, 148, 232, 413, 464n19
Calderón, President Felipe, 278

carbon budget, 19, 277, 280, 194, 297, 362, 366, 396-97, 402
carbon capture and storage (CCS), 367-68
carbon price, 265, 280-83, 286, 292-94, 409
carbon tax, 49, 148, 214, 218, 222, 278, 281, 282, 283-87, 293, 294, 310, 332, 406, 414, 462-06n105, 474n98
Carbon Tracker, 237
Carleton, Andrew, 77-78
Carr, David, 344
Carter, President Jimmy, 216-17
Cassandra, 206
Cato Institute, 165, 213, 344, 346
cement, 416-17
Chait, Jonathan, 424
Chandler, Raymond, 125
Charles, Prince, 14
Chellaney, Brahma, 130
Cheney, Dick, 128, 187, 219, 220, 379
Chevron: poor citizenship of, 220, 231, 380-82, 388; exploiter of tar sands, 386; Hurricane, 63; low taxes of, 289; refuses to pay for Amazon disaster, 380-82; wealth of, 231, 363, 382
China, 409; a chief emitter, 21, 22, 235, 310, 353, 365, 393, 402; clean energy development by, 308, 310-11, 312, 313, 314, 322, 325, 329, 338, 339, 343, 344, 346, 348, 354, 356, 358, 366, 392; co-operation with U.S., 21, 365, 398, 422; cumulative emissions of, 235; problems exacerbated by climate change, 35, 39, 50, 52, 57, 69, 79, 91, 96, 97, 100, 101, 111, 130, 367, 395; solving climate problem, 21, 22, 202, 422-424
Choi, Yong-Sang, 170-71
Chomsky, Noam, 14, 232, 299
Chowdhury, Saber Hossain, 112
Christy, John, 165-66, 168-69, 187
Chu, Secretary Steven, 100, 341

Churchill, Winston, 122

Citizens for a Sound Economy, 214, 218

civilization: beginning of, 11-12, 17, 22, 68, 184, 262; saving, 264, 272, 276, 295, 298, 300, 310, 366, 391, 393, 396, 399, 404, 410, 413, 421; global warming threat to, 13-16, 17, 20, 21, 24, 92, 94, 104, 105, 143, 149, 153, 178, 183, 198-99, 204-05, 206, 225, 227, 241, 261, 273, 370, 279, 393, 395, 399, 401; suicide of 13, 14, 109, 263, 264, 300, 366

Cizik, Richard, 250-51, 252, 253, 254, 467n22

Clark, Tony, 80

Clark, William A., 215

Clarke, Garry, 82

clean energy: 100% by 2050: 304, 334, 349, 354-56, 360; energy efficiency as, 304-05; interchangeable with 'green energy', 303; not interchangeable with 'renewable energy', 303, 318, 330-32, 334; and biomass, 303

climate change, 20, 28-29, 59, and passim; anthropogenic (human-caused), 17, 148, 164, 167, 172; denial, 20, 153-180; global warming and, 11, 13-15, 27; other terms for, 16-17, 24; weather and, 15

climate collapse, 16

climate departure, 38

climate disruption, 14, 16-17, 18, 19, 20, 24, 27, 28, 116, 118, 119, 121, 132-33, 166, 178, 182, 190, 198, 199, 208, 224, 233, 235, 237, 247, 264, 269, 276, 362, 365, 376, 394, 395, 418

climate complacency, 245-46

climate economics, 264, 267, 268, 271, 273, 279, 299, 300

Climategate, 174-75, 187, 191, 209, 211

climate sensitivity, 19, 170-71, 190, 276

Cline, Martin, 157

Cline, William R., 173, 273-74, 280, 300

Clinton, President Bill, 95, 166, 202, 214, 218-19, 343

Club of Rome, 265, 300

CO2 (carbon dioxide): concentration of, 17, 18-19, 23, 25, 52, 137, 169, 202, 276, 396, 402; ppm (parts per million), 17-19, 23, 38, 45, 52, 103, 203, 396

CO2e (carbon dioxide equivalent), 424n32

coal: "clean," 365, 367; cost of, 309-10, 356, 365, 368-69, 370; destructiveness of, 365-67, 370; elimination of, 314, 318, 323, 365, 370, 412, 422; exports of, 223, 366; power plants based on, 222-23, 315, 318, 360, 365, 370

Cobb, John B., Jr., 266, 300

Cohen, Sacha Baron, 407

Colbert, Stephen, 78, 402, 407

Collins, Gail, 215

Collins, Senator Susan, 414

Condon, Bradly J., 264

Confucianism, 260

Conway, Erik, 17, 75, 154-67, 172, 184, 185

Cooney, Philip, 219

Copenhagen climate summit, 109, 187, 191, 203, 207, 221, 234, 296

corals, 102-04

Cornwall Alliance, 169, 246, 251, 252-53

Cox, Julian, 341, 342

Cramton, Peter, 292, 293, 294

Crist, Governor Charlie, 344

Crowe, David, 249

Crutzen, Paul, 13, 135, 143, 162

Cruz, Ted, 209

Cuomo, Andrew, 24

Curry, Judith, 77

cyclones, 54, 60-61, 63, 98, 112, 434n37

D

Dai, Aiguo, 41, 52

Daly, Herman, 266, 299-300
Darwin(ism), 255, 256
Davenport, Coral, 369
Davidson, Osha Gray, 388
De Blasio, Mayor Bill, 412
de Châtel, Francesca, 129
Deffenbaugh, Noah, 35, 88
Dei Filippone, Glori, 419
Del Genio, Tony, 63
denialism, 153, 154, 176, 178, 186-88,
    198, 214, 244, 251, 402
denialist, 77, 87, 153-54, 158, 168, 170,
    171, 172, 175-76, 178, 188, 189,
    191, 211, 212, 401, 407
Descartes, René, 247
Dionne, E.J., 250
dirty energy, 264, 289, 303, 304, 310,
    331, 360, 362, 363, 365, 366, 367,
    418
Dismal Theorem, 271-72, 300
divestment, 236-39, 362, 403, 410, 422
Dobriansky, Paula, 219
Dobson, James, 251
Donors: Capital Fund, 177; Trust, 177,
    208
Donziger, Steven, 381-82
Doppelt, Bob, 394
dust-bowlification (desertification),
    43, 90
Dyer, Gwynne, 118, 125-27, 130

E

Earle, Sylvia, 418
economism, 266, 299-300
Ehrlich, Paul and Anne, 14
Eilperin, Juliet, 194, 250
electric vehicles, 336-42; battery
    electric vehicles (BEVs), 337-39;
    fuel-cell electric vehicles (FCVs),
    339-42
Eliot, T.S., 178
Elsner, James, 65-66
Emanuel, Kerry, 66
emergency, 14, 363, 391, 393, 394,
    396, 397, 400, 401, 411, 420
energy efficiency, 212, 242, 278, 304-

06, 325, 352, 357, 399, 400, 408,
    412, 413
Engelhardt, Tom, 14, 183, 187, 364,
    421
Environment America, 58, 224, 311,
    355, 372, 374
Environmental Justice Foundation,
    233-34
EPA (Environmental Protection
    Agency), 157-60, 162, 174, 214,
    216, 222, 223, 318, 329, 333, 335,
    341, 351, 365, 367, 369, 374, 384,
    408, 414
Epstein, Paul, 65, 369-70
equilibrium, 265-66
equity, 211, 234-36, 294-96
Erickson, Millard, 245
ethanol, 334; cellulosic (advanced),
    335-36; crop-based (traditional),
    334, 335, 336
evolution, 248-49
ExxonMobil: bad citizenship of, 207-
    08, 219-20, 289, 363-64, 377-80,
    386-87; Hurricane, 63; origin of,
    163-64; tobacco strategy of, 164-
    69, 171-72, 176-78, 200, 208, 210,
    213-14, 219-20, 223, 231, 252-53,
    260, 289, 345, 353, 363, 377

F

Falk, Richard, 206-07
Fallin, Governor Mary, 408
Faris, Stephen, 131-32
Farley, Andrew, 252
Faust, Drew, 236-37
Femia, Francesco, 128, 129
Fenner, Frank, 142
Ferrell, Will, 407
Figueres, Christiana, 208
FitzGerald, Frances, 250
Fitzpatrick, Ryan, 360
Flannery, Tim, 153
Flavelle, Christopher, 423
Fogarty, John, 186
fossil-fuel industries: 164, 200, 236-42,
    363-64, 370, 372-79, 388-89, 409,

414, 419
fracking (hydraulic fracturing), 91, 92, 223, 327, 340, 370, 372-79, 388, 389, 414, 419, 493-94n75
Francis, Jennifer, 30, 46
Francis, Pope, 263, 377, 417
Freeman, Andrew, 125
Friedman, Thomas, 128, 223, 283, 299
Froomkin, Dan, 192, 290, 364

G

Gates, Bill, 286, 408, 474n98
Geertz, Clifford, 258
Gelbspan, Ross, 13-14, 183, 184, 188, 205, 282, 391
geoengineering, 105, 143-48, 198
geothermal energy, 313, 325-29, 330, 357; enhanced (EGS), 326-27; traditional, 326
Gillis, Justin, 28-29, 54, 171, 225, 236, 296
Gingrich, Newt, 252
Gitlin, Todd, 195
glaciers, 22, 70, 73-74, 76-77, 80, 81-88, 91, 92, 100, 101, 113, 130-32, 149, 175-76, 196, 205, 235, 277, 295, 395, 396, 439n7. *See also* Kilimanjaro glaciers
Global Climate Coalition (GCC), 163, 164, 167, 219-20, 379, 453n65
global warming: anthropogenic (human-caused), 20, 23; as hoax, 120, 172, 183, 195, 208-09, 245; climate change and, 11-18, 27, 153, 189; consensus on, 59-60, 105, 121, 123, 137, 166, 168, 169, 171, 172, 182, 185, 186, 187, 198, 206, 209, 248, 251, 270; definition of, 15, 27; ocean acidification and, 101-04; runaway, 67, 140, 205, 237, 394; self-amplifying, 73, 74, 140 (*see also* runaway); "tragedy of the commons" writ large, 292; unhappiness with term, 16-17; weather and, 25-33
Goldenberg, Suzanne, 28, 61, 203, 214

Goldmark, Peter, 392
Goodall, Jane, 418
Goodell, Jeff, 69, 224
Goodman, Mayor Carolyn, 412
Google, 406
Gore, Al, 14, 15, 27, 85, 111, 122, 153, 210, 219, 221, 238, 419
Gould, Stephen Jay, 255, 257
Graham, Senator Lindsey, 211
Grantham, Jeremy, 415
Green Climate Fund, 234, 293, 295
Greenland, 70, 72-75, 76, 79, 87, 195, 267, 270, 396
Greenpeace, 176-77, 219, 308, 367, 404, 453n67
grid, 307, 308, 309, 314-16, 320, 322, 323, 325, 329, 339, 340, 349, 354-55, 358-61, 397
Guerra, Alberto, 382

H

Habermas, Jürgen, 245, 259
Haeberli, Wilfried, 84
Hagee, John, 249
Hamilton, Clive, 22, 143, 145, 148, 149
Hanemann, Michael, 287
Hansen, James, 11, 18-19, 22, 25, 33, 46, 68, 75, 94, 135, 136, 168, 170, 181-82, 185, 202-03, 217, 225, 227, 232, 233, 243, 277, 278, 279, 286, 365, 397, 403, 413, 415, 419
Happer, William, 189
Harman, Gilbert, 257-58, 261
Harper, Prime Minister Stephen, 50, 388
Harris-Perry, Melissa, 195
Hartmann, Thom, 142, 181, 191, 199
Hartshorne, Charles, 260, 261
Hatch, Sen. Orrin, 210
Hawken, Paul, 290, 393
Hayes, Chris, 402
Hayes, Denis, 201
Hayhoe, Katherine, 351-53
Hayward, Jeremy, 261
Healey, Ben, 291
Heartland Institute, 157, 165, 167, 170,

178
Hedges, Chris, 421
Heinberg, Richard, 378
Hemmingway, Ernest, 85
Hertsgaard, Mark, 120, 154, 166, 182, 187, 188, 204, 205, 206, 208, 389
Hirayama, Takeshi, 155-56
Hodel, Donald, 162
Hoeppe, Peter, 29
Holdren, John, 16, 169
Holocene, 11-12, 17, 68, 135-36, 140, 141, 249, 262-63
Holtz-Eakin, Douglas, 414
Homer-Dixon, Thomas, 125
Hoofnagle, Mark, 153
Horgan, John, 194
Huckabee, Mike, 250
Hudson, Drew, 208
Hume, David, 258
Hunter, Joel, 250
Hunter, Rep. Duncan, 210, 251, 254
Huntsman, Jon, 211, 248, 414
Huq, Saleem, 220
Hurricane Sandy, 24, 28; as Frankenstorm, 62
hydropower, 49, 85, 88, 130, 131, 308, 313, 318-19, 328, 354, 355, 356, 357

I

Ice Age, 11, 71
ice sheets, 70; Antarctic, 70, 72, 75-76, 78, 79; Greenland, 70, 72-75, 76, 79, 87, 195, 267, 396
idolatry, 266, 300, 362
Idso, Craig, 165, 166
Idso, Fred, 165
Idso, Sherwood, 165, 166
IKEA, 406
Ikle, Fred, 144, 145
India: aquifer depletion in, 91, 108, 129; climate refugees and, 111; coal and, 366-67; contribution to global warming of, 235, 365, 398; drought in, 50-51; EVs in, 339; food insecurity and, 97, 101,

130; rain storms in, 8; sea-level rise threat for, 69; solar energy in, 308-09, 311, 313; water scarcity and, 130-32
infallible revelation, 246-47
Inglis, Congressman Bob, 284, 414
Inhofe, Senator James, 171-72, 208-09, 245-47, 251
intergenerational justice, 227, 231-33, 239, 295, 298, 413
interglacial, 11, 71
International Energy Agency (IEA), 38, 278, 289, 304, 305, 324, 361, 371
IPCC (Intergovernmental Panel on Climate Change), 13, 19, 26, 32, 62, 68, 71, 75, 85, 87, 95, 99, 101, 119, 122, 163, 164, 166, 169, 170, 172, 173, 175, 176, 184, 186, 195-96, 201, 202, 204, 211, 217, 219, 220, 252, 268, 270, 277, 287, 296, 305, 371, 392, 404
Iroquois, 231
Islam, 244, 260

J

Jackson, Jeremy, 142
Jackson, Wes, 405
Jastrow, Robert, 160
Jefferson, President Thomas, 231-32
jet stream, 31, 46
John Birch Society, 213
Johnson, President Lyndon, 206, 343
Johnson, Senator Ron, 210
Jones, David, 33, 49
Jones, Phil, 174
Jotzo, Frank, 423
Judaism, 244, 260
Justice, Charles, 239, 243

K

Kammen, Daniel, 238-39, 403
Kaplan, Judge Lewis, 381-82
Kasper, Matt, 409
Keller, David P., 146, 147
Kennedy, President John F., 198

Kernen, Joe, 189
Kerry, Secretary John, 118, 246, 341, 398
Kilimanjaro glaciers, 85; sublimation theory of retreat, 440n22
Kim, Jim Yong, 282
Ki-Moon, Ban, 11, 56, 98, 127, 200, 208, 393
Klare, Michael T., 118, 225-26, 378, 387, 389
Klein, Ezra, 194
Klein, Naomi, 221, 235, 299
Koch brothers, 176-78, 213-16, 231, 345, 386, 402; Charles Koch, 176, 286; David Koch, 176, 214-16, 218, 286; and Tea Party, 213-15; William (Bill) Koch, 286, 317
Koch Industries, 176-78, 200, 208, 213, 386
Kolbert, Elizabeth, 13, 142, 204, 205, 218, 220, 388
Kormann, Carolyn, 83
Kramon, Glenn, 192
Krauthammer, Charles, 190, 194, 423
Krugman, Paul, 206, 278, 407
Kudlow, Larry, 189
Küng, Hans, 228
Kyoto Protocol, 164, 202, 203, 207, 218, 219, 220, 234-35, 281, 292-93, 351, 379

L

Lacy-Swing, William, 116
Laffer, Art, 284, 414
lag time, 424-25n34, 436n63
LaHood, Ray, 344
Lakes, Osprey, 417
Lakoff, George, 18
Leakey, Richard, 142
Leifer, Ira, 142
Lemonick, Michael, 55
Leno, Jay, 195
Lenton, Timothy, 270
Letterman, David, 195
Lewandowsky, Stephan, 187
Lewinsky, Monica, 218

Lewis, Charles, 215
Lewis, Joanna, 130
Lewis, Rep. John L., 198
Lewontin, Richard, 256
Light, Malcolm, 143
Likens, Gene, 161
Limbaugh, Rush, 246
Limits to Growth, 265-66, 299-300
Lin, Justin, 344, 348
Lincoln, President Abraham, 159, 225, 240, 243, 466n67
Lindzen, Richard, 165-66, 169-71, 173
Liu, Jipling, 77
Locke, John, 231
Locklear, Admiral Samuel, 119
Loorz, Alec, 419
Lovins, Amory, 423
Lubchenco, Jane, 101
Luers, Amy, 243
Luntz, Frank, 164
Lyons, Oren, 231

M

Ma Jun, 50
MacKenzie, Craig, 238
Mackie, John, 257-58, 260, 469n55
Madison, President James, 231
Madoff, Bernard, 298-99
Majidulla, Kamal, 132
Mankiw, Gregory, 286, 414
Mann, Michael, 11, 12, 173, 174-75, 190, 209, 232, 415
Mantel, Nathan, 156
Marcott, Shaun, 12
Marsden, William, 200, 203-05, 207
Marshall, Andrew, 120
Marshall Institute, 160, 163, 166, 169, 171, 189
Martin, Michael, 205
Masters, Jeff, 24, 26, 28, 35, 59, 61, 62, 64
Mayer, Alden, 207
Mayer, Jane, 213-15
McCain, Senator John, 211, 414
McConnell, Mitch, 423, 424

McGinn, Michael, 237
McGinn, Vice Admiral Dennis, 413
McKibben, Bill, 18, 19, 22, 24, 28, 32,
    39, 54, 61, 62-63, 72, 200, 220,
    221, 222-23, 224, 226, 228, 236-
    37, 363, 371, 380, 387, 390, 393,
    403, 408, 421, 422, 424
McKinsey and Company, 304
McPherson, Guy R., 143
Medvedev, Dmitri, 29
Merchant, Brian, 130
Merkel, Angela, 235
methane (CH$_4$), 72, 138–43, 223, 333,
    371-74, 377, 395, 404, 491n38
Michaels, Patrick, 165-69
Mill, John Stuart, 230
Miller, Kenneth, 68
Milloy, Steven, 157
mitigation, 117, 233, 236, 267, 277-79,
    295-97, 407
mobilization, 20, 21, 22, 51, 78, 150,
    236, 263, 391-420; Joe Romm
    and Lester Brown on, 391;
    leadership for: academic, 403;
    activist, 403-04; agricultural and
    forestry, 404-05; business, 405-06;
    congressional, 406; economists',
    406-07; entertainment, 407-08;
    financial, 407-08; gubernatorial,
    408-09; legal, 410; mayoral,
    410-12; media, 400-02; military,
    412-13; presidential, 392-400;
    religious and moral, 413-14;
    Republican, 414-15; scientific,
    415-16; technological, 416-17;
    women's, 417-18; youth, 418-20
Modi, Prime Minister Narendra, 311,
    313, 424
Molina, Mario, 162
Monaghan, Andrew, 76
Monbiot, George, 16, 95, 200, 203,
    205, 214, 226, 350, 421
Moniz, Ernest, 167, 176
Mooers, Arne, 137-38
Mora, Camilo, 106
morality, 20, 53, 93, 94, 115, 117, 227-
    43, 244-45, 249-50, 254-55, 257-

62, 264, 266, 280, 288, 290, 295,
    298, 299, 303, 362, 390, 410, 413
Moran, Daniel, 130
Morningstar, Cory, 425n40
Mouhot, Jean-François, 239, 240, 241
Murdoch, Rupert, 188, 189, 408
Murphy, Jeffrie, 258
Murray, Robert, 367

N

Nash, Michael, 112
Nasheed, Mohamed, 108-09
National Climate Assessment, 211, 213,
    225
National Academy of Sciences, 23, 77,
    90, 166, 169, 171, 225, 371
National Science Foundation, 40, 139,
    170, 174
natural gas, 223, 229, 241, 281, 288,
    305, 307, 309, 312, 315, 327, 333,
    340, 341, 363, 367, 370-78. *See
    also* fracking
Natural Resources Defense Council,
    224, 353, 365
Nelson, Ken, 304-05
Neo-Darwinism, 255-57, 261
New Climate Economy Project, 278
Nickel, James, 229
Nierenberg, Bill, 159-60
nihilism, 257-61
Nixon, President Richard, 216
NOAA (National Oceanic and
    Atmospheric Administration), 37,
    52, 62, 63, 101, 102, 104, 127,
    193, 204, 211, 260, 275
Norcross, Bryan, 61-62
Nordhaus, William, 222, 265-88, 299,
    300, 369, 407; Nordhaus era, 266
Nutter, Mayor Michael, 411

O

Obama, President Barack: and
    Snowmageddon, 59; criticized
    by Republicans and Libertarians,

190, 212, 213, 214, 423, 424; statements about slowing climate change, 195, 220-21, 225, 240, 401, 406; statements vs. behavior, 220-26, 389; all-of-the-above energy policy, 224-26, 389; on carbon tax, 283, 287; on coal power plants, 365-66, 367, 369; on energy efficiency, 304; on fossil-fuel subsidies, 288; on fuel-cell autos, 342; on grid, 359-60; on high-speed rail, 344-45; on Keystone XL Pipeline, 387-88; on natural gas, fracking, 371, 375; working with China, 398, 423; ocean acidification, 101-04, 105, 134, 135, 142, 147, 149, 276, 287, 395

ocean energy, 318, 319-25. *See also* tidal energy, wave energy

oil: must remain in ground, 238, 379; pollution by, 221, 229, 236, 379, 380-88; tar sands, 385-88; oil shale, 388-89; derived from fracking, 389

oil industry: disinformation campaign by, 163-71, 219; influence on U.S. policy, 202, 208, 209, 211, 219-26; influence on media by, 188; lying by, 220; risking civilization for its profits, 243

Oliver, John, 186, 402, 407

Olson, Julia, 419

omnipotence, 245-46

Onion, the, 407

Oppenheimer, Michael, 27, 209

O'Reilly, Bill, 196

Oreskes, Naomi, 74, 85, 154-67, 172, 184, 185

Orr, David, 16, 403

Ostro, Stu, 62

P

Pachauri, Rajendra, 82, 202, 392

Panetta, Leon, 119

Parris, Mayor Rex, 412

Paulson, Secretary Henry, 407, 408, 414

Pearce, Fred, 91, 203

Pennock, Robert, 256

Perkins, Tony, 251

Permafrost, 50, 72, 138-40, 142-43, 395

Pershing, Jonathan, 205

Petition Project, 166-67

Pfund, Nancy, 291

phytoplankton, 102-04, 146, 147

Piltz, Rick, 219

Pimlott, Ken, 40

Pimm, Stuart, 138

Pindyck, Robert S., 272, 407

plankton, 102-04, 135, 146, 147

Plato, 247

Plumer, Bradford, 291

Podesta, John, 95, 422

polar bears, 71, 244, 437n20

Polk, William R., 128, 129

Ponzi scheme, 298-99, 378

Pooley, Eric, 182-83, 276, 297

Pope, Vicky, 21-22

Powell, James, 172

process philosophy and theology, 245, 261, 466n2

Provine, William, 255, 257

Q

Qiu, Jane, 86, 87

Qureshi, Shah Mahmood, 131

R

Rabatel, Antoince, 80

Rahmstorf, Stefan, 12, 436n4

railroads, 342-50; high-speed rail (HSR), 342-49; maglev (magnetic levitation) trains, 348-50

Rakova, Ursula, 107

Rand, Ayn, 178

Ranney, Sally, 417

Reagan, President Ronald, 144, 156, 159-62, 217, 284, 400, 414

Reason Foundation, 344, 345

Redden, Molly, 250, 251, 252
Redfearn, Jennifer, 108
Reese, William, 260
Reid, Senator Harry, 406
religion, 20, 228, 243, 244-63, 264, 266,
   300, 362, 413
Remnick, David, 225
renewable energy, 242, 291, 298, 303,
   304, 313, 315, 318, 319, 320,
   324, 326, 334-35, 341, 355; not
   equatable with 'clean energy,'
   303, 318 , 330-32, 334, 476n4; not
   equatable with 'good,' 318
Republican politicians, 118, 164, 195,
   208, 209, 217, 219, 248, 284, 286,
   287, 312, 345, 384, 387, 412, 414-
   15, 422, 423; stampede toward
   absolutist denial, 211-13, 214,
   215, 216
Rich, Frank, 215
Richter, Burton, 368
Ridley, Matt, 189
Ritter, Governor Bill, 224
Roberts, David, 22, 290, 310
Robinson, Mark, 77
Robinson, President Mary, 417
Rocky Mountain Institute, 424
Rockström, Johan, 135-36
Romm, Joe, 22, 24, 25, 30, 31, 35, 38,
   40, 42-43, 46, 52, 53, 55, 58, 60,
   62, 66, 67, 74, 75, 78, 90, 95, 97,
   102, 118, 138, 139, 144, 182, 183,
   187, 189, 190, 193, 194-95, 196,
   220, 225, 240, 260, 275, 290, 291,
   298-99, 304-05, 341, 342, 368,
   371, 391, 423, 424
Romney, Mitt, 212, 414
Roosevelt, President Franklin (FDR),
   225, 393, 397, 399, 400
Rosenthal, Elisabeth, 350, 351, 358
Roth, Kevin, 63
Rowland, Sherwood, 46, 162, 204, 421
Rubio, Marco, 209
Ruckelshaus, William, 160
Russell, Bertrand, 153, 205

S

Saad, Aaron, 106
Sachs, Jeffrey, 126-27, 189, 221
Sagan, Carl, 256
Sandell, Clayton, 197
Sanders, Senator Bernie, 406
Santelli, Rick, 189
Santorum, Rick, 195
Sassoon, David, 192, 215, 386
Satterfield, Dan, 62-63
Sax, Joseph, 410
Scambos, Ted, 72
Schade, Leah, 239, 241, 243,
Schellnhuber, Hans Joachim, 135
Schmidt, Gavin, 415-16
Schwarzenegger, Arnold, 46, 48, 414
Scott, Governor Rick, 344
Scribbler, Robert, 242
Searching, Tim, 330
Seitz, Frederick, 155, 157, 160, 163,
   165-67, 170, 171, 172
Sensenbrenner, Rep. James, 210-11
Serreze, Mark, 71
Shah, Jamaat Ali, 131
Shahan, Zachary, 355
Shepherd, Andrew, 68
Shimkus, Rep. John, 211
Shiva, Vandana, 50, 417
Shue, Henry, 229, 230-31
Shultz, Secretary George, 414
Sierra Club, 224, 367, 387, 404
Singer, S. Fred, 157-58, 160-63, 165-67
Sinha, Tapen, 264
Skuce, Andy, 139
Sloan, Lisa, 46
Smith, Adam, 298
Smith, Jennifer, 44
Smith, Rep. Lamar, 212-13
snowpack, 81, 88, 90, 92, 100, 130,
   295, 395
social cost of carbon, 280-81, 286-87,
   290, 369
solar energy, 109, 217, 281, 291, 295,
   306-11, 313, 314, 325, 330, 349,
   355, 356, 357, 358-59, 360, 406,
   408, 409, 412; concentrated

(CSP), 307-08, 309, 477-78n20;
   photovoltaic (PV), 306-11
solar radiation, 11, 12, 74;
   management (SRM), 143-45, 171
Solnit, Rebecca, 234
Solomon, Susan, 209
Soon, Willie, 165, 166, 171
Soros, George, 215, 408
Spencer, Roy, 165, 166, 168-69, 175
Spinoza, Benedict, 247
Spratt, David, 277
Stager, Curt, 24
Stallone, Sylvester, 157, 452n24
Stanton, Elizabeth A., 264, 267-71,
   276-77, 287, 290, 295, 297, 300,
   369, 407
Staudt, Amanda, 43
Stavins, Rob, 200
Steffen, Will, 135
Steiner, Achim, 134, 264
Stephenson, Wen, 199
Stern, Sir Nicholas, 121, 200, 203, 206,
   266, 267, 268, 267, 270, 273,
   274-77, 280, 284, 286, 288, 295,
   296, 300
Stern era, 266-67
Stern Review, 121, 265-69, 271, 273,
   280, 287
Stern, Todd, 234, 296
Stewart, Jon, 195, 402, 407
Stewart, Rep. Chris, 212
Steyer, Tom, 238, 408
Steyn, Mark, 175
Stiglitz, Joseph, 288, 292, 293
Stipp, David, 120
Stoermer, Eugene F., 423n7
subsidies: for fossil fuels, 229, 243,
   265, 288-91, 309, 310, 312, 315,
   317, 321, 324, 330, 347, 364,
   369-70, 396, 407, 422; for green
   energy, 243, 286, 288- 91, 312,
   321, 324, 331, 364, 396
suicide, 14, 51, 109, 263, 264, 300,
   366
Sullivan, General Gordon, 121-22, 133,
   412
Sullivan, Margaret, 192

Sullivan, Walter, 185
Suomi, Victor, 23
supernaturalism, 245; extreme, 249;
   modified, 249-55

T

Tapper, Jack, 196
Taylor, Graeme, 231
Tea Party, 209, 213-15, 251, 253, 345,
   435
Teller, Edward, 144
Tertrais, Bruno, 125-26
theism, 244; evolutionary,
   255-57; naturalistic, 262;
   supernaturalistic, 245, 247, 248,
   249-56, 260, 261
Third Pole, 86-88
Thomas, Chris, 135
Thompson, Lonnie, 13, 82, 83, 85, 86-
   87, 225, 415
Thornton, Paul, 190
threat multiplier, 121, 123, 124, 127,
   129
tidal energy, 319, 322-25, 355, 357;
   based on tidal barrages, 322-23;
   based on tidal stream turbines,
   323-25 *See also* ocean energy
Tillich, Paul, 261, 266
tipping point, 73, 77, 79, 120, 136,
   270-72, 394
Trenberth, Kevin, 25, 41, 55, 65, 168,
   170-71, 174, 209
Trent, Steve, 117
Tutu, Bishop, 227, 236, 244
Twain, Mark, 215
typhoons, 54, 56, 63, 434n37
Tyson, Neil deGrasse, 415

U

U.N. Framework Convention on
   Climate Change, 202, 208, 217
Union of Concerned Scientists, 40, 99,
   164, 188, 203, 207, 327

V

Vaks, Anton, 140
Van der Hoeven, Maria, 304
Vidal, John, 26, 111, 143
Vincent, John, 230
Voltaire, 256

W

Wadhams, Peter, 71-72, 140
Wald, Matthew, 360
Walker, Governor Scott, 345
Wallich, Henry, 265
Wallis, Jim, 244
Walsh, Bryan, 30
Walzer, Michael, 228, 229
Warren, Rachel, 52-53
Warren, Rick, 250
Watson, Harlan, 219
Watson, Robert, 219
wave energy, 320-22, 357. *See also* ocean energy
Weber, Max, 245
Weinberger, Mayor Miro, 412
Weiss, Elizabeth Brown, 410
Weitzman, Martin, 271-72, 283, 287, 294, 300, 407
Werrell, Caitlin E., 128, 129
West, James, 43
Weyant, John, 281
White, Bill, 358
Whitehead, Alfred North, 230, 261, 262, 466n2
Whitehouse, Senator Sheldon, 406
Wicker, Senator Roger, 210
Will, George, 189-90, 194
Williams, Bernard, 259
Williams, Jody, 417
wind energy, 311-17
Windom, Dr. Robert, 156
Wines, Michael, 89-90
Winston, Andrew, 241, 243
Wood, Lowell, 144, 148
Wood, Mary Christina, 410
Woolsey, James, 133

World Bank, 33, 39, 96, 131, 253, 266, 278, 282, 296, 318, 327, 344
World Meteorological Organization, 24, 189, 201
Worm, Boris, 102
WWF (World Wildlife Federation), 290, 350, 356-57

X

Xi, President Jinping, 422, 424

Y

Yao, Tandong, 86, 87
Years of Living Dangerously, 46, 223, 252, 283, 402
Young, Rob, 68, 70, 99

Z

Zeller, Tom, 192-93
Zinni, General Anthony, 127